3r2 - 2133

PITT LATIN AMERICAN SERIES

CUBA BETWEEN EMPIRES, 1878–1902

Louis A. Pérez, Jr.

CUBA

BETWEEN

EMPIRES

1878–1902

UNIVERSITY OF PITTSBURGH PRESS

Published by the University of Pittsburgh Press, Pittsburgh, Pa. 15260
Copyright © 1983, University of Pittsburgh Press
All rights reserved
Feffer and Simons, Inc., London
Manufactured in the United States of America

Library of Congress Cataloging in Publication Data

Pérez, Louis A., 1943–
   Cuba between empires, 1878–1902.

   (Pitt Latin American series)
   Bibliography: p. 449
   Includes Index.
   1. Cuba—History—1878–1895.   2. Cuba—History—Revolution,
1895–1898.   3. Cuba—History—1899–1906.   I. Title.
II. Series.
F1785.P47   1982   972.91′06   82–11059
ISBN 0–8229–3472–8

For Amara and Maya

Do tell my children please, in black on white,
that once, when I was young and close to them,
I loved them as a god must love his fantasies
and laid my hands upon them while they slept,
willing my love to fashion in my hands
such rainbow sprays of covenanted time
as reached one season when, flower-like, they wilted
into the . . . women who do not know me.

—Nathaniel Tarn

Contents

Acknowledgments

The completion of this manuscript has provided moments to reflect back on nearly a decade of research and writing—moments given unabashedly to nostalgic retrospection and detached introspection. I recall many years ago, in one of my first research seminars, the late Professor Russell C. Ewing warning the new and uninitiated graduate students that the enterprise of history was very much a solitary endeavor. There is, I have learned in the intervening years, considerable truth to this observation. But I have come to appreciate more the extent to which the pursuit of the past draws on the resources, talents, and wisdom of others. The completion of this book leaves me very much in the debt of friends and colleagues, individuals upon whose professional assistance, scholarly counsel, and moral subsidy I came to depend. This enterprise of scholarship is, in the end, truly a collaborative undertaking.

In the course of this research I received complete cooperation from a number of libraries and archives. I am especially mindful of the courtesy and assistance provided by the staffs of the National Archives, the Library of Congress, the New York Public Library, the Alabama Department of Archives and Records, the Pennsylvania Historical Society, and the University of Florida Library. I owe a special dept to María A. Lastayo and her staff at the Biblioteca Nacional "José Martí" in Havana. Vital bibliographic materials otherwise unavailable to me originated from that cluttered second floor office of the Biblioteca Nacional.

Most of all, I owe an enormous debt to the staff of the University of South Florida Library. From Donna M. Asbell, Julia L. Schwartz, and Dorothy N. Tiemann I received unflagging cooperation. On many occasions they rescued me from aimless and time-consuming wanderings through labyrinthine stacks of government serials. My debt to Mary Kay Hartung and Florence Jandreau is not repaid here—it is simply acknowledged. My appreciation of the importance of their assistance has deepened over the years. Much of the research for this study would have been impossible to complete without their help. No amount of appreciation can return to them their contribution.

It becomes necessary, also, to acknowledge the enormity of my debt to Michael G. Copeland, Lucia Grimaldi, Gregg B. Gronlund, Marian E. Pittman, and Cecile L. Pulin—but most especially to Robin L. Kester, who with great attention to detail and passion for perfection presided over the **xi**

xii **Acknowledgments**

final draft of the manuscript. They all suffered in stoic silence (and some-times not so silently!) countless drafts of this manuscript—again, again, and again. My appreciation of their efforts on my behalf is most heartfelt. Without them I would still be hopelessly struggling somewhere between the first and second draft.

A special debt of gratitude is owned to Peggy Cornett, who occupied the front trenches of the Department during the period in which the manu-script was undergoing final revisions. A special thanks is due to Travis J. Northcutt, Jr., and Susan M. Stoudinger who between 1977 and 1980 pro-vided the support and contributed to creating the environment that made the final writing of this book possible.

I am especially grateful to the American Philosophical Society for a grant that allowed me to complete the final research for this study. I am indebted, too, to the Office of Sponsored Research under A. Riley Macon at the University of South Florida for support in the form of a Research and Creative Scholarship Grant.

These past years have allowed me to share with friends and colleagues the ideas developed in the forthcoming pages. Since this book has been so long in preparation, drafts of the manuscript and chapters thereof have circulated frequently and in various stages of completion. Cecil B. Currey, Sue Fernández, and Robert P. Ingalls offered helpful advice on various portions of the manuscript. George H. Mayer read an early draft of the complete study and found many soft areas where my enthusiasm exceeded my evidence. The gentility of his criticism and the erudition of his argu-ments made subsequent reconsideration of my own case a valuable under-taking. Jorge I. Domínguez read a later draft of the manuscript and pro-vided many thoughtful suggestions. I owe a large debt of gratitude to Thomas P. Dilkes, a friend and colleague, who read the completed manu-script and offered suggestions and advice. In the course of those many glorious Florida days we spent together along the Gulf, he passed more time sharpening my arguments than improving his fishing. I also owe much to Steven F. Lawson, a friend and selfless collaborator, who a long time ago believed in the premises that inspired this book and who, from those early research trips together, provided continual support and encouragement. He has been a sympathetic listener and a critical reader. He offered in-sightful comments and constructive advice at every stage of research and writing.

The aforementioned individuals provided gratifying response to and stimulation for many of the arguments that follow. At times their disagreements forced me to reconsider particular formulations and rework ambiguous constructions. They picked up flaws, challenged dubious propositions, and saved me from egregious errors. Many of their comments no doubt emerge in modified form, with perhaps a different emphasis here and there, but nonetheless began as their thoughts. Not everyone has agreed with the propositions advanced in the pages that follow. Indeed, some have already conveyed their vigorous disagreement. Without their help, however, this book would not have taken the form it has. Their assistance is acknowledged with gratitude. Hard as they tried to eliminate the faults that may remain, and there were some mighty efforts, I did not heed their suggestions every time. Their sustained efforts on my behalf free them of any responsibility for particular statements and arguments that I have stubbornly refused to delete. And, of course, their generosity does not make them in any way responsible for whatever errors persist in the following pages.

There were, too, over the years, listeners—mostly good friends, of course, for upon whom else would one routinely inflict the desultory laments that are so much a part of this thing we call scholarship. They provided the love, moral nourishment, and understanding that reinforced my resolve and sustained my spirits. I realize now, with hindsight, how often I abused their forbearance. Though they did not participate directly in the preparation of this book, it is entirely possible that without them it would not have been completed. A special thanks to Etta Bender Breit, Stephanie Lawson, James W. Silver, and Brenda and G. Kelly Tipps. I am grateful, too, for the encouragement and affection of J.A. Domínguez and Ramón Pi y Castella. The knowledge that the faith can be kept for seventy years is a source of enduring comfort and recurring inspiration.

There is, finally, I have recently concluded, no mystery to completing a book. It simply involves diverting attention, moral resources, and commitment to the task of research and writing. But this is the stuff of love, too—the substance of parenting. This book is dedicated to my daughters, Amara and Maya, who sometimes unknowingly and often unwillingly gave up something of their future to my present study of some other past. In a very real sense, this is their book. They are correct in their expectation that things will now be different.

Tampa, Florida
March 1982

Introduction

I Cuban independence arrived as something of an anticlimax. On May 20, 1902, at noon, the American flag was lowered, the Cuban flag raised —a properly orchestrated and orderly inauguration of the new republic. But something had gone awry, Cubans sensed after 1902. Somehow the twentieth-century republican reality had fallen short of the nineteenth-century separatist ideal. It was not only that the Platt Amendment had compromised the integrity of the republic: it was more. Something else troubled the national mood. The outcome of the separatist enterprise was unequal to the magnitude of the effort. A default was in the making, a promise remained unkept. It was left to the mutterings of the old general in chief to give expression to Cuban disillusionment: "This is not the Republic we fought for," a crestfallen Máximo Gómez brooded in 1902, "it is not the absolute independence we dreamed about, but there is no gain in discussing that now. . . . What we must study with profound attention is the manner to save what remains of the redemptive Revolution."

II Decades earlier, the first of many summons had stirred Cubans to dramatic action. The call to revolution served as a recurring referendum of arms, periodic outbursts of rage registering Cuban inconformity with the Spanish colonial regime. The war launched on February 24, 1895, was a renewal of an earlier war, which was in turn a continuation of a previous conflict. In all, three decades of revolutionary activity, spanning the years between 1868 and 1898, involved two generations of Cubans in three major wars and, in between, a greater number of tentative starts and abortive endings. The Ten Years' War (1868–1878), known also as "La Guerra Grande," was the longest sustained separatist effort. "La Guerra Chiquita" (1879–1880) was among the shortest. They both failed.

The war of 1895 was different not only because it succeeded. It succeeded because it was different. Much had changed in Cuba between the "Grito de Yara" in 1868 and the "Grito de Baire" in 1895. Cuban society was different, more complex. Property relations and production modes were in transition. So were social relationships. Allegiances were in flux. The pull of geography had finally overcome traditional ties of colonialism as the United States replaced Spain as Cuba's principal trade partner and primary guarantor of the status quo. And in 1895, discontent with that status quo was everywhere on the increase.

It was inevitable that the "Grito de Baire" would be different from its predecessors. Cuba had changed, and the sources of Cuban grievances no longer emanated exclusively from the rule of the distant metropolis. By the late nineteenth century, Spain was neither the primary nor the principal beneficiary of empire. Madrid would strain to preserve the island not so much for colonial profits as for national pride.

The principal beneficiaries of empire were local elites, Creole and *peninsular* (Spaniard) alike, whose privileged position in Cuban society was also becoming increasingly anomalous and ambiguous. For decades colonial elites had relied on Spain for the suppression of social challenges to their political preeminence while counting on the United States for the expansion of the economic sources of their political power. Local elites found themselves between two metropolitan centers upon whom they relied for defense against colonial revolution. They feared social upheaval more than they opposed colonial rule, and they preferred security to change, not being willing to risk the loss of privilege to gain independence. What reforms elites did advocate were always conceived within the colonial framework. Politics in the colony may have pitted Creole reform against *peninsular* reaction, but both Creoles and *peninsulares* remained united in their preference for empire and defense of privilege.

It was perhaps inevitable that separatism would reflect the contradictions and the anomalous character of Cuban society in the late nineteenth century. The forces that coalesced around Cuba Libre in 1895 were extraordinarily diverse. The revolutionary enterprise was a coalition of Cubans who shared one—and often, only one—sentiment: a consuming desire to end Spanish rule. But even the sources of this common purpose were varied. Cubans embarked on their mission with a mixture of motives, a conflict of interests, and a diversity of objectives. Some were annexationists, some were *independentistas*. Some wanted automomy, others wanted social revolution. Some wanted a new country, others a new society. Patricians joined with peasants; the proletariat collaborated with the bourgeoisie; black officers commanded white troops; socialists and capitalists, anarchists and liberals shared positions of leadership; and all rallied around this mystical sentiment called Cuba Libre.

Cuban separatism was many things to many people, and these differences acquired institutional form early in the war. Conservative separatists, principally annexationists and those who advocated a protectorate status for Cuba, served the cause of Cuba Libre abroad, in the Cuban Revolutionary party (PRC) and patriotic juntas in the United

States, Europe, and Latin America. *Independentismo* flourished in the armed camps of Cuba Libre.

But armed separatism was more than independence, for it subsumed a social imperative into its vision of a free Cuba. Inequity in Cuba in 1895 had a peculiarly home-grown quality. That the sources of oppression in Cuba were more internal than external, more social than political, served as the premises around which armed separatism took shape in the 1880s and 1890s. Not that these developments were entirely new; they had always been elements of the Cuban insurrectionary tradition of the nineteenth century. What was different in 1895 was the recognition that inequity was not caused principally by Spanish colonial rule, for which independence was the obvious panacea, but, rather, was the effect of the Cuban social system, for which the only remedy was a transformation of Cuban society. After 1895, Cubans continued to speak of independence, but they spoke also of the war as a method of redemption and a means of social revolution. Political separatism had expanded into revolutionary populism, committed as much to ending colonial relationships within the colony as to ending colonial connections with the metropolis.

III Diversity was the insurrection's principal source of strength. It sustained Cuban resolve. For the duration of the war it was enough that all Cubans agreed on the necessity to separate from Spain. But diversity was also the revolution's principal weakness. The mixed social origins of Cuban separatism gave rise to divisive political conflicts. Ambiguity of purpose produced an ambivalence in policy. Leadership fragmented. In the end, the institutional agencies around which the forces of Cuba Libre had organized were more competitive than complementary, and the only real unifying bond was the will to wage war against Spain.

The will to wage war served Cubans well and in the end carried them to victory over Spain. By the time the United States decided to intervene militarily, the outcome of the war was predictable: Spain was defeated and doomed. But the separatist triumph produced not Cuban independence but American intervention. Once local elites were convinced that Spain could no longer guarantee privilege and property, they were prepared to shed traditional colonial relationships. The call for American intervention came loudest from the representatives of a beleaguered social order on the verge of collapse; elites, Spaniards and Creoles alike, appealed to the United States for salvation against the revolution.

Once the war against Spain was over, the Cuban coalition collapsed.

Contradictions surfaced, conflict ensued, and consensus ended. The forces of Cuban separatism were thrown into disarray and confusion. Cuba Libre spoke with too many voices, and the sounds were unintelligible, the message garbled. Americans chose to listen selectively. Divided, exhausted, and impoverished, the revolutionary coalition came apart. The United States skillfully exploited these conditions, and while the American intervention may have exacerbated the contradictions within the separatist polity, it did not create them. What was remarkable about developments after 1898 was the absence of anything like organized resistance to the United States. A revolutionary movement, for three decades devoted to armed struggle as a means of national liberation, did not challenge the American presence in Cuba. In the end, Cuban separatism collapsed as much from overweighing internal contradiction as from overwhelming external forces.

IV   Far from stumbling into war against Spain, the United States followed a policy that was shrewd, purposeful, and calculated. American policy was directed as much against Cuban independence as it was against Spanish sovereignty: 1898 was a climax to a hundred years of policy. For almost a century, the United States had covetously pursued the acquisition of Cuba. The proposition that Washington would suddenly renounce annexation in 1898 is untenable. In fact, it did not. Rather, the specific circumstances under which the American intervention in 1898 unfolded —both in Cuba and the United States—required new ways to achieve old objectives.

For almost four years, between 1898 and 1902, the United States militarily occupied Cuba, officially to discharge the terms of the Teller Amendment, ostensibly for the purpose of preparing Cuba for independence. But other objectives guided its policy toward quite a different direction; the organization of self-government in Cuba was not a means to promote sovereignty but a way to advance annexation. The military occupation was not preparation for independence but the prelude to annexation. The vast resources and authority of the military government were mobilized for this end. The intervention in 1898 blocked the ascendancy of the Cuban revolutionary forces and preserved intact the prevailing social order. The military occupation between 1898 and 1902 created a national system designed to promote dependency and ultimately facilitate annexation. No aspect of Cuban society was spared in this endeavor. Pro-American political parties were organized; elites who earlier had depended on Spain to guarantee their positions of privilege transferred their allegiance to the United States; a colonial army was created; the national economy was restructured around one export product for one market. And under the auspices of the military government, an annexationist naturalized American citizen was elected as Cuba's first president.

V For decades the Cuban insurrection of 1895 has been viewed as simply the last in a series of New World rebellions in which disgruntled colonial subjects resorted to arms to end European colonial rule. This schema stressed the standard causal factors as precipitants of the Cuban insurrection, including the traditional Creole-*peninsular* schism, the excesses of Spanish colonial administration, and the presentiment of nationality. Focus centered principally on the political aspects of Cuban separatism, chief among which figured the goal of independence. With independence identified as the purpose of Cuban arms, the objectives of the war seemed rather self-evident and fulfilled. The Cuban struggle acquired a one-dimensional form, seemingly conventional in its objectives and successful in its purpose: the last of the nineteenth-century wars for independence in Latin America.

But Cuban separatism was possessed of more than a desire for nationhood. It was not the last of a kind but the precursor of a genre: a guerrilla war of national liberation aspiring to the transformation of society. The Cuban insurrection had more in common with the Mexican revolution fifteen years later than it did with the South American wars for independence seventy-five years earlier. Independence served as the cutting edge of separatist politics, a purpose that found universal endorsement among the diverse social groupings that had organized around Cuba Libre. But the vision went beyond free Cuba, for independence was a means, not an end. Cuba Libre contained elements of anti-imperialism, political radicalism, agrarian reform, racial equality, and social justice.

This was Cuba's first revolution, one crushed by American military intervention. There were portents in these developments, for it would not be the last time the Cuban revolutionary impulse would be thwarted by the United States.

The experience of 1895–1898 cast a long shadow across twentieth-century Cuba and left a legacy of expectations unfulfilled and promises unkept. The revolutionary endeavor of 1895–1898 remained unfinished and incomplete. Cubans had been summoned to dramatic action but failed to produce dramatic change. What remained of the "redemptive Revolution," to return to Máximo Gómez's lament, was the ideal, and the ideal was so indelibly impressed on the collective Cuban consciousness that it would serve the same function in the twentieth century that it had in the nineteenth: the call to revolution. Out of the frustration and dashed hopes of 1898 were released the forces that would give structure and substance to Cuban politics for the next sixty years. The political labor of the next three generations of Cubans would be devoted to redeeming the "redemptive Revolution."

CUBA BETWEEN EMPIRES, 1878–1902

1 The Fateful Interlude

The general feeling is that no remedy or relief is possible, except through annexation to the United States. They might prefer it, for there is no particular love for the United States in Cuba. The desire for annexation is purely selfish . . . but . . . in the fullness of time, when Cuba and Spain and we should all be of one mind—without discussion, or revolution, or war,—Cuba would doubtless be added to the Union.
—Adam Badeu, U.S. Consul, Havana, 1833

The country does not have, as it ought to have with the struggle so close upon us, a unification plan to unite it, and a political program to allay its fears. Cuba's resolve to fight will be far stronger than it is today, and the revolutionary work much easier, when the enemies of the revolution can no longer uphold—as they are now doing for lack of expressed declarations against it—the argument that the war will be nothing but an arena for the hatreds and ambitions of rival military leaders.
—José Martí, 1887

I A gentle rain mourned the dawn. Few Cubans gathered at an abandoned farm at Zanjón found more than fleeting comfort in the symbolic gesture of divine commiseration. The ill-fated events scheduled for the morning of February 10, 1878, placed most Cubans assembling in Camagüey province beyond the reach of any expression of consolation—whatever its origins.

Some ten years earlier, not too distant from Zanjón, many of the very same Cubans had unfurled the banner of rebellion against Spain. But a war launched with national objectives failed to move beyond provincial operations. At no time in the course of the Ten Years' War did insurgent Cubans manage to sustain a drive much beyond the eastern third of the island. Insurgent armies remained effectively contained east of Spanish military fortifications constructed along the Júcaro-Morón *trocha*, (a fortified military trench), there falling prey to internal conflict and strife. A rebellion of such long duration, patently meager in insurgent successes, quickly turned on itself with disastrous consequences for the separatist cause. Recurring military-civilian disputes, racial tensions, and regionalism wracked the insurgent movement. By the end of the decade, desertions, defections, and the depletion of morale dealt the final body blows to the separatist effort. Almost ten years after the euphoric "Grito de Yara," prostrate insurgent forces succumbed easily to the newly arrived Spanish military reinforcements under General Arsenio Martínez Campos.[1]

The arrival of the Cuban peace delegation to Zanjón on the morning of February 10, 1878, served simply to signify the formal, if only ceremonial, acknowledgment of the failure of insurgent arms. After a decade of conflict, disheartened insurgent leaders accepted Spanish peace terms as the most honorable arrangement through which to extricate themselves from a cause hopelessly doomed to failure. By the terms of the Pact of Zanjón, Spain pledged to institute a wide range of administrative and political reforms. A general amnesty pardoned insurgent Cubans and guaranteed unconditional freedom to all African slaves and Asian indentured workers registered in the ranks of the Liberation Army in February 1878.[2] An exchange of signatures and an exchange of salutes brought the conference to a close and the war to an end.

But not all separatist chieftains concurred with either the decision to surrender at Zanjón or the terms of the peace. Meager concessions for such a mighty effort, some Cubans said bitterly. The Pact of Zanjón generated as much dissension among Cubans in arms as any other single issue in the decade-long war. The more intransigent separatists rejected outright any peace settlement that sanctioned the continued presence of Spanish au-

4

thority in Cuba. For other *insurrecto* chieftains, a formal peace pact that confined the emancipation to only those African slaves formally enrolled in separatist armies fell far short of satisfying a central and long-standing insurgent demand for the complete abolition of slavery.

Many ranking insurgent chieftains denounced the Zanjón settlement. News of Zanjón reached General Ramón Leocadio Bonachea on field operations in the western extremity of Camagüey. Bonachea ignored the peace settlement and defiantly continued his westward advance into Las Villas province. In the southeastern Oriente village of Baraguá, General Antonio Maceo assembled the 1,500 officers and men under his command to repudiate publicly the peace protocol and renew the insurgent commitment to armed struggle. In March 1878 a new provisional government, committed to continued fighting, was organized around the irreconcilable elements of the separatist movement.[3] And for ten more weeks the Ten Years' War continued.

This renewed commitment to arms after Zanjón, Cubans knew, was more symbolic than substantive: a demarcation so they would know where to begin the next time. By May, weakened by deaths and desertions and wholly reduced to desultory operations in scattered pockets of territory in the remote eastern interior, the armed protesters of Baraguá, too, grudgingly made their peace with Spain and left Cuba.

II   Until the Ten Years' War, Spain had administered Cuba as an overseas territory, principally for the benefit of metropolitan society. In the colony there had been little significant and less sustained political activity. Administration prevailed in the place of politics. If problems were recognized it was for—not by—the island population; attempts to resolve - colonial questions came from above and abroad. Outside of an occasional and short-lived armed protest, a general consensus had prevailed on both the premises and propriety of this arrangement—until the Ten Years' War.

Between 1868 and 1878, Madrid confronted in Cuba the longest and most serious challenge to Spanish colonial rule since the South American wars for independence fifty years earlier. The Peace of Zanjón, to be sure, ended the revolutionary challenge, but only after Madrid had agreed to concede reforms and sanction colonial politics. The war had forced Spain to renounce the principle of metropolitan absolutism; the Pact of Zanjón provided the standard against which to measure the performance of Spanish administration.

The Ten Years' War released political forces that survived long after the insurgent armies of Yara had abandoned the field. Even as separatist arms faltered in 1878, the question of Cuba's future political status and its relationship to Spain became the subject of intense public debate well beyond the confines of the war zones of the eastern provinces. Politics in post-Zanjón Cuba organized around the central questions raised by the separatist war. The failure of insurgent arms and the subsequent departure of the most ardent separatists did not quiet the central political issues. On the contrary, a decade of armed struggle had catapulted both the objectives of the separatist war and their means onto the central arena of Cuban politics. The abeyance of the armed expression of Cuban separatism after Zanjón and the end of the extralegal challenge to Spanish authority, followed by the exodus of the most intransigent advocates of Cuba Libre, only eliminated the most untenable proposition of the separatist dispute from political consideration—Cuba's complete and immediate independence from Spain.

After Zanjón, the issues of Cuba's future political status surfaced in established and prescribed political forums. Lest Spanish intransigence again drive advocates of change to the outer fringes of legality and into armed rebellion, the issue of reform acquired legitimacy and centrality in an arena of sanctioned political debate. In the Pact of Zanjón, Spain sought reconciliation with the rebellious colony in a spirit of reform and compromise, committing itself to an institutional resolution of outstanding colonial grievances. Zanjón represented Spain's attempt to renew the imperial lease over the colony by offering colonial reforms to Creole dissidents and promising political participation to Creole loyalists. The unsuccessful revolution made reform possible.

Politics in Cuba after 1878 organized around the prospects and promise of Zanjón. Preparations for the 1878 municipal elections and the selection of forty Cuban representatives to the Spanish parliament as outlined in the peace settlement immediately established the political delineations emerging in postwar Cuba. Zanjón served as the summons to politics for Creole planters, an opportunity to step into the colonial breach and assert leadership over the shattered colonial polity. Metropolitan policies had driven the colony into rebellion, but rebellion had failed to expel the metropolis. Neither revolution nor reaction proved capable of resolving colonial grievances. Zanjón created the conditions for a third alternative—reformism. Planters did not hesitate: not that planters were immune from the appeals of *cubanidad*, and indeed, some believed that it could be fulfilled through an independent nationality. Most, however, believed that its fulfillment could be best guaranteed within the existing, albeit modified, structures of empire.

Thus it was that the first political party to organize after Zanjón embodied the reformist principles long associated with the Creole planter elite. Established in July 1878, the new Liberal party (Autonomist) proclaimed its commitment to actualizing the promises of Zanjón and offered advocates of reform a sanctioned institutional structure within which to pursue the transformation of the colonial regime.[4]

In its charter manifesto published on August 1, 1878, the party outlined the bases of its political, social, and economic program. On the matter of political reform, the manifesto demanded immediate equal rights for Cubans under the Spanish constitution of 1876, the uniformity of *peninsular* laws for all the constituent components of Spain, and the separation of military and political authority in Cuba.[5] On a long-term basis, Autonomists advocated preserving the structure of empire with Cuba in full possession of local institutions leading to self-government.[6] On social issues, liberals supported the gradual abolition of African slavery with indemnification to the planters and the organization of an apprenticeship system for former slaves. The party urged an increase in the white population of the island through unrestricted family immigration and the abolition of all restrictions of white immigration to Cuba. In economic matters, Autonomists advocated far-ranging reform proposals, including the abolition of all duties on Cuban exports, tariff reforms, reduction of Spanish custom fees, and the negotiation of commercial treaties with foreign countries, principally the United States, on the basis of reciprocal tariff reductions.[7]

Early strength of the new party, and ultimately the Autonomist constituency, consisted of *hacendados* (landowners), planters, and professionals—Creoles anxious to steer a course between the uninspired colonial policies of the metropolis and the uncertainties associated with complete separation from Spain. These were the Creole elites, drawn to colonial politics as a result of separatist excesses and metropolitan abuses; this was the Cuban aristocracy, men who presided over Cuba's principal economic institutions, including the Círculo de Hacendados y Agricultores, Centro de Propietarios, Círculo de Abogados, and the prestigious Sociedad Económica de Amigos del País, Cubans who placed their considerable wealth and prestige at the service of reformist politics. The Autonomist party offered Creoles the opportunity to gain political power in pursuit of the reforms promised at Zanjón.

Membership in the Autonomist party was not, however, confined to Creole planters. The reformist banner also attracted the support of liberal sectors of the *peninsular* community in Cuba, Spaniards for whom reform offered the only means through which to preserve empire by a reconciliation of the rebellious colony with the refractory metropolis. Prominent liberal *peninsulares*, men like journalist Manuel Pérez de Molina and property owner Ricardo del Monte, enrolled in Autonomist ranks in the belief that reformism offered the most promising if not the only solution to the colonial problem.

Autonomism also attracted the conservative wing of the separatist polity. The bitter experience of the Ten Years' War persuaded many *insurrecto* veterans of the futility of further appeals to arms. Indeed, for these insurgent leaders the peace of 1878 signaled the bankruptcy of the armed strategy. Disillusioned separatists saw in autonomism the means to achieve peacefully—if admittedly only in modified form and on a gradual basis—the objectives that had eluded them during the Ten Years' War. For conservative separatists, principally those with origins in the Creole planter elite, the failure of Cuban arms in 1878 offered no reasonable alternative to the pursuit of reform within the newly sanctioned arena of political competition.[8] Many of the most prestigious leaders of the unsuccessful insurrection abandoned separatist ranks to embrace autonomism, including José María Gálvez, one of the original conspirators of 1868, Miguel Bravo y Sentiés, formerly secretary of foreign relations in the insurgent provisional government, Emilio Luaces, a member of the separatist junta that negotiated the settlement of Zanjón, and Juan Spotorno, formerly the president of the insurgent provisional republic.

But the enrollment of dissident Cubans and loyal Spaniards into the ranks of the Autonomist party did not announce the emergence of a new colonial consensus. Nor did it signal the triumph of planter leadership. On the contrary, it served to deepen the divisions in the colony and open new political fronts of an old war.

Reformism split separatist ranks, dividing the veterans of 1868 into two distinct groups. Autonomism served to fix institutionally the ill-defined division shattering the separatist consensus after Zanjón—between those veterans, on one hand, who, heartened by the terms of the peace settlement, remained in Cuba to seek fulfillment of the separatist agenda within the autonomist program (legal) and those veterans, on the other, who, unreconciled to the post-Zanjón order, chose expatriation to prepare for a renewal of the armed struggle (extralegal).[9] It was in this process, too, that Cuban separatism lost its affiliation with and became disassociated from the island's traditional Creole elites, who after Zanjón found autonomism considerably more convivial to their ideological temperament, if not to their class interests.

If the Pact of Zanjón precipitated a rupture within separatist ranks, the emergence of a liberal reformist party in the aftermath of the 1878 peace settlement shattered the loyalist consensus. For the better part of the Ten Years' War, Spanish sentiment in Cuba remained uncommonly united around steadfast opposition to the central tenets advanced by the separatists in arms. The inadmissibility of the separatist objectives, including the abolition of slavery and the independence of the island, together with the singleness of purpose occasioned by the war, shaped the conservative community in Cuba into an uncompromising and unyielding upholder of permanent Spanish sovereignty.

The Pact of Zanjón contributed as much to shattering the *peninsular* consensus as it did to disrupting the separatist unity. The failure of insurgent arms and the repudiation of the most untenable separatist objectives after Zanjón led to a relaxation of the wartime *peninsular* solidarity. Indeed, the restoration of peace encouraged Spaniards and their Creole allies to reexamine, with disinterest and dispassion, the colonial policies that had led to Yara. The willingness, too, of key insurgent leaders to come to terms with Spanish reformers encouraged many *peninsulares* to seek some type of reconciliation with the more moderate representatives of the abortive separatist cause.

Debate over the most efficacious means through which to guarantee the survival of Spanish sovereignty over Cuba divided the *peninsular* community on the island. Within a year of Zanjón, Martínez Campos's emphasis on reform and the subsequent emergence of a liberal party dedicated to the pursuit of comprehensive colonial change aroused a mixture of rancor and resentment among the most intransigent supporters of Spanish authority in Cuba. Having defeated the insurgent armies in the field, Spaniards were ill-disposed to support a policy of reconciliation that involved granting in peace concessions opposed during war. Few were prepared and fewer predisposed to compromise in any form with representatives of the rebellious colony. Quite the contrary. By the end of the 1870s, many resident *peninsulares* had emerged as uncompromising advocates of stronger metropolitan authority in Cuba. The conciliatory tenor of Zanjón and the subsequent organization of the Autonomist party offended the sensibilities of those *peninsulares* for whom victory over the rebellious Cubans in 1878 announced only the prelude to a harsher regimen of metropolitan authority and a rigorous reaffirmation of Spanish sovereignty. Never fully trusting their liberal compatriots, Spanish conservatives viewed the new Liberal party with no small horror and no less amount of misgiving and mistrust. The organization of the Autonomist party, joining liberal Spaniards with Cuban Creoles and former separatist leaders in the pursuit of reforms, aroused the fear among many conservatives that the extralegal dispute of the previous decade had found a spurious if not sinister legality in post-Zanjón Cuba. The large number of former insurgent chieftains enrolling in the ranks of the new party served to confirm the conservatives' worst fears. Indeed, the new party was seen as little more than a legal political fiction behind which lurked the malevolent force of Cuban separatism.

Peninsular reaction to autonomism was not long in coming. Nor was it equivocal. In the autumn of 1878, the conservative response to liberal reformism gave post-Zanjón Cuba its second political party—the Partido Unión Constitucional. Unabashedly metropolitan in its sympathies, overwhelmingly *peninsular* in its composition, the Unión Constitucional attracted to its ranks the most ardent advocates of "Cuba española." Into the ranks of the new party flocked conservative *peninsularss*, most notably former officers who had served Spain in the Corps of Volunteers during the Ten Years' War and whose dedication to "Cuba española" was at once deepened and consecrated by blood spilled in the defense of Spanish sovereignty against Cuban separatism. Distributed in Havana and throughout the larger provincial cities of the interior, this intransigent *peninsular* party organized its constituency around merchants, businessmen, traders, and members of the professions as well as government employees at the colonial, provincial, and municipal levels. Wealthy and influential industrialists, moreover, together with financiers, importers, and exporters, found in the Unión Constitucional a cause worthy of their allegiance and support. *Peninsular* sugar magnates and powerful *hacendados*, men like José Eugenio Mora and the Marquis de Apezteguía, provided leadership and financial subsidy.

The Unión Constitucional sought, in clearly defined and categorically stated terms, both the preservation and regeneration of Spanish authority in Cuba. Like their Autonomist counterparts, Unionists advocatd uniform laws and the expansion of commercial relations with the United States. Unlike the Autonomists, the Unión Constitucional sought these changes without assimilationist objectives; Cuba was to continue as a colonial entity, subservient to and for the benefit of metropolitan interests.

Whatever else may have separated the two new political parties in post-Zanjón Cuba, they shared two central and reciprocally binding premises. Representatives of both the Autonomist party and the Unión Constitucional rejected outright the means and the objectives of the insurgent separatists. An appeal to arms was as unacceptable as Cuba Libre was unthinkable. Second, and closely related, both parties accepted the legitimacy of the Spanish colonial regime and the desirability of empire as the central and unchallenged tenets of colonial politics. For Autonomists, reforms were the best guarantees of empire; for Unionists, empire was the best guarantee against revolution.

III Excluded from the new political alignments in post-Zanjón Cuba were the irreconcilable veterans of the Ten Years' War. Indisposed to accept the implied finality of Zanjón, many insurgent Cubans chose expatriation as an alternative preferable to submitting to continued Spanish rule. The Ten Years' War had permanently changed the character of Cuban separatism. There could be no reconciliation with Spain, there would be no compromise of the ideal of independence. Exile attracted the most irreconcilable members of the separatist polity. An expatriate community acquired its definitive character around the central proposition that reconciliation with Spain on any basis other than independence was unacceptable and that independence through any means other than arms was unattainable. Separatist sentiment remained intact abroad, a vigorous force immune from the compromise associated with political affiliations in the post-Zanjón colonial regime. The ranks of exiled separatists were held together by a persisting vision of Cuba Libre and an enduring commitment to armed struggle. In émigré centers abroad, the ideal of Cuba Libre endured and received its earliest institutional expression in the form of expatriate revolutionary clubs and patriotic juntas. Throughout exile communities in Latin America, Europe, and the United States, patriotic associations nurtured the notion of a free homeland. Expatriation was a political statement, at once a rejection of the surrender at Zanjón and a reaffirmation of the sentiment of Yara. But in 1878 no one envisioned anything more than a short exile, a momentary pause abroad during which the patriots prepared for their return and the renewal of the armed struggle. Unrepentant, unyielding in their conviction that Zanjón represented only a truce, expatriate separatists refused to renounce armed struggle as the means of securing Cuba's independence from Spain. Indeed, their very presence abroad signified a singular inconformity with the post-Zanjón regime in Cuba and a persistent commitment to arms. No tenet was so central to separatist sentiment after Zanjón as the belief that a new war of liberation was as imminent as it was inevitable.[10]

Nor were separatist expectations unfounded. Only months after Zanjón, separatist leaders abroad completed plans for a new war. In early 1879 veteran General Calixto García organized expatriate separatists into the Cuban Revolutionary Committee of New York and prepared for a new uprising. Several months later, García returned to Cuba at the head of an expeditionary force. "La Guerra Chiquita," as the short-lived war of 1879–1880 became known, fell prey immediately to many of the mishaps and misfortunes that had frustrated the separatist effort a decade earlier. Veterans returned to Cuba only to find anticipated local support nonexistent. Important conspiratorial centers in Camagüey and Oriente had been uncovered well before the exiled military chieftains had arrived in Cuba. The communication network among coordinating centers of separatist activity collapsed. Racism again shattered the separatist consensus when General Antonio Maceo, earlier promised command of the eastern army corps, was passed over for fear that the presence of a black general at the head of the Liberation Army would discourage support of whites in the west. The political infrastructure in exile, moreover, lacking both organization and leadership, failed to support the military venture adequately.[11]

Military disarray in Cuba and civilian disunity abroad sealed the fate of "La Guerra Chiquita." By August 1879, only weeks after his arrival to Cuba, Calixto García fell captive to Spanish military authorities. Pursued by superior enemy forces, without support within Cuba, and lacking supplies from abroad, insurgent chieftains in the field again made peace with Spanish authorities and, once more, returned to exile to prepare for the next war.

The setbacks of the Ten Years' War and "La Guerra Chiquita" had not been without their lasting impact. Two successive military failures had dealt body blows to expatriate morale. For many exiled patriots, the patently meager accomplishments of insurgent arms offered little basis on which to sustain reasonable optimism for the immediate success of Cuba Libre. At times peace produced as much if not more rancor and dissent among separatists than the differences during the war. Recrimination swept through expatriate communities as exiles sought to fix the responsibility for the failures and reversals of the previous decade; the dispute wracked separatist ranks in exile and served as a measure of the depth of despondency and demoralization developing within the separatist polity abroad.[12]

Few saw more clearly the prevailing disorganization settling over the separatist movement than the young writer in exile José Martí. Born in Havana in 1853, Martí entered separatist politics modestly enough. Anti-Spanish statements in Cuba during the Ten Years' War had led to his arrest and exile to Spain in 1871. During the better part of the next decade, Martí traveled throughout Europe, Latin America, and the United States. In January 1880, he arrived in New York and immediately volunteered his services to the Cuban Revolutionary Committee during "La Guerra Chiquita." Irresistible in his rhetoric, compelling in his prose, Martí quickly distinguished himself as the outstanding propagandist of the ill-starred separatist war of 1879–1880. Even before the conflict had come to its infelicitous end, Martí had assumed interim presidency of the committee and had emerged as a central force among separatists exiled in the United States.[13]

Martí drew the correct lessons from the Ten Years' War and "La Guerra Chiquita." Cuban separatists were ill prepared to mount, much less sustain, a successful drive for independence. Both wars revealed the most exposed frailties and contradictions of separatist politics, symptomatic of larger problems that ran the full depth and breadth of the patriotic movement. Martí was convinced that the sources of Cuban failures in the past were to be found within the separatist movement itself, most notably in the lack of political organization through which to promote the purposes of separatist arms. A "war of massive effort," Martí wrote in retrospect about the Ten Years' War, was "lost only through a lack of preparation and unity."[14] The struggle for Cuban independence could not be based on quixotic military adventures organized around well-meaning and dedicated men and women who believed that justice and virtue were sufficient reasons to expect the triumph of Cuban arms. "The revolution," Martí insisted in 1882, "is not merely a passionate outburst of integrity, or the gratification of a need to fight or exercise power, but rather a detailed understanding dependent on advanced planning and great foresight."[15] Cuban independence, Martí argued, was a process, not an event—a process in which final victory would proceed from patient preparation, dedicated organization, and enduring commitment. By 1880, two heroic but ill-conceived attempts at independence had taken an enormous toll on separatist lives, treasure, and morale.[16] Further vindication of Martí's contention was not long in coming. In 1883, veteran General Leocadio Bonachea led his followers into a disastrous uprising in Oriente. Two years later, a short-lived rebellion under Generals Limbano Sánchez and Panchín Varona met a similar fate.

Instead of healing the breaches among contending expatriate factions, Martí's arguments in the early 1880s had the net effect of deepening existing splits and opening new ones. Martí was a relative newcomer to separatist political forums, something of an outsider without a history of revolutionary affiliation. He had not participated directly in either the Ten Years' War or "La Guerra Chiquita," the moral fountainhead of separatist leadership.

But he had a following—enough of a following to justify his participation in preparations for a new war. In 1884, Martí met in New York for the first time with the two prestigious generals of the Ten Years' War, Antonio Maceo and the Dominican-born Máximo Gómez. Gómez unveiled plans for a new rebellion in Cuba—a scheme conceived wholly by the veteran military chieftains, organized entirely by army commanders, and directed solely by Commander in Chief Gómez. General Gómez's military autocracy, his intolerance if not unabashed scorn for civilian sensibilities in the decision-making process, and the arrogance with which he appropriated the direction of the separatist struggle had a sobering impact on Martí.

Martí's awe of the great generals turned quickly to horror. If the soldiers unilaterally ruled the struggle for nationhood, who could be expected to govern the nation? Martí had before him the infelicitous history of Spanish America—new republics in which caudillos, rapacious army chieftains, and military tyrants of all species had preyed on their countries after independence.

Days after his meeting with the generals, Martí denounced military preeminence within and army dominance over the separatist movement. The struggle for Cuban independence, Martí chided Gómez, was not his "exclusive property"; a republic was not founded in the manner of organizing a military camp. Martí returned again to the theme of organization and preparation, stressing the need to coordinate all sectors of Cuban society in and out of the island in order to insure ultimate success. Martí's denunciation of militaristic tendencies within the movement was categorical: "It is my determination not to contribute one iota . . . to the establishment in my land of a regime of personal despotism that would be more shameful and evil than the political despotism that currently exists."[17]

The Martí-Gómez split plunged the separatist polity into still deeper crisis. But it touched on considerably more than a conflict of personality or a struggle for power within the separatist movement. These were, to be sure, some of the unspoken issues of the 1884 controversy. In spurning the Gómez plan of action, however, Martí challenged the traditional and un-questioned military leadership and, in so doing, alienated many of the most prestigious military chieftains of previous separatist campaigns, including the ranking veterans of 1868 whose collaboration was essential to all future separatist strategies.[18] In a larger sense, the break between Martí and Gómez signified a rupture between Martí and the ranking hierarchy of the separatist movement in exile—a rather exclusive circle in which certification of membership was largely a function of participation in the Ten Years' War and "La Guerra Chiquita." Martí had scandalized the separatist establishment that was linked to the Dominican general by ties of sentiment, politics, and shared experiences; he had challenged the military monopoly on the separatist cause. By the late 1880s, the estrangement was all but complete. In the Dominican Republic, Gómez confided to his diary his dismay over Martí's apparent determination "to eliminate the military" from the separatist movement.[19] In 1888, General Flor Crombet, a close friend of Antonio Maceo, denounced Martí for his overly zealous *civilista* position.[20] Throughout the late 1880s, Martí fell victim to a propaganda campaign that condemned his posture as divisive and impugned his patriotism.[21]

The rupture of the mid-1880s also set off in relief tensions of a different sort developing within the separatist polity. More than twenty years had passed since the debate on Cuban separatism had first erupted into armed conflict in 1868. In the intervening years, the councils deliberating on the fate of Cuba Libre had become the exclusive domain of the veterans of 1868; access to these councils turned on previous service in arms. In many ways, Martí's dispute in the 1880s was as much a sign of generational conflict as it was of political disagreement. A generation of Cubans too young to have responded to the call of Yara, and Cubans born after October 10, 1868, in and out of Cuba, found few opportunities to participate in debates of the decade. The civil-military dispute contained a quarrel between the generation of 1868—military—and the post-Yara generation—civilian. Through political organization Martí hoped to offer the new generation of separatists an affiliation with a patriotic organization devoted to Cuba Libre, one that functioned in parallel fashion to membership in the Liberation Army. In 1891, Martí had found an apt allegory inspired by the Florida pine forests to give form to the new generation: "The sun suddenly broke through a clearing in the forest and there, in the dazzling of unexpected light, I saw above the yellowish grass rising around the black trunks of fallen pines, the flourishing branches of new pines. This is what we are: new pines."[22]

Censured, rebuked, and all but formally expelled from established separatist forums, Martí appealed directly to the expatriate separatist constituency as compensation for the lack of support from the exile leadership. From this point it was a logical and perhaps natural step for him to take the views repudiated by the established leadership directly to the rank and file. By the late 1880s, Martí's early emphasis on organization acquired new strategic urgency as he turned his attention away from attempts to unite the leadership to efforts to organize the rank and file.

For decades, Cuban communities in exile had labored faithfully in behalf of Cuba Libre. They had served as the wellspring of moral and material support into which the leadership had dipped freely in time of need. Indeed, for all practical purposes, civilian expatriates were expected solely to provide the funds to allow the military chieftains to pursue the war. And the leadership, despite the importance of the expatriates to separatist strategy, professed and real, had made little effort to build the institutional framework to integrate the far-flung exile communities into a structured separatist movement. Nor was there, in fact, any urgent need to do so. The very function of their exile made Cuban expatriates a captive constituency of the separatist leadership. Their support of Cuba Libre had been as unqualified as it had been uncomplaining.

For the better part of two decades, however, the idea of Cuba Libre had not moved beyond an essentially undefined and wholly ambiguous sentiment. The schism of the mid-1880s served at once as the cause and effect of a debate to define separatist issues in a manner that transcended factional politics. Martí found it necessary to initiate two simultaneous processes: a broadening of the social base of the movement and a reordering of the central separatist propositions. The first was a tactical necessity so he could appeal to the popular sector of the expatriate community. And the second would attract a following. Both required defining the ideological character of Cuban separatism and unifying program with praxis. It was simply inadequate, if not perhaps impolitic, for Martí to appeal for expatriate support on the basis of political credentials exclusively derived from his advocacy of Cuba Libre. The strength of his patriotic credentials was not enough to rival his detractors. Since the names of Máximo Gómez, Antonio Maceo, and Flor Crombet were virtually synonymous with Cuba Libre for the vast majority of Cubans in exile, he was forced to appeal to a wider cross section of exiles and to introduce broader issues into separatist politics. By the end of the 1880s, Martí had taken the first tentative steps toward giving ideological meaning and political organization to the mystic patriotic sentiment to which all separatists found themselves devoted.

By the early 1890s, Martí had discovered in Florida's cigarworkers' clubs and juntas a wellspring of patriotic sentiment with a distinct affinity for his version of Cuba Libre. Clearly the most radical sector of the expatriate centers in the United States, the proletarian communities of cigarworkers in Key West, Tampa, Ocala, and Jacksonville brought decades of labor militancy, political activism, and an enduring sense of *cubanidad* to the separatist cause.[23] Moreover the cigarworkers, long in the vanguard of the trade union movement in Cuba, brought organizational experience to Martí's political designs.[24]

In selecting the cigarworkers as the constituency around which to begin the organization of a political movement, Martí at once broadened the social base of Cuba Libre and introduced a conspicuous if only vaguely defined populist current into separatist ideology.[25] The separatist movement directed in the 1860s by slaveowning Creole patricians, revived in the 1890s under the impetus of an expatriate proletariat.

Martí had long understood the need to organize a revolutionary party. The party would serve as the principal unifying agent and provide a common set of objectives around which to organize all sectors of the independence movement—the army veterans of 1868 and the civilian separatists of the post-Yara generation, Cubans from the provinces of the east and west, Cubans who lived inside and outside Cuba, blacks and whites, and Cubans of all classes—brought together in one front of national liberation.[26]

By the early 1890s, Martí's efforts had reached fruition. In November 1891 in Tampa, Martí announced the "Resolutions" of a proposed political party, a statement defining the organizational basis around which the separatists would pursue the liberation of the homeland.[27] April 1892 marked the formal establishment of the Cuban Revolutionary party (PRC). The central goal of the PRC, Martí indicated, was to mount "common revolutionary action" to win Cuban independence. Indeed, the issue of unity continued to be of paramount importance to Martí. The new party represented first and foremost an attempt to organize all patriotic Cubans in one party for one purpose: the liberation of Cuba. The PRC renewed the traditional commitment to armed struggle and summoned all Cubans to participate. It was to unite Cubans in exile with patriots in Cuba for the common purpose of waging war for independence and provide the moral and material support in exile for the revolution in Cuba.[28] Martí had transformed a revolutionary movement into a revolutionary party, and by the end of 1892 the third post-Zanjón political party had taken definitive form.

IV   More than politics changed in the colony after Zanjón. It was not readily apparent in 1878, but the Ten Years' War announced the passing of an age. Colonialism had been shaken at its foundation—and survived, in a fashion. It was colonial society that was measurably different ten years after Yara; for the million and a half inhabitants of the island, life soon returned to normal, but it would never be the same.

The war spanned a changing era in Cuban history, and by the following decade that time of transition was coming to an end. The war had profoundly disrupted the island economy and, while everyone was hurt, Cuban planters were hurt more than most. Estates operating before the war on marginal profits and planters lacking either the finances or the foresight to modernize their mills were among the earliest casualties. Of the 41 mills operating around Sancti Spíritus in Las Villas province in 1861, only 3 survived the war. The 49 mills in Trinidad were reduced to 16. In Santa Clara, only 39 of 86 survived. The Cienfuegos mills were reduced from 107 to 77. In Güines, almost two-thirds of the 87 mills operating before the war had disappeared by 1877.[29]

The disruption of Cuban sugar production was particularly acute in the eastern provinces. Throughout the latter half of the nineteenth century, Oriente and Camagüey had remained impervious to the modernizing currents that had transformed the west into the bastion of the sugar latifundia. Sugar estates in the east, by comparison, were private family enterprises, without the capital reserve and technological resources of the west, and singularly incapable of participating in the modernization drive of the early nineteenth century. The sugar system in Oriente was backward and primitive. The estate in the east was more traditional than commerical, more family than corporate. Life on the *oriental* estates was turned inward, isolated, and largely self-contained, conferring on their owners more prestige than profits.

The Ten Years' War, during which the eastern provinces had served as the principal theater of military operations, had dealt a body blow to agriculture in that area. In some districts the collapse of sugar production was all but complete. None of the twenty-four mills in Bayamo and the eighteen mills in Manzanillo survived the war; the sixty-four mills of Holguín were reduced to four. Of the one hundred *ingenios* (mills) operating in the district of Santiago de Cuba in 1868, only thirty-nine resumed operations after Zanjón. In Puerto Príncipe, only one of a hundred survived the war.[30]

But the destruction wrought by the conflict went beyond sugar. No facet of agriculture in Oriente survived untouched:[31]

Date	Ingenios	Coffee Farms	Tobacco Farms	Livestock Farms	Other Small Ranches and Farms
1862	1,362	782	11,550	8,834	34,546
1887	1,191	192	4,515	3,172	17,906

Those estates fortunate enough to escape the ravages of the Ten Years' War survived only to discover capital scarce and credit dear. Prevailing rates of interest, fluctuating typically between 12 percent and 18 percent—with highs often as much as 30 percent not at all uncommon—foreclosed any possibility that local credit transactions would contribute significantly to the economic recovery of post-Zanjón Cuba.[32]

The war and the attending destruction of Cuban estates set the stage for the next series of afflictions to descend upon Cuban planters. Expansion of sugar cultivation elsewhere in the world, as a result of the disruption of Cuban cane production during the war and the subsequent decline of sugar exports, led to the development of new sources of competition. In the United States, new varieties of cane were introduced in Louisiana, while experimentation with beet sugar in the west and southwest expanded under the encouragement of state and federal governments. In 1876, sugar from Hawaii entered the U.S. market duty free. Responding to the opportunity created by faltering Cuban production, European beet sugar growers, protected and underwritten by government subsidies, made enormous strides between the late 1870s and early 1880s. Within a decade, France, Austria, and Germany had become the largest suppliers of sugar for the world market. Beet sugar, accounting in 1853 for only some 14 percent of the total world production, had by 1884 come to represent 53 percent of the international supply.[33] Even Spain was not immune to the lure of beet sugar profits. In 1882, two beet factories commenced operation in Granada and Córdoba; another two opened ten years later in Zaragoza and Aranjuez. Spanish beet production increased from 35,000 tons in 1883 to 400,000 in 1895.[34]

As planters prepared to resume production after Zanjón they discovered that they faced not only new competition and loss of old markets, but a precipitous decline in the value of their principal product and an increase in taxes. A rise in public spending during the 1870s to finance the cost of war and an increase in the circulation of paper money in the 1880s brought on the first of a series of devastating inflationary spirals. After Zanjón, Madrid transferred the war debt directly to Cuban producers and consumers. In 1884, the price of sugar plummeted to an unprecedented low, dropping from eleven cents a pound to an all-time low of eight. The collapse of sugar prices occurred at the precise moment Spain levied a series of harsh taxes on Cuban planters and just as they were trying to adapt to the abolition of slavery and the expiration of the *patronato*.[35] All at once, Cuban planters were hit with declining sugar prices, increased taxes, mounting debts, and shrinking markets. "Out of the twelve or thirteen hundred planters on the island," the American consul in Havana reported in early 1884, "not a dozen are said to be solvent."[36]

In 1883 the American vice-consul in Matanzas, David Vickers, wrote of "the impoverished condition of sugar" in central Cuba:

Through want of frugality and foresight and with enormous taxation, added to the competition of other sugar countries, the planter, to meet all demands, has discounted his crops at such ruinous rates of interest, piling mortgage upon mortgage, that to-day he finds himself irrevocably involved in debts equal to at least one year's excellent crop and in some instances much more. In the event of a poor crop, he would not have enough money either to pay current expenses or even to commence grinding his cane when the harvest begins, and no one to loan it to him.[37]

Beyond this, Vickers added, planters were forced to endure a crushing tax system. Heavy taxes assessed against agriculture and livestock, municipal taxes on land, sales taxes, transportation taxes, duties on imported equipment and food—"everything that the people eat comes from abroad," Vickers noted—threatened the planter class with extinction. The Cuban landowner, the vice-consul predicted, "is a man of determination and courage and will not submit to it much longer. At times his mutterings can be heard even above the tramp and bustle and pomp of the military occupant, and someday he will rise up in his might, and the Spanish functionary and his compadre—the military incumbent—will be hurled into the sea, and Cuba will go under a kind of temporary autonomy, which will end in its admission to the United States."[38]

Adversity after Zanjón affected all Cubans. Members of the Creole gentry who had opposed Spain during the Ten Years' War paid dearly for their separatist affiliation. The war provided *peninsulares* and their supporters with the opportunity to enlarge their property and expand their power at the expense of Creoles. Landowners who enrolled in separatist ranks or were suspected of separatist sympathies lost their property through a series of punitive expropriation decrees. The decline of sugar production in Oriente announced the collapse of the eastern planter class, a position that the traditional *oriental* elite would never recover. Many Creoles, further, lost administrative positions and public office for displaying insufficient ardor for the *peninsular* cause. Out of the ranks of the impoverished Creole planters and the displaced civil servants emerged an enduring constituency for Cuba Libre, while those who benefited from the expropriation of lands and jobs rushed to fill the party ranks of the Unión Constitucional.[39]

But Creole separatists were not the only Cubans to lose their property. Many small planters had resumed production after the war on a precarious footing. Heavily in debt, without capital to modernize, and lacking the resources to renovate their mills, small planters engaged in marginal production were perched at the brink of disaster. The end came in the mid-1880s. The combination of rising taxes, increased operating costs, declining sugar prices, and mounting debt forced small planters to abandon sugar production. Property changed hands at accelerating levels as planters desperately sought to stave off insolvency. As early as 1883 the American consular agent in Cienfuegos reported that all the mills in his jurisidiction had changed ownership at least once as a result of debt and foreclosures.[40] It was in Cienfuegos that New England financier Edwin Atkins foreclosed on the mortgage of the Soledad estate in 1884. By the end of the decade, the Atkins family had secured possession of nearly a half dozen estates in central Cuba.[41]

Farmers and peasants, too, suffered a loss of property. The wartime practice of relocating rural families into urban centers left the countryside depopulated and the cities overcrowded. Few farmers were successful in reclaiming their lands. Many farms were destroyed during the war; others were simply seized outright by unscrupulous landowners. Dispossessed of their lands, rural families remained crowded in the cities, there to form part of an impoverished displaced population forced to resort to begging and dependent on public charity for survival.

This generally bleak picture of post-Zanjón Cuba was confirmed by foreign visitors. English historian John Anthony Froude, visiting Havana in the mid-1880s, described the legions of beggars crowding the capital's streets. Squalor and distress were everywhere manifest, Froude wrote.[42] Much the same conditions greeted American tourist Richard Davey during his visit to Havana. "Never," Davey wrote " . . . have I seen such terrible beggars as those of Cuba. They haunt you everywhere, gathering round the church doors, whining for alms, insulting you if you refuse them and pestering you as you go home at night, never leaving you till you either bestow money on them, or escape within your own or some friendly door."[43] Not long after, another tourist, Maturin M. Ballou, traveled across the island east to west. In Santiago de Cuba, Ballou found the local gas monopoly "on the verge of bankruptcy, like nearly everything else of a business character in Cuba." In Cienfuegos, Ballou met a local sugar planter in crisis. The planter was preparing to spread his molasses on canefields as fertilizer, he informed Ballou, rather "than send it to a distant market and receive only what it cost." The planter further indicated that he would allow "thousands of acres of sugar cane to rot in the fields this season as it would cost more to cut, grind, pack, and send it to market than could be realized for the manufactured article." "Mercantile credit may be said to be dead," Ballou noted upon his arrival to Havana, "and business nearly at a standstill." And as he prepared to leave Cuba: "Financial ruin stares all in the face."[44]

By the mid-1880s, all of Cuba was in the throes of a severe depression. Business houses closed and banks collapsed. Seven of the island's largest trading companies failed. Credit, dear after Zanjón, was almost nonexistent a decade later. In October 1883, the Bank of Santa Catalina closed. In March 1884, the most important savings institution in Havana, the Caja de Ahorros, suspended payments, ostensiby in response to the suicide of the bank's president. "It is more probably," the American consul in Havana speculated tersely, "that the Director committed suicide because the bank was unable to meet its engagements."[45] Two weeks later, the Caja de Ahorros went into liquidation. In the same month, panic runs on the Banco Industrial and the Banco de Comercio forced both institutions to close. Two months later, the Banco Industrial went into liquidation. The crisis also affected provincial institutions. In March 1884 the prestigious house of Rodríguez in Sagua la Grande and its correspondents in Havana, Miyares and Company, failed. Government revenues declined and municipal authorities in Havana fell hopelessly behind in meeting municipal payrolls.

The central office of the Spanish-American Light and Power Company in New York threatened to suspend gas service for Havana street lights if the city did not speedily and satisfactorily settle its dept of some $400,000. In the first three months of 1884, business failures totaled $7 million. "The entire population is reduced . . . to blank despondency and universal ruin," the American consul reported in 1884.[46]

At the same time, the destruction of Cuban agriculture and livestock during the war and the subsequent depopulation of the countryside crippled domestic food production. The number of cattle had increased in absolute terms from 1 million head in 1827 to about 2 million in 1894. But the population, too, had increased, quadrupling in approximately the same period. The availability of fresh milk and meat declined. Goats and sheep decreased from some eighty-three thousand head in 1846 to seventy-eight thousand in 1894. There were 50 percent more hogs in 1827 than in 1894; a ratio of three pigs per person in 1827 had changed by 1894 to three persons per pig.[47] Cuban dependency on imported foodstuffs increased. So did prices. Jobs were few and competition fierce. An increase in Spanish immigration to Cuba after Zanjón, in part to maintain the colonial policy of "racial equilibrium," meaning white superiority, further exacerbated unemployment. In 1886, Madrid announced a policy of underwriting the cost of passage to Cuba for all Spanish workers desirous of seeking employment on the island. Between 1882 and 1894, a quarter million Spaniards arrived in Cuba.[48] The crisis in the sugar industry and business failures contributed still further to unemployment. Against this generally bleak economic landscape, the abolition of slavery was completed. Two hundred thousand former slaves joined Cuban society as free wage earners at a time of a stagnating economy, rising prices, and decreasing wages. The decline of the standard of living for former slaves after emancipation was as immediate as it was dramatic.[49] By 1888, upon the completion of emancipation, unemployment reached desperate proportions. Thousands of rural workers migrated to the already overcrowded cities in search of jobs, only to join the swollen ranks of the urban unemployed. Vagrancy and mendicancy developed into major social problems by the end of the decade. In late 1888, Havana authorities passed a severe antivagrancy law, pledging to rid the city of all but the gainfully employed.[50] From the cities, thousands of Cuban workers extended their search for employment to the United States. Another constituency for Cuba Libre took shape in the cigar factories of Key West and Tampa.

V   The decline in the number of sugar mills after Zanjón signified more than the disappearance of inefficient *centrales* (mills). A new stage of sugar capitalism was about to transform Cuban society. The demise of small mills contributed at once to the development of a new regimen of property organization and the rise of a new system of production. Smaller sugar enterprises, lacking capital, unable to keep pace with technological and production advances, passed ultimately under the control of larger estates. Planters unable to meet the growing capital requirements of sugar manufacturing abandoned the industrial end of sugar production altogether and devoted themselves exclusively to agricultural pursuits. The prevailing system whereby the grower milled his own cane gave way to a new specialization in which large mill owners concentrated on the manufacturing of sugar and the farmers tended to the planting and harvesting of cane. Many formerly independent planters survived the crisis of the 1880s only to find themselves as *colonos* (farmers) subservient to the larger and more successful *centrales*. The *colono* was reduced to dependence on the mill, was frequently in debt and typically without an alternative marketplace for his product.[51] The disappearance of mills after the Ten Years' War compounded the *colono*'s plight, for fewer *centrales* signified at once the collapse of the Cuban planter class and fewer potential buyers of sugar cane.

While the number of mills decreased, the size of the surviving estates increased. The war and the economic crisis of the mid-1880s provided a powerful boost to new concentrations of land and the expansion of the sugar latifundia. Not since the early third of the nineteenth century had the Cuban estate expanded so aggressively and with such speed as it did in the decade after Zanjón. Military operations during the war destroyed farms and estates; damaged property was cheap land. Farms vacated by the relocation of rural families, as well as property whose owners were killed in the war, provided further opportunities for alert landowners to expand their holdings. So did the expropriation of separatists' property. Then, too, many of the small estates that failed after Zanjón were acquired by larger estates.

During the war years these expansions had been haphazard and fortuitous: land seizures had been sporadic and scattered, more in response to opportunity than the result of organization. This changed by the mid-1880s. Mobilized into action in response to international sugar developments, Cuban planters undertook far-reaching changes that foretold a profound transformation of the sugar system, changes that were as sweeping as they were systematic. Greater efficiency was needed to market the sugar profitably under the prevailing low prices. By the mid-1880s, production strategies shifted from increasing the number of sugar mills to increasing the production capacity of existing *centrales*. New credit, fresh capital, and expanding ownership, largely American, provided larger enterprises with the resources to expand. Improved varieties of cane, innovations in processing techniques, and technological and industrial advances became generally available to Cuban planters by the 1880s and provided planters the opportunity to respond aggressively to new conditions. New machinery to extract maximum sugar from improved strains of cane and grind the increased volume of harvested cane efficiently was introduced. New vacuum pans and centrifugal equipment were installed to distill and crystalize more sugar from new strains of cane. These requirements, in turn, placed additional pressures on supporting production capabilities, including fuel and transportation. Railroad facilities expanded. So did wharf and pier construction. But most of all, land—and more land—was essential to derive optimum advantage of the technology that was transforming sugar production.

In the eastern provinces, sugar production revived around the new latifundia. In Puerto Príncipe, surviving sugar estates absorbed local cattle ranches. Three *centrales* (Senado, Congreso, and Lugareño) dominated sugar production by 1891. On the north Oriente coast, a joint Spanish-French venture acquired enormous tracts of land around Nipe Bay. To the south, around Manzanillo, new land concentrations revived the moribund local sugar industry. In two years three newly organized *centrales*, Dos Amigos (1884), Niquero (1884), and Isabel (1886), had converted vast tracts of land to sugar production.

In central Cuba, too, the sugar latifundia expanded its boundaries at the expense of other agricultural units, sugar and nonsugar alike. In the region of Remedios in Las Villas province, the new regimen of land concentration proceeded swiftly to establish the preeminence of the sugar latifundia. In Yaguajay, the new *central* Narciso (1891) absorbed older and less efficient *centrales*, including Soberano, Oceano, Encarnación, Aurora, Urbaza, and Luisiana. In the rich sugar zones of Matanzas-Cárdenas-Colón, the sugar estate expanded at a frenetic pace. The sugar revolution of the 1880s also transformed the region around Sagua la Grande. Technological improvements and cultivation of new land increased the production of Sagua's six major *centrales* by 50 percent. Nowhere, however, did land concentration occur as quickly or as spectacularly as in Cienfuegos. Between 1884 and 1891, some thirteen new *centrales* were organized. These new mills, destined to dominate Cuban sugar production for the next quarter century, included Constancia, Soledad, San Lino, San Agustín, Lequeito, Caracas, Hormiguero, Parque Alto, and Cieneguita.[52] By the end of the 1880s, the Cuban sugar system had revived under the aegis of the corporate latifundia.

This economic recovery was not, however, without far-reaching consequences. The expansion of the sugar estate after war had converted only the more fortunate farmers into *colonos*. In fact, the increased production capabilities of the larger mills and the attending expansion of zones of cultivation had forced the wholesale displacement of the rural population. The process of relocating rural families from the countryside continued through the 1880s, no longer as a military imperative but an economic expedience. The concentration of land into the sugar latifundia uprooted the farmer, destroyed the rural landowning and independent farming class, and impoverished the rural population. Scores of small farmers and peasants, maintaining a precarious existence on marginal farms, found themselves displaced, landless, and unemployed. The cane field spilled out of the traditional regions, laying claim to all land in its path. Old estates passed under new management; traditional holdings, family farms, and unincorporated rural property disappeared under sugar cane. Expelled from the land, deprived of an independent livelihood, many farmers and peasants channeled their rage into banditry. To be sure, the Ten Years' War had given powerful impetus to life outside the law, but formal peace provided former farmers little incentive to resume peaceful pursuits. Many insurgent veterans had little to return to. If their farms had not been destroyed during the war, they had been expropriated. Even in those instances where Cubans could reclaim their land, the destruction of crops, livestock, and equipment was so complete and the cost of a new beginning so great that all but the most determined were discouraged from returning to the farm. *Pacíficos*, too, returned from their wartime internment in the cities only to find their former world in shambles. Without land, without employment, the dispossessed peasant joined outlaw bands in the interior, living outside the law in the inaccessible swamp regions and mountains of the Cuban countryside.[53]

By the late 1890s, entire regions of the Cuban interior had fallen more or less under the control of bandits. In Havana province, Juan Vento, Gallo Sosa, José Plasencia, and Manuel García had virtually free range in the countryside. José "Matagás" Alvarez, Nicasio Matos ("El Tuerto Ro-

dríguez"), Regino Alfonso, Desiderio Matos, and Aurelio Sanabria dominated the Matanzas interior. In Las Villas, Florentino Rodríguez, the
Machín brothers, and Bruno Gutiérrez eluded Spanish authorities for over
a decade. Jesús González, José Muñoz, Lino Mirabal, and Alvaro Rodríguez operated almost at will in the Camagüeyan countryside. In
Oriente province, Isidro Tejera, Onofre de la O. Rodríguez, and José de la
O. Rodríguez moved through the interior with impunity.

Bandits combined a defiance of Spanish colonial authority with social
protest. In its most prominent manifestations, this sentiment found expression in bandit attacks against all forms of property and wealth. In
Havana province, Manuel García terrorized planters. His exploits of hold-
ups, train robberies, and the kidnapping of *hacendados* converted him into
a figure of legendary proportions throughout the Cuban countryside and
earned him the title of "El Rey de los Campos." In Matanzas province, José
"Matagás" Alvarez exacted annual tribute from *colonos* and *hacendados* in
exchange for "protection."

Spanish colonial authorities were powerless to contain bandit activities,
and by the late 1880s banditry reached epidemic proportions. In 1888 Governor General Sabas Marín, in a desperate measure to combat rural lawlessness, declared a state of war in Pinar del Río, Havana, Matanzas, and
Las Villas and relinquished the administration of justice to military authorities.[54] Two years later, another governor general, Camilo Polavieja,
mounted a new and more formidable military offensive against Manuel
García. Some ten thousand troops were mobilized in fruitless operations in
the southern part of Havana province.[55] By the 1890s, bandits in the interior ranged over the countryside virtually at will and without serious or
sustained obstruction from colonial military authorities.

VI   The forces that expelled the peasants from the land also displaced
planters as owners of the estates. An inexorable reciprocity joined both
ends of the island social order. The forces that uprooted the peasant and
transformed the independent farmer into a *colono* served as portents of
the fate about to befall the *hacendado*. The old planter elite survived the
crisis of the 1880s, but only at the cost of its traditional supremacy over
sugar production. The price of solvency had been dependency. Indeed, the
privileged position of the planter elite in Cuban society grew increasingly
tenuous as its dependency upon American capital and U.S. markets increased. The landed aristocracy guaranteed its survival by exchanging
titles of property for ownership of stocks in American corporations and

positions as land owners for places on corporate boards of directors. And even this salvation was to be illusory, and brief. In practice, planters would henceforth function as the local agents of American capital and the instruments of American economic penetration of Cuba. Their well-being now depended on the success foreign capital enjoyed in extending control over the island's strategic production sectors—a pursuit that would engage the active collaboration of the newly displaced bourgeoisie.

The transfer of property, further, was accompanied by a transformation of nationality. In the decades following the Ten Years' War, scores of Cuban planters found it convenient to acquire American citizenship. Class interests transcended national allegiances. In more than symbolic ways, American citizenship offered planters a hedge against local instability and protection against property destruction. Cuban planters used American nationality as an instrument to defend their economic interests and enlist the support of the U.S. government in the defense of local privilege and property. Through naturalization planters acquired a powerful foreign ally, a protector to be summoned on those occasions when colonial government demonstrated inefficiency or indifference to the needs of property now owned by new American nationals. Equally important, as American citizens planters were in a position to demand reparation and receive indemnification for property losses stemming from local political disorders. A new habit developed in Cuba, one soon to stand as an enduring source of national emulation, in which Cubans appealed to Washington to intercede in their behalf in the resolution of local conflicts. These developments served, further, to internationalize Cuban politics and, in one more fashion, provide the United States with an entree into the internal affairs of the island. In the closing decades of the nineteenth century, the transfiguration of planter nationality placed the object of planter allegiance above national interests and located the sources of planter patronage outside the island. In still another manner, property owners came to identify their well-being with the United States.[56]

By the end of the 1880s, the reorganization of the Cuban economy was nothing less than spectacular. Some 94 percent of Cuban sugar products, the American consul general in Havana reported in 1886, found their way to American markets. The implications were far-reaching. Consul Ramon O. Williams suggested:

The Island is now entirely dependent upon the market of the
United States, in which to sell its sugar cane products; also that

the existence of the sugar plantations, the railroads used in transporting the products of the plantations in the shipping ports of the island, the export and import trades of Cuba based thereon, each including hundreds of minor industries, such as the agricultural and mechanical trades, store-houses, wharves, lighters, stevedors, brokers, clerks and bankers, real estate owners, and shop-keepers of all kinds, and holders of the public debt, are now all directly related to the market of the United States, to the extent of 94 percent for their employment.[57]

Growing dependency on U.S. markets had two immediate consequences. First, it intensified Cuban demands for greater local control over trade regulation and commerce. Secondly, increased Cuban-American trade created considerable colonial pressure on Madrid to negotiate a commercial treaty with the United States.

The availability of North American credit, even on an unlimited scale, would have been insufficient to revive the languishing sugar estates without preferential access to the American market. In 1890, the newly enacted McKinley Tariff Act placed Cuban raw sugar on the free list. Article III (Aldrich Amendment) of the new tariff law, however, required the president of the United States to impose high duties on primary products, including sugar and molasses, against countries that denied American exports concessions commensurate with those offered by the McKinley bill.

Developments in the United States presented Cuban producers with the opportunity they had long awaited. They did not hesitate. The effect of the Aldrich Amendment in Havana was immediate. A series of public meetings throughout 1890 and 1891 galvanized public opinion and resulted in Cuban appeals to Spanish authorities to negotiate a reciprocal trade agreement with the United States. Petitions from all regions of the island were forwarded to the Spanish Cortes; protests flooded the Council of Ministers.[58] In late 1890, representatives of key economic sectors of Cuba organized to demand Spanish tariff concessions to American products. Known as the Movimiento Económico, the coalition was led by Círculo de Hacendados y Agricultores, representing the most powerful producers of sugar, and included the Commerce League, the Association of Cigar Manufacturing, the Chamber of Commerce, and the Economic Society of Cuba. In July 1891, the Central Committee for Economic Propaganda of the movement issued its "Manifiesto Económico," a lengthy denunciation of past Spanish economic policies that concluded with a demand for a treaty with the United States to provide Cuban sugar with preferential access to American markets.[59] Never had Cuban producers aligned themselves against Spanish policies with such purposeful unanimity. In protesting one of the more onerous features of the colonial system, the Movimiento Económico identified interests that were peculiarly Cuban and demanded concessions that benefited primarily Cuba. The first hairline fracture of the colonial consensus had appeared. "Public opinion here among the laboring, agricultural, proprietary and manufacturing classes," American Consul Ramon O. Williams in Havana had written a month earlier, "sides generally with the Board of Planters." Williams added prophetically;

This state of things shows that the present ties connecting Cuba with Spain are based more on historic custom than on economic necessity, for while the United States, the great consumer of Cuban products, facilitates the commercial development of this colony through the legislative abolition of import duties on its sugars, the Mother Country difficults that development by increasing their cost of producting, diminishing, in like ratio, their competitive power with the similar products of other countries in its only market, the United States, and exposing the colony, withal, from the loss of industries, to future social dangers.[60]

Within the year, partly as a result of economic pressure at home but chiefly in response to the clamor from Cuba, Spain acquiesced and relaxed long-standing protectionist trade policies. In June 1891, under the auspices of the McKinley Tariff Act, Washington and Madrid negotiated the Foster-Cánovas agreement whereby Cuba and Puerto Rico received the full benefits of the 1890 bill in exchange for Spanish tariffs concessions to U.S. exports.

The results of reciprocal trade arrangements between Cuba and the United States were as dramatic as they were instant. Sugar production revived in spectacular fashion. From some 632,000 tons in 1890, sugar production approached 976,000 tons in 1892, reaching for the first time the historic 1 million ton mark in 1894.

However great the impact of the McKinley tariff on Cuban sugar production, and, indeed, it was by no means inconsiderable, the long range effects of reciprocal trade went far beyond sugar. By 1893, Cuban imports from the United States accounted for just under half of total American exports to Central and South America ($24 million out of $62 million). Cuban exports to the United States increased from $54 million in 1890 to $79 million in 1893. Indeed, by 1893, imports from Cuba represented almost half the total Central and South American imports to the United States ($79 million out of $111 million). In 1893, Cuban exports to the United States were some twelve times larger than its exports to Spain ($79 million to the United States and $6 million to Spain). By 1894, the United States received almost 90 percent of Cuba's total exports ($98 million out of $116 million) and provided 40 percent of its imports ($39 million out of $97 million). Metropolitan Spain, on the other hand, accounted for some $10 million of Cuban exports while providing the island with $34 million of its imports.[61]

Trade statistics underscored the direction of Cuba's new economic orbit. In the short space of two years, the Cuban economy had taken a giant stride toward deepening its dependence on the capital, imports, and markets of the United States. Colonial political grievances receded quietly into the background as Spain's trade and commercial policies conformed to the demands of all key economic groups on the island. Pressure on the cost of living eased as the reduction of duties lowered prices on foreign imports. The sugar system, in a central and strategic relationship to all other sectors of trade and commerce, prospered and expanded and with it the entire economy.

VII Celebration of prosperity proved premature. Within three years, Cuba's prosperity ended as quickly as it had begun, and with less warning. In 1894, the United States rescinded its tariff concession to Cuban exports. By establishing a new duty of 40 percent *ad valorem* on all sugar entering the United States, the Wilson-Gorman Tariff Act of 1894 dismantled the cornerstone of previous reciprocal trade arrangements between Washington and Madrid. In that same year, the Foster-Cánovas agreement expired. Spanish authorities responded swiftly to U.S. tariff legislation in 1894 and canceled duty concessions extended earlier to American imports. An impenetrable protectionist wall reappeared around the island in mid-1894, reviving memories of the worst features of Spanish commercial exclusivism.

The sudden disengagement of Cuba from its prosperous but brief privileged participation in international trade had jolting consequences on the island. Cuba lost preferential access to the only market with the capacity to absorb its sugar exports and insulate the island from the uncertainties of world competition. The restoration of Spanish tariffs, further, raised the spectre that the United States would retaliate by banning Cuban sugar from American markets altogether.

Profits declined immediately. Production followed. Sugar exports valued at $64 million in 1893 plummeted to $45 million in 1895 and $13 million a year later. The 1 million ton sugar harvest of 1894 collapsed to 225,000 tons in 1896. No less daunting to sugar producers, after 1894 planters also faced the grim prospect of losing preferential access to the equipment, machines, and spare parts around which the sugar industry had reorganized after the mid-1880s. In Santiago de Cuba, new duties on American materials after mid-1894 raised the prices on all imports:[62]

	1891–1893	1894
Iron bridge material	free	$48.00 per ton
Iron or steel rails	free	20.00 per ton
Iron or steel tools	free	25.00 per ton
Machinery	free	15.00–60.00 per ton

The loss of preferential access to American markets, moreover, occurred simultaneous with a sudden drop in world sugar prices. For the first time in the history of Cuban sugar production, the price of sugar dropped below two cents a pound.

Reaction in Cuba to Spain's retaliatory levies was immediate. For the second time in almost as many years, Cuban producers joined together against Spanish policy. In November 1894, the Círculo de Hacendados y Agricultores convened in an extraordinary session to protest Madrid's tariff policies. In the largest attended meeting of its history, the Círculo petitioned the Ministry of Colonies to rescind the duties assessed against American products entering the island. After adjournment, the planter elite took to the streets and converged on the Governor General's palace for a public meeting that one Havana newspaper described as a "peaceful protest."[63] Several weeks later, the Centro de Propietarios in Santiago de Cuba met and seconded the Círculo's protest.

Beyond the immediate and apparent consequences of the retaliatory duties decreed by Madrid, many Cubans feared that Spain's actions threatened to lead to an all-out tariff war in which the principal casualty would be Cuba's access to U.S. markets. The loss of the American market, Cubans predicted soberly, would precipitate the complete collapse of the Cuban sugar system and, with it, the entire island economy. "Has the government stopped to reflect what would be the situation of the Island of Cuba without an open market in either the Metropolis or Europe, without the market of the United States?" the Havana daily *Diario de la Marina* asked editorially. "What future would await us?" The loss of markets accounting for 90 percent of the island's exports, the editorial concluded, would signal the complete and immediate ruin of the Cuban economy.[64]

The impact of the crisis of 1894, however, went far beyond the sugar system. No facet of Cuban society was unaffected. Merchants, traders, and retailers who had replaced their traditional commercial ties with Spanish suppliers in the metropolis for dealers in the United States faced ruin. Unemployment rose, commodity goods decreased, prices increased. The price on foodstuffs imported from the United States, and upon which large sectors of the population had come to depend, soared. Government duties passed directly onto consumers and prices reached unprecedented heights. Higher duties led directly to increased prices. The restoration of colonial custom duties meant that all Cubans would henceforth pay higher prices for vital food imports:[65]

	1893–1894	*1894–1895*
Wheat	$ .30 per 100 kilos	$3.95 per 100 kilos
Flour	1.00 per 100 kilos	4.75 per 100 kilos
Corn	.25 per 100 kilos	3.95 per 100 kilos
Meal	.25 per 100 kilos	4.75 per 100 kilos

As costs increased, even the availability of the higher priced goods decreased. American imports dropped, shipping declined. By October 1894 half the American steamers serving Santiago had been withdrawn from service.[66]

The implications of the events of late 1894 were apparent to all Cubans. The passage of a decade had not dimmed Cuban memories of the crisis of 1884. A unanimous outcry of indignation and protest rose across the island against Spain. "The worst of all is that we have to go against our Government and take sides with the yankees," *La Lucha* complained with incredulity. "We need, in effect, American flour entering Cuba under reasonable conditions and Cuban sugar entering American ports under similar conditions. . . . It is out of order for us to be the ones to launch a tariff war, for our sugar has no market other than the United States. Every one of our tariff measures should have the dual purpose of facilitating the entrance of American goods into our ports and doing nothing to encourage our neighbor from impeding the importation of our sugar."[67]

Frustrated by their inability to influence the direction of policy decisions in Madrid, planters, merchants, and businessmen in Cuba sought to enlist the assistance of the United States. Cubans appealed directly if only privately to Americans to intercede with Spanish authorities in Washington on their behalf. American consular agents in Cuba were approached on several occasions by planters soliciting Washington's support in their struggle against Spanish colonial policy.[68] This turn of events, too, had portentous implications. Cubans "are slowly accustoming themselves to think that their capital is not at Madrid but at Washington," *La Lucha* discerned perceptively. "And once such a belief takes hold, the effects of such a short-sighted [tariff] policy will be such that appeals to patriotism will no longer be able to alter the course of events."[69]

Cuban sense of economic deprivation served to underscore a growing cognizance of political powerlessness. As Cubans grew dependent on trade with the United States, they grew increasingly subject to the vagaries of the international marketplace and the economic policies of two metropolitan centers—one political, the other economic. The well-being of the island more and more depended on forces over which the Cubans had little control. Throughout the crisis, Cubans found themselves reduced to passive onlookers of a momentous economic drama involving the very solvency of the Cuban economy and powerless to control the vital forces governing their lives. "The residents and commercial interests here," the American consul in Santiago reported, "are protesting loud and strong against being thus summarily cut off from their natural commercial allies, and this action on the part of the home government adds greatly to the feeling of unrest that pervades all classes."[70]

Once again the question of Cuba's status and the nature of its relationship with Spain resurfaced as topics of political debate and public discussion. An enormous sense of uncertainty and uneasiness settled over the island. Prosperity required the expansion of trade, and that in turn required the reduction of Spanish control over the Cuban economy. The brief cycle of prosperity resulting from close economic ties with the United States made the prospect of returning to the regimen of Spanish exclusivism as inconceivable as it was inadmissable. Planters, merchants, and traders had visited the promised land and there gazed covetously at an economic destiny in which Spain had no visible place. Spain's arbitrary and unwelcomed intrusion in Cuban affairs in 1894 served to remind Cubans in dramatic form of the economic liabilities attending continued political association with Madrid. Cuba had experienced in palpable form the fruits of close economic collaboration with the United States in the 1890s—and the possibilities seemed infinite.

VIII The year 1895 began on a note of despair and frustration. Madrid had turned a deaf ear to Cuban appeals. "Here we are tired of protesting against the exhorbitant levies used to keep yankee goods out of Cuba," *La Lucha* lamented in Havana. "In vain, too, have been our efforts against the imposition of prohibitive duties on American goods. We have not been heard in Madrid; because we are miserable and long-suffering colonists, our clamors are undeserving of the attention of those who govern and misgovern."[71] Without warning, without attention to and, apparently, without concern for the interests of the island, Spain abruptly and arbitrarily disengaged Cuba from the American economic system and reimposed a regimen of retrogressive and potentially catastrophic economic policies. "What road," the *Diario de la Marina* asked portentously in December 1894, "would we have to take to avoid falling into the abyss of bankruptcy and misery?"[72]

Spain's economic policies offered dramatic if not final proof of the insolvency of the Spanish colonial system. But the uneasiness settling over the island economic elites reflected only the upper reaches of tensions that ran the full depth and breadth of Cuban society.

At about the same time, the socio-economic crisis in the Cuban countryside merged with political tensions of the mid-1890s. Indeed, it was a short and perhaps inevitable step to move from defiance of Spanish authority to the support of Cuban separatism. Many bandit chieftains had acquired a vague and shadowy devotion to the cause of Cuba Libre. Several had emerged from the separatist armies of the Ten Years' War. In the intervening years, bandits had kept disaffection against Spain alive in the Cuban countryside.[73] Throughout the period, communication between bandit chieftains in the countryside and separatist leaders in the cities and abroad increased. In 1890, Antonio Maceo met with Manuel García and secured from "El Rey de los Campos" a commitment to support separatist arms against Spain.[74] Open class warfare in the Cuban countryside acquired separatist overtones. Bandit activities increased in direct relationship to PRC preparations for a new war. In the mid-1890s, Manuel García stepped up his activities against Spanish authorities. In 1894, he scandalized Havana society by kidnapping Antonio Fernández de Castro, a wealthy *hacendado* and brother of the prominent Autonomist Rafael Fernández de Castro. More than half of the 15,000 pesos in ransom paid for Fernández's release found its way to the PRC cell in Havana.[75] In early 1895, García announced his intention to increase attacks on the sugar estates of Havana province as a way of guaranteeing the payment of tribute money from the planters. In January of that year, Portugalete, one of the largest sugar mills in Havana province, owned by the Spaniard Manuel Calvo, was set ablaze. On the eve of the outbreak of the war, García had donated some $75,000 to the PRC junta in New York in behalf of the separatist cause.[76] The devotion of bandits to the cause of Cuba Libre served to broaden the social base of the separatist movement. Dispossessed and displaced peasants, living during the 1880s and 1890s outside the reach of Spanish authority, saw in a war of liberation the opportunity for securing redress against the authorities that had sanctioned the alienation of their lands.[77]

Economic distress revived demands for a political solution of colonial grievances. By the 1890s, the much heralded promises of Zanjón remained largely unfulfilled. Even the most devoted autonomist had little to sustain the faith that inspired the creation of the party in 1878. The planter bid for political leadership in the colony after Zanjón had situated the propertied elite directly between the crossfire of the contentious extremes of the colonial polity. This middle position earned Autonomists the enmity of separatists and the suspicion of loyalists. It was a position that reflected accurately the anomalous social reality of planters and the inevitable ambivalence of a class dependent on American markets for prosperity but relying on Spanish military for security. It was a position, too, of immense vulnerability, one that had neither the support of the leadership of the colonial body politic nor the following of the colonial body social.

That planters were willing to risk this exposure in no small way underscored their devotion to and faith in the possibility of reform within empire. But more than imperial belief was involved. The planter bid for political leadership over the colonial polity occurred concurrently with the decline of their local economic prominence. In fact, during the decade between the economic crisis of 1885 and the political crisis of 1895, more and more planters had less and less to lose. Increasingly, autonomism attracted growing numbers of indigent planters, Creoles who sought to combat growing economic impoverishment through political sinecures and parlay social prominence into political preeminence. Public office became an adequate if admittedly uncertain means of reversing declining economic fortunes. Reform politics promised to create new economic opportunities for the new entrants into the colonial bureaucracy, displacing *peninsular* office holders with Creole office seekers. Colonial politics acquired a particular distributive quality, one in which Creoles competed with *peninsulares* not only on ideological grounds but also for control over the public means of acquiring and expanding economic power. For the first time, Creoles as a class, possessed of prestige and some resources, representing principally local property interests, challenged the traditional *peninsular* monopoly over public office.

Whatever else may have separated the Creole planters from the Creole politicos, they were united in their defense of local privilege and their fear of colonial revolution. Empire guaranteed both. It was the post-Zanjón euphoria, the belief that autonomism would lead at once to collective economic expansion through the liberalization of trade arrangements and to individual mobility through the liberalization of colonial politics and that both would eliminate the sources of future colonial instability, that rallied the planter elite to the side of metropolitan authority.

The fact was, however, that Autonomists had not fared well after Zanjón. Liberals had performed poorly at the polls in the years following Zanjón but not, they insisted, because of a lack of popular support but rather as a result of official intimidation and fraud. Census irregularities, ballot stuffing, and certification frauds were only the most blatant of the abuses routinely practiced by the Spanish officialdom in Cuba. Autonomist politicians frequently ran afoul of local authorities and found these political transgressions punishable by imprisonment. Provincial autonomist newspapers were harassed and often suspended. As early as 1890, the official autonomist newspaper, *El País*, conceded failure. "After twelve years of painful struggle against the combined action of intrigue and violence . . . .," *El País* complained editorially, "the Cuban people find themselves in worse condition than in 1878, their spirit hurt by disillusionment, their patience worn out by suffering."[78] In 1892, in the face of official indifference to liberal charges of intimidation and fraud, Autonomists withdrew from insular elections. In January 1895, the provincial autonomist committee in Santiago dissolved in protest of Spanish policy.

The failure of Autonomist politics signified fundamentally the failure of both the Creole bid for political mobility and the planter drive for political representation. Nor was this entirely the unintended result of *peninsular* politics. In a very real sense, political competition between Creoles and *peninsulares* represented a deepening economic conflict between the colony and the metropolis, between those who promoted Cuban interests and those who served Spanish needs. The relationship between property and politics cum nationality was a fixed feature of the colonial landscape. Decrying the preponderance of *peninsular* candidates for a seat on the Havana *diputación* in 1889, *El País* discerned: "All but one are *peninsulares*, in the main industrialists and merchants; none represent real property, that is, landed property and permanence."[79] Of the composition of the whole *diputación*, *El País* noted: "Three quarters of the representatives of the most populous province of the island are made up of *peninsulares* and of these the majority are without landed property; most represent industry and commerce, that is, the transient element."[80]

After nearly two decades, the record of Spanish reform in Cuba remained singularly inauspicious. The economy had begun to contract and the promised political reforms remained unfulfilled. Suffrage manipulation and election rigging favored the Unión Constitucional. The participation of Creoles in the Spanish *cortes* and the insular government of the island remained wholly token in nature.[81] Spain's allies had been estranged and its opponents emboldened.

2 From Reconciliation to Reconcentration

Even if we win in the field and suppress the rebels, since the country wishes to have neither an amnesty for our enemies nor an extermination of them, my loyal and sincere opinion is that, with reforms or without reforms, before twelve years we shall have another war.
—Arsenio Martínez Campos, July 1895

If I failed the unique responsibility is mine. The government has in no way restricted my action, neither political nor military. I happened not to have used the means and the full powers which have been conceded to me.
—Arsenio Martínez Campos, January 1896

I see only one way of ending definitively disturbances in Cuba—war.
—Valeriano Weyler, February 1896

I On Sunday morning, February 24, 1895, Havana awoke to the customary echoes of church bells. But this was a special Sunday morning, a day awaited expectantly by all *habaneros*. The echoing sounds of church bells descended into the city below, mixing there with the noises rising from Havana streets. Even as churchgoers made their way to early mass, the streets of the city were filling with venders, strolling musicians, and peddlers hawking their merchandise. It was to be a day of festivities, highlighted by bullfights, cockfights, concerts, and banquets. February 24 was the first Sunday of Carnival.[1] To be sure, unconfirmed reports of scattered incidents of lawlessness in the interior cast a distant pall over the capital in the early hours of Carnival Sunday. In the early morning, however, these were only unsubstantiated rumors circulating among friends and families who lingered to socialize after mass. On this particular morning, moreover, *habaneros* were indisposed to allow bad news to interfere with the festivities planned for the day. In any case, nearly a decade of bandit depredations in the interior had all but totally inured *habaneros* to accounts of recurring disquiet in the Cuban countryside. Nor did rumors that the disorders of February 24 had separatist origins provoke extraordinary concern. Uprisings in the name of Cuba Libre in the 1890s had become as commonplace as they were short-lived. A separatist uprising in Guantánamo in 1892 ended ingloriously after only days of fighting. Another rebellion in April 1893 collapsed in a matter of weeks. Six months later, an uprising in Las Villas ended with the quick capture of the principal insurgent leaders.[2] On February 24, 1895, therefore, reports of new disturbances in the eastern interior failed to arouse in most *habaneros* anything more than renewed self-satisfaction and thanksgiving for the security offered by urban life.

Habaneros who attended mass at the Cathedral of Havana, however, sensed that something more than simple and unrelated incidents of lawlessness were absorbing the thoughts of Governor General Emilio Calleja. The usually gregarious and always engaging governor rarely lost the opportunity afforded by Sunday mass to commingle among and ingratiate himself to ranking representatives of Havana society. On this Sunday morning he seemed unusually preoccupied and lost in his thoughts. He arrived at mass a bit later than usual and remained solemnly distant through the service. It seemed to provide little comfort. And on this Carnical Sunday morning, a day famous for social gatherings and conviviality,

Calleja dispensed with the social amenities that had charaterized the Sunday morning routines of his two years in Havana and returned to the Governor's Palace immediately.

II News of political disturbances on February 24, 1895, came as little surprise to ranking Spanish authorities in Cuba. The governor, during his eighteen months in Havana, had presided helplessly over the collapse of the Cuban economy. Rising public discontent and growing popular dissatisfaction, much of it coming from those sectors of Cuban society traditionally loyal to Spain, presented colonial authorities with some unsettling political portents. Nor was Calleja unmindful that Cuban disaffection extended deeper in private than was expressed in public. Known, too, was the growing disaffection within Autonomist ranks. Political discontent in the provinces was mounting. After 1894, Spanish authorities had new problems. The economic crisis had produced a political crisis and both had shaken the confidence of the colonial elites. Loyalties were in transition, evidenced by Cuban appeals to American authorities for assistance against Spanish policy—"we have to go against our Government and take sides with the yankees," in *La Lucha*'s words. Traditional allegiances were shaken. Class interests clashed with long-standing ties of culture and sentiment. "Many are already talking of resistance [to Spain] and annexation to the United States," the American consul in Matanzas had written almost a decade earlier; "not that they love Spain less, but their interests more."[3] Nothing had changed but everything was different. The Cuban elites inhabited a nether world where friends and foes appeared to have exchanged identities, a condition complicated by increasingly unrealizable expectations of both protection from Spain and profits from the United States. Cubans in the past loyal to Madrid now questioned the efficacy of continued association with Spain. Many were reluctantly arriving at the conclusion that Spain no longer possessed the means—or the desire—to accommodate the expanding needs of Cuban society within the framework of traditional colonial relationships. The economic crisis of the mid-1890s served to underscore in dramatic terms the liabilities attending Cuba's continuing relationship with Spain. But in 1895, the Cuban elites were spared the agony of a painful decision. The outbreak of a new separatist war forced the disgruntled bourgeoisie to return instinctively to the metropolitan fold. Not that planters' sudden reconciliation with the colonial regime in February 1895 signaled conformity with colonial policies; rather, that the separatist alternative was wholly unacceptable. Whatever doubts may have sapped elite morale, whatever grievances may have weakened elite loyalties, planters were neither so desperate nor so reckless as to confuse the separatist cause with their own. In 1895, the Cuban elite had nowhere to go but back.

Spanish authorities in Madrid were not totally unaware of the political undercurrents swirling around the colony. Even as separatists completed plans for the February uprising, the Spanish Cortes prepared to approve a series of colonial reforms in the hope that political concessions would partially offset economic grievances. In Havana, Governor Calleja repeatedly warned Madrid that shortsighted metropolitan policies were edging Cuba ineluctably toward revolt. The question was not *if* Cubans would rebel, but *when*.[4]

III   The deepening economic crisis of the mid-1890s and the attending political tensions augured well for separatist plottings. By 1894, the PRC had brought unity and consensus to separatist ranks.[5] The party had provided an effective institutional structure within which to raise funds for a new war. Organized around patriotic juntas and revolutionary clubs in hundreds of expatriate Cuban communities, the PRC enjoyed early success in securing donations and contributions for Cuba Libre.[6] It also had provided the means for effecting a reconciliation between the army veterans of 1868 and the post-Zanjón generation of civilian separatists. In 1892, in his official capacity as the chief delegate of the PRC, Martí had journeyed to the Dominican Republic to persuade Máximo Gómez to assume command of the Liberation Army.[7] In agreeing to serve the Cuban cause and by proclaiming his adhesion to the PRC, Gómez paved the way for the reconciliation of the old military leadership with the new civilian PRC organizers. His adherence in 1892 to the *pinos nuevos*, followed in 1893 by a pledge of support from Antonio Maceo, completed the unification phase of separatist politics. Preparations for war could now proceed.

Eighteen ninety-three was not the best time to undertake revolution. Cuba was enjoying the first flushes of a dazzling prosperity, and few beneficiaries of the 1890s boom showed any disposition to welcome an interruption of the island's new economic fortunes. But the Cuban indifference to politics was shattered by the economic crisis of 1894, and for the first time in almost thirty years Cuba was susceptible to separatist appeals. Prosperity ended as quickly as it had begun; the Cuban economy approached disaster and only the most intransigent loyalist believed Spain capable of restoring prosperity. The political reforms promised at Zanjón had been disappointingly few and patently specious.[8] Not all Cubans, to be sure, rushed to rally around the newly unfurled separatist banner; it would take more than this crisis to produce mass defections among Spain's supporters. But many Cubans, previously unmoved by separatist entreaties, were now disillusioned and disappointed and increasingly receptive to political change. They may not have been prepared to believe the best about the separatist project, but they were predisposed to believe the worst about Spanish policy.

IV   The uprising on February 24 began inauspiciously—in fact, ingloriously. A month earlier, from New York, the PRC had issued the call for a new war, sometime "during the second half of, not before, the month of February." The call to arms stressed the necessity for simultaneous uprisings in the east and west, an uprising of island-wide proportions to preclude the concentration of Spanish forces at one given point at any one moment.[9]

On that day the "Grito de Baire" in Oriente was echoed immediately by the "Grito de Ibarra" in Matanzas—but nowhere else. Original hopes for the establishment of insurgent operations in the western half of the island proved illusory. In Havana, Spanish authorities learned of the conspiracy and moved swiftly against the conspirators. The rebellion in Matanzas collapsed within days of the arrests in Havana. The capture and death of key leaders delivered a powerful body blow directly to the *matancero* uprising and indirectly to the entire western campaign. Nor had separatists fared much better in Las Villas and Camagüey. Early arrests deprived local organizations of central direction, and survivors, who scattered into the countryside, established only a tenuous hold over remote regions of the interior.

Only in Oriente did the summons to arms receive immediate and extensive support. Almost every town responded; insurgent zones of operations arose immediately around Santiago de Cuba, Manzanillo, Guantánamo, Las Tunas, El Cobre, Bayamo, Holguín, El Caney, and Baracoa. Within a month, some three thousand *orientales* had taken to the field.[10]

V   Insurgent successes in Oriente could not offset the dismal separatist prospects elsewhere on the island. Initial hopes that the rebellion would simultaneously take hold on both sides of the Júcaro-Morón *trocha* vanished by early March. Separatists' worst fears, that the rebellion would be localized in one province, had come to pass. Many principal civilian leaders and key military chieftains had been either captured or killed in the early days of the insurrection. The insurgent bands that survived the initial weeks eluded capture only by seeking refuge in the remote interior regions, there to face a precarious existence and uncertain future. Early reversals also had the net effect of generating self-fulfilling defeatism, persuading many separatist sympathizers, committed to but not yet compromised by the conspiracy, to delay any pronouncement against the government.

Even the most disappointed separatist, however, found some ground for cautious optimism. The success of the rebellion in Oriente provided some compensation for failures elsewhere. However faint rebellion flickered elsewhere, the success in Oriente guaranteed that the insurrectionary flame would not be extinguished altogether. Not auspicious, to be sure, but adequate—providing a provincial base from which to regroup and renew. In any case, the most prestigious revolutionary leaders had not yet arrived in Cuba. Their return, separatists predicted confidently, would breathe new life into the moribund movement.

VI   April 1895: The contrast could not have been sharper. Antonio Maceo sailed to Cuba in an undersized schooner, buffeted by strong winds and high waves. He washed ashore on the north Oriente coast, near Baracoa, after the wreck of his vessel. Pursued by the Spanish immediately upon his arrival, Maceo took refuge in the inhospitable wilderness of the Oriente interior. Some nights later, the crew of a German fruit ship lowered a small row boat gently into frenzied swells three miles off the southeastern Cuban coast. Through driving rain and six-foot waves, the party of six rowed determinedly toward the mountain landscape etched against the northern night. Hours later, the crew washed ashore, wet and cold but otherwise euphoric. After some fifteen years of exile, José Martí and Máximo Gómez had returned to Cuba.

At the other end of the island, and at the same time, Havana completed lavish preparations for the arrival of the new governor general. Week-long formal ceremonies and official receptions greeted General Arsenio Martínez Campos. Much optimism surrounded the return of the Spanish hero of Zanjón. He was a distinguished soldier and skilled negotiator—he spoke the separatists' language, many were convinced. Many believed, too, that the new governor general would repeat in short order his triumph of 1878.

In April 1895, the leading protagonists of a thirty-year-old drama had returned to Cuba. The arrival of Gómez, Maceo, and Martí had an immediately uplifting impact on insurgent morale. By late spring, an uprising of such palpably inauspicous beginnings had taken a firm hold in the east. Languishing revolutionary fervor revived. So, too, did the resolve of insurgents in the field.[11] The 1895 sugar harvest had just ended, and thousands of sugar workers completing the cycle of semiannual employment found the call to arms in behalf of Cuba Libre an irresistible summons. The rainy season had begun, and unfavorable weather conditions hampered Spanish military operations. Restrictions on government military activities facilitated insurgent movement in the countryside, allowed new incorporations into separatist ranks, and favored the arrival of filibustering expeditions from abroad.[12] Preoccupied with disturbances in the interior districts of the east, government authorities neglected surveillance of the coastal regions of central Cuba. In late spring, an expedition under the direction of Generals Carlos Roloff, Serafín Sánchez, and José María (Mayía) Rodríguez landed in Las Villas. In a matter of weeks, key regions of central Cuba joined the east in rebellion. By the summer, virtually the entire eastern third of the island was up in arms.

If Gómez, Maceo, and Martí arrived in Cuba to make war, Martínez Campos arrived to make peace. Not that the new Spanish governor general lacked the resources to prosecute the war. On the contrary, he had sailed into Havana at the head of an expeditionary force of some thirty thousand officers and men, equipped with new arms, supplies, and additional ships to strengthen coastal defenses. But war was not Martínez Campos's purpose. His part at Zanjón had established Martínez Campos as a political defender of the colonial commonweal. No one represented more, either in his person or in his politics, the spirit of reform and concession; no one was more associated with a conciliatory approach to the Antillean problem than Martínez Campos.[13] He arrived with his saber sheathed at his side and an olive branch in his hand.

VII
Autonomists welcomed this change in colonial administration. The outbreak of a new colonial rebellion made reforms obligatory, Autonomists insisted.[14] Spain must either concede reforms to end the Cuban rebellion or confront a revolution that would end Spanish rule. Autonomists greeted Martínez Campos's appointment as a favorable augury—evidence that Madrid now intended to deliver long overdue reforms.[15] Long the object of official harrassment, Autonomists now represented a potential solution to the Cuban problem. Or so they believed. The rebellion conferred on the Autonomist party a new respectability, and these conditions, liberals were certain, made autonomist policies irresist-

ible if not inevitable. Autonomists were no longer perceived as situated along the subversive fringe of the island's political spectrum. If the rebellion had bestowed a new respectability on Autonomists, the appointment of Martínez Campos provided them with a new legitimacy. No Spanish official of comparable stature had been more favorably predisposed to the tenets of autonomism than Martínez Campos. Indeed, the Autonomists, having acquired official favor under Martínez Campos, figured to play an important role in the restoration of peace.

That it was Martínez Campos who arrived in Cuba to assume supervision of the Spanish war effort contributed powerfully to prolonging the flagging Autonomist faith in a reformist solution to the colonial crisis. At the critical juncture of the war, Creole elites chose to persist in the middle position between the embattled extremes of the colonial polity. This lingering faith would last long enough to discredit liberals among loyalists and estrange Autonomists from armed separatists.

Autonomists had consistently advocated a pacific end to the rebellion. Soon after the "Grito de Baire," party leaders appealed to insurgent chieftains to abandon the path of armed struggle. As early as March 1895, the Junta Central of the Autonomist party dispatched a commission to meet with Bartolomé Masó in an unsuccessful effort to secure the insurgent chieftain's surrender. A second Autonomist peace delegation a short time later, this one headed by the former insurgent president during the Ten Years' War, Juan Spotorno, fared little better.[16]

But these unsuccessful peace overtures, Autonomists insisted, had been undertaken under the auspices of the old regime, one that lacked both credibility among separatists and confidence among Autonomists. Nor was it certain that these early discussions had official sanction. Too much was too vague in these, the early weeks of the insurrection.

In April 1895, the occasion to renew the quest for reforms seemed properly auspicious and sufficiently urgent. As the natural political allies of the new governor general, Autonomists quickly announced their commitment to a negotiated peace. A peace settlement, particularly an early and speedy peace, one to which liberals were party, promised at once to advance the political fortunes of the Autonomist party and increase its effectiveness in the pursuit of the colonial reforms.

Coincident with the arrival of Martínez Campos, the Junta Central drafted a lengthy exposition outlining its opposition to the insurrection. Signed by the ranking members of the party in Havana, the Autonomist manifesto denounced the insurrection as "criminal" and urged insurgent leaders to return to a legal resolution of colonial grievances. Autonomists also took advantage of Martínez Campos's return to Cuba to urge Madrid to adopt reform and concession as a means of demonstrating good faith with the colony—measures seen preliminary to a larger reorganization of colonial government.[17]

VIII The new governor-general confronted two distinct but inter-related problems upon his arrival. First, he understood immediately the necessity of arresting the growth in the insurgent armies. Second, and related, the revolution had to be contained to the east if reforms were to have any chance of success.

The solution to the first problem was obvious. Mindful of the politico-military implications of the *tiempo muerto* (dead season), government authorities rushed to provide relief work for the swelling ranks of the unemployed sugar workers. In early spring, Martínez Campos organized a variety of public works programs in Oriente and Camagüey designed to cushion the economic repercussions of *tiempo muerto*. In Santiago de Cuba, municipal authorities inaugurated the construction of a series of public buildings and new streets. In Manzanillo, workers found employ-ment in military construction projects. Various railroad projects linking Manzanillo to Bayamo, Puerto Príncipe to Santa Cruz and Júcaro to Ciego de Avila employed thousands of workers in Oriente and Camagüey. Pier and wharf construction in several eastern port cities, including Santiago de Cuba and Manzanillo, also provided jobs for unemployed workers.[18]

The resolution of the second issue was more complicated. To be sure, Martínez Campos adopted the necessary military measures to quarantine the insurrection in the east. Immediately upon his arrival, he transferred 10,000 troops to the eastern war zones and established his military head-quarters in Santiago de Cuba. At the same time, military authorities rein-forced Spanish defenses along the Júcaro-Morón *trocha*, so effective two decades earlier in containing the insurgency in the east.

But the governor-general sensed that Spanish arms alone could not settle the Cuban conflict. In fact, military measures served only as corol-laries to Martínez Campos's larger purpose. Any hope of confining the insurrection to Oriente necessarily involved ending the conflict altogether, and only a speedily negotiated political settlement, one based on met-ropolitan concessions, offered any likelihood of restoring peace to the troubled eastern end of the island.

Nor were these newly discovered truths. For two decades Martínez

Campos had acted as the reformist conscience of Spain, reminding national leaders of the promises he had made in their name at Zanjón. But these were the decades of the Restoration Monarchy, a period of revived reverence for things traditional, not the best of times to be seeking adjustments of historic colonial relationships—no matter what had been promised at Zanjón. In 1895, however, Cuba resurfaced in Spanish domestic politics. Metropolitan attention was again directed to disaffection on the Ever-Faithful Isle. The time was both right and short for reform. Urgent military considerations made political concessions an essential if not an indispensable—and immediate—requisite of a peace settlement. However much Martínez Campos the statesman may have believed in the virtue of colonial reforms, it was Martínez Campos the soldier who appealed for compromise and concession. Only reform, he warned soberly, held any promise of ending revolution. Repeatedly the governor-general appealed to Madrid to offer the rebellious colony immediate and far-reaching concessions.[19] Fifteen years of shortsighted policies and broken promises had placed disaffected Cubans beyond the pale of a negotiated settlement based only on metropolitan pledges of future reforms. Deeds, not promises, were an essential and minimum demonstration of metropolitan good faith—the only type of demonstration Martínez Campos believed capable of restoring peace to Cuba.

The insurrection had transformed a political expedient into a military imperative. Martínez Campos appealed for reforms while the rebellion was still comparatively weak and insurgent leaders and their followers were susceptible to a negotiated compromise based on metropolitan concessions. It was necessary to end the insurrection in the east before separatist chieftains had developed the capacity to extend the war to the west. But from the outset, he feared that the insurgents possessed the capacity to cross the Júcaro-Morón *trocha* at will. "If [Máximo Gómez] wants to pass, he will pass," Martínez Campos predicted in July 1895.[20] Peace depended on ending the insurrection while it floundered in Oriente. In the spring of 1895, the rebellion involved only the leadership of a traditionally dissident sector of the *oriental* body politic, followed by the dispossessed of the eastern body social, and confined to a region of comparative political, military, and economic insignificance.

Martínez Campos also appreciated the delicate and precarious balance between metropolitan authority and colonial politics. The disastrous consequences of Spanish economic policies of 1894-1895 had estranged the colonial elite. Only the outbreak of internal war in February 1895, and the attending spectre of economic disruption and social chaos, had arrested the erosion of Cuban support for Spain. The reserve of planter goodwill toward Spain was all but exhausted when the insurrection broke out. If planters could not reasonably expect enlightened economic policies from Madrid, they felt minimally justified in demanding protection of their property from the ravages of colonial disorders. Planter support was not unconditional, however. The exigencies of war persuaded property owners to subordinate outstanding economic grievances with Spain to immediate political concerns. But they desired neither a costly war, one that would be financed out of Cuban revenues as in 1878, nor a protracted war, one that would disrupt the economy and destroy property.

The political dimensions of the conflict were self-evident. By ending the insurrection before it reached the rich sugar-producing districts in the west, Martínez Campos protected the economic base of Spain's local allies. But there were other considerations. The expansion of the war westward, he understood, would also have far-reaching international implications. With so much property in the west in the possession of North American investors, an extension would inevitably serve to draw the United States directly into the conflict. Moreover, new insurgent operations in the west would necessitate the deployment of Spanish forces on numerous fronts and require patrolling an additional thousand miles of coast while facing internal political discontent and international diplomatic pressure.

IX Martínez Campos was never unduly sanguine about Spain's prospects in Cuba. As early as May 1895, only a month in Cuba, he predicted that it would probably become necessary to concede the Cubans autonomy—"and even the island if they want it."[21]

By the end of the summer, however, the issue of political reforms was a moot question. In Madrid, Spanish authorities steadfastly balked at all suggestions of colonial reforms so long as Cubans remained in arms. In Cuba, the insurgent command refused to discuss any terms for a peace settlement based on anything other than independence.[22]

In late summer, Spanish efforts to contain the rebellion to Oriente suffered a jolting blow when insurgent armies crossed into Camagüey province. Several weeks later, Máximo Gómez and Antonio Maceo crossed the *trocha* and passed into Las Villas.

The presence of insurgent armies in central Cuba in the autumn of 1895, coincident with preparations for the 1896 sugar harvest, stunned western planters and evoked the spectre of the apocalypse so long the nightmare of the west. Insurgent operations in the west now created pressures of a new sort for beleaguered Spanish military authorities. Political considerations weighed heavily on military planning. Mindful of the economic coefficient of colonial politics, the Spanish army command hastily reorganized military operations around planters' needs, reassigning field units to garrison duty on the western estates, guard detail along main railroad lines, and supervision of the sugar harvest.[23] The presence of insurgent columns in Las Villas in September forced Martínez Campos to assign the majority of the 25,000 officers and men arriving in Cuba that autumn to the sugar estates of central Cuba.[24] And inevitably, plainly political decisions were not without military consequences. After August, he all but officially conceded the eastern countryside to the swelling insurgent armies.

Behind these decisions lay a dismal assessment of politico-military conditions in Cuba. The failure to negotiate a political settlement while the revolt faltered in Oriente, followed by the spread of the insurrection into central Cuba, ended all chances of a negotiated reconciliation. Central to Martínez Campos's calculations was the conviction that if Spain remained indisposed to settle the conflict politically, it was incapable of ending it militarily. He never underestimated the gravity of the Cuban revolt. Disaffection that could not be relieved by reforms would not be subdued by repression. The insurrection, the governor general wrote in July, had assumed in six months far more serious proportions than the Ten Years' War had achieved at its apogee.[25] In April 1895, Martínez Campos was skeptical; in August, he was pessimistic.

If the expansion of the insurrection placed the Cuban conflict beyond the pale of a negotiated political settlement, it also enormously raised the requirements of a military solution. Only the most severe of military campaigns offered Spain any prospect of success. And any military plan that failed to include the resettlement of the rural population was doomed to defeat.

Martínez Campos was neither enthusiastic to pursue the type of campaign necessitated by the Cuban insurrection nor optimistic that it would in the end produce a victory of Spanish arms. "We would need," he wrote prophetically in the summer of 1895, "four years, 400,000 soldiers, and 4,000 million *pesetas*."[26] When asked by a reporter later that autumn if his policy of conciliation should be replaced with more rigorous measures, he responded that any such change would involve minimally some 150,000 troops and three years of war. He did not, moreover, want to assume "responsibility for the burial of 75,000 *peninsular* Spaniards."[27] The insurrection, Martínez Campos sensed with foreboding, represented a total war, a struggle that found virtually the entire Cuban population arrayed against Spain. The population outside the cities "hates Spain," the governor-general reported. "Even the most timid are quick to follow the orders of the insurgent chieftains.[28] "They want independence," he wrote, "even though the land is left razed and sterile."[29]

It was a war without a clearly identifiable enemy.The support of the insurgency by the rural population, if only passively, converted a difficult situation into an impossible one. Allied to the insurgents by persuasion and proximity, the peasantry provided shelter, supplies, medicine, and food. Rural families cared for the wounded; peasants served as guides and scouts and always a ubiquitous source of intelligence. It did not take Martínez Campos long to understand the depth and significance of this collaboration. "When passing peasant huts in the countryside," he wrote in despair, "men are not to be seen; and the women, when asked for the whereabouts of their husbands and sons, respond with a frightful frankness, 'in the woods with so and so' . . .; on the other hand, they see a [Spanish] column pass, they count it, and voluntarily pass the information on with astonishing spontaneity and speed."[30] Any hope of a victory of Spanish arms, Martínez Campos concluded grimly in mid-1895, would require the relocation of the entire rural population away from the zones of insurgent operations to specially constructed fortified centers under Spanish control. But, he hastened to warn, the conditions of hunger and misery in these centers would be incalculable. A reconcentration program not only promised to visit untold grief and suffering on innocent noncombatants, but it would also require a considerable increase in Spanish troops and expenditures. Spain could neither adequately feed nor properly shelter the hundreds of thousands of civilians that such a program would relocate into fortified centers. And even if this policy proved successful in the short run, he predicted, the continued unwillingness of metropolitan authorities to provide the necessary colonial reforms in Cuba would make an outbreak of a new war within another decade all but inevitable.

These propositions were advanced as theoretical responses to the Cuban problem. In fact, they were formulations Martínez Campos knew to be very much under consideration in senior military circles in Spain. He never missed an opportunity to underscore the deficiency and, ultimately, the futility of such a plan. From the outset, the governor general disassociated himself from the reconcentration program. If Madrid desired to institute such a policy, he wished to be relieved of command; his sense of honor and professional ethic would not permit him to prosecute a war of such ruthless proportions against the civilian population of Cuba, preferring, he wrote, to resign rather than "subject the island to a reign of terror."[31]

X   Martínez Campos's offer to resign was a grand but empty gesture. Developments in the field had already sealed his fate. On Christmas Day, 1895, a beaten Martínez Campos returned to Havana. His arrival in the capital completed an odyssey of defeat. Two months earlier, in September, he had transferred his headquarters from Santiago de Cuba to Santa Clara. From this point, insurgent columns marched implacably westward, forcing Spanish units to retreat along the front line of the *insurrecto* advance. The site of Martínez Campos's headquarters served to mark, in more than symbolic terms, the forward point of the insurgent drive westward: from Santa Clara to Cienfuegos in November, to Colón in December, to Jovellanos in the middle of the month, further west to Limonar four days later. On December 23, at Coliseo in Matanzas, the combined forces of Antonio Maceo and Máximo Gómez outmaneuvered Martínez Campos. Two days later, the governor general moved his headquarters to Havana and immediately readied the capital for the expected insurgent attack. On January 2, Martínez Campos proclaimed a state of war for Havana and Pinar del Río.[32]

Havana was stunned. Alarm increased to panic, and ultimately the city passed under martial law. The capital waited tensely. On January 6, Antonio Maceo paused at Hoyo Colorado, a Havana suburb. But instead of laying seige to the capital, the *Ejército Invasor* (Invading Army) bypassed the capital and continued westward toward Pinar del Río. A week later, the invasion of the west was complete.

The presence of insurgent forces in the western extremities of the island gave palpable expression to the bankruptcy of the policy of reconciliation. In the course of some ten months, the insurrection had dramatically outgrown its provincial dimensions and acquired the characteristics of a full-scale national uprising. By early 1896, every province in Cuba reported insurgent operations. As the insurgency approached the completion of its first year, travel and communication across the island had broken down. Planters despaired. The prospects for the 1896 *zafra* (harvest) were now bleak. Trade and commerce declined as uncertainty increased.

The invasion signaled more than the failure of Spanish military policy. In a very real sense, it announced the insolvency of Autonomist politics. Not a few rushed to fix responsibility for Spanish reversals on those officials, principally Martínez Campos, who had neglected, in their zeal to arrive at a political settlement of the Cuban problem, to attend adequately to the military requirements of the Spanish war effort. But more than the governor-general suffered ignominy. Upon Autonomists generally fell the weight of metropolitan wrath and *peninsular* ire. The military and political setbacks of late 1895 and early 1896 confirmed among conservatives the futility if not folly of metropolitan efforts to seek reconciliation with the rebellious Cubans through compromise and concession.

The failure to restore order to the troubled regions of the east by pacific means, followed by the expansion of the insurgency into the west, galvanized conservative sentiment against Martínez Campos. Never sympathetic with the liberals' approach to pacification, the Spanish community and its supporters on both sides of the Atlantic denounced the governor general and clamored for a change of colonial administration. An irresistible swell of conservative opinion demanded a change of policy and the adoption of aggressive military measures against the growing insurrection.[33] Criticism of the governor-general increased through the end of 1895. By late fall, the policies of Martínez Campos were openly attacked in senior government circles in Spain.[34] "What is happening is really inconceivable," the Madrid daily *El Heraldo* announced. "It is incomprehensible that experienced generals . . . can be mocked in the manner now occurring. It is no longer a surprise, it is an astonishment, in fact, a stupefaction. The Government must already understand that this situation cannot be prolonged."[35] In Cuba, the governor general was the object of public censure for having permitted a regional uprising to assume island-wide proportions. The *Boletín Comercial* described a "desperate situation in . . . provinces desolated by the war." "We foresaw this some time ago," the editors intoned, "and advised the authorities to take measures for the mitigation of the disastrous effects of the crisis."[36] The *Avisador Comercial* denounced, through sarcasm, the "generosity and chivalry" of a military policy that failed to contain the rebellion.[37] "A desolating war is sweeping away the wealth of the Island," the *Diario de la Marina* editorialized, "perturbing the public mind, impeding the functions of economic forces of the country, and destroying the lives and fortunes of its inhabitants."[38] In late 1895, the executive board of the Unión Constitucional cabled a lengthy denunciation of Martínez Campos to Spain that concluded with a demand for his removal.[39] In late December, Madrid relieved Martínez Campos of his command.

XI   In 1896 attention centered on General Valeriano Weyler. Never discreet in his opposition to Martínez Campos's approach to pacification,

Weyler had emerged as the leading advocate of a military solution to the Cuban problem. A veteran of previous Antillean campaigns, Weyler had earned the reputation as a ruthless and tenacious campaigner.[40] The appointment of Weyler represented more than a reaction against Martínez Campos. In its broadest sense, it signified Madrid's repudiation of any policy that had as its goal anything less than a total victory of Spanish arms. By early 1896 conservative Prime Minister Antonio Cánovas del Castillo had committed his ministry to winning the war militarily, without concession and reform.[41] Both in his person and policies, Weyler represented a military solution to the Cuban problem. Martínez Campos had sought to end the war by negotiating peace; Weyler sought peace by waging war. "I believe," Weyler announced upon his appointment as governor-general, "that war should be answered with war."[42] "Even the dead will rise against him," Martínez Campos predicted grimly upon learning of Weyler's appointment.[43]

Weyler arrived in Cuba in February 1896 and immediately set about the task of waging war. The Júcaro-Morón *trocha* in the east was reinforced. The fifty-mile clearing, some 200 yards wide through tropical forests, was fortified by new blockhouses at fifty-yard intervals guarded by some twenty thousand Spanish soldiers. Weyler constructed a second *trocha* between Mariel and Majana, dividing Havana province from Pinar del Río. The Mariel-Majana *trocha*, extending some twenty miles north to south, was garrisoned by some fifteen thousand troops. By partitioning the island into three regions, Weyler hoped to isolate and contain *insurrecto* armies at both ends of the island, thereby defeating insurgent units province by province.[44]

The reorganization of Spanish defenses around the Júcaro-Morón and Mariel-Majana *trochas* marked the first in a series of new military measures. The renewed emphasis on the *trochas* system announced the inauguration of a much more aggressive Spanish campaign. By mid-1896, Weyler had gone beyond the *trocha* strategy and paid increasing attention to enhancing the combat capabilities of Spanish armed forces. New arms were distributed to Spanish troops. Greater attention was paid to the security of communication and transportation systems. Troops assigned earlier by Martínez Campos to the sugar estates were withdrawn from garrison duty and reassigned to combat units. To replace them, Weyler authorized planters to hire and arm private guards at their own expense.[45] To the more than one hundred fifty thousand Spanish troops in Cuba, Weyler added several auxiliary military units recruited locally. The Corps of Volunteers was revived, recruiting officers and men from the resident *peninsular* population on the island. Commanded by colonels, the senior ranks of the officer Corps of Volunteers represented the *peninsular* elite, the owners and managers of commerce, industry, and agriculture in Cuba. Volunteer troops were recruited among *peninsulares* in the civilian employ of their commanders.[46] From among the Cuban-born population, Weyler organized guerrilla units to serve with Spanish army patrols and municipal police forces.[47]

In late 1896, Weyler undertook the final measure of his "war with war" strategy—the decree ordering the reconcentration of the rural population. Even before his appointment to Cuba, Weyler had advocated reconcentration as a measure necessary to the defeat of the insurgents.[48] Weyler early acquired an understanding of the nature of the Cuban insurgency and the requirements of a military victory. Any campaign strategy that did not first deprive the insurgents of their support in the countryside, Weyler insisted, and distinguish combatants from the noncombatant population, was doomed to failure. So long as the rural population remained free to move between the cities and the countryside, at liberty to transport medicine, supplies, and food across government lines, so long as farmers remained free to tend to their crops and livestock, Spain would find itself in an impossible war against insuperable odds.

In the autumn of 1896, Weyler issued the first in a series of decrees ordering the rural population to relocate to designated fortified towns. All agricultural activities without specific authorization were prohibited. Spanish forces scoured the countryside, destroying all fields under unauthorized cultivation and removing all supplies and equipment of potential use to insurgent armies.[49] Ranchers were ordered to drive their livestock herds to the cities.[50] All unauthorized trade and commerce between the cities and the countryside were banned.

By the end of the year, a stillness had settled over the Cuban countryside. Rural Cuba had been converted openly into a war zone where the presence of life signified a struggle to the death. For countless thousands life in the interior war zone seemed to have turned into an incomprehensible nightmare. Reconcentration camps filled the cities with distant sounds of women wailing, children shrieking, and men praying for deliverance, or else swearing vengeance on their tormentors. Hundreds of thousands of Cubans, the young and old, men, women, and children, were crowded into hastily and poorly constructed resettlement camps. With only scant attention to housing and less to diet, the overcrowded reconcentration centers became breeding grounds for disease, epidemics, and, ultimately, death. The *reconcentrados*, without adequate medical attention, sanitation, and food, died by the tens of thousands.[51]

The stage was set for a grim confrontation. Spain had embarked on a policy committed to total victory of Spanish arms, and insurgent Cubans vowed to accept nothing less than total independence. Insurgent military achievements and Spanish policies after 1896 sharpened and clarified the issues. Weyler's total war strategy affected the island totally. So, too, did the invasion. There were no longer enclaves of Cuban society immune from the effects of the war. Politics hardened and polarities sharpened.

3 Intuitive Certainty

The American Government could not consent to any change in the political situation of Cuba other than one which should place it under the jurisdiction of the United States.
—Alexander H. Everett. U.S. Minister to Spain, 1825

The policy of the Government of the United States in regard to Cuba, in any contingency calling for our interpretation, will depend in a great degree upon the peculiar circumstances of the case, and cannot, therefore, now be presented with much precision. . . . Nothing will be done on our part to disturb its present connection with Spain, unless the character of that connection should be so changed as to affect our present or prospective security.
—William L. Marcy, Secretary of State, 1853

Every rock and every grain of sand in that island were drifted and washed out from American soil by the floods of the Mississippi, and the other estuaries of the Gulf of Mexico. The island has seemed to me . . . to gravitate back again to the parent continent from which . . . it sprang. . . . The acquisition of Cuba is a question of time, of necessity, and of opportunity.
—William H. Seward, 1859

I am thinking a great deal about Cuba, but I am as far as ever from seeing the place when we can get in.
—Grover Cleveland to Richard Olney, July 1896

I December 7, 1896. Curious coincidence, the events of December 7, 1896: "Spanish authorities reported this morning that Antonio Maceo, the Cuban commander, was killed in battle at Punta Brava," an Associated Press dispatch from Havana read. On December 7, 1896, American newspapers carried front-page accounts of new Spanish military operations in western Cuba. On that day in December, the *New York Times* published a letter from a concerned reader in Brooklyn lamenting "the burning of sugar plantations, the shooting of prisoners, and the wrecking of railroad trains." Throughout "this bloody year," the writer concluded, "there has not been a single stand-up battle. It is all a 'stab-him-in-the-back' kind of fighting, ruthlessly cruel, but unproductive of results save the utter desolation of the island."[1] Also on that day, Grover Cleveland submitted his last presidential message to Congress. He, too, commented solemnly on the "immense destruction of property" and the "utter ruin of an adjoining country." Indeed, Cleveland dwelled at length on the conflict in Cuba— almost a quarter of the annual message centered on what the president called "the Cuban problem."[2]

The events of December served to set in relief a dramatic climax to 1896, a year of growing preoccupation in the United States with the deepening conflict in Cuba. By the end of the year, the two-year-old war on the island had catapulted Cuba onto the front pages of American newspapers and into the center stage of national debate. On December 7, 1896, it no doubt appeared perfectly normal to most members of Congress that the president's overview of the state of the union should also include a lengthy review of the state of Cuba. The requirements of partisan politics and public opinion made it perhaps obligatory. On December 7, Congress assembled expectantly to receive Cleveland's message, especially mindful of those sections of the presidential text outlining the White House response to conditions in Cuba. The *New York Times* correspondent in Washington reported that the Senate had paid "very little attention . . . to the other portions of the message."[3] The press, too, for its part, featured those sections on Cuba as the most newsworthy items of Cleveland's address. "By far the most important part of the President's message," the *New York Times* asserted editorially, "related to the Cuban question."[4]

The anticipation greeting the president's message reflected more than fleeting preoccupation with "the Cuban question." A growing sense of historical climax had stirred the national imagination. It was with no small sense of prescience that Americans detected in the events of 1896 the signs announcing the fulfillment of one of the central prophecies of nineteenth-

58

century America: the long expected annexation of Cuba. These were truly portentous moments. A national policy pursued by three generations of American statesmen over three quarters of a century seemed in late 1896 to be approaching its predestined denouement.

II   Over the course of some seventy years, through the century of American history Robert Kelley described as the age of "bi-polar politics," an uncommon consensus had developed around the fate that destiny had fixed for Cuba: at some indeterminate point in the future, Cuba would be part of the American union.[5] To many, the destinies of the two countries seemed not merely intertwined, but indissoluble. This fascination with Cuba was only in part economic. Other factors played more prominently on the early nineteenth-century imagination. Even Americans who suspected the potential agricultural wealth of the island failed to appreciate its full economic significance. National security needs were invoked regularly. So, too, was the need to civilize. Sentiment, culture, and race played their part. In the end, Cuba was simply there, and so close as to confer on geographical nearness divine sanction for political intimacy. It was only the means by which Cuba would become an American possession that remained beyond the powers of divination of nineteenth-century Americans. All were certain, however, that history would respond to the summons of manifest destiny.

The process was inexorable, the end inevitable. Indeed, this belief held such a powerful grip on the nineteenth-century American mind that it was perhaps only natural that this policy premise assumed the full proportions of an axiomatic imperative. Certainty of Cuba's destiny rested not on any particular prophetic gift but, rather, on an understanding of very predictable, if perhaps not self-evident, truths of nature. Just as there were incontrovertible laws of nature, nineteenth-century Americans posited, so too were there self-evident truths of politics. "There are laws of political as well as of physical gravitation," John Quincy Adams discerned in 1823, "and if an apple, severed by a tempest from its native tree, cannot choose but fall to the ground, Cuba, forcibly disjoined from its own unnatural connexion with Spain, and incapable of self-support, can gravitate only towards the North American Union, which, by the same law of nature, cannot cast her off from its bosom."[6]

Repeated and refined in the course of the nineteenth century, the notion of "political gravitation" became the central and enduring feature of American Cuban policy.[7] This construct, however, rested on a number of assumptions, chief among which was continued Spanish sovereignty over Cuba for an unspecified but not unlimited period of time. To be sure, Spain's intrusion into the Western Hemisphere had upset the natural order of the geo-political universe, and, no doubt, its continued presence postponed the restoration of the balance. But by the first quarter of the nineteenth century the tide of the Spanish empire in America had receded to the outer Caribbean rim. It was a weak and exhausted Spain that shared Gulf shipping lanes with the United States and whose very state of torpor made its presence in Cuba tolerable if not perhaps even desirable.[8]

This Spanish weakness, however compatible with immediate American national interests, remained a constant source of potential calamity to long-term American designs. A weak Spain could uphold only the most tenuous claim of sovereignty over Cuba. And while this state of affairs may have offered encouragement to the seers of the Cuban-American union, it also served to arouse unwelcomed European interest in the Caribbean. A derelict Spain was an invitation for a resurgence of colonial rivalries in the Caribbean, and this spectre of renewed European intrusion in the Antilles was an uncertainty from which the United States required release—something possible only when Cuba passed securely under American control.

For many Americans, the withering of Spanish sovereignty in Cuba represented the last act of a historic drama, one predestined to climax with the annexation of Cuba. For its part, the United States committed itself to guaranteeing the process by which Spanish sovereignty would continue to attenuate, at the end of which the United States would assert control over Cuba. Meanwhile, nothing could be permitted to deflect again the course of natural laws; this nineteenth-century drama would be played out wholly in the Western Hemisphere and without the intrusion of outside men and nations. Until such moment as Spain proved incapable of maintaining its authority over Cuba, at which time the United States would claim possession over the island, Spain's declining sovereignty in the Caribbean would be underwritten by the United States.

Throughout the nineteenth century, all matters affecting the political status of Cuba passed under the policy purview of the United States. As guardians of the status quo, Americans pursued a policy designed at once to guarantee Spanish sovereignty and prevent any modification of the island's political status that did not have as its end the cession of Cuba to the United States.[9] Guaranteeing Cuba's "independence against all the world *except* Spain," Thomas Jefferson had insisted in 1823, ". . . would be nearly as valuable to us as if it were our own."[10] John Forsyth, James Monroe's minister to Spain, had repeatedly assured Spanish authorities that the United States' "interest required, as there was no prospect of [Cuba's] passing into our hands, that it should belong to Spain."[11] The American commitment to Spanish sovereignty over Cuba included a national resolve to resort to arms to maintain the prevailing order. In 1823 Jefferson had counseled James Monroe to "oppose, with all our means, the forcible interposition of any power, either as auxiliary, stipendiary, or under any other form or pretext, and most especially [Cuba's] transfer to any power, by conquest, cession or in any other way."[12] Twenty years later, Martin Van Buren's Secretary of State John Forsyth had authorized the American minister in Madrid to reassure Spanish authorities "that in case of any attempt, from whatever quarter, to wrest from her this portion of her territory, she may securely depend upon the military and naval resources of the United States to aid her in preserving or recovering it."[13] Secretary of State John M. Clayton had stated this policy succinctly in 1849: "The news of the cession of Cuba to any foreign power would, in the United States, be the instant signal for war."[14]

Nor was American support of Spanish sovereignty in Cuba confined solely to a defense of the status quo against external threats. Any internal attempt by Cubans to end Spanish rule, and thereby alter the island's political status, posed a threat no less menacing to the United States. The Haitian experience loomed large over American policy calculations. The prospect of Cuban independence immediately raised the spectre of another black republic in the Caribbean. For John Adams, the thought of a free black population in Cuba, so close to American shores, offered sufficient grounds to oppose any independence movement on the island.[15] "Other considerations," Martin Van Buren had warned in 1829, "connected with a certain class of our population, make it the interest of the southern section of the Union that no attempt should be made in that island to throw off the yoke of Spanish dependence, the first effect of which would be the sudden emancipation of a numerous slave population, the result of which could not but be very sensibly felt upon the adjacent shores of the United States."[16]

The prospect of Cuban independence aroused other fears. American policymakers believed Cuba incapable of successfully sustaining self-government. The central premise of Adams's "law of political gravitation" rested on the belief that Cubans were "not competent to a system of permanent self-dependence."[17] In 1825, Henry Clay had given explicit and enduring form to American opposition to Cuban independence. The United States, Clay had stressed, in possession of guaranteed access to Cuban trade and commerce, was eminently satisfied with Spanish sovereignty over Cuba. "This government desires no political change of that condition," Clay insisted. "The population itself of the island is incompetent at present, from its composition and amount, to maintain self-government." Indeed, should Cuba become the theater of revolution, Clay had concluded in a thinly veiled warning, the "possible contingencies of such a protracted war might bring upon the government of the United States duties and obligations, the performance of which, however painful it should be, they [sic] may not be at liberty to decline."[18] Throughout the Ten Years' War, the Grant administration had resisted public pressure to support the Cubans' struggle. Secretary of State Hamilton Fish made no effort to conceal his low esteem of the intellectual and moral quality of the Cubans, believing a population consisting of Indians, Africans, and Spaniards singularly incapable of self-government.[19]

American refusal to extend recognition of belligerency to the insurgent republic between 1868 and 1878, a status that would have enhanced the rebel cause immeasurably, also had stemmed from the hope that the Cuban conflict would advance American designs over the island. Certainly Fish had contemplated, with more than casual interest, the possible benefits accruing to the United States as a result of a prolonged, costly, and destructive war in Cuba. The Cuban insurrection, the secretary of state commented at a cabinet level meeting in April 1869, promised to expose the "madness and fatuity" of Spain's continued sovereignty over Cuba; ultimately, the war would produce "a condition of affairs, and state of feeling that would compel all the civilized nations to regard the Spanish rule as an international nuisance, which must be abated, when they would all be glad that we should interpose and regulate the control of the Island."[20] By 1875, however, as Spain appeared to have regained its mastery over the island, Grant reaffirmed the traditional American commitment to Spanish sovereignty in Cuba. Recognition of Cuban independence, Grant indicated in his 1875 message to Congress, was "impracticable and indefensible"; similarly, extending belligerent status to insurgent Cubans was "unwise and premature." Grant offered, instead, the good offices of the United States to bring about a reconciliation between the rebellious colony and the mother country.[21]

III   American support of Spanish sovereignty over Cuba in the nineteenth century also imposed on Spain the tacit obligation to retain possession of the island. A curious, if only vaguely understood, reciprocity had emerged in the course of the nineteenth century, one in which the United States upheld Spanish sovereignty in return for a future preferential access to ownership of Cuba. This was a conscious policy of patience and watchful waiting, one in which Americans expected that their support of Spain, as well as their forebearance and restraint, would ultimately be rewarded with Spain's cession of Cuba. "Desirable . . . as the possession of this Island may be to the United States," James Buchanan as American minister in Spain had proclaimed, "we would not acquire it except by the free consent of Spain. Any acquisition not sanctioned by justice and honor, would be too dearly purchased." The United States was confident, the future president added, "that in the natural course of events the time is not very distant when it will become part of our Union by peaceful negotiation."[22] Continued Spanish sovereignty in Cuba served American interests—a necessary if only temporary condition until such time as circumstances permitted the expected transfer of the island. Spanish rule represented the only acceptable alternative to U.S. possession. Spain had forfeited effective sovereignty over its colony, losing everything but the right to retain possession of the island. In 1840, Secretary of State John Forsyth outlined the American position. "Should you have reason to suspect any design on the part of Spain to transfer voluntarily her title to the island," Forsyth had instructed the American minister in Madrid, "whether of ownership or possession, and whether permanent or temporary, . . . you will distinctly state that the United States will prevent it at all hazards."[23] The United States, the American minister in London explained to Lord Palmerston, could not permit Spain to cede Cuba to any European power: "That of the right of the United States to interfere in relation to these islands . . . there could be little doubt; that whilst the general rule of international law which forbids the interference of one State in the affairs of another was freely admitted, there were yet *exceptions to the rule, in relation to the laws of defense and self-preservation*, which all nations acknowledged, and that the present was precisely such a case."[24]

Seduced by a sense of historic inevitability, Americans had never quite defined the means by which the United States would acquire Cuba. The auguries that were to announce the momentous occasion remained unrevealed to nineteenth-century policymakers. The United States approached the acquisition of Cuba timidly, reconciled to a predestined if not inscrutable rhythmic order of a geo-political universe that would, Americans were certain, at some undetermined moment in the future, deliver

Cuba into the union. The one attempt to take the initiative in 1854, through the Ostend Manifesto, had resulted in an embarrassing diplomatic debacle. For the remainder of the nineteenth century, the United States chose to await passively the development of conditions propitious for the annexation of Cuba.

The American commitment to continued Spanish sovereignty in Cuba, always the calculated and central means by which to promote American policy designs in the Caribbean, had not, of course, precluded efforts to hasten Cuba's self-evident destiny. Whatever else may have separated Whigs, Democrats, and Republicans, all agreed that at least one precondition to annexation was necessary: demonstration of Spain's inability and/or unwillingness to uphold its sovereignty over Cuba. Three generations of American statesmen had repeatedly seized occasions of Spanish political misfortunes as the moments in which to mount diplomatic initiatives for the purpose of acquiring the island. In 1809, as French troops overran the Iberian peninsula, Jefferson had proposed purchasing the island from Napoleon. The peak period of American filibustering activity in Cuba in 1848 had provided the occasion for President James Polk to offer Spain some $100 million for the island. Six years later, Franklin Pierce had taken advantage of a political crisis in Spain to renew Polk's earlier offer, raising the American offer to $130 million. Secretary of State Hamilton Fish seized the occasion of the Ten Years' War to propose again the purchase of Cuba.[25]

IV   In 1895, the antecedents of the American Cuban policy reached deep into the nineteenth century. They were possessed of a singular mystique—articles of faith as much a part of the national experience as the Articles of Confederation. The Cuban policy, too, had its origins with the Founding Fathers and, in time, acquired a peculiar inviolability. If no American president had found a moment favorable to consummate the prophetic imperative, neither had any found a reason to repudiate its essential assumptions. Nor, in fact, had there been cause to do either. Until 1895, the Cuban policy of the United States had required only the maintenance of the status quo and the preservation of Spanish sovereignty.

In 1895, however, the Cuban revolution challenged the status quo. It mattered not that the threat to Spanish rule originated internally from disgruntled colonial subjects harboring grievances universally perceived as legitimate. Few in Washington saw in the events of 1895 any reason to depart from the time-honored policy canons of the nineteenth century. On the contrary, insofar as the Cuban insurrection posed a direct challenge to Spanish sovereignty, it also jeopardized the long-standing American design to succeed Spain in the Caribbean and required of Washington a reaffirmation of the central tenet of its Cuba policy.

Not since Napoleon's invasion of Spain had the future of Spanish sovereignty in Cuba appeared as uncertain as it did in 1895. As early as September 1895, Secretary of State Richard B. Olney warned the White House that the insurrection in Cuba had assumed serious proportions. "While the insurrectionary forces to be dealt with are more formidable than ever before," Olney informed Grover Cleveland, "the ability of Spain to cope with them has visibly and greatly decreased. She is straining every nerve to stamp out the insurrection within the next few months. For what obvious reason? Because she is almost at the end of her resources." To the point, Olney concluded: "Spain cannot possibly succeed."[26] Nothing in the remaining two years of his service as secretary of state would alter Olney's initial impressions. The passage of time served only to corroborate his early judgments. Throughout late 1895 and early 1896, the insurrection had gathered momentum and expanded beyond the confines of the eastern provinces, and by the end of the year, it had been extended deep into the rich agricultural districts of the west. A year later, Olney reiterated his earlier conviction, this time directly to the Spanish minister. "It can hardly be questioned," he chided Enrique Dupuy de Lôme, "that the insurrection, instead of being quelled, is today more formidable than ever and enters upon the second year of its existence with decidedly improved prospects of success."[27] Reports from Cuba confirmed these fears. In June 1896, reinforcements from Spain brought the total number of Spanish troops in Cuba to a high of some two hundred thousand. "From these figures," American Consul Fitzhugh Lee in Havana noted disingenuously, "I deduce the fact there must be opposition to Spanish rule on the island, and that *war* is a fact accomplished."[28]

It was perhaps inevitable, if not predictable, that the insurrection in Cuba would surface immediately in American politics. Indeed, the long-standing national preoccupation with the island would have all but guaranteed eventual public debate; however, in 1895, a new urgency surrounded the Cuban question. Unsettled conditions in Cuba had immediate implications for the vastly augmented American capital stake on the island. With some $50 million invested in Cuba, official concern for the well-being and security of U.S. owned sugar estates, mines, and ranches, as well as for the safety of American citizens, became of paramount importance in Washington and added one more source of tension to the complicated policy issues of the mid-1890s.

The spectacle of a war in Cuba, early noteworthy for its fratricidal excesses, threatening American lives and property, and daily the subject of an aroused press, translated immediately into political pressure on incumbent Democrats. The Cuban insurgency showed early signs of capturing the public imagination and winning widespread popular sympathy. The presidential campaign of 1896, moreover, served to elevate the Cuban question as the central foreign policy issue in national politics. By late 1895, U.S. Cuban policy had moved into public forums. Much to the horror of the Cleveland administration, the legislative branch, responding to and motivated by public opinion, threatened to challenge the White House for the initiative and direction of American policy approaches to the conflict. For Cleveland, the Cuban policy represented a sacred legacy, the function of a historical mandate beyond the purview of partisan politics and above the changing tides of public opinion. Concern grew in the White House that a prolongation of the Cuban crisis would compel the administration to act either in a manner contrary to long-standing policy commitments or in a way that would threaten immediate American interests. As early as September 1895, Secretary of State Olney submitted for "the careful consideration of the Executive" a prophetic warning:

The contest [is] attracting the attention of all our people as well as enlisting their sympathies, if for no other reason, than because the insurgents are apparently the weaker party— politicians of all stripes, including Congressmen, either already setting their sails or preparing to set them so as to catch the popular breeze—it being not merely probably but almost certain that next winter Washington will swarm with emissaries of the insurgents demanding at least recognition of their belligerency.[29]

In his annual message several months later, Cleveland appealed for national calm and reiterated the American commitment to its "international obligation" to Spain.[30]

The president's appeal fell on deaf ears, however. The press denounced the president's December address as timid and without direction. In April 1896, only four months after Cleveland had appealed for national prudence,

Congress defiantly passed a joint resolution calling for the recognition of Cuban belligerency.

The April congressional resolution notwithstanding, Cleveland adhered steadfastly to existing policy procedures in Cuba. The White House rejected outright the congressional demand for recognition of belligerency as an infringement of the president's prerogative in foreign policy.[31] By the mid-1890s, moreover, American property owners opposed recognition of belligerency, fearful that this would induce Spain to adopt retaliatory measures against American interests on the island.[32] In his 1896 message to Congress, Cleveland noted that belligerency rights to the insurgents were "clearly perilous and injurious to our own interests."[33]

Recognition of Cuban belligerency also promised to uplift insurgent morale and boost the separatist war effort, complicating Spain's task of pacification. From the very outbreak of the Cuban conflict, the Cleveland administration remained steadfast in its commitment to Spanish sovereignty. Of all the possible alternatives to Spanish rule in Cuba, none aroused greater misgivings in Washington than Cuban independence. Indeed, only the prospect of a Cuban victory seemed to trouble Washington more than the likelihood of a prolonged war. For many, the withdrawal of Spain would be the signal for the onset of civil strife, racial conflict, and economic chaos. Opponents of Cuban independence found palpable confirmation of their worst fears in the separatist conflict. Many detected uncomfortable portents of Cuba Libre in the social heterogeneity of the insurgent ranks and in the ferocity of the war. The racial composition of the insurgent armies, the general availability of arms to the population at large, and the Cubans' growing experience in warfare seemed to set the stage for interminable civil havoc in the wake of the Spanish withdrawal. Even the "most devoted friend of Cuba" and the "most enthusiastic advocate of popular government," Olney insisted, could not look at developments in Cuba "except with the gravest apprehension." Olney continued:

There are only too strong reasons to fear that, once Spain were withdrawn from the island, the sole bond of union between the different factions of the insurgents would disappear; that a war of races would be precipitated, all the more sanguinary for the discipline and experience acquired during the insurrection, and that, even if there were to be temporary peace, it could only be through the establishment of a white and black republic, which, even if agreeing at the outset upon a division of the island be-

tween them, would be enemies from the start, and would never
rest until the one had been completely vanquished and subdued
by the other.[34]

Pending an acceptable and peaceful adjustment of the Cuban crisis, U.S.
support of Spanish sovereignty was deemed necessary—if only to forestall
the calamity Americans expected would follow the independence of Cuba.
In Madrid, correspondent James Creelman reported learning confidentially from officials of the Spanish court that Cleveland had "intimated to
the Monarchy, through more than one channel, his desire to prevent Cuba
from achieving independence."[35] Whatever else may have separated the
administration and its critics on Capitol Hill, they remained united by a
commonly held conviction of the inefficacy of a free Cuba. Indeed, for
many, belligerency was perceived as a means of hastening the separation
of Cuba from Spain, thereby setting the stage for the much-anticipated
annexation of the island. Senator Don Cameron, the sponsor of the April
1896 congressional resolution, saw the acquisition of Cuba as "not only
desirable but inevitable." "Civil and servile war" would follow independence, Cameron argued, "and Cuba would present, as Haiti now does, no
traces of its former prosperity, but the ruins of its once noble mansions."[36]

By 1896, the Cleveland administration was involving itself more directly
in assisting Spain to resolve the Cuban conflict. It had become apparent
that Spain lacked the military means to end the rebellion soon. On the
contrary, the first anniversary of the "Grito de Baire" found insurgent
forces operating across the full breadth of the island virtually unchecked.
Spanish efforts to end the insurrection, most notably Weyler's reconcentration policy, served only to intensify the debate in the United States and
inflame American public opinion without demonstrating much success.

The patently meager success of Spanish arms convinced the Cleveland
administration that only sweeping reforms in Cuba, including autonomy,
held any promise of bringing the insurrection to an end while preserving
Spanish sovereignty intact. Cleveland advocated reform as a means to end
the revolution and autonomy as an alternative to independence. In
January 1896, Secretary of State Olney asked two American planters in
Cuba, Oscar B. Stillman and Edwin F. Atkins, to contact insurgent leaders
in the field and ascertain their willingness to accept autonomy as a satisfactory arrangement for ending the conflict. Olney was subsequently led to
believe that insurgent separatists would consider Spanish concessions and
autonomy as sufficient terms to bring them to the peace table.[37] In the

following months, Olney approached Spanish authorities for the purpose of persuading Madrid to offer the rebellious colony substantive reforms. On March 20, Spanish Minister Enrique Dupuy de Lôme reported to Madrid the purport of a conversation with Secretary Olney. Officials in Washington, de Lôme wrote, had concluded that it would be "impossible for Spain to win, short of a protracted war." This pessimistic prediction notwithstanding, the Cleveland administration remained committed to Spanish sovereignty in Cuba. To guarantee continued Spanish rule, however, and retain American support, de Lôme reported learning from Olney, would require Madrid to institute a series of far-reaching reforms that, in Washington's judgment, would serve as the minimum conditions for peace based on continued sovereignty in Cuba. De Lôme added:

[Olney] wished to help Spain bring peace in Cuba; that he would oppose any step which might be considered as unfriendly to our sovereignty . . . but that he was sure that if Spain would put into effect reforms of a sort which the American public should regard as adequate, and which should evoke a declaration to this effect by this [the American] Government—in that case the insurrection would be shorn of the moral support it now has in this country, and the task of suppressing it would be made easier, because public opinion in the United States would be arrayed against it, and would force abandonment of arms by the Cubans, or facilitate their complete rout.[38]

Several weeks later, as Congress was preparing to vote favorably on the Cameron resolution, Olney increased American pressure on Spain. It had become apparent, the secretary of state suggested, that the insurgent armies were in command of a greater part of the island with a greater number of men and a greater quantity of modern weapons and equipment. Spain was losing the war, Olney suggested, and seemed incapable of arresting and reversing insurgent momentum. He offered the good offices of the United States to mediate a settlement based on Spanish reforms. "What the United States desires to do . . . .," Olney assured the Spanish minister, "is to cooperate with Spain in the immediate pacification of the island on such a plan as, leaving Spain her rights of sovereignty, . . . shall yet secure to the people of the island all such rights and powers of local self-government as they can reasonably ask." It did not seem reasonable, Olney concluded, that Spain could refuse the American offer; certainly the insurgents could not because "anything assented to by this Government which did not satisfy the reasonable demands and aspirations of Cuba would arouse the indignation of our whole people."[39]

Nothing in Washington's actions belied Cleveland's assurances of support of Spanish sovereignty. The administration continued to resist mounting congressional pressure to recognize Cuban belligerency. At the same time, Washington strictly enforced American neutrality laws. Cleveland had vowed in 1895 to "enforce obedience to our neutrality laws and to prevent the territory of the United States from being abused as a vantage point from which to aid those in arms against Spanish sovereignty."[40] A year later, Cleveland again enjoined American citizens, particularly "Cubans at heart and in all their feelings . . . [who] have taken out papers as naturalized citizens of the United States," to honor United States neutrality laws.[41] Within weeks of the outbreak of the insurgency, Washington had pledged to Spain to combat Cuban filibustering expeditions organized in the United States.[42] Between 1895 and 1896, American authorities had successfully intercepted over half of the Cuban expeditions fitted in the United States and vigorously prosecuted offenders. Of the seventy U.S. organized expeditions during the course of the war, only a third reached Cuba.[43]

American support of Spanish sovereignty in 1896 rested on the expectation that Spain would reestablish its authority over the rebellious colony—if not immediately through arms, then ultimately through reforms. Both Cleveland and Olney believed that autonomy would serve at once to placate dissident Cubans and discredit those separatist leaders who spurned the Spanish offer. In either case, the insurrection would quickly come to an end with Spanish sovereignty essentially intact. This had served as the central assumption of Cleveland's Cuban policy. This had been the purport of Olney's conference with Minister de Lôme in March, 1895. And it was repeated by President Cleveland later that year. "It would seem," Cleveland speculated in his 1896 message, "that if Spain should offer to Cuba genuine autonomy—a measure of home rule which, while preserving the sovereignty of Spain, would satisfy all rational requirements of her Spanish subjects—there should be no just reason why the pacification of the island might not be affected on that basis."[44]

By the early summer of 1896, however, Spain had all but formally rejected the American offer to mediate a peace settlement based on reform and autonomy. Speaking for the Spanish court, the minister of state, the duke of Tetuán, disputed Washington's version of the Cuban situation, arguing that Cuba already enjoyed, even before the rebellion, "one of the most liberal political systems in the world." Any resolution of the Cuban rebellion based on anything other than a triumph of Spanish arms, Tetuán suggested, promised only to doom all future efforts to establish peace on a long-standing basis and condemn the island to a recurring cycle of periodic uprisings. For the moment, Madrid insisted, conditions in Cuba were simply not conducive to such an undertaking. If an opportune occasion arose for Madrid to consider new reforms, Tetuán added tersely, Spain fully possessed the means of undertaking such a program without participation of the United States.[45] For the time being, the government of Prime Minister Cánovas del Castillo flatly refused to consider extending new reforms as long as Cubans remained in arms.[46]

As Cleveland approached the end of his term, the administration despaired of any solution of the Cuban conflict. The policy on which Washington had earlier placed so much hope, peace through reforms, had failed to win support in Madrid. In the closing days of his administration, Cleveland made one last effort to arrange a solution consistent with American interests—this one through the purchase of Cuba. As early as June, when it had become apparent that the mediation offer had failed, Consul General Fitzhugh Lee had suggested the purchase of Cuba. Within a month, as the Democratic convention prepared to nominate a presidential candidate, Lee urged the White House to support a party platform containing a commitment to the purchase of Cuba.[47] In his 1896 message to Congress, Cleveland publicly announced that the purchase of Cuba was a suggestion "worthy of consideration if there were any evidence of a desire or willingness on the part of Spain to entertain such a proposal."[48] Nor were Cleveland's utterances merely for popular consumption. On the eve of the Democratic party convention, Cleveland informed Olney that the purchase of Cuba was indeed "perhaps worth thinking of"—not, however, for the purpose of preparing for Cuban independence. "It would seem absurd for us to buy the island," Cleveland commented, "and present it to the people now inhabiting it, and put its government and management in their hands."[49] But time ran out and the expiration of his term prevented Cleveland from formally offering Spain the proposed $100 million for the island.[50]

V   So it was that on December 7, 1896, a disheartened and frustrated Cleveland used his last message to Congress to reflect at length on the Cuban conflict. The president chided Spanish authorities for their unwillingness to concede "genuine autonomy" to the rebellious colony. In Washington's view, autonomy offered the only basis upon which to end the conflict and restore order and stability to the strife-ridden island. "It would," Cleveland predicted confidently, "keep intact the possessions of Spain without touching her honour." Nor, Cleveland argued, was it reasonable for Madrid to demand of the insurgents unconditional surrender as a preliminary requirement for reform. Speaking directly to the insurgents, the president offered to guarantee the reform program in "a way not objectionable to Spain." Once again Cleveland offered the good offices of the United States for the purpose of "healing the breach between Spain and the insurgent Cubans."

By the end of 1896, however, Cleveland was no longer optimistic about the prospects of peace on the island under Spanish rule. Accordingly, he served notice on Spain that the United States expected some resolution of the conflict within a fixed but indeterminate period of time. "It cannot be reasonably assumed," Cleveland warned reproachfully, "that the hitherto expectant attitude of the United States will be indefinitely maintained." A continuation of the Cuban conflict would create "such an unusual and unprecedented condition as will fix a limit to our patient waiting for Spain to end the contest, either alone and in her own way or with our friendly cooperation." To the point:

With the inability of Spain to deal successfully with the insurrection has become manifest and it is demonstrated that her sovereignty is extinct in Cuba for all purposes of its rightful existence, and when a hopeless struggle for its reestablishment had degenerated into a strife which means nothing more than the useless sacrifice of human life and the utter destruction of the very subject matter of the conflict, a situation will be presented in which our obligations to the sovereignty of Spain will be superseded by higher obligations, which we can hardly hesitate to recognize and discharge.[51]

The year 1896 ended with Spanish authority in Cuba on the decline. The outgoing Democratic administration had found little in the Cuban conflict to justify any notable departure from the established policy approaches to Cuba. The assumptions of the nineteenth century survived the two-year conflict almost intact—but not entirely. Already, a sense of climax settled over Washington. An "unusual and unprecedented condition," in Cleveland's words, had created circumstances beyond the reach of the old policy formulations and had fixed "a limit to our patient waiting for Spain to end the contest."

4 Exhaustion of the Passions

We have not changed clothing in sixteen days. The marches are wearisome. By night the rain robs us of our rest. There is no food. For days at a time all we eat is corn meai mixed with water.
—Ricardo Burguete, Spanish soldier, 1895

Our soldier is a martyr for his sufferings, the most disciplined in the world, the most tractable, with good direction and fine chiefs, the most valiant. . . . If I could only feed them!
—General Arsenio Martínez Campos, 1895

Without doubt, the insurgents are stronger today than at any time since the inception of the insurrection; yet little of this gain is due to the Cubans themselves, but is attributable to the growing weakness of the Spanish army.
—Walter B. Barker, U.S. Consul, Sagua la Grande, September 1897

I A military tour of duty in Cuba was an unwelcome assignment. Periodic political disturbances, chronic rural instability, and, above all, the constancy of an oppressive climate combined to make Cuba one of the least desirable posts in Spain's remaining empire. Compensation for service in the Caribbean was notoriously meager. Spanish soldiers in Cuba traditionally suffered from privation, neglect, and abuse.[1] Men of any means, career officers and draftees alike, went to considerable lengths to avoid service in Cuba. Those who lacked the appropriate political connections to secure more congenial assignments had, as last resort, the option of buying their exemption from a tour in Cuba by paying the Ministry of War a fixed sum of money.[2]

This was before the war. In early 1895, Spanish regiments in Cuba languished underofficered, undermanned, poorly trained, poorly fed, and poorly housed—the fate of those too poor to purchase more felicitous assignments. Seriously below strength, the army was also short of essential supplies of every type. Conditions deteriorated rapidly in the early months of the insurrection. When Martínez Campos arrived in Havana in April 1895, he found all the military services in disarray, housing in short supply, and hospital facilities woefully inadequate to care for the needs of the sick and wounded.[3] These conditions had deteriorated further by the time of Weyler's arrival. The destruction of communication facilities and interruption of transportation had all but completely isolated Spanish forces across the island. It took days for Weyler to inform the provincial commands of his arrival in Havana and weeks to account for the whereabouts of the forces listed under his command.[4] In the months that followed, the rapid buildup of Spanish forces—from 20,000 on the eve of the insurrection to 200,000 at the height of Weyler's campaign—served only to compound Spanish difficulties.

If insurgent armies were the only source of adversity awaiting *peninsular* troops in Cuba, the odds against Spanish success would conceivably have been less skewed. In fact, enemy bullets were not the only—or, for that matter, the most formidable—hazard confronting the Spanish army in Cuba. *Insurrecto* chieftains had settled upon a guerrilla strategy calculated to deplete Spanish resources, undermine enemy morale, and break the metropolitan will. Most important, and central to the purpose of separatist arms, the insurgent command had committed itself to a war wholly impossible for Spain to win militarily so as to make Spain's defeat politically inevitable.

74 In this enterprise, Cubans had an array of formidable allies. For the

better part of the three years of war, the Spanish army was undermined by disease and overwhelmed by climate. The rigor of campaigning in the tropics, and the attending heat prostration, fatigue, and malnutrition, increased the susceptibility of *peninsular* soldiers to a variety of tropical diseases and illnesses, including malaria, yellow fever, dysentery, tuberculosis, smallpox, anemia, enteritis, and beriberi.

By the end of 1897, Spain was losing the war—not only on the battlefields of rural Cuba but in the hospitals and infirmaries of the cities. Between March and December of 1895, the Spanish army reported some forty-nine thousand hospital cases from noncombat illness. This increased to some two hundred thirty-two thousand in 1896, and reached two hundred thirty-one thousand cases in the first six months of 1897.[5] Of the thirty-two thousand troops participating in Weyler's western campaign in Pinar del Río in early 1896, some nine thousand required hospitalization for malaria in the first ten days; thereafter, some one thousand soldiers entered Havana hospitals daily.

Nor were the Spanish successful in periodic efforts to improve their capabilities to care for the sick. Woefully understaffed, without an adequate number of physicians and nurses, overcrowded and poorly provisioned, military hospitals in Cuba soon earned the reputation among Spanish troops of being a "slaughterhouse of soldiers." Disease fed on poor hygiene, poor diet, and overcrowding, but most of all on negligence. Neglect of elementary sanitary conditions in army camps, neglect of patients in hospitals, turned crisis into disaster. Indeed, very little distinguished the condition of the Spanish soldier in military hospitals from that of the Cuban *pacífico* (noncombatant) in reconcentration camps.[6]

The shortage of hospital facilities and the inability to evacuate the ill and wounded and adequately treat disease-stricken troops contributed to the deaths of thousands of Spanish soldiers.[7] By the second year of the war, the mortality rate in the Spanish army had reached staggering proportions. In 1897 alone, some thirty-two thousand soldiers perished in Cuba from disease. This did not include soldiers who died from combat-related wounds and troops who returned to Spain in various stages of terminal illnesses. Another five thousand perished in combat, and an estimated three thousand died upon their return to Spain.[8] Over the three years, Spanish officials estimated a mortality rate of one hundred soldiers a day, approximately thirty-five thousand a year, and one hundred thousand for the entire conflict.[9]

Soldiers escaping disease and illness survived only to face the horrors of field operations in the tropics. The Cuban environment punished Spanish forces unmercifully. Torrential rainfalls, cold evenings, scorching days—often weeks at a time without an opportunity to change into dry clothes—made the Cuban campaign a nightmare. Alligators, leeches, insects, and, above all, the omnipresent mosquito—the transmitter of yellow fever—tormented Spanish troops relentlessly and served "as the unsung allies of Cuban separatism. Troops on operations often found it impossible to keep warm and protect themselves against mosquitos through the use of campfires for fear of drawing the gunfire of insurgent snipers; they typically slept in wet clothing, through chilly evenings tormented by disease-carrying mosquitos.[10]

The rainy season in particular had a devastating effect on government military operations in Cuba. The summers paralyzed the Spanish. Rivers became impassable and solid land masses were transformed into mud flats. The movement of men and beasts of burden alike became impossible. The rains filled the *trochas* with water and converted Spain's principal lines of defense into miasmatic canals of stagnant water.[11] The rainy season was also the breeding season for mosquitos, and they multiplied and ravenously preyed upon Spanish soldiers. Once asked to name his three best generals, Máximo Gómez responded unhesitatingly: "June, July and August"—the peak months of the rainy seasons.[12] Every summer the pattern repeated itself: the rains, an increase of illness and death, a reduction of Spanish operations, gains for the Cubans.[13]

These conditions soon brought the Spanish war effort in Cuba to a virtual standstill. By 1897, government operations were confined to limited daily forays into the countryside from fortified towns and cities. Spanish forces could not move too far or remain away too long from their base of supplies. Quartermaster, commissary, ordinance, and hospital supplies were all carried by pack animals; few units on operations received shelter or ambulance service for the sick, exhausted, and wounded. And at dusk, everyday, Spanish forces rushed to return to the security of the cities.[14]

The nature of Spanish field operations underscored the essential quality of the Cuban campaign. Weyler's withdrawal of soldiers from estates did not substantially alter the purpose of *peninsular* forces. The vast bulk of the Spanish forces in Cuba remained on garrison duty, protecting the provincial towns and cities, safeguarding principal lines of communication, including railroad lines, bridges, and roads, and assigned to the more than two thousand forts distributed throughout the island—"a feature of the landscape hardly second to the royal palm," one visitor commented.[15] Some additional twenty to thirty thousand troops were assigned to the block houses along the Júcaro-Morón and Mariel-Majana *trochas*. "I have over there," Máximo Gómez would say pointing figuratively to the Júcaro-Morón *trocha*, "some 10,000 Spaniards prisoner."[16] Spain had effectively relinquished control over the countryside to insurgent forces, choosing to remain behind fortified lines in the cities and *trochas* and confining military operations to daytime marches into the surrounding countryside.

These developments set the prospects of Spanish arms in Cuba in bleak relief. Of the some two hundred thousand *peninsular* troops on the island, fully half served on garrison detail. At any given time, another fifty thousand were hospitalized for disease, illness, and battle wounds. Only a quarter of the total number of Spanish forces in Cuba, some fifty thousand officers and men, were available for field operations against an estimated fifty thousand Cuban troops.[17] There were, in short, only slightly more Spanish soldiers on their feet and able to bear arms than there were in insurgent ranks. This parity between Spanish military forces and Cuban *insurrectos* had ominous implications for the Spanish war effort in Cuba.[18]

Nor did Spanish authorities seem unduly preoccupied with efforts to improve the odds for survival of *peninsular* soldiers in Cuba. On the contrary, military officials displayed a supine indifference to conditions in the army. Arbitrarily conscripted into military service in Spain, new adolescent recruits arrived in Cuba poorly trained, poorly disciplined, and ill-equipped; inadequately acclimatized, new troops were immediately ordered into the field. Their collapse was not long in coming. A chilling consensus emerged around the condition of the Spanish army from observers on the island. "The Spanish army is in a deplorable condition," a long-time English resident in Havana wrote in late 1897, "a very large percentage of the soldiers being unfit for service. They are scarcely clothed, and what uniforms they do receive are quite unfit for campaigning work. The average age of the rank and file is from 15 to 18. They are mere boys—recruits who, immediately on their arrival in Havana, are despatched to the interior without drill of any kind. Naturally they soon fall victim to the climate, for it is not Cuban bullets that have carried off the majority of the Spanish army."[19] The American consul in Havana, Fitzhugh Lee, likewise observed: "One of the most pitiable conditions existing here, is the fact that so many of these young men of Spain are transported to this Island for soldiers, without drill, without discipline, and un-acclimated, a thin blue uniform is put on their bodies, a straw hat on their heads, a gun in their hands and they are sent out in the interior to get alternately wet and dry and die of fever. One half of them will never get back to Spain."[20] In Puerto Rico, the American consul reported that Spanish soldiers passing through San Juan en route to Cuba were "mostly boys, very young and poorly equipped." "They are extremely filthy," Edwin F. Uhl reported, "poorly conditioned, and little attention is apparently given to their care and comfort."[21]

New recruits fared poorly in field operations. Ill-prepared to undertake the rigors of the campaign in the tropics, the Spanish soldier was even less prepared for combat encounters with Cuban *insurrectos*. The lack of training and experience made the young *peninsular* soldier easy prey for seasoned veterans of the insurgent Cuban army. Many "gave up," one *insurrecto* later recalled, "because they were very green and young. The conscripts, for instance, were only sixteen or seventeen, fresh out from Spain. Most of them had never fought before. When they got into a serious fix they would drop everything, even their pants."[22]

Nor did officers provide much by way of leadership and command. The resistance of regular army officers in Spain to tours of duty in Cuba forced Spanish authorities to dip into *peninsular* reserve units to find commanders. And this, too, was difficult without adequate inducements. Reserve officers received automatic promotions for volunteering for Cuba. Some 80 percent of the lieutenants who served in Cuba came from reserve units. [23] Similarly, sergeants in their terms of enlistment were commissioned second lieutenants upon volunteering for duty in Cuba. In 1897, as conditions on the island worsened, new teenage cadets were induced to volunteer in Cuba by offers of commissions in the army. Second lieutenants sixteen years of age began arriving at about the moment insurgent armies prepared to mount serious offensives.[24]

Corruption, too, weakened the effectiveness of the Spanish army. Officers often privately leased their battalions to planters for garrison detail on the estates in direct violation of Weyler's order.[25] Charges of speculation, padded personnel rolls, and substitute purchasing were frequently leveled at Spanish officers.[26]

When not exposed to climate, mosquitos, and enemy ambushes in the field, the Spanish soldier faced a precarious existence in the cities. *Peninsular* troops in Cuba endured chronic shortages of food, supplies, and provisions. Poor civilians of Spain were transformed into indigent soldiers in Cuba. Accounts of starvation in the Spanish army were not uncommon.

Suicides among officers were not unknown. Reports of Spanish soldiers dressed in tattered clothing increased as the war moved into its third year.[27] In Sagua la Grande, the American consul reported that Spanish troops had taken to the streets to beg. By 1897, begging had become a common sight in Havana. "You go into the streets of Habana any hour of the night," Frederick W. Lawrence, the *New York World* correspondent in Cuba reported, "and if you look like a man of any means at all you will be asked for alms by Spanish soldiers."[28] At the same time, charges of theft against Spanish soldiers were lodged with increasing frequency by Havana merchants and provincial shopkeepers.[29]

The pathetic spectacle of Spanish soldiers as beggars and burglars was symptomatic of a larger and more serious problem: soldiers' pay was hopelessly in arrears. The rapid military buildup in Cuba between 1895 and 1896 had exceeded Spain's capacity to administer efficiently or support finanacially swelling army payrolls. As early as August 1895, Martínez Campos had complained to Madrid of severe problems meeting army payrolls.[30] In 1896, pay schedules for troops in Havana had fallen some five months in arrears. By 1898, some Spanish units in Oriente had not been paid for nearly a year.[31]

Nor did the celebration of payday, on those solemn and increasingly rare occasions, provide more than fleeting relief for the hapless *peninsular* soldier. On the contrary, the despair over delinquent pay envelopes was eclipsed by the disappointment with their contents. From the beginning of the Cuban conflict, Spanish authorities sought to defray the expense of the war by resorting to the wholesale issuance of paper money. Resistance in Cuba to the new paper money victimized first the Spanish soldier who had little choice but to accept his earnings in whatever form Madrid dictated. Cuban merchants were under no such constraints, however, and across the island shopkeepers refused to accept Spanish notes at face value. As the war continued, the amount of paper currency steadily increased and its value, just as steadily, decreased. Repeated government decrees enjoining shopkeepers to accept paper money on a par with gold and silver, periodically enforced by the arrest of an uncompliant merchant, failed to lessen Cuban resistance to Spanish notes. Spain financed its deficit by simply issuing more pesos. In large measure, Madrid fought the colonial war on credit—and the Cubans found themselves submerged in a glut of debased currency. As the crisis deepened and uncertainty about the future increased, paper currency depreciated precipitously. By 1897, paper money, when accepted, was universally discounted by 50 percent.[32]

Ordinary retail transactions between the storekeeper and the soldier became, in more than symbolic terms, a microcosm of the larger conflict—growing colonial disaffection with metropolitan policy. The embattled Spanish soldier, when paid, found his meager earnings depreciating rapidly and routinely discounted by local merchants. Frustration turned to anger. Arguments and quarrels between storekeepers and soldiers increased. Shops were frequently plundered; merchants were often physically beaten and their property destroyed. In mid-1897, the local Spanish army commander in Sagua la Grande ordered local merchants to contribute food for a battalion of some one thousand soldiers. Shopkeepers refused. Angry soldiers responded by sacking local shops and, with official sanction, met their needs through looting.[33]

The estrangement was complete. *Peninsular* troops reacted to Cuban burghers with injured sensibilities and aroused indignation. Conflicts with the civilian population contributed further to declining morale and added one more grievance to the growing list of soldiers' complaints. Palpable signs of ingratitude, Spanish soldiers concluded bitterly, from the very people for whom they risked their lives—certainly not much incentive to inspire enthusiasm among *peninsular* conscripts. Shopkeepers and merchants, for their part, resented Madrid's poorly veiled attempts to pass the cost of the war on to Cuba's commercial community. Rising tensions between the local business establishment and the *peninsular* army command served at once to fix the limit of Cuban patience with deteriorating conditions on the island and increase local impatience at the meager results and great cost of Spanish pacification efforts. The price of Spanish redemption was gradually exceeding the cost of the Cuban rebellion.

II   By late 1897 and early 1898, as senior military commanders prepared for the grim campaign of the approaching rainy season, the Spanish army in Cuba was in serious crisis. The inablity of Spain to end the war contributed to the deterioration of Spanish morale and increased the unwillingness of *peninsular* soldiers to continue fighting. Spanish soldiers found little in either the island or its population worth fighting and dying for. Most were in Cuba against their will. Reports of desertions, mutinies, and, with increasing frequency, wholesale surrenders to insurgent forces appeared to announce the imminent collapse of the Spanish army in Cuba. "Disaffection is rapidly on the increase," the American consul in Sagua la Grande reported as early as mid-1896.[34] In early 1897, a gunboat crew mutinied and defected to insurgent forces operating in Pinar del Río. A year later, the better part of the prestigious Imperial Battalion of Madrid operating in Nuevitas deserted to the local insurgent force. "Hunger is driving Spanish soldiers into the insurgent ranks," the *New York World* correspondent in Havana reported.[35] By mid-1897, conditions had deteriorated so far that Fitzhugh Lee privately predicted a total collapse of the Spanish army: "Everything points to a break up of the present conditions here in 60 days. Private letters from different parts of the Island tell me of the great dissatisfaction of the poor Spanish soldier, who gets no pay, whose rations have become scanty and whose comrades fall at his side from pestilential fevers. This condemnation is beginning to take organized shape, and today I heard on the streets, that a riot is very possible here on the part of the soldiers, for bread and money."[36]

Where Spanish troops did not desert or mutiny, they simply ceased to fight. As early as mid-1895, the Cuban army command had detected a marked unwillingness among Spanish army authorities to engage separatist forces. Even the transcendental military accomplishment of the insurrection—the invasion—had been conspicuous for the virtual absence of Spanish resistance and the limited number of encounters between the opposing armies. "The countryside is ours," a euphoric Antonio Maceo had written his wife in August 1895.[37] In November, Maceo wrote his wife again: "There is hardly any fighting in this revolution; it has been two months since I have had serious battles."[38] Later that month, Maceo wrote his brother: "The enemy appears to be terrified, for notwithstanding the announcement of the departure of the *Oriental* contingent by our very own press, we have crossed all of Camagüey without firing a shot, and, what is more, passed the *trocha* without the least resistance."[39] In December 1895, as the *Ejército Invasor* passed through Havana province, one of Maceo's officers had recorded in his campaign diary his surprise at the absence of Spanish resistance.[40] Between 1895 and 1896, insurgent columns had marched through central Cuba, destroying railroad lines, burning cane fields, and destroying sugar mills for weeks at a time without once encountering enemy forces.[41] By early 1898, insurgent forces could cross the *trochas* at both ends of the island at will. One visitor to the Júcaro-Morón *trocha* reported that Spanish troops did "not care whether Spain owns an island eighty miles from the United States or loses it."[42] Spanish officers, Consul Walter B. Barker reported from Sagua la Grande in June 1897, "manifest a supreme indifference, as to the situation, duration, and final outcome. . . . This complete revulsion has been wrought within the past sixty days."[43] A similar tone was struck by Fitzhugh Lee two months later:

"With the exception of the seaports and a few interior towns, the Insurgents occupy the whole island. Their camps and bivouacs are located in plain view of the Spanish garrisoned towns, but the Spanish troops do not seem disposed to molest them."[44]

By the winter of 1897–1898, insurgent military operations had reached a critical threshold. Holding undisputed control of the Cuban countryside, the insurgent military command prepared for the final phase of the insurrection—the assault on the cities, the last remaining stronghold of Spanish power in Cuba.[45] In mid-1897, the insurgent army completed organizing artillery units and prepared to carry the war to urban centers. In early summer insurgent forces in Oriente laid siege on Bayamo, a city of some twenty-one thousand inhabitants. In August, General Calixto García mounted a stunning artillery attack on Victoria de las Tunas, a city of eighteen thousand people. The Cuban victory at Las Tunas had a jolting impact on the Spanish military command, contributing ultimately to Weyler's recall.[46] In the succeeding six months, town after town in eastern Cuba fell to insurgent forces, including Guisa, Guáimaro, Jiguaní, Loma de Hierro and Bayamo. In early 1898, Manzanillo was threatened. In April 1898, as the U.S. Congress concluded debate on the war resolution against Spain, Calixto García was engaged in final preparations for an assault against Santiago de Cuba.[47]

The Spanish army in Cuba was approaching desperate conditions. In an exhaustive internal study of conditions in the Spanish army, concluded in December 1897, General José Fernández Lozada arrived at some grim conclusions. "The soldier is exhausted, fatigued, and poorly fed," Fernández Lozada wrote. Not only were hospital facilities for the 32,000 patients woefully inadequate, but, Fernández Lozada discovered, the vast number of troops on operations were unfit for service. The type of campaigning undertaken by the army command, moreover, was contributing directly to exhaustion and fatigue, thereby converting the soldier into easy prey for disease. The combination of disease, climate, poor diet and dress, and the rigors of campaigning in the tropics, Fernández Lozada concluded, had reduced the Spanish army in Cuba to a moribund state.[48]

III   In August 1896, an incredulous Spanish public, weary of the eighteen-month war in Cuba, learned that the unthinkable had occurred: another colonial insurrection against Spain, another war in the tropics— now on the other side of the world—this one in the vast Philippine archipelago.

For many thousands of Spanish families, this frightful news from the Pacific had little meaning. Their anguish had already been spent on the tragedy in the Caribbean. By the summer of 1896, a deep melancholia had settled over the peninsula. There were few households in Spain untouched by the events in Cuba. The countryside, the towns and villages, the farms and factories had become places of inconsolable grief. The land had filled with the sounds of bereavement—voices of mothers, wives, sisters, and daughters mourning for their men and the mutterings of old men seeking meaning in the loss of their sons; churches filled alternatively with hushed undertones of supplicants in prayer in search of solace and the open weeping of the disconsolate. In the cities, the funeral procession, winding haltingly through city streets and announced by rising murmurs of grief, had become a daily feature of Spanish urban life. One American visitor in Madrid in 1896 described an "indescribable pathos" throughout Spain. "The people are broken-hearted over the tragedy which they see in the shipping of their young sons by the tens of thousands to death in Cuba. . . . Crowds assemble everywhere along the routes to Cadiz, and as they witness the departure of the troops, they weep and groan and pray."[49]

Few remained unaffected by the Cuban insurrection. Some regions suffered more directly than others. In Catalonia, the war had devastating economic consequences. Two decades of Catalan prosperity, based in large part on trade with the Caribbean colonies, ended abruptly. Only a year before the war, Cuba had accounted for more than 60 percent of Catalonia's exports, but the political disturbances resulted immediately in production slowdowns. Before the end of 1895, over half the Catalan textile mills had shut down; those that remained open operated on shorter work days with fewer workers. In the space of a year, some ten thousand Catalan workers lost their jobs, while many more found themselves reduced to part-time employment.[50]

All of Spain, in one fashion or another, suffered from the effects of Antillian war. Taxes increased, food prices rose, rents went up, and unemployment mounted. Increasing numbers of Spaniards faced hunger without work. Thousands of families abandoned farms and flocked to the cities in search of food and jobs. The grim consequences of war deaths in Cuba were not long in coming. The "widows and orphans of the thousands of brave youths who lost their lives in Cuba," one American journalist reported from Madrid, "are dying slowly of starvation."[51]

The news in August 1896 of another colonial war sent shock waves across the peninsula. Incredulity gave way to rage, and throughout Spain an aroused public took its grievances to the streets. By late summer, civil strife had broken out in Spanish cities as demonstrators and protestors clashed with public security forces. In Saragossa, Seville, and Madrid, street fighting became daily occurrences. In Málaga, thousands of unemployed workers rioted to protest the scarcity of food and the lack of jobs. From the countryside, local authorities reported peasant uprisings, land seizures, and widescale rural violence.[52] In Catalonia and the Basque provinces, the economic crisis combined with political discontent and infused a new vigor into long-standing separatist nationalism. The war designed to preserve the integrity of empire abroad was threatening to cost Spain national unity at home.[53]

By 1896, both colonial order and domestic stability had become the principal concerns of the Spanish army. Once in the vortex of the national crisis, the military also became the center of political intrigue—the object of anti-government conspiracy from above, below, and within from both the right and the left. National frustration against the government's colonial policies expressed itself first in the form of direct popular appeals to the Spanish army. Antiwar protesters enjoined civilian men to resist military service and encouraged those in uniform to desert and mutiny. In late 1896, antiwar riots erupted across Spain. In Barcelona, every embarcation of troops for Cuba provided an occasion for armed confrontation between demonstrators and government forces. Anonymous manifestos circulated throughout the city, urging departing troops to resist service in Cuba and calling on the Barcelonans to block the sending of reinforcements to Weyler; placards and banners calling upon soldiers to mutiny were placed along the streets through which they marched to their ships. Three hundred miles away, in Logroño, women marched to protest the departure of local draftees. To the south, in Cádiz, another women's demonstration, this one designed to block the embarcation of troops, ended only after the protesters were set upon by a local detachment of cavalry.

Opposition to military service was almost universal. Rural Spaniards protested that conscription threatened to depopulate the countryside and ruin agriculture. In the cities, protesters denounced the inequities of a system that drafted only those too poor to buy their way out of military service. Catalan nationalists charged that the provincial quota assigned to Catalonia was proportionally higher than those assigned to other regions, further proof, Catalans decried, of Castile's maltreatment of the provinces.[54]

Across Spain, families were consumed in the sorrowful labor of raising sufficient money to buy their sons' exemption from military service. Many sold whatever they owned of value; other families exhausted their savings.[55] In one instance, several families of a rural community appealed for public donations to buy local youths out of military service.[56]

If Spanish troops succeeded in resisting civilian importunings to desert, they could not remain unaffected by the tales told by soldiers returning from Cuba. Indeed, nothing demoralized Spanish troops more than the horror of war stories from Cuba. Mere sight of the broken condition of returning veterans sent tremors of apprehension rippling among new recruits in Spain. Veterans from Cuba returned with hair-raising accounts of jungles, mountains, disease, insects, and the everywhereness of death.

With every passing month, fewer soldiers were willing to risk death in the malarial wastes of the tropical colonies. Desertions increased. In several provinces, antiwar organizers established "desertion agencies" to assist deserters in finding safety.[57] By late 1896, members of the Cuban junta in Paris reported that some eight thousand Spanish soldiers had deserted to the French Pyrennean province of Rousellon.[58] Countless young men escaped military service by emigrating from Spain altogether.[59]

And—with increasing frequency—insubordination, and outright mutiny. In late 1896, soldiers fraternized openly with antiwar demonstrators in Barcelona. In October 1897, an army unit in Cádiz refused to board a troop transport ship destined for Cuba.[60]

If the army was threatened with disintegration from below, it was also in danger of coming apart from the top. Exasperated by the military stalemate in the colonies, disgruntled over civilian misconduct of the colonial conflicts, senior military commanders edged the army closer to political action against the government. Officers returning from Cuba gave vivid corroboration to the worst accounts of government mismanagement and ineptitude. Returning army chiefs came to form something of a disillusioned fraternity of veterans and emerged as a focal point of antigovernment plotting. Officers, too, like the troops they commanded, began to question government colonial policies and voiced increasing disinclination to serve overseas. Spanish officers instinctively opposed and consciously resisted overseas commands. That Spanish authorities were forced to seek line officers from the aged in reservist pools and the young in military academies gave dramatic corroboration of the success regular officers enjoyed in avoiding service in Cuba. But exemption from overseas duty did not lead immediately to a reduction of army agitation. The domestic repercussion of the colonial conflicts also had an unsettling effect on the army command. Officers' displeasure increased over the government's growing use of the military to suppress civilian demonstrations at home.[61] By 1897, with military discontent rising, government authorities lived in daily fear of military intervention.[62]

Growing discontent within the army command made the military especially susceptible to conspiratorial overtures from civilians opposed to the government of Prime Minister Antonio Cánovas del Castillo. Committed to the monarchy, Cánovas found King Alfonso of little value as a political ally. Alfonso had completed his ninth birthday at the time of the outbreak of the Cuban insurrection and passed the better part of the following years isolated at the court, protected against the currents raging about his kingdom. Nor was Queen Regent María Cristina much of an asset to the conservative ministry. A foreigner in Spain, daughter of Hapsburg Archduke Charles of Austria, María Cristina enjoyed only limited popularity with the Spanish public.

The Spanish colonial crises in the 1890s revived debate over the institution of the monarchy. Throughout the war, conspiracy and plotting overshadowed an unoccupied throne awaiting the majority of a boy-king. The regency of María Cristina was stalked on the right by Carlists and on the left by republicans. Carlists established conspiratorial liaisons with a number of disaffected groups in Spain, most notably Catalan and Basque nationalists and disgruntled senior officers of the army. Key conspiratorial centers formed in Madrid, Catalonia, Valencia, and Aragón. Several premature and abortive Carlist uprisings in 1897 served as auguries of the political turmoil to come.[63] Later that year, several ranking Carlists visited members of the Cuban junta in Paris seeking financial assistance to overthrow the Spanish government, in exchange for which they committed themselves to Cuban independence after their triumph.[64] At the other end of the Spanish political spectrum republicans actively plotted the overthrow of the monarchy. For republicans, the real war was in Spain against royal autocracy. Like their conservative counterparts, republicans established conspiratorial networks within the military. As popular sentiment against the war in Cuba mounted, republicans increased their attacks on Spain's colonial policy; by 1897, many republicans had made Cuban independence a central part of their program.[65]

IV   As the war in Cuba entered the third year, Spain found itself at the edge of an abyss. Demonstrations paralyzed urban life. Conspiracy and political intrigue haunted the Cánovas government. Food riots, antiwar protests, and army mutinies, together with the looming spectre of Catalan and Basque separatism, threatened to plunge Spain into civil war. A population of sixteen million Spaniards groaned under the weight of an expanding and seemingly interminable colonial military commitment. By the end of 1896, Spain had sent 200,000 soldiers to Cuba and another 40,000 troops to the Philippines. In early 1897, rumors of separatist plottings in Puerto Rico impelled Madrid to send 6,000 soldiers to San Juan. Effectively under seige at home, Spanish authorities were forced to distribute another 126,000 soldiers across the peninsula.[66]

The financial burden of 400,000 men in arms and two colonial wars at opposite ends of the world all but totally exhausted the national treasury. Bankruptcy and economic collapse appeared imminent. Spanish credit in the great money markets of Europe plummeted. Spending a million pesetas a day on the Cuban conflict, Spain found itself confronted with shrinking sources of credit and a collapsing treasury. In early 1897, Madrid learned that French bankers, on whom Spain had become dependent, had canceled Spanish credit pending a resolution of the Cuban conflict.[67] On Wall Street later that year, Spanish indemnity certificates failed to secure more than eleven cents on the dollar.

Events in Spain, in turn, could not help but have a salutary effect on the insurgent cause in Cuba. It was not necessary to defeat Spain militarily. That the rebellion itself could precipitate a political crisis in Spain and potentially bring to power a government sympathetic to Cuban independence was an eventuality separatists frequently contemplated.[68] Certainly developments in 1897 were promising.

By the end of 1897, Spain was engulfed in social turmoil, political intrigue, and at the brink of economic chaos. Cuba had plunged Spain into crisis and only the end of the war in Cuba, many Spaniards argued, promised to restore peace in Spain. Pressure to recognize Cuban independence mounted. Carlists were involved in a number of conspiracies, having committed themselves in private to relinquishing Cuba. Republicans clamored for an end to the war and recognition of Cuban independence. In early 1898, several ranking members of the Catholic church in Spain, including the bishop of Barcelona, called for the independence of Cuba. In Havana, Fitzhugh Lee learned from a recent visitor to Spain that "the peasants and people of Spain are all anxious for the Government to let go of its hold on Cuba."[69] In late 1897, the American minister in Madrid portrayed Spain as unable to continue the war and on the verge of internal collapse: "There is quite general apprehension here that Spain may be on the eve of social disorders, possibly of revolution. The Carlists are evidently plotting and the Madrid papers have for some days stated that ten or twelve thousand rifles have been smuggled across the Pyrenees into the Basque provinces for Carlist use. Bread is rising in price; work is scarce; and there is certainly much popular discontent. The common people are tired of the Cuban and Philippine wars."[70]

5 An Imperfect Consensus

While the war lasts, there must be only soldiers and swords in Cuba, or at least men who know how to prosecute the war and how to achieve the final redemption of our people. When this is achieved, which is the objective to which our efforts are directed, the time will then be ripe for the forming of a civil government.
—Antonio Maceo, November 1895

If you do not submit unconditionally, the Government is disposed to remove you.
—Secretary of War Rafael M. Portuondo to Máximo Gómez, October 1896

The old general with the star on his forehead was sitting in his hammock under a guásima *and a carob tree, dictating a letter. He was informing their delegate in New York about the war, and ended with a comment on the fact that the troops had nothing to do, now that the enemy was retreating and almost the whole province was under rebel command. "We've become fat cats," he dictated, "and if this continues I'm coming over there to work with you, since there's more danger on Broadway than there is here." The aide-de-camp, who was taking down the letter, asked how to spell Broadway.*
—G. Cabrera Infante, *View of Dawn in the Tropics*

I "I called up the war," José Martí wrote to Federico Henríquez y Carvajal in March 1895; "my responsibility begins rather than ends with it."[1] Two months later, José Martí was dead, a casualty of an early battle at Dos Ríos.

Martí's death created an enormous vacuum in separatist ranks. The blow to insurgent morale was incalculable. But more was involved, for in a very real sense Martí had defined the ideological character and developed the political structure of Cuban separatism. And because this was so much the fruits of his labor, he alone possessed the political skills necessary to balance the diverse and heterogeneous social groupings organized around the most exalted notion of Cuba Libre. His death early in the war left a host of issues unresolved. Separatist agencies, both on the island and abroad, had attracted supporters from all levels of Cuban society united only by a common and consuming desire to end four hundred years of Spanish rule. Martí had transformed a movement into a party, one representing various political tendencies, organized around a vague devotion to an ambiguous objective. The separatist call to war had attracted supporters in and out of Cuba who had conflicting goals and divergent purposes, for whom even the meaning of Cuba Libre possessed few commonly shared attributes.

II The separatist enterprise, in all its institutional manifestations, organized for the purpose of armed struggle. No tenet held such a central position or enduring vigor in separatist thought as the commitment to armed struggle. From the first national summons to war at Yara in 1868, an uncommon consensus had developed within separatist ranks around the necessity of arms to achieve independence from Spain. To be sure, the adherence of many insurgent veterans in 1878 to the reform promises of Zanjón and the subsequent organization of the Autonomist party created a schism in separatist ranks. The protest of Baraguá, however, served to set off two tendencies in sharp relief—a resident reformist party and an exiled revolutionary movement. The dedication to arms deepened in the ensuing years and was properly consecrated by the anguish of expatriation. After Zanjón, Cuban separatism acquired an irredentist quality in which the expulsion of Spain and the recovery of the homeland was possible only through an appeal to arms. Irredentism gave rise to adventurism, but no matter, for not even the series of short-lived and ill-fated uprisings of the 1880s and early 1890s had dampened the separatist devotion to arms.

90   For Martí, no less than his predecessors, armed struggle was at once a

necessary and indispensable prelude to independence. Whatever else may have separated the civilians and the soldiers between wars, all agreed on the requirements of arms. The genius of Martí lay in his understanding of the necessity to organize for war. Organization, Martí insisted, promised not only to increase the efficiency of the separatist effort but also guaranteed a rational war, a conflict free of the rancor and vengeance that had corrupted the abortive independence movements earlier in the century. In the three basic separatist documents of the 1890s authored by Martí—the "Resoluciones" (1891), the "Bases of the Cuban Revolutionary Party" (1892), and the "Manifiesto de Montecristi" (1895)—armed struggle acquired a political and moral function. Martí alluded variously to a "just conflict," "a cultured war," and a "healthful and vigorous war"—a campaign that would at once end the regimen of Spanish rule and serve to forge values indispensable to the new republic. Indeed, for Martí the war of liberation promised to ennoble its participants, purge the vices of the colony, and promote the virtues of the republic.[2]

III If an appeal to arms as the means of independence enjoyed general endorsement among separatists, the precise meaning of independence failed to achieve comparable consensus within the insurgent polity. Beyond a commonly shared notion that independence minimally involved separation from Spain, the final structure of Cuba Libre remained vaguely, if not often incompatibly, defined by the various sectors of the separatist movement.

For many Cubans, independence from Spain signified the preliminary act of a larger drama in which Cuba would ultimately find fulfillment in union with the United States. Indeed, for the better part of the Ten Years' War, annexationist sentiment occupied a central position within the body of separatist thought.[3] Annexationism received most support from patrician separatists, Creoles for whom annexation offered the most practical resolution of the contradictions arising from Cuba's growing economic dependence on the United States within a context of political dependence on Spain. Moreover, detecting a source of future unrest in the social heterogeneity of the Liberation Army, annexationists sought in union with the United States the salvation of a socio-economic system threatened by the political forces released by the armed struggle against Spain. United States sovereignty, many reasoned, promised at once to fill the vacuum created by the expulsion of metropolitan Spain and guarantee the status quo.[4] Annexationists, further, doubted the Cuban capacity for self-government. Cuba Libre raised the spectre of the apocalypse and evoked images of race war, chronic political instability, and economic chaos. The "independence of Cuba is the unknown, with all its illusions, and all its terrors," one Cuban wrote. The separatist proposition to organize a nation out of "elements so heterogeneous and complicated would be an insensate preposterous idea." To the point, the writer continued: "Independence will put in our hands—utterly inexpert—an organization most delicate and complicated, such as the democratic Republic must be; and it is not rash to predict that before acquiring the experience necessary for its management we shall have broken the organism in pieces, and crippled ourselves with the fragments."[5] Francisco Figueras, vice-president of the Cuban-American league, expressed his fears succinctly: "Independence in the social order threatens us with chaos and in the political order with anarchy or a dictatorship, in the economic order, it would bring besides to the soil of Cuba, barrenness, like the deserts of Africa."[6]

The sentiment for annexation was not confined solely to Cubans who feared chaos and tumult in the aftermath of independence. Many separatists had developed an abiding respect and deep admiration for American institutions. For many Cubans, as for many Latin Americans generally, the United States at the close of the nineteenth century offered an appealing model of modernity, progress, and economic development. Many supporters of Cuban separatism in the 1890s were the children of the exiles of the 1860s, born and raised in the United States. Others, the sons and daughters of Creole families residing in Cuba between the wars, had been sent to the United States to complete their education. Many separatists, either as a result of birth or through naturalization, held U.S. citizenship. Many had repudiated Roman Catholicism as the state religion of the oppressor and embraced various denominations of Protestantism as the new faith of the enlightened North.[7]

It was a short and natural step for admirers of the United States to desire to introduce into Cuba the benefits of the American system. Annexation offered Cubans the means to unite their nostalgic homeland with their adopted homeland. To be sure, this view also rested on implicit assumptions of Cuban incapacity for self-government. But its primary inspiration emanated from the hope that Cuba would partake of the opportunities and advantages offered through union with the United States and enjoy the fruits of American civilization.

Other separatists shared many of the fundamental assumptions of the annexationists but were loath to disavow entirely the individuality of Cuba or renounce the vision of a separate nationality. Like their conservative counterparts, moderate separatists acknowledged the perils attending premature nationhood. But inexperience was not confirmation of incapacity. Cuba needed only experience in self-government under the watchful eye of the United States. A period of apprenticeship in home rule, moderates insisted, one in which Cuba submitted itself to the United States as a protectorate, would suffice as proper preparation for independence. "Ten years," one Cuban separatist predicted confidently, "will give Cubans an opportunity of learning how to govern—how to handle their country. They have had no chance to learn it."[8]

Like their conservative counterparts, moreover, moderates were not unmindful of potential economic benefits attending close political relations with the United States. Special treaty arrangements promised to guarantee a market for Cuban products while allowing the island to advance in measured and calculated terms toward complete political sovereignty.

Tomás Estrada Palma, president of the insurgent provisional government during the Ten Years' War and Martí's successor as head of the PRC, gave clearest expression to protectorate sentiments within the separatist polity. During the Ten Years' War, Estrada Palma had been an unabashed advocate of outright annexation. Four hundred years of servile dependence to Spain, he insisted, together with the dismal example of uninspired government in Latin America and the laws of nature, made annexation to the United States necessary, if indeed not inevitable.[9] In the years following Zanjón, as the independence sentiment within separatist ranks crystalized, Estrada Palma modified his views. It is not certain that the former Cuban provisional president abandoned his annexationist sentiments altogether. In his public utterances and private correspondence, however, Estrada Palma emerged as a strong advocate of a dependent relationship to the United States—for many of the same reasons that he had earlier advocated annexation. If annexation in the 1890s was both impracticable and immediately unattainable, it was nevertheless essential to extend to the United States, in some form, a measure of supervision to guarantee political stability and economic solvency. Conceding in 1898 that annexation had few supporters among the Cuban people, Estrada Palma nevertheless remained steadfast in his conviction that a period of apprenticeship under the United States was the necessary preliminary phase of Cuban independence, a time during which Cubans would acquire the skills necessary for successful self-government. In the meantime, the "American government [would] in some manner serve to guarantee the internal peace of our country so that the Republic of Cuba will inspire sufficient confidence among foreign capitalists to encourage them to invest large sums in our bonds and to promote the financial development of our industries and public utility undertakings."[10]

Separatist ranks included, lastly, those Cubans for whom the ideal of independence represented an inviolate absolute. For the *independentista* wing, sovereignty necessarily involved independence from the United States as much as it required separation from Spain. Independence as an uncompromising ideal moved into a position of central importance during the late 1880s and early 1890s largely as the result of the efforts of José Martí. "To change masters," Martí repeatedly insisted, "is not to be free."[11] Martí directed almost as much energy toward combating sentiment for the annexation of Cuba to the United States as he did promoting support for its independence from Spain. The war against Spain and opposition to annexation represented the opposite poles of a single process. Martí believed Cubans capable of winning the war against Spain over the short run and maintaining a republic over the long run. He was not, however, as sanguine over the prospects of Cuba's ability to resist annexationist pressures. "The [annexationist] current is strong," Martí warned in 1889, "and the blind annexationists of the island have never been nearer to joining forces with the Yankee annexationists than they are now. This would be death for me and for our country."[12]

Martí was deeply troubled by the prospect of Cubans winning the battle for separation from Spain only to lose the larger struggle for independence. Years of residence in the United States had alerted him to the perils attending the long-standing American designs on the island. As early as 1886, Martí warned his compatriots that the United States had "never looked upon Cuba as anything but an appetizing possession with no drawback other than its quarrelsome, weak, and unworthy population." Anyone who "had knowingly read what was thought and written in the United States," Martí insisted, could not entertain any illusions about American intentions in Cuba.[13] Time was short. Already in the 1880s, Martí sensed that the forces driving Cuba into union with the United States were well advanced. "For the island to become North American," Martí wrote from New York in 1889, "it would be unnecessary for us to do anything; if we do not take advantage of the little time that remains for us to impede the inevitable, through the island's own disintegration, it will come to pass. That is what this country expects, and it is that which we must oppose."[14]

Martí's repeated injunction during the 1880s and 1890s on the necessity for a correctly organized war for independence stemmed in large measure from his fear that a prolongation of the armed struggle, one that would continue indefinitely without the immediate prospect of Cuban success, would create the conditions leading to American intervention and ultimately annexation. As early as 1886, Martí alerted his compatriots to the danger that "annexation might become a fact and that perhaps it may be our fate to have a skillful neighbor let us bleed ourselves on his threshhold until finally he can take whatever is left in his hostile, selfish and irreverent hands."[15] Separatist "words and acts" should be guided by the necessity "to prevent annexationist propaganda from undermining the strength which the revolutionary solution has been gathering."[16] A quick and successful war was necessary to forestall U.S. intervention. A premature war, Martí warned prophetically, a protracted war, would provide the Americans with the pretext to intervene—"and with the credit won as a mediator and guarantor, keep [Cuba] for their own."[17]

Fears of American intervention in a new Cuban war preoccupied Martí. The essential feature of Martí's "just war" was its brevity, a short war that would eliminate the pretext for and necessity of American intervention and would present Washington with Cuba Libre as *fait accompli*. The conditions that would invite U.S. mediation of the Cuban conflict, he feared, would also create the opportunity for American control. Intervention would serve as the prelude to annexation. "Once the United States is in Cuba who will drive it out?" Martí asked rhetorically.[18] He planned a separatist war wholly free of U.S. participation, relying exclusively on the moral and material resources of Cubans for the expulsion of Spain.[19]

The death of Martí early in the war consecrated *independentismo*. His martyrdom and the doctrines he forged in life had given independence its most compelling expression. Not that annexationist sentiment disappeared completely; on the contrary, discredited and all but formally banished from patriotic forums, annexationists and advocates of a protectorate relationship sought alternate means through which to influence the course of events.

IV   By the 1890s, the ideological diversity within the separatist coalition had acquired demographic dimensions. A peculiar broadcast came to fix the distribution of the separatist polity. The Pact of Zanjón in 1878 had brought to an end one cycle of immigration that had started ten years earlier at the outbreak of hostilities and precipitated the onset of another. Well before Zanjón insurgent sympathizers had sought refuge abroad, expectantly awaiting the outcome of the war.[20] Separatists unable to participate directly in the armed struggle, together with thousands of sympathizers seeking to escape the anticipated wrath of Spanish colonial administration, scattered throughout Europe, Latin America, and the United States. By the end of the first year of armed struggle, some one hundred thousand Cubans had sought refuge abroad.[21]

Political unrest in Cuba unfolded against a larger economic drama. Mid-century economic dislocation in the United States reverberated directly, and often with calamitous repercussions, in Cuba. The U.S. panic of 1857 precipitated pressure for higher tariff duties on items manufactured abroad.[22] During the American Civil War, moreover, a succession of acts raised the average rate of tariff on dutiable goods to an all-time high of 40.3 percent. The crisis of 1857, followed by higher tariff rates on foreign manufacturers, had a catastrophic effect on the Havana cigar industry. Panic gripped cigar manufacturers, and, in the course of the following decade, many factories failed.[23]

The disruption of the Havana cigar factories in the mid-nineteenth century resulted in a major reorganization of the industry. Several of the more resourceful manufacturers in Cuba, seeking to penetrate the American tariff wall, relocated their factories in the United States. As early as the 1830s, Key West had served as a site of modest cigar manufacturing.[24] In the 1860s, the city provided Cuban manufacturers an ideal setting for the production of cigars, easy access to the tobacco regions of western Cuba and to the commercial and transportation centers of Havana. This nearness, moreover, allowed manufacturers to tap directly into the Cuban labor market for the skilled labor required to produce the much-coveted Havana cigar. In 1869, as the war in Cuba deepened, the Spanish cigar manufacturer Vicente Martínez Ybor left Havana and established El Príncipe de Gales factory in Key West.[25] Within two years, eighteen thousand workers had established residence there.[26] Within a decade, the city emerged as the major cigar manufacturing center in the United States.[27] During the late 1880s and early 1890s, manufacturers expanded production facilities to Tampa, Ocala, and Jacksonville.[28]

The emergence of this population center of Cuban exiles in the southeastern United States was concurrent with the development of other émigré centers in Boston, New York, and Philadelphia. In the years following Zanjón, increasing numbers of Cuban Creole middle-class families sent their children to the United States for their education and professional training, adding to the expanding expatriate community. Thousands of

Cubans took up residence in the northeastern cities to study law, engineering, and medicine and to organize businesses.

Many other veterans of the Ten Years' War, together with the participants of subsequent uprising during the 1880s and 1890s, emigrated to various Latin American countries. In Mexico, Central and South America, and the West Indies, communities of Cuban exiles grew, dedicated to the continuing struggle for Cuba Libre.[29]

Paris emerged as another site of Cuban expatriation. As early as the 1860s, France had become the second home for increasing numbers of the planter class. For these Europeanized Creoles, Paris served as the distant core of their social and cultural universe, passing the tumult of the 1860s and 1870s in felicitous residence abroad. Many remained in Paris after Zanjón as absentee landowners and later served as the center of a Cuban colony around which the separatist community in France grew after the renewal of the conflict in 1895.

The distribution of the Cuban emigration between 1868 and 1895 acquired distinctive social characteristics. The *hacendado* and propertied elite took up residence in Paris. Sectors of the Cuban educated and professional middle class settled in the northeastern cities of the United States and Latin American capitals. Cuban proletariat communities emerged in Key West, Tampa, and Ocala. Collectively, these communities served as the three components of the expatriate constituency of Cuba Libre.

The social determinants of expatriation also tended to fix the place of Cubans of the separatist political spectrum. The advocates of annexation and the protectorate tended to serve the separatist cause abroad. Exiles functioned as the politico-diplomatic representatives of the insurgent provisional government abroad and headed the various exile patriotic organizations responsible for raising funds, making propaganda, and winning diplomatic support. The Cuban propertied elite in France, organized around the Paris junta, provided the financial support.

The political strength of annexation and protectorship sentiment resided abroad and in the leadership of the PRC. Martí's death early in the war removed the most outspoken and intransigent advocate of uncompromised independence and resulted immediately in a general moderation of the party's leadership. Gonzalo de Quesada, a naturalized American citizen and graduate of Columbia University School of Law, served as chargé d'affaires in Washington. Benjamín Guerra, a naturalized American citizen and owner of several cigar factories in Key West and Tampa, was appointed secretary-treasurer of the PRC. Tomás Estrada Palma replaced Martí as head of the PRC. A resident of some thirty years in the United States, Estrada was a converted Quaker and naturalized American citizen who advocated close relations with the United States.

By the time of Martí's death, the effort to create some consensus within separatist ranks as to the precise meaning of Cuba Libre had lost impetus. Cuban patriots had united around little more than an unsettled notion of independence. The exigencies of the war required immediate attention to the means of the separatist struggle rather than to the precise definition of the ends. For the time being, it was sufficient only to agree that Cuba Libre generally meant separation from Spain.

After Martí's death, annexation/protectorate sentiment resurfaced in expatriate separatist forums. "Thousands of Cubans have joined or helped on the revolution," several Cubans wrote to the *New York Herald* in 1897, "only because they thought and still think that independence would pave the way to annexation. If there are some who oppose it, it is because they lack a full knowlege of the American constitution and of the spirit of American institutions, and have been led to believe that annexation would mean only a change of masters."[30] One southern journalist reported in 1898 that virtually all the Cubans interviewed in Atlanta favored annexation, quoting the head of the local patriotic junta, Francisco Pla: "I have always believed that annexation meant the salvation of Cuba."[31]

While annexationist and protectorate sympathies came to be lodged within the PRC, *independentista* sentiment came to reside largely in the politico-military agencies of the armed struggle in Cuba—specifically, the insurgent provisional government and the Liberation Army. It was in the *manigua*, the insurgent-held interior, along the front lines of the armed struggle in insurrectionary Cuba, that Martí's version of Cuba Libre had found the most emphatic endorsement: neither autonomy nor annexation—nothing less than complete independence. "No fighting Cuban I ever met," Grover Flint wrote from Cuba, "favored annexation nor have I seen a fighting Cuban who distrusted Cuba's ability to govern herself peacefully."[32] Steven Bonsal writing from Oriente reported in 1898 that the "rank and file of Cuban army" knew "very well what they want, and what they have been fighting for so many years, and not two percent of these men want annexation to the United States, and a very large percent of them are ready and willing to carry on the struggle for independence of the island as resolutely and determinedly against the power of the United States as they did against the sovereignty of Spain."[33]

V   By the end of the first year of the war, the essential institutional manifestations of the separatist polity had assumed definitive form. In September 1895, a constituent assembly convened in Jimaguayú and established a provisional government headed by a Council of Government. Endowed by the new constitution with supreme authority over all separatist agencies, the Council of Government consisted of a president, a vice-president, and four cabinet members representing war, interior, treasury, and foreign relations.[34] The provisional government was responsible for the establishment of the services of state, including administration of law, the organization of public finances, and the dispensation of justice. Toward this end, the Council of Government appointed civilians as provincial governors in those territories under the control of separatist armies. Provincial governors, in turn, established a system of prefects and sub-prefects who functioned as local justices of the peace.[35] The Assembly of Jimaguayú, lastly, gave definitive form to the Liberation Army. Máximo Gómez was confirmed as general in chief. Within two years Gómez presided over an army of fifty thousand officers and men, organized into five army corps operating in every province of the island.

VI   But all was not well in the *manigua*. United by a common commitment to the most exalted view of Cuba Libre, the civil-military agencies of the *independentista* sector split early over matters of authority and leadership. From the inception of the insurrection, soldiers and civilians differed sharply on the character and function of the provisional government. This quarrel was not, to be sure, without precedent. The civil-military dispute had wracked separatist ranks during the 1880s. The reconciliation of 1892 had united Cubans in exile during peace. But the war in Cuba changed everything. In May 1895, Gómez, Maceo, and Martí had met at La Mejorana in southern Oriente to plan the character of the provisional government. Maceo insisted upon the formation of a government headed by a junta of generals, invested with complete authority over the politico-military direction of the war, and responsible directly to the armed forces. Martí balked, insisting upon the participation of all sectors in a government directed by civilians. The conference ended inconclusively, without a formal resolution of the dispute.[36]

Martí could not, however, have reflected over developments at La Mejorana without experiencing some dismay and foreboding. It was with no small sense of uneasiness that he watched the consensus laboriously forged in exile unravel under the exigencies of war. In the last entries of his diary, Martí scribbled private misgivings and growing despair over the course of events in the early months of war.[37] Only days before Dos Ríos, he wrote pessimistically for prospects of "respectable republican representation" in the revolution. "I put aside the authority given to me by the emigration and acknowledged here on the island," Martí wrote a friend on May 18. "The revolution desires complete freedom in the army, without the obstacles previously raised by an assembly without real authority."[38]

The death of Martí two weeks after La Mejorana weakened civilian influence within separatist councils. There was no successor of his stature capable of either articulating the *civilista* position or rivaling the prestige of such military chieftains as Gómez and Maceo. The Jimaguayú Assembly, to be sure, later dutifully proclaimed the doctrine of civil supremacy. But the 1895 constitution did not provide the means nor did the war permit the occasion to enforce this principle.

VII   It was an unequal struggle, one which civilians could not hope to win—not, at least, as long as the quest for independence remained primarily an issue of arms. But neither was it a principle with which there could be compromise. For members of the provisional government, the issue of civilian supremacy was as important as Cuban sovereignty. For Martí, a decade earlier, it had been worth the price of separatist unity. These were the *pinos nuevos*, the post-Yara generation, schooled in the principles of civilian authority, liberals who distrusted the army, public men of laws who feared the public men of arms.[39]

For three years, civilians demanded army allegiance to the constitution and acquiescence to the authority of provisional government. And for three years, insurgent military chieftains dutifully swore allegiance to the constitution—and ignored the provisional government. For three years, Máximo Gómez resisted civil authority over the armed forces. The war was a military affair, Gómez frequently chided civilians, subject only to direction of army chieftains charged with the responsibility for its conduct. The Dominican generalissimo tolerated the existence of the provisional government as a necessary nuisance, a structure required to give the revolution a measure of juridical legitimacy to the outside world. In private, however, the army command held the government in disdain, often denouncing civilian leaders and challenging their policies.[40] "They believe they constitute a real and effective government," Gómez wrote mordantly, "and they speak of constitution and laws, when in my judgment we have desired only to present a simple basis of government for higher political ends abroad, and nothing more. . . . It's ridiculous. In whose name do those men believe they govern?"[41] General Calixto García, deputy commander in chief in Oriente, was openly scornful of civilian authorities—a "miniscule clique," García sneered, "that entertains itself by playing at government."[42]

A fateful flaw, this civil-military breach, one that would deepen as the war widened: two centers of rival authority within the *independentista* wing of the separatist polity. At times the dispute threatened to paralyze the entire insurgent war effort. Military chieftains ignored provincial governors, prefects, and sub-prefects. Local civil authorities, for their part, frequently undertook programs and implemented policies totally independent of and often in opposition to provincial army commands.[43] Ambiguous and overlapping spheres of authority fueled the civil-military enmity. Army commanders often issued decrees that at once contravened the authority of civilian leaders and contradicted the laws of the provisional republic. The dispute at times played havoc with the internal governance of the army. In 1896, in an effort to weaken the army command, the provisional government began the practice of awarding commissions to civilians occupying administrative positions or possessing academic degrees. Thus the president was also the generalissimo of the army, the vice-president and cabinet ministers were major generals, subsecretaries were brigadier generals, and provincial governors were appointed colonels. University graduates were routinely commissioned as captains and lieutenants.[44] The Council of Government favored army chieftains known for their devotion to the primacy of civilian rule. In several instances, officers court-martialed for violating military codes in defense of civil laws were subsequently exonerated by the government.[45] Gómez responded in kind. Commissions awarded by the government were nullified; promotions and changes of command made without prior army approval were countermanded.

The provisional government struggled unsuccessfully throughout the war to subordinate the army command. In September 1896, the Council of Government amended the Organic Military Law in an effort to restrict the authority of the general-in-chief. Henceforth, Gómez could dictate only "military dispositions and general orders of the army that referred to the internal governance of the army and the technical parts of war operations." In all instances, including projects relating to operational plans, salaries, and recruitment, the army chief was ordered to submit his proposal in advance to the Council for approval.[46] In December 1897, the Council revised the Law of Military Organization to increase the authority of the Secretary of War over the army command. The amended law required the army chief to report on a regular basis to the Council of Government. More important, the revision sanctioned the direct intervention of the government in military affairs.[47]

The civil-military dispute continued unabated throughout the war. From time to time, the conflict erupted into open confrontation. On at least six different occasions between 1895 and 1898, Gómez was summoned by the Council of Government to defend himself against charges of insubordination. Twice the government contemplated removing Gómez, once by asking outright for his resignation and another time by abolishing the rank of general-in-chief. On three different occasions Gómez submitted his resignation.[48]

Gómez's personality certainly did not make the civilians' task simpler. Impetuous, petulant, and irascible, the seventy-three-year-old Gómez conducted the affairs of war imperiously. That he was a Dominican in command of Cubans did not make it any easier for civilian leaders to indulge his excesses. "General Gómez forgets," the secretary of war complained in 1896, "that he is only a foreigner who we have honored by offering him the command of the army."[49] More than one visitor to army headquarters commented on Gómez's overbearance. One writer traveling with the insurgent army command in 1897 commented that he was a "stern disciplinarian" and "something indeed of a martinet."[50] Later that year war correspondent Sylvester Scovel reported that Gómez had "become so uncontrolled as to endanger good feeling among his officers, and act as a disorganizing element."[51] George Bronson Rea, a correspondent for the *New York Herald*, reported an incident in which Gómez assaulted one of his staff officers:

Gomez leveled blow after blow on him. This exhibition of
Gomez's temper had a startling effect on the officers of his staff,
who belong to the most aristocratic families of Cuba, and they
all agreed then and there to recall the old fellow to his senses. . . .
Whether Gomez was aware of this attitude on their part it is
hard to state, but he showed his contempt for them by repeat-
ing the offense on the persons of various other officers during
the same afternoon. . . . Calling me to come nearer, one of the

the officers said: "Mr. Rea, we have decided to make the general understand once and for all, that we are not common soldiers or slaves, to be beaten and insulted at every change of his whim or disposition, and that in the future, if he has any just complaint against an officer, he must lay his charges in due form before a court convened for the occasion, who will punish or acquit him in their verdict."[52]

Only the prevailing Cuban belief that Gómez's military leadership was essential to the ultimate success of the separatist enterprise prevented an outright civil-military rupture during the war. As long as the separatist effort was primarily an affair of arms, civilian leaders were grudgingly obliged to share power with army chieftains. For the duration of the war, the army command and government leaders coexisted uneasily, pursuing Cuban independence in muted conflict and mounting tension.

VIII
The issues underlying the deepening civil-military schism went beyond simply a conflict over the direction of the insurgency. In a real sense, the dispute represented a struggle to define the very character of Cuba Libre. The *independentista* wing of the separatist polity contained conflicting versions of independence: one, represented by civil authority, commited to a liberal, statist, and bureaucratic model of Cuba Libre; the other, lodged within the Liberation Army, devoted to an authoritarian, populist, and charismatic version of free Cuba. Even as the war progressed, army chieftains perceived members of the provisional government to be more concerned with building the political apparatus of state —the edifice through which to advance civil supremacy over the separatist polity—than with ending the colonial regime. Insurgent army chieftains detected motives in civilian policies that were neither simple nor pure, maneuvers inspired by a desire to enhance the authority of the provisional government over the army and contain the social forces of the revolution.

The provisional government had been unenthusiastic—often uncooperative—about the invasion. On two occasions in 1896, relief suplies destined to the west were diverted by the government without approval of the army command. Military leaders suspected that civilians now feared that the insurrection had gone too far, that the war had acquired social currents that had to be harnessed.[53] And, indeed, there was some substance to army perceptions. Civil agencies of the revolution were dominated by representatives of the Cuban bourgeoisie, men with academic degrees, professional titles, and property—lawyers, engineers, doctors, teachers, and impoverished planters—who detected in the inchoate apparatus of the provisional government the device to control the diverse socio-political forces of free Cuba and the means by which to redistribute political power and economic wealth to disenfranchised Creoles. Ideologically devoted to Cuban nationalism, civilians approached Cuban independence in a legalistic and constitutional fashion. They defined the Cuban insurrection in essentially political terms, a struggle to wrest political power from a distant metropolis and its local representatives and establish in Cuba the state agencies capable of guaranteeing their ascendency in the future republic. The state in postwar Cuba would serve at once to institutionalize this new power and contain the social forces released by the revolution.

This commitment to legality, the demand for conformity to rules legally correct and imposed by accepted procedures, provided the basis for wartime political authority and, Creole civilians hoped, the source of future legitimacy. Civil officials derived their authority from constitutional legality and demanded, in turn, strict adherence to the laws of the provisional government. But it was more than a dedication to law—it was a commitment to legality and a legal system as the ultimate justification of the state, an authority based on an impersonal norm rather than upon the name of a personal authority. The principle of legality was intimately linked to and served as the foundation of the statist perception of Cuba Libre. The conflict within the *independentista* sector represented civilian efforts to develop a constitutional system to defend against the arbitrary authority represented by the army. The rule of law offered the institutional structures within which to establish the legitimate foundations of the state. Authority exercised according to and in the name of the law served to establish the supremacy of civilian politicians.

The world view of civilian leaders led inexorably to a national view of Cuba Libre. For the members of the government, patriotism pointed the way to salvation. Patriotism was pride of nation and love of liberty, self-assertion, and respect for the law. Liberty joined with rationalism and constituted the definition of Cuban nationality—the central justification for the state. Nationalism served as the means to transform nationality from a cultural phenomenon into a political ideology and the central principle upon which to establish the legitimacy of the state. Hypothetical imperatives were converted into categorical ones. The liberation of Cuba was the end and justification of the state.

But for many in the armed ranks of the *independentista* sector, patriotism had little direct relationship to national consciousness or political allegiance. Separatists in arms rarely lost sight of social and racial dimensions of the revolution and were not typically susceptible to the appeals of a national view of *patria*. Throughout the war, armed insurgents intuitively resisted the ideological transfiguration of separatist populism and consciously rejected the national transformation of patriotism. The national version of *patria* was a view associated with the western regions of Cuba, a view preeminently cosmopolitan in nature, *habanero* in origins, and colonial in its sources. It was a view that generated little enthusiasm in the east, certainly not one for which *orientales* would willingly sacrifice their lives.

The Júcaro-Morón *trocha* represented something more than a fortified line of Spanish military defenses. In fact, it gave palpable form to a boundary demarcating the eastern provinces from the rest of Cuba, fixing militarily a long standing politico-cultural division between east and west. The very construct of the separatist offensive in the west, designated as the "invasion"—one region of Cuba "invading" another—offered dramatic expression of the deep regional distinctions existing in the minds of nineteenth-century Cubans. This construct pitted primitive, parochial, economically backward Oriente against modern, cosmopolitan, and wealthy Occidente. The west viewed the approach of eastern insurgent armies as nothing less than an onslaught of barbarians, threatening the very foundations of civilization in Cuba. *Orientales*, for their part, had an equally low esteem of the west, a region they perceived as the bulwark of metropolitan authority, estranged from the historic traditions of the island over which *orientales* felt a peculiar custodial responsibility.

Ties of local attachment in the east ran deep. If *orientales* rejected a national view of *patria* ideologically, they also resisted the operational transformation of *patria*, namely taking the war to the west. To be sure, insurgent chieftains understood the tactical importance and the strategic necessity of carrying the insurrection to the west. But it was not without significance that one of the most resolute advocates of the invasion, Máximo Gómez, was not Cuban. The army command encountered considerable resistance among eastern chiefs to the preparations for the invasion. *Oriental* troops balked at operations that would take them away from their homes, out of their province, and into new and unfamiliar zones. Antonio Maceo had difficulty persuading his brother to contribute men and equipment to complete the organization of *Ejército Invasor*.[54] Early during the westward march, many *oriental* troops under Gómez abandoned the Dominican chieftain in Camagüey and returned to Oriente.[55] Desertions in Maceo's column reached such alarming proportions that Maceo was compelled to order the summary execution of all soldiers abandoning the *Ejército Invasor*.[56]

IX A fundamental and, indeed, profound difference separated *independentista* agencies in the *manigua*. For the army command the issue was not merely the form of political power but, rather, its purpose and scope. Insurgent army chieftains were less concerned with formal structures of power than with the function of power. The cause of Cuba Libre had attracted to the armed ranks the socially dispossessed, Cubans for whom the armed struggle—rather than the state—offered the means through which to redress long-standing grievances against the colonial regime. No less committed to the *independentista* version of Cuba Libre, armed separatism subsumed a social imperative into its vision of independence. The army was commanded by officers of humble social origins, frequently men of color, men like Jesús Rabí, Flor Crombet, Quintín Banderas, Antonio and José Maceo, and Guillermo Moncada, for whom the old regime was as much a social anathema as it was a political anachronism. The Liberation Army consisted principally of peasants and rural workers, with blacks well overrepresented in insurgent columns and accounting for some 40 percent of the senior commissioned ranks of the army.[57] They had pledged themselves to a movement that promised not only to free them from the old oppression but to give them a new place in society and a new country to belong to. Independence was at once a means—a necessary means, to be sure—and a prelude to the fulfillment of a social vision.

The struggle for Cuba Libre signified considerably more than the pursuit of independence. Nationhood was only an aspect of Cuban fulfillment. José Martí's republic was as much a function of his social vision as it was a product of his political aspirations. The separatist effort joined all classes and both races in a common cause. Rich and poor, black and white, were summoned to participate in the construction of the new republic.[58] The Cuban enterprise was as much committed to ending colonial relationships within the colony as it was determined to end the colonial connection with the metropolis. Indeed, the rebellion against Spanish political rule was a revolution against the Cuban social order.

Martí spoke of insurrection and revolution as two distinct but interrelated processes. Within the context of the insurrection against Spanish rule, he described a revolution against the values and beliefs of the colonial system. "The war is but only the expression of the revolution," Martí wrote in 1885.[59] Cuba Libre signified a Cuba free from racism and oppression, a republic responsive to the needs of all Cubans. "The revolution will be for the benefit of all who contribute to it," he vowed. "Through the gates we exiles open . . . ," he predicted in 1892, "will enter Cubans with a radical soul of the new country." A change only in the form of government was inadequate compensation for the sacrifices separatist leaders were demanding of patriots. "Nor would a single war," he insisted, "suffice to complete a revolution whose primary success was only a change of location of an injust authority."[60] Independence represented only the preliminary political phase of a larger process, one in which Cubans would labor to eliminate the socio-economic vices of the colony. "In my view," Martí wrote Antonio Maceo in 1882, "the solution to the Cuban problem is not a political but a social one."[61] A decade later, he reiterated his conviction: "Our goal is not so much a mere political change as a good, sound, and just and equitable social system without demagogic fawning or arrogance of authority. And let us never forget that the greater the suffering the greater the right to justice, and the prejudices of men and social inequities cannot prevail over the equality which nature has created."[62]

The armed struggle was to be nothing less than a war of redemption and redistribution. Martí repeatedly invoked the concept of redemption to characterize the separatist enterprise. "The war is planned abroad," he wrote in early 1892, "for the redemption and benefit of all Cubans."[63] Martí spoke both of a "holy revolution" and the "redemptive virtue of just wars that would join all Cubans around the burning idea of decent redemption."[64] But social and cultural equality was impossible within a system of economic inequality. The vision of the new republic included a commitment to national economic development based on diversified agriculture. "Exclusive wealth," Martí wrote in 1878, "is unjust. . . . A nation with small landowners is rich. A country with a few rich men is not rich—only the country where everyone possesses a little of the wealth is rich. In political economy and good government, distribution is the source of prosperity."[65] Fifteen years later, Martí again addressed himself to the issue of distribution of property. Cuba possessed vast expanses of uncultivated land and had "obviously just to make it available to anyone desiring to work it." With an equitable system of land distribution, he predicted, "a simple matter upon the inauguration of a sovereign state, Cuba will accommodate many good men—a counterbalance for social problems and foundation for a Republic . . . should be one of enterprise and work."[66]

Martí's vision of the republic remained always ambiguous and imprecise. He spoke more to aspiration than action, promise rather than program; his concerns were expressed in thematic rather than programmatic terms. Martí did not develop a program as much as he identified the problems and committed the future republic to their resolution. But these vague commitments established the ideological premises of the separatist cause, the central if ambiguous creed and articles of faith around which Martí mobilized support from those sectors of Cuban society most susceptible to appeals for a new order. Martí was not merely attempting to overthrow Spanish rule; he aspired to nothing less than a fundamental change in Cuban politics by creating new ways of mobilizing and sharing power. Independence was to produce the republic and the republic stood for political democracy, social justice, and economic freedom. He added a social agenda to the historic program of national liberation and instantly converted a movement devoted to the establishment of a new nation into a force dedicated to shaping a new society. Martí transformed rebellion into revolution.

It was for these reasons that the effects of Martí's death were incalculable. His revolutionary formula was a conglomeration of national pride, social theory, anti-imperialism, and personal intuition. He rationalized it all into a single revolutionary metaphysic and institutionalized it into a single revolutionary party. Like a master weaver, Martí pulled together all the separate threads of Cuban discontent, social, economic, political, racial, historical, and wove them into a radical movement of enormous force. After his death, it began to unravel.

So it was that the dispossessed and disinherited on both sides of the Florida Straits responded to this summons. An expatriate proletariat, a dispossessed peasantry, blacks and whites, the landless and the poor, ratified Martí's vision of free Cuba—"with all and for the well-being of all" to end "the malevolent regime of the Creole oligarchy."[67] For Martí, the goal of the war of independence was "not a change in forms but a change of spirit." To this end, it was "necessary to make common cause with the oppressed, to secure the system opposed to the interests and habits of the rule of the oppressors."[68] For the many thousands who early enlisted into the ranks of the insurgent armies, the armed struggle against Spain represented a struggle for social justice, racial equality, and economic well-being possible only through the redemptive struggle for Cuba Libre.[69]

6 Convergence and Divergence in Cuban Separatism

I believe if left alone we will achieve our own independence unaided, and I am loath that we should be robbed of any share in the honor of the expulsion of the Spaniards.
—Máximo Gómez, December 1897

I have on this date authorized Juan Pedro Baró, Fernando Pons, and Mariano Ortiz to proceed with this year's harvest.
—Tomás Estrada Palma, November 1895

The proprietors of mills who go on milling . . . will be immediately hung. Identification only is necessary.
—Máximo Gómez, January 1896

I   The first anniversary of the "Grito de Baire" found Cuban separatists united around little more than vague if not incompatible definitions of Cuba Libre. As the war deepened, so too did the contradictions in the revolutionary coalition.

The change of leadership of the PRC after the death of Martí fundamentally transformed the purpose of the revolutionary party. The PRC had united Cubans behind the armed struggle, raised war funds, and generally underwritten the insurgency in Cuba. Martí's party was, in both design and function, the political wing of the armed struggle. The purpose of the PRC, Martí insisted in May 1893, was "to unite all the elements of emancipation both in and out of Cuba" and "save the war . . . from the natural but correctable mistakes of the first [provisional] republic and to organize, with the approval of the island, the vigorous and total insurrection that will finally convert the wretched and miserable colony into an equitable and industrious nation." The party was "to accumulate resources for the war of independence" and assemble "willing adherents and necessary resources to gain the independence Cuba desires."[1] Later in 1893, Martí reiterated: "The Revolutionary Party was created for a judicious and democratic war and it will not abandon its objective to wage the war of independence democratically and judiciously."[2]

Under Martí, the role of the PRC was clearly defined: support of the armed struggle. This was the principal mission of the party, the purpose for which it was created. Upon the PRC rested the responsibility for delivering war materiel to the *manigua*. In this unequal contest between the Spanish Mauser and the Cuban machete, supplies from abroad would mean the difference between victory and defeat. The only thing worse than a quick defeat was a delayed victory, one creating the conditions for an American intervention.

After the death of Martí, the PRC passed under the direction of Tomás Estrada Palma. Almost immediately the party underwent a significant transformation. By the end of 1895, the PRC had been reorganized into a consular agency. This was more than a change in form. In a very real sense it was a redefinition of purpose, one in which diplomatic considerations overshadowed political objectives. Not that the PRC abandoned its original mission. Many of the party's original activities continued more or less uninterrupted throughout the war. But the expansion of the party's function signified a reordering of expatriate emphases, a change whereby PRC delegates constituted themselves as the diplomatic representatives of the provisional government rather than the political agents of the Liberation

Army. This conversion also transformed the PRC constituency from the communities of exiled Cubans to the courts of foreign governments. In November 1895, Estrada Palma assumed the title Minister Plenipotentiary of the provisional Cuban republic. The title Martí had used—Chief Delegate of the Cuban Revolutionary Party—was abandoned. By early 1896, Estrada Palma had appointed thirty diplomatic representatives to head PRC missions abroad. Distributed thoughout some twenty countries in Latin America and Europe, PRC envoys were charged with the task of representing the insurgent provisional government to foreign capitals and working for recognition of Cuban belligerency.[3] In January 1896 Minister Plenipotentiary Estrada Palma left the center of the Cuban expatriate community in New York to establish himself at the center of the U.S. government in Washington.[4]

This transformation of the PRC underscored the conflicting tendencies emerging within the separatist polity after the death of Martí. Many within the organization doubted the Cubans' ability for self-government, just as there were those who doubted—and feared—the Cubans' ability to win the war unassisted. The effort of the expatriate representation in the United States after 1896 toward securing recognition of Cuban belligerency was but a means, a way to achieve a mediated political settlement of the military conflict. Belligerency was conceived more in terms of diplomatic pressure directed against Spain than as an expression of military support for the Cubans. Not that belligerency would have been without its positive effect on the insurgent fund of morale and materiel. Such status would have immediately legitimized the acquisition of arms and their transshipment to Cuba. But there was another aspect to belligerency. American recognition of the Cuban cause would have directly involved the United States in the conflict. It was this involvement, the PRC leadership calculated, clearly serving to tip the scales in favor of the Cubans, that would force Spain to the negotiation table at which the United States would preside.[5] Martí's abhorrence became Estrada Palma's aspiration. American participation in a negotiated peace promised to provide both the means and the justification for the establishment of the protectorate.

For the duration of the war, PRC policy centered on seeking American support to end Spanish rule and guaranteeing the United States a part in that settlement. The expanding insurgency did not increase expatriate support of Cuban military efforts as much as it increased PRC pressure on Washington to secure a mediated political settlement. American involvement was designed both to save the island from the continued adversity of Spanish sovereignty and the unknown perils of Cuban independence.

Having failed to secure American mediation to settle the war politically, the PRC appealed for American intervention to end the war militarily. By 1897, the expatriate representation had emerged as unabashed advocates of U.S. military intervention. Only the interposition of American armed forces, Estrada Palma concluded, promised to bring the conflict to a satisfactory end. In mid-1897, the PRC junta joined New York bankers with interests in Cuba in petitioning Washington to intervene to end the conflict.[6] By 1898, Estrada Palma publicly advocated American intervention. "I think," he pronounced in January 1898, "the time has come for the American government to intervene."[7]

II   Army chieftains in Cuba viewed the activities of the emigration leadership with growing alarm. From the start of the insurrection, military leaders shared none of the expatriate enthusiasm for American involvement in the conflict. For them the energy and resources directed abroad toward securing American recognition of Cuban belligerency represented misplaced if not misdirected efforts. The priority assigned by the PRC to recognition confused the issues, often obscuring among separatists the sharp distinction between recognition as a means and recognition as an end. Much too much emphasis, army leaders complained, had been placed abroad on securing assistance from the United States. They insisted that separatist arms were sufficient for the task of Cuban liberation. "I expect nothing from the Americans," Antonio Maceo confided to a friend in exile. "We should entrust everything to our own efforts. It is better to rise or fall without help than to contract debts of gratitude with such a powerful neighbor."[8] In May 1897, General Calixto García wrote to Gonzalo de Quesada in New York: "I have always expected little from the Americans, choosing instead to rely on our efforts; I believe that we can defeat the Spaniards fighting exactly as we have been up to this moment."[9]

At a much more fundamental level, insurgent chieftains in Cuba questioned the utility of the expatriate diplomatic mission abroad. Ranking army chieftains were not unmindful of the potential benefits accruing to the cause of Cuban arms as a result of belligerency status. But they remained unconvinced that belligerency status was essential if at all relevant to the final outcome of the war. "The official recognition of our belligerency," Antonio Maceo wrote Alberto J. Díaz in United States, "does not seem to me a matter of such importance." The secret of "our definitive triumph," Maceo insisted confidently, "is contained in the efforts of the Cubans who work for a free homeland."[10] Máximo Gómez, too, had misgivings. "Much is spoken here about recognition of belligerency," he wrote as early as November 1895, "but without preoccupying ourselves unduly about events still to come, we trust everything to the labor of our effort and our determined resolution."[11] Six months later, the Dominican generalissimo again returned to this theme. "Much is spoken and written of the recognition of belligerency by the American government," he wrote Estrada Palma in March 1896, "and such an event would be advantageous, but since we counted only on the strength of our effort and an unalterable resolve when we started, we will continue our march undaunted—what will happen will happen."[12] By early 1897, his patience with the Cuban fixation on recognition had grown thin. "I have a mind to forbid any man's speaking that word in camp," an exasperated Gómez confided to correspondent Grover Flint. "Recognition is like the rain; it is a good thing if it comes, and a good thing if it doesn't."[13]

Insurgent military chieftains also opposed direct U.S. armed intervention in the Cuban conflict. Behind insurgent military lines in Cuba, American intervention was as unwelcomed as it was unwanted. Cubans did not need foreign involvement to win its independence, Maceo insisted. The war would be won without any help other than that provided by the Cuban freedom fighters.[14] "We shall not ask for interference by the United States," General Julio Sanguily asserted confidently in early 1897. "We don't need that. We can end this war ourselves and that before the year is out."[15]

Nor were insurgent military chieftains unmindful of the perils attending American intervention. "We sincerely believed," one insurgent officer later wrote, "that . . . intervention would result in danger for Cuba and many of us preferred not to have this help and keep fighting without it since sooner or later we would have had to defeat Spain."[16] Advocates of belligerency status and U.S intervention, Máximo Gómez explained to an aide in March 1897, as well as those who expected the United States to give Cuba its independence, were not to be trusted. "There are two types of turncoats," Gómez mused, "those who join the Spanish camp and those who are morally in the Spanish camp, the latter being those who long for an end to the war and dream of recognition and who believe that the new president of the United States will give us independence."[17] He feared that the "North American republic's absorbing tendency" would overwhelm the cause of Cuban separatism. "Cuba must not be," he insisted, "beholden for its independence in any way to foreign good graces."[18]

III The reordering of the PRC mission abroad, most notably the new emphasis given to belligerency, enormously complicated expatriate activities in the United States. In a very real sense, the position of the party had become untenable. Separatist representatives found themselves, on one hand, seeking to win American support for the recognition of belligerency while, at the same time, engaging in filibustering activities in direct violation of U.S. laws. Exiles holding naturalized American citizenship feared arrest; Cubans feared deportation. All feared that continued filibustering would threaten what the PRC leadership perceived to be the more important task of securing belligerency status. And from time to time, expatriate Cubans were reminded of their precarious position. As early as June 1895, President Cleveland issued a proclamation ordering all "citizens and other persons" to abstain from violating American neutrality laws.[19] "It would be well for Cubans in this country," the *New York Tribune* chided exiles editorially, "[those] who have been going as close to violation of the laws of the United States as they possibly could in safety, to understand that they are under great obligations to this Nation for its hospitality and forbearance. . . . If they have done what they profess to have done, they are candidates for imprisonment for breaking the laws of the land that shelters them."[20] There was some sentiment within the New York junta to relocate PRC headquarters to a country more favorably disposed to Cuban activities. The decision to remain in the Unied States resulted in greater circumspection given to organizing filibustering operations.[21] This translated into further decreasing support of the armed struggle in Cuba.

These developments had far-reaching consequences in Cuba. If the expatriate leadership had patently little to show for its diplomatic labors abroad, it had less to show for its efforts in behalf of the armed struggle in Cuba. The PRC pursuit of recognition and intervention had substantially reduced the expatriate effort in behalf of tactical support of the separatist war effort. Indeed, after January 1896, Estrada Palma divested himself entirely of the responsibility for organizing filibustering expeditions to Cuba. A reorganization of the PRC in late 1895 had created a separate Department of Expeditions under the direction of General Emilio Núñez, thereby allowing Estrada Palma to devote more time to diplomatic activities in Washington. The added emphasis on the diplomatic mission further reduced Cubans' access to equipment. The shipment of arms, ammunition, and supplies to Cuba, originally the central responsibility of the PRC, diminished markedly; filibustering expeditions decreased.

The repercussions were felt immediately in Cuba. Insurgent chieftains repeatedly appealed for arms and supplies. The message from the *manigua* was clear: Cubans needed neither recognition nor the assistance of foreign soldiers—just arms. Arms had always been the primary need; back in April 1895, only two weeks in Cuba, Martí had written: "Arms, and quickly, is definitive and imperative—that is all that is needed here." Popular support had exceeded original expectations, Martí exulted, and with proper supplies and equipment, "This time the war will not be frustrated."[22] "Arms, arms, and arms," General Francisco Palomares urgently appealed to his compatriots in New York later in 1895, "is what we need to finish soon—very soon!—with our oppressors."[23] "We need arms and ammunition," Colonel Fermín Valdés Domínguez wrote in 1896. "We do not need expeditions of men; there are many here and very brave ones. What the leaders who work abroad should do is dispatch small boats with few crewmen and much arms and ammunition. In that way we could make ourselves masters in Oriente and support the efforts in Camagüey and Las Villas."[24] "Arms, my friend," General José María Rodríguez exhorted Gonzalo de Quesada in New York. "Many arms, much munitions, and the definitive victory will not be long. . . . Rush the shipment of war materiel that we need so much and forget everything else."[25] Only the chronic shortages of supplies, insurgent chieftains repeatedly exhorted, delayed the Cuban triumph. "If we had fifty percent of the people well armed," José Maceo insisted to Benjamín Guerra in New York, "independence would already be a fact."[26]

The reordering of PRC activities had particularly adverse effects on insurgent military operations in western Cuba. At the precise moment Estrada Palma was moving the center of expatriate activities from New York to Washington, Antonio Maceo was completing the insurgent drive from Oriente to Pinar del Río. The invasion had been conceived in the expectation that supplies from abroad would support the operations on the *Ejército Invasor* in the west. Indeed, one of the central strategic objectives of the western campaign was to secure control of coastal regions in Havana province and Pinar del Río, points closer to exile centers in the United States, and thereby facilitate the flow of arms and ammunition to Cuba.

Once in Pinar del Río, however, Maceo found himself all but completely isolated, distant from the base of supplies in the east and no closer to support from the north. Immediately, insurgent columns in the west encountered a severe shortage of arms, ammunition, and supplies. Through 1896, Maceo urgently appealed for supplies from abroad. In March 1896, an impatient and frustrated Maceo wrote to Estrada Palma: "Since I organized the contingent for the invasion with the resources allowed to me by the conditions of the army in Oriente, sufficient for the campaign until now . . . I resent that you people have not yet taken advantage of the facilities that this whole west coast offers you to undertake small and frequent expeditions which would be of the greatest use to me. Accordingly, I expect that you will do everything possible to urgently send small landing parties to said coast."[27] A month later, Maceo reacted angrily upon hearing of the continuing expatriate maneuvers in Washington to secure American intervention. "We do not need such an intervention to triumph sooner or later," an exasperated Maceo wrote Estrada Palma. "If we want to shorten the triumph to a few days, bring to Cuba twenty-five thousand rifles and a million rounds of ammunition in one or, at most, two expeditions."[28] In June, Maceo complained again, this time to Máximo Gómez: "Until now I have received no resources, absolutely none; I am making the war with the supplies I have on different occasions taken from the enemy."[29] Throughout the summer campaign, the insurgent leadership in the west continued to appeal abroad for relief. After the death of Maceo, General Juan Rius Rivera assumed command of the *Ejército Invasor* and renewed earlier insurgent pleas. "We do not need men, and above all we do not want foreigners to come," he insisted in January 1897. "An army of 50,000 could be placed in Havana province before the winter is over if we had but the arms and ammunition." Rius publicly chided his compatriots abroad for their inattention to the needs of the western armies: "I do not wish to criticize our friends in the United States, for I believe [members of the New York Junta] patriotic men and striving to do their best for Cuba, but we here in Pinar del Río have been somewhat neglected. . . . Some of my friends may criticize me for speaking so plainly, but I wish the Cubans of New York, Philadelphia, Jacksonville, and Key West to know that we here in Pinar del Río, like our brothers in Oriente, are willing to die for Cuba to win. We cannot fight alone with our hands, nor even with machetes, against an enemy that is fully equipped, fed and drilled."[30]

IV The presence of insurgent armies in the west in 1896 sharpened the ideological tensions within the separatist polity and delineated the substantive issues of Cuban separatism. Indeed, the success of the armed struggle exposed the conflicts and contradictions within the revolutionary coalition.

On January 22, 1896, Antonio Maceo led a triumphant procession of the *Ejército Invasor* into Mantua, the westernmost extremity of the island of Cuba. The completion of the invasion gave dramatic expression to the vitality of the year-old insurrectionary war. Insurgent forces had accomplished in ten months what the separatist armies of Yara had failed to achieve in ten years. The completion of the invasion thus settled the central military issues of the Cuban conflict. The essential and perhaps critical military objective of insurgent strategy—the extension of the revolution across the full breadth of the island—had been achieved by the first anniversary of the separatist war.

The invasion changed everything. Within a period of three months, insurgent columns had penetrated Spanish defenses with impunity and launched military operations in central Cuba. In five months, much to the horror of the Spanish authorities, insurgent forces operated in every province. Indeed, the *Ejército Invasor* served as something of a lightning rod, attracting recruits across the island into insurgent ranks; new recruits produced new military operations. By the end of the westward march in January, insurgent armies, strengthened by local recruits, had launched operations in Las Villas, Matanzas, Havana, and Pinar del Río.[31] Only days after arriving at Mantua, Maceo estimated that the size of the Liberation Army had increased 25 percent, with his own army reaching some ten thousand officers and men.[32]

Shock waves reverberated across the Atlantic. No longer could Spain dismiss the rebellion as an insignificant provincial affair. The presence of insurgent armies in western Cuba transformed a regional conflict into a national war of liberation, integrating all of the island into the armed struggle and involving all social classes. Those provinces traditionally immune to the havoc attending past separatist conflicts, together with property owners who found in that immunity sufficient justification to pay homage to Spanish sovereignty, found themselves after 1896 in the eye of the separatist storm. Much of Spain's traditional support, indeed, its very claim on the allegiance of the planter class, rested historically on its ability to confine the recurring separatist maelstrom to the east and protect western Cuba from tumult and disruption. This was the tacit understanding between officials in the metropolis and property owners in the colony, an understanding with origins early in the nineteenth century and upon which the fidelity of the Ever-Faithful Isle had since depended.

The basis of Spain's claim to Cuban loyalty was shattered. The inability of colonial authorities to protect property and bring the war to a hasty end deprived Spain of the single most compelling basis upon which to retain the support of the planters and eliminated the most powerful bond between the propertied elite and metropolitan authorities.[33] Planters who earlier had depended upon Spain for the security of their estates found themselves after 1896 at the mercy of forces over which the metropolis had no control.

The effects were immediate. The invasion hampered the 1895–1896 harvest, threatened preparations for the 1896–1897 crop, and resulted generally in the disruption of the western economy. Over the longer run, and more important, it served to disabuse those who expected that the insurrection of 1895, like so many of its abortive predecessors in the previous decade, would expend its destructive energies in the east and sputter ingloriously to a quick end.

The arrival of Antonio Maceo in Pinar del Río ended the premise of Creole collaboration with metropolitan Spain and shattered the colonial consensus. By early 1896, the insurrection threatened to destroy the wealth-producing regions and plunge the island into a monumental economic crisis. Far from showing signs of abating in 1896, the rebellion gave every indication of gaining strength and momentum, causing many to reconsider their attitude toward insurgent separatism. Planters lost confidence in Spain's ability to restore order and reestablish its authority over the island. Persuaded that a settlement of the Cuban crisis necessarily lay with a separatist solution, many planters embraced the cause of Cuba Libre. If, indeed, this was to be Cuba's fate, many reasoned, it behooved them to participate in the process and thereby have some influence on the outcome of events.[34] "It appears to me," one Autonomist concluded in 1896, "that those of us who failed to end the revolution now have no other recourse but to join it so that it may end soon."[35] A movement initially endorsed by an exiled proletariat in Florida, and seconded on the field of battle by the dispossessed of the east, underwent a profound social transformation as insurgent armies swept across the western provinces. As the invasion moved westward, it carried the impact of the insurgency upward through the class structure of the island.

Hacendados of central Cuba were among the first to accommodate themselves to the emerging separatist ascendancy. Planters who enrolled in separatist ranks were typically owners of property in regions that had fallen more or less under insurgent control and for whom the value of Spain's traditional commitment to security had effectively lapsed with the success of Cuban arms. These planters hoped to parlay newly acquired separatist credentials into security for their estates and exchange financial contributions to separatist coffers for insurgent permission to plant and harvest. Planters who supported the separatist cause after 1896 joined secret patriotic juntas in Cuban cities. Many *hacendados*, like Perfecto Lacosta, abandoned the Autonomist party to support the PRC in Havana. By early 1896, many of Cuba's wealthiest planters had enlisted in the separatist cause. Marta Abreu and her husband, Luis Estévez, Fernando Pons, Juan Pedro Baró, and Emilio Terry, among the most prominent, abandoned their estates in central Cuba and joined the PRC junta in Paris.[36]

V   The invasion was the first of two events that transformed the balance of politics in the colony. It set the stage for the second blow: the arrival of Valeriano Weyler. Separatist military successes signaled the political failure of Martínez Campos and, with him, the end of any hope that reform could produce a negotiated settlement of the Cuban crisis. The presence of insurgent forces in western Cuba, moreover, announcing the bankruptcy of liberal approaches to pacification, resulted directly in the adoption of Weyler's "war with war" policy. His appointment announced in rather unequivocal terms Madrid's repudiation of "la vía autonomista." Spain's commitment to suppression of the insurgency through force of arms left little room for compromise and concession. The liberal failure to secure a negotiated settlement served to discredit Autonomists among *peninsular* authorities. But it was also true that the inability of the colonial government to protect the estates discredited Spanish authorities among Cuban planters. On both counts, Creole elites were the victims.

Weyler's appointment in 1896 signaled the ascendancy of the intransigent pro-Spanish sectors for whom there was little substantive distinction bewteen autonomism and separatism. Weyler indiscriminately situated Autonomists with separatists at opposite ends of the same political spectrum, separated only by the means they employed to subvert metropolitan authority. The appointment ended any likelihood of a peace settlement based on reconciliation and sharpened the polarities of colonial politics. Cuban liberals now had to choose between separatism and Spain.

News of Weyler's appointment in Cuba had a profoundly unsettling political effect in Cuba. Almost immediately, it precipitated a new wave of emigration. Scores of Cuban families departed for the United States. In February 1896, in the space of one month, some thirteen hundred people left for Tampa. In the first three months of Weyler's government, another two thousand families emigrated to Europe.[37]

Nor were the fears that propelled thousands of Cubans into exile entirely unfounded. Under Weyler, Autonomists were all but formally banished from political forums in Cuba. The rigor with which Weyler pursued separatists in the field was surpassed only by his persecution of Autonomists in the cities. Public criticism of government policies was banned. The opposition press was silenced. This was calculated terror, a measured program directed against the Cuban upper classes that claimed hundreds of victims. Waves of arrests resulted in the imprisonment and deportation of thousands of Cubans suspected of separatist sympathies, the majority of whom were Autonomists. Within days of Weyler's arrival, provincial authorities made some 50 arrests in Pinar del Río. By July, consul Fitzhugh Lee reported 720 political prisoners in Havana alone.[38] In the small Matanzas city of Jovellanos, 600 people fled after a wave of government arrests led to the imprisonment of some 40 people in two days. Hundreds of Cubans were deported to Spain to serve prison terms in *peninsular* jails; many others were sent to Spain's African penal colonies in Ceuta, Chafarinas, and Fernando Poo. In December 1896, several hundred Cuban political prisoners disembarked in Cádiz; this particular group of prisoners included property owners, businessmen, lawyers, and several Cubans who had previously served in the provincial government of the island.[39] In September 1896, the Russian consul in Havana had written of the "daily executions of prisoners of war, the numerous arrests and the deportations to Africa." Arrests, he reported, "have become more frequent in this city within the last fortnight. . . . Lawyers and university professors have joined their numerous imprisoned colleagues."[40] Gilson Willets, an American traveling in Cuba in 1896, noted that "every ten days or so crowds of handcuffed men are driven through the streets of Havana, which they will never tread again, on their way to the transport ships which will convey them to penal settlements on the African coast. Many of these men represent the elite of Cuban society." In all, Willets estimated, some ten thousand prominent citizens "had been shipped to overseas penal colonies."[41]

Weyler's appointment signaled the demise of the Autonomist party. From the very outset of the war, *peninsular* authorities and their Creole allies had viewed Autonomists with great suspicion, detecting in the ranks of the party the natural allies and potential collaborators of insurgent Cubans. To be sure, many Autonomists, particularly at the provincial level, had indeed responded to the separatist call with some ambivalence, if not outright sympathy. That many Autonomists joined the insurgent armies, particularly the younger impatient members of the party and the elders with separatist antecedents who were frustrated and despondent over the slow pace of metropolitan reform, confirmed the worst forebodings of the Spanish officialdom. As the insurgency spread westward, it attracted the support of ranking Autonomist provincial leaders. After 1896, the prospects of autonomism could not rival the promise of separatism. In the provinces, Autonomists who earlier had served in separatist forces during the Ten Years' War, together with liberals exasperated by metropolitan inattention to colonial grievances after Zanjón, joined local insurgent armies. In Las Villas, Francisco Suárez, Francisco López Leyva, and José Alemán, all provincial Autonomist officeholders, assumed command of insurgent forces operating in central Cuba. Spanish loyalists pointed to these defections as evidence of Autonomist sympathy for the separatist cause.

These developments, in turn, justified the continued harassment of Autonomists. Throughout the island, local civil and military authorities attacked them at every opportunity. Party officials, including ranking provincial leaders, were arrested, beaten, and subjected to house searches; many were deported without trial. Autonomist meetings were banned and party newspapers suspended.[42]

Before 1896, the excesses against Autonomists in the provinces could be dismissed as the misconduct of overzealous local authorites, peccadillos for which there existed in Havana appropriate mechanisms of appeal and redress. "As long as we have hopes that they will pay attention to us," one Autonomist stubbornly persisted as late as February 1895, "we will continue to struggle in good faith."[43] When Martínez Campos arrived in Havana later that year, not a few Autonomists interpreted the occasion as the vindication of liberal policies and the end of party harassment.

Weyler's policies after 1896, however, served to disabuse all Autonomists of such continued expectations. What had been sporadic and local harassment became systematic and island-wide. It was soon apparent that there was no room and less tolerance in the Weyler regime for politics based on compromise with and concession to the rebellious colony. In early 1896, Weyler threatened to dissolve the party altogether.

For decades Autonomists had struggled against the abuses of colonialism rather than the system of colonialism. In 1896 they were disoriented and disillusioned. Their debut in Cuban politics was as inglorious as their performance was short-lived. The island's natural elite had failed in its quest for political power. It now faced political extinction by *peninsular* loyalists from above and economic ruin by Cuban separatists from below. Having failed to establish political preeminence, the shattered elite settled into the role of a pressure group—a part it would play for the next sixty years.

A combination of separatist military success and Spanish repression forced many Autonomists to side openly with the revolution. The choices were difficult, but decisions were necessary. Scores, including key members of the party's Junta Central, deserted the party and left for exile, many to join separatist agencies abroad. By the end of 1896, virtually every ranking Autonomist had either enrolled in the separatist cause or was in prison.[44] In New York and Paris, former Autonomists denounced the Spanish regime and proclaimed their support of the separatist cause. Eliseo Giberga, Raimundo Cabrera, Carlos de Zaldo, Carlos Párraga, Gabriel Millet, Fernando Freyre de Andrade, José Antonio González Lanuza, and Emilio Terry were only a few of the most prestigious members of the Autonomist party who embraced the separatist cause between 1895 and 1896. Diego Tamayo, a member of the Autonomist Junta Central in 1895 was serving in 1896 on the PRC revolutionary council in New York. Autonomist landowner José de Zayas joined the Cuban junta in Paris. Evilio Rodríguez Lendián, an Autonomist law professor, emigrated to New York after Weyler's arrival to Havana, there to join the junta. Adolfo de Aragón left Havana in 1896 and became active in the political clubs "Oscar Primelles" and "Patria" in New York. Fernando Freyre de Andrade, an Autonomist magistrate in Havana, left Cuba upon learning that Weyler had issued orders for his arrest; Freyre emigrated to New York and offered his services to Estrada Palma. Alfredo Zayas, a member of the Autonomist Junta Central, was arrested by Weyler in 1896 and joined separatist groups after his release a year later.

Two powerful sectors of Cuban society, formerly allied to Spain, had enrolled in separatist ranks. Autonomists who advocated reforms and planters who demanded repression discovered that Spain could neither offer reforms sufficient to conciliate the insurgents nor apply repression enough to dominate the insurrection. The triumph of the invasion persuaded many previously unsympathetic to separatist goals that the insurrection could indeed succeed; the ruthlessness of Weyler's regime convinced them the insurrection had to succeed. Continued Spanish sovereignty promised only to prolong Cuban difficulties. Indeed, metropolitan authority represented the single largest obstacle to order and stability, making it all but impossible to bring a recurring cycle of war and rebellion to an end once and for all.

The new wave of recruits to the separatist cause boosted insurgent morale.[45] At the same time, however, the influx of Autonomists, filling as they did the ranks of the emigration, tended to become one more moderating force on Cuban separatism. It was toward the most conservative wing of the separatist political spectrum that Autonomists gravitated, that sector with which Autonomists had the greatest affinity. They did not suddenly abandon the central tenets around which their party had developed during the preceding twenty years; on the contrary, it was simply that after 1896 there was little inducement to remain in Cuba and less likelihood that autonomism would find a sympathetic audience in Cuba. The decline of Autonomist political fortunes after Weyler's appointment left liberals no alternative to the separatist option. Many continued to defend Autonomist policies and programs in exile.[46] Indeed, all that really divided conservative separatists from liberal Autonomists was the choice for the role of Cuba's protector: the United States or Spain. After 1896, however, after Weyler, even the most devoted Autonomist found little in Spanish policy to sustain the traditional liberal faith. In the ensuing political realignment, Autonomists abandoned their preference for autonomy under Spain for support of a protectorate under the United States. The annexationist/protectorate expatriate sector of the PRC found new allies in the most recent converts to separatism.

Autonomists wasted little time in proselytizing their old faith in new temples. "I see but one hope of salvation," Autonomist planter Cristóbal N. Madan predicted, "and that is autonomy through American intervention, and without this, there is nothing but ruin."[47] Just before leaving Cuba, a delegation of Autonomists headed by Raimundo Cabrera presented the American consul general in Havana with a lengthy assessment of insurrection. These views, Consul Ramon O. Williams informed the State Department, deserved serious consideration, for they represented the propertied and commercial classes of the island. The United States, the Autonomists insisted, had to "induce insurgent leaders to give up the idea of political independence, for which Cuba is utterly unprepared." The Autonomists continued:

It is a mad dream to imagine that this island may now become an independent nation. . . . The more conservative and responsible part of the Cuban population looks most anxiously, in the present emergence, to the United States, as the only available power to extricating this unfortunate Island from her present difficulties. . . . The more enlightened and responsible part of the Cuban population thinks of American mediation or intervention as the only possible or practical means of saving this island.[48]

Several weeks later, Cabrera took up residence abroad and proclaimed his adherence to the separatist effort.

VI   If Weyler's political policies forced Autonomists into PRC ranks abroad, his military operations propelled thousands of peasants into insurgent army ranks in the interior. Spain's reconcentration policy signified not only the forced relocation of peasant families, but also destruction of their homes and farms, the expropriation of their livestock, and, in the end, caused a profound disruption of life in the Cuban countryside. The order of reconcentration had the net effect of converting much of the peasantry from passive allies to participating combatants.[49] Weyler's reconcentration policy vastly accelerated the deterioration of economic conditions in the countryside, and this abrupt break with continuity helped enroll a hitherto passive peasantry in the separatist ranks.[50]

Not for the first time in the struggle, a policy of deliberate terror proved ill-contrived. Forced to abandon their land, witness to the destruction of their homes and farms, peasants by the thousands across the island joined the swelling columns of the insurgent armies. Insurgent military chieftains throughout the island reported the marked increase. "The sending here of ferocious Weyler," General José María Rodríguez wrote from Oriente in March 1896, "has been a counterproductive measure for Spain: great numbers of Cubans who had remained pacific, in the countryside as well as in the towns, are found today swelling our ranks."[51] From the west, Maceo wrote that Weyler's policies had redounded to the benefit of the insurrection. "The Revolution," he exulted, "does not have a better ally than Weyler himself."[52] "The time for the definitive division has arrived," Colonel Fermín Valdés Domínguez recorded in his diary. "Those who are with the Spanish will go to the cities and our supporters will be with us in the countryside. Weyler works for us. The *good* result of his method of directing military operations will soon be seen."[53] The American consul general in Havana concurred. Weyler's policies, Fitzhugh Lee wrote, "has had the effect of filling up [insurgent] ranks and binding them together in stronger union, as well as increasing the spirit of their resistance."[54]

The swelling of separatist ranks at the other end of the Cuban social order deepened contradictions within the revolutionary polity. New demands were made on Cuban separatism. Social issues were now lodged deeper and more directly into the armed populist sector of the separatist coalition.[55]

The invasion and Weyler's policy served to define the issues of the war. The Cuban offensive and the Spanish counteroffensive polarized the island and, inevitably, sharpened the polarities within the separatist polity. The Creole elite, many former Autonomists who earlier had denounced the rebellion, passed into exile and reinforced the conservative wing of Cuban separatism. At the same time, thousands of peasants strengthened the social base of the insurgency and reinforced the populist wing.

Maceo and Weyler together precipitated a severe dislocation in Cuban politics. From both ends of the island's social order, thousands sought refuge in separatist ranks. The process that the invasion had started, Weyler completed. Political repression in the wake of the invasion drove moderates into the PRC centers abroad; the military policy of reconcentration drove thousands of peasants across the island into the insurgent armies in the interior. The net effect of the invasion was to produce concurrently within the structure of Cuban separatism a reaction in the revolution and a revolution within the revolution. As the social base of the insurrection in Cuba broadened, the social base of the PRC in exile narrowed; as social expectations associated with separatism rose among the former, political misgivings over separatism increased within the latter.

VII   The clash between the politico-diplomatic goals abroad and social-military objectives in Cuba set the stage for the next dispute between the emigration and the *manigua*. The nature of the armed struggle—indeed, the very strategy pursued by the insurgent army command—represented the specific means chosen to achieve specified separatist ends. The conflict over the ends of the struggle inevitably spilled over into dispute over the means.

In Cuba, the armed struggle remained possessed of much of its original purpose. Martí's vision of Cuba Libre survived in the insurgent camps and found widespread endorsement within the swelling ranks of the Liberation Army. The invasion and Weyler's reconcentration policy not only expanded the scope of the separatist conflict but, in fact, added a new impetus to the social purpose of Cuban arms. The events that contributed to moderation abroad led to radicalization in Cuba. In early 1896, the Cuban conflict had assumed the full proportions of a revolutionary struggle with distinct, if imperfectly formulated, socio-economic objectives.

The invasion gave palpable form to the revolution against the colonial system. The encounter of the west by the east set in sharp relief the issues of the armed struggle and the central task before the Liberation Army. Insurgent columns were now at the very center of the source of Spanish power on the island, face to face with the most powerful allies of the Spanish regime in Cuba. No longer would the *insurrectos* be dealing with bankrupt planters in the east presiding over languishing estates, operating on the outer fringes of the island's sugar system, and generally sympathetic toward the separatist struggle. After January 1896, the insurgent columns found themselves in a position of toppling the twin pillars of the colonial system in Cuba: sugar and the planter class. The emphasis of the campaign turned away from challenging the military defenders of Spanish authority and toward destroying the politico-economic sources of Spanish power in Cuba—the colonial economy. The insurrection was now "an economic war," Fermín Valdés Domínguez wrote in his diary, "against capital and production."[56] This was to be the central function of the invasion: penetrate the wealth-producing provinces and lay siege to the economy. Emphasis was not so much on engaging enemy forces or liberating territory but, rather, on the destruction of property and the disruption of the economy.

Insurgent chieftains had initially lacked a coherent policy toward property. In various pronouncements before the war, the separatist leadership had pledged to respect property.[57] On April 26, 1895, Gómez and Martí gave public expression to a slightly modified statement of separatist strategy, one that promised only to avoid "unnecessary devastation and futile violence."[58] A third variant appeared only days later. "With regard to property," Martí and Gómez announced on April 28, "all properties that respect us will be respected and . . . only those that serve or habitually support the enemy will be destroyed."[59]

Even as the war stalled in Oriente in early 1895, individual insurgent commanders pursued independent and often conflicting policies. The practice of levying a surcharge on authorized planting and harvesting, adopted originally during the Ten Years' War, continued in Oriente through 1895. Antonio Maceo had independently contracted a schedule of payments with several landowners in exchange for permission to plant and harvest.[60] This practice was associated with the early phase of the war, typically confined to Oriente, and reserved to the discretion of local army commanders. Then, too, many planters in Oriente had long been sympathetic with past separatist struggles and found in the ranks of the insurgent leadership the congenial if not reassuring companionship of distinguished representatives of the eastern propertied class.[61]

Even during the initial phase of the war, however, Máximo Gómez opposed financial settlements with landowners. Gómez had always maintained that property represented Cuba's principal enemy and the greatest obstacle to independence. Before returning to Cuba in 1895, he had attributed the failure of Cuban arms during the Ten Years' War directly to the insurgents' inability to carry the war to the west and destroy the economic sources of colonial authority.

In 1895, Gómez grudgingly approved the early settlements between Cuban commanders and eastern planters. In August of that year, he informed Estrada Palma that he would honor one such contract—not, however, without communicating to the PRC representation his disdain for such settlements. "I value much the Cuban blood that is being shed as a result of sugar," Gómez warned, "and it is necessary to collect quickly, and if not, the torch will adjust everything."[62] It was essential, he wrote to Estrada Palma, to prevent the harvest and destroy the *ingenio* as a means of assuring the triumph of the revolution in the shortest possible time.[63]

With the completion of the invasion, the need to lay seige to property assumed strategic urgency. Contact between the primitive noncapitalist eastern periphery and the developed, capitalist, western center brought insurgent armed forces face to face with the enduring source of metropolitan power and determined the function of Cuban arms. After 1896, the insurgent command turned on the colonial economy and the social and political structures it supported. The war of liberation was transformed from a struggle against colonial government to a war against the colonial system.

The assault on property emanated directly from the army command's perception of the function of the armed struggle. The success of the western campagn and, with it, the fate of the revolution, depended directly on the ability of the insurgents to disrupt the island's economic system, the bedrock of the colonial regime. Separatists would wage war on the economy, destroy the agricultural wealth of the colonial regime, and disrupt the supporting transportation and communication system.[64] By attacking property, moreover, the insurgents sought to mobilize the traditionally apathetic planter class. Any hope of a return to normal production and former prosperity, separatists announced, was to await the independence of Cuba.[65] Indeed, this served as a vital coefficient to insurgent strategy: demonstration that Spain had lost its ability to provide adequate security for the Cuban economy and that separatists now controlled Cuba's destiny.[66]

The assault on property represented at once a means and an end—a method of ending Spanish sovereignty while leveling the inequities of the colonial system. Insurgent chieftains announced their intention to reduce the island to a mound of charred debris rather than allow Spain to use Cuban wealth against the insurrection—the island would be independent or worthless. Deny Spain the wealth produced in Cuba, Gómez predicted confidently, and the island would have its independence at once. "It is necessary to burn the hive in order to disperse the swarm," he mused.[67] After the invasion, Cubans declared war without quarter on the colonial economy—a strategy that now precluded the continuance of financial settlements with planters. The very word *zafra* was held synonymous with "counterrevolution." "Work is a crime against the revolution," Gómez proclaimed.[68]

Three separate military decrees between 1895 and 1897 gave definitive form to insurgent strategy. In July 1895, Máximo Gómez had ordered planters, farmers, and ranchers to discontinue all work activities and suspend trade and commerce with towns occupied by enemy forces. All estates found in violation of this order, he had vowed, would be destroyed and the owners tried for treason.[69] Five months later, concurrent with the invasion of the west, Gómez had ordered chiefs of operations to enforce the July manifesto. Economic activity was to come to a halt. "All sugar plantations will be totally destroyed, the standing cane set fire and the factory buildings and railroads destroyed," he proclaimed in November 1895. "Any worker assisting the operation of the sugar factories will be considered an enemy of his country . . . and will be executed." Sugar, he insisted, was the "principal enemy of independence."[70] In January 1897, in the third pronouncement, Gómez reminded his officers of earlier decrees and enjoined army chieftains again to destroy all estates found in defiance of the insurgent moratorium.[71] Sounding the recurring insurgent exhortation, he vowed to raise the flag of the independent republic—"even over ashes and ruin."[72]

VIII   Insurgent strategy against property in Cuba aroused immediate opposition abroad. The army moratorium on sugar production coincided with the swelling of expatriate ranks with planters and their autonomist allies. Many had gravitated toward exile centers predisposed to support the separatist cause, if only in exchange for security for their estates. Others had emigrated to escape Weyler's excesses. But whatever the reason, separatists ranks abroad were filling with property owners at the precise moment that insurgent policies in the *manigua* turned against property.

For the PRC leadership, the adhesion of the planters was a welcome development. For many it was the most positive result of the invasion. A vast new source of revenue was now available. Such planter notables as Juan Pedro Baró (*ingenios* Conchita and Asunción), Marta Abreu (*ingenios* San Antonio and Santa Rosa), Antonio Terry (*ingenios* Juraguá and Teresa), Mariano Ortiz (*ingenio* Narciso), and Andrés Terry (*ingenio* Cayajabos) had emigrated and proclaimed their loyalty to the separatist cause. Even before the insurgent columns had completed their westward march, at about the exact moment Gómez was drafting his November decree, Estrada Palma was authorizing Juan Pedro Baró to complete the harvest in exchange for an initial contribution of 5,000 pesos, to be followed by 2,000 pesos every month for the duration of the harvest.[73]

For PRC leaders abroad, insurgent operations in western Cuba created an opportunity to tap into new sources of revenue. Throughout 1895, early settlements between the insurgent command and *hacendados* in Oriente had filled separatist coffers. In the first nine months of the insurrection, tens of thousands of dollars had been transferred from planters' accounts in Paris and New York to the PRC treasury.[74] Donations from planters in 1895 had contributed powerfully to separatist funds and enormously simplified the PRC task of raising revenue. Under Estrada Palma the PRC shifted its original emphasis from small donations by the many to large donations from the few. Just as the social base of the PRC abroad had narrowed, so too had its source of financial support. From its inception, and through the early months of the war, the PRC had relied almost exclusively on modest funds collected from local revolutionary clubs.[75] By the end of 1895, however, the PRC had become dependent on planters' contributions. In the process, the expatriate leadership had come to identify the well-being of property with the success of the separatist war. Even before the year ended, separatist centers abroad had come to represent and defend the interests of the planter class and emerge as a bastion of the Creole property owners.

But the insurgent army command had different plans. Already Gómez's decrees had taken their toll. As planters donated money to the PRC in New York, their property in production was being attacked.

As early as August 1895, weeks after Gómez's first decree, Estrada

Palma urged the insurgent army command to respect property and permit the *zafra* to continue, if only on a selective basis. The expatriate leadership saw the planter class as a potentially valuable, if not perhaps totally willing, ally in the struggle against Spain. The threat of the torch would persuade recalcitrant planters of the efficacy of cooperating with the separatist cause. To tap into planter wealth, however, it was necessary to accommodate planter needs. By levying a tax on *hacendados* and authorizing planters to plant and harvest, Estrada Palma insisted, separatists would be guaranteed of large and steady revenues every year. "This money," he pledged, "would be used religiously for arms and munition that would be sent regularly."[76] Ramón Emeterio Betances, the head of the Cuban junta in Paris, also argued the planters' case. It would be foolish, he wrote, to "destroy the chicken of the golden egg—without benefit to anyone."[77]

There was, further, some urgency to expatriate appeals in 1896. The western estates, historically beyond the reach of past separatist conflicts, had ignored insurgent injunctions against planting and harvesting. The invading columns surprised planters in the west, most of whom were fully engaged in normal operations in defiance of the separatist moratorium. "If anyone had told us four months ago," one planter wrote from the capital in February 1896, "that [Gomez] would be able to stop the crushing of the cane in the Province of Havana, or even in Matanzas, we would have laughed in his face. Today not a planter disobeys his orders."[78] Suddenly, for the first time, the western estates were exposed to the insurgent torch.[79]

In mid-1896, frustrated by Gómez's indifference to earlier pleas, the New York junta appealed directly to the provisional government. The interrruption of the *zafra*, Estrada Palma complained to President Salvador Cisneros Betancourt, had made it all but impossible to secure funds from planters. Indeed, the army ban threatened to deprive the PRC of a major source of revenue and had a generally adverse effect on the party's treasury and its ability to continue to subsidize the separatist war effort. To relieve the precarious financial situation, Estrada Palma urged, it was necessary to permit planters to prepare for the 1896–1897 harvest.[80]

Initially, the provisional government favored the expatriate position. In 1896, the Council of Government periodically ordered the army command to respect property of planters who had donated funds to separatist coffers. And, just as often, the army ignored the government. In August, the government ordered the army to permit Senado estate in Camagüey province, owned by a pro-Spaniard Creole, to prepare for the upcoming *zafra*.

Gómez ignored government instruction and within weeks destroyed the estate.[81]

One other factor influenced expatriate calculations. The PRC quest for American recognition of belligerency required consideration of the political aspects of the armed struggle. The policy of the *manigua* against property struck directly at the heart of the PRC mission abroad. As its emphasis shifted increasingly toward the task of securing belligerency status, the diplomatic repercussions of insurgent policies in Cuba increased in importance abroad. Through 1896 and 1897 insurgent military policies in Cuba played havoc with expatriate diplomatic efforts.

The destruction of American property did the separatist cause little good in the United States. The injunction against planting and harvesting, as well as the destruction of estates, won Cubans the lasting enmity of American property owners. Many American landowners, often men with direct access to the White House and congressional offices, had initially used their influence to promote the separatist cause in Washington. Insurgent policy toward property strained relations between expatriate representatives in the United States and American property owners. Indeed, the destruction threatened to deprive expatriate representation of the support of powerful U.S. allies. As early as October 1895, the head of the Cuban junta in Philadelphia complained that the *insurrectos* had destroyed mines and railroad property owned by George McCreary. The Cuban cause in Philadelphia, Juan Guiteras wrote, relied heavily on the support of McCreary and, lest separatists lose McCreary's support, it "would, perhaps, be convenient to dispense some considerations to that property."[82]

Throughout 1896, Estrada Palma repeatedly complained that the destruction of American property had antagonized some of Cuba's closest U.S. friends. One property owner, he informed Antonio Maceo, had worked diligently among congressmen in behalf of recognition of Cuban belligerency only to have his efforts rewarded by the destruction of his property. "The burning of cane fields attached to American properties," Estrada Palma wrote in January, "has excited the ire of some owners influential in Washington."[83] Indeed, by early 1896, several American property owners informed Estrada directly that unless the insurgents modified their policies, they would use their influence against the Cuban cause.[84]

Insurgent military policy in Cuba against property aggravated relations between separatist representatives and authorities in Washington. The

Cuban cause had few friends in Washington, Estrada Palma complained to President Salvador Cisneros; no other issue had inflamed official sentiment against the separatist cause as much as the destruction of property. In mid-1896, Estrada Palma reported experiencing rebuffs on several occasions and hostility from officials in Washington, antagonism he attributed directly to the insurgents' policy in the *manigua*.[85] Edwin F. Atkins later recounted the details of an 1895 meeting between the leaders of the New York junta and Secretary of State Richard Olney:

Among those who called upon Secretary Olney in December were Palma . . . Gonzalo de Quesada . . . and Benjamin Guerra. . . . Mr. Olney, who was always an outspoken man, later listening to what they had to say, asked Palma if he was an American citizen. Palma replied that he was proud to acknowledge his citizenship. Mr. Olney then asked the same of the others, and received the same reply. He then asked if they had given orders to destroy the property of other American citizens in Cuba, to which Palma answered that while he had not done so, he knew and approved of such orders as a war measure in their struggle against Spain. Mr. Olney said: "Well, gentlemen, there is but one term for such action. We call it arson." With that he terminated the interview.[86]

IX   Expatriate appeals had little impact on insurgent strategy in Cuba. What happened in the United States, Máximo Gómez informed a New York reporter in 1896, and the resolutions made by American politicians, "influence neither our plans nor the manner of making war; we will continue to destroy the land—which is ours—without preoccupying ourselves with anything more than that which will favor the revolution."[87] Except for the dispensations extended earlier to property owners in Oriente, Máximo Gómez remained steadfast in his determination to enforce the decrees of July and November 1895 uniformly and without respite. No strategy figured as prominently, and no tactic was as central to insurgent goals, as the moratorium on all economic activity.

The dispute over property strained relations between the army command and the expatriate leadership. "The rich have congregated there in New York," Colonal Fermín Valdés Domínguez noted with some bitterness, "they want to dominate Estrada Palma and from there impose upon us their self-interests. They want us to permit the harvest, they want us to allow a few privileged *hacendados* to grind and 'patriotically' collect funds for our delegation . . . . Those in New York pursue these ends with two evil intentions: either they are deceiving us and take advantage of the patriotism they proclaim but do not feel, or they are trying to maneuver Estrada Palma into a difficult position leading to a break with our government. The conduct of these merchants has always been vile, first in the slave traffic, and now with false *cubanismo*."[88]

Nevertheless, throughout the western campaign, Estrada Palma continued to press Gómez to modify his policy.[89] In July 1896, the Dominican generalissimo reiterated his position: "The zafra . . . causes us great damage. . . . Work implies peace and in Cuba we must not permit work. When a people embark on a war for their emancipation, they must not be permitted to think in anything other than the war. . . . The chains of Cuba have been forged by its own riches and it is necessary to put an end to this in order to finish soon."[90] In August, Gómez repeated to Estrada Palma his opposition to the *zafra* and added: "I do not want you to speak to me of it again." "It seems that I must always speak of sugar when I answer your letters," wrote Gómez wearily a month later; again Estrada's petition to permit work on the estates was denied.[91] The loss of planters' contributions mattered little to the insurgent field command. In a cover letter forwarding the November 1895 decree, Gómez informed Estrada: "As you will see in the copy of the 'Circular' I am enclosing, I have resolved to prevent the *zafra*, although we will be deprived of the collection of some funds. An acceptable loss, given that our enemies would have obtained more and, what is worse: the Revolution would have appeared patently weak, appearing incapable of destroying the resources and manifestations of its enemy's power." The western campaign, he concluded, would "make every sacrifice" to deal the mortal blow to Spain.[92] Some months later, Gómez returned to this theme: "The collection of funds does not worry me, since, if the loans and emissions from the exterior fail, the radical means used here give us greater probabilities of ultimate triumph."[93] He was categorical: under no circumstances, and for no amount of money, would he sanction the harvest. "There is no reason to fear the complaints of the superficial and the ignorant," he sought to console Estrada. "What is necessary is to triumph and the most efficacious and effective means to reach this end, even though they might appear severe, are always the best, the most decent, and the most noteworthy. The evil, the misfortunate, the dishonorable is not to triumph, and the evil, the cruel, and the disgraceful is to delay the triumph."[94]

Nor was the army command susceptible to Estrada Palma's appeal for circumspection as a means of obtaining U.S. belligerency status. The military leadership found recognition of belligerency inadequate compensation for abandoning a policy central to its objectives. Even if the army command had been disposed to respect foreign property, it was virtually impossible to make the distinction between property owned by Cubans and Spaniards, on one hand, and foreigners on the other. By the end of 1895, scores of Cuban and Spanish planters had transferred their property to American citizens and corporations organized specifically for this purpose.[95] It was often impossible to distinguish between foreign ownership and Cuban/Spanish ownership. In any case, the army command was not inclined to make such distinction. Anything that could complicate Spain's international relations, Cubans argued, particularly the destruction of foreign property, promised to redound to the benefit of the insurgent cause.[96] Of more immediate concern, Gómez sought to deprive the Spanish government of the revenue generated by foreign capital. "We want no foreign capital or any capital in Cuba," he announced, "that pays tribute to a country other than that from which it derives its revenues."[97]

The insurgent command also declined to distinguish between foreign property and the policies of their government. In August 1896, a delegation of French, British, German, and American planters met with Gómez in Camagüey to protest the destruction of the estates. "It does no good to proclaim your foreign nationality . . . ," Gómez insisted, "because for us there are only Cubans,"—a nationality, he reminded the foreign planters, that their governments had refused to recognize. "Take your complaints to the Spanish government," he taunted his visitors.[98]

By late 1896, the military policy had prevailed. In September 1896, the provisional government, under pressure from the army command, had enacted into law the substance of earlier army decrees.[99] Eusebio Hernández, the Sub-Secretary of war, announced:

Property is the true enemy of the Revolution, for on it rests the
power of the Spanish government, and on its defense rests all
[Spain's] effort. . . . While Cuba is not independent, it is necessary to paralyze the social, political and economic life of the
country; our attacks should be directed principally against property that comforts and supports the Spaniard—the essential
means of securing that paralysis. Once this is obtained, Spain,
its army notwithstanding, will de facto no longer exercise its

sovereignty over Cuban territory and will have no recourse but to end a futile war and abandon the island.[100]

X The destruction of sugar estates reflected considerably more than a strategy calculated to assure military success. Army policy gave dramatic form to the social currents within the insurrection. In attacking sugar, Cubans consciously and deliberately struck at the very foundations of the colonial system. The latifundia, monoculture, and labor relations symbolized the inequities and injustices running through the depth and breadth of Cuban society. The assault on property at once pushed a war of national liberation beyond the politico-military objectives of the insurrection and lay seige to the very socio-economic foundations of Cuban society. The "centers of our sugar production," Colonel Fermín Valdés Domínguez wrote in early 1897, "contain great evils, participate in criminal negotiations, and contribute to the degradation of our people. Work . . . there is the humiliation and exploitation of the weak." It was necessary, he insisted, for the "redemptive revolution" to show "the weak how the people express their protests." The destructive mission of the war could not be delayed. "It is necessary to destroy the idols before which those stained with blood fall to their knees." The war was for the redemption of dignity and justice. "This is a social revolution in which the bureaucrat, the corrupt and cruel, rich, and coward . . . are the only ones who have any reason to feel vanquished. When we are free, then we can be and will be truly rich, our *ingenios* and *centrales* will be centers of work and schools of virtue, and the Cuban family will occupy the position of honor that it deserves."[101]

For Máximo Gómez, too, the separatist war was as much a struggle for social justice as it was a quest for political independence. The difference between the Ten Years' War and the war of 1895, he insisted, was that the former originated from "the top down, that is why it failed; this one surges from the bottom up, that is why it will triumph." The dispossessed and the disinherited making up the revolutionary force would be sufficient "to raise high the banner of a true democracy, of a Republic by the people and for the people."[102]

Gómez consciously seized the war against Spain as a means of remedying the inequities of the society he was seeking to liberate. This concern deepened as insurgent armies moved through the western sugar regions. The striking contrast between the prosperity of the *hacendados* and the poverty of the workers had an unsettling impact on the army chieftain.

Some type of equity was required, Gómez insisted, between the owner of the *central* and the farmer, between the industrial unit and the agricultural sector. "I have not been able to understand the fundamental cause of such an unjust disproportion between the farmer and the *central*-owner," Gómez confessed to a friend. He was deeply troubled and very much disturbed by these conditions. "I signed the decree to destroy the sugar wealth as a means justified by the war," he wrote. Passing through the western sugar properties, however, he came into increasing contact with the living conditions on the estates: exploited farmers, families clothed in rags, existing on the edge of starvation, without schools, without health care, living on someone else's land in squalor and ignorance. "At that moment," the general wrote, "I felt indignant and profoundly predisposed against the upper classes of the country, and in an instant of rage, at the sight of such a sad and painful disparity, I exclaimed: 'Blessed be the torch.'"[103]

The attack on property gave expression to the social dimensions of the war. To be sure, the strategy had as its immediate goal the end of the Spanish regime. However Gómez had also a vision of an independent republic without the trammels of class privilege. Property relations loomed large in his calculations, both as the immediate enemy of independence and the future source of injustice. In attacking property, he sought to achieve two goals, one serving as the means to the other. The sugar system, with its enormous concentration of wealth, the monopolization of land, and regimen of dependent labor, was an anathema to him. He advocated the creation of a class of small independent farmers, with each farmer deriving independence and dignity from the fruits of his labor on land that he owned.[104] In what was tantamount to a sweeping land reform decree in July 1896, the insurgent army command brought both purposes of insurgent arms into alignment. Exhorting Cuban forces to "burn and destroy all forms of property" as "rapidly as possible everywhere in Cuba," Gómez pledged:

All lands acquired by the Cuban Republic either by conquest or confiscation, except what is employed for governmental purposes, shall be divided among the defenders of the Cuban Republic against Spain, and each shall receive a portion corresponding to the services rendered, as shall be provided by the first Cuban Congress, after Cuban Independence has been recognized by Spain, and this shall be given to each in addition to

cash compensation for all services previously rendered, and as a
special bounty and reward. . . . All lands, money, or property in
any and all forms, previously belonging to Spain, to its allies,
abettors or sympathizers, or to any person or corporation acting
in the interest of Spain or in any manner disloyal to the Cuban
Republic are hereby confiscated, for the benefit of the Cuban
Army and of all the defenders of the Cuban Republic.[105]

XI The deepening contradictions within the separatist polity had
far-reaching consequences. For many expatriates, the destruction of
sugar property evoked the spectre of the apocalypse, evidence that the
war against Spain had released powerful social forces well beyond the
control of the declining metropolis. A division over tactics gave way to a
conflict over the strategy and, in the end, a disagreement over goals.
Increasingly, the exile representation came to look at developments in
Cuba with an ambivalent mixture of misgiving and horror. By late 1897,
the social system in Cuba was on the verge of collapse. With the failure of
Weyler in mid-1897, Spain had exhausted any reasonable likelihood of ending the insurrection and containing the revolution. Planters who had relied
on Spain for security in 1895, and who later appealed unsuccessfully to
separatists for protection in 1896, were forced to turn elsewhere in 1897.

The revolutionary content of the insurrection did not pass unnoticed.
Planters and Autonomists alike sensed uneasily that this uprising was
unlike any of its predecessors. It aspired to more than political independence. This war was different. "Without question," Raimundo Cabrera
wrote in late 1896, "this has not been like the Ten Years' War—not in its
origins, or in its means, or in its expansion, or much less in its social,
political, and economic aspects. Cuba today is revolutionary. . . . Everything is undone and in transition."[106]

Finding Spain incapable of protecting property and insurgents indisposed to accommodate property interests within the separatist polity,
detecting in the ranks of the Liberation Army the source of future social
turmoil, planters appealed to the United States for assistance. Any hope of
redeeming the socio-economic order rested on the intervention of a power
superior both to the declining authority of metropolitan Spain and the
rising strength of insurgent Cuba.

7 Rebellion of the Loyal

No solution of this war can be thought of for an instant that is not based upon the absolute independence of the island. . . . We have accomplished too much to accept anything short of absolute freedom. The Cubans really control all of Cuba but the fortified towns, and the more artillery we receive the more of these will we take. . . . Why, then, should we lay down our arms for anything but the end for which we took them up–the freedom of the island and the people of Cuba?
—Máximo Gómez, March 1897

All autonomists feel hopeful over the situation but the public generally does not feel so, because the insurgents hold out. I found no opposition to autonomy anywhere, but a general sentiment now pervades the whole community for annexation. . . . All the better class Cubans fear independence.
—Edwin Atkins, January 1898

When Spain will admit defeat no mortal, in my humble judgment, dare predict. That her plan of settlement–autonomy–is a failure; and with this failure Cuba passes from under her domination, is not to be questioned.
—Walter B. Barker, U.S. Consul, Sagua la Grande, January 1898

I A new impatience settled over Washington in 1897. The two-year-old war in Cuba had assumed special significance in the United States. For three-quarters of a century, the question of Cuba had absorbed the official mind and aroused the popular imagination. The distinction between those issues properly defined as domestic and those concerns traditionally foreign had ceased to apply to Cuba.

By 1896 the Cuban question had emerged as a central political issue in the United States. Cuba found a place in every major party platform and surfaced repeatedly in the presidential campaign.[1] "Every Congressman [has] two or three newspapers in his district, most of them printed in red ink, shouting for blood," one legislator complained.[2] As long as the Cuban conflict continued, the spectre of war with Spain darkened the American horizon, causing financial instability and economic uncertainty.

It was this intrusion of Cuba into American domestic affairs, and the unsettling internal effects of the Cuban conflict, that initially preoccupied the new Republican president. William McKinley was sensible to conditions in Cuba and mindful of potential repercussions of those conditions in the United States. During a visit with the president-elect in Canton, Ohio, in December 1896, Senator Henry Cabot Lodge found McKinley very much troubled by the continuing political and economic reverberations of the Cuban war. Cuba was "very much on his mind and I found he had given it a great deal of thought," Lodge later recounted to Theodore Roosevelt. The president's great ambition was "to restore business and bring back good times." But the Cuban insurrection was distractive to the main domestic issues at hand and the continuing prospect of war with Spain promised only to thwart his efforts to revive the economy.[3] The early months of the new administration were given to approaching the Cuban conflict as a domestic issue rather than a matter of foreign policy. As late as July 1897, one cabinet official conceded that McKinley had "formed no Cuban policy. . . . The President's desire is for the country to enjoy quiet in order that business prosperity may be established. His chief thought is given to securing this one desideratum—quiet."[4]

McKinley's worst fears were confirmed soon after his inauguration. In early May, McKinley found his administration embroiled in a political conflict with the Senate over a congressional resolution proposing the recognition of Cuban belligerency. Early in his term, he became guarded toward Congress, suspicious of legislative maneuvers capable of infringing on traditional executive prerogatives.[5]

140   Domestic concerns also served as one of the focal points of Washington's

instructions to the new American minister to Spain, Stewart Woodford. These instructions, formulated directly by the White House, outlined the new administration's preoccupation in precise and concrete form:

Not only are our citizens largely concerned in the ownership of property and in the industrial and commercial ventures which have been set on foot in Cuba through our enterprising initiative and sustained by their capital, but the chronic condition of trouble and violent derangement in that island constantly causes disturbance in the social and political condition of our own people. It keeps up a continuous irritation within our own borders, injuriously affects the normal functions of business, and tends to delay the condition of prosperity to which this country is entitled.[6]

II   That the new administration had "formed no Cuban policy" reflected Republican conformity with enduring national assumptions of the nineteenth century. The Cuban policy in 1897 remained possessed of the essential objectives that had characterized American diplomacy in the preceding seventy-five years. "I anticipate no departure from the policy of my predecessor," McKinley announced in mid-1897.[7] Like his predecessors, McKinley, too, supported continued Spanish sovereignty in Cuba—a sovereignty, the new president believed, that would be best assured through colonial reforms. American interests would also be best served, the administration insisted, by a negotiated political settlement based on a program of far reaching reforms. "I do not believe the United States Government should interfere in the Cuban trouble," Secretary of State John Sherman explained in early 1897. The granting of "extensive reforms in Cuba," including autonomy, Sherman predicted, would immediately have a salutary effect. "If this is done, as I am led to believe it will be, that is all that is necessary. The war will be settled."[8]

If, however, reform failed to restore order to the troubled island, and if Spanish arms continued unequal to the task of pacification, the United States was invested with a historical mandate to relieve Spain of its sovereignty over Cuba. Many close to the new administration were already arguing that the Cuban state of affairs in early 1897 had created the conditions for the fulfillment of the nineteenth-century prophecy. Henry Cabot Lodge urged McKinley simply to declare war on Spain and annex Cuba.[9] Whitelaw Reid, Republican owner of the *New York Tribune* and friend of McKinley, urged the new president to prepare himself for the momentous occasion to fulfill the American destiny. "Some day we will have Cuba," a confident Reid predicted to McKinley in December 1896; to secure the island "in your administration," Reid exhorted the president, "would put it beside Jefferson's in popular mind, and ahead in History." Nor did Reid believe a war necessary to acquire Cuba. Keep Congress in check for four months, he counseled, and resist all congressional attempts for the "recognition of independence" until the "next sickly season, suspending Spanish operations again, might bring them so near exhaustion as to be willing to consider parting with 'the ungrateful island' in payment of our claims or otherwise." In the meantime, Reid advised, the administration should commit itself to upholding Spanish sovereignty.[10]

The appointment of Stewart Woodford as the new minister to Spain in July 1897 provided the administration with the occasion to review in detail the course of American policy. "Before you go to your post," Secretary of State John Sherman explained to Woodford, "it is proper to state to you the President's views on the relation of your Government to the contest which is now being waged in Cuba. The same occasion requires that you should be made acquainted with the course which has been deemed best for the United States to follow under existing conditions." The two-year war, the secretary of state continued, had wrought havoc and destruction from one end of the island to the other. "Day by day the conviction gathers strength that it is visionary for Spain to hope that Cuba, even if eventually subjugated by sheer exhaustion, can ever bear to her anything like the relation of dependence and profit she once bore." The U.S. government faced increasing domestic pressure to participate in a settlement of the Cuban conflict. American property interests on the island suffered, neutrality laws were difficult and costly to enforce, the American public demanded action, and Congress clamored for recognition of belligerency. "It may not be reasonably asked or expected that a policy of mere inaction can be safely prolonged," Sherman warned obliquely. The time had arrived to "put a stop to this destructive war and make proposals of settlement honorable to herself and to her Cuban colony and to mankind." Only the granting of meaningful reforms held any promise of reestablishing peace and restoring Spanish authority over the island. "The methods which Spain has adopted to wage the fight give no prospect of immediate peace or of a stable return to conditions of prosperity which are essential to Cuba in its intercourse with its neighbors." If, however, Madrid pledged to concede to Cuba the reforms necessary to restore order and revive prosperity, the United

States would commit itself "to assist her and tender good offices to that end." Otherwise, Sherman threatened, the United States would be obligated to assume unilateral responsibility for resolving the conflict between Spain and its rebellious colony.[11]

Sherman's instructions contained recurring allusions to the consequences attending Spain's rejection of American "good offices." "Assuredly Spain cannot expect this Government to sit idle, letting vast interests suffer, our political elements disturbed, and the country perpetually embroiled, while no progress is being made in the settlement of the Cuban problem," Sherman speculated portentously. At another point in Woodford's instructions: "You will not disguise the gravity of the situation, nor conceal the President's conviction that, should his present effort be fruitless, his duty to his countrymen will necessitate an early decision as to the course of action which the time and the transcendent emergency may demand." And, lastly, the invocation of the ultimate recourse— intervention and war: "It is with no unfriendly intent that this subject has been mentioned, but simply to show that this Government does not and cannot ignore the possibilities of duty hidden in the future, nor be unprepared to face an emergency which may at any time be born of the unhappy contest in Cuba."[12]

Woodford was more than the American minister to Spain—he also served as a trusted personal representative of the president. He communicated directly with McKinley in dispatches marked "To be handed unopened to the President by his direction." En route to Madrid, Woodford visited London and Paris where he conferred with the American ambassadors to England, France, and Germany to learn of possible European responses to several eventualities, including war with Spain and the forceful annexation of Cuba.[13] The occasion was momentous. The administration detected in the state of affairs in Cuba the portents of annexation. Woodford's instructions revealed only in part the state of expectancy with which Washington followed developments in Cuba.

Even as Woodford was completing the details of his mission abroad, events in Spain were approaching a dramatic climax. By the summer of 1897, an embattled Prime Minister Antonio Cánovas de Castillo, stalked by tumult at home and insurrection abroad, privately acknowledged the bankruptcy of the conservatives' colonial policy. He needed a rest, he explained to a friend, time away from Madrid to review the state of the kingdom and contemplate the future policy of his government. Even before the prime minister had departed for his planned vacation at the resort baths of Santa Agueda in Vizcaya, he had decided to reorganize his ministry upon his return and make one last appeal for national unity. If, at the end of a year, the Cuban war continued, Cánovas vowed, he would relinquish power to liberals and allow them to restore peace in Cuba through autonomy.[14]

But such was not to be. On the morning of August 8, Antonio Cánovas del Castillo was shot three times in the face at point blank range. He died within the hour. After a late-summer cabinet crisis, Queen Regent María Cristina asked Liberal party leader Práxedes Mateo Sagasta to form a new ministry.

III The new Liberal government hardly had time to complete the distribution of ministerial portfolios when the new American minister arrived in Madrid. Liberals now had a new problem. The failure of Spain to bring the Cuban insurrection to an immediate and satisfactory end threatened to lead to serious international complications between Spain and the United States. This was the message the American minister delivered to the new Liberal government. On September 18, Woodford verbally communicated the purport of his instructions to the Spanish foreign minister, the Duke of Tetuán. Madrid had "underrated the strength of the rebellion," Woodford began bluntly, and Spain's performance in Cuba "gave no apparent hope of an early peace." Woodford insisted on a speedy conclusion to the conflict and offered the Spanish government the "good offices of the Untied States to secure this result." In a thinly veiled ultimatum, Woodford demanded by November 1 "such assurances as would satisfy the United States that early and certain peace can be promptly secured . . . otherwise the United States must consider itself free to take such steps as its Government should deem necessary to procure this result, with due regard to our own interests and the general tranquility."[15] Five days later, he forwarded the full text of his instructions to the Spanish government, adding one clause: "It is sincerely hoped that during the coming month of October the Government of Spain may either be able to formulate some proposal under which this tender of good offices may become effective or may give satisfactory assurances that peace in Cuba will, by the efforts of Spain, be promptly secured."[16]

IV Liberals needed little additional incentive to inaugurate their long-advocated program of colonial reforms. But in the autumn of 1897, outside pressure, including domestic turmoil and diplomatic tensions, added a new urgency to reform. Between October and November, Madrid instituted a number of measures designed to liberalize colonial administration. On October 9, the Liberals relieved General Weyler of his command and appointed moderate General Ramón Blanco as governor-general. Two weeks later, Madrid committed itself to a more humane conduct of the war. On November 6, the government announced full amnesty for all political prisoners. In the days that followed, the promulgation of a series of decrees prepared the way for the establishment of a new autonomist government in Cuba. All powers except foreign relations and war were to be vested in a Cuban parliament. Budgetary matters, trade regulations, and administrative authority would henceforth fall wholly under the purview of Cuban authority.

Governor-General Blanco arrived in Havana in late October and immediately turned to implementing metropolitan reforms. Blanco spent the better part of the closing months of 1897 undoing the effects of two years of Conservative policies. All political prisoners were released. Relief supplies were distributed throughout the island's reconcentration camps. In early November, Cuban insurgents were offered a general amnesty. In a gesture to mollify planters, Blanco ordered the 1898 *zafra* to commence and pledged full military protection to all estates participating in the harvest. By the end of the month, tobacco exports to the United States resumed. In late December, Blanco decreed the new autonomist constitution in force.[17]

Liberal reforms gave dramatic expression to the insolvency of Spanish pacification efforts. Whatever other virtues Madrid may have wished to confer on its gestures of colonial reforms, nothing could obscure the central politico-military reality of 1897: Spain could not continue the war. Before leaving for Cuba, Blanco had learned that the Liberal government would oppose new war expenditures and resist further military increases in Cuba. Blanco knew too that the reforms he carried to Havana represented Spain's last hope for preserving sovereignty over the Antillean colony.[18] Liberals hoped to convert the impending military debacle into a political triumph.

American pressure to offer reforms provided Spain with the opportunity to breathe life into the moribund pacification program. By conceding reforms ostensiby in response to American requests, moreover, Madrid sought to enlist U.S. support of Spain's new colonial policy. On October 23, the Duke of Tetuán requested Washington to increase its vigilance against insurgent filibustering expeditions.[19] Several weeks later, Minister of the

Colonies Segismundo Moret asked the United States to dissolve the Cuban junta in New York.[20]

Nor were liberals totally disappointed with American responses to Spain's new pacifications attempts. While declining to outlaw the activities of the Cuban junta, Washington did agree to issue a public statement endorsing Spanish reforms.[21] In November 1897, Woodford pledged that the United States would seek to induce separatist leaders to accept the Spanish compromise as the basis of a political settlement to the conflict. Woodford also assured Madrid that the United States would "refrain from interference in Cuba for a reasonable time so that the effect of what Spain is now trying to do might be clearly seen."[22] A month later, the American minister reiterated Washington's satisfaction with Spain's new course. "Spain may reasonably look to the United States," Woodford informed the government, "to maintain an attitude of benevolent expectancy until the near future shall have shown whether the indispensable condition of a righteous peace . . . is realized."[23] This optimism was echoed in Havana. "I am satisfied," Consul General Fitzhugh Lee wrote in November, "that this new administration of Insular officers intends to remove all cause of complaint on the part of the United States and reduce to a minimum the issues between the two countries."[24] In Washington, Secretary of State Sherman praised the "laudable paths" of Spanish policy and offered "to render effective assistance toward a speedy, just, and honorable termination of the devastating war." He communicated official pleasure that the "institution of true self-government shall give to the Cubans their own local government, whereby they shall be at one and the same time the initiators and regulators of their own life while remaining within the integral nationality of Spain."[25]

American diplomacy in late 1897 remained wholly consistent with the established contours of the nineteenth-century policy. In renewing the American commitment to Spanish sovereignty, McKinley upheld the central feature of a policy that Americans earlier in the century believed would lead directly to Spain's cession of the island. American endorsement of liberals' pacification schemes was not entirely unconditional, however. Washington linked its support of Spanish sovereignty directly to the success of proposed autonomy within an unspecified but fixed period of time. Minister Woodford spoke of restraint from interference in Cuba for "a reasonable time" and later of an attitude of "benevolent expectancy until the near future." Indeed, American support of Spanish reforms—and, concomitantly, respect for Spanish sovereignty—were contingent on

Spain's ability to restore peace to the troubled island. If, after proffering reforms, Spain still found itself incapable of restoring order in Cuba, the United States reserved the right to pursue an independent course of action.[26] In his first annual message to Congress in December 1897, McKinley urged that "Spain be left free to conduct military operations and grant political reforms, while the United States for its part shall enforce its neutral obligations and cut off the assistance which it is asserted the insurgents receive from this country." The president pleaded with Congress to extend to Spain a "reasonable chance to realize her expectations and to prove the asserted efficacy of the new order of things to which she stands irrevocably committed." But American patience was not inexhaustible. McKinley concluded ominously:

The near future will demonstrate whether the indispensable condition of a righteous peace, just alike to the Cubans and to Spain as well as equitable to all our interests so intimately involved in the welfare of Cuba, is likely to be attained. If not, the exigency of further and other action by the United States will remain to be taken. When that time comes that action will be determined in the line of indisputable right and duty. It will be faced, without misgiving or hesitancy in light of the obligation this Government owes to itself, to the people who have confided to it the protection of their interests and honor, and to humanity. . . . If it shall hereafter appear to be a duty imposed by our obligations to ourselves, to civilization and humanity to intervene with force, it shall be without fault on our part and only because the necessity for such action will be so clear as to command the support and approval of the civilized world.[27]

But even success of Spanish autonomy was not without its potential benefits to the United States. Many in Washington believed that over the long run, the United States would emerge as the principal beneficiary of a successful autonomist government in Cuba. If Madrid detected in autonomy the immediate means through which to restore Spanish sovereignty over Cuba, Washington expected autonomy over time to weaken Spanish authority and serve as a prelude to annexation. As early as November, a self-satisfied Woodford informed McKinley that American pressure had maneuvered Spain beyond the point of no return. If Madrid broke its pledge or abandoned its commitment to reform, Woodford concluded virtuously, "her last attempted defense against our immediate and effective intervention [would] be gone.[28] Some days later, he predicted the imminence of the inevitable: "If (Spaniards) now secure pacification through the realization of humane methods and efficient reforms, I do not see any possible ultimate result except that Cuba will gradually become accustomed to self-government and so will fully be fit for self-government." And to underscore the implications of these developments, Woodford calculatingly invoked a familiar policy metaphor: "When the apple is ripe it will drop from the tree."[29]

V   On January 1, 1898, Spain installed the new Autonomist administration in Havana. The Cuban government consisted of a cabinet and an insular parliament made up of two branches, one elected and the other appointed by the governor general. In December, many leading Autonomists returned from exile to assume positions in the new government. More returned to Havana in the early weeks of 1898. In some instances, Autonomist officeholders moved directly from prison cells to palace offices. The cabinet consisted of ranking members of the old party leadership, including José María Gálvez, Antonio Govín, Rafael Montoro, Eduardo Dolz y Arango, and Francisco Zayas. At the provincial level, Autonomists assumed the offices of governors, mayors, and aldermen. Some separatist veterans of the Ten Years' War also assumed key posts in new Autonomist governments at the local level.[30]

Expectations that Spanish reforms would lead to settlement of the conflict were short-lived. Separatist leaders in Cuba and abroad immediately denounced autonomy and repudiated any proposed accommodation with Spain based on anything less than complete independence. On this issue, in 1898, all Cuban separatists were united. Civil and military leaders in Cuba unanimously and immediately rejected the concession of autonomist administration. "You may make it known to the American people . . . ," Máximo Gómez instructed *New York Herald* correspondent John Caldwell, "that it is the firm resolution of the army and people of Cuba, who have shed so much blood in order to conquer their independence, not to falter in their just cause until triumph or death crowns their efforts."[31] Indeed, as early as January 1897, upon learning of American maneuvers designed to induce Spain to concede reforms to Cuba, Gómez had rejected outright anything less than independence. Only weeks after Cleveland's last annual message asked Spain to liberalize colonial administration in Cuba, Gómez spurned any Spanish plan for home rule, including one supported by the United States:

We recognize that we are in this fight for life or death; that even
the strongest suggestion of peace which Spain can make is only
for the purpose of gaining advantage. If Spain today should
offer us the most complete home rule, backed by the United
States, she would fail to keep the promise. Then we would have
to wait for the United States to enforce the agreement and that
enforcement would never come, for there will always be commercial and other interests strong enough to keep the rulers of
nations in cohesion with each other.[32]

Two weeks later, Gómez reiterated the insurgent position: "We no longer
ask concessions. . . . Even were Spain's proposals bona fide, nothing could
tempt us to treat with her. We are for liberty, not for Spanish reforms."[33]
Again in March, he reaffirmed his decision to reject any solution "that is
not based on the absolute independence of the island."[34] President Salvador Cisneros Betancourt rejected autonomy, pledging to "reduce the
island to ashes" before accepting a continuation of Spanish rule in any
form.[35] In January 1898 Gómez wrote Estrada Palma privately indicating
that the Liberation Army would not accept autonomy; the war would
continue until the last vestiges of Spanish colonialism had been expelled.[36]
    The expatriate representation also joined the *manigua* in rejecting
Spanish reforms. As early as December 1896, learning of Cleveland's proposal of autonomy, Estrada Palma dismissed as "idle" all discussion of
reforms as the basis of peace.[37] Three months later, he reiterated the
separatist position on autonomy: "The time has passed when even real
reforms would be accepted at the hands of the Spanish Government. Cuban
arms have enabled us to dictate our own terms, and our terms now are
absolute independence—'Cuba Libre' in fact as well as in name—nothing
less, nothing else."[38] In Key West and Tampa, Cubans marched in mass
torchlight demonstrations demanding "Independence or death."[39] Under
orders from the Council of Government, expatriate leaders were directed
to disabuse American authorities of the belief that Cuban insurgents would
accept Spanish reforms. "As the representative of the Cubans in arms, and
under their instruction," Estrada Palma informed Secretary of State
Sherman, "it is my duty to again announce that nothing short of absolute
independence will be accepted by us on the basis of peace. . . . We will
never lay down our arms until we have freed ourselves from the
sovereignty of Spain. . . . We will not renounce our object."[40] Several
weeks later, Gonzalo de Quesada restated the provisional government's
position: "I am instructed by the . . . government to which all our military

forces are subordinate, to announce the unalterable determination of the Cubans in arms to continue the war until complete independence from Spanish rule is achieved."[41]

But, privately, insurgent chieftains passed through anxious moments in late 1897 and early 1898, fearful that the lure of reforms and the promise of amnesty would, like Zanjón twenty years earlier, divide separatist ranks and result in defections.[42] And, in fact, the promise of autonomy and the offer of amnesty, together with Spain's distribution of large cash bonuses to insurgent chieftains who surrendered, induced several insurgent army leaders to abandon the armed struggle.[43] Even before the installation of the new Autonomist government in Havana, insurgent chieftains revived earlier separatist policy concerning negotiations with Spain. All public and private discussions of autonomy in separatist camps were outlawed; the death penalty was decreed for anyone in communication with Spanish envoys seeking a peace on any basis other than complete independence.[44]

Overall, however, Cuban fear that Spanish concessions would lead to a weakening of insurgent resolve proved groundless. On the contrary, Spanish reforms had generally a salutary effect on the separatist esprit. Insurgent leaders universally interpreted the liberalization of the Spanish pacification program as palpable evidence of Spain's impending defeat— nothing less than an augury announcing the imminent triumph of Cuban arms. Insurgent morale soared. Separatist determination to press toward what was now seen as the inevitable collapse of Spain hardened. "Spain's offer of autonomy is a sign of her weakening," President Bartolomé Masó proclaimed.[45] This view was shared by military chieftains. "I regard autonomy," General Calixto García wrote in December 1897, "only as a sign of Spain's weakening power and an indication that the end is not far off."[46] Spain's offer of autonomy, Máximo Gómez wrote a friend in Santo Domingo, is a "clear confession that [Spain] is incapable of defeating us through force of armies"; the war, Gómez predicted euphorically, was approaching its climax.[47] "The insurgents . . . are every day more hopeful of forcing Spain to deliver the island to them, and the fact is that they are also more and more encouraged, seeing that Spain demonstrating by offers of reforms and autonomy her tendency of weakness," American consul Walter B. Barker in Sagua la Grande reported in late 1897.[48]

VI   The reforms in 1897 leading to autonomy in 1898 were not, however, without their demoralizing effect. The ascension of Liberals in Spain had a deeply unsettling impact on conservatives in Cuba. In many ways, the formation of the Sagasta ministry served as an ominous denouement to a long series of setbacks. Two years earlier, *peninsulares* and their Creole allies had repudiated outright Liberal attempts to pacify the island through reforms and concessions. Conservatives had enthusiastically greeted Weyler's appointment on two counts: first, it brought to Cuba a governor general determined to crush the revolution through force rather than compromise; second, Weyler's appointment offered reassuring evidence of Spain's commitment to uphold traditional authority. To be sure, the war under Weyler would be hard, but, *peninsulares* believed, it would also be short and, in the end, Weyler would firmly reestablish peace upon the unchallenged primacy of metropolitan rule.

Weyler's policies initially enjoyed the unanimous endorsement of Spain's most zealous supporters in Cuba. If the appointment of Weyler united conservatives around the singleness of purpose of Spanish arms, however, it also shattered Spain's base of moderate supporters committed to a political settlement of the conflict. Weyler's policies drove Autonomists into prison and exile and banished moderates from the island's political forums—measures, conservatives insisted, justified by the need to unite the island around the cause of Spanish arms. Conservatives had long viewed Autonomists with suspicion, detecting in the ranks of the reformers the political surrogates of separatist arms. The repression of Autonomists, as well as repudiation of the policies they represented, were viewed as preliminary steps necessary to the restoration of Spanish authority.

But the new conservative consensus did not fare much better than the old moderate regime. On the contrary, the Weyler years were disappointing ones for Spain's supporters in Cuba. Original optimism gave way first to doubt and soon to despair. By late 1897, Spanish achievements in Cuba fell woefully short of the expectations that had greeted Weyler's arrival two years earlier.

Even as early as the end of Weyler's first year in Cuba, many conservatives had lost confidence in Spain's ability to end the war. The fury of the insurgency continued unabated, with Spain patently powerless to prevent the destruction of property and incapable of restoring order. Property owners found themselves caught hopelessly between the excesses of contending armies. The insurgents prohibited the movement of livestock into the cities, the government ordered all cattle and horses out of the countryside. Gómez threatened to destroy all estates engaged in the *zafra*, Weyler threatened to destroy all estates not working on the harvest. In

May 1896, Weyler prohibited the export of leaf tobacco to the United States.[49] A measure designed to weaken separatist cigar centers in Florida threatened instead to precipitate the collapse of the tobacco industry in Havana. Weyler's decision to withdraw Spanish troops from garrison duty on the estates left property owners vulnerable to insurgent attacks and forced planters unable to afford private guards to suspend operations. In either case, the cost of the war passed directly on to planters.

Much to the dismay of Spain's supporters in Cuba, a year of Weyler's policies had failed to improve conditions on the island. On the contrary, the military situation for Spain continued to deteriorate and the economy moved closer toward total collapse. Trade and commerce between the cities and the countryside ceased. The resettlement of the rural population in reconcentration centers had brought agricultural activity in the countryside to a standstill. The dispersal of the rural population into insurgent camps in the interior and reconcentration camps in the cities also signified the loss of the large rural labor force upon which planters had traditionally depended for the *zafra*. Sugar production, which had reached an all-time high of 1 million tons in 1895, dropped to a fifty-year low of 212,000 tons in 1897. The scorched earth policies of insurgent armies in Pinar del Río and Weyler's decree banning tobacco exports to the United States crippled the *vegas* (tobacco farms) of the west. Unemployment increased. Taxes went up. A relentless price spiral buffeted all sectors of the population. Between January and March 1897 the price of food increased by some 30 percent; by May, the price of bread, milk, and flour had doubled. Eggs sold at three for twenty cents. Yams and plantains were up five times their normal price.[50] Currency approached collapse as the government printed paper money with reckless abandon. In one month alone, the Bank of Spain printed some $20 million in paper currency. Weyler's decree mandating face value to paper currency on pain of arrest for treason strained relations between the government, on one hand, and merchants, shopkeepers, and businessmen on the other. Resentment increased and by 1897 merchants and shopkeepers began refusing altogether depreciated script as payment for goods and services. The result was a new wave of arrests and imprisonments; many had their shops looted and their goods expropriated under military decree. "Weyler has touched the merchants' pockets once too much," an American correspondent in Cuba reported in May 1897. "Provision dealers who a year ago built welcoming arches for the troops to march under will no longer contribute supplies without hope of compensation, and few of them are willing to exchange food stuffs for Weyler's depreciated scrip."[51]

In the provinces, Weyler's "war with war" policy affected Cubans in still other ways. The arrival of Spanish troops thoroughly disrupted community life, converting provincial towns and cities into armed camps and interrupting normal social and commercial activities. Martial law preempted locally elected government officials. Families were required to quarter and feed Spanish troops in their homes.[52] The war penetrated every aspect of Cuban life and now, in 1897, even the calamity many expected to follow a Cuban victory appeared somewhat diminished by the consequences attending an indefinite postponement of a Spanish defeat.

By the end of 1897 many who only a year earlier had celebrated Weyler's arrival with enthusiasm despaired at his inability to provide a satisfactory solution of the crisis. His military policies lost popularity in Cuba. No one less than the Marquis of Apezteguía, the president of the Unión Constitucional and passionately devoted to the Spanish cause, found Weyler's methods as excessive as they were ineffective. In 1897, he broke with Weyler and returned to Spain. Conservatives were initially prepared to endure the hardships of Weyler's "war with war" policy as the necessary and inevitable consequences of the insurrection—as long as they believed these measures capable of ending the conflict. Sacrifices and hardships they had been led to expect. But defeat was still a novelty. Weyler's failure to deliver the decisive military blow to the separatist insurrection raised doubts among even Spain's most ardent supporters that the metropolis possessed either the means or the capacity to defeat the insurgent armies. The Spanish war effort was going nowhere—and at great cost. The price of Pax Hispánica taxed even the most affluent supporter of the Spanish rule. After almost two years under the regimen of the "war with war" strategy, conservatives were suffering as much at the hands of their Spanish allies as they were from their Cuban adversaries. With no prospect of a military end to the conflict in sight, and economic conditions continuing to deteriorate, the foundations of Spain's narrow political base in Cuba began to crack under the strain.

By 1897 the spectre of a protracted war had become as unbearable as a separatist victory was unthinkable. As early as April 1896, the *Avisador Comercial*, representing business and commercial interests in Cuba, had complained of burdensome taxes and apparent metropolitan indifference to the well-being of the island's producing classes:

It would be highly unjust for the public burden to be heavier on those who with patriotic zeal have devoted themselves to the

work of pacification, when our merchants have become the first
victims of the ruined planters; when our manufacturers have
lost the greater part of their consuming Markets and are . . .
deprived of staple articles . . . for the maintenance of their relations with foreign countries, when the paralyzation of business
and three quarters of the clerks and workmen are being thrown
out of occupations; and when, too, from the forced emigration of
many families, property holders are so much injured in their
interests.[53]

Three months later, Consul Fitzhugh Lee had reported that new taxes
were having a powerfully unsettling effect in Cuba. "This action," Lee
informed Washington, "has given intense dissatisfaction to all engaged in
business or who are property owners, whether Cuban or Spaniard, and
adds greatly to the many disturbing elements already in force and which
must sooner or later produce disaster."[54]

Disaffection among those sectors traditionally identified with Spain
mounted steadily through the first half of 1897. One American journalist
reported that the "Spanish element" in Havana was "condemning with
more and more emphasis the fruitless exhausting policy of General
Weyler. . . . They see that Weyler is making no progress."[55] In Sagua la
Grande, the American consul reported that the very class of Spaniards
who originally had supported Weyler "now silently but bitterly denounce"
him.[56] In October 1897 an English resident in Havana wrote that Weyler's
policy "has been an absolute and entire failure. What sympathy may at one
time have been has been alienated."[57] One Spanish merchant in Havana,
claiming to represent the views of the Cuban business community, acknowledged that disaffection was "growing more serious daily" and concluded bluntly that "Weyler must go."[58]

The inability of Weyler to end the war and restore Spanish authority
over the rebellious island came as the latest in a series of rude blows to
pro-Spanish sectors in Cuba. So much depended on Weyler's success—the
very solvency, many sensed, of Spanish rule in Cuba. Those who had been
public in their confidence that Weyler represented Spain's best hope for
restoring order also acknowledged in private that he was Spain's last hope.

For the better part of the nineteenth century, and as early as the wars of
independence in South America, the *peninsular* elite and its Creole allies
in Cuba had embraced Spanish sovereignty as the most effective guarantee
of property, order, and privilege. Confirmed in this conviction by periodic

disorders and uprisings in the latter half of the nineteenth century, conservatives had seen no alternatives to the prevailing political order underwritten by and dependent upon Spanish arms. The elites preferred security to change and were not disposed to risk their social predominance for the sake of independence. Many had been inspired less by loyalism than by fear of social upheaval and the collapse of law and order. If in times of war the *peninsular*-Creole elites looked to Spain to uphold their privilege in the political order, in times of peace they looked to the United States to underwrite the prosperity of their economy. Under more or less normal conditions, the apparent contradiction of the Cuban political economy in the nineteenth century had posed little difficulty to the local elites, for whatever else planters may have been, they were preeminently pragmatic. In 1895, elite disaffection at metropolitan economic policies subsided only after the shadow of civil war had passed over the island. More immediate concerns now took precedence. The necessity of having to appeal to Spain for protection against the ravages of civil strife forced property owners to subordinate outstanding economic grievances to immediate politico-military needs. The earlier clamor against Spanish economic policies was muted by the distant rumblings of colonial insurrection. Led by a sector outside the traditional elite, the revolution posed as much a threat to the economic interests of property owners as it did to the political authority of Spain. Overriding concerns for property and privilege had forced planters to retreat again into the safety of the metropolitan fold—a place where they would remain unless or until Spain defaulted on the only remaining rationale for Spanish colonialism: order and security for property and privilege.

By 1897 the conservative consensus began to unravel. The inability of Martínez Campos to confine the insurrection to the east and the incapacity of Weyler to expel the insurgent armies from the west exposed the bankruptcy of the Spanish colonial regime. The apparent futility of Spanish arms gave rise to doubt, and this uncertainty served to undermine the prevailing *peninsular* unanimity of purpose. A sense of despair settled over the conservative community in Cuba. The crisis continued to deepen, seemingly unaffected in the slightest by the mightiest of Spain's efforts. The moral in 1897 was painfully clear: neither in peace nor in war could Spain protect the interests of Cuba's producing classes.

Within two years of Weyler's appointment, *peninsulares* and their Creole allies had abandoned all hopes of salvation from Spain. In 1897 the propertied classes faced an unprecedented situation. Their traditional source of security, upon which they had historically depended for protection against local dissidents, approached exhaustion and, for the first time, Spain gave evidence of defaulting on its security responsibilities to the colony. Spaniards in Cuba, consul Walter B. Barker reported tersely in June 1897, "are now convinced that the Mother Country is powerless to protect their interests."[59]

Admission of Spain's impotence in Cuba forced conservatives to confront the heartsickening prospect of the unthinkable—a victory of Cuban arms. The very interests that obliged planters in 1895 to appeal to Madrid for military assistance made them reconsider in 1897 the efficacy of continued political ties with Spain. Indeed, growing more certain in their conviction that Spain's hold over Cuba was slipping, the insular elites were not indisposed to abandoning a doomed cause if assured of an alternative source of protection and patronage. Weyler's faltering in 1897 served as the signal to begin the search for a new political arrangement, one optimally capable of preserving local preeminence or minimally capable of blocking the ascendency of those new forces in Cuban society that threatened the old order. Those groups who before 1895 had powerful economic reasons to seek union with the United States had, after 1897, powerful political reasons to do so.

It was in the face of the apparent impotence of the political metropolis that the propertied elites appealed to their economic metropolis for assistance. Only U.S. intervention, many concluded, leading eventually to annexation, held any promise of ending the insurrectionary challenge and redeeming the beleaguered social order. Through late 1896 and early 1897 property owners had grown increasingly predisposed to sacrifice traditional colonial relationships to preserve the local socio-economic system. To be sure, annexationist sentiment had long possessed a measure of respectability within patrician circles in Cuba. Until the late 1890s, however, it had functioned principally as a manifestation of political dissidence, in its own way a striving for modernity advanced primarily by disgruntled liberal Cubans seeking to sever ties with the backward colonial metropolis in order to join the progressive republic to the north. To this group was added, in 1897, disillusioned conservatives who saw U.S. intervention and annexation as the only acceptable alternatives to Spanish rule. Before the 1890s, annexationism had represented reform and the promise of modernity; by the end of the decade, annexationism also represented reaction and the defense of tradition. As early as June 1896, nearly one hundred planters, lawyers, and industrialists petitioned President Cleveland for American intervention to resolve the crisis. "We cannot," the petitioners wrote, "express our opinion openly and formally, for he who should dare, whilst living in Cuba, to protest against Spain, would, undoubtedly, be made a victim, both in his person and his property, to the most ferocious persecution at the hands of the Government." Spain, the petition continued, had defaulted on even the most modest promise of reform and could offer Cuba nothing for the future except continued destruction and ruin:

The property-holders are perfectly well aware that if Spain triumphs, they would be foolish, if, having saved anything from the catastrophe, they reinvested in reconstructing their property; are also aware, that no one would lend them a cent for that purpose. Capital in Cuba, being once lost, Spain would not be able to refurnish it, not having any herself. Neither would foreigners because, besides having lost all confidence of continued peace and apart from the natural fear of renewed revolts, the Government which would forcibly have to reign here, the immense burden that Spain would impose on us, would smother all future hope for Cuba.

Neither could the petitioning property owners find much comfort at the thought of independence. If the prospect of continued Spanish rule threatened to result in ruin, independence would lead to havoc. "Can there be no intermediate solution?" the petitioners asked somewhat plaintively. Without confidence in Spain, and uncertain about the future under Cuban rule, property owners asked Washington to intercede in their behalf: "We would ask that the party responsible to us should be the United States. In them we have confidence, and in them only."[60] "The worst thing that could happen to Cuba," another planter wrote a year later, "would be independence, if that implies the domination of the Gómez band over the civilized inhabitants. . . . They impounded, pillaged, and wantonly destroyed everywhere. Such a band cannot bring a firm and stable government to the island. Instead of that, devastation, riot, and rebellion might become permanent."[61] In early 1897, an American correspondent in Havana had reported that planters, merchants, and businessmen had concluded that Cuba was lost to Spain and hoped for American intervention and, ultimately, annexation of the island.[62] Later that year, William H. Calhoun, appointed special agent in Cuba by President McKinley, reported to the White House that "Cuban planters and Spanish property holders are now satisfied that the island must soon slip from Spain's grasp, and would welcome immediate American intervention."[63]

In 1897, deep political dislocations had worked their way upward through the social substructure of the colonial regime. Disaffection remained tentative, however, expressed always in private anonymity. A delicate balance of interest was all that supported the colonial equilibrium in Cuba in 1897. While *peninsulares* and their Creole allies may have questioned Spain's ability to defend their interests, they had never doubted Spain's will to do so—until late 1897.

VII The colonial regime was tottering on a narrow and precarious base when it received a series of external shocks. First, news of the Cánovas assassination. It stunned conservatives. No other person was more clearly identified with or more firmly committed to the defense of Spanish sovereignty in Cuba. Arguably, Cánovas's oft-repeated vow that Spain would fight in Cuba "until the last man and the last *peseta*" weighed heavily on war-weary ears in 1897. Arguably, the meager results of the "war with war" policy made skeptics of many supporters. But there was no argument that Cánovas represented reassuring comfort to conservatives that Spain would never abandon its loyal supporters in Cuba.

The months of political crisis in Spain after the Cánovas assassination further heightened uncertainty and misgiving in Cuba. When liberals finally emerged at the head of the new government, uncertainty in Cuba gave way to dismay and revulsion. The final shock was not long in coming.

News of Liberal reforms and the appointment of a reformist governor general offended conservatives. Rage followed. Summarily displaced, repudiated by a new regime in Madrid, conservatives in Cuba discovered to their horror that a shift of political fortunes in Spain had placed their fate at the mercy of traditional foes. Loyalists felt betrayed, but worse still, they felt discarded. Values long defended by conservatives in Cuba were suddenly pronounced by Liberals in Spain as misguided, if not misbegotten. The thought of a Liberal government in Spain and the spectre of Liberals spreading their odious doctrines in Cuba appalled those *peninsulares* and Creoles for whom the defense of traditional authority and persecution of Autonomists had been virtues of singular propriety. Conservatives received word of each new reform with anguished disbelief. Political prisoners jailed by Weyler were released. Newspapers earlier banned returned to legality. The party outlawed one day catapulted into power the next.

For those conservatives for whom the distinction between autonomism and separatism had little more than specious significance, metropolitan reforms assumed proportions of disgraceful treason. For the vast majority of *peninsulares*, the Autonomist party served only as the political front behind which stalked insurgent separatists. That scores of Autonomists had enrolled in separatist ranks after the appointment of Weyler served to confirm these long-standing suspicions. Taking note of the scores of high ranking Autonomists who had earlier joined separatist organizations, *peninsulares* could not help but respond to Spain's proclamation of an Autonomist regime with numb incredulity. The direction of Spanish policy could have been dismissed as folly if it did not point to calamity. It was madness.[64] Loyalists denounced the establishment of an Autonomist government, insisting that reforms served only to pave the way for revolution and open the back door to the triumph of Cuban arms and the eventual independence of the island. Conservatives freely predicted that radical separatists would quickly overrun moderate Autonomists and convert autonomy into independence. "There may be a revolution in the revolution," Fitzhugh Lee predicted soberly.[65] Richard Weightman, the *Washington Post* correspondent in Havana, reported *peninsular* fears graphically. Autonomy promised to relinquish "property to the rule of the ignorant rabble," Weightman wrote. "It would be the death knell of civilized society in Cuba. . . . The Spanish residents, who conduct nearly all the commercial and industrial enterprises in the island, are afraid to have the governing power confided to the multitude."[66]

The end of *peninsular* exclusivism over matters of state was sufficient cause to arouse conservative misgiving. For many the distinction between autonomists and separatists was further blurred by the issue of nationality. It mattered not that autonomists were politically moderate, often men of means, and, by tradition, ideologically allied to the metropolis. The *creole-peninsular* schism persisted unabated to the very end of the colonial regime. "All classes of the Spanish citizens," Consul Lee reported, "are violently opposed to real or genuine autonomy because it would throw the control of the island into the hands of the Cubans and rather than that, they would prefer annexation to the United States or some form of an American protectorate."[67]

The organization of the Autonomist government, finally, convinced conservatives that Spain had lost the will to retain sovereignty over the war-torn island. An ominous portent, *peninsulares* feared. Many believed, too, that Madrid only awaited the opportune moment in which to abandon the island altogether. Certain now that Spanish authorities no longer controlled events at home or abroad, convinced that Spain possessed neither the means nor—after 1897—the will to defend the status quo, *peninsulares* and their Creole allies resolved to shed a metropolis incapable of protecting their interests. Conservatives found themselves caught between the ebbing of metropolitan authority and the advancing tide of colonial rebellion. Political separation from Spain became necessary to forestall independence.

Discarded and disgraced, converted from allies to adversaries, conservatives reacted immediately. News of the formation of the Autonomist government and the appointment of Ramón Blanco as governor-general provoked protest demonstrations and marches across the island. Through November and December 1897, rallies and mass meetings in all major cities denounced Madrid's decision to concede the island autonomy. In December 1897, a statement published in Havana and signed by businessmen and property owners claiming to represent 80 percent of the island's wealth, denounced the new regime.[68] So casual an act as a change of governors in Havana was a traumatic shock to the only forces in Cuba who, apart from the insurgents, still retained loyalty and the will to win. Planters, businessmen, and soldiers long constituting the lynch pin of the colonial regime were abandoned by Madrid and, alone, they had little to offer as an alternative to the rising swell of colonial revolution.

The Liberal reforms had a particularly unsetling effect on Spanish armed forces. Soldiers who had not been paid in months could not react with anything less than undisguised bitterness and rage at the generous bounties offered to pardoned insurgent leaders. Disaffection in the army increased incrementally, measured responses to each newly announced reform. While many in the army may have been willing to continue to defend traditional authority in Cuba, few were disposed to support an Autonomist regime. By early 1898, entire units of the Spanish army had ceased to fight. Officers publicly demanded to be returned to Spain.[69] After autonomy, many officers no longer considered Cuba a Spanish possession. "No one understood the motive for continuing to fight," one Spanish officer later recalled, "for from the moment Autonomy was proclaimed, the troops should have . . . left the Cubans with their 'Cuba Libre.'"[70]

Nowhere was this sentiment more vividly manifested than in the Corps of Volunteers. Made up exclusively of *peninsular* residents in Cuba, commanded by Spanish officers from local business, commerce, and agriculture, the Volunteers vigorously denounced the new government. Perhaps no sector of the Spanish population was so intransigent in its opposition to Liberal reforms or so vocal in its denunciation of autonomy as the officers. Fearful of future reprisals, unwilling to defend a regime they did not support, scores of officers resigned. Many immediately liquidated their property and left for Spain. José Gener y Batet, Pedro Murias, Leopoldo Carvajal, Calixto López, Segundo Alvarez, Perfecto López, Gumersindo García, Manuel Valle, and Julián Alvarez, men who also served as the ranking officers of the Volunteers, left for Spain. They were also some of the largest cigar manufacturers, owners of La Flor de Murias, Henry Clay, Punch, La Corona, Cabañas, La Flor de Cuba, and La Rosa de Santiago.

Officers in the Corps of Volunteers and the Spanish army took umbrage at the decision to establish an autonomist regime. Weyler's substitution by Blanco in particular provoked widespread revulsion within the predominantly pro-Weyler officer corps. By late 1897 and early 1898, numerous conspiracies against the new governor-general and the Autonomist government unfolded in senior military circles across the island.[71] The army that had ceased to fight in the countryside had become the focal point of political intrigue in the cities.

Caught between the Scylla of metropolitan reform and the Charybdis of colonial revolution, *peninsulares* and their Creole allies charted an independent course of action. By late 1897, conservatives appealed directly to the United States for deliverance. In November 1897, the American vice-consul in Matanzas reported that "nearly all Spaniards, businessmen, and property holders in this province wish and pray for annexation to the United States."[72] "Property holders, without distinction of nationality, and with but few exceptions," Consul Pulaski F. Hyatt cabled from Santiago, "strongly desire annexation, having but little hope of a stable government under either of the contending forces."[73] Fitzhugh Lee reported similar conditions in Havana. "A large majority of the Spanish subjects," he wrote in November 1897, "who have commercial and business interests and own property here will not accept Autonomy, but prefer annexation to the United States, rather than an independent republic or genuine autonomy under the Spanish flag."[74] Two months later, Lee forwarded to Washington a brief transcript of a conversation: "I talked with a rabid violent (at one time) Spaniard last night, a colonel of volunteers. He said he 'tried to be a Reformist at first' and then told the Palace people he 'would try and be an Autonomist.' What next, I asked. 'Yankee,' he replied."[75] From the provinces American consular agents reported receiving individual letters and private petitions denouncing autonomy and appealing for American intervention and annexation. By the end of the year sentiment for American intervention had become public. In December, a meeting of property owners in Cienfuegos concluded plans to forward a petition to President McKinley asking the United States to establish a protectorate over Cuba. In February, at a meeting of ranking members of the Unión Constituciónal, conservatives established a formal commission for the purpose of securing American assistance. "The Mother country cannot protect us," one spokesman insisted. "Blanco will not protect us. If left to the insurgents our property is lost. Therefore, we want the United States to save us."[76] A similar mood existed among the officers of the Volunteers. One journalist reported that in Sagua la Grande officers of the Corps of Volunters insisted that "if Spain cannot protect them, they desire American rule, but that they will never submit to be ruled by the Cubans."[77]

On January 1, 1898, members of the new Autonomist government were installed in office. Outside the rank and file of the Autonomist party, few in Cuba had cause to celebrate the occasion. A Liberal government had been summoned into existence to preserve metropolitan sovereignty and thwart colonial revolution. It failed on both counts. Instead, reforms had the net effect of alienating the most tenacious supporters of Spain without reconciling the most ardent opponents to Spanish rule. The two groups upon whose support the success of autonomy depended—loyalists and separatists—spurned metropolitan reforms and arrived at one common goal if not different objectives—the separation of Cuba from Spain.

VIII   From the insurgent army command in central Cuba, Máximo Gómez renewed his determination to continue the war against Spanish rule, whatever form it took. In Havana, political intrigue slowly edged the new government toward crisis. On January 12, 1898, *peninsular* despair gave way to violence when several units of Spanish soldiers and volunteers mutinied and stormed editorial offices of two Havana newspapers sympathetic to the Autonomist government. With cries of "Death to Blanco," "Long Live Weyler," and "Down with Autonomy," rioting troops destroyed the presses of *El Reconcentrado* and *La Discusión*.[78]

In mid-January, an uneasy tension had settled over the capital. Rumors of conspiracy within the armed forces in Havana raised doubts that the new administration possessed the capacity to govern effectively for anything more than a brief period. Reports of insurgent military operations kept Havana in a continual state of unrest. In Washington, the State Department prepared itself for the after-shocks of the Havana riots. Reports from Havana, Assistant Secretary of State Alvey A. Adee informed his superiors confidentially, "suggests the beginning of the end in Cuba." He continued:

I fear that the Volunteers will rise, and by a counter-revolution, overthrow not only the professed autonomists government, but also what little vestige of power remains to the Peninsular authority in Cuba; much as they rose and expelled General Dulce early in the ten years' war. I think it would be well for our naval squadron in the Gulf to be ready for immediate action, for which the emergency may arise any moment. . . . These movements in Cuba are very contagious, and Santiago and Matanzas are likely to follow suit. Cienfuegos is more conservative, being the headquarters of the sugar interest which is largely American.[79]

A day after the Havana riots, Consul Fitzhugh Lee wired an urgent request for the prompt presence of American warships in Havana.[80] On January 25, the U.S.S. *Maine* arrived in Havana harbor.

8 The Passing of Spanish Sovereignty

A year ago we received a proposal to agree to an armistice. We refused then and we must refuse now. The rainy season is at hand, and Spain's troops would like an armistice until it is over. We will not, however, throw away the advantage. I am anxious that hostilities should cease, but it must for all time. If Spain agrees to evacuate Cuba, taking her flag with her, I am willing to agree to an armistice to last until October 1, when loyal Cubans shall come into their own again.
—Máximo Gómez, April 1898

Don't worry about Oriente. Here nobody even speaks about autonomy, but on the contrary so many people come out of the towns to unite with us that we don't know where to put them.
—Calixto García, March 1898

I "Autonomy is already a dead issue," the American consul in Santiago wrote on February 1, 1898.[1] No one in Cuba in early 1898 would have disputed this conclusion. Prime Minister Sagasta's appeal to autonomy had fared no better than Cánovas's application of arms. Reforms had failed. Spain at last resort had made the ultimate concession to empire and found it wanting. Autonomy instead had compounded Madrid's difficulties by estranging what little remained of Spain's support on the island. But, then, few knowledgeable observers in Cuba had ever really been sanguine about the prospects of reforms. As early as November, American officials in Cuba had predicted outright that autonomy would fail. "I cannot help to foresee," Consul Walter B. Barker wrote prophetically from Sagua la Grande, "that far from improving the actual conditions of things, it will make it more and more critical."[2] In a personal letter to Assistant Secretary of State William R. Day some weeks later, Fitzhugh Lee had predicted that both Cuban insurgents and Spanish loyalists would reject autonomy.[3] In December, even before the formal establishment of the Autonomist government, Secretary of State John Sherman had informed the White House that autonomy had failed to satisfy insurgent demands. Separatist leaders, Sherman wrote, had reiterated their determination "to fight until the independence of Cuba is achieved."[4] In mid-January 1898, Fitzhugh Lee summarized the Cuban situation succinctly:

1. The great mass of the Spaniards here are opposed to Autonomy.
2. The Governor General is powerless to force its adoption.
3. Large numbers of the officers and men of the Spanish Army, more particularly, the Volunteers, cannot be depended upon to obey General Blanco's orders, when issued in the interest of Autonomy.
4. The Spanish merchants and property holders generally favor some form of intervention on the part of the United States. . . .
5. The Cubans bearing arms want an Independent Republic and the intelligent and educated Cuban citizens desire Annexation to our Republic.[5]

In a personal letter to William R. Day, Lee was briefer still: "Autonomy is not cutting any ice."[6]

The failure of reforms fixed politically what earlier had been settled militarily: the bankruptcy of the colonial regime. The end of the Cuban conflict was in sight and the outcome a foregone conclusion. In Spain, the pressure to evacuate *peninsular* forces and recognize Cuban independence mounted. "Spain is exhausted," former President Francisco Pi y Margall insisted. "She must withdraw her troops and recognize Cuban independence before it is too late."[7] The failure of autonomy, the Madrid daily *El Nuevo Régimen* editorialized, left only one alternative: "negotiate on the basis of independence."[8] Another Madrid daily reached similar conclusions. "In reality," *La Epoca* suggested, "Cuba is lost to Spain."[9]

Separatists, too, sensed the end near. At new optimism lifted insurgent morale to an all-time high. Never before had separatists been as certain of the triumph of Cuban arms as they were in early 1898. "This war cannot last more than a year," Máximo Gómez predicted euphorically in January 1898. "This is the first time I have ever put a limit to it."[10] The newly elected president of the provisional government agreed. "The war for independence of our country is nearing the end," Bartolomé Masó proclaimed confidently in late 1897.[11]

Well before political reforms delivered the final body blows to the resolve of Spanish armed forces, insurgent army commanders had detected a sharp decline in Spanish morale and operations. "The Spanish are tired," Máximo Gómez had reported back in July 1897, "and in these days when the heat suffocates even us, I do not see how those troops move."[12] In the summer of 1897, Spanish forces lay prostrate, weakened by illness and disease, sapped to the point of exhaustion by the unrelieved tropical heat. Reports from various zones of insurgent military operations arrived independently at a striking consensus: Spanish armed forces had lost the will to fight.[13]

This was before the proclamation of autonomy. After January 1898, after the installation of the Autonomist government, Spanish military operations came to a virtual standstill. It was now the turn of Spanish forces to avoid combat.[14] Across the island, the Spanish army had ceased to fight. *Peninsular* units abandoned smaller interior towns to concentrate in the larger provincial cities. Preparations for the last desperate battles had begun. "The enemy," Máximo Gómez wrote from Las Villas in March, "has departed, ceasing military operations and abandoning the garrisons and forts which constituted his base of operations. Days, weeks and months pass without a column of troops appearing within our radius of action." He now wrote confidently about preparations for the final assault against the Spaniards in the cities. With "cannons and a great deal of dynamite," a self-assured Gómez predicted in March 1898, "we can expel them by fire and steel from the towns."[15]

January was customarily the month in which the Spanish army command launched vigorous field operations—traditionally the beginning of the winter campaign. Insurgent army chieftains braced themselves for what many believed to be the last and, perhaps, the most desperate enemy offensive. But nothing happened. In January 1898, Máximo Gómez wrote of a "dead war."[16] The collapse was all but complete. "The enemy is crushed," Gómez reported with some surprise, "and is in complete retreat from here, and the time which favored their operations passes without their doing anything."[17] Spain's failure to mount a new winter offensive confirmed separatists' belief that the enemy was exhausted and lacked the means and the will to continue the war. One more rainy season, insurgent chieftains predicted confidently, would suffice to deliver the *coup de grace* to the moribund Spanish army.[18]

American officials, too, had acknowledged what in early 1898 was evident in Spain and Cuba: the failure of reforms ended any likelihood that Madrid would reestablish sovereignty over the rebellious colony. Cuba was lost to Spain. In January 1898, it had become apparent that the insurrection had at once undermined Spanish sovereignty and neutralized American efforts to underwrite that sovereignty. Indeed, there effectively ceased to exist in Cuba any Spanish sovereignty for Washington to uphold. Spain was simply powerless to overcome the rebellion, American authorities conceded. The days of Spanish rule were numbered. "Spain herself has demonstrated she is powerless either to conciliate Cuba or conquer it," former American Minister to Spain Hannis Taylor had written in late 1897; "her sovereignty over [Cuba] is . . . now extinct."[19] Secretary of State John Sherman: "Spain will lose Cuba. That seems to me to be certain. She cannot continue the struggle."[20] Assistant Secretary of State William R. Day concurred. "The Spanish Government," he wrote to Minister Woodford, "seems unable to conquer the insurgents."[21] In a confidential memorandum, Day went further:

To-day the strength of the Cubans [is] nearly double . . . and [they] occupy and control virtually all the territory outside the heavily garrisoned coast cities and a few interior towns. There are no active operations by the Spaniards. . . . The eastern provinces are admittedly "Free Cuba." In view of these statements alone, it is now evident that Spain's struggle in Cuba has

become absolutely hopeless. . . . Spain is exhausted financially
and physically, while the Cubans are stronger.[22]

When asked if Spanish authorities possessed the means of ending the
insurrection, Consul Fitzhugh Lee responded unequivocally: "I do not
think there is the slightest possibility of their doing it at all in any way."[23]
In December 1897, Lee had summarized Spain's condition in Cuba graphically for the State Department:

1. In my opinion there is no possibility of Spain terminating
    the war here by *arms*.
2. Or by *Autonomy*—real or pretended.
3. Or by *purchasing the insurrection leaders*, as recently at-
    tempted.
4. Or, as far as I can see, in any other way.[24]

And with the rainy season approaching, Americans feared that Spain's
collapse was imminent.[25]

II   In fact, the failure of autonomy surprised no one. Even as McKinley
applied pressure on Madrid to concede reforms, few in Washington believed the proposed concessions capable of providing anything more than a
temporary postponement of Spain's inevitable collapse. As early as September, only days after his arrival in Spain, Minister Woodford had acknowledged that whatever reforms Liberals could be persuaded to adopt
in Madrid faced bleak prospects in Havana. "Events are apparently moving so rapidly in Cuba," Woodford conceded to the State Department,
"that the conditions may come at any day when the insurgents might reject
any suggestion of autonomy and mediation and insist upon absolute independence."[26]
    American policy in 1898 now moved toward the final act of the
nineteenth-century drama in which the United States upheld its commitment to Spanish sovereignty in Cuba. Madrid had received ample warning
that there were fixed limits to this commitment. Cleveland in 1896 and
McKinley in 1897 had alluded to those conditions that would compel the
United States to respond to higher obligations. "When the inability of
Spain to deal successfully with the insurrection has become manifest,"
Cleveland had proclaimed, "and it is demonstrated that her sovereignty is
extinct in Cuba for all purposes of its rightful existence, . . . a situation

will be presented in which our obligations to the sovereignty of Spain will be superceded by higher obligations."²⁷ "The United States," Cleveland warned in conclusion, "is not a nation to which peace is a necessity."²⁸ In 1897, McKinley, too, had spoken of a higher commitment, "the obligation this Government owes to itself" and "a duty imposed by our obligations to ourselves."²⁹

In early 1898, American officials were united in their conviction that Spanish sovereignty over Cuba had lapsed. There, set against the landscape created by the receding tide of Spanish sovereignty, the United States confronted the anathema of all American policymakers since Jefferson—the spectre of Cuban independence. The implications of the "no transfer" policy were now carried to their logical conclusion. If the United States could not permit Spain to transfer sovereignty over Cuba to another power, neither could the United States permit Spain to cede sovereignty to Cubans.

III   The insolvency of Spanish sovereignty in Cuba transformed the traditional function of American policy. McKinley, like Cleveland before him, had adhered scrupulously to the central policy tenets that for almost a century had obliged the United States to defend and uphold Spanish sovereignty. The lapse of Spanish sovereignty in 1898 released the United States from any further obligations to Spain. Washington ceased its efforts to secure reforms designed to restore Spanish authority. Indeed, failure of Spanish arms and rejection in Cuba of Spanish reforms left little ground upon which to reestablish colonial rule. In 1898, the United States recognized the futility of pressuring Madrid into offering reforms foredoomed to failure to Cuba. The obstacle to reforms lay in the fields of insurgent Cuba, not in the courts of Madrid. Spanish authoriteis had acquiesced on all substantive American requests, Woodford informed McKinley in February. "They cannot go further in open concessions to us without being overthrown by their own people."³⁰

American policy acquired a new purpose. Few in Washington believed reforms and autonomy capable of providing a long-term solution to the Cuban conflict. But, then, long-term goals were not American objectives. McKinley was bargaining for time, fixed on short-term goals through which to create the conditions leading ultimately to the acquisition of Cuba. "If, in spite of all they do," Woodford counseled the president in November 1897, "it shall be found that their action has come too late and the war shall continue, you must be absolutely free to do hereafter what shall seem to you wise and right."[31] By 1898, Washington abandoned its commitment to Spanish sovereignty and sought to persuade Madrid to transfer sovereignty over the war-torn island to the United States.

The Cuban rejection of autonomy added a new gravity to the American purpose. Washington now applied pressure on Madrid to settle the status of Cuba politically with the United States before insurgent Cubans settled the island's future militarily with Spain. A new urgency accompanied American efforts to resolve the Cuban conflict before May 1, the official start of the rainy season. Autonomy, American officials had hoped, would lead to a truce through the rainy season, thereby preventing the anticipated triumph of Cuban arms. Few in Washington believed Spain capable of surviving the 1898 summer campaign. The failure of autonomy to forestall the renewal of summer operations, a key American objective, and the inability of the Spanish army to withstand the expected insurgent offensive, announced the end of Spanish rule in Cuba. "It now seems almost certain," an anxious Woodford explained to McKinley, "that autonomy cannot succeed before the rainy season begins."[32] In Madrid, Woodford exhorted Spanish authorities to resolve the Cuban crisis before the summer. "I beg you," Woodford pleaded with Colonial Minister Moret, "not as the American Minister but as a man, urge your Government to finish this rebellion, no matter what your Government is required to do, before the rainy season begins. . . . No thoughtful American can tell how long the conscience and humanity of the American people can be held in check."[33]

In early 1898 the alternatives were manifest: either the Cubans would force Spain militarily to cede the island its independence or the Americans would force Spain politically to transfer the island to the United States. American policy in 1898 was designed to forestall the former to facilitate the latter. But if a satisfactory diplomatic settlement was unobtainable before the onset of the summer rains, Washington, too, was prepared to appeal to force to establish its claim over Cuba. If Spanish sovereignty was untenable, Cuban pretensions for sovereignty were unacceptable. "I do not believe that the population is to-day fit for self-government," Woodford mused from Madrid in March, "and that acceptance of a practical protectorate over Cuba seems to me very like the assumption of the responsible care of a madhouse."[34] This conviction persuaded Woodford to conclude: "I have at last come to believe that the only certainty of peace is under our flag. . . . I am, thus, reluctantly, slowly, but entirely a convert to the early American ownership and occupation of the Island. If we recognize independence, we may turn the island over to a part of its inhabitants against the judgment of many of its most educated and wealthy residents."[35]

Efforts to negotiate a peace with Spain based on a transfer of the island to the United States began in earnest in early 1898. In February, the White House informed ranking members of the Senate of administration plans to purchase the island.[36] The president asked Whitelaw Reid to undertake the negotiations with Madrid.[37] At about the same time, Woodford had arrived at the conclusion that the transfer of the island had to be made as soon as possible—peacefully if possible, with Spanish honor preserved if it could be, but above all quickly, and absolutely. The moment seemed auspicious, Woodford counseled from Madrid. "The feeling here is despondent," the American minister reported to the State Department in mid-March. "Bread grows dearer; business more stagnant; public securites fall."[38] Woodford reaffirmed his optimism in private communications with the president. Spain was "tired and exhausted," he reported in March, "threatened with practical famine and confronted with the immediate necessity of tremendous outlay." The time had come to pursue the acquisition of Cuba vigorously.[39] On the day of this communique, Woodford discussed the Cuban situation at length with Colonial Minister Segismundo Moret. Spain had lost Cuba, Woodford stressed to Moret. Autonomy had failed to restore peace, and Spanish arms had failed to defeat the insurgents. But Cuban independence was not an acceptable alternative. There were no prospects that the "insurgents can secure peace and good order in Cuba under a free or independent Government." The conclusions, hence, were inescapable. Woodford affirmed: "I see nothing ahead except disorder, insecurity of persons and destruction of property. The Spanish flag cannot give peace. The rebel flag cannot give peace. There is but one power and one flag that can secure peace and compel peace. That power is the United States and that flag is our flag." "Some way must be found," he urged Moret, "by which Spain can part with Cuba without loss of self-respect and with certainty of American control so that we may give that protection to loyal Spaniards and rebels alike." Woodford proposed that the United States would pay Spain a "fixed sum for the purchase of the Island," part of which would be retained as fund for the payment of all war claims.[40] On March 19, Moret pledged to work personally with Woodford toward these ends.[41]

IV   By mid-March, however, it was no longer possible for the McKinley administration to continue to insulate private diplomatic discussions abroad from mounting political pressure at home. The publication of the de Lôme letter on February 9, vilifying McKinley, followed a week later by the destruction of the *Maine*, produced a national outcry demanding action. Aroused further by an impassioned press and urged on by mounting public opinion, the pro-Cuban Congress seized the initiative from the ostensibly inactive chief executive and directly challenged the president for leadership over foreign policy.[42] On March 9, a rebellious Congress voted unanimously to appropriate $50 million for war preparations. In the weeks that followed, members of both houses of Congress introduced a series of resolutions variously favoring belligerency to the Cuban insurgents, recognizing Cuban independence, and declaring war on Spain. Administration supporters on Capitol Hill rallied successfully on each occasion to thwart hostile legislative initiatives but reported to the White House that each victory proved more difficult than the one before. By late March, Congress seemed prepared to ignore the president altogether and pass a war resolution without his authority. "Don't your president know where the war-declaring power is lodged?" one angry senator asked Assistant Secretary of State William R. Day. "Well tell him . . . that if he doesn't do something Congress will exercise the power and declare war in spite of him! He'll get run over and the party with him!"[43]

In early spring, the administration found itself in a race to negotiate a peace settlement to facilitate the transfer of the island before Congress declared war on Spain in behalf of Cuban independence. A new political urgency in Washington now joined previous administration concerns about the approaching rainy season in Cuba. The insurgents were nearing the end of their war while Congress threatened to start a new war—both in the name of Cuba Libre. A congressional declaration of war against the will of the president, moreover, threatened a political crisis of monumental proportions. At the same time, recognition of Cuban belligerency or Cuban independence threatened to undermine McKinley's attempt to negotiate the acquisition of the island. Even as McKinley enjoined his minister in Madrid to press forward with negotiations, the *Chicago Tribune* denounced administration policy. "The people want no disgraceful negotiations with Spain," the *Tribune* editorialized in late February. "Should the president plunge his administration into that morass, he and his party would be swept out of power in 1900 by a fine burst of popular indignation. An administration which stains the national honor never will be forgiven."[44]

Elections were also on the mind of Senator Henry Cabot Lodge, himself facing reelection in 1898. "If the war in Cuba drags on through the summer with nothing done," Lodge warned the White House, "we shall go down in the greatest defeat ever known . . . , it will be deadly. I know that it is easily and properly said that to bring on or even threaten war for political reasons is a crime and I quite agree. But to sacrifice a great party and bring free silver upon the country for a wrong policy is hardly less odious."[45]

Congress grew restive. Administration congressional supporters warned the White House that it would be impossible for the president to keep Congress in check much longer. Congressman Joe Bailey outlined the Democrats' position: "If the President of the United States wants two days, or if he wants two hours, to continue negotiations with the butchers of Spain, we are not ready to give him one moment longer for that purpose."[46] After a particularly stormy session of the Senate, Vice-President Garrett Augustus Hobart informed McKinley that he could not longer restrain the Senate from declaring war. "They will act without you if you do not act at once," Hobart informed the president bluntly. McKinley was startled. "Do you mean that the Senate will declare war on its own motion?" McKinley asked incredulously. Hobart repeated his warning. "Say no more!" the president exclaimed and lapsed into silence.[47] At a subsequent White House meeting on March 22, McKinley informed the assembled members of his cabinet that his hopes for ending the Cuban conflict were rapidly diminishing.[48]

V   Political pressure in Washington passed directly on to the negotiation tables in Madrid. Only hours after McKinley's March 22 cabinet meetings, Woodford was instructed to inform the Spanish government that "unless some satisfactory agreement is reached within a few days, which will assure immediate and honorable peace in Cuba, the President must at once submit the whole question of relations between the United States and Spain . . . to the decision of Congress"—a decision, Washington intimated, that all but formally guaranteed intervention and war.[49] Woodford bluntly warned Madrid to sell Cuba or face war with the United States.[50] Spanish authorities reacted with surprise "at the apparent change in the attitude of the United States" but expressed a day later a willingness to empower the insular government to proclaim a peace. A way out of the impasse had been reached, Woodford reported euphorically; once again Spain had acquiesced. It had the effect of an immediate truce, Woodford insisted. "It also admits and even invites possible intervention by the United States"—palpable proof, Woodford suggested, that Spain wished to relinquish control over Cuba.[51] On March 25, seeking still another way to forestall the summer campaign, Woodford proposed a truce to last until the following fall. "I believe," he wrote confidently, "that if immediate peace can be assured now lasting until September 15 Cuba will become peacefully the property of the United States."[52] Two days later, on March 27, Assistant Secretary of State Day formally instucted Woodford to secure from Spain: (1) an armistice until October 1; (2) immediate revocation of the *reconcentrado* order and authorization to distribute American relief supplies among needy Cubans and, "if possible," Day inserted, (3) acceptance of the president as arbiter if the conflict resumed after the expiration of the cease fire. "If Spain agrees," Day promised, the "President will use friendly offices to get insurgents to accept the plan." Prompt action, Day concluded, was vital.[53]

Political tensions in Washington increased. Diplomatic pressure on Madrid mounted. On March 28, Day cabled: "Important to have prompt answer on armistice matter."[54] On March 29, Day again wired from Washington: "Feeling here is intense."[55] A day later the assistant secretary again cabled: "You should know and fully appreciate that there is profound feeling in Congress, and the gravest apprehension on the part of most conservative members that a resolution for intervention may pass both branches in spite of any effort which can be made."[56] Woodford immediately communicated this new threat of war to Spanish authorities.[57]

By early April, however, events were overtaking the White House. In the face of mounting political pressure, McKinley was losing time to negotiate a political settlement with Spain. Nor had Madrid offered many diplomatic concessions of any political use to the president at home. Congressional clamor for the recognition of Cuban independence grew daily more difficult to resist. Spain had capitulated on every demand on the March 27 note—except for the armistice. If, however, the insurgents would ask for a cease-fire, Sagasta had indicated earlier to Woodford, "it would be granted at once."[58] Delicate domestic political considerations, Woodford explained to McKinley two days later, made it very difficult for Spain to proclaim a unilateral armistice. "I am told confidentially that the offer of armistice by the Spanish Government would cause revolution here," Woodford wrote. "I believe the Ministry are [sic] ready to go as far and as fast as possible as they can and still save the Dynasty here in Spain." Conceding that the Spanish response to the American note "was a sorrow to me," Woodford nonetheless expressed a guarded optimism. "They know that Cuba is lost," he explained. "Public opinion in Spain has moved steadily toward peace. No Spanish ministry would have dared to do one month ago what this Ministry has proposed today."[59]

Private diplomatic optimism, however, had little effect on political demands in the United States. On April 2, the State Department wired Woodford: "Matters serious. Action by Congress seems probable by the middle of next week."[60]

On April 5, Woodford cabled stunning news: the queen regent had personally interceded and was at that very moment preparing a proclamation ordering a unilateral cease-fire in Cuba, effective immediately, and lasting through October. "Can you prevent hostile action by Congress?" Woodford asked McKinley urgently. "I believe this means peace which the sober judgment of our people will approve long before next November, and which must be approved at the bar of final history."[61] The administration made one more attempt to restrain Congress. Pro-administration forces in Congress were asked to assume their places at the political barricades on Capitol Hill one more time. The White House took the offensive. An administration spokesman chided Congress for holding "a stop-watch over the head of the President" and demanding action "on a certain day and at a certain hour or suffer the humiliation of having Congress act without waiting for his recommendations."[62]

On April 10, Washington received Spain's formal acceptance of the essential provisions of McKinley's March 27 ultimatum.[63] On the same day in Havana, Governor-General Blanco ordered all Spanish forces to halt operations.[64] Also on April 10, Woodford appealed to McKinley: "I hope that nothing will now be done to humiliate Spain, as I am satisfied that the present Government is going, and is loyally ready to go, as fast and as far as it can. With your power of action sufficiently free you will win the fight on your own lines."[65]

VI   McKinley had scored a diplomatic victory on all fronts. But as he must have known in early April, it was a hollow triumph. The administration had already tried but failed to make good on the American part of the March 27 ultimatum: "use friendly offices to get insurgents to accept plan." In early April, McKinley summoned Horatio Rubens to the White House to discuss with the Cuban junta's legal counsel the terms of impending settlement. Rubens later recalled the meeting:

"You must," he clipped out at me, "accept an immediate armistice with Spain."

"To what end, Mr. President?"

"To settle the strife in Cuba," he cried.

"But is Spain ready to grant Cuba independence?" I asked.

"That isn't the question now," he exclaimed, his voice rising. "We may discuss that later. The thing for the moment is an armistice."

Rubens rejected outright McKinley's terms of the cease-fire. Such an arrangement, Rubens countered, would benefit only Spain and have calamitous consequences on the Cuban war effort:

The reason is a practical one, Mr. President. Nothing you could propose would be so beneficial to Spain and so detrimental to Cuba as an armistice. If an armistice is carried out in good faith, it means the dissolution and disintegration of the Cuban army. There is no commissary for it even now; it must live, poorly and precariously, on the country. If armistice is accepted the army cannot obtain its food supplies; it will starve. Furthermore, in the natural uncertainty pending negotiations, the men would scatter, going to their homes. . . . If, on the other hand, having accepted the armistice, the Cubans continued to live on the country, they would be loudly charged with breach of faith.[66]

In Cuba, separatist army chieftains denounced the cease-fire and ordered insurgent forces to continue operations.[67] "They have to be hit hard and at the head, day and night," General Calixto García exhorted his troops. "In order to suspend hostilities, an agreement is necessary with our Government and this will have to be based on independence."[68] More than ever before," Máximo Gómez proclaimed, "the war must continue in full force."[69]

Cuban rejection of the Spanish cease-fire ended American hopes that the 1898 summer campaign could be averted. Spain had attached only one condition to its agreement: that Cubans honor the cease-fire.[70] Spain, American officials feared, now had no choice but to resume military operations and face inevitably final defeat.

Many close to McKinley would later insist that the president had come very near to a peaceful settlement of the Cuban crisis. "Do you realize," Secretary of the Navy John Davis Long wrote privately to the editor of the *Boston Globe* in April 1898, "that the President has succeeded in obtaining from Spain a concession upon every ground which he has asked." Long continued: "You cannot expect [Spain] to get up and get out in five minutes; but, if the history of the last six months means anything, it means constant steps towards her retirement. In this direction the President has gone with the most thorough decision, persistance and fidelity." Long concluded with the familiar metaphor: "I honestly believe that if the country and Congress had been content to leave the matter in his hands, independence would have come without a drop of bloodshed, as naturally as an apple falls from a tree."[71] James Boyle, McKinley's private secretary, later recalled McKinley lamenting: "The declaration of war against Spain was an act which had been and will always be the greatest grief of my life. I never wanted to go to war with Spain. Had I been let alone, I could have prevented the war. All I wanted was more time."[72]

In the early spring, events were being determined by forces outside Washington and Madrid, beyond the reach of traditional diplomacy. Spain and the United States moved closer to war as a result of their failure to control developments in Cuba. The inability of Madrid and Washington to persuade the embattled extremes of the Cuban polity—the two groups to which they had some access—to accept a middle compromise position really left little for Spain and the United States to discuss. Peninsulares and their Creole allies had spurned Liberal reforms; separatists rejected both autonomy and the armistice. Once Spain refused to transfer sovereignty over Cuba to the United States, once Cubans rejected the continuation of Spanish sovereignty in any form, the Americans faced two prospects: independence or intervention. Intervention in 1898 was directed as much against Cuban independence as it was against Spanish sovereignty.

9 Shades of a Shadow

I am convinced that the nearer the war comes to an end by force of arms the more difficult it will be to resist American intervention.
—Valeriano Weyler, June 1897

[Congress] argued that though the people of Cuba had not driven the Spaniards out of the Island, yet they had resisted the Spanish arms successfully, that Spain was no longer attended with a reasonable hope or expectation of success in her effort to regain her lost sovereignty, and that our whole proceeding was based on the theory that Spain, by her misgovernment and bad conduct, had forfeited, not only her sovereignty, but also her right to regain it; for which reason we were proposing to drive her out.
—Senator Joseph B. Foraker, April 1898

Side by side in this evening's paper appear the President's declaration that the war in Cuba must be stopped and Spain's declaration that she has stopped it already.
—*London Times,* April 12, 1898

A shadow has fallen over us.
—Máximo Gómez, May 1898

I The United States prepared for intervention, as alarmed at the prospect of a Cuban victory as it was exasperated at Spain's inability to end the war. Neither the force of Spanish repression nor the concession of Spanish reforms had checked the advance of Cuban arms. Spanish sovereignty had slipped beyond recovery. The failure of the United States to forestall the anticipated Cuban victory through diplomacy left only American arms.

It was with no small sense of horror that the White House received congressional resolutions calling for the recognition of Cuban independence. The cause of Cuba Libre had won much popular support in the United States. Both major parties had sensed the national mood and adopted free Cuba planks in the 1896 party platforms. For much of the American press and the vast body of American public opinion, the struggle for Cuba Libre was a sacred and noble cause not unlike the American revolutionary experience. Indeed, so close was the identity in the public mind between the Americans of 1776 and the Cubans of 1898 that opposition to Cuba Libre appeared as nothing less than a betrayal of national ideals. Congressional sentiment could not fail but to respond to these national stirrings. The de Lôme letter and the destruction of the *Maine* served to fix in the American mind the Cuban charge of Spanish villainy.[1]

In early April, the White House recognized that it could no longer stem the congressional tide.[2] The Cuban rejection of the American-inspired cease fire, moreover, left no reason to postpone intervention. Every moment the president delayed affirming his leadership over Congress increased the likelihood of congressional obstruction of White House objectives and the forfeiture of executive claim over foreign policy. Caught between Cuban rejection of the armistice and the approaching rainy season on the one hand, and a rebellious Congress determined to recognize Cuban independence on the other, McKinley countered to affirm his leadership and embarked purposefully on an interventionist course.

On April 11, the president forwarded the long awaited war message to Capitol Hill. McKinley asked Congress for authorization "to take measures to secure a full and final termination of hostilities between the Government of Spain and the people of Cuba, and to secure in the island the establishment of a stable government, capable of maintaining order and observing its international obligations, insuring peace and tranquility and the security of its citizens as well as our own, and to use the military and naval forces of the United States as may be necessary for these purposes."[3]

180   McKinley's decision to intervene climaxed deliberations begun as early

as the first months of the new Republican adminisration. The structure and purpose of McKinley's proposed intervention were not the hurried results of an administration under siege but, rather, the products of careful and deliberate calculation. As early as August 1897, the State Department had outlined four interventionist options available to the president: (1) amicable intervention to restore peace and the status quo ante; (2) interposition of effective office to keep the peace while belligerent parties negotiated a settlement; (3) intervention to protect American interests in the face of Spain's inability to do so; and (4) intervention on behalf of one side against the other. Only the last two provisions, the State Department advised the White House, had any direct relevance to the Cuban situation. "We may either intervene . . . for the protection of our own endangered interests against the malice or impotence of the contending parties in Cuba," the State Department counseled, "or we can intervene as a political act to ally ourselves with the Cubans and aggressively engage Spain."[4] McKinley endorsed the State Department judgment but soon thereafter substantively modified options two and four. The president, too, allowed as admissable only two actions, but in slightly different terms. In his first annual message to Congress that following December, McKinley alluded to an "intervention in favor of one or the other party," omitting, however, any reference to an intervention specifically to assist the Cubans as the State Department version had originally proposed.[5] The second available interventionist option, the president indicated, was a "neutral intervention to end the war by imposing a rational compromise between the contestants."[6]

The "neutral intervention" had early captured the policy imagination of the White House. A "neutral intervention" allowed the United States to impose a settlement without obligation, real or implied, to any particular solution or party. More specifically, a "neutral intervention" had the virtue of allowing Washington to undertake intervention without a prior commitment to Cuban independence while conferring on the United States complete freedom of action to determine the ultimate fate of the island in whatever manner it saw fit.

By early April, the purpose of American intervention emerged in sharp relief. Washington viewed the "neutral intervention" as a means through which to establish, by virtue of conquest, American claims of sovereignty over Cuba. "The forcible intervention of the United States . . . ," McKinley announced to Congress on April 11, "involves . . . hostile constraint upon both the parties to the contest."[7] Indeed, McKinley's war message, directed at both Spaniards and Cubans, sought to establish the grounds upon which to neutralize the two competing claims of sovereignty in order to establish a third by force of arms. This was the outstanding virtue of the "neutral intervention" to which the administration had committed itself by April. "We have already canvassed recognition of independence," the State Department reported on April 7, "with an adverse conclusion." The "neutral intervention" would effectively concede to the United States control of the island. "It would make a notable difference in our conduct of hostilities in Cuba," the State Department advised, "if we were to operate in territory transiently ours by conquest, instead of operating in the territory of a recognized sovereign with whom we maintain alliance." Nor was the State Department unmindful of the long-term advantages that transient conquest would confer on the United States:

We would be free, if successful, to dictate the terms of peace and control the organization of an independent government in Cuba. We could hold the Cuban territory in trust until, with restored tranquility a government could be constitutionally organized which we could formally recognize and with which we could conclude a treaty regulating our future relations to and guarantee of the Republic.[8]

By early April, the cornerstone of the intervention policy had been set in place. Even as McKinley worked to complete the final draft of his message, the administration disclosed the key features of official thinking. On April 5, a White House spokesman acknowledged that President McKinley opposed recognizing "a people of whom we know practically nothing." Once in Cuba, the administration argued, the United States would decide "whether the insurgents are capable of a government of their own. If they are not, then we can establish a government we think will be stable and which will continue peace and order on the island. . . . We do not think it advisable to grant independence to the Cubans until we get to Havana and know more about the condition of affairs and the men now running the insurgent government."[9] Two days later, the proadministration *New York Tribune*, owned by Whitelaw Reid, reflected White House thinking editorially. "It must be frankly stated," the *Tribune* insisted, "that they have not yet sufficiently established their authority to entitle them to recognition." The insurgents, the *Tribune* continued, represented only a small minority of the population—a minority guilty of acts "which this Government could never approve." The destruction of property, the Cubans' conduct of the war, and separatist indifference to foreign interests, concluded the *Tribune*, hardly "inspired confidence in Washington that they possess the attributes necessary to qualify for independence."[10]

Even if the Cubans, in the end, proved worthy of U.S. support, the administration was unwilling to forfeit in advance American control over the island. As early as February 1897, Secretary of State John Sherman had privately predicted the necessity of American intervention in Cuba. This intervention, Sherman counseled McKinley, should be "controlled by commercial interests rather than by sympathy with a people struggling for liberty."[11] Premature recognition of Cuban independence, Washington feared, promised to deprive the United States of the leverage necessary to establish later a government consistent with American interests. Republican Senator Thomas Carter, a defender of McKinley's policy and a frequent visitor to the White House during the April deliberations, insisted that "the United States ought to take the island out of the hands of the Spaniards, and then arrange for its future government, reserving to itself the right to establish a protectorate, if need be, in order that no harm may come to American capital that will certainly be attracted to the island."[12] Other proadministration senators communicated White House fears that the insurgent republic was not "capable of [bringing] stability and power" to Cuba. Another government might be required, one which "would guarantee to the United States the tranquility and security which we are seeking." To wit:

If the United States is to intervene for the pacification of Cuba
it should do so free-handed; it should not tie itself fast to a form
of government which afterwards may prove an impediment to
those reforms which ought to be effected in the island. The
United States ought to be free to insist upon such a government
as will be of practical advantage to the United States, not by
way of annexation, but in those matters of commercial advantages which, from the location of the island and the relations of
this country to it, we ought to expect. If we recognize the independence of this government now, it is free to grant us those
privileges or to deny them. If it denies them when we think we
are entitled to them, we can only get them by the assertion of
force, which certainly would be embarrassing.[13]

On April 11, 1898, the long-awaited presidential message outlined the administration's policy in detail. "Nor from the

standpoint of expediency," McKinley insisted firmly, "do I think it would be wise or prudent for this Government to recognize at the present time the independence of the so-called Cuban Republic." McKinley continued:

Such recognition is not necessary in order to enable the United States to intervene and pacify the island. To commit this country now to the recognition of any particular government in Cuba might subject us to embarrassing conditions of international obligations toward the organization so recognized. In case of intervention our conduct would be subject to the approval or disapproval of such government. We would be required to submit to its direction and to assume to it the mere relation of a friendly ally.

The American purpose in Cuba, McKinley concluded, consisted of a "forcible intervention . . . as a neutral to stop the war."[14] Having submitted his message, the president let it be known that he would veto any congressional resolution providing for the recognition of Cuban independence.[15]

II   Even before the president's message reached Congress, the substance if not the details of the administration's proposed intervention had been the subject of informed speculation among pro-Cuban forces in Washington. The Cuban representation in the United States reacted first and made no attempt to conceal its astonishment and ire. What possible reason could the United States have for withholding recognition of Cuban independence, separatists asked suspiciously, unless it was for the purpose of annexation. McKinley's message aroused separatist misgivings and suggested the presence of sinister motives. Horatio S. Rubens reported learning from a "reliable authority" that in the course of the intervention in Cuba, a "pretense will . . . be made of seizing the Philippines and Puerto Rico," but that the "real object" was to be the annexation of Cuba.[16] "The very fact that recognition is expressly withheld now," Rubens warned, "implies the possibility that it may be permanently withheld." The Americans would defeat Spain, he predicted, occupy Cuba, and organize a plebiscite in which the "presence and pressure of federal force would determine the election in favor of annexation."[17]

The intervention proposed by the White House, Cubans stated flatly, was unacceptable. "We will oppose any intervention which does not have for its expressed and declared object the Independence of Cuba," Gonzalo de Quesada proclaimed.[18] Horatio S. Rubens's comments were direct and unequivocal. Speaking for the insurgent provisional government and the Liberation Army, Rubens announced the necessity of having "to go a step further" and bluntly warned American authorities that an intervention along the lines suggested by the White House would be regarded as "nothing less than a declaration of war by the United States against the Cuban revolutionists." Rubens detailed the implications of the president's policy:

> If intervention shall take place on that basis, and the United
> States shall land an armed force on Cuba soil, we shall treat
> that force as an enemy to be opposed, and, if possible, expelled,
> so long as the recognition of a free Cuban republic is withheld. I
> do not mean to say that the Cuban army will assemble on the
> coast to resist the landing of Federal troops, but that it will re-
> main in the interior, refusing to cooperate, declining to ac-
> knowledge any American authority, ignoring and rejecting the
> intervention to every possible extent. Should the United States
> troops succeed in expelling the Spanish; should the United
> States then declare a protectorate over the island—however
> provisional or tentative—and seek to extend its authority over
> the government of Cuba and the army of liberation, we would
> resist with force of arms as bitterly and tenaciously as we have
> fought the armies of Spain.[19]

III   McKinley's proposed intervention did not fare much better on Capitol Hill. His refusal to recognize Cuban independence, long a sacred and emotional cause in Congress, made the administration's motives immediately suspect.[20] Days of intense politicking and maneuvering followed. Administration opponents made repeated attempts to secure congressional approval of resolutions recognizing Cuban independence. Throughout the floor battle in Congress, the White House sustained its determination to oppose Cuban independence.

By mid-April, McKinley grudgingly accepted a compromise. In the course of congressional deliberations, a House-Senate conference committee agreed to forego recognition of Cuban independence for the administration's acceptance of the amendment introduced by Senator Henry M. Teller of Colorado. The final Joint Resolution represented a compromise of all parties concerned. Article I proclaimed that the "people of the island of

Cuba are and of right ought to be free and independent"—but did not provide for recognition of the Cuban republic. Article II demanded that Spain immediately relinquish control of Cuba, and Article III directed the president to use military force if necessary to achieve this end. Article IV, the Teller Amendment, specified that the United States "hereby disclaims any disposition of intention to exercise sovereignty, jurisdiction, or control over said island except for pacification thereof, and asserts it determination, when that is accomplished, to leave the government and control of the island to its people."[21]

A variety of factors converged to thwart the "neutral intervention" proposed by the White House. McKinley's silence on the question of Cuban independence aroused in the minds of many legislators the fear that the administration planned to annex the island. Opposition to annexation drew support from many quarters for many reasons. Many legislators supported the ideal of Cuban independence out of personal conviction and in response to their constituents' concerns. Other factors intervened, however. Racial considerations influenced congressional resistance to annexation. "There was," one McKinley biographer wrote, "a general repugnance to the idea of admitting to the Union an alien and insubordinate people Roman Catholic in faith, with a large admixture of Negro blood."[22] Advocates of Cuban independence, moreover, as well as members of the Cuba lobby, held bonds in the Cuban republic. An examination of the Estrada Palma papers a decade later revealed that during congressional deliberations in April the Cuban junta had freely distributed bonds valued at $50 million to "persons of influence and position" in Congress, redeemable only at the time of Cuba's independence.[23]

At stake too, was the fate of the fledgling but important domestic beet sugar industry. The Cuban insurrection in 1895 and the subsequent sharp decline of Cuban sugar imports had given the beet sugar industry in the United States a powerful boost. The Dingley Tariff of 1897, levying a duty on refined sugar, provided additional incentives to expand beet sugar production. Some twenty states, including California, Utah, Oregon, Colorado, Michigan, Pennsylvania, New York, and New Jersey, had developed substantial beet sugar industries. Many state legislatures had invested considerable public funds through subsidies and bounties in beet sugar production. In March 1898, even as Congress debated about Cuba, the New Jersey legislature appropriated $50,000 to subsidize its beet growers. Only weeks before the Joint Resolution, New York lawmakers passed a five-year plan providing for an annual $50,000 bounty for beet sugar producers.[24] As early as 1893, the Mormons had invested nearly three-quarters of a million dollars in Utah beet sugar production. One new beet sugar factory in California cost $2.7 million.[25] By 1899 there were thirty-one factories in twenty states representing $21 million, producing 80,000 tons of sugar.[26]

Beet sugar had become a flourishing enterprise in the United States, an industry that would not survive the onslaught of cheap cane sugar following the annexation of Cuba. "The effect on our own beet would be disastrous," one worried observer wrote.[27] Only months before Congress debated McKinley's war message, domestic beet sugar producers had suffered a major setback as a result of the annexation of Hawaii. The "beet sugar industry," one sugar trade journal reported in January, "of momentously increasing importance in the States, has sent its agents to Washington, who are lobbying against the admission of Hawaii as a State or territory, on the ground that the free import of Hawaiian sugar will help spoil their markets."[28] In Salt Lake City, the *Desert Evening News* followed the debate on the Hawaiian annexation with great apprehension, fearing that "competition with the cheap native product, made from cane," would do great injury to Utah beet.[29]

Few had any illusions about the economic consequences attending the annexation of Cuba. In January 1894, Senator Henry M. Teller had proclaimed bluntly: "I am in favor of the annexation of Cuba."[30] In the four years that followed, beet sugar had rapidly developed into a major industry in Colorado, a consideration that no doubt contributed to Teller's zeal in supporting the Cuban independence in 1898. Three years later, Teller was equally ardent in his opposition to the reciprocity treaty with Cuba for fear of its adverse effects on Colorado's beet sugar industry.[31]

The Dingley Tariff on refined sugar also protected the interests of the Sugar Trust. The prospect that Cuba would be annexed, and thereby allow refined Cuban sugar to enter the United States duty free and in unlimited quantity, threatened the Sugar Trust with ruin. The powerful sugar lobby, thus mobilized, vigorously opposed any war resolution that did not specifically subject Cuba to continued tariff regulation.[32]

The commitment to Cuban independence rested fragilely on a fleeting but convenient convergence of special interests. The administration's initial hostility to the final form of the Joint Resolution gave way to approval as the White House recognized that, in the end, the Teller Amendment created no serious obstacle to larger policy objectives.[33]

IV   The debate over the question of American intervention had been an enduring source of dispute between the separatist leasdership abroad and the insurgent command in Cuba. The institutional entities around which the forces of Cuba Libre had organized between 1892 and 1895 existed in an unstable coalition, united only by a common but vague commitment to Cuba's independence from Spain. The PRC abroad, on one hand, and the Liberation Army and the provisional government on the other, had not resolved the disparate and contradictory versions of Cuba Libre. Nor had the civil-military agencies in Cuba reconciled their outstanding differences. In 1898, only the most tenuous consensus, held intact by the exigencies of the war, had prevented discord from openly shattering the separatist polity.

The American intervention upset the fragile separatist politicl equilibrium. Most immediately, the American presence introduced into separatist ranks one more power contender advancing one more version of Cuba Libre. To be sure, the American version remained, in mid-1898, undefined and incomplete. But if Washington was unwilling to continue to tolerate Spain's incomplete claim of sovereignty over the island, neither was it prepared to permit Cubans to complete their claim. McKinley's intentions were clear: a declaration of war on both parties of the Cuban conflict and the assertion of a third claim to rule Cuba. This repudiation of the *independentista* version of Cuba Libre, moreover, made the Americans the natural allies of the conservative expatriate representation. One more moderating force had been admitted into separatist circles abroad.

The Joint Resolution consolidated the new alliance. For the émigrés, the war resolution represented a triumphant climax to three years of diplomatic efforts abroad. Cuba's independence from Spain was now a foregone conclusion. Expatriate leaders could not conceal their satisfaction at having achieved what their compatriots in arms had failed to attain in three years. American intervention promised to end the war quickly, while the Joint Resolution appeared to commit the United States to the separatist goals.[34]

The Joint Resolution received the enthusiastic endorsement of the expatriate representation. In New York, the Cuban junta proclaimed its support of the congressional resolution.[35] Days after the passage of the Joint Resolution, Estrada Palma pledged Cuban support of the American war effort. In the name of the Republic of Cuba, but without authorization of the provisional government, Estrada Palma placed the Liberation Army under American military command.[36] In this act, one of far-reaching consequences, the expatriate representation effectively placed the armed *independentista* sector of the separatist polity under the control of a powerful anti-independence third party.

In Cuba insurgent chieftains received the prospects of the American intervention with a disagreeable mixture of misgiving and foreboding, uncertain of the meaning of the Joint Resolution and unconvinced that American intentions in Cuba were entirely free of ulterior motives. The spectre of American intervention had loomed ominously over the insurgent command throughtout the conflict. For the better part of the war, *insurrecto* chieftains had instinctively opposed and consciously resisted direct American participation in the Cuban conflict. Nothing had changed in 1898. American silence on the question of recognition had generally an unsettling impact on many Cubans, and few insurgent chieftains were free of suspicions about American intentions. "The Yankee purpose is not clear to me," provisional President Bartolomé Masó confided to a friend, "I have always seen them as a people who do not work for nothing."[37] Not a few army chieftains confided to private letters and diaries their concern for the ability of Cuban independence to survive the American intervention.[38]

V The American intervention deepened existing tensions within the separatist polity and created new ones. Throughout 1898, the PRC representation had labored abroad without once consulting the separatist leadership in Cuba. Official communication between exile representatives in the United States and the separatist war agencies on the island had all but totally ceased. To be sure, news of developments abroad reached insurgent camps, but through private correspondence and newspaper reports, and was frequently contradictory and always incomplete.[39] It was not until May 10 that insurgent authorities in Cuba learned officially of the American war resolution. It was in this same communication, much to their astonishment and shock, that Cubans learned of Estrada Palma's decision to place the Liberation Army under the command of American authorities.[40]

Indignation was immediate and widespread. Sentiment to annul the PRC commitment led to acrimonious debate, but no agreement. In the end, the provisional government grudgingly accepted the fait accompli, choosing to uphold the ideal of "revolutionary unity" rather than repudiate a commitment made in the name of the provisional republic by accredited representatives abroad. The Council of Government, however, censured Estrada Palma for exceeding his authority. On May 10, Secretary of Foreign Relations Andrés Moreno de la Torre forwarded a detailed set of instructions to the PRC delegation, enjoining Estrada Palma to learn of the "total politics of the United States with respect to Cuba." Moreno also communicated the Cubans' annoyance at the American refusal to recognize

the provisional government. Estrada Palma was instucted to secure clarification of the nature of relations to exist between the United States and
separatist agencies.[41] The provisional government, lastly, voted to dispatch Vice-President Domingo Méndez Capote to the United States to
supersede Estrada as the ranking Cuban representative in the United
States and report directly to the Council of Government.[42]

If Estrada Palma's decision to place Cuban armed forces under American command opened a breach between the Council of Government and
expatriate representation, the government's acquiescence to that decision
deepened the schism between civilian leaders and military chieftains.
Without consultation with the insurgent army command, on May 12, the
Council of Government ordered military chieftains to submit themselves to
the authority of the United States.[43]

Army leaders reacted angrily to the government's decision to elevate
American commanders over Cubans. The civil-military dispute flared
anew. For the insurgent military command, the May 12 decree represented the latest in a long series of affronts to army sensibilities and the
most recent usurpation of military authority.[44]

The army command challenged the government's authority to make this
decision. The provisional government, Máximo Gómez reminded Vice-
President Méndez Capote on May 14, derived its authority from the Army
of Liberation, the body to which it was responsible. It was absurd, Gómez
suggested, for the Council of Government to act as if it derived its authority from some mythical mandate of the people: "This Government is not the
work of an assembly of the people, but one of the army."[45] Government
leaders, Gómez complained to Estrada Palma a month later, "do not constitute anything more than the government of the revolution, and not the
government of the Republic." He concluded: "To me, it has always appeared foolish when I read 'Republic of Cuba.'"[46]

VI   Army complaints to the expatriate representation foretold an
emerging realignment within the separatist polity. Relationships changed
after April. If the provisional government relinquished its authority over
the Liberation Army to the United States, to whom were military chieftains now responsible? Relations between the government and the army,
tenuous throughout the war, underwent new strains. If the military leaders obeyed the May 12 decree, they accepted also the proposition that the
provisional government no longer exercised authority over the army. For
many army chieftains, the government decree corroborated the long-

standing military contention that the supreme authority of the revolution properly resided in the Liberation Army. The provisional government was superfluous and no longer had any reason to exist. "If we accept the intervention," General Calixto García insisted to Estrada Palma, "we accept also that there does not exist in Cuba a Government of the type which the Americans desire to establish, that is to say, we have to recognize with them that we do not have a government given that the Council of Government is incapable of fulfilling the most elementary duties." The provisional government, he added emphatically, no longer had any purpose: the moment the government accepted intervention, it also accepted the American proposition that there did not exist in Cuba an authority capable of effective government. The provisional government, García concluded, "not only . . . accepts the intervention, which is its death sentence signed by McKinley, but also, in fact and without right, renounces its authority over the Chiefs of the Liberation Army."[47] The government, he insisted, represented nothing more than an "oligarchy that never should have been formed."[48] The prospects of American intervention, moreover, now placed the burden of defending Cuban interests and redeeming the cause of Cuba Libre entirely on the Liberation Army. Immediately after the American war resolution, García assumed the task of organizing local government in eastern towns and cities under the control of the *oriental* army.[49] "My only preoccupation," he explained to Estrada Palma, "is to strengthen my good relations with this allied army, and I have no doubt that before the campaign ends, all the people of the United States will be convinced that we do not lack the conditions to govern ourselves and to organize all the institutions necessary to achieve all the requirements of an independent state." Upon the termination of the war, García proposed, the Cubans should convene a national assembly to establish a government that would meet the conditions outlined in the Joint Resolution.[50]

There were deepening problems, too, between the provisional government and the PRC leadership. Estrada Palma reacted with surprise and anger that his activities had met with disapproval and censure in Cuba. The appointment of a special delegation to supersede the authority of the PRC representation angered all expatriate leaders. Many received news of this mission as an expression of no confidence and a usurpation of PRC authority. Emilio Núñez denounced the Méndez Capote mission and urged Gonzalo de Quesada in Washington to "use all the means at your disposal to prevent this man from placing himself in contact with the official element in Washington." Núñez scorned this mission: "He brings ideas that are as puerile as they are troublesome to our interests, for he believes that Cuba does not need the actual cooperation of the Americans."[51]

On the eve of the American intervention, Cuban separatism was a house divided. The estrangement between the Liberation Army and the Council of Government had widened. Placed under the command of American military authorities, insurgent army chieftains now looked directly to the expatriate representation for information concerning American policy. This led inevitably to a growing isolation of the provisional government and the development of closer ties between Cuban representatives abroad and the insurgent army command in Cuba. The provisional government was, indeed, emerging as a superfluous entity of the revolution. The decision to place the Liberation Army under American command, further, blurred lines of separatist authority. In relinquishing its authority over the insurgent armed forces the Council of Government added to the conditions that allowed the United States to continue to ignore the provisional government and deal directly with individual military chieftains. The dispute between the provisional government and the PRC leadership reinforced pro-American sentiment among the exiles. Spurned by the government they had served, exile leaders moved closer to the United States. By late spring, the expatriate leadership and the army command had arrived at similar conclusions—the provisional government represented an obstacle to the resolution of the Cuban question. This, too, was the central assumption of American policy in 1898.

VII   Not a few army chieftains sensed uneasily that the issue of Cuban independence had been swept up in and obscured by larger American policy calculations. The Cuban-American alliance rested on the Joint Resolution, specifically Articles I and IV. Insurgent leaders did not conceal their displeasure at cooperating with a government that denied the recognition of Cuban independence in policy and practice. Only confidence in the stated congressional pledge, outlined in the Joint Resolution, encouraged separatists to believe that the American intervention shared something in common with the Cuban struggle.[52] In Washington, Vice-President Méndez Capote spoke unofficially with members of McKinley's cabinet and received full assurances that the United States intended to honor the Joint Resolution.[53] Gonzalo de Quesada reassured Máximo Gómez that the purpose of the American intervention was defined by the Joint Resolution. "Cuba will be for Cubans," Quesada predicted confidently.[54]

The Joint Resolution served to calm separatist misgivings. Satisfied that the intervention made common cause with separatist goals, Cubans prepared to coordinate joint military operations with their new allies. No matter that the Americans refused to recognize the republic, as long as Washington endorsed the goals for which the republic stood. "It is true," Calixto García conceded, "that they have not entered into an accord with our government; but they have recognized our right to be free and independent and that is enough for me."[55] Whatever else may have separated the Cubans and Americans in April 1898, the Joint Resolution established the common ground upon which collaboration between the two allied armies would rest.

10 The Infelicitous Alliance

Don't ask about the Cubans! The regular army has not use for them. Probably they are capable of any vandalism of which they are accused, but this is not the point. What they want is to see us do the work and themselves reap the fruits.
—Major James M. Bell, First Cavalry, July 1898

The Americans continually fill their newspapers with sympathy for our cause, but what do they do? They sell us arms at good round prices,— as readily as they sell supplies to the Spaniards, who oppress us; but they never give us a thing,—not even a rifle.
—Máximo Gómez, June 1898

The Cubans who have made a pretense at fighting with us have proved worthless in the field and unappreciative of modern conditions and humanity and justice in war. It would be a tragedy, a crime, to deliver the island into their hands.
—*New York Times*, July 29, 1898

I "Our situation is extremely difficult here," an alarmed Estrada Palma wrote Máximo Gómez from Washington in May 1898. The United States, Estrada complained, refused to recognize the Cubans who had fought for three years "as an army or a people or a government." The Americans perceived the insurgent armies as "simply bands, more or less dispersed in conformity with the topography and special circumstances of the land. . . . They expect little to come from the cooperation of those bands, and hardly include them in their campaign plans."[1]

Estrada Palma's concerns were well founded. By mid-May, the cornerstone of American policy had been set in place. Beyond grudging acceptance of the congressional resolution of April 20, the McKinley administration declined to make any further concessions to the separatist cause. The intent of the Joint Resolution notwithstanding, McKinley's preparation for war conformed entirely to the purpose of the policy construct outlined in the original presidential message of April 11. McKinley continued to ignore scrupulously the official agencies of the separatist movement, careful to avoid conceding in practice that recognition that the Americans denied in policy. Having steadfastly resisted the adoption of separatist ends as the basis of the intervention, it was hardly conceivable that the administration would now collaborate with Cubans in any manner that would imply official recognition of separatist politico-military agencies. Indeed, in declaring war on Spain, the United States acquired de facto an ally it refused to recognize with objectives it declined to endorse.

Communication with separatist representatives remained unofficial and informal. American commanders coordinated military plans with individual army chieftains in Cuba. This policy allowed the United States both to ignore the political authority of the provisional government and to disregard the military authority represented in the person of General in Chief Máximo Gómez. In Tampa, American authorities bypassed local separatist agencies in the recruitment of Cubans to serve as pilots and navigators for forthcoming expeditions. In May, Washington despatched Lieutenant Andrew S. Rowan to Oriente to confer directly with General Calixto García and arrange for military cooperation between the American and Cuban armies.[2] In central Cuba, Máximo Gómez held himself in readiness, waiting to learn what his role would be in joint operations. By mid-June, an impatient Gómez protested directly to Estrada Palma, complaining at being kept in ignorance of American war preparations.[3]

A month later, General William R. Shafter, commander of the Fifth Army Corps, conferred with General García at Aserradero, some fifteen miles west of Santiago, to arrange for joint Cuban-American military operations. Shafter and García selected Daiquirí and Siboney as the sites of disembarcation, and García committed Cuban forces to protect the American landing. The two generals also completed the details of the joint Cuban-American operations against Spanish forces in Santiago de Cuba. The two-day conference ended with Shafter promising to relinquish control of Santiago to insurgent Cuban authorities.[4]

II Only the most improbable circumstances and the most tenuous affinity united Cubans and Americans. The two allies shared only an enemy in common—and even the sources of this common enmity divided the allies. Americans entered the war amidst great excitement and enthusiasm. That the national imagination could persuade itself that the call to arms represented a crusade to deliver an oppressed New World people from the clutches of Old World tyranny served further to consecrate the American purpose in Cuba with lofty and selfless motives. Off to war Americans went, for Cuba Libre they believed, in a spirit of elevated purpose, certain of the virtue of the Cuban cause, convinced of the nobility of the Cuban *insurrecto*, confident in their mission of liberation.

Nothing in the preceding three years had prepared Americans for the Cuban reality. This latest Western Hemisphere rebellion against European colonialism, some ninety miles off American shores, could not help but receive anything less than the enthusiastic popular support of the first independent nation of the Americas. For the better part of the Cuban conflict, Americans had indulged themselves with fanciful if faulty historical analogies, detecting in the Cuban struggle a drama not unlike the American war for independence. Not a few Americans found in these apparent similarities the perspective from which to derive meaning and understanding of the Cuban struggle.[5] Cubans, for their part, skillfully and deliberately—and not always in dissimulation—played on these assumptions. The propaganda of expatriate agencies in the United States consciously evoked the affinity of the Cuban struggle for independence and the American revolutionary war. In appealing for popular sympathy, Cubans spared no effort to flatter American historical sensibilities. These analogies fell on receptive audiences. Indeed, both the personalities and the issues of the Cuban conflict were understood through the use of historical surrogates and appeals to the national hagiography. Máximo Gómez evoked George Washington, Tomás Estrada Palma in the United States corresponded to Benjamin Franklin in France. The Assembly of

Jimaguayú in 1895 found its counterpart in the Continental Congress in 1776. To those who charged that the Cubans lacked a fixed site for a permanent government, John Sherman responded that in this detail, too, the Cubans were reminiscent of the Founding Fathers "who assembled at Philadelphia, adjourned to Baltimore, fled to Lancaster, and convened at Yorktown."[6] "The fight for Cuban independence is similar to our own," Congressman William Sulzer of New York proclaimed. Representative James B. McCreary from Kentucky agreed: "The Cuban patriots are fighting for the same rights and independence and home government that our ancestors fought for and won."[7] Senator John W. Daniel spoke of the "gallant revolutionists" engaged in the very cause "which made America a free and independent Republic. It is the cause which threw the tea into Boston Harbor. It is the cause that makes the name of Concord and Lexington ring throughout the world."[8] Senator Benjamin R. Tillman concurred: "They have resisted oppressive taxation and tyranny in the same manner that the American people resisted it in 1775 and 1776."[9]

The American press made its contribution to the process, exalting the Cuban struggle and raising the embattled *insurrecto* to larger than life proportions. For the better part of three years, newspapers had reserved the right half of the front page for moving accounts of Cuban valor and bravery. It soon became difficult for the popular imagination to resist the appeal of the Cuban cause or disregard its overdrawn affinity to the American experience without repudiating something central to the national ethos.

So much had been left unsaid, however. Few Americans perceived the social undercurrents of Cuban separatism or appreciated the tactical imperatives behind insurgent strategy. Few appreciated the terrible toll of three years of guerrilla war on *insurrecto* armies. Somehow, also, through some extraordinary oversight, the matter of race remained unmentioned. For race conscious Americans who championed Cuba Libre, the racial composition of insurgent armies was an inconvenient detail, something best to ignore lest such revelation alienate popular support and lend credence to Spanish claims that portrayed the Cuban insurrection as a race war. Nor had the expatriates in the United States, the Cubans with whom the American public had the greatest contact, offered any hint of what awaited Americans on the island. This was, after all, the most Americanized group of Cubans, educated in the United States, fluent in English, frequently naturalized American citizens, and white. Indeed, these similarities gave the analogies with 1776 a compelling credibility.

"Why, they are just like us," Congressman Sulzer exulted in 1896.[10] Then, too, few American war correspondents had penetrated into the eastern zones of operations, those regions subjected longest to the cruel conditions of a guerrilla war, where insurgent armies consisted of proportionally more Afro-Cubans, where the *independentista* sentiment flourished in its most vigorous form—and the site of the disembarcation of the Fifth Army Corps.

III   The Cuban-American alliance did not survive the first weeks of joint operations. At the front lines of eastern Cuba, along the trenches around San Juan, El Caney, and Santiago de Cuba, initial American contact with Cubans immediately shattered three years of illusions. Expecting to meet the idealized legions of Cuba Libre, Americans found instead bedraggled throngs of war-weary guerrillas. They did not even look like soldiers. "Our first sight of our Cuban allies was not reassuring," one Rough Rider later recalled. "They were the dirtiest, most slovenly looking lot of men I had ever seen."[11] Theodore Roosevelt later remembered Cuban insurgents as "a crew of as utter tatterdemalions as human eyes ever looked on."[12] "There was hardly a suggestion of a uniform in the whole command," correspondent George Kennan reported; "most of the men were bare-footed, and their coarse, drooping straw hats, cotton shirts, and loose, flapping cotton trousers had been torn by thorny bushes and stained with Cuban mud."[13] The Cubans "wore clothes something like Adam and Eve wore," one American observed; another soldier compared Cubans to "cave-dwellers."[14] "Half-starving ragamuffins" and "a collection of real tropic savages," war correspondent Stephen Crane wrote; "a queer lot," an American soldier confided to his diary. "Dirty, torn, and ragged . . . barefooted, emaciated and apparently half starved," a correspondent reported. "I think that 80 percent of them are the worst specimens of humanity I ever saw," one astonished army medic asserted; "a majority of them are ignorant and very filthy." "A motley crew they were," one infantryman later wrote, "ragged and half starved." The Cuban "soldiers go around half-naked," a correspondent noted disconcertingly. Another writer remarked that his "innate modesty was somewhat shocked at a comparative nudity that did not seem to worry the native." George Kennan, earlier sympathetic to the Cubans, could not conceal his disillusionment: "The Cubans disappointed me, I suppose, because I had pictured them to myself as a better dressed and better disciplined body of men, and had not made allowance enough for the hardships and privations of an insurgent's life."[15]

And then, the issue of race. "They are nearly all half-naked," one soldier exclaimed, "and a large proportion are of negro blood."[16] Upon first encounter with Cubans in Tampa, one American soldier remarked that "all coons looked alike."[17] One American officer later recalled that insurgent forces in Daiquirí "were all negroes and the most ragged, hungry and motley looking crowd we had ever seen."[18] "The Cuban soldiers were almost all blacks and mulattos and were clothed in rags and armed with every kind of rifle," Roosevelt noted.[19] "The valiant Cuban!" and American lieutenant scoffed. "He strikes you first by his color. It ranges from chocolate yellow through all the shades to deepest black with kinky hair." But color was only the first in a series of features that struck this American officer: "The next thing you notice is the furtive look of the thief. . . . Next you notice that he is dirty. . . . He is infested with things that crawl and creep, often visibly, over his half-naked body, and he is so accustomed to it that he does not even scratch."[20]

Americans arriving in Cuba in 1898 also lacked an understanding of the nature of insurgent military operations and failed to appreciate the particular genius of the Cuban war effort. The palpably few military achievements registered by separatist arms were attributed immediately to the deficiency of the insurgent operations if not of Cuban character. "After they had been fighting for three years," one correspondent commented derisively, "they held no important city, had captured no important stronghold, had won no important battle."[21] These impressions would later encourage Americans to believe that the Cubans had accomplished nothing in three years and that the intervention alone determined the outcome of the war.

If separatist strategy passed by unappreciated, insurgent guerrilla tactics earned the Cubans universal and unqualified contempt. Cuban reliance on ambush and sabotage, the destruction of property, and the severity of *insurrecto* justice offended the conventional military sensibilities of the American allies. "They are obviously a wretched mongrel lot," one writer asserted, "devoid of any idea of what civilized warfare means."[22]

Americans drew a number of early conclusions from these initial contacts with Cubans. Roosevelt determined "at a glance" from the appearance of Cubans that insurgent troops "would be no use in serious fighting."[23] Devoted to conventional warfare, American soldiers and the accompanying war correspondents deprecated the qualities of the insurgent armies. "They are the most worthless . . . a lot of bushwackers extant," Captain Frank R. McCoy wrote his parents.[24] Lieutenant J. W.

Heard believed the Cubans "untrustworthy" while correspondent Richard Harding Davis concluded that Cubans were "worthless." If not all Americans agreed with a cavalry major who denounced the Cubans as of "no use," most seemed to agree with Stephen Bonsal's contention that the Cuban did "not understand discipline" and, hence, could not be relied upon.[25]

And when the fighting ended, most Americans were unanimous: the Cubans had contributed nothing to the victory over Spain. "While the freedom of Cuba was being decided under their very eyes," one reporter wrote with undisguised scorn, "they stood by, inefficient, inactive. The rewards were theirs, but the Americans made the sacrifice. By the blood of the Americans the victories were won."[26] "There is one point on which the officers of the Fifth Army Corps are unanimous," the *New York Tribune* correspondent cabled, "and that is in pronouncing the so-called Cuban army an utterly useless ally."[27] "The Cubans did little or no fighting," the *New York Times* reporter wrote in early August. "The insurgent army, therefore, has borne no testimony to its desire for a free Cuba. If it wants it, it was not willing, in the presence of a magnificent opportunity to fight for it, or make any sacrifice for it."[28] When asked later to evaluate the contribution of the Cubans during the war, General Samuel B. M. Young, a cavalry brigade commander in Santiago, responded categorically: "They were of no use to me whatever."[29] Theodore Roosevelt agreed. "We should have been better off if there had not been a single Cuban with the army," Roosevelt later insisted. "They accomplished literally nothing, while they were a source of trouble and embarrassment."[30] General William R. Shafter privately concurred. "I have not said anything about the action of Cuban troops," Shafter informed the adjutant general, "because I knew the feeling in the United States about the *poor* Cubans; but I will say to you that they were of no earthly service to me."[31] Commenting on the "little aid" the Americans had received from the Cubans, one writer later determined that racial factors explained why Cubans made such "very weak allies." "They were of another race and the greater part of them were unable to understand the steady nerve and the businesslike habits of their American rescuers."[32]

Neither the condition of Cuban troops nor the organization of the insurgent army, however, had as much to do with the displacement of separatist forces from the front lines as did the American determination to minimize Cuban participation in military operations. In fact, the decision to restrict Cuban participation in the war effort to a subordinate support role, giving expression in practice to what the Americans were already calling the

"Spanish-American War," was made in Washington soon after the passage of the Joint Resolution. The American command determined to limit Cubans to ancillary roles, including rear guard detail, scouts, messengers, trench diggers, pack carriers, and sentries.[33] By denying insurgent forces the opportunity to take part in major operations, Washington also minimized the Cuban contribution to the final defeat of Spain and reduced in advance the Cuban claim to participate in the postwar ordering of the island. The American appropriation of the Cuban struggle against Spain served to guarantee uncontested postwar American mastery of Cuba. Washington's determination to avoid establishing formal command over the insurgent armies was based on the fear that such a relationship would extend formal allied status to the Cuban army and confer on insurgent army chieftains formal recognition that would later require the United States to share authority with Cubans. War correspondent Stephen Crane correctly understood the implications if not the cause of these developments. If the Cuban "stupidly, drowsily remains out of these fights," Crane asked rhetorically, "what weight is his voice to have later in the final adjustments? The officers and men of the [American] army, if their feelings remain the same, will not be happy to see him have any at all. . . . It is the worst thing for the cause of an independent Cuba that could possibly exist."[34]

Cuban cooperation was eagerly solicited but never formally ordered. At Aserradero, García pledged to support American forces and informed General Shafter that he and his officers awaited orders. Shafter quickly sought to disabuse the Cuban general that any official relationship existed between the two armies. The United States, Shafter stressed, could not exercise any formal authority over Cuban forces, but, Shafter hastened to add, he would be delighted to accept the Cubans' "voluntary services." To establish some form of parity in this anomalous relationship, Shafter insisted, the United States would compensate Cubans for their "voluntary services" with rations and supplies. Shafter accepted García's offer of assistance conditionally, he later wrote, "impressing it upon him that I could exercise no military control over him except such as he would concede, and as long as he served under me I would furnish him rations and ammunition."[35]

In both policy and practice, the United States refused to recognize the Cuban army, denying the existence of the formal Cuban military organization to which it was allied. Instead, the War Department coded commands as informal expressions of "wishes" and "preferences" and dealt with

Cuban army leaders as individual chieftains who, in return for supplies, volunteered their services to the American command.[36] Adjutant General Henry C. Corbin specifically warned Shafter "against putting too much confidence in any persons outside your own troops."[37] Colonel Arthur L. Wagner, a cavalry officer at Santiago, later wrote that he was "enjoined to be extremely careful to avoid in every way anything that might be construed as a recognition by my superiors of the Cuban forces as the army of an independent power or belligerent nation."[38]

American actions quickly antagonized Cubans. Calixto García early feared the displacement of the insurgent army and understood its implications. "We must fight side by side the Americans on the front lines," García insisted as early as June 1898, "and not ever permit the American flag to fly without having at its side the Cuban flag."[39]

Denied participation in military operations, Cubans rejected their assigned roles as hirelings and orderlies toiling behind American lines for a daily allotment of rations. Cubans balked at assignments that would have converted the Liberation Army into a gang of unskilled workers dependent on American handouts. "My men are soldiers, not laborers," García protested.[40] Displaced at the front lines, unwilling to perform the menial tasks assigned to them by Americans, it soon appeared to many American observers that the Cubans had taken advantage of the American presence to retire from the war altogether. Resentment among American soldiers mounted. "You observe the intense pride of this Cuban libre," one American officer wrote sarcastically in his diary. "It is manifested the very first time you suggest anything like manual labor—even for such purpose as camp sanitation, carrying rations, or for any other purpose. His manly chest swells with pride and he exclaims in accents of wounded dignity, 'Yo soy soldado!' Still his pride does not get him knowingly under fire."[41] Reporters, too, joined the troops and openly denounced the Cubans in their despatches. "The suggestion that they help build roads was received with haughtiest scorn," the *New York Tribune* correspondent wrote mockingly. "Soldiers of Cuba Libre felling trees, shoveling earth and moving stones! The idea was not to be entertained."[42] James Langland, writing for the *Chicago Daily News*, captured the prevailing mood of Americans in Cuba: "So while the United States regulars and volunteers have been straining their muscles to the utmost and risking their health, if not their lives, . . . the natives, many of whom are stout, able-bodied men, have stood by idly watching them or have been busy in drawing rations for themselves and their families."[43]

Scorn for the Cuban insurgents turned quickly to suspicion of Cuban motives. Piqued American sensibilities could not admit that Cubans, who neither conformed to American standards of soldiering nor discharged even the most fundamental tasks of the joint military operations, were possessed of genuine patriotic sentiment. Cubans were not, as the Americans had been led to believe, inspired by love of liberty but by the lure of looting. Cuban actions, Americans deduced, betrayed the presence of self-serving if not sinister aims lurking behind separatist arms. Cubans had embarked on revolution simply for the opportunity to sack and plunder, some Americans concluded. Or perhaps, other Americans believed, the insurgent leadership represented nothing more than a disgruntled political clique in search of jobs. "From the highest officer to the lowliest 'soldier,'" one American wrote, "they were there for personal gain."[44] Another American took note of the "villainous-looking face" of the Cuban army and concluded: "Patriots! Oh, yes, but on either side of the fence."[45]

The ultimate American scorn was not long in coming: Cuban soldiers had discredited their sex—they had not properly earned their gender. In the "qualities which make for manhood," one American correspondent wrote, "their organized forces seemed mean in comparison with American regiments."[46] "I have seen degradation in negro slaves," one returning artillery officer remarked, "but never have I seen such degradation as a Cuban exhibits in everything that means manhood."[47] "In courage," correspondent George Kennan wrote from Santiago, "in honesty, in capacity, and in all that goes to make true manhood, . . . American soldiers were immeasurably superior to Cubans."[48] The Associated Press correspondent in Santiago summed up American attitudes succinctly: "The more our commanding officers see of the Cubans the less they appear to think of them as soldiers or as men."[49]

The apparent absence of Cubans from the front lines, further, produced the final transfiguration of separatism: a denial that Cubans existed at all. "The Cuban soldier is a myth," General H. S. Lawton proclaimed in July, "an evanescent dream."[50] Stanhope Sams, the *New York Times* correspondent in Cuba, played on this theme in several lengthy despatches. On July 29: "There is *no* Cuba. There is no Cuban people. There are no freemen here to whom we could deliver this marvelous land."[51] On August 7: "There is no 'Cuban people'; no Cuban aspiration; no Cuban sentiment. Indeed, there could be discovered no 'Cuban people' where the United States sent its fleets and armies to find them, to liberate them, and to aid them in establishing another free republic among the nations of the world. . . . I ask where is the Cuban Nation, and if there really is or can be a Cuban people."[52]

IV   But disenchantment with the alliance was not confined exclusively to American camps. For the *insurrectos*, contact with Americans confirmed their worst fears. Far too many American officers, the Cubans sensed uneasily, moved in their midst brusquely, preemptively, and, worst of all, indifferent if not unsympathetic to the separatist cause. Máximo Gómez had never concealed his distrust of the United States. The Dominican generalisimo had denounced Americans as hypocrites, a people pleading, on one hand, public sympathy with the Cuban cause and, on the other, intercepting relief expeditions originating in the United States.[53] American troops were unnecessary, Gómez had insisted from the outset. The insurgent command had asked only for arms and supplies to complete the task of liberation.[54] Why, insurgent army leaders asked cynically, did the United States wait so long to come to their assistance? The intervention at the precise moment many Cubans believed the end near made American motives suspect.[55]

The insurgent army chieftains had neither desired nor asked for U.S. intervention. Cubans greeted the arrival of the Americans without enthusiasm. Americans were irked by the coolness of the Cuban reception. Anticipating adulation, they found indifference; expecting homage they encountered hostility. Weary after some three years of war, wary of the American purpose in Cuba, Cuban troops conveyed little of the gratitude their would-be deliverers deemed appropriate to the circumstances. One American reporter commented on the "sour and sullen" mood of Cuban *insurrectos*. Another writer noted that "the men we came to free from Spanish thraldom, silently threaded their way through our soldiers.[56] "One must not suppose that there was any cheering enthusiasm at the landing of our army here," Stephen Crane cabled from Cuba. On the contrary, the Cubans looked at the Americans "stolidly, almost indifferently."[57] One correspondent found Cubans "vain and jealous"; another described the insurgents as "conceited."[58]

Conscious of the self-proclaimed role of liberators, Americans took umbrage at this sullen reception greeting their arrival in Cuba. "The American soldier," Stephen Crane wrote, "thinks of himself as a disinterested benefactor, and he would like the Cubans to play up to the ideal every now and then. . . . He does not really want to be thanked, and yet the total absence of anything like gratitude makes him furious."[59] These injured sensibilities soon turned to anger. "You would expect them to be filled with gratitude towards us who are about to redress their wrongs," one writer asserted plaintively. "But that is not so."[60]

By mid-summer, outright contempt for Cubans had become common-place behind American lines. "The Cubans are a dirty, filthy lot," one American officer complained to a friend at home.[61] Cuban insurgents "hear nothing but words of scorn from our men as they pass," the Associated Press correspondent in Santiago reported. "Even our officers no longer conceal their disgust for their allies, and it is understood that the warm friendship displayed toward them at first has now turned to contempt. . . . The name of Cuban is usually wreathed with camp profanity, and rarely is a kind word spoken of them.[62] "A wretched mongrel lot," one reporter wrote contemptuously. "Mango-bellied degenerates," an American officer uttered in disgust. At the Fifth Army Corps headquarters, the *New York Tribune* correspondent overheard American officers describe Cubans as "a pack of wingless vultures."[63] "He is a treacherous, lying, cowardly, thieving, worthless, half-breed mongrel," one American officer of the Fifth Army Corps concluded; "born of a mongrel spawn of Europe, crossed upon the fetiches of darkest Africa and aboriginal America."[64] From the outskirts of Santiago, Stephen Crane wrote: "It becomes necessary to speak of the men's opinion of the Cubans. To put it shortly, both officers and privates have the most lively contempt for the Cubans. They despise them. They came down here expecting to fight side by side with an ally, but this ally has done little but stay in the rear and eat army rations, manifesting an indifference to the cause of Cuban liberty which could not be exceeded by some one who had never heard of it."[65]

V   The surrender of Santiago de Cuba in mid-July brought the developing estrangement between the allied armies to the breaking point. American operations against the Spanish-held eastern capital had not fared well. By the end of the first week in July, the American army faced a setback of major proportions in the first significant operation of the war. Shafter was himself virtually incapacitated by the heat and illness; throughout the siege, the 300-pound American general did not venture much beyond walking distance of his tent. Conditions among American troops had become desperate. Shortages of food, medicine, and supplies were critical; inadequate hospital facilities compounded the crisis. The daily tropical rains, too, demoralized and disabled. The rain pelted American forces unmercifully, filling the trenches with water ankle-deep. In early July, the enemy was no longer the Spanish army but, instead, time and the elements. Wholly vulnerable to the climate, without proper food rations and adequate medicinal supplies, American troops succumbed swiftly to disease and illness. Malaria, typhoid, and dysentery took their toll on American lives. And on July 6 the dreaded quarantine flag was raised ominously behind American lines—yellow fever had struck.[66] One writer gave graphic description to conditions behind American lines:

The sultry air grew still sultrier. From the trampled, beaten, crushed, tropical undergrowth rose sickening odors and heavy miasmatic mists. As the heat grew fiercer, the odors and mists grew heavier. Every life-giving quality of the air seemed to be squeezed out of it, and even the myriad insects and crawling reptiles were quieted. Then, just as the sizzling heat reached a spot where it apparently could go no further and be bearable, a zigzag flash, a thunderclap, and a cataract of ice-cold rain came simultaneously, and every man was soaked and shivering. If the men were marching, they found themselves suddenly wading through swift running streams of cold muddy water. . . . If the men were in camp or the trenches, their fires were put out and every ditch became a mud pool. For two or three hours the icy water fell, until all the hillsides were moving with a floating mass of mud and leaves, and the muddy water in the trails had risen from sole to ankle and from ankle to legging top. Then, as suddenly as it had begun, the storm would come to an end, the sun came out hotter than ever, the wet ground steamed; horrible crawling, flying things filled the muggy air, and from shivering the men passed to gasping.[67]

By mid-summer, war in eastern Cuba had come to a grim standstill outside Santiago—a contest of wills pitting the determination of the beseiging army against the durability of the beseiged. The scales quivered in the balance, each army weighed down with a sense of disaster. A prolonged siege had calamitous implications for the United States. On July 3, Theodore Roosevelt urgently appealed to Washington for help. "We are within measurable distance of a terrible military disaster," Roosevelt cabled. "We *must* have help—thousands of men, batteries, and *food* and ammunition."[68] Four days later, the tone of Roosevelt's despair deepened: "The lack of transportation, food and artillery has brought us to the very verge of disaster."[69] Alarm swept through the American command. After some ten days, Shafter contemplated withdrawing to a new position some five miles south of Santiago—palpable admission of American failure.

But pressure, too, was building behind Spanish lines in Santiago. Weeks of artillery bombardments had reduced much of the city to rubble; a scarcity of food, medicine, and supplies had created desperate conditions for both Spanish armed forces and the civilian population.[70]

In mid-July, the opportunity to convert a disaster into a triumph presented itself unexpectedly to the United States. On July 13, General José Toral, the Spanish commander in Santiago, communicated his willingness to negotiate a conditional surrender. He offered to surrender Santiago and all the forces under his command with the proviso that the officers and men be permitted to retain possession of their personal property and side arms. Spanish troops and Cubans in the service of Spain, moreover, were to be assured of the opportunity to remain in Cuba after the war if they desired. Lastly, he asked for guarantees of safety for his soldiers and the civilian population against the insurgent armies.[71]

Spanish conditions for surrender were not initially satisfactory to the War Department. But neither were the alternatives. By American intelligence estimates, Spanish forces had sufficient provisions to last some two months. Spain's terms, General Nelson O. Miles cabled the Secretary of War, were not unreasonable. Conditional surrender, more important, obviated the necessity of a prolonged siege that had potentially disastrous repercussions for the United States.[72] On July 15, negotiations commenced.

By the proposed terms of the surrender, the United States would assume control of key cities and towns in Oriente province. Incumbent civil officials and local constabulary authorities were to be ratified in their positions. All residents of the province passed directly under the authority and protection of the United States.[73] On July 17, a joint Spanish and American commission completed the terms of capitulation.

VI   The exclusion of Cuban representatives from the negotiations leading to the surrender of Santiago was the first in a series of interrelated incidents that brought the brewing dispute between the allies into full public view. On July 14, García learned that the Cubans would neither share in the municipal administration of Santiago, as promised at Aserradero, nor receive control of liberated Cuban territory, as promised in the Joint Resolution. Stunned at this news, García demanded from

Shafter a clarification of the status of Santiago and learned, to his horror, that Cuban troops would not be permitted into the city, now considered by the American command as territory conquered by the United States and "part of the Union."[74]

To have been excluded from the negotiations and denied the opportunity to participate in the ceremonies attending the formal surrender of Santiago injured already bruised Cuban sensibilities. To have been prohibited from entering the eastern capital, however, a city of powerful emotional significance for the *oriental* insurgent command, and denied a part in municipal administration in favor of incumbent Spanish office-holders, negated the very purpose of Cuban arms. That Santiago was now considered by the Americans as "part of the Union" was the final outrage to the eastern insurgent command. "I will never accept," General García vowed angrily, "that our country be considered as conquered territory."[75]

The final insult was not long in coming. Several days after the surrender, Shafter publicly justified his decision in terms reminiscent of Spanish colonial truths, namely, that Cubans could not be restrained from massacring unarmed Spanish soldiers, murdering women and children, and plundering the city. Cubans, the Americans insisted, could not be trusted with the security of civilian life and property in Santiago de Cuba.[76]

A wave of indignation and anger swept across insurgent army camps. For many Cubans, Shafter's disposition of Santiago represented an ominous augury. Cuban suspicions about American motives were confirmed; what happened at Santiago offered insurgents a portent of American plans for Cuba.[77] Offended by American actions and accusations, García denounced Shafter and broke publicly with the Americans. The *oriental* army commander assailed Shafter's decision to retain in power the "very same Spanish authorities against whom I have struggled these three years as enemies of Cuban independence." The Cuban general dismissed as "absurd" Shafter's reason for prohibiting his soldiers from entering Santiago. "Allow me to protest against even a shadow of such an idea," García asserted indignantly on July 17. "We are not savages who ignore the principles of civilized warfare. We respect too much our cause to stain it with barbarity and cowardice."[78] Later that day, García forwarded to Máximo Gómez an official protest of American actions accompanied with his resignation. American actions in Santiago, García wrote bitterly, made continued cooperation with the United States impossible. "I am no longer disposed to continue obeying the orders and cooperating with the plans of the American Army, and I do not want it said that I disobey the orders of my government. I have no other form to protest against the attitude of the American government other than to offer my resignation."[79] García encouraged the officers and men under his command to continue to prosecute the war and alerted the insurgent forces against relinquishing any authority to the "army of the intervention."[80] By late July, the allied armies in Oriente had broken relations. The issues of the intervention for both Cubans and Americans had been defined.

VII On August 12, 1898, the United States and Spain formally ended the "Spanish-American War." Again, the Americans purposefully neglected to include their Cuban allies in the peace negotiations. For the second time in as many months, the United States had negotiated an independent and unilateral settlement with Spanish authorities. Since Cubans were not signatories to the peace protocol, however, insurgent armies in Cuba continued military operations. On August 12, the War Department appealed unofficially to the PRC representation in Washington to secure the Cuban ratification of the armistice. Hinting of its desire to move ahead with the pledge contained in the Joint Resolution, Washington stressed the necessity of ending hostilities in Cuba as quickly as possible.[81] Three days later, Estrada Palma accepted the Spanish-American peace protocol, an accord subsequently ratified in Cuba by the provisional government.[82]

The war was over. But it was not certain who had won what. Insurgent army chieftains made no effort to conceal their ire over the provisional government's unilateral decision to accept the peace protocol. For three years, the insurgent command had declined to accept a peace based on anything other than Cuban independence. And in mid-August, too much remained unsettled and undefined. In August 1898 many Cuban army chieftains asked publicly if the central proposition of the armed struggle had not been somehow betrayed.[83]

11   From Allies to Adversaries

The situation has now reached a point where there is practically no communication at all between the two armies, and their relations border on those of hostility rather than the relations which one would suppose would exist between allies.
—*New York Times*, July 20, 1898

We will soon be back to Cuba to thrash the Cubans.
—Anonymous, U.S. Officer, July 1898

None of us thought that [the American intervention] would be followed by a military occupation of the country by our allies, who treat us as a people incapable of acting for ourselves, and who have reduced us to obedience, to submission, and to a tutelage imposed by force of circumstances. This cannot be our ultimate fate after years of struggle.
—Máximo Gómez, June 1899

Peace came and with it our incapacity was declared by the allies, who in time of danger found us competent and treated with us, disposing of our forces and our blood. We now see ourselves relegated to an inferior condition, our banner lowered, our treasury occupied, our men ostracized as useless, our people despised, and our army condemned to misery and to live on charity which the new and victorious master throws to the gutter.
—Enrique Collazo, December 1899

I The August 12 peace protocol formally ended the purpose of the Cuban-American collaboration. It was also true that well before the end of the war, the alliance of virtuous New World forces against the iniquitous Old World power had lost its innocence. It was not simply a matter of victors quarreling over spoils. There was, to be sure, some element of this. But spoils for the interventionist army was home for the revolutionary army. The capitulation of Santiago seemed to suggest that the Cuban war of liberation had been transformed into an American war of conquest. The ensuing dispute served only to confirm this perception among Cubans, giving lie to the presumed common purpose of the Cuban-American collaboration. In the course of these events, the allied armies discovered that they were, in fact, divided by differences of the most insoluble kind. And because, Cubans sensed, relative power capabilities would decide matters absolutely, their continued participation in what was now being called the "Spanish American War" served to tilt the scale against the old enemy only to raise a new one. The sense of betrayal was not long in coming.

But García's denunciation of the United States, followed by the abrupt withdrawal of Cuban forces from joint military operations, encouraged Americans to perceive themselves deserted by the very people whom they had come to rescue. More grist for the worst of American suspicions. Insurgent actions served to fix in the minds of Americans the view of Cubans as an ungrateful rabble.

A new American consensus took shape after Santiago. The Cubans had forfeited all claims to American goodwill, proving themselves unworthy of further American sympathy and undeserving of continued American support. Finding few redemptive qualities in their allies, enthusiasm among American commanders for Cuba Libre and their affection for its advocates in the field waned noticeably. Disillusionment gave way to bitterness. Increasingly, Americans in Cuba perceived themselves victims of a hoax, duped into an unnecessary war to fight for an unworthy cause in behalf of an undeserving people. "Poll the United States troops in the province of Santiago de Cuba today," one correspondent advocated rhetorically two weeks after the fall of Santiago, "and 99 out of 100 will say in almost so many words: "We have brought a gold brick in Cuba Libre.'"[1] American officers reported that the insurgents were "looked upon by all our men who have seen them in their native land as a huge fake."[2] "If they do not get us away from here," one American officer wrote in late July from Santiago, "I fear many more of our brave boys will be left in Cuban soil. Too many have been left already we feel for such a cause which everybody here is satisfied was the result of mistaken sympathies at home."[3] And by the end of the war, most Americans agreed with one correspondent's conclusion: "the Cubans themselves were not worth one gill of the good American blood spilled for their benefit."[4]

As the breach between the allies widened, a new bond between the former enemies developed. If only to enhance the achievement of American arms, the United States conferred newly discovered virtues on the recently vanquished foe. Spanish troops had fought courageously against insuperable odds, Americans proclaimed, displaying throughout the hopeless war courage, valor, and honor. They had been, indeed, worthy opponents, overcome in the end only by a vastly superior army.[5] During negotiations at Santiago, American commanders had developed a new respect for their Spanish counterparts. These were the men to whom the Americans were naturally and inexorably linked by a universal code of the profession of arms and military etiquette. They had negotiated through interpreters but spoke the same professional language. The Spanish had fought fairly and lost honorably—canons of warfare readily understood and appreciated by the victors. These, the Americans discovered, were real soldiers and honorable men, fully entitled to American respect and worthy of admiration.[6]

Nor did generous terms of surrender conceded by the United States pass unappreciated by Spanish authorities. Indeed, Spanish officers and men offered Americans what the Cubans had withheld—gratitude. A sense of solidarity immediately developed between the soldiers of both armies. Spanish soldiers, one observer wrote from Santiago de Cuba, "shook hands with their captors, expressing admiration and respect for those with whom they had so desperately fought."[7] After the surrender of Santiago, fraternization between Spanish and American troops became commonplace. "I met many of the Spanish officers in the restaurants of the city," and American officer later recalled, "and I must admit they were, as a rule, capital fellows, kindly disposed, hospitable, and very gentlemanly."[8] The former enemies commingled cordially, trading souvenirs and exchanging war stories over mixed drinks. The narrow streets of Santiago, the *New York Times* correspondent cabled, were "crowded from morning till night by chattering groups of uniformed Spanish soldiers and crowds of laughing, rollicking men belonging to General Shafter's army. In the numerous airy cafes the officers of the opposing armies lounge through the day."[9] "As I entered Santiago," another reporter wrote, "strolling almost alone among the thousands of Spanish soldiers, I did not hear a single angry or disparaging word against the Americans. I heard only courteous and appreciative expressions."[10]

Goodwill toward American forces spread throughout the entire *peninsular* population of the Oriente capital. American troops marching into Santiago received a warm reception from adulating crowds, of the type characteristically reserved for a victorious army returning home. The *Philadelphia Enquirer* correspondent, James Gordon Bennett, described the "cordial feeling between conquered and conquerors. Their friendship seems to increase rather than diminish." Throughout the city, Bennett wrote, Americans and Spanish walked arm in arm while the exclusive Spanish Club opened its door to American officers. "The invaders are treated more like guests than enemies," he noted.[11] The *New York Tribune* correspondent, too, was struck by the reception Santiago accorded to American forces. "It is hard to tell whether there is more rejoicing among the victors or the vanquished."[12]

It was in the spirit of mutual admiration that Spaniards and Americans discovered they held one last attitude in common: a lively contempt for the Cubans. One departing Spanish infantryman published an open letter to his new friends in the American army, warning the United States against the Cuban "descendants of the Congo and the Guinea" who had "mingled with the blood of unscrupulous Spaniards and of traitors and adventurers."[13] Cubans became easy targets for the disillusioned would-be liberators and the embittered former defenders of colonial rule. The former allies became the object of American scorn—and such easy targets they provided for the culturally imperious and morally superior Americans. "Enterprising American soap-manufacturers," one American writer suggested with scorn, "could obtain splendid advertisement by the cleaning of the Cuban army—officers and men alike—and having pictures of 'before and after' used as illustrations."[14] Spaniards charged—and Americans agreed—that Cuban soldiers were "cowards and freelooters," "pillagers . . . who find living on the country easier than working in the fields or the shops."[15] Spanish and American commanders ridiculed the officer ranks of the insurgent army, scoffing at Cuban commissions as ostentatious displays of misbegotten military authority.[16] Racial slurs became commonplace. "They used to shout 'Nigger, nigger,' and burst out laughing," one Cuban soldier later recalled.[17] In fact, virtually everything about Cubans became objects of ridicule and scorn. "If you were here," one American soldier wrote home, "you would probably laugh yourself to death at the customs of the Cuban people. They live in houses made of palm leaves and bark from coconut trees and they and their children, their horses, goats, chickens, hogs, dogs, cats, parrots, cows, lizards, and furniture all stay under one roof and just as you have seen from photos the children go naked."[18] Writing from Santiago de Cuba in August, the *New York Tribune* correspondent summed up these new developments succinctly: "So great has been the change of feeling here that it seems as if the Spaniards and not the Cubans had been the allies of the United States in the recent campaign around this city."[19]

II The cordiality of the Spanish welcome represented more than simply an expression of grace among the vanquished. For many, the U.S. victory signified a triumph of order over chaos, stability over uncertainty, continuity over disintegration. The new military presence represented the protective interposition of the United States between the Spanish population and their Creole allies, on one hand, and the insurgent Cubans on the other. It mattered little that this was the army of a foreign nationality—and a conquering one at that—for order had its own peculiar universality. The Spanish knew what the Cubans only suspected: the American victory signified a Cuban defeat. As long as the American army remained, Cuban goals were unattainable. The arrival of the United States was greeted in Santiago as nothing less than a God-sent deliverance from the separatist armies and, many hoped, from Cuban independence itself. That the Americans received treatment "more like guests than enemies" gave public expression to Spanish recognition that the United States represented the last hope against Cuban independence—the Americans were indeed guests who the local elites had no desire to see leave; these were liberators to be indulged and befriended, for they represented the only salvation left to the socio-economic order threatened by the forces of Cuba Libre. "Wearers of American uniforms," one percipient correspondent discerned, "are treated with a cordiality as if they had rescued the city from the Cuban army."[20]

In five months, the purpose of the American intervention underwent a dramatic transformation. What began in April as the liberation of Cuba from Spain ended in August as the rescue of Spaniards from Cubans. In more than symbolic terms, the responsibility of protecting the existing colonial order had passed from the Spanish army to the American army. "As I view it," General Shafter acknowledged in late 1898, "we have taken Spain's war upon ourselves."[21]

A striking consensus greeted Americans at the end of the war. Spanish residents immediately transferred their loyalties to the United States and emerged as advocates of indefinite American sovereignty over Cuba. Fearful of Cuban insurgents, at times hysterical in their opposition of Cuban independence, the old loyalist element consistently denied that the Cubans possessed the aptitudes necessary for the rigors of self-government. Spaniards freely offered grim predictions of pillage, race war, and endless vendettas against *peninsulares* by vengeful insurgents—all certain to follow in the wake of independence. "The insurgents demand independence," the Associated Press correspondent in Santiago reported, "but the better classes, the merchants and land owners, dread such a possibility and fervently hope that the United States will retain the reins of government in the island as the only guarantee of stability and prosperity."[22] The *New York Times* reporter discovered that the "higher classes" were "in favor of American annexation, or at least of a permanent American protectorate." Businessmen were opposed to a Cuban government, fearful that independence would result in a "long reign of terror in which all who opposed the insurrection will suffer greatly."[23] The "producing element" in Cuba, a wire service report indicated, had concluded that annexation offered the only alternative to a "selfish ambition, social disorders and political perturbation and conflict" certain to attend self-government.[24]

Immediately after the occupation of Santiago, Spanish merchants and businessmen appealed to American authorities for guarantees of order and stability. In late July, a delegation of businessmen met with General Shafter to learn if the United States planned to retain control of Cuba. If not, the merchant indicated, they would close their shops and businesses and return to Spain. "I have assured them," Shafter wrote to Washington, "that I did not believe that the United States was going to relinquish their [*sic*] hold on Santiago or leave it without a stable and sufficient garrison and suitable government."[25] Several weeks later a delegation of seven of the most prominent merchants of Santiago asked for assurances of a continuation of American rule before committing millions of dollars to replenishing their inventory. "Unless these men are assured of protection," the *New York Tribune* correspondent learned, "they will take no steps in this direction."[26] In Havana, Nicolás Rivero, the editor of the pro-Spanish daily *Diario de la Marina*, delivered a petition signed by several hundred planters, appealing directly to McKinley for the annexation of Cuba.[27] The Marquis de Apezteguía, the head of the Unión Constitucional, insisted that in expelling Spain, the United States had contracted a "moral duty" to guarantee order and stability in Cuba. And the first and necessary step in this direction, Apezteguía insisted, was the "destruction beforehand of all insurgent or insurrection elements."[28]

III In the weeks and months following the fall of Santiago, sentiment against Cubans mounted. Contact with the Spanish served to confirm many of the worst opinions that Americans had formed earlier of the insurgent Cubans. Throughout the remaining weeks of summer and into the early fall, as Spanish and American diplomatic representatives in Paris completed the details of a formal treaty of peace, the two foreign armies in Cuba drew closer to one another. Together the victors and the vanquished commingled felicitously in the last remaining bastions of Spanish colonialism in Cuba—the cities. Both agreed on the necessity of keeping the ravenous insurgent hordes at bay and confined to the interior wilderness. In these twilight hours of the Iberian empire in the New World, the ideological constructs that Spain had employed to justify its rule in war-torn Cuba found renewed vigor in a new occupation authority. Indeed, the ideological baggage of colonial rule survived the transfer of authority and was passed on intact. As early as mid-July, one State Department official predicted bluntly that the United States would soon "be occupying the same attitude toward the Cubans that Spain has maintained for the last two years."[29]

The rupture between the United States and Cuban insurgents was almost complete by the end of August. But for many Americans, the alliance with the insurgent army had one redeeming virtue: it had allowed the United States to discover the true nature of the Cubans. Earlier disparagement of Cubans as soldiers gave way to increasing skepticism that Cubans as citizens possessed the virtues necessary for self-government. "One of the results of the war," one American noted, "is the insight we have gained as to their real qualities, their still underdeveloped capacity for self-government and the kind of treatment they require." Indeed, this "better knowledge" of the Cubans raised "very serious doubt about their being as yet properly qualified for self-government, or being able to maintain a stable government among themselves."[30] The implications of these new revelations were clear. "It is, perhaps, a good thing," a correspondent reported, "that the Cubans have displayed their worthlessness this early in the struggle. Their conduct may furnish an easy solution of the Cuban problem. While our Government disavowed a purpose of conquest, it may be absolutely necessary for us to keep Cuba and make it a part of the United States."[31] One American officer detected divine intervention in these revelations, with unmistakable sanction for the obvious: "Providence has reserved a fairer future for this noble country than to be possessed by this horde of tatterdemalions. Under the impetus of American energy and capital, governed by a firm military hand with even justice, it will blossom as the rose and, in the course of three or four generations, even the Cuban may be brought to appreciate the virtues of cleanliness, temperance, industry, and honesty."[32]

In the weeks that followed the peace protocol, the American supposition of Cuban incapacity for self-government became an imperative for policy. Conditions in Cuba and the insight the Americans claimed to have acquired into the character of the people they had presumed to liberate, factors previously unknown, made consideration of Cuban independence something little short of criminal. It would be at least another generation, General William Ludlow, military governor of Havana, informed President McKinley, before Cubans would be sufficiently fitted for the responsibilities of self-government.[33] General Leonard Wood, military governor of Santiago, agreed and predicted "quite a period of time" before Cubans could assume control of a stable government.[34] Admiral William T. Sampson, a member of the American Evacuation Commission, insisted that the Cubans had no idea of self-government—"it will take a long time to teach them."[35] Some American officials believed Cubans incapable of self-government at any time. "Self-government!" Shafter responded intemperately to a reporter's query. "Why those people are no more fit for self-government than gunpowder is for hell."[36] General Samuel B. M. Young concluded after the war that the "insurgents are a lot of degenerates, absolutely devoid of honor or gratitude. They are no more capable of self-government than the savages of Africa."[37] For Americans like Major Alexander Brodie, the necessity for a protectorate or outright annexation was as self-evident as it was irrefutable. "The Cubans are utterly irresponsible," Brodie insisted, "partly savage, and have no idea of what good government means."[38]

American authorities had given full credence to Spanish allegations. If the Cubans could not be trusted to enter Santiago for fear of plundering, neither could Cubans be entrusted with the responsibilities of self-government—an opportunity, many predicted, the Cubans would use to exact vengeance on their former foes. "If we are to save Cuba," one *New York Times* correspondent exhorted, "we must hold it. If we leave it to the Cubans, we give it over to a reign of terror—to the machete and the torch, to insurrection and assassination."[39] To relinquish the government of the island to the Cubans, one American officer predicted, "would mean to turn over the island to a worse condition than that from which we are seeking to rescue it."[40] The Cuban desire for self-government, Americans suspected, was motivated by a desire to plunder, pillage, and exact reprisals. Cubans, one observer reported, were possessed by the "sole active desire to murder and pillage."[41] The United States, officials proclaimed, would simply not turn the island over to the insurgents for plunder and pillage.

By late summer, the United States discovered another Spanish truth: the insurgents represented only a minority of the population. The corollary to this discovery was immediately self-evident. The United States, professing its commitment to democratic rule, simply could not relinquish the future government of Cuba to a minority faction of the population. "The inhabitants of Cuba," the *New York Tribune* asserted editorially, "are not all insurgents, nor in sympathy with the insurrection. The United States will find it impossible to ask that the . . . insurrectionists only . . . be the future government of the island. . . . They are not the only inhabitants and in all probability not the majority of the permanent inhabitants of Cuba."[42]

One more distinction had to be made: not only were insurgent Cubans a minority, they were a propertyless minority. "We must discriminate between the insurgents and the Cubans," one American counseled. "The Cubans as a whole—meaning all those who have any property, or who expect to live by industry instead of politics—desire annexation to the United States."[43] Only a tiny handful of malcontents, desirous of laying siege to the public treasury and violating private property advocated independence, Americans discovered. Cubans of the "better class," the Associated Press reporter in Cuba wrote, preferred to live under the protection of the United States but were under the influence of a "certain class of rabid orators and breeders of sedition and rebellion against anything smacking of law and order."[44]

Nor were Americans unmindful of the racial dimensions of Cuban separatism. Here, too, Americans discovered one more imperial verity. Madrid's protestation that only Spanish rule prevented the Cuban insurgency from assuming the full proportions of a race war now acquired full credibility among American authorities. If Spain's presence had indeed represented the margin between civilization and chaos, the Americans could morally do no less than to continue to uphold that burdensome responsibility. It was by no means certain, the *New York Times* reporter posited, that a "majority of the people" would submit to an insurgent government; certainly the "producing classes" preferred annexation to "an irresponsible government of half-breeds. The negroes, too, who, in various degrees of mixture, constiture nearly one-half of the population are another uncertain element. . . . We cannot afford to have another Haiti."[45] "Have we any reason to believe," one writer asked rhetorically, "that the insurgents and their sympathizers constituted a majority, or even a strong minority, of the inhabitants of the island? Where is the proof of their numerical preponderance. . . . We could not impose on the inhabitants of Cuba complete political independence . . . if the result of such an act upon our part were the eventual experience by Cuba of the fate of Haiti, we should be held responsible for a crime against civilization."[46] One American resident in Cuba predicted that the "lawful land-owning interest" in Cuba would vote for protectorate status. He continued:

The "Cuba Libre" of the blacks would be a veritable hell upon
earth, a blot upon Christian civilization. Cuba the fair and fer-
tile, to take her place in the family of Nations, must have law,
order, and peace guaranteed by the United States. Cuba to be a
creditable part of the earth must be ruled by a firm hand. A rebellious, beggarly minority, largely the criminal elements of the
island, must be taught that the great law abiding majority have
rights that must be respected.[47]

To concede independence to Cubans, American authorities feared, and allow insurgents to take revenge on their former enemies, would result inevitably in a mass exodus of whites and create in Cuba conditions not unlike those that led to the creation of a black republic in Haiti.[48]

IV   The disenchantment of Americans in Cuba with the insurgents was not long in reaching the United States. During the war, disillusionment among American military authorities was expressed in private official reports to Washington. American correspondents concurred in public. Caught up in the passions of the moment, journalists chronicled in great detail the defects of the Cuban allies. Newspaper editorials reflected despatches from the field. Visitors returning from Cuba and soldiers released from military service denounced the insurgents. Letters from Santiago decrying Cuban treachery appeared in hundreds of newspapers across the country. "The White House," the *New York Evening Post* reported, "is visited daily by men of high stations in public life. . . . The friends and relatives of the American soldiers who have given their lives to the war are being gradually undeceived by their advices from the front, and discovering that the war was not begun for a holy purpose, but for a mixture of self and politics. . . . In plain terms, it has been discovered that there is no Cuban republic outside of the vivid imagination of the Junta."[49] The newspapers that had contributed so powerfully to mobilizing public opinion behind a war in behalf of Cuba Libre discovered after the war that free Cuba was, after all, a dubious proposition. Indeed, the public opinion that had earlier supported Cuban independence underwent remarkable transformation. Months of rising anti-Cuban sentiment had effectively muted popular support for free Cuba.

By the end of the summer the reassessment of the Cubans was completed. Those at home soon shared the opinions of those at the front. Speaker of the House Thomas B. Reed expressed shock upon learning that the much vaunted Cuban army was nothing but an "armed rabble as unchivalrous as it was unsanitary." Former President Grover Cleveland denounced the American alliance with the "most inhuman and barbarous cutthroats in the world." From Emporia, Kansas, editor William Allen White found little to distinguish the Cubans from the Spanish: "Both crowds are yellow-legged, garlic-eating, dagger-sticking, treacherous crowds—a mixture of Guinea, Indian, and Dago. . . . It is folly to spill good Saxon blood for that kind of vermin."[50]

In Washington, the White House congratulated itself for its prescience. Revelations from Cuba, administration spokesmen exulted, had vindicated the president's policy. And, of course, this new information now required reconsideration of American policy toward Cuba. The *Hartford Herald*, published by McKinley's private secretary, John Addison Porter, railed against the Cubans and gave the clearest expression of administration sentiment:

Our Cuban Allies—would we have been saved from calling them such!—are utter failures. They will neither fight nor work. . . . Lucky, indeed, was it for the United States to have as a wall between them and their recognition as an independent government so acute an observer and stanch a statesman as President McKinley. Had it not been for our Chief Magistrate, these good-for-nothing allies of ours would have been made superior in the command of fighting forces to our gallant Miles. . . . Strange it is that for three long years these ingrates have been able to hold off many thousands of Spanish troops. Skulking in inpenetrable morasses is the only tactics that have made this possible. The Government long ceased to put the slightest confidence in anything the insurgents say. . . . President McKinley was right when with all his power he successfully resisted the demand of Congress and of a large section of people that these cowardly, good-for-nothing insurgents be recognized as an independent government.[51]

The conduct of insurgent Cubans, administration officials predicted at the time of the fall of Santiago, would require the United States "to change its plans and purposes."[52] Indeed, the pledge outlined in the Joint Resolution underwent official reexamination. On the very day of the peace protocol, the *New York Times* reflected administration thinking editorially:

We are bound by a pledge which we must observe in good faith to allow the people of the Island of Cuba to set up Government of their choice. They are obviously incapable of doing this at once. . . . When the time comes we shall withdraw and leave them to work out their own destiny. If that time never comes we shall continue to control the island, and ultimately, in all probability, it would be annexed to the United States. The pledge we made by no means binds us to withdraw at once, nor does full and faithful compliance with its spirit and letter forbid us to become permanent possessors of Cuba if the Cubans prove to be altogether incapable of self-government. A higher obligation than the pledge of the resolution of Congress would then constrain us to continue our government of the island.[53]

The pro-administration *New York Tribune* insisted that the American commitment to Cuban independence was made in good faith. But it was not unconditional, for it was a pledge made in the belief that Cubans were prepared for self-government. "The 'civil government' of the 'Cuban Republic' is found . . . to be practically non-existent," the *Tribune* commented indignantly, "and its large, fully organized army dwindles under inspection to a few scattered guerrilla bands." The conclusions were inescapable. "If thus the basis and foundation of our pledge be found false and unsubstantial," the *Tribune* asked rhetorically, "with what grace can it be demanded that the pledge itself stand?" The *Tribune* editorial foretold administration policy:

The master-factor of the whole problem lies in the [Joint Resolution] phrases . . . "except for pacification" and "when that is accomplished." We have gone into Cuba to pacify it, and we are under no obligation, legal or moral, expressed or implied, to leave it until it is fully pacified. On the contrary, we are under the strongest possible obligation, legal and moral, expressed and implied, not to leave it until it is fully pacified. . . . As soon as the Cubans show themselves able and ready to govern the island in accordance with American principles of order, liberty, and justice, it is to be assumed this Government will be ready to fulfill its pledge and relinquish control to them. It is not to be assumed that it will do so one day before that time.[54]

Ten days later, the *Tribune* elaborated further on the implications of the pacification clause of the Joint Resolution. The United States did not intend to repudiate its pledge, the *Tribune* explained. On the contrary, it intended to fulfill its obligations "scrupulously and exactly." Washington had not recognized the independence of Cuba or the sovereignty of the insurgent republic; "it did not promise to establish that republic, or to put the insurgents in control of the island." The United States pledged only to pacify the island. Only after the Spanish army has left and the Cuban insurgents "return to ways of peace," the *Tribune* concluded, would the United States begin "to consider the question of turning the island over to the control of the inhabitants."[55] The *Philadelphia Inquirer*, too, insisted that the central issue turned on pacification. To be sure, the *Inquirer* asserted editorially, the United States had declared war against Spain with the intention of securing Cuban independence. But the Joint Resolution carried other responsibilities. The United States intended to see "that a stable government should be formed." And portentously: "Who can deny that the very height of freedom would come under American rule?"[56]

By early fall, Americans had subscribed to still one more Spanish proposition. By ending Spanish sovereignty over Cuba, the United States had assumed moral responsibility for order and stable government. The displacement of Spain, the White House insisted, left only the superior authority of the United States standing between civilization and chaos. The president, administration spokesmen reminded Americans, had originally asked Congress on April 11 for authority to use American armed forces specifically to establish "a stable government, capable of maintaining order and observing its international obligations insuring peace and tranquility and the security of its citizens as well as our own."[57] Nothing between

April and August had altered White House thinking. On the contrary, the revelations from Cuba strengthened the administration's contentions. If the Cubans showed themselves capable of presiding over such a government, one writer insisted, the United States would honor its commitment. "If not, we shall have to continue to regard ourselves as their guardians."[58] The United States was obligated to establish a government guided by "equity and common sense," the *New York Times* insisted. "The sacrifices of treasure and life that we have made clearly entitles us to fix the conditions under which the observance of these principles shall be secured, and to retain whatever power is requisite to enforce these conditions."[59] One member of the cabinet asserted bluntly that the United States did not intend to expel Spain only to turn the island "over to the insurgents or to any other particular class or fraction." The American purpose in Cuba was not to be guided by the political issue of independence but by the moral necessity to establish a "stable government for and by all the people."[60] Robert P. Porter, McKinley's special agent in Cuba, insisted that it was necessary to create conditions that promised to allow the "whole population" to vote and "select a definite government."[61] A great moral responsibility had descended on the United States. "We must lift them up by a generous and noble Christian series of efforts," General Oliver O. Howard insisted. "It is our God-given mission, and the whole Christian world is watching to see if the great American republic is equal to the strain."[62]

Officials in Washington, who before the war had desired a free hand to decide the future of Cuba, discovered in the autumn that developments in Cuba had all but formally eliminated restraints on administration policy. The ambiguity of the pacification clause of the Joint Resolution provided considerable latitude in determining if and when Cuba met conditions justifying independence. Indeed, as members of the administration must have realized, the Joint Resolution provided a rationale for an indefinite occupation of Cuba. This, a McKinley advisor recorded in his diary, "under conditions now and hereafter to exist in Cuba means ultimate annexation."[63]

V   Cubans detected ominous portents in changing American attitudes. Uneasiness swept across insurgent camps as separatist leaders witnessed the growing cordiality between Spaniards and Americans and learned of mounting American attacks on Cuba Libre. Resentment among separatists increased as they became the objects of American slander. In the United States, the PRC representation followed rising anti-Cuban sentiment closely and with no small sense of dismay. Cubans, too, junta spokesman Lincoln de Zayas insisted in New York, desired a permanent and stable government on the island. "The Cubans do resent, however," Zayas protested, "the slurs that are being cast upon them. They are made to appear despicable while the Spaniards are suddenly being pictured as heroes."[64] Not a few observers detected in changing American attitudes the presence of sinister designs. "There seems to be in the process of development," N.G. Gonzales charged, "a systematic scheme to depreciate and misrepresent the Cubans in arms with a view to the preparation of public sentiment for an evasion of the terms of the congressional resolution recognizing the independence of Cuba. It looks to me as if the foundations are being laid—in lies—for the indefinite control of the island by the United States, on the ground that Cubans favoring independence are a small and weak minority and have failed to contribute to the redemption of the island."[65]

Cuban bitterness toward the United States mounted steadily. Insurgent army leaders resented American appropriation of victory over Spain. Preparations for peace proceeded without the participation of Cubans; insurgent leaders were reduced to bystanders during the peace negotiations and spectators to the victory celebrations. "The war was declared and the peace signed," Máximo Gómez complained to Estrada Palma, "without my receiving even the slightest official attention from the Americans. The Americans have been very rude to me."[66]

The issues transcended injury to Cuban sensibilities, however. By the end of the summer, American actions foretold an ominous change of policy. American intentions were no longer clear and this uncertainty contributed powerfully to the general uneasiness among insurgent leaders. Cubans detected in American actions and attitudes indications that the United States planned to disavow its commitment to Cuban independence. Cuban anger mounted as insurgent leaders saw themselves victims of American duplicity, despoiled of victory over their adversaries, and denied mastery over their country.[67] "It is necessary that the American government define its attitudes," an impatient Calixto García warned Estrada Palma weeks after the peace protocol. "Cuban patriots are suspicous; they are fearful because they see the horizon dark." García demanded to learn American plans and the length of time the United States proposed to occupy the island. "We are not reconciled to this ambiguous situation in which they have placed us."[68]

The dispute over Santiago served as a microcosm of the larger contradictions of the Cuban-American alliance. Events at Santiago confirmed Cubans' worst fears. The commitment of the Joint Resolution and the promise of Aserradero notwithstanding, American plans did not include relinquishing the island to Cubans. Shafter, too, sensed the compelling implications of the estrangement. The "Cubans are feeling very sore," Shafter reported only days after the Santiago dispute, "because they were not permitted to take part in the conference leading to the capitulation and because I will not permit them to go into the city armed. They expected and claim as their right to take possession of the city and control affairs."[69] The "trouble with General García," Shafter wrote with growing impatience a week later, "was that he expected to be placed in command at this place; in other words, that we would turn over the city to him." The American commander reported that he had "explained fully that we were at war with Spain, and that the question of Cuban independence not be considered by me."[70]

Peace did not reduce tensions between both armies. On the contrary, the armistice exacerbated relations. While the United States had occupied Santiago and the larger cities in the east, Cuban forces remained in control of the small towns and the countryside. By mid-August, two armies representing rival claims of authority had divided Oriente province between them. "A dual government can't exist here," Shafter anxiously warned Washington in mid-August; "we have got to have full sway of the Cubans." Otherwise, Shafter predicted, there would inevitably be a war between the former allies to resolve competing claims of sovereignty over Cuba.[71]

Indeed, the spectre of war between the Cubans and Americans loomed increasingly as a distinct possibility. Disgruntled insurgent chieftains made no effort to conceal their resentment over the course of late summer events. In central Cuba, Gómez accused the United States of having broken faith with the Cubans. During the negotiations for the surrender of Guantánamo several days after Santiago, American officials again ignored Cuban military authorities and ordered the insurgent forces under General Pedro Pérez to remain outside the city. "If our independence is not secured now," and angry Pérez warned the *New York Herald* correspondent, "I am willing to continue the fight for another thirty years, if necessary. The Cuban army has not fought for annexation or American control of our affairs. Our fight has been for independence, and the army will not be satisfied with anything else."[72] Talk of renewing the war, this time against the United States, increased among insurgent officers throughout the late summer and early fall. General Juan Elogio Ducasse acknowledged to an American correspondent that the Cuban army was stockpiling arms, ammunition, and supplies.[73]

Nor were American authorities unmindful of the implications of mounting disaffection among Cubans. "I don't wish to be an alarmist," General Shafter wrote in late July, "but if I am not very much mistaken, we will have trouble with the Cubans before we get through with it." Shafter described the Cubans as a "menace to the peace of the country," asserting that the insurgent forces could not be permitted to garrison any town or city.[74] "The Cubans had no love for the Americans," Lt. J. W. Heard warned. "They expected after the present war ended a conflict between themselves and the United States; and, further, they expressed a readiness to participate in such conflict when it did come."[75] The concentration of Cuban forces in Oriente, Shafter warned, "may lead to complicatons of grave character."[76] Several days after the Peace Protocol, Shafter advised Cubans that continued operations against Spain would be considered as "an attack upon the United States and will be treated accordingly."[77]

By late summer, the United States had come to perceive Cubans as the single largest threat to order and stability on the island. And in the months following the peace protocol, the United States increased the strength of its military forces on the island. In late August, the United States reinforced the American garrison in Santiago. Fifteen regiments of infantry volunteers, one of volunteer engineers, and four artillery batallions were sent to Cuba after the signing of the peace treaty with Spain. There were more American soldiers in Cuba after the peace than during the war. Washington outlawed all Cuban filibustering expeditions from the United States. American authorities proclaimed a blockade of the island and announced that any vessel captured attempting to deliver war supplies to Cubans would be treated as a "blockade runner." The wartime practice of distributing arms, ammunition, and supplies to Cuban forces was halted. American military authorities announced their intention to withhold rations, food supplies, and jobs to all Cubans as long as they remained under arms.[78] The old allies were now new enemies.

12 Peace Without Victory

The Cuban Army is dying of hunger. . . . We have in the towns and fields of Cuba all that is needed in the way of food, but . . . we are forbidden to touch it by reason of the peace order. . . . What shall we do? The time will come when we cannot bear it any longer, and then what will be the result?. . . . If by misfortune we are driven by the necessities of our army to get by force what we need so as not to die of hunger will the President of the United States condemn us, or will the nations of the world, which do not know what is happening, judge us unworthy of the sympathy of the American people?
—Lieutenant Colonel Edgar Carbonne, Cuban Liberation Army, October 1898

The policy now is to put the Cubans "in a hole"; to slight them and sneer at them and neglect them as if they were vagabond dogs; to "foresee" trouble with them and to promote this "trouble" by exciting their suspicion of our motives and letting the "immediate" evacuation of the island by the Spaniards, provided for in the protocol, take effect five months after. An excuse is wanted for sending a great army to Cuba, where it is not needed; an excuse is wanted for a long occupation. If the starving Cubans in their extremity attack a Spanish garrison and try to loot a town of its food supplies, there will be an illustration of the necessity for a big force of American troops to keep down this banditti and for a long delay in permitting the formation of a government of the people in Cuba.
—*The State* (Columbia, S.C.), November 5, 1898

The Spaniards, we are told, are to go by December 1, or soon after. Then is to come an American "army of occupation," some saying that it is to be 50,000 strong. It is but natural that we should ask, Why is this great army sent to Cuba? When the Spaniards are gone, who is it going to fight?
—Bartolomé Masó, November 1898

I On October 8, 1898, a devastating hurricane struck eastern Cuba. For the next two days, the storm slowly battered its way westward across the island and, during those days, life in Cuba came to a standstill. A portent, a superstitious few concluded. Cubans for whom October 10 had special meaning found little to celebrate in 1898, and the thirtieth anniversary of the "Grito de Yara" passed without much formal observance. The storm did much to mute public enthusiasm to commemorate this, the most solemn, date of the patriotic calendar. But other circumstances contributed to this subdued Cuban mood.

In the autumn of 1898, a tempest of a different sort was brewing. Something was wrong, or not quite right, Cubans sensed. In those weeks after the war, the forces of Cuban separatism found themselves disoriented and in disarray. A spectre of uncertainty stalked separatist camps. The American presence in Cuba continued as a disquieting reminder that the status of the island remained unresolved. The undefined goals of American intervention during the war, the unstated purpose of the American military occupation after the war, and, above all, the unknown intentions of the American government in peace had an unsettling impact on Cubans.

Peace played havoc with the revolutionary polity. Adjusting to peace proved almost as difficult as adapting to war. In many ways, it was. As long as the war against Spain continued, the separatist consensus remained more or less intact, united around one central objective: the overthrow of Spanish rule. Military considerations guided separatist policy and arms governed the separatist purpose. Peace created new conditions, however. Gone now was the unifying purpose around which the heterogenous constituencies of Cuba Libre had organized. Gone, too, was the principal source of Cuban unanimity. After the peace protocol, no one person possessed authority to represent all separatist agencies; no one agency possessed authority to formulate separatist policy.

The cessation of hostilities established an ambiguous peace in Cuba. Spain had been defeated, to be sure, but it was not certain that this signified the triumph of Cuban aspirations. The peace for which the Cubans had so long yearned had arrived, but the objectives to which the separatists had committed themselves remained unfulfilled. The status of the island was further obscured when later in 1898 Spain and the United States, without Cuban participation, concluded in Paris a treaty formally transferring control over Cuba to the United States.

The meaning of the peace in 1898, just as earlier the meaning of war, 230 remained vaguely and incompatibly defined by various sectors of the separatist coalition. For the vast majority of Cuban exiles, the peace protocol of August 12 signified the end of Spanish rule, cause enough to persuade them that the struggle for independence had at last come to a successful end. The anguish of expatriation was over. Years of brooding homesickness and personal sacrifice had been vindicated. Convinced that the objectives of the insurrection had been achieved, Cubans saw no further reason to continue their expatriation. Even as Santiago passed under American control in July, separatists abroad readied themselves to return to Cuba.[1] In the period immediately following the peace protocol, thousands of exiles returned to the island.

Nor did Cubans abroad now see any further reason to maintain in peace the organizations established for war. Contributions to PRC coffers declined after the surrender of Santiago, then ceased entirely after the peace protocol. The return of expatriates to Cuba depleted the membership of local PRC juntas, forcing many patriotic clubs to dissolve altogether. "The end of the war," José Dolores Poyo wrote to Estrada Palma from Key West two weeks after the peace protocol, "the belief that the Americans will give us everything, and preparations to return to Cuba at any moment is what absorbs the attention of Cubans here."[2] In October, General Emilio Núñez dissolved the Department of Expeditions, the agency responsible during the war for delivering arms, ammunition, and supplies to the *manigua*.[3] In December, the New York Delegation announced the dissolution of the PRC and enjoined patriotic juntas to disband all local organizations.[4]

II   Peace also had immediate and calamitous repercussions in Cuba. The August protocol resulted in dividing control of the island's urban centers between Spanish and American forces, leaving fifty thousand Cuban officers and men confined to a countryside devastated by three years of war. Throughout the war, the insurgent forces had lived off the land, dependent on supplies and provisions arriving from abroad and levies exacted locally. Separatist armies had survived through extralegal measures sanctioned more or less by the exigencies of the war, taking what they needed, whenever needed, wherever found. Livestock, fruits, and vegetables were seized as required from farms and estates. After August, relief expeditions from abroad ceased. The end of the war also ended foraging. Under American rule, private property returned to its inviolable prewar status. The end of the war signaled the end of the insurgents' ability to meet their needs by simply seizing supplies wherever and whenever necessary.

The peace that relieved the grief of Cuban communities abroad visited anguish upon the Cuban camps in the *manigua*. Life, precarious during the war, became untenable in the peace. In the months that followed the August protocol, food, medicine, clothing, and supplies all but disappeared in the insurgent camps. Living conditions were appalling, and they never improved. Idle army veterans passed the autumn months in constant, sometimes desperate, want. Cuban troops, particularly in the western provinces, found themselves distant from their homes and without the means of returning to their families. Nor did many have much to look forward to upon their return. The vast majority of Cuban soldiers found themselves without land to work and without prospects of employment.[5] Without funds and credit, those insurgent veterans fortunate enough to own property could not purchase needed equipment and supplies to return to productive pursuits. After the war, the sires of Cuba Libre depended on local charity organizations and voluntary donations. Supplies from the cities, at best haphazardly organized and always uncertain, provided only partial relief and this only to units having had the good fortune to have established camps near the larger urban centers.[6] But the cities, too, suffered from privation, and urban dwellers were not in a condition to offer the countryside much relief for any length of time. "From glorious soldiers with heroic aspirations," General Enrique Collazo later recalled, "we saw ourselves transformed into beggars, living off public charity and depending on the generosity of friends in order to shed the rags of war."[7]

By early fall, conditions had become desperate for the *insurrecto* army. Illness, malnutrition, and starvation swept through army camps across Cuba. Insurgents sold their equipment and horses for money to buy food. By early winter, veterans were forced to search for edible roots and slaughter horses and pack mules for food.[8] Soldiers who had lived through the severest difficulties of the war failed to survive the peace. "Our soldiers are dying at the gates of the city for lack of food," one Cuban officer wrote in despair from an insurgent army camp outside of Havana.[9] "The men are dying because they cannot get medicine, or establish a hospital," a Cuban merchant reported from Sagua la Grande. "The day I left a lieutenant died, and there are six or eight dying every day."[10] In Sancti Spíritus, reports of dying soldiers were forwarded daily to insurgent army headquarters. In Havana province, one correspondent reported a dozen Cuban soldiers dying daily.[11] "Before the war ended," one American officer in the Cuban army wrote from Guanabacoa, "we lived better, as the enemy's provisions were at our mercy. The orders are now to discontinue foraging. . . . Last week the death in town was twenty to thirty daily."[12] "Hunger causes in our ranks more casualties than enemy bullets caused," one Cuban officer despaired. "If we do not receive more food within a month, more than a third of the Cuban Army and rural population would have ceased to exist. In another month, it will be too late to avoid the death of thousands by starvation. I am horrified by the scenes I am witnessing."[13]

III   The end of the war transformed, too, the nature of civil-military relations within the revolutionary polity. For three years civilian authorities had acquiesced grudgingly to the army command, deferring unenthusiastically to the dictates of insurgent chieftains, subordinating constitutional prerogatives to military imperatives. The principle of civilian supremacy, asserted first in the Bases of the PRC in 1892 and ratified later by the Assembly of Jimaguayú in 1895, had been one of the first casualties of the insurrection. As long as the fate of the separatist cause resided in Cuban arms, military considerations and, with them, army leadership prevailed. Only the overriding need to maintain a united separatist front during the war had prevented mounting grievances from erupting in full public view.

Peace released civilians from these constraints. A backlog of ill will and accumulated enmity surfaced immediately. No longer were government authorities obliged to acquiesce to army dictates. On the contrary, the time was now right for the men of laws to reassert their constitutional authority over the men of arms. For members of the provisional government, the mission of the insurgent armed forces had been completed on August 12 and, in the judgment of many, there no longer existed any reason to retain the organization of the Liberation Army.

Government leaders emerged from the war determined to recover the authority that had earlier ebbed to the army command. Peace provided the occasion to reestablish the civil supremacy mandated by the constitution. But more than bruised civilian sensibilities animated the Council of Government. For too long the separatist coalition had spoken with too many voices—with the faintest voice being that of the supreme civil agency of revolution. The PRC representation negotiated independently with American officials in Washington; army chieftains, too, freely treated with American officers in Cuba. Unrecognized by the United States, ignored by the expatriate leadership, disregarded by the army command, the provisional government awoke to the necessity of asserting its constitutional authority over the revolutionary coalition. The Méndez Capote mission to Washington in May represented the first attempt to subordinate the PRC delegation to the authority of the provisional government. It was not until August, however, that the Council of Government could contemplate measures to establish its authority over the insurgent armed forces. If conditions of peace made this possible, the circumstances of the American intervention made it necessary.

IV   The first government blow against the army was not long in coming. "The voice of patriotism and a spirit of conciliation," Secretary of the Interior Manuel Silva announced on August 13, "have prevented me until now from forwarding to the Council [of Government] grave accusations against General García." A day after the peace protocol, and after only two hours of discussion, the provisional government dismissed Calixto García. Abusive of his authority, the government indictment charged, publicly scornful of civil authority, García had repeatedly violated the constitution by establishing in Oriente province a virtual military dictatorship. This behavior could not be sanctioned, Silva insisted, demanding that the government relieve the *oriental* general of his command and consider future legal action against him.[14]

The dismissal of García was possessed of more than symbolic meaning. The *oriental* army chieftain had long been a caustic and constant critic of the provisional government. Government charges were substantially correct. García had permitted little civil participation in the administration of insurgent-held zones in Oriente. It was also true that General García held civil authorities in contempt. But this was true of all *oriental* chieftains. The Oriente command had a long tradition of defiance of civil authority. Like Antonio and José Maceo before him, who also made little effort to conceal their disdain for the men of government, García had ignored civil authorities throughout the war. In moving against General García, the provisional government struck at both the symbol and the person most clearly identified as an opponent to civil authority.

The ouster of García produced shock waves within the insurgent armed forces. The second highest-ranking chieftain of the Liberation Army, outraged officers charged, the successor of Maceo, had been the victim of a political vendetta by a group of ungrateful politicians. The firing of García caught the military chieftains of the eastern army corps by surprise and served to exacerbate civilian-military tensions. Indignant over late summer events, officers of the eastern army corps organized a junta to protest the government decree. Ranking officers in Oriente denounced the government and voluntarily followed their chief into retirement.[15] Several weeks after the dismissal of García, and in the face of mounting criticism and attack from the eastern army, the government authorized the disbandment of the entire eastern army, traditionally the corps most hostile to civilian authority.[16]

In the following weeks, an emboldened Council of Government moved to expand its authority over other regiments of the Liberation Army. Each army corps passed under the supervision of civilian commissioners, appointed directly by the provisional government and responsible only to President Bartolomé Masó. Each civil agent received a military grade commensurate with professional and/or academic title.[17] In late September, lastly, the Council of Government called for a national assembly to convene the following month in Santa Cruz del Sur in Camagüey. On October 23, the Council of Government formally dissolved itself and invested in the Santa Cruz Assembly the supreme authority of the provisional republic.[18]

V The Santa Cruz Assembly convened in an atmosphere surcharged with tension. The long-brewing civil-military conflict, muted during the war, erupted into full view. That citizen Calixto García had won election as a delegate to the Assembly certainly did not make matters easier. Army chieftains and civilian leaders took their quarrel to the public and openly exchanged epithets on the front pages of local newspapers. Early sessions of the Assembly were given to charges and counter-charges. Attacks on the army increased. Senior officers of the insurgent armed forces, including General in Chief Máximo Gómez, became the objects of criticism and censure. "The army today," delegate Porfirio Valiente charged, "is an obstacle to the well-being and prosperity of Cuba."[19] Delegate Manuel Sanguily went so far as to suggest that a formal army had never really existed—only a "handful of patriots who rose up in armed struggle." This "handful of patriots," Sanguily now demanded, should simply be ordered to dissolve and return to their homes.[20]

Two issues loomed immediately before the Santa Cruz Assembly in the closing months of 1898. The first concerned the posture of the provisional government toward the United States. Preeminently concerned with the necessity of legitimizing its claim to represent the supreme governing authority in Cuba, the Assembly reasserted its constitutional mandate and claimed jurisdiction over those areas administered by separatist agencies.

From the outset, the Assembly announced its intentions to constitute itself as the legitimate governing authority in Cuba. To this end, it created an executive commission to coordinate all activities under one authority.[21]

The second question involved the status of the insurgent armed forces. In early November, the Assembly voted to disband the Liberation Army—but not without first providing partial back pay to facilitate the veterans' adjustment to civilian life. The Assembly established a second commission charged with the task of negotiating a loan in the United States to be guaranteed by the future revenues of the republic.[22]

Both issues were inextricably interrelated. Dissolving the Liberation Army promised to eliminate the major rival to civilian authority. The two conflicting *independentista* versions of free Cuba remained unresolved. If civilians were suspicious of the populist character of army leadership, they were in terror at the social forces contained in the insurgent armed forces. After the war, the doctors, engineers, and lawyers of government perceived the peasants, workers, and blacks in the army as the single largest threat to a peaceful and stable republic. The army represented a source of immediate political rivalry and potential social disorders, upon whose dissolution depended the solvency of civilian government and the future stability of the republic.

Disbanding the insurgent forces, further, promised to demonstrate the government's authority within the revolutionary polity, thereby affirming the Assembly's claim as supreme governing agency in Cuba. By seeking to negotiate a loan to pay the army veterans, the Assembly sought to establish its credentials as legitimate bargaining agent of both the provisional government and the future republic. To establish itself as the undisputed bargaining agent of Cuban separatism, capable of organizing a government as outlined in the Joint Resolution, the Assembly recognized the necessity of first having to assert its authority over the army, long the most defiant and unabashed opponent of civilian administration. Any likelihood of fixing the legitimacy of the provisional government in the official American mind and establishing as definitive its claim of supremacy over all revolutionary sectors depended first on the government's success in attaining credibility within the separatist polity. This immediately and inevitably meant civilian control over the Liberation Army.

VI In early autumn, Cuban military leaders found themselves between an army disintegrating from below and a government seeking to displace them from above. Peace had nullified the importance of separatist arms and reduced the influence of the men who bore them. The war was over, the Assembly exhorted, and the separatist cause had triumphed; there was no longer any reason for Cubans to continue under arms or remain in military organizations. The time had arrived to replace the gun with the plowshare and return to peaceful pursuits. The dissolution of the army, the Assembly insisted, would go a long way toward the restoration of normality and fulfill the conditions of pacification as outlined in the Joint Resolution. But the Assembly was not unmindful that the dissolution of the army also eliminated a political rival. And if the Assembly succeeded in establishing its authority over the army by presiding over its dismantling, civilian political fortunes would certainly increase.

Army chieftains, however, were unreconciled to the course of events in the early autumn. Discontent in the army increased. The military command again perceived itself victimized by self-serving politicians claiming authority in peace that army chieftains had consistently refused to recognize during the war. Unlike the period of the war, however, when the military requirements of the separatist struggle guaranteed the soldiers a place of influence in separatist councils, peace converted the army presence into an unwelcomed spectre.

In late September, Calixto García responded publicly to his dismissal. Asked for his opinion of the provisional government, García disdainfully waved his hand and dismissed the question: "Provisional Government! What government? There is no government," he sneered. "I deny the legality of the action of the present so-called provisional Cuban government." Claiming to speak for the army leadership, García scorned claims made by civil authorities. "In the army we do not pay much attention to this little clique playing at government. So long as they keep quiet and do not interfere with us it is all right, and they may sit up at Camagüey and make laws, but we pay no attention to them." García also personally attacked President Bartolomé Masó and Vice-President Domingo Méndez Capote: "They are not fighters, and the real revolutionary party in Cuba is the fighting party. Have you ever heard of Bartolomé Masó as a fighter, or Señor Capote in a battle? . . . Faugh! These men are not the leaders in Cuba." García spurned civilian claims of authority over the Liberation Army. "We deny the power and authority of the provisional government in any way to interfere with the actions of the commander in chief. The provisional government has been and is a figurehead, nothing more."[23]

Military leaders rejected outright civilian attempts to exclude the army from participating in the formulation of postwar separatist policy, particularly since so many of those decisions affected the army directly. Veterans scoffed cynically at the Assembly's injunction to return to peaceful pursuits: go back to what—with what? More than this, however, army leaders were troubled by what appeared to many as undue haste to dissolve the insurgent army forces. Unlike the Assembly, army chiefs remained unconvinced that American intentions in Cuba were either simple or pure. An ambiguous peace settled over Cuba after August. The army command had already received from Shafter the astonishing news that the United States considered Cuba as "conquered territory." The American military buildup after the peace protocol had ominous implications and further aroused Cuban suspicions. The allied army that had arrived to free Cuba now appeared transformed into a conquering army preparing to occupy Cuba. It was precisely this American military presence in Cuba that troubled army chieftains most. Discussions in early fall about dissolving the Liberation Army, the military command insisted, were premature. True, the peace protocol had effectively achieved the immediate objectives of Cuban arms. But the larger separatist goal, army leaders argued, the independence of the island, remained unrealized.

Máximo Gómez passed the months following the peace protocol secluded in cental Cuba. News of peace had failed to arouse more than subdued celebration among the senior army commanders in Las Villas. "This moment of joy fills me with fear," Gómez confided to an aide. The war had come to an end, to be sure, and Spain had suffered the final defeat; but it was not clear that the Cubans were the victors.[24] The unstated purpose of the continued American presence troubled Gómez. Months had passed since U.S. military forces had arrived in Cuba and not once had the Americans communicated officially with the insurgent general in chief. Gómez's sensibilities had been offended and his suspicions aroused.[25]

Nor had relations between Gómez and civilian authorities after the war fared much better. Communication with representatives of the provisional government had been haphazard and infrequent.[26] An accumulation of three years of grievances surfaced in government councils, and Gómez became the object of growing criticism and attack. Indeed, Cuban neglect of the Dominican-born generalissimo after the peace protocol was all but complete. The message from Santa Cruz was clear: the war was over and Cubans were no longer in need of his services.[27]

In Remedios, Gómez brooded in anxious isolation. Uncertainty filled him with a frustration bordering on despair. He presided over a disintegrating army, helplessly watching the officers and men who had successfully braved the ravages of war fall victim to the uncertainties of peace. He confronted a foreign government unwilling to recognize his military authority and a Cuban government indisposed to sanction his continued exercise of that authority. The seventy-three-year-old Dominican, weary of war, found himself alone, something of an outcast in central Cuba, unceremoniously discarded by the people for whose liberation he had toiled, and rebuffed by the foreigners he had once called allies. "I remain . . . abandoned by the Cubans and the Americans," a disconsolate Gómez wrote his wife late that autumn.[28] To a close friend in the Dominican Republic, Gómez likened himself to Prometheus, thwarted by forces beyond his control from completing his mission.[29]

Uneasiness settled over army headquarters in Remedios as fear increased that the Americans planned to disavow their commitment to Cuban independence.[30] Nor did Assembly proposals inspire much confidence. On the contrary, army commanders reacted with dismay and disbelief upon learning of the Assembly's call for the dissolution of the Liberation Army. If there had been little consultation between the Assembly and the army about this summons, there was less concurrence. Neither the official policy of Americans in Washington since the war resolution nor the public actions of the Americans in Cuba since the peace protocol, army leaders insisted, had given even the slightest credibility to the Joint Resolution. As long as the purpose of the American military presence in Cuba remained unknown, as long as the status of the island remained unclear, the army command refused to comply with government orders to dissolve the Liberation Army. Military leaders instinctively opposed and consciously resisted the call to demobilize without first receiving formal assurances of Cuban independence. "We will not lay down our arms," General Pedro Betancourt vowed, "until Cuba is, absolutely, independent."[31] At army headquarters, senior officers resolved to remain under arms until independence was assured. In the meantime, the army command began to think the unthinkable—a new war, this one against the United States.[32]

Gómez ignored the Assembly's injunction and ordered his officers to hold the army together until further notice. "We came to the country to secure the independence of Cuba," he reminded his officers. "Where is independence? I do not see it. . . . An affirmation from the American congress is not sufficient; it is necessary that the organized Cuban people, that is, the Liberation Army, remain prepared to reclaim the promise." Gómez was adamant. "While we are not assured of independence, our mission is not yet finished." Anyone leaving the ranks of the Liberation Army without military authorization, the army command announced, would be guilty of treason and tried as a deserter.[33]

Gómez was deeply troubled by the course of events in late 1898. He confided his anguish to an aide:

I am worried and offended. I can shake off my being offended, but not my preoccupation with the plight of the army and independence. What is going to be done about independence? The Americans, it seems, are not thinking about it. . . . Even if finally they give it to us, it will be as a gift, while we have gained it, and more than gained it with continuous efforts during more than half a century. The Americans have had an easy campaign because we have exhausted Spanish soldiers and resources. I am obliged to be grateful to the Americans, but only when they fulfill their promises, and if they fulfill them with decency and without aggravation to the Cubans. . . . The Cuban Army cannot dissolve itself unless I receive assurances, honorably promised, that independence will be given to Cuba and that it will be given as just reward of Cuban efforts, suffering, constancy, and spilled blood.[34]

But Gómez's opposition to demobilization was not without complications. Most immediately, in more than symbolic terms, it signified open army defiance of civil authority—insubordination tantamount to mutiny, the Assembly would later charge. More important, the decision to keep Cubans organized under arms could lead only to the continued deterioration of already desperate conditions in the army. Gómez's dilemma was real: the thought of dissolving the army before securing a guarantee of independence was unacceptable, but the prospect of keeping the army intact without relief was unthinkable. Gómez confided privately to his diary a despairing conscience over the sight of battalions of soldiers transformed into legions of beggars, dependent on public charity to survive, while the fate of Cuba continued unresolved.[35]

To the Assembly, Gómez publicly appealed for assistance. But the provisional government showed little interest in the plight of the army and remained impassive if not indifferent toward the postwar needs of the insurgent veterans. Army appeals for relief elicited only perfunctory repetitions of the Assembly's injunction to disband.[36]

News in the late fall that the Assembly contemplated disbanding the armed forces without full compensation, moreover, aroused army ire. Two years earlier, the provisional government had approved an army pay schedule based on time in rank and service and payable upon the conclusion of the war. The Assembly proposal in 1898 to disregard this commitment further encouraged insurgent commanders to keep the army intact until conditions permitted demobilization to conform to original plans. Gómez opposed any demobilization plan that did not provide veterans with compensation to facilitate their transition to civilian life. His work was "only half done," Gómez pledged in September 1898. "I cannot desert these soldiers now. If I cannot obtain at least part of the arrears of pay for them from customs receipts or other sources, I must do my best in every possible way to restore them to a self-supporting condition and place them in positions such as they abandoned to take up arms for independence."[37]

Conditions after the war worked powerfully against Gómez's efforts to retain the Liberation Army intact. The destitute condition of insurgent forces made the order to remain under arms difficult to justify and virtually impossible to enforce. The precarious condition of the troops was only one problem. The distress of soldiers' families added further pressure on the army command to allow veterans to return to their homes. By early October, Gómez was compelled to authorize the issuance of furloughs to heads of families.[38] Conflicting orders between the army command and the Assembly, moreover, blurred lines of separatist authority and plunged separatist camps into confusion and disarray. Who did insurgent officers obey? This conflict contributed to fragmenting the revolutionary polity further, as some officers complied with the orders of the provisional government and others obeyed the army command.[39]

VII   By early autumn, the anomalous condition of Cuban separatism had emerged in sharp relief. Separatist agencies of war had passed into the period of peace intact. They had been neither dissolved by defeat nor institutionalized by victory. At the same time, separatist agencies had been preempted, superseded by a superior power possessed of unknown intentions. What Cubans did recognize, however, was that after August 12 the United States was the authority with which they would have to settle the future of the island. But there was no consensus around who would speak for Cuba Libre or what version of free Cuba would prevail. The survival of the institutional structures of Cuban separatism, moreover, also guaranteed the persistence of the diverse ideological constructs of Cuba Libre. There was more than symbolic significance to the early dissolution of the Department of Expeditions and the PRC. The weakest exponent of national liberation, the expatriate sector, was the first to shed separatist trappings and end its revolutionary affiliation. In Cuba, the mounting civil-military dispute plunged the *independentista* sector of the separatist polity into crisis. More important, it announced an emerging realignment within *independentista* ranks, with each wing searching for advantage and allies against the other. The Santa Cruz Assembly sought to secure funds for the purpose of dissolving the armed forces; the military command sought the resources with which to keep the army intact. Neither the Assembly nor the Liberation Army, however, had independent access to resources. The American blockade immediately after the war and the subsequent dissolution of the expatriate support agencies deprived separatists in Cuba of resources from abroad. The establishment of American rule in Cuba also blocked the politico-military ascendancy of separatist forces and placed government resources beyond the reach of Cubans. Control over the island's customs receipts, governmental revenues, and administrative sinecures passed wholly under the jurisdiction of the American government.

Very early, the competing sectors of the separatist polity turned to the United States for assistance. The Santa Cruz Assembly established a commission to visit Washington to secure approval for an American loan with which to dissolve the armed forces. Gómez, too, appealed to the United States to relieve the suffering in insurgent camps. In September, the army command dispatched General Rafael Rodríguez to present to the members of the American Evacuation Commission an army request for food and supplies.[40] A month later, Gómez appointed Enrique Conill to deliver a personal message to President McKinley, urgently appealing for supplies to relieve the suffering in the Cuban countryside.[41] In control of vast resources and having appropriated the functions of state, the United States had established itself as a power broker between rival political groupings on the island.

VIII
Nowhere were the forces shaping Cuba's future more vividly in evidence than in Oriente province. Indeed, developments in the eastern province after the fall of Santiago represented at once a microcosm of conditions in postwar Cuba and a foreglimpse of Cuban-American relations during the occupation. Six months before assuming formal and full control over Cuba, while the rest of the island remained under Spanish rule, Oriente had passed completely under American administration.

Nowhere was the hold of formal separatist authority weaker than over the insurgent forces in Oriente province. Neither the Council of Government nor the general in chief had ever exercised more than token authority over insurgent chieftains in the east. Calixto García, and before him Antonio and José Maceo, functioned as regional caudillos whose authority emanated more from a status derived locally than from a position within the larger separatist hierarchy. Antonio Maceo's independent negotiations with Oriente planters in 1895 and Calixto García's cooperation with Americans in 1898 were actions taken without prior sanction of either the provisional government or the army command and were typical of the authority that the *oriental* chieftains arrogated to themselves during the war. There was indeed substance to the charges the Council of Government leveled against Calixto García in August 1898. Like Maceo, García was openly scornful of civil authority. But it was more than this: García resented all outside interference in Oriente.[42]

Nothing could have offended *oriental* sensibilities more than the American seizure of Santiago. To learn, too, that the Americans considered the eastern capital as "conquered territory" added outrage to insult. The most rebellious province of the Ever-Faithful Isle could no more accept American rule than it could tolerate Spanish administration. If *oriental* traditions could not admit to American authority, neither could separatists in Oriente accept American aims. The arrival of American armed forces in Oriente in 1898 shattered insurgent military preeminence in the province. Not only had larger separatist objectives been thwarted by the American seizure of Santiago, but the authority of the insurgent provincial command had been superseded by an outside military power.

García's break with the Americans, followed a month later by his dismissal by the provisional government, left the fifty-nine-year-old general in an ambiguous situation. These quarrels had no adverse effect on García's local prestige. A veteran of three separatist wars, a patriot of impeccable credentials, he commanded enormous respect within the ranks of eastern separatism. His unceremonious dismissal in August had scandalized the *oriental* army corps and reinforced his moral authority over insurgent forces of the east. The action by the provisional government confirmed the worst cynicism of a province traditionally skeptical of all outside authority. Government officials had shown themselves to *orientales* as a rabble of ungrateful and ambitious politicians who rewarded García's three decades of patriotic labor with an inglorious ouster from the separatist family. The expulsion of a man of enormous local prestige and influence, one of the most venerated leaders of thirty years of armed struggle, produced across eastern Cuba a wave of indignation against the provisional government.

The dispute between García and the United States had similar repercussions. García's denunciation of the United States made American intentions immediately suspect. The meaning of the old general's break with the Americans was not lost on *orientales*. Something was wrong, Cubans sensed. Suspicion increased to hostility. The establishment of occupation rule in Santiago proceeded uneasily as Americans peered nervously over their shoulders in fear of an armed challenge from their erstwhile eastern allies. "The attitude of the pronounced Cubans," General Shafter cabled the War Department in mid-August, "is hostile. They so far show no disposition to disband . . . and until they do there will be trouble."[43] The newly appointed military governor, General H. W. Lawton, expressed similar apprehensions. Only days after the peace protocol, Lawton urgently appealed to Washington for instructions as to the policy to be pursued toward the insurgent army of the east. Cuban troops still maintained their organization, Lawton explained, and were "threatening in their attitude, keeping the inhabitants stirred up and panicky by threats and acts of violence."[44] Washington telegraphed its response to Lawton within hours. Interference with the exercise of American authority, Lawton was instructed, could not be tolerated. Washington demanded that Cubans "with all others" be required to recognize the military occupation and the authority of the United States.[45]

Washington's instructions may have been reassuring, but not especially helpful. The continued presence of armed Cubans disaffected with American authority caused officials in Santiago considerable uneasiness. "The main problem in Cuba today, that is, the immediate one," General Leonard Wood, the governor of the provincial capital, warned the War Department in early September, "is the disbanding of the Cuban Army."[46] American authorities perceived themselves sitting atop a powder keg capable of exploding at any moment without warning.

At the same time, however, Americans had not been unmindful of the schisms developing within separatist ranks. The Assembly's dismissal of García was the subject of much official correspondence in the late summer of 1898; these events, too, had received extensive coverage in the American press. Nor were García's attitudes toward the provisional government—not unlike American views—unknown in official circles in Washington. Indeed, many Americans detected in the dispute between García and the provisional government at least one area in which the

United States and the *oriental* army chieftain were in substantial agreement. Both refused to recognize the authority of the provisional government; both saw the Assembly's pretensions as potential obstacles to order and stability in postwar Cuba.

By late summer the United States had recognized the value of securing the support of the ousted insurgent chieftain. When General H. L. Lawton replaced Shafter as provincial governor, he had specific instructions from Washington to improve relations with García and actively seek his advice and counsel.[47] In the following weeks, American authorities conferred continually with García, assuring him that the United States fully intended to honor the terms of the Joint Resolution. But Cuban cooperation, Lawton hastened to add, was essential to the success of the congressional pledge. This support would greatly facilitate the American mission and remove all obstacles to Cuban independence. More importantly, the assistance of Cubans would go a long way toward demonstrating to authorities in Washington that the Americans had not misplaced their original confidence in Cubans.

By early fall, the breach had been healed. On September 27, Lawton could inform the War Department that General García was "warmly in accord with our policy, and is giving me the support of his influence." To assure continued support, moreover, Lawton urged Washington to enlist García's services formally. "He is destitute," Lawton explained. "He cannot accept a subordinate place under my control, but I think he should be on commission and invited to the United States. His influence is great, and we will purchase it cheap by giving him a good salary and a position commensurate with his former rank and dignity."[48] Two weeks later General García was appointed to the board of directors of the Cuban Educational Association at a modest salary.

García's support of American rule was not unconditional, however. He was satisfied with American assurances that Washington intended to honor the terms of the Joint Resolution. The alternative to American government—the Assembly—was unacceptable to García. He insisted that American rule was a useful transition to orderly government and eventual independence. Certain the Americans would honor their pledge, García summoned Cubans to assist the United States in the reconstruction of the island. "I believe," he wrote to Estrada Palma, "that the United States will not disavow its given work; but if this should come to pass, there would always be time to die, if not to win."[49]

García's support of the United States all but formally eliminated the most serious obstacle to American rule in Santiago. More than this, it provided an enormous moral boost to American administration in the eastern province. The rift within the separatist polity had provided the opening through which the Americans secured an unchallenged foothold in eastern Cuba. Divided separatists could offer only the feeblest resistance to American authority. García's denunciation of the provisional government, moreover, and his subsequent endorsement of American administration, served to legitimize further the American refusal to recognize the authority of the Assembly. General García's words were "plain and direct," the *Philadelphia Inquirer* said, editorially reflecting official thinking. García's statements demonstrated "the precise estimation in which the so-called Cuban Government is held by one of the brainiest of all the Cuban leaders." The conclusions were inescapable: "Now that the fact is clear to all that there is no government in Cuba to be recognized, it follows logically that this country must place in control of the island an administration strong and stable enough to bring out the reconstruction and regeneration of the land. That government should be an American government, and once in power it should never be withdrawn."[50]

García, too, supported the disbandment of the eastern army corps. The dissolution of the insurgent army, he insisted, was necessary to meet the conditions of pacification as outlined in the Joint Resolution. With García's moral endorsement, and the Americans making appropriate use of resources, the United States moved to eliminate the potential threat of an armed insurgent challenge in Oriente.

Like units of the Liberation Army elsewhere, the insurgent forces in the east had also found the transition from war to peace difficult to make. But in Oriente, conditions were particularly desperate. No contingent of the Liberation Army had endured the privation of the war as long as the *orientales;* no other region had experienced as much devastation for as long a time as the eastern province. Starvation, illness, and unemployment in Oriente, however, unlike the condition of Cuban army units further west, had a remedy. The establishment of American rule in Santiago in July 1898 allowed the United States to make effective political use of superior resources. From the outset, American officials announced their willingness to exchange rations and jobs for Cuban arms. "As the war is practically over and further resort to arms cannot be contemplated," Lawton informed General Agustín Cebreco in September 1898, "an early disbanding of the forces . . . seems desirable, and I will gladly aid you in any way to bring this about." Lawton issued the insurgent commander rations for his forces with an accompanying admonition: "I shall not be at liberty to continue the issue. I will be glad, however, to aid any of the soldiers of the Cuban Army, after disbanding, by the issue of rations to them individually until they can secure employment or mature a crop on their plantations."[51] Leonard Wood stated the matter bluntly: "No Cuban bearing arms should have work or food."[52] His administration, Wood informed the White House, had one central objective: "Getting [Cubans] to disband, getting them to work, and impressing upon them the necessity of recognizing the absolute authority of the civil law."[53] To this end, Wood promoted the expansion of public works programs in Oriente. American authorities in charge of municipal and provincial posts and revenues created jobs and positions throughout the province and offered destitute veterans public employment in exchange for their arms. Wood also encouraged local merchants, businessmen, and planters to provide work for needy veterans— always under the same proviso: work for guns.[54] By the end of October 1898, the 11,000 officers and men of the eastern army corps had completely dissolved. The challenge to American authority in Oriente had been eliminated.

13 Dissent and Dissolution

We have not fought for a change of masters. We have fought for liberty, and not for a new ownership. Our army is still in the field. They shall not lay down their arms until we find out whether we are to be slaves or free.
—Colonel Juan Federico Centenalles, December 1898

I have talked with the American generals and high authorities, and am deeply, truly convinced that the United States will loyally keep its promise and that Cuba will be free and independent.
—Máximo Gómez, March 1899

The old commander in chief entered the capital with his right hand dislocated and in a sling—as one president would say in the future, "a casualty of popularity," so many times had it been shaken by the multitudes who crowded around him as he passed. His entry into the capital was a moment of glory and the old commander in chief couldn't get over his amazement, remarking: "Good God, if we had succeeded in having as many troops as admirers, we would have finished off the Spaniards at the drop of a hat," and he added: "Goddamn it, at the drop of a hat!"
—G. Cabrera Infante, *View of Dawn in the Tropics*

I The separatist consensus had always been a fragile body of opinion. Even in the best of times, which is to say the worst times of the war, the unanimity of the Cuban purpose was sustained by little more than the collective instinct for survival. Peacetime proved disastrous. The internecine feud of the war became a fratricidal struggle of the peace.

Much of this was endemic, with a history. But the American intervention exacerbated old tensions. Army leaders watched with distrust and dismay as the provisional government cooperated with the United States, suspecting civilians of using the American intervention as the occasion to promote dubious claims as the supreme and legitimate political authority in Cuba. Collaboration with the Americans had never been especially popular within the army, so civilian efforts to win American approval did little to enhance the esteem of the government among military chieftains. Indeed, the extent to which the provisional government seemed prepared to submit to American authority troubled army leaders. To the recurring dismay of the army command, the Council of Government had submissively endorsed the American intervention, relinquished control over the Liberation Army, sanctioned the Santiago accord, and ratified the peace protocol. Too many decisions, disgruntled military chieftains charged, were made to accommodate American needs rather than advance Cuban objectives. In late 1898, a brooding sense of betrayal settled over insurgent army camps. Government officials in Cuba, General Enrique Collazo later wrote, as well as the separatist representation abroad, appeared as "instruments of the American government that had deceived the Cuban Army in order to secure its cooperation."[1]

Civilian attempts to dissolve the Liberation Army after the war confirmed the military's worst fears. The dismissal of García, too, had devastating repercussions within armed separatist ranks. Many military chieftains shared García's early suspicions about American intentions in Cuba; that the provisional government remained silent during the García-Shafter dispute created in the army the impression that civilians had become timid on the matter of independence. The dismissal of García for an action universally endorsed in the armed forces shattered army confidence in the provisional government and made all future government actions suspect. "The men who on May 12 relinquished control of the Cuban Army," Enrique Collazo lamented, "delivered the final blow, dismissing the only Cuban chieftain in a position to protest the deceit the Americans had practiced in Santiago de Cuba."[2]

250   Army leaders feared, too, that the Assembly's intention to press its

claim as the legitimate political authority and, by implication, its demand
to govern the island, threatened to complicate Cuban-American relations
and delay independence interminably. Few ranking army chieftains believed the provisional government, still unrecognized in Washington, capable of enjoying any more success as an advocate of Cuban objectives in
peace than it had in war. The provisional government was now perceived
as a potential obstacle to independence, whose persistent pretensions to
supremacy offended army chieftains as much as it antagonized the Americans.

In civilian circles, on the other hand, it was the army that posed the
threat to independence. The military represented a potential challenge
both to the constitutional supremacy of the provisional government and
the authority of the United States in Cuba. On this one point the Assembly
and the Americans were unanimous: order and stability—"pacification," in
the language of the Joint Resolution—could not be attained until the dissolution of the insurgent armed forces was completed. This was the unspoken issue of García's dismissal in August. The provisional government
shrank in horror at the army challenge to the United States in Santiago—a
challenge that confirmed in civilian circles the existence within the Liberation Army of uncontrollable and potentially dangerous social forces. By
advancing uncompromisingly the most exalted view of the separatist ideal
and demanding authority over Santiago, García at once threatened to precipitate an armed confrontation with the Americans and gave vivid expression to the military's political ambitions. García's dismissal resolved
both concerns: a civilian assertion of a monopoly claim to political power
and the banishment from the separatist polity of a popular army chieftain
potentially a liability in Cuban relations with the United States.[3]

Consensus had collapsed. Both sectors of the *independentista* wing of
the separatist polity looked at each other with suspicion. While the army
subscribed to the American view that there did not exist in Cuba a legitimate government, the provisional government supported the American
determination to dissolve the army. Civilians and soldiers feared each
other far more than they distrusted the foreign power that had intervened
in their affairs.

II Months had passed since the end of the war—months of unrelieved
disquiet in army headquarters. Orders to keep the insurgent veterans
under arms had enjoyed mixed results. By November, the Americans in
Oriente had dissolved nearly a quarter of the Liberation Army. In Novem-

ber, too, the Assembly was preparing to dispatch its commission to Washington to negotiate a loan to disband the insurgent armed forces. But the army's adherence to Gómez's injunction did not provide the military command with more than fleeting consolation. Where insurgent units remained under arms, they endured under wretched conditions, and with no prospects of relief in sight. Meanwhile, the Assembly proposed to buy the dissolution of the army while the Americans prepared to starve the army out of existence. Time was running against the army leadership. Both the Assembly and the Americans continued to ignore the authority of the military command. Uncertainty about American intentions caused anxiety in army headquaters. Would the Americans honor their promise? Would the Assembly's actions jeopardize that promise? Could, lastly, the insurgent army remain sufficiently intact and the soldiers survive long enough to see these issues resolved satisfactorily?

In the autumn of 1898, the army command turned to the expatriate representation for answers to these questions and assistance in their resolution. A new alignment within the old revolutionary coalition was taking shape. Army leaders were not the only ones who nursed grievances against the provisional government. Like the army command, the expatriate representation, too, had suffered at the hands of the provisional government. Exile leaders were offended by unwarranted government intermeddling in their sphere of authority. They resented the inadequate expatriate representation on separatist councils in postwar Cuba. Also, like the army command, the exile leadership resented the indifference the government had displayed toward expatriate sensibilities after the peace protocol. "Those of us in exile," Emilio Núñez warned Gonzalo de Quesada in November 1898, "have to unite but we cannot count on support from any one."[4] Two months later Núñez struck a slightly more alarming note. "Those of us who have struggled abroad," he lamented in January 1899, "have no friends. They embrace us and they flatter us when they need us and in the end, they scorn us." What was worse, he complained, the emigration was being held responsible for the American intervention. "New Quixotes—they perceive themselves as the victors and accuse us of having betrayed them to the Yankees when the aurora of victory was just upon them."[5] Lastly, like army chieftains, expatriate authorities feared that Assembly politics and intrigue would complicate Cuban-American relations. "In my view," Núñez wrote, "the Americans have worked more to take us toward independence than we have." He complained that "puerile politics" had exaggerated suspicions and placed "Cuba's future in the concert of free and sovereign countries in grave danger."[6]

Circumstances soon after the American intervention contributed much to the affinity developing between the emigration and the army. The exile sector occupied a strategic position between the insurgent command in Cuba and the War Department in Washington. Communication to and from Cuba passed through the expatriate delegation. Washington relied on émigré representatives to communicate American plans to Cuban field forces and relay information from insurgent camps to authorities in the United States.

Rebuffed by the Assembly, ignored by the Americans, the army command appealed directly to the overseas delegation for support. The expatriate leaders had developed direct access to and, the army command sensed, influence with the authorities in Washington shaping Cuba's future. They offered a way, independent of the Assembly, of reaching American authorities. More importantly, the emigration offered the army an opportunity to participate directly in a Cuban settlement at a time when the Assembly was committed to excluding the military altogether. Only days after his dismissal, Calixto García appealed to Estrada Palma to assist the eastern army command in arriving at some understanding with American authorities in Santiago. Restating his lack of confidence in the provisional government, García announced his substantial concurrence with Americans' plans to organize a stable government in Cuba and the need to dissolve the army.[7] Throughout the fall a disconsolate Máximo Gómez corresponded frequently with Cuban agents in the United States. Often in eloquent anguish, he bared his despair over the destitution of the idle insurgent veterans and appealed to his compatriots abroad for assistance in finding an honorable solution to the Cuban problem. "Most of the officers and soldiers went into the field obeying my orders," a conscience stricken Gómez wrote in October. "I cannot abandon them until their future is assured. They have lost everything they had, they have a right to some compensation and, above all, their salaries; the new government must secure them." He appealed to the emigration to secure from Washington a statement of purpose of American intentions and to demand evidence of Washington's sincerity. "I have full confidence in the solemn promise made by the Congress of Washington," Gómez wrote in October, "and for that reason I do not have any fear as to the independence of Cuba. Some time must elapse before our ideal will be realized, but after so many struggles and privations we can wait a little longer." Before doubting the faith of the American people, Gómez concluded, "we must wait for acts which shall give lie to their solemn pledge."[8] A month later, he communicated his growing impatience with the Assembly and informed Estrada Palma that "on almost every stand you take we are in perfect accord." The only notable difference, Gómez hastened to add, was on "the manner in which you counsel the disbandment of the Army." For reasons of "public order, high politics, and morality," he opposed any plan that would have the soldiers return to their "destroyed homes and wasted countryside without a cent in their pockets."[9]

By the autumn of 1898, the expatriate representation had emerged as a broker between the army leadership in Cuba and policymakers in Washington. No other group in the separatist coalition had as current information or were in as frequent and direct communication with American authorities as the exiles. Washington had found the expatriate representation a congenial group, sharing assumptions not dissimilar to the premises of the intervention. This compatibility made the exile delegation the natural ally of the United States. Its members provided the United States access to the upper ranks of the insurgent leadership at a time when it was necessary to communicate with Cubans but inexpedient to recognize separatist agencies. In the process, over time and imperceptibly at first, the expatriate mission underwent a transformation, from representing the Cuban cause to the United States to representing American objectives to separatists.

Expatriate relations with Washington after the war transformed separatist politics. Most immediately, this connection translated into an enormous source of authority for the exiled separatists in postwar Cuba and conferred on the leadership a new influence within the revolutionary coalition. Reduced during the insurrection to the margins of the separatist polity, possessed of fewer legitimate claims to power and influence in separatist councils, the exterior representation emerged from the war with a new-found prominence. From a position of relative obscurity, expatriate leaders came to occupy a strategic place in postwar politics, holding the balance of power between the competing *independentista* sectors on the island.

Appeals from the army command in Cuba fell on a receptive audience abroad. Injured by the Assembly's indifference to exile sensibilities, the expatriate leadership responded favorably to the military call for assistance. This offered the emigration the opportunity to outmaneuver the politicians perceived by both the diplomats and soldiers as potentially pernicious to the cause of Cuba Libre.

But more than the exigencies of the intervention worked to unite the military command and the expatriate leadership. Whatever else may have earlier divided the army and the emigration, they were united by bonds of sentiment and history. Past political differences could not negate the ties of a generation born of common struggle. The old leaders, men like Máximo Gómez, Tomás Estrada Palma, Calixto García, Emilio Núñez, among the most prominent, shared experiences that reached deep into the formative years of separatist politics. These were the *pinos viejos*, the prestigious elders of the revolutionary polity who had kept the separatist faith for thirty years of struggle. Between 1895 and 1898, they had displayed something of an avuncular indulgence toward the activities of the youngers in the provisional government. "Figurehead," Calixto García charged with blunt scornfulness, a "little clique playing at government." But after the war, the old veterans had been dealt with rudely by the *pinos nuevos* dominating the provisional government and the Assembly. The *pinos nuevos* were behaving with an inordinate highhandedness and seemed determined to purge other sectors from the revolutionary coalition. These were ominous portents. "If [the Americans] deal with us," Calixto García reminded Estrada Palma in June, "the chiefs of the army, it is because they see that we have prestige and support in the country. You find yourself in a similar condition and if they listen to both of us it is because they see we have the people behind us, not because the Council of Government has given us the positions we occupy. That is the pure truth, my esteemed friend, the truth and nothing more."[10]

After the war, a new urgency served to bind the army to the emigration. The displacement of Estrada Palma by Méndez Capote and the ouster of Calixto García represented in more than symbolic terms the generational dimensions of the separatist dispute. These were not the moments to stand fast on ideological ceremony. The moment was urgent, and the brewing crisis threatened to undo thirty years of patriotic labor. The expatriate delegation possessed attributes perceived by the military as complementary to rather than competitive with those of the army. Each had something to contribute to a satisfactory resolution of Cuba's postwar problems.

By late fall the realignment was complete. The armed wing of Cuba Libre had separated from the political wing. A fragmented revolutionary polity awaited developments in occupied Cuba.

III   In November 1898, the Assembly commission arrived in the United States. The mission was ill-fated from the outset. Made up of José Antonio González Lanuza, Manuel Sanguily, José Miguel Gómez, José

Ramón Villalón, and Calixto García, the delegation represented a curious mix of civilians and soldiers. Dissent surfaced immediately. During preliminary briefings with expatriate leaders, the Cubans split on the nature of their mission in Washington. Several members insisted on negotiating a loan to secure funds adequate to meet all back pay owed to the army veterans. García demurred, proposing instead funds sufficient only to permit the immediate disbandment of the army.[11]

These differences were unresolved when the commission visited the White House in early December. In the course of an hour-long meeting, members of the Cuban delegation sought to learn from President McKinley the purpose of the American occupation, stressing their desire to cooperate as fully as possible to hasten the evacuation of American forces and facilitate an orderly transition to Cuban rule. Central to these calculations, the Cubans emphasized, was the swift demobilization of the insurgent armed force. It was necessary first, the commission indicated, to negotiate a loan in the United States. When asked by McKinley the amount of money required for the demobilization of the army, García answered immediately, "$3 million."[12]

García's response stunned other members of the commission. At no previous time had the Cubans discussed among themselves the figure of $3 million. Committee members reacted incredulously to García's figure and, in the presence of McKinley, a heated argument erupted. "I do not agree with General García!" one commissioner angrily retorted. "We really need at least $7 million." To which McKinley countered: "As I understand it, General García does not agree with you." Upon which, the president announced the end of the meeting.[13]

The sum of $3 million was not a random figure. At some point—probably to García through the expatriate leadership—the McKinley administration communicated its willingness to provide $3 million for the purpose of dissolving the insurgent army. The $3 million was the exact balance remaining from the $50 million Congress had appropriated in April for the war against Spain, discretionary funds entirely at the disposal of the president, money the Americans were prepared to distribute outright to the Cubans. This arrangement had the singular virtue of thwarting the Assembly's plan to negotiate a loan while, at the same time, expediting the disbandment of the Liberation Army. With this single measure, the United States would deal a body blow to both wings of the *independentista* sector.

News of the commission's troubles in Washington and García's part in those troubles quickly reached Cuba. The Assembly reacted immediately and directed its ire evenly toward the United States and García. The *oriental* chieftain never learned of the new vilification to which he was subjected in Cuba, however. In early December, the fifty-nine-year-old general succumbed to the rigors of the American winter and died in New York of pneumonia.

IV The Assembly's new attack on the United States was only one source of mounting tensions in Cuba. By early winter, a series of controversies brought Cubans and Americans to the point of an open rupture. In early December, an American decision to ban a veterans' march in Santiago commemorating the death of Antonio Maceo precipitated large scale anti-American demonstrations. And when days later the United States concluded the Treaty of Paris with Spain, insurgent chieftains across the island protested the absence of Cuban representation in Paris and the treaty's silence on the question of Cuban independence. Later that month, another dispute brought both armies to the brink of armed conflict. The American decision to exclude the Liberation Army from the formal ceremonies marking the end of Spanish sovereignty aroused enormous bitterness among senior Cuban officers and a wave of discontent within insurgent ranks. Public protests erupted in Havana; American flags were torn from public places and throughout the city American troops were hooted and taunted on the streets.[14] Concern in Washington was sufficiently high to prompt authorities to order four battleships to Cuban waters.[15] In early January, Cubans and Americans were again embroiled in dispute, this time over the position of an insurgent delegation at the funeral of Calixto García. Inadvertently assigned to the rear of the funeral procession, the offended Cuban representation protested without securing redress and there upon promptly withdrew from the procession.[16]

Throughout the late fall, moreover, tensions between American occupation forces and Cuban soldiers increased. Hungry insurgent veterans had broken ranks and returned to the ways of war. Foraging resumed and thefts of crops and livestock increased; merchants and shopkeepers in the towns reported a rise of thefts and break-ins. "Most of them," Cuban General Porfirio Valiente explained apologetically, "were good soldiers during the war, but many have since been virtually bandits out of sheer hunger as they could not get rations because they were armed and refused to disband."[17] Set within the larger context of mounting Cuban-American tensions, the actions of desperate veterans threatened on several occasions to precipitate a full-scale armed clash between the former allies. Leonard Wood denounced the "restless and disorderly spirits" who had resumed "their irregular and lawlives lives" and constituted "a serious menace to public order, life, and property."[18] The American response to postwar lawlessness further served to exacerbate deteriorating relations with the Cubans. Summary executions became an early feature of occupation justice. In Santiago, Leonard Wood authorized the execution of captured suspects without trial or hearing. "I issued [an order] that the brigands be brought in dead or alive, preferably dead," Wood later recalled.[19] In his official report of 1899, he explained the high number of deaths as the result of "attempts to resist arrest."[20] "Both [Governor General John] Brooke and [Adjutant General Adna] Chaffee," General James H. Wilson, military governor of Las Villas later wrote, "tell me that Wood is in very deep water. They knew personally that he has been hanging a lot of people without trial. . . . Chaffee says that Wood told him in person that he was having alleged bandetti killed without trial."[21]

V   In central Cuba, General in Chief Máximo Gómez approached the end of the year in despondent isolation, watching events in late 1898 with growing uneasiness. If Gómez had indeed been waiting for "acts" to give evidence to the sincerity of American intentions, he could not have found developments in December particularly reassuring. The Treaty of Paris, concluded without Cuban participation, had transferred control of the island to the United States without as much as a hint of Cuban independence. The Dominican army chieftain watched the mounting tensions between insurgents and Americans with growing apprehension. The slightest incident, Gómez worried, the smallest altercation between the former allies, would substantiate American charges of Cuban incapacity for self-government and provide the pretext through which to abrogate the pledge of the Joint Resolution. The fear that Americans would exploit the trivial incidents to achieve dramatic ends haunted the army command.[22] Certainly the deepening dispute between the Assembly and the Americans did little to allay these concerns. The controversies between separatist army leaders and Americans in Santiago and Havana in December, further, had created much ill feeling among the Cubans and seemed to announce an open break between the former allies. Much to the dismay of the insurgent army command, moreover, Washington had commenced the organization of the occupation government without consultation with ranking separatist leaders. Uneasiness swept across insurgent camps as destitute veterans witnessed public office and administrative positions distributed to nonparticipants in—if indeed not outright opponents to—the liberation struggle.

The army, meanwhile, continued to languish in desperate condition in the interior countryside. The failure of the Cuban commission in Washington in late 1898 ended any reasonable likelihood that relief would be forthcoming soon from the efforts of the Assembly. On the contrary, all indications suggested that relief for the army would be hopelessly delayed as the result of the brewing political dispute between the Assembly and the Americans. In late December, confrontations between occupation authorities and hungry veterans foraging for food resulted in several shooting incidents and the death of two Cuban soldiers. Tensions flared anew in insurgent army camps and disgruntled officers and restless troops asked impatiently how long they would have to tolerate passively existing conditions. By the end of the year, the incidents Gómez had come to fear most had the greatest likelihood of originating from the Liberation Army. The decision to keep the veterans organized under arms as a guarantee of Cuban independence had also the potential of creating the conditions jeopardizing that independence.

On December 29, Gómez broke his long silence to address the Cuban armed forces. "The moment has arrived to give public expression of my conduct and my objectives," he announced. Cuba was living under perilous conditions, he warned, and it was necessary to eliminate as quickly as possible all the causes that gave rise to the American intervention. "The Americans—tacitly—our allies, have completed the war with Spain and signed a treaty of peace." The period of transition was about to end, but, Gómez paraphrased the Joint Resolution, Cuba was "not yet free or independent." As long as the task to which he had devoted his life remained incomplete, the army chief vowed cryptically, he remained "always ready to help the Cubans finish the work."[23]

In another communication a week later to the Assembly, Gómez appealed for reconciliation and unity. A "rational necessity and complete urgency," he insisted plaintively, compelled him to speak on a issue of "transcendent gravity." He urged the Assembly to convoke immediately a national constituent assembly to establish the basis for a legitimate government—"the only means of terminating the labor and dismissing the foreign power, for me unjustifiable and that in the long run constitutes a danger to the absolute independence of Cuba."[24]

Gómez's effort to close separatist ranks evoked only civilian suspicion and a restatement of the Assembly's position. In condescending language, the Assembly reassured the Dominican chieftain that matters were securely under control. The Assembly expressed its appreciation of Gómez's interest in the affairs of state but insisted that these issues properly fell under the purview of the Assembly and would, in due time, be satisfactorily resolved.[25]

VI   Cuba entered the new year formally under the sovereignty of the United States. But it was not an uncontested sovereignty. As long as the Assembly claimed to represent legitimate authority of Cuba, American political control remained incomplete. But it was the Liberation Army that posed the primary threat to American rule in Cuba. As long as the insurgent army retained "its organization and its rifles," the *New York Times* editorialized in early February, "we could never measure the difficulties in our path."[26]

At the end of formal Spanish sovereignty in 1899, some forty thousand Cubans remained under arms. Their presence had an unsettling effect on Americans in Cuba. General James H. Wilson, the American commander in Las Villas, complained in early 1899 that Cuban troops considered "themselves exclusively under the control of the military chiefs, not subject to the alcalde or other civil authorities."[27] From Pinar del Río, Fitzhugh Lee wrote that the soldiers "still kept their guns, and were massing around the cities and towns producing more or less unrest in the public mind, with the fear that many of them unaccustomed to work for so long, would be transformed to brigands."[28] This uncertainty discouraged many farmers and planters from returning to the land. From Puerto Príncipe, Colonel L. H. Carpenter reported that "people were afraid to go into the country and make any start with cattle or in other directions without being assured protection."[29] From Oriente, General H. L. Lawton had reported similar conditions. "The material interests of the country suffer," Lawton wrote, "and planters hesitate to reclaim their farms, fearing loss from pilfering of the crops by these bands."[30]

Nor had American silence on the question of Cuban independence contributed to allaying separatist misgivings. On the contrary, formal American rule over Cuba commenced in 1899 amidst insurgent suspicions and distrust. Six months had passed since the cessation of hostilities and Cubans remained in ignorance of their fate. This silence represented a sinister augury. The closing months of Spanish sovereignty found the United States publicly belittling its former allies, impugning their capacity for self-government, and openly engaged in a military buildup for which there could be no other possible use except against the Cubans.

VII   In central Cuba, a disillusioned Máximo Gómez brooded alone. News of the ceremonies on January 1 in Havana ending four hundred years of Spanish rule aroused nostalgic memories in the crestfallen old general. The principal purpose of his adult life, the consuming vision of thirty years, and he had not been present. Gómez despaired. "I dreamed of peace with Spain," he confided to his diary. "I had hoped to bid the valiant Spanish soldiers, with whom we always found ourselves face to face on the fields of battle, farewell. . . . But the Americans, with a tutelage imposed by force, have soured the joy of the victorious Cubans."[31]

But personal disappointment did not blind him to political realities. The Americans now controlled Cuba, and the matter before the Cubans was to end the occupation as quickly as possible. For Gómez, the Cuban task was self-evident: eliminate the conditions that served as the pretext for the continued American presence. The military occupation, he believed, represented something of a transitory arrangement sanctioned in the very Joint Resolution that also promised Cuba its independence. Order and peace functioned as the necessary preconditions to Cuban independence. It was the task of Cubans, the army chieftain reasoned, to facilitate the labor of pacification as much as possible. This was the purport of his January communication to the Assembly—urging Cubans to cooperate so as to make the American stay as short as possible. Any contemplated abrogation of the congressional pledge, he sensed, could find justification only within the context of the Joint Resolution. Any condition that would delay pacification threatened also to postpone indefinitely the fulfillment of the American promise.

VIII   The United States inaugurated formal rule over Cuba without direct access to the leadership of the Assembly or the Liberation army. The death of Calixto García had deprived Washington of the support of an ally possessed of impeccable patriotic credentials and universally venerated within armed separatist ranks. More than ever before, the Americans needed an ally of sufficient stature and influence to counter the authority of the Assembly and through whom to resolve the problem of the Liberation Army. In January 1899, Estrada Palma suggested to the White House that some official attention to General Gómez, together with American recognition of his authority, would go a long way toward resolving the impasse in

Cuba. Estrada also wrote directly to Gómez, alluding to the perils that unsettled conditions in Cuba posed to the cause to which they had devoted their lives. The time had arrived, he counseled, to join together to establish Cuba on a "firm base of peace, tranquillity, and public order."[32]

Washington reacted immediately to Estrada's suggestion. In late January, McKinley announced the appointment of Robert P. Porter as his special representative to meet personally with Máximo Gómez in Cuba. "I want you to go to Cuba and find Gómez," the president instructed Porter. "I am informed he feels hurt because he was not recognized in the peace negotiations, and is in doubt regarding our intentions towards the Cubans. We must get him to cooperate in the disbandment of the Cuban army."[33]

Porter arrived in Havana on January 30, accompanied by Gonzalo de Quesada and in possession of two letters of introduction, one from Secretary of War Russell A. Alger to Governor General John R. Brooke and the other from Estrada Palma to Máximo Gómez. "Mr. Porter has the entire confidence of the President," Alger informed Brooke, "who directs that any subject he may bring to your attention shall receive your careful and immediate attention and cooperation."[34] The United States, Porter explained to Brooke, was prepared to renew the offer of $3 million, this time to Gómez, as a means to facilitate the disbandment of the insurgent armed forces and assist the veterans' return to civilian life. A personal invitation to Gómez to visit Havana, Porter suggested to Brooke, one showing proper respect and appropriate deference to the generalissimo's status, would contribute enormously to the success of this mission.[35]

In early February, Porter traveled to army headquarters in Remedios. This was the first official American contact with the Cuban army chieftain. More than this, Porter's visit signified, at long last, American recognition of Gomez's authority.

Upon his arrival, Porter delivered Estrada Palma's letter. The expatriate leader urged Gómez to accept the American offer of assistance as the basis upon which to begin to restore conditions of stability and peace.[36] Quesada reiterated verbally Estrada's views.

In his discussions with Porter, Gómez sought clarification of American intentions in Cuba, specifically the American view on Cuban independence. Porter reassured him that the United States intended to honor fully the terms of the congressional commitment. The military occupation, Porter pledged, would not last one moment longer than the time required to complete the task of pacification, as stipulated by the Joint Resolution. "The President's idea," he explained, ". . . was to build up the new government from the foundations. . . . Under such conditions, the President needed and was entitled to the friendly cooperation of all interested in the future welfare of Cuba"—especially that of the insurgent army chieftain. An important step toward meeting the conditions outlined in the Joint Resolution necessarily involved the release of the forty thousand Cubans still under arms. Porter asked Gómez to assert his leadership in peace as he had during the war and assist the United States in creating the conditions that would at once facilitate pacification and hasten Cuban independence. The "first problem to be confronted," Porter concluded, was the immediate disbandment of the Cuban army and the return of the veterans to peaceful pursuits.[37] After several days of discussions, Gómez accepted the American offer. "Gómez will cooperate fully with United States authorities in disbandment of army and distribution of relief funds," Porter cabled the White House. "He will go to Havana and confer with Brooke."[38]

Máximo Gómez emerged from these discussions euphoric, wholly persuaded that the issue of Cuban independence had been successfully resolved. Indeed, for Gómez, Porter's visit in his capacity as the personal representative of President McKinley achieved what until then had eluded insurgent agencies in Cuba: American recognition of separatist authority. This official attention, too, did much to lift the old general's spirits. He was now assured of playing as large a role in establishing the republic as he had in ending the colony. Gómez was also convinced that his agreement with the United States had definitively guaranteed Cuban independence. He had received from the president of the United States a solemn and personal pledge. "The United States," a confident Gómez exulted some weeks later, slightly paraphrasing Porter's comments, "has intervened only for the pacification of Cuba and the establishment of a stable independent government and . . . it does not intend to exercise any control or sovereignty over Cuba."[39] With these words, Gómez believed Cuba's future independence secured. In that moment, the overwhelming weight of anxiety he had carried so long began to lift from his shoulders. "I confess to you," he wrote exuberantly to his wife, "that I felt like the happiest man in the world, thinking that I helped the Cubans in peace as I had helped them in war, . . . bringing to a quick end the period of reconstruction and ending through these means the unnecessary foreign military occupation with Cuba emerging as an independent Republic, free, felicitous and well-ordered."[40]

IX   Gómez's happiness was short-lived. News of the Porter-Gómez agreement plunged the separatist polity into a new crisis. The Assembly reacted with a mixture of incredulity and shock. Deliberately ignored at Remedios, the Assembly had been neither privy to nor a participant in the negotiations. More was involved than injured sensibilities, however. The Remedios settlement directly threatened the authority of the Assembly. If left unchallenged, it promised to reduce the supreme deliberative body of the revolution to a position of impotence.

The Assembly denounced the Remedios accord and reaffirmed its determination to negotiate independently a loan with which to dissolve the army. Within several weeks, the Assembly met with C. M. Cohen, a New York banker, who offered the Cubans sixty-two cents on the dollar for a $20 million bond issue, redeemable at face value in thirty years bearing 5 percent interest semiannually. These funds, Cohen stressed, were to be used exclusively for the "payment and disbanding of the Cuban Army which must be carried out promptly in a manner satisfactory to the U.S. Government." Further, the contract could not be ratified without the approval of the president of the United States which he and his associates pledged to "obtain without the Assembly having any work to do in that line."[41] As these negotiations drew to an end, the Assembly ordered General Gómez to endorse the new settlement. He declined. An agreement had already been made with the United States, Gómez answered, and he was bound to honor his earlier commitment.[42]

Disbelief over Gómez's accord with the Americans turned to dismay at the general's open defiance of the Assembly's authority. Rafael Portuondo, president of the Assembly's Executive Commission, invoking the principle of civil supremacy, denied the legitimacy of Gómez's agreement with Porter. "General Gómez is only the General-in-Chief of the Army," an angry Portuondo insisted, "and, like the Army, is subject to the decisions of the Assembly."[43] Shock gave way to anger and acrimony. Several members of the Assembly recommended that Gómez be sentenced to death by a firing squad—and volunteered their services as executioners.[44] "It has come to pass," José Lacret Morlet announced, "that the General-in-Chief has disobeyed this Assembly, . . . from which he has voluntarily separated himself to join the side of the interventionist power."[45] "It is necessary," Manuel Sanguily exhorted, "to disabuse the Government of the United States that the General-in-Chief is the authority who represents the Revolution. . . . The American Government is a victim of a deception or illusion by treating with the General-in-Chief as if he were the sole legitimate representative of the revolution."[46] To end this confusion, the Assembly charged Gómez with insubordination and abolished the rank of general in chief, a measure effectively relieving the Dominican chieftain from his command of the Liberation Army.[47] The Assembly also censured the expatriate representation and deposed Gonzalo de Quesada as chargé d'affaires for his part in the Remedios settlement.[48]

X The Assembly's dismissal of Gómez and Quesada, as well as the repudiation of the Remedios accord, was as much a challenge to American authority in Cuba as it was an affirmation of civil supremacy within the separatist polity. The Assembly's action, allowed to stand unchallenged, threatened to deprive Gómez of the moral, if not the military, authority necessary to implement the terms of the Remedios agreement. Indeed, control over the army under these circumstances would pass directly to the Assembly. A hostile Assembly, contesting the authority of the American military government, with its prestige at a new high and in control of the insurgent army, promised to place an endless series of obstacles in the path of the consolidation of American rule in Cuba.

Washington responded swiftly. In Cuba, Governor General John Brooke completed preparations to dissolve the Assembly by decree and tensely awaited final authorization from the War Department.[49] In the United States, President McKinley reappointed the ousted Quesada as the Cuban representative in Washington at an annual salary of $5,000. Quesada now represented the United States. Secretary of War Russell A. Alger instructed Governor General Brooke to "let it be known" that the United States "would not recognize any financial obligations entered into by any person claiming to represent the people of Cuba without authorization of the President."[50] Washington reiterated again its refusal to recognize the Assembly. "The Secretary of War," Army Adjutant General Henry C. Corbin cabled Havana, "directs me to say that the so-called Assembly or any part of it will not receive recognition by this Government under any conditions whatever."[51] The United States also reaffirmed its support of the deposed Gómez. The general's authority in Cuba, Washington announced, did not flow from the Assembly but, rather, from the American military government. Washington informed Gómez that he retained the full support of the United States. "President McKinley and General Brooke," an aide of the American governor general informed Gómez, "recognized no other person or entity but himself, with him they had dealt, with him they had entered into and concluded negotiations;—that was finished business. All that remained was the execution of that contract."[52] Brooke later wrote to the adjutant general:

As you know, the Assembly deposed General Gómez. I have consistently refused to acknowledge the Assembly as having any authority, as you know. General Gómez admitted the authority of the Assembly by accepting its act deposing him. I still maintain that he is the Commander-in-Chief of the Cuban Army and as such had been in communication, through Mr. Porter, with the President. Therefore I considered that the act of the President should be upheld and that no party or parties could, under any circumstances, interpose between General Gómez and myself in connection with the distribution of this money to the Cuban soldiers.[53]

Gómez left Remedios in early February to meet formally with Brooke in Havana. He traveled westward at a leisurely pace, stopping along the way to address the crowds that assembled in the towns and cities along the parade route. The trip to Havana as well covered by the Cuban press and attracted thousands of spectators and well-wishers; every town greeted the Dominican chieftain with a tumultous welcome.[54] It was at the height of this public acclaim, as the seventy-three-year-old general neared Havana riding a crest of national popularity, that Cubans learned of the Assembly's decision to oust Gómez. Disgraceful, many felt; outrageous, others protested. In deposing Gómez, the Assembly appeared to the public as a group of quarrelsome and self-serving malcontents, devoid of the gratitude appropriate to the general chosen personally by Martí to lead the insurrection and who had devoted the better part of his adult life to the cause of Cuban independence. The ouster of Gómez earned the Assembly immediate public enmity. Newspaper editorials denounced the Assembly.[55] A wave of indignation swept across the island. Rallies, mass demonstrations, and public processions protested Gómez's ouster. Leading members of the Assembly were hung in effigy; thousands of telegrams decried the Assembly's act.[56] Brooke, who earlier had sought official authorization to dissolve the Assembly, now relaxed; American action was no longer necessary. "There seems to be an outbreak of indignant protest against the action of the Assembly and expressions of confidence in Gómez," Brooke cabled Washington. "Gómez seems in the ascendant."[57] In late March, under constant attack and without popular support, the Assembly dissolved.[58] Some months later, without further obstructions, the Liberation Army disbanded.[59]

The corporate expressions of Cuba Libre, the institutions summoned into existence to secure independence, had failed to survive the early months of the American occupation. Successively, the PRC, the provisional government, and the Liberation Army disappeared. The agencies through which Cuba had sought independence passed out of existence at the precise moment the new formal foreign rule commenced.

14   Purpose Without Policy

I am speaking for myself alone, but speaking thus, I say that for the good of Cuba . . . a separate government over Cuba uncontrolled by the American Government should never have been promised. Cuba is a mere extension of our Atlantic coast line.
—Senator Albert G. Beveridge, September 1898

Personally . . . I have always regarded the resolution of Congress, at the outbreak of the war, a grave mistake. Seventy-five years of our diplomacy on this subject had pointed steadily to one thing—the absolute necessity of controlling Cuba for our own defense. To announce at the outset that we were going to drive Spain out and then preclude ourselves from this control was a self-denying ordinance possible only in a moment of national hysteria.
—Whitelaw Reid, September 1900

We will control Cuba. It makes little difference now whether or not the insurgents can maintain a stable government. In less than twenty years the United States will practically own the island.
—Senator Mark Hanna, August 1898

I cannot believe it an evil for any people that the stars and stripes, the symbol of liberty and law, should float over them.
—David J. Hill, Assistant Secretary of State, December 1898

I On January 1, 1899, John R. Brooke became the 167th governor-general of Cuba. Like the 166 Spaniards who preceded him, the new governor-general assumed responsibility for the fundamental well-being of the island. "The object of the present Government," he proclaimed on January 1, "is to give protection to the people, security to person and property, to restore confidence, to encourage the people to resume the pursuits of peace, to build up waste plantations, to resume commercial traffic, and to afford full protection in the exercise of all civil and religious rights."[1]

Unlike his predecessors, however, Brooke arrived in Havana without benefit of a sense of policy. Indeed, all he had learned from Washington was that "the foundation of our authority in Cuba is the law of belligerent right over conquered territory." President McKinley encouraged him to "mingle with the leading men of all parties in social and public functions" and to "show a ready sympathy in all things that truly concern the welfare of the island."[2] Beyond these vague instructions, however, Brooke arrived to his position in Havana without policy directives or official knowledge of American intentions in Cuba. General James H. Wilson, military governor of Matanzas and Las Villas provinces, in frequent communication with Brooke during the first year of the occupation, later recalled that the governor-general often complained about the absence of instructions from Washington. "When I asked Brooke," Wilson wrote a decade later, "as I did frequently during that year, what our Government's policy and ultimate purpose were in all that it was doing, in short, what was the law under which we were acting, he frankly confessed that he did not know, 'except by induction.' " Whatever information he possessed, Brooke confessed to Wilson, had reached him by way of published orders. He disclosed to Wilson that he had not received any "private intimation from those in the confidence of the President or the administration."[3] In the absence of "private intimation," Brooke accepted published orders at face value. But public instructions reflected more the political discretion of his superiors than the policy directions of the government—something Brooke failed to realize until too late. He did sense, however, contradictions. As a result, he governed haltingly, incapable of giving either his administration in Havana direction or his subordinates in the provinces directives. "He . . . gave me no special instructions," Wilson later reminisced, "but left me to make my own way through the maze which surrounded us both."[4]

270   Those in possession of the president's confidence were no wiser. Senator

Joseph Benson Foraker also bemoaned the confusion in the White House. "Instead of determining upon a policy," Foraker complained impatiently in mid-1899, "and indicating to them what it is, the President carefully abstains from allowing any Cuban, or any American for that matter, so far as I can learn, to know what his policy is, or whether he has any policy whatever, except only to hold on by military force to the control of the Island, including the Custom Houses and all other sources of revenue."[5] "The government lets everything drift," Henry Adams observed from Washington in January 1899. "It professes earnestly its intention to give Cuba its independence, but refuses to take a step towards it, and allows everybody to act for annexation. It supports Wood at one end and Brooke at the other, pulling different ways."[6] A month later, Adams again noted: "A dozen Major Generals are all pulling in different ways . . . on totally different lines and only by the greatest effort has a grand dissolution of all ties been avoided thus far, although it is nearly certain to occur.[7]

II In fact, the United States began the military occupation without a coherent policy or defined objectives. The lack of policy did not, however, signify the absence of purpose. On the contrary, the organization of the military government in occupied Cuba was itself a clear expression of purpose. Well before 1899, the administration had committed itself to a course leading ultimately to the annexation of Cuba. Few if any in Washington questioned the fundamental premises or the inexorable logic of the policy roots of "political gravitation." Annexation was inevitable, more so after 1898 as a result of the newly discovered deficiencies in the Cuban character. The task before the United States in 1899, and the function of the military government during the occupation, was to realize these objectives and prepare the way for the ultimate annexation of the island.

The military government was organized around several assumptions. First, and from which all others would flow, was the enduring nineteenth-century conviction that the establishment of an independent and sovereign Cuba was incompatible with American interests. Doubts about Cuban fitness for self-government raised early in the nineteenth century were confirmed by American soldiers in the trenches outside El Caney and Santiago. The epithets of war were transformed into articles of faith in peace. Indeed, attacks on Cuban qualifications for independence assumed a new virulence after the establishment of the military government. Whatever self-serving purpose these allegations may have concealed, it was nonetheless true that this perception seized both the official mind and popular imagination in the United States and offered Washington encouragement and justification to contemplate ways of contravening the Joint Resolution. "To fully understand their deficiencies and vices," the former American consul in Sagua la Grande wrote the White House, ". . . it is necessary to live among them." Walter B. Barker continued:

They are not only dishonest but weak minded; this, of course, is due to the lack of training, for Spain did not allow them to *think* for themselves. Even those who have had advantage of more or less education are totally unenlightened with the history of their own or any other government. The best of them are not practical, but improvident and wholly lacking in executive ability. . . . They are indolent and manifest no further interest than to secure a lucrative position with little or no work. . . . They are innately dishonest with a low standard of morals. Their chief virtue is that they are not of a turbulent nature, and can (when understood) be made as tractable as a child, controlled as a child with kindness but firmness. Thus, it is that I hold the present generation will not prove equal to self-government.[8]

Senator Orville H. Platt agreed and in a striking coincidence invoked the same metaphor. Having earlier deprived Cubans of their "manhood," presumably all that remained was "childhood." "In many respects they are like children," Platt noted. "They are passionately devoted to the sentiment of liberty, freedom and independence, but as yet have little real idea of the responsibilities, duties and practical results of republican government."[9] The Cubans, insisted Major George M. Barbour, the American sanitary commissioner in Santiago, "are stupid, given to lying and doing all things in the wrong way. . . . Yet I find them docile, willing, and careful. . . . Under our supervision, and with firm and honest care for the future, the people of Cuba may become a useful race and a credit to the world; but to attempt to set them afloat as a nation, during this generation, would be a great mistake. We must wait until the children of to-day are old enough to think for themselves, and absorb American ideas."[10]

The consensus was striking. No public official of any influence in the administration, civil or military, in Cuba or in the United States, conceded any possibility that Cubans could, over the long run, succeed at self-government. In mid-1899, Leonard Wood, as military governor of Santiago, insisted "that the mass of the people are ignorant. . . . As yet they are not fit for self-government."[11] A year later, as governor-general of Cuba, Wood reiterated his conviction that Cubans were "not ready for self-government." "We are going ahead as fast as we can," he informed the White House, "but we are dealing with a race that has steadily been going down for a hundred years and into which we have to infuse new life, new principles and new methods of doing things."[12] Governor-General Brooke agreed. "These people cannot *now*," he counseled at the end of his one year term, "or I believe in the immediate future, be entrusted with their own government."[13] "The present generation will," predicted General William Ludlow, military governor of Havana, "in my judgement, have to pass away before the Cubans can form a stable government."[14]

These conclusions corroborated initial assumptions, namely, that Cuban independence was as unthinkable as it was impossible—the Joint Resolution notwithstanding. Annexationist sentiment increased throughout the first year of the occupation. In June 1899, Robert P. Porter, who only months earlier had solemnly reassured Máximo Gómez of American intentions to honor its commitment to Cuban independence, spoke openly of annexation. "The future of Cuba, in my opinion," Porter proclaimed, "can only lay in annexation, and the longer the Cubans in Cuba and the anti-expansionists in the United States continue to deceive themselves and the people by suggesting any other solution, the longer capital and enterprise will hold back from the island."[15] Fitzhugh Lee, formerly the consul general in Havana and during the occupation the military governor of Pinar del Río, predicted exultantly in 1900 that the American flag was over Morro Castle "to stay and will never be pulled down."[16]

Even the most zealous and unabashed advocate of annexation, however, recognized the necessity to acknowledge the constraints of the Joint Resolution. Whatever justification existed for disavowing the Teller Amendment—and, indeed, many argued that mitigating and previously unsuspected circumstances not only warranted but demanded annulment of the congressional pledge—most American authorities were loath to move in blatant and flagrant violation of Congress's promise.[17]

Nor did Americans detect in Cuba in 1899 much popular support for annexation. On the contrary, most observers conceded that the prevailing expectation of independence among Cubans would not allow annexation during the occupation. Any scheme contemplating a denial of the congressional pledge, Americans in Cuba warned, any plan to revoke the American commitment contained in the Joint Resolution, threatened to provoke a crisis of monumental proportions. As early as August 1898, Calixto Gar-

cía admitted that annexation could sometime in the future be Cuba's ultimate destiny. If that resulted in a "natural form," he was prepared to
accept it. Any attempt by the United States to seize Cuba by duplicity or
force, however, would serve as the instant signal for rebellion.[18] "Nothing
could provoke a conflict," Bartolomé Masó cautioned General James H.
Wilson, "except continued and indefinite delay on the part of the United
States in complying with the Fourth Section of the Joint Resolution."[19]
The outbreak of rebellion in the Philippine Islands only a month after the
inauguration of American rule in Havana, moreover, caused Washington
to move with great caution in Cuba. "A series of disasters at the very
beginning of our colonial policy," Roosevelt warned Secretary of State
John Hay, "would shake this administration, and therefore our party. . . .
If some political cataclysm was the result, it might mean the definite abandonment of the course upon which we have embarked—the only course I
think fit for a really great nation."[20] Rumors in Cuba during the autumn of
1899 that Washington contemplated replacing the military government,
avowedly temporary in its mandate, with a civilian administration, possessed of an unlimited charge, plunged the island into political crisis. Denouncing the rumored change as a thinly disguised annexationist plot,
Cubans organized mass demonstrations and protests across the island.
Americans in Cuba, startled by the magnitude of the protest, openly predicted that the establishment of a civilian government in Havana would
precipitate open rebellion. By early November, one American wrote,
guerrilla bands had "taken to the woods" across the island.[21] In Santiago,
Leonard Wood wrote his wife that the local press was "preaching blood and
war and talking of the revolution sure to come in the near future."[22] Governor General Brooke, who only weeks earlier had approved a reduction of
American military forces in Cuba, immediately called a halt to further
withdrawal of troops.[23]

Whether the rumors were groundless or, in fact, as Cubans suspected, a
device employed by the administration to test public opinion in Cuba toward proposed schemes to govern Cuba indefinitely, the conclusions were
irrefutable. Any plans in Washington to use the military occupation as the
bridgehead of annexation were abandoned.[24]

III   Neither the congressional proscription against annexation nor
Cuban opposition to American rule could dissuade Washington to abandon
century-long designs on Cuba. Indeed, no goal was so central to American
calculations during the four years of military occupation as the eventual

annexation of the island. If the Joint Resolution prohibited immediate annexation, one imposed on Cuba by the United States by virtue of force, it did not preclude future annexation based on mutual consent, a merger resulting from Cubans voluntarily suing for admission into the Union. These calculations gave the American military government in Cuba a goal and officials in Washington a policy. The American purpose in Cuba was not, as the administration proclaimed during the occupation years, to prepare the island for independence, but, rather, to prepare Cuba for eventual annexation. A period under American rule, Washington reasoned, during which time the United States would have an opportunity to Americanize the island, organize national institutions compatible with the American political system, and recruit local allies, would suffice to create the conditions setting into motion the forces leading to annexation after the cessation of formal military rule. Properly prepared, Cuba would be predisposed for annexation at some undetermined future date.

The Joint Resolution was not, however, without policy value or relevance to American calculations. To be sure, the spirit of the congressional resolution served as a powerful moral deterrent to annexationist impulses after the war. But, with equal moral force, Congress had also outlined the preconditions necessary to the fulfillment of the American commitment to Cuban independence. The United States had assumed before the world a sober responsibility by intervening in the Cuban conflict, administration officials explained after 1898; central to this responsibility was the obligation to establish in Cuba a government, in the words of the Treaty of Paris, capable of "protecting life and property."[25] Those who had earlier demanded intervention as a duty to the Cubans now insisted on retaining control over Cuba as a duty to the world.

American rule in Cuba found continued sanction in the pacification clause of the Joint Resolution. "The United States," the Teller Amendment pledged, "hereby disclaims any disposition or intention to exercise sovereignty, jurisdiction, or control over said island except for pacification thereof." It soon became apparent that Washington construed pacification to mean something considerably more than merely a cessation of hostilities. "What does 'pacification' mean in that clause?" Senator Orville H. Platt asked rhetorically in May 1900. "We became responsible for the establishment of a government there, which we would be willing to indorse to the people of the world—a stable government, a government for which we would be willing to be responsible in the eyes of the world. Until that time occurs, no patriotic American will ask that our troops and our government be withdrawn from the island of Cuba."[26] "We could not impose on the inhabitants of Cuba complete political independence," one writer intoned soberly; ". . . if the result of such an act upon our part were the eventual experience by Cuba of the fate of Hayti, we should be held responsible in history for a crime against civilization. Having delivered Cuba from the Spanish yoke, we are accountable for her tranquility and prosperity."[27] President McKinley, too, in his annual message of 1899, reminded Americans of the sober burden the United States had assumed in Cuba. "This nation has assumed before the world a grave responsibility for the future of good government in Cuba," McKinley stressed. The president continued:

We have accepted a trust the fulfillment of which calls for the sternest integrity of purpose and the exercise of the highest wisdom. The new Cuba yet to arise from the ashes of the past must be bound to us by ties of singular intimacy and strength if its enduring welfare is to be assured. . . . Our mission, to accomplish when we took up the wager of battle, is not to be fulfilled by turning adrift any loosely framed commonwealth to face the vicissitudes which too often attend weaker states.[28]

In Havana, Governor-General Brooke emphasized to Cubans that the United States was determined first to "establish a stable government in the island, then to deliver it to the Cubans themselves."[29] "There was a qualification to the [Congressional] pledge," one writer noted, ". . . which is contained in the promise made to the world at large, that Cuba should always maintain a stable government."[30]

A general consensus emerged in Washington early into the occupation, namely, that the requirements of "pacification" involved, specifically, stability. But "stability" and "stable government," too, were many things to many people. Whatever else stability may have meant, Washington had long before determined that an independent and sovereign Cuba could not meet conditions of stability. The ideal of order that required intervention against Spain also justified indefinite control over Cuba. If, indeed, the United States was morally obligated to relinquish "the government and control of the island to its people," it was equally obliged to establish in Havana a government mindful of its responsibilities to the United States and conscious of the solicitude necessary for the well-being of American interests. When asked during congressional hearings if Cubans should be "entirely independent in the administration of their own local affairs," General James H. Wilson responded unequivocally: "Only so far as they are willing to bind themselves to manage their own affairs, in a way that would be acceptable and agreeable to us."[31]

The need to establish stable government in Cuba, all quite properly within the context of the "pacification" clause of the Joint Resolution, provided the justification for a period of prolonged American rule, an adequate if only temporary prelude to annexation. The clause designed to guarantee Cuban independence provided the opportunity to prepare the island for annexation. Having successfully subsumed "stability" into the meaning of the Teller resolution, the McKinley administration acquired political license in both Cuba and the United States to resolve the status of Cuba in virtually any manner it deemed appropriate over however long it proved necessary. Few disputed the necessity of stability as a precondition for self-government. But "stability," like pacification, underwent repeated ideological transfigurations, and it soon became apparent that the logical if not inevitable conclusion of "stable government" was American government. "We propose to establish a stable government on that island," Senator Mark Hanna announced in August 1898, "but what constitutes a stable government, has not yet been defined. I think, however, Cuba will be an evolution, and in about twenty years, it will be so thoroughly Americanized that there will be no question as to what a stable government means."[32] Stability, too, was an economic condition and necessarily involved the creation and maintenance of an atmosphere conducive to American investment and hospitable to American capital—a condition, Washington insisted, Cubans alone and unassisted could not attain. "They are utterly unfit to be masters of themselves or of anybody else," one writer argued. "They are by inheritance unfit for responsibility. . . . Americans in Cuba have seen this so clearly that, although there are magnificent opportunities for profitable business, they are not making investment; for cheap as most of the land is now, it would be worthless if Cuba should be handed over to its inhabitants."[33] For Leonard Wood, the establishment and maintenance of stable government necessarily depended first upon creating "business confidence." "The people ask me what we mean by a stable government in Cuba," Wood explained to Secretary of War Elihu Root in January 1900. "I tell them that when money can be borrowed at a reasonable rate of interest and when capital is willing to invest in the Island, a condition of stability will have been reached."[34] A month later, Wood wrote to McKinley: "Business is gradually picking up, but capital is still very timid in regard to Cuban investments. When people ask me what I mean by stable government, I tell them 'money at six percent'; this seems to satisfy all classes."[35] Major Duncan B. Harrison, inspector general on Wood's staff, summarized official thinking in late 1899. "If the proper kind of a government could be guaranteed," he speculated wistfully, "hundreds of Americans and their dollars would go to the island, thereby giving numerous teachers and exponents of republics and republican principles."[36]

Stability also had international dimensions. An unsupervised Cuban government, one given to periodic disorders, Americans feared, promised to make the island again a source of international tension. To withdraw from the island without establishing first some restraints on Cuba's conduct of its foreign relations, Wood predicted, would be tantamount to inviting European powers to occupy every harbor in Cuba.[37] Whitlaw Reid acknowledged that the Joint Resolution had obligated the United States "to give Cuba a chance to see what she can do in the management of her own domestic affairs." On the matter of Cuban foreign relations, however, Reid was unequivocal: "Under no circumstances, however, do I think it would be wise of the United States ever to relinquish control of her foreign relations. To do that would be to insure more dangerous embarrassments immediately on our coast than we had under the rule of Spain." This meant, ultimately, placing Cuba in a protectorate relationship to the United States.[38] American interests, Senator Platt insisted, required ironclad assurances that Cuba would indeed be "an independent and self-governing power" from all other nations but the United States. The United States demanded some definition and acknowledgment of this special relationship as a precondition for the completion of pacification. "In no other way," Platt insisted, "could a stable government be assured in Cuba, and until such assurance there could be no complete 'pacification' of the island, and no surrender of its control."[39]

IV   Washington concluded early in the occupation that annexation remained beyond the direct reach of the military government. While American authority in Cuba may have indeed rested on, as McKinley informed Brooke, "the law of belligerent right over conquered territory," it was also apparent that it was impolitic if not impossible to pursue annexation as a function of that authority. This determination did not dissuade the administration from pursuing annexation by alternative means, however. Washington correctly sensed that it had little choice but to go through the motions of preparing Cuba for independence as outlined in the congressional resolution of 1898. But independence in this instance was designed to be qualified and short-lived. After 1899, the authority and the resources of the occupation government were committed to prepare Cuba for future annexation. After a brief period of independence and self-government, one that allowed the United States to acquit itself of its obligations and honor long-standing Cuban aspirations, the island would voluntarily sue for admission into the Union. Proper preparation for independence, Washington reasoned, and introduction to American ideas and methods, would serve as the formal antecedents for annexation.[40] Leonard Wood from the outset opposed forceful annexation. After a brief period of self-government, he divined, one that would satisfy Cubans' sentiment for "theoretical liberty," the island would eventually petition the United States for annexation. "Forcible annexation he had refused to consider," wrote Wood's biographer; "annexation by guile he had effectively opposed; but annexation by acclamation had been his dream from the beginning."[41] Wood hoped, in fact, to secure "annexation by acclamation" during the period of American rule. Writing in 1899 to Henry Cabot Lodge, Theodore Roosevelt communicated Wood's thinking on Cuba: "Wood believes that we should not promise or give the Cubans independence; that we should govern them justly and equitably, giving them all possible opportunities for civic and military advancement, and that in two or three years they will insist upon being part of us."[42] Wood hoped to complete the task of Americanization before the end of occupation, at which point annexation would respond to a rising, if not perhaps orchestrated, clamor from Cubans. "Go we must," Wood wrote to Roosevelt in 1900, "when the time comes, if they want us to." But, Wood hoped, Cubans would not ask Americans to leave.[42] Secretary of War Elihu Root drew the moral by analogy: "It is better to have the favors of a lady with her consent, after judicious courtship, than to ravish her."[43]

By far the most comprehensive formulation of official thinking on the status of Cuba originated with General James H. Wilson, the military governor of Matanzas and Las Villas. A prolific and indefatigable correspondent, Wilson was in constant communication with ranking and influential members of the official Republican family in Washington, including Root, Roosevelt, Reid, Lodge, and Foraker. In lengthy policy expositions, Wilson emerged as the outstanding advocate of Cuban independence as the means to Cuba's annexation. "I am an out and out Annexationist," Wilson proclaimed to Lodge in late 1899. "I believe in 'Expansion' and 'Empire,' and that neither can wait."[44] For Wilson, the Teller Amendment was "an unnecessary and serious mistake," an impediment that forced the United States to seek a "different course" through which to acquire Cuba. Any attempt to prolong the occupation indefinitely, or seek the forceful annexation of Cuba, Wilson warned, threatened to provoke resentment and resistance. And with the Filipino insurrection approaching the one year mark, Washington could hardly afford additional disorders in any other of the newly acquired colonies.[45] A solution to the impasse was readily available, however. "Inasmuch as we are prohibited from taking Cuba into the Union," Wilson reasoned, "and giving her the advantages of the Constitution, for the present, it seems to me that we should find some other way to take care of her and safeguard our interests in respect to her." "I would not sully the American name by endeavoring to hold Cuba against our solemn pledge that we would 'not exercise sovereignty, jurisdiction or control,'" Wilson insisted. "I would have Cuba come into the Union freely and voluntarily, and yet I would take mighty good care to . . . establish such conditions as would stimulate her activities and her honorable sentiment."[46] He urged the establishment of special relations with Cuba, relations that would serve at once to bind the island to the United States and guarantee the stability of Cuban government. Wilson also recommended negotiating a treaty to create a customs union with Cuba and the establishment of one or more American naval stations on the island: "This would practically bind Cuba hand and foot, and put her destinies absolutely within our control; it saves the amour propre of her leaders, . . . it keeps our own good name clean and unspotted; it gives us all the business this island can develop; it secures a firm and faithful ally." Obviously, however, Wilson acknowledged, "in order to carry this scheme into effect, an independent government in Cuba is necessary. We must have somebody to negotiate with." It behooved Washington to establish as soon as possible as independent Cuban government in Havana as a means of at once fulfilling the Joint Resolution and bringing Cuba to the negotiating table.[47] Independence under these circumstances, Wilson predicted optimistically, would "give time for the Cubans to show that they are not tropical and revolutionary, not a mongrel and vicious race, and not disqualified by religion or impaired social efficiency from carrying on a peaceful stable government, or becoming American citizens." Nor would Cuba's aspiration for independence be sacrificed. Cubans would "never reach the highest freedom and independence of which they are capable until they are free to enter the Great Republic on a just and equal footing."[48] Independence under American treaty supervision would prepare Cuba for the long-prophesized union. Political stability and economic prosperity, Wilson predicted, "would Americanize the Island and would ultimately compel its annexation to the United States."[49] In the end, everyone would be satisfied. "That it would put matters on the best possible footing of the ultimate absorption of [Cuba] into the Union," Wilson was certain; "by natural, voluntary and progressive steps, honorable alike to both parties seems to be . . . probable."[50] "If my views are carried into effect," he predicted confidently to Theodore Roosevelt in 1899, "Cuba will be in the Union within Ten Years."[51]

V The broad purpose of American policy had been defined by the end of Brooke's one-year term as governor-general: prepare Cuba for independence cum annexation. This was the meaning of Wood's replacement of Brooke. An unabashed annexationist, politically atuned to the policy signals emitted from the White House, Wood assumed the governor-general's position committed to the nineteenth-century proposition that Cuba's destiny remained unfulfilled as long as the island remained outside the American union. Prevented by the Teller resolution from seizing Cuba outright, Wood used the resources and authority of the military government to prepare Cuba for eventual annexation. The necessary precondition to immediate independence was a predisposition for eventual annexation. It was necessary to create during the military government, while the island remained under American rule, the conditions leading to "annexation by acclamation."

15 Collaboration and Conflict

*We must remove every pretext which may be alleged in order to delay
the coming of that independent government for which three generations
of Cubans have struggled and sacrificed themselves. We now invite all
classes to join us in forgetting that the war ever divided the people of the
island. I hope that we will never again speak of victors and vanquished.*
—Máximo Gómez, May 1899

*He said this was only for convenience, but I'm telling you, that word
"convenience" does not impress me. . . . I never have and never will
understand why Máximo Gómez said, in his last speech at Quinta de
los Molinos at the end of the war, that in Cuba there were neither victors nor vanquished. That was what he said. I heard him say it, because
I was there at the time. It didn't go down well with anyone there.*
—Esteban Montejo, *The Autobiography of a Runaway Slave*

I "Personally," General James H. Wilson wrote from Matanzas in May 1899, "I see no reason why we should not have set about making friends with all the leading men and interests of the Island from the date we first came here, for the purpose of inducing them to cooperate with us."[1] At the other end of the island, Leonard Wood entertained similar thoughts. "Clean government," Wood predicted optimistically to Theodore Roosevelt later that year, "quick decisive action and absolute control in the hands of trustworthy men . . . and I do not believe you could shake Cuba loose if you wanted to.[2]

No consideration was so central, nor any goal so vital, to the mission of the military government in Cuba and the long-range success of American policy objectives as the winning of local political allies. As early as August 1898, President McKinley confidentially instructed the American Evacuation Commission to confer "prudently" and "in an unofficial manner" with "leading citizens of Cuba . . . to ascertain their sentiments toward the United States and their views as to such measures as they may deem necessary or important for the future welfare and good government of the island."[3] A similar directive was issued to the new American governor-general four months later. "I advise you to mingle with the leading men of all parties in social and public functions," McKinley instructed General Brooke in December.[4] One reason the president found it necessary to relieve Brooke a year later was his inattention if not indifference to the need to promote the creation of the local political alliances desired by Washington. Brooke was too detached, too much the professional observer who saw every side of the issue and chose none. "It is true," Brooke conceded apologetically to McKinley late in 1899, "that I have been unable to mingle with the leading men of all parties as much as I could wish for many reasons, the principal of which is that I found so many factions that it was deemed better to stand somewhat aloof."[5] If, as Washington pledged, the United States contemplated the eventual withdrawal of American military forces from Cuba and relinquishing control to Cubans, it behooved the administration to establish in Havana a local political coalition both sympathetic to long-term American policy objectives and capable of implementing those goals after the American departure. A policy predicated on voluntary union and "annexation by acclamation" necessarily required some guarantee of Cuban concurrence. Nor, of course, could this be left to chance. Even as the American military government set about the task of ostensibly preparing Cuba for some form of eventual self-government, 284 considerable attention was given to subsuming into the emerging Cuban national system an annexationist infrastructure. No element was so essential to larger American goals as the need to create in independent Cuba the conditions that would facilitate the ascendancy of a local clientele political class upon whose national preeimence American hegemony—and eventual annexation—would depend.

II From the outset of the occupation, the Americans had a captive constituency in the Spanish population of the island. Hostile to Cuba Libre, Spaniards emerged as early collaborators of American military government. Few Spaniards could look forward to an independent Cuba with any measure of equanimity. Indeed, the expulsion of Spain left resident *peninsulares* only the superior authority of the United States behind which to seek protection from the retribution expected from Cuban separatists. Unreconciled to an independent Cuba, fearful of their fate in free Cuba, Spaniards sought to influence the United States against independence. Steadfast in their opposition to Cuba Libre, *peninsulares* became outspoken advocates of annexation. Businessmen, merchants, property owners, and officials of every type flocked around the military government in search of salvation from Cuba independence.[6] After the war, Spaniards volunteered their services to military authorities and received early local appointments; many incumbent officials were ratified in their positions pending later reorganization.[7] In Las Villas, General John C. Bates, the first American military governor of the province, retained incumbent Spanish officeholders in positions of provincial and municipal administration. In Sagua la Grande, Cienfuegos, and Santa Clara, the majority of municipal officials were Spaniards. Indeed, in February 1899, Bates scandalized separatist sensibilities by appointing as mayor of Corralillo a former captain of Spanish guerrillas.[8] With the transfer of sovereignty on January 1, 1899, it was natural, if perhaps not inevitable, that resident Spaniards would also transfer their allegiance.[9] In return, they sought assurances that the United States would guarantee the security and protect the property of the *peninsular* population in Cuba. The experience of their countrymen in South America earlier in the century, when the newly organized republican governments despoiled Spaniards of their property and deported them from their homes, foreshadowed the fate awaiting the *peninsular* community in Cuba. For the Spanish in Cuba in 1898 it was enough that the American presence guaranteed their well-being and security among the former colonial subjects.

American authorities initially welcomed Spanish support. Washington detected in Spanish property owners, businessmen, and merchants the bedrock of future Cuban stability—the foundation upon which to rebuild Cuban society. The *peninsular* community passed under protection of the United States, the position it held earlier under Spain. More than this, however, American authorities sought to guarantee Spaniards a future place in the Cuban polity as active participants in the island's political processes and to organize this community into a constituency for order and stability.

Few Americans, however, seriously contemplated restoring Spaniards to positions of political preeminence. On the contrary, from the very beginning of the occupation, American authorities recognized the necessity of appointing Cubans to civil positions under the military government.

The military government applied the vast resources and authority at its command to promote the ascendancy of local political allies. Government positions offered a vast source of patronage, the means by which to recruit allies and reward local supporters. Appointment to public office, the distribution of governmental sinecures, and the disbursement of public revenues formed a complex network through which the military government established in occupied Cuba the substructure of American authority. It used public institutions and public resources to promote a pro-American consensus. Patronage operated on a grand scale. Jobs became a major political weapon, the means through which to reward supporters and punish opponents. American control of public administration, the largest single source of employment in postwar Cuba, served to solidify support and discourage dissent. Monopolization by the United States of national, provincial, and municipal administration, set against the backdrop of a devastated economy and widespread unemployment, where private employment opportunities remained largely under the control of foreigners—mainly Spaniards and Americans—pre-eminently sympathetic to American policies, worked powerfully to align a war-weary and work-starved population behind American rule.[10] The military government elevated to positions of national, provincial, and local preeminance those representatives of Cuban society most sympathetic to American rule. Employment in occupied Cuba was very much the function of American largess, and only those Cubans sharing views consistent with—or at least not hostile to—U.S. goals enjoyed the patronage of the military government. Indeed, jobs also became the central means through which to eliminate centers of rival authority. Through a skillful manipulation of the public treasury and administrative sinecures, the American authorities in

1898 had disbanded entire regiments of the insurgent army. The distribution of $3 million to the Liberation Army in 1899 repeated on a grand scale the policy applied earlier at the local level. Jobs provided the best antidote to disaffection and dissent, American officials argued. "The whole problem today in Cuba is work," Leonard Wood insisted in 1899. He continued:

Put the idle people who are now reading the incendiary press to
work, relegate to a back seat the politicians, whose present importance rests solely on the attentions they are receiving from
our people, and they will not have followers enough left to give
them the slightest importance or weight in the community.
Agitators have tried to stir up the people of the province, but
they cannot do it, simply because we have given the people
something to do and put them in a condition so good that they
will not leave it for a lawless life unless absolutely forced to.[11]

Provide Cubans with jobs, a confident Leonard Wood predicted in 1899, and "you couldn't stir up an insurrection in the province with the aid of the best agitator in Cuba."[12] Colonel L. H. Carpenter, military governor of Camagüey province, similarly reported that public works projects "gave many who had no resources a way of earning a living, and who would, in the end, have given trouble if not provided for." Indeed, Carpenter reported that the activity of "certain agitators" in the province had little effect on the population. "These demagogues can not induce the people who have work and whose families are provided for to embark in any uprising or adventure that would jeopardize their present condition. If they were out of work and in consequence much discontented, perhaps more could be done with them."[13]

For appointed positions in the occupation Americans turned to Cubans of property, education, and social standing. While Cubans with separatist antecedents were not specifically excluded from consideration, neither were they initially given preference. Indeed, Washington instructed provincial commanders to appoint residents of the island "without reference to their connection with the revolution."[14] At the provincial level, American military commanders organized advisory committees consisting of local property owners, businessmen, and professionals to recommend nominees for local political office. In Santiago, Wood organized a commission of fifty of "the most prominent and reliable men" to advise him on appointments.[15] General Wilson established a similar commission in Matanzas and Las

Villas. Both Wood and Wilson also solicited nominees for political office from American planters in the provinces.[16]

These appointments tended to reflect the antiseparatist bias of local elites. Few separatists received the endorsement of these provincial committees of local notables. The majority of Cubans who became mayors in Matanzas and Santa Clara provinces originated from local planter and professional ranks.[17] The political origins of provincial and local committees, moreover, further served to join representatives of the ancien regime with the new colonial administration. Made up in the main of Autonomists and their sympathizers, advisory committees returned members of the old Liberal party to positions of political prominence. Indeed, during the first year, American authorities dipped freely into the ranks of the former Autonomist party for political appointments. Many of the incumbents of the short-lived Autonomist regime under Spain in 1898 were confirmed in their positions under the Americans in 1899.[18]

Separatist antecedents did not, to be sure, disqualify Cubans out of hand from consideration for office. On the contrary, during the first year of the occupation, separatists were well represented in virtually every agency of national, provincial, and local administration. But these appointments reflected a striking pattern: the vast majority of separatist officeholders originated from the ranks of the expatriate representation. From the very outset of the occupation, American authorities turned to the Cuban emigration in the United States for assistance in staffing administrative positions on the island. Exile leaders served as power brokers of the occupation, intermediaries between Cubans and their prospective American employers. Patronage during the first year of the occupation, particularly those appointments involving Cubans with separatist antecedents, was directed by the expatriate representation in the United States in collaboration with the American government. General William Ludlow, military governor of Havana, before departing for Cuba in late 1898, visited expatriate leaders in New York to obtain lists of Cubans for consideration in political appointments.[19] In Washington, the War Department in consultation with Cuban exiles recommended specific appointments to military authorities in Cuba.[20] In many cases, the department made appointments directly from expatriate ranks in New York, Philadelphia, and Washington. In other instances, returning exiles arrived in Cuba in possession of letters from American senators and congressmen recommending the bearers for positions in the military government.[21]

The appointment of expatriate separatists offered the United States a number of advantages. The expatriate return to Cuba began immediately after the peace protocol in August 1898. By late fall, an estimated fifty thousand exiles had arrived in Cuba in search of positions in the rapidly expanding occupation bureaucracy. Men and women of the liberal professions, lawyers, engineers, and physicians, with skills very much in demand in Havana in 1899, often experienced in administration, quickly filled civil positions under the military government. After years of residence in the United States, moreover, expatriate separatists returned to Cuba holding American citizenship, in possession of varying degrees of fluency in English, and familiar with American methods—assets of immediate practical value to the occupation and accounting in large part for the exiles' quick inroads into government and administration.[22] In Santiago, Wood extended preference to Cubans speaking English in making appointments to office.[23] In Havana, civil positions were filled with naturalized Americans holding degrees from American universities and conversant in English.

But above all, returning expatriates were sympathetic to the American presence in Cuba. In selecting Cubans from the expatriate ranks, Americans recruited allies from within the most ideologically compatible sector of the separatist polity. The ranks of exiles returning to occupied Cuba in search of political positions included conservatives for whom the American military government represented the preliminary phase to the establishment of a protectorate and eventual annexation. "If the American government desires to rule Cuba temporarily with as much tranquility as possible," Estrada Palma suggested a day after the peace protocol in August, "the best way would be to dismiss from office every native Spaniard and put conservative Cubans in their places."[24] And, indeed, advocates of dependency status quickly occupied strategic places in the civil administration. Charles M. Pepper, correspondent for the *Washington Evening Star*, learned that the leaders of the expatriate juntas, "the politicians," were among the first to return to Cuba. The majority were from New York and other large American cities—"all men of means," Pepper wrote. Their presence in Cuba would have, Pepper predicted, "a decidedly beneficial effect," for their influence "will be conservative, and will be one of the guarantees of stable government."[25] George Reno, the correspondent of the *Philadelphia Inquirer*, arrived at substantially similar conclusions:

"The Annexationists include a large number of respectable and intelligent Cubans, many of whom have spent the greater part of their lives in the United States, and who, keenly aware of the financial and other advantages that would accrue from annexation, are in favor of it and will vote for it at the first opportunity. They compose a worthy element in society, and are practically American in everything but birth.[26]

Exiles filled positions in civil agencies almost as quickly as they were organized. By early 1899, the majority of civil positions in the occupation had been distributed to the returning exiles.[27] As late as 1901, of the twenty-four Cubans employed in the Bureau of Statistics in the Havana Customs House, twenty-two had passed the war years in exile.[28] Expatriates who secured positions as chiefs of administrative units, in turn, proceeded to staff subordinate posts with employees also drawn from the old emigration representation.

Expatriate separatists quickly dominated the upper reaches of the civil government. Of the four departments of state organized by the military government in 1899, three were directed by Cubans who had served in separatist agencies abroad. Adolfo Sáenz Yáñez, secretary of agriculture, a former member of the Autonomist party, joined the separatists in exile after the arrival of Weyler. Secretary of Finance Pablo Desvernine received his law degree from Columbia University and during the war worked for the PRC in New York. José Antonio González Lanuza, secretary of public instruction, served under Estrada Palma in New York until June 1898, when he joined Shafter's staff en route to Cuba. A year later the position of *Gobernación* was filled by Diego Tamayo, a former Autonomist who served as president of the Revolutionary Council in New York. Other positions in the national administration awarded to expatriate representatives included Leopoldo Cancio, assistant secretary of finance, a former Autonomist and member of the PRC in New York; José Eliseo Cartaya, inspector of customs, a naturalized American citizen serving in the Department of Expeditions; José María García Montes, assistant secretary of *Gobernación*, a member of the Autonomist central committee who joined the PRC after the appointment of Weyler; Nicolás Heredia y Mota, director of public instruction, a member of the New York junta; Luis A. Baralt, secretary of civil government, a lawyer who served in the Philadelphia junta; Rafael Cruz Pérez, a supreme court justice, had worked for the junta in St. Augustine, Florida during the war; Federico García Ramis, chief clerk of the supreme court, was a naturalized American citizen with an American law degree; Juan Antonio Lliteras, chief of registry in the Department of Justice, served as a member of the New York junta.

Expatriates also occupied key provincial and municipal positions. The governor of Pinar del Río, Guillermo Dolz y Arango, a prominent property owner in the province, served as member of the New York junta. Emilio Núñez, chief of the Department of Expeditions, was appointed governor of Havana province. Fernando Figueredo y Socarrás, appointed chief of customs in Cienfuegos, was a naturalized American citizen, had studied at the Charles French Institute, and graduated from the School of Engineers in Troy, New York; during his exile in Florida, Figueredo served as superintendent of schools and mayor of West Tampa. Carlos M. de Rojas, mayor of Cárdenas, studied at Harvard. The secretary of the governor of Camagüey, Alcides Betancourt, studied commerce in New York. Alberto Barreras Fernández, the secretary of the Havana board of education, had served as a PRC organizer in the United States. Scores of Cubans chosen as mayors served as the separatist cause abroad, including Emilio Bacardí (Santiago), Martín Casuso Roque (Batabanó), Juan Antonio Garmendía (Colón), Domingo Lecuona (Matanzas), Fernando Méndez Capote (Cárdenas), Ignacio Pizarro (San Nicolás), and José María Zayas (Jaruco). Heads of provincial *audiencias* and courts, mayors, chiefs of local administrative bureaus, and advisors to American military commanders were drawn from expatriate ranks.[29]

The most striking feature of these developments was the sudden political ascendency of the members of the old expatriate representation. The military occupation provided exile representatives dramatic entry to the top of the postwar political pyramid. The secondary separatist elite received positions much out of proportion to either its role in the separatist polity or its contribution to the revolutionary struggle. American administration catapulted into political prominence and placed in positions of administrative authority the most conservative representatives of Cuban separatism.

But the influence of the expatriate representation went beyond its own meteoric rise in the civil administration of occupied Cuba. Indeed, expatriate access to the Washington overseers of the occupation increased the postwar authority of emigration within the old separatist polity. Separatist representatives abroad emerged as intermediaries between their compatriots on the island and the occupation officialdom in Washington. Very quickly, émigrés emerged as the effective if perhaps indirect source of patronage. For many separatists in Cuba, public employment was now possible only through the intercession of the Cubans in the United States. Throughout late 1898 and early 1899, Estrada Palma in New York and Gonzalo de Quesada in Washington received scores of requests and petitions from ranking separatists in Cuba asking for expatriate assistance in securing positions in Cuba, appealing to the emigration leadership to intercede on their behalf with authorities in Washington for positions in the expanding occupation administration. Others asked expatriates to use their influence with American property owners in Cuba to provide jobs.[30]

Separatists who served in the *manigua* during the war were not, to be sure, entirely ignored. Early appointments to civil positions, however, also reflected American preference for Cubans who were at once familiar with and sympathetic to American methods. General Pedro Betancourt, appointed civil governor of Matanzas, was a member of a prestigious local family and held a degree in medicine from the University of Pennsylvania. Betancourt "has all the qualities of an American gentleman," James H. Wilson noted approvingly upon Betancourt's appointment.[31] General Demetrio Castillo Duany, civil governor of Oriente province, a naturalized American citizen, owned a school of commerce in New York and possessed controlling interests in the Juraguá iron mines. General Mario G. Menocal, appointed as the chief of police of Havana, had received engineering degrees from the Maryland College of Agriculture and Cornell University. José Ramón Villalón, appointed by Wood as secretary of public works, had received a degree in civil engineering from Lehigh University. Perfecto Lacosta, the annexationist president of the patriotic junta in Havana during the war and appointed mayor of Havana in 1899, was a naturalized American citizen graduated from the University of Pennsylvania, owning some three-quarters of a million dollars worth of sugar estates and ranches in central Cuba.

By early 1900, American officials could derive some satisfaction from their handiwork. In February 1900, a self-satisfied Wood could report to Elihu Root that it was "safe to say that eight out of ten people are our friends; by our friends I mean the friends of good government and of what we are doing."[32]

III   The rapid ascendancy of the expatriate sector in the early months of the occupation underscored the nature of the fragmentation occurring within separatist ranks. The successive dissolution of local juntas, the Department of Expeditions, and, lastly, the PRC in 1898 signified expatriate conformity with the state of affairs in Cuba. The dissolution of expatriate agencies released thousands of Cubans to return to the island in search of jobs under the military government. In Cuba, however, separatist politico-military agencies remained intact. Indeed, the decision of separatist leaders in Cuba to retain their organizations in the defense of the ideal of independence pending clarification of American policy created the conditions whereby members of the Liberation Army and provisional government were by-passed in the initial distribution of public office and administrative posts. To be sure, ranking representatives of both the army and the government did make their way into civil positions under the occupation government. But typically candidates for these positions, in order to qualify for the appointment, were required to sever ties with separatist agencies—something many Cubans in 1898 were loathe to do.[33] In fact, as a matter of separatist policy, politico-military agencies enjoined Cubans to decline all positions under the American military government until the issue of Cuba's status was resolved.[34] "Certain classes," one correspondent learned, "refused to work or serve the Government until a clear statement of the freedom and independence of their country is made."[35]

The decision of Máximo Gómez to cooperate with the United States, and the subsequent dissolution of the Assembly and the Liberation Army, brought most separatists into more or less conformity with the American presence in Cuba. Gómez emerged from his discussions with Porter wholly persuaded that the United States planned to honor the congressional pledge of April 20. From this central conviction, the Dominican generalissimo sought to assure the salvation of Cuban independence through acquiescence to American authority. Knowledge that Washington looked upon the Liberation Army with suspicion encouraged Gómez to accept the $3 million to facilitate its dissolution. Conscious that the Americans feared Cuban reprisals against Spanish residents, he emerged from his meeting with Porter as the advocate of national reconciliation as a means toward independence. Aware that the Americans had little confidence in the Cubans' ability to govern themselves, he exhorted his followers to seek positions in the military government to demonstrate that they indeed possessed the aptitudes necessary for independence. Personally convinced that the United States planned to honor the Joint Resolution, and fully sensitive to the obstacles still before the realization of Cuba Libre, he dedicated his peacetime energies to the elimination of all conditions capable of obstructing independence. In his zeal for independence, in his conviction that independence now depended on the performance and behavior of Cubans in the course of the American occupation, Gómez emerged as the outstanding advocate of national reconciliation and collaboration.[36]

In this sentiment, Máximo Gómez came ever closer to the exile perception. By early 1899, ranking separatist leaders had accepted the proposition that only collaboration with the United States and reconciliation with their former adversaries, Spaniards as well as Autonomists, could guarantee Cuban independence.[37] Cuba would receive its independence, Gonzalo de Quesada predicted, but whether independence would be sooner rather than later depended on the behavior of Cubans. To challenge American authority and resist the military occupation promised only to delay independence indefinitely.[38] Gómez agreed: "We should aid by every pacific means in completing the work of the Americans. We must forget past antipathies and disagreements and unite all elements completely. . . . We must make the presence of foreigners on our soil unnecessary by our behavior—that is to say, to demonstrate to them the legitimate desires and sufficient capacity to govern ourselves. . . . We should assist the Americans to complete the honorable mission they assumed by force of circumstances."[39]

If collaboration with American authorities offered a means of winning U.S. support for independence, reconciliation with Spaniards and former Autonomists offered a means of ending local opposition to independence. It was necessary to reassure old adversaries they would be safe and secure in the new Cuba. "Neither victors nor vanquished," Gómez proclaimed in the course of his subsequent peregrinations across the island. "Spaniards and Cubans should embrace, forgetting the rancor that has passed never to return, all united around the goal we propose: make Cuba free and independent." Gómez invited "all classes to join us in forgetting that the war ever divided the people of the island."[40]

The attempt at rapproachement between separatists and loyalists met one key American objective. Cuban reconciliation with their former adversaries, particularly the Spanish, guaranteed the solvency of the *peninsular* community in Cuba, a sector of the population that by virtue of its composition and affinity would always be properly and primarily allied to the United States. This solvency, in turn, promised to serve as a moderating force in Cuban national life. Very early the military government urged General Gómez to explore the possibility of alliance with the Spanish community. Major John Kennon, a member of Brooke's staff, informed Gómez that Washington was pleased with the new Cuban attitude toward the Spanish community. There were real political advantages to this collaboration. "The policy of conciliation between the Cubans and Spaniards," Kennon stressed, ". . . ought to be accomplished as soon as possible." Kennon continued: "The Spaniards represent a great deal of wealth and would be a factor which would be necessary to take into consideration. They would be in a position soon to hold the balance of power, and the faction of Cubans, which would unite with them, would probably be able to control the destinies of the Island."[41]

IV Gómez's adhesion to the military government exerted a powerful influence on the approach separatists in postwar Cuba would take on the road to independence. For many, collaboration with American authorities promised both to hasten the end of the intervention and place in positions of influence a body of opinion underrepresented in the military government. As defined by Gómez, collaboration with the United States emerged as an act of singular patriotic virtue; resistance to American rule, on the other hand, threatened to jeopardize the independence to which the United States had already committed itself.[42]

The injunction to seek positions under the miliary government, however, signified considerably more than a political strategy calculated to hasten the end of the occupation. The early organization of civil administration in the island had inspired enormous disquiet among separatist chieftains. Many individuals appointed to political office in 1899 were well known for their opposition to Cuban independence. Insurgent veterans watched in disbelief and reacted with dismay as public office and positions of influence were distributed to people opposed to or altogether outside of the separatist polity. Pressing economic concerns, moreover, had heightened the urgency of employment for the many thousands of veterans still in the ranks of the Liberation Army. Conditions in the army in 1899 had reached desperate proportions, and the imminence of demobilization promised to turn a crisis into a disaster. The release of thousands of officers and men into the labor market of an economy devastated by three years of war forced veterans to turn to public administration for employment.

The release of the army veterans created new tensions in the already splintered separatist polity. They arrived comparatively late to the long employment lines. By early spring of 1899, the time when the army command began to issue official furloughs preliminary to complete demobilization, the task of staffing civilian agencies under the military government had been all but completed.

An intense struggle for jobs and positions pitted Cubans against one another. Economic issues were joined to political grievances, and the crisis within Cuban separatism deepened. Competition for administrative positions created one more source of conflict within the old separatist polity.

Disgruntled military chieftains challenged the patriotic credentials of those Cubans who had served the separatist cause in exile, imputing lesser patriotic virtue to duty abroad than service in arms. Army veterans reacted with no small resentment and rancor at the number of expatriate appointments to public office. "To me," Major Walter B. Booker wrote from Cienfuegos in mid-1899, "the most difficult matter is to harmonize the several factions of the island." He continued:

A large proportion of the better educated Cubans refugeed in various lands during the rebellion; many of these self-appointed, perhaps, were agents or members of the so-called Cuban junta. Most of these have returned, and are eager for recognition. As they speak English they have more readily found employment and appointment at the hands of United States officers. The fact that they have been recognized, which I do not pretend was ill-advised, has created friction between them and the Cuban soldier.[43]

In Sagua la Grande an American officer reported widespread anger at the appointment of the local tax collector. "I find here," Major John A. Logan wrote, "a great deal of feeling over the appointment of the present sub-collector, on the grounds that he was a Cuban who went to the United States in 1868 and did not return until December 27, 1898, when he arrived with appointment of sub-collector from the government in his pocket, it having been given to him at Washington."[44] This practice, too, of making political appointments in Washington incurred the ire of army veterans in Cuba. The Society of Veterans of Independence denounced appointments originating in Washington. "Only those having influence with Secretary [of War Russell] Alger through Washington connections," one army leader complained, "are able to secure appointments, and there are some of those who were not in Cuba during the War." This practice, the Society warned "will eventually lead to trouble. Those who defended the country deserve recognition and will tire of being consistently ignored."[45]

Separatists turned on each other with unrestrained acrimony. By early 1899, military chieftains were demanding preferential employment of army veterans.[46] Many went so far as to demand the ouster of all Cuban officeholders without wartime service in the *manigua*. A groundswell of discontent spread across the island as economic issues fused with political grievances. Colonel Tasker H. Bliss, chief of customs in Havana, had completed the staffing of his agency well before dissolution of the Liberation Army. "With the disbandment of the army," an embattled Bliss later wrote, "there immediately came tremendous pressure from all quarters for appointments. Had I yielded to that demand I could, during the last three months, have discharged and appointed the personnel of the Habana custom houses ten times over."[47] Confidential reports from the American-run postal system, a key patronage agency subjected to unusually heavy pressure from office-seeking veterans, specifically warned of potential political problems arising from employment frustrations. In Oriente province, insurgent army officers unsuccessful in securing positions were said to be "engaged in serving the seeds of discontent by saying that the United States never intended to give the Cubans freedom and independence."[48] If the United States refused to distribute public offices to army veterans, Julio Sanguily insisted, Cubans should again take to the field and drive the Americans out.[49] José Antonio González Lanuza, a member of the New York junta, warned the United States that it was necessary to reach an accommodation with the veteran chieftains, lest they lose control of the "lower classes" of the army and create a "truly grave danger for everyone in Cuba."[50] Governor-General Brooke conceded in mid-1899 the existence of an "active effort on the part of agitators to create trouble . . . The main body of agitators," he reported, came from "the Cuban army officers. These men are without an occupation. They are unfitted for any civil work, and may be relied upon to stir up strife by all means in their power." As a precautionary measure, Brooke appealed to Washington to halt the withdrawal of American forces and send reinforcements armed with machine guns and Hotchkiss mountain guns.[51]

By the time Leonard Wood replaced Brooke as governor-general, the issue of patronage had acquired considerable urgency. In late 1899, Horatio Rubens, the former legal counsel for the New York junta, met in Washington with Wood and Elihu Root and agreed to travel to Cuba to seek a reconciliation between the army veterans and the expatriate officeholders.[52] Even before Wood assumed his new post in Havana, General James H. Wilson recommended reconsideration of McKinley's earlier order and urged that "officers of the successful revolution should have preference for civil employment."[53] Tasker H. Bliss, too, pledged to use the resources of the customs houses to accommodate the demands of army veterans. "Knowing the duty of this department of the administration to assist in the solution of the political problem before the government in the conciliation of conflicting opinions," Bliss indicated, "I have recognized this latter element as far as it has been practical to do."[54] Fred E. Bach, chief of the Bureau of Statistics, also acknowledged the necessity of displacing the vast majority of employees of expatriate origins with "Cubans more patriotic."[55]

The intense struggle for jobs shattered what remained of a separatist consensus. Antagonism between civilian expatriates and army veterans deepened as each challenged the patriotic credentials of the other. For army veterans, the readiness with which expatriates served the interventionist government, even as the soldiers remained in arms defending the ideal of independence against the uncertain designs of the occupation army and refusing to disband until the intentions of the Americans were made known, represented a breach of patriotic faith. The returning exiles, for their part, detected in the attitude of the soldiers confirmation of their worst fears, which aroused further expatriate fear of Cuban independence. Rejected by former comrades in arms, their patriotic credentials and revolutionary labor all but wholly impugned, expatriates received from Americans the reward and recognition that the insurgent separatists withheld.[56] The divisions in the old revolutionary coalition deepened.

Over the short run, postwar conditions in Cuba contributed to the further unraveling of the separatist consensus. Over a longer period, these circumstances transfigured the very nature of Cuban separatism. Public office was a life and death issue, the only available hedge against total impoverishment in a wholly impoverished environment. Means became ends. Employment became an adequate substitute for independence. Immediate concerns prevailed over abstract ideals. In these moments of desperate want, *libertadores* were preoccupied less with political independence than physical survival. "My family has been with me for a month," General Carlos Roloff complained to Gonzalo de Quesada, "and I have to find work to support it. If I had money, I would pursue any job other than public office; but today I am obligated to find employment."[57] Two months later, General Alejandro Rodríguez wrote in similar despair: "I who have served my country, for which I have sacrificed everything, cannot even have my family at my side for a lack of means to support it; I cannot embark upon any business nor reconstruct my farm for a lack of funds. I see myself perhaps forced to emigrate to search for bread in a strange land, when here there are individuals in high office who were indifferent or hostile to Cuba and always remained on the side of Spain."[58] Seeking to escape the destitution of postwar Cuba, without funds to restore their estates and farms, lacking the means to start new businesses, the impoverished *libertadores* vied with each other to win the beneficence of the foreign occupiers who controlled resources. "Employment-mania," one Cuban charged in early 1899.[59] Former provisional President Salvador Cisneros Betancourt denounced the military government for making "extensive use of patronage" for the purpose of "political bribery."[60] "We are growing to be a nation of petty office-seeking," General Enrique Collazo lamented in early 1899; "we have no more political personality."[61]

The separatist war had been long and ruinous. It had been successful as a means but failed to attain its ends. Peace was announced by a thunderous anticlimax, for independence from Spain had not provided Cubans access to the principal and ultimate prize of the successful war of liberation—control over the apparatus of the state. Unlike the leadership of independence movements elsewhere in Latin America, the Cubans had failed to secure control of the machinery of state. Once in power, the separatist polity would have found itself strategically placed to consolidate its control still further and reward the triumphant liberators. The interposition of American rule after Cuba's separation from Spain, however, at once thwarted the separatist ascendency and denied the revolutionary forces direct access to the state structures capable of giving wartime separatism postwar institutional vitality. The separatist amalgam constituted a polity organized for war around the goal of establishing claims to national sovereignty; the end of a successful war without providing Cubans control of the state plunged separatists into a crisis from which they never recovered.

The separatist polity, rather than being the expression of the economic interests of any one class, was itself expected to produce the opening to security and economic opportunity. For Creole Cubans, wealth and position typically derived from political power—they did not create it. Other means of acquiring wealth, prestige, and power in postwar Cuba were severely limited. These were Cubans of humble origins, men of moderate incomes and precarious occupations, historically resentful of Spanish monopolization of local administration. Spain had correctly suspected the subversive undercurrents of Creole clamor for public office, for what Cubans demanded was control of the island: they wanted offices in their country and they wanted all of them. Cubans of humble origins before the war were destitute after the peace. To a political objective was now added an economic imperative. Public office was a need, not a luxury. But the United States, not the Cubans, seized control of the state. As the military occupation penetrated every area of social life, the American government—not the separatist polity—became the principal avenue of advancement for the ambitious and the aspiring. When the revolutionary coalition lost its potential to provide advancement, indeed, when membership in the separatist amalgam was itself a liability to advancement, separatism lost its claim on the allegiance of all but the most passionate advocates of *independentismo*.

A casual survey of the political landscape after 1899 revealed a pattern of administration not unlike the Spanish regime. Important political positions were held by official representatives appointed by a distant authority, allocating in judicious and measured calculation lesser political office to those deserving recognition by virtue of political compatability. In the bleak and devastated countryside, uncompensated and unthanked veterans, now perceived as rabble and potential troublemakers, muttered aimlessly about the countryside asking impatiently, "What have we gained by this war?"[62] All that remained for the unemployed and penniless separatist legions was a scramble for jobs—work simply to exist.

Converted into applicants for positions and supplicants for resources, separatists accommodated themselves to the prevailing political orthodoxy. Cuban officeholders swore allegiance to the United States.[63] The Americans held an exclusive franchise, and all would-be political entrepreneurs understood the unspoken restrictions on continued employment. Few critics of American policy remained long on government payrolls. In 1900, Wood summarily fired three Havana aldermen after they criticized his conduct of municipal elections. A year later, six mayors across the island were dismissed as a result of their opposition to the Platt Amendment. Newspapers were controlled and censored and, on occasion, suspended for criticism of American methods.[64]

Position and income in the military government typically corresponded to rank in separatist organizations. Occupation authorities were not unmindful of the necessity of bringing influential separatists into the American fold. Co-optation was an essential if not conscious policy of the occupation, a policy enormously facilitated by poverty of resources and the absence of alternatives. Never a hint of deliberate conspiracy—simply a vast and efficient system without conscious central coordination into which was subsumed a set of assumptions about the function of the American purpose in Cuba. Calixto García had early received preferential American treatment. A year later, Secretary of War Elihu Root secured a post office position for General Carlos García, the son of Calixto.[65] Conscious efforts went into finding appropriate sinecures for the staff officers of ranking separatist generals.[66] When the Assembly dismissed Gonzalo de Quesada in early 1899, Washington retained his services as the official Cuban representative in Washington at an annual salary of $5,000. Máximo Gómez was given Quinta de los Molinos, formerly the summer residence of Spanish Captain-Generals. In 1899, the Dominican general also received $10,000 to meet, as Brooke noted at the time, "his pressing wants and to put him in funds for a year."[67] Over the course of the next two years, Gómez obtained from the United States some $26,000.[68] The disbursement of these funds to General Gómez, the War Department later conceded, was dictated by political considerations. "It is believed," a War Department spokesman explained with disarming candor in 1902, "that but for this assumption of the costs of Gómez's living expenses, the conditions in Cuba might have paralleled those in the Philippines, and the United States Government, after fighting Spain to secure freedom for the Cubans, might have been obliged to turn on them the forces of her armies."[69] Gómez, in turn, using his new influence with American authorities, secured positions for his supporters in the Cuban army. In late 1899, even before assuming office, Wood prepared to distribute government positions to officers recommended by Gómez. "These men," he explained to Root, "have a great influence with the army and great influence among the people."[70]

16 The Electoral Imperative

I could not take in "Tom, Dick and Harry," and thus promote the organization of a peculiar political party, which would consider itself the ruler of Cuba, etc. This would not do, as the conditions would be intolerable to the people, and would defeat the purposes of the United States in its efforts to establish in this Island a stable form of government.
—John R. Brooke, September 1899

The individual who on reaching twenty-one has not shown enough energy to accumulate $250, nor to have learned to read and write, nor to have defended his country in a state of war, is a social element unworthy to be counted upon for collective purposes. Let him not vote!
—Leonard Wood, January 1900

It is possible . . . that there is a deeper design in the idea of now giving the municipalities of Cuba an American form of government than is apparent from surface indications—that it is thought that by so doing the Cubans will be enraptured with the American methods and begin to clamor for annexation before they have attempted an independent general government.
—Major Arthur Murray, Judge Advocate's Office, July 1899

I The appointment to public office and administrative positions of Cubans sympathetic with American goals was only the preliminary phase of a larger process. Cubans appointed to public office during the occupation owed their positions entirely to the U.S. military presence, an arrangement that offered only a partial and short-term expedient through which to promote American interests. The decision in late 1899 to proceed with preparations for self-government in Cuba presented American policymakers a new set of problems. Ultimately, Cubans favored by the United States to lead the island into independence and govern the new republic and, eventually, promote annexation would be subject to the vagaries of electoral politics, forced to compete for public office against political opponents, and be required to appeal for the support of an uncertain if not perhaps unsympathetic electorate. Hopes for future annexation depended directly on the continued political preeminence of those Cubans who shared with Washington the central goals of American policy.

In anticipation of independence, the military government devoted increasing attention to promoting the political fortunes of local allies. This took two forms: first, attempts to shape the leadership of a pro-American political coalition into cohesive and competitive political contenders; and, second, to fashion out of the national electorate a sympathetic constituency possessed of the resolve and resources capable of providing the conservative coalition with an electoral mandate. The United States could not contemplate ending military rule without first seeking to guarantee that the bias built into the Cuban national system during the occupation would survive after the evacuation. Annexation depended on the endurance of both the political and institutional structures created during the occupation. Very early, the United States identified the *independentista* sector, largely the army veterans of the old separatist polity, as a threat to be politically neutralized and quarantined.

This would be no easy task, however. A central reality confronted the United States in Cuba in 1900: most Cubans, by substantial margins, Americans conceded, opposed annexation and favored independence. *Independentista* leaders had a ready-made numerical superiority. American authorities in Cuba sought periodically to reassure their superiors in Washington that annexation enjoyed widespread support on the island. "The sentiment for our remaining forever," Wood wrote McKinley in April 1899, "is becoming very strong in this part of the island and I think we should have hard work to get away."[1] "The people who are talking 'Cuba Libre' and the total withdrawal of the American Army in the daily press,"

304

he again assured McKinley five months later, "represent at most not over five percent of the Cuban people."[2] But occasional attempts at self-serving dissimulation notwithstanding, the Cuban reality persisted; simply, the absence of popular support for annexation. Most Americans on the island acknowledged, even if only in private, that a majority of Cubans opposed annexation. "I believe," the military governor of Havana, General William Ludlow, conceded in 1900, "that the proposition of annexation would be voted down by an overwhelming majority if presented now to the Cuban people."[3] An American journalist in Cuba concurred: "Cubans were overwhelmingly opposed to the annexation of the island to the United States."[4]

But Americans were unimpressed with either the size or the sentiment of the majority. On the contrary, that Cubans in large numbers opposed annexation was itself a cause for suspicion and sufficient grounds to discredit public opinion. If there were people who opposed U.S. rule, they were probably led by wicked men, or knew no better. In either case, opposition to the United States was itself evidence of the Cuban incapacity for self-government. Only the "ignorant masses," the "unruly rabble," and "trouble makers,"—"the element," in Wood's words, "absolutely without any conception of its responsibilities or duties as citizens"—could have any grounds to oppose the American presence in Cuba.[5] "The only people who are howling for [self-government]," Wood wrote derisively, "are those whose antecedents and actions demonstrate the impossibility of self government at present."[6] Having subsumed into the American presence in Cuba a civilizing mission, opposition to the United States could not be seen as anything other than evidence of the continuing existence of the forces of anarchy and chaos. Numbers alone, then, could not be permitted to influence unduly the course of American policy—especially when majority sentiment was associated with disorder, instability, and turmoil. Americans, too, were confident that over time, under the protection and encouragement of the United States, the call for annexation would rise above the clamor for independence. There existed in Cuba a yet-unrevealed majority, Americans were certain, silent in its preferences but steadfast in its desire for union with the United States. "The real voice of the people of Cuba," Wood reassured the White House in late 1899, "has not been heard because they have not spoken and, unless I am entirely mistaken, when they do speak there will be many more voices for annexation than there is at present any idea of."[7]

If the United States found no support in the Cuban majority, it derived some consolation in the quality of the pro-American minority. The "better classes," the propertied, and the educated—those sectors of Cuban society most deserving of American attention—were desirous of close and permanent relations with the United States. There was, no doubt, "much plausibility," correspondent Herbert P. Williams learned during his visit to Cuba in 1899, that the large majority of the "half-barbarous rabble in a vote would request us to leave the island." It was also "probably true that the Cubans who want us to go outnumber those who want us to stay." But mere numbers were inconsequential, Williams insisted. Conceding that Americans "ought not go into the business of government without the consent of the governed," Williams nevertheless concluded: "The point is that if all, or nearly all, the people whose convictions deserve respect are on one side, mere numbers should not be allowed to decide the matter."[8]

In fact, however, as all American officials knew only too well, "mere numbers" would indeed decide the matter. Leonard Wood arrived in Havana in late 1899 bound by specific instructions from the White House: "go down there to get the people ready for a republican form of government . . . and to get out of the island as soon as we safely can."[9] The establishment of a Cuban government, one organized around political competition and dependent upon electoral mandates, presented the military government with an obvious dilemma. An electoral system based on popular suffrage threatened to displace the "better classes" and result in the political ascendancy of those sectors of Cuban society most hostile to annexation. A stable form of government, General Brooke confided to a friend in late 1899, "does not seem to be practicable in the early future." Those who would "naturally be the leaders" had not fully developed the proclivities for electoral competition and the skills for political success. More to the point, he concluded: "They are very few and could not expect to cope in an election with the 'Liberating Army' leaders, who are clamorous for places for which they manifested no capacity during the war, and have demonstrated by their acts since their utter incapacity for any leadership which would benefit the people."[10] Leonard Wood, who in 1899 as governor of Oriente wrote insouciantly to the White House about "five percent," warned in 1900 as governor-general that liberal suffrage posed a "menace to Cuba" and would result in "serious alarm among [the] better class."[11] There was a feeling of "genuine alarm among the educated classes," Wood explained, "lest the absolutely illiterate element be allowed to dominate the political situation." Such a development "would be fatal to the interests of Cuba and would destroy the standing and influence of our government among all thinking intelligent people in the island. . . . Giving the ballot to this element means a second edition of Haiti and Santo-Domingo in the near future."[12] General William Ludlow agreed. "To give universal suffrage to such a people," he predicted in an address to the New York Chamber of Commerce, "would be to swamp the better class. We might just as well retire and let it drift to Hayti No. 2."[13]

The spectre of Haiti—more specifically, race—loomed over preparations for self-government. Black suffrage set in relief all the political perils attending Cuban independence. The prospect that the numerically large Afro-Cuban population would emerge as a decisive factor in future national politics, if not, in fact, dominate provincial elections, was unacceptable to many. Independence leaders had early made universal manhood suffrage an issue central to the separatist program. At the end of the war, Afro-Cubans occupied ranking positions in all separatist politico-military organizations. The war had provided blacks considerable social mobility and catapulted Afro-Cubans into the highest positions of leadership within the separatist polity. From these positions separatist leaders could challenge the traditional colonial elites, defeated and discredited in the war, for political ascendency in free Cuba—until the American intervention. The intervention blocked the ascendancy of the insurgent political leaders and contained the social forces released by the insurrection. The American presence also guaranteed that the colonial elite would survive more or less intact into the republic, and, with it, the social order of the colony. The price for this survival, and the cost of continued local hegemony, was allegiance to the new metropolis. Nevertheless, this allegiance was not unqualified, for local elites demanded American assistance against all internal challenges to traditional positions of privilege and power.

In 1900, the system of government contemplated in Washington for Cuba, one organized around electoral competition, caused considerable anxiety among the "better classes." "The possible ascendancy of the blacks," one American correspondent wrote soon after the war, "especially in Santiago province, is already a cause of uneasiness. They are a majority there, and under the leadership of shrewd men of their own race who had won distinction as soldiers they would surely become important factors."[14] An electorate organized around universal manhood suffrage, in which blacks represented a sizeable proportion of voters, threatened to overwhelm the traditional political elite. At best, local elites feared, Cuba would find itself interminably beset by political tumult and social turmoil. At worst, the island would follow the example of Haiti and, in short time, emerge as a black republic. Self-government, under these conditions,

Wood predicted direly in 1899, would lead to the "establishment of another Haitian Republic in West Indies"—and that "would be a serious mistake."[15] T. Bently Mott, the adjutant general in Havana, feared that the enfranchisement of blacks would create "hereafter a knot to untie no less difficult than the one which the sword of our country has so recently cut."[16]

The potential challenge to the traditional authority of the "better classes" also had direct implications for American policy. If, in fact, the United States planned to entrust its interests in an independent and self-governing Cuba to the political representatives of the "better classes," a challenge to the rule of American surrogates represented no less a direct challenge to the United States. The prominence of Afro-Cubans in insurgent ranks allowed opponents of independence to malign *independentismo* if not discredit the sentiment altogether—palpable evidence that independence was as unworthy an ideal as its proponents were unfit to govern. Like the Spanish before them, Americans sought to discredit Cuba Libre by identifying independence sentiment with race. "The negroes," one American writer noted, "who number at least one third, and possibly one half of the population, are said to belong to the party which clamors for independence."[17] Governor-General Brooke reported in mid-1899 that "the lower, or negro, element is talking about matters in such way as it places it in opposition to annexation and in favor of independence."[18] In central Cuba, Lieutenant A. P. Berry, an aide to General James H. Wilson, reported the existence of three general political groupings in Matanzas. The annexationists represented Spaniards, Americans and "many of the better educated Cubans." A second group, consisting of "the better class" of Cubans, favored a republican form of government under an American protectorate. "The Independents," Berry concluded, "wanting a government republican and democratic in form and entirely independent of the United States, . . . is made up of the turbulent, the ignorant and the negroes and is the largest party."[19]

American authorities feared, too, that a liberal suffrage, raising the spectre of political instability, would serve to discourage economic development and all but formally deter foreign investment. Unrestricted suffrage, one Havana merchant warned, would lead to a black republic and, ultimately, a flight of white capital.[20] Several potential American investors informed Charles M. Pepper, the Havana correspondent for the *Washington Evening Star*, that they "didn't know how they were to get their money back if they had to depend on the 'lazy niggers.' "[21] Leonard Wood, too, was mindful of the economic implications of unrestricted suffrage. "I believe," Wood warned Secretary of War Elihu Root, "that if it were known to be a fact that we were going to give universal suffrage it would stop investments and advancement in this island to an extent which would be disastrous in its results."[22]

II   Few Americans believed the colonial elite capable of remaining long in power after the military occupation or surviving an electoral onslaught of the majority. This realization required the Americans to forge an electorate that posed minimal threat to elite rule. Otherwise, the antiannexationist majority, with a full voice in political affairs, would overwhelm the pro-American minority. For those Americans like Leonard Wood who sought "annexation by acclamation," it was apparent that a great number of Cubans would have to be silenced. It was of little value to establish the "better classes" in power during the occupation only to see them displaced by the "ignorant masses" in the republic. The political solvency of the "better classes" required a constituency organized around a consensus in which the defense of social interests formed the single most important unifying element. By 1900, close relations with the United States, leading eventually to annexation, had become synonymous with property, privilege, and prosperity. There could be no place in this constituency for those sectors of the Cuban society opposed to union with the United States. One certain way to foreclose the rise of the unruly masses was to deny *independentista* leaders the opportunity of mobilizing the vast political force of the national majority. And the surest way of keeping the "better classes" in power was to exclude the "rabble" from the electorate. "We are dealing here in Cuba," William Ludlow explained to his superiors in 1899, "with a relatively uninstructed population, whose sensibilities are easily aroused but who lack judgement, who are wholly unaccustomed to manage their own affairs, and who readily resort to violence when excited or thwarted. . . . The whole structure of society and business is still on too slender and tottering basis to warrant putting any additional strain upon it."[23]

In early 1900, Washington undertook a census of the island preliminary to fixing final suffrage requirements for municipal elections scheduled later in June. The decision to limit suffrage had been made months earlier in Washington; all that remained was to establish the nature of the voting qualifications. General James H. Wilson dismissed Cuban demands for universal manhood suffrage as "rot." "Suffrage," Wilson insisted, "like any other privilege of citizenship, should be based upon qualifications, and its exercise not permitted merely because one happens to belong to the male species."[24] There was, indeed, some talk of universal suffrage, Wood conceded, but "almost all the educated people are in favor of restricted suffrage."[25] In Washington, Elihu Root predicted confidently that restricted suffrage would exclude the "mass of ignorant and incompetent," promote "a conservative and thoughtful control of Cuba by Cubans," and "avoid the kind of control which leads to perpetual revolutions of Central America and other West India islands." Opposition to restricted suffrage was immediately suspect. "I think it is fair," Root suggested, "that the proposed limitation is approved by the best, and opposed only by the worst or the most thoughtless of the Cuban people." Root hoped, too, that the exclusive nature of the franchise would serve to legitimize the electoral mandate, making "suffrage respected so that there would be acquiescence in its results."[26]

In Cuba, however, Wood anticipated widespread opposition to a restricted suffrage. A literacy requirement, he knew full well, would disenfranchise outright the vast majority of army veterans. Recognizing the political imprudence of denying the franchise to the *libertadores*, Wood proposed a "soldier clause," waiving the literacy requirement for officers and noncommissioned officers.[27] But this, too, Wood feared on second thought, would perhaps prove inadequate. After several months of further reflection, and anticipating the ire of the former enlisted ranks of Liberation Army, the occupation government expanded the "soldier clause" to include all veterans, removing, in Wood's words, "the only elements which would be dangerous."[28]

In early spring the military government announced the suffrage requirement. Voters for the June 1900 municipal elections were required to be Cuban-born males or sons of Cuban parents born while in temporary residence abroad or Spaniards who had renounced their citizenship. All voting males were to be twenty years of age, free of felony conviction and residents of the municipality in which they intended to vote at least thirty days preceding the first day of registration. In addition, the voters were required to possess one of the following: ability to read and write, real or personal property worth $250, or honorable service in the Liberation Army prior to July 18, 1898.[29]

Wood's fears of Cuban reactions proved correct. Protest was immediate. For many Cubans, American actions represented an abridgment of a key separatist ideal—the commitment to universal manhood suffrage. Led by veterans' organizations, Cubans across the island denounced the military government. "By ordering a restricted suffrage for the people of Cuba," the *Partido Republicano Democrático* protested, "the Government of the *United States* not only exercises a sovereignty right over a people it has not conquered . . . but violates (be it said with all due respect) the people's sovereignty, and unduly disregards the most numerous classes, although they may be poor and illiterate, of our Society."[30] The veteran's Territorial Council of Matanzas petitioned Wood to permit unrestricted suffrage. The *ayuntamientos* (town councils) of San Luis, San Juan, Jiguaní, Manageia, Ceiba de Aguainin, Güines, Alquizar, and Los Palacios registered formal protests. Veterans associations, patriotic clubs, and civic organizations in Santiago de Cuba, Manquito, Manzanillo, Sagua la Grande, Santa Clara, Remedios, and Jovellanos demanded universal manhood suffrage. Ranking separatist leaders, including Bartolomé Masó, Enrique Collazo, and Salvador Cisneros Betancourt publicly denounced the proposed basis of suffrage.[31]

By early spring, the military government had completed the work of the census. By Root's calculations, there was a total of three hundred fifteen thousand Cuban males over twenty-one—one hundred eighty-eight thousand whites and one hundred twenty-seven thousand blacks—and some fifty thousand Spanish males over twenty-one entitled to Cuban citizenship. Suffrage restrictions reduced the Cuban electorate to some one hundred five thousand males—two-thirds of all adult Cuban males were excluded from the franchise. It was with no small relief, Root wrote Wood, that he learned that "whites so greatly outnumbered the blacks." Root expressed satisfaction also that Spaniards constituted a minority, thereby foreclosing any charges that the proposed basis of suffrage "would result in turning the island over to the control of Spain."[32]

In Cuba, Wood ignored Cuban protests. "I have not heard of any criticism anywhere," Wood reassured Root with something less than complete candor. "Its approval has been little short of remarkable."[33] Suffrage restrictions reduced the electorate to some 5 percent of the population.[34] From Washington, Root offered his congratulations:

It was a great thing to secure the peaceful adoption of the basis of suffrage upon which we had agreed and to carry the Cubans through their first real election so quietly and satisfactorily. Of course, most people will assume that this is one of the things which happens as a matter of course, but we know better here, and when the history of the new Cuba comes to be written the establishment of popular self-government, based on a limited suffrage, excluding so great a proportion of the elements which have brought ruin to Haiti and San Domingo, will be regarded as an event of the first importance.[35]

III Congratulations were a bit premature, however. The results of the June 1900 municipal elections did not fulfill American expectations. The military government may have been successful in denying the "illiterate and ignorant masses" the vote, but Americans surveying the political landscape after the municipal elections could not derive anything more than fleeting consolation from the results. The *independentista* sector, organized into the National party, generally enjoyed more success at the polls than did conservatives. Not that Wood was totally disappointed with the outcome; many pro-American candidates had triumphed.[36] Still, the military governor could not conceal his unhappiness over the strong showing of Cuban nationalists at the polls and the victory, as Wood despaired, of "the extreme and revolutionary element."[37] Nor were victorious Cubans reluctant to bring the moral of the election results to the attention of American authorities. "The Cuban National Party," an exultant General Alejandro Rodríguez taunted McKinley, "victorious in the election, salutes the worthy representative of the North American Nation, and confidently awaits an early execution of the Joint Resolution."[38]

The municipal elections represented something of a personal defeat for Wood. For months preceding the June balloting, he had labored diligently behind the scenes in behalf of conservative pro-American candidates. The elimination of the "illiterate and ignorant masses" from the voter registration lists was only the first step, a means to a larger end. Wood worked tirelessly in early 1900 to forge conservatives into a political coalition capable of competing successfully with the "extreme and revolutionary element" at the polls. He consulted "with all classes," Wood explained to Root, "the Spanish and the conservative element; property holders as well as foreigners" to promote a conservative consensus. "I am preaching but one policy," Wood wrote to Root in February, "and that is for all people to get together and unite for good government."[39] The military governor gave conservatives private encouragement in their quest for political office, repeatedly reassuring them of American goodwill and support while seeking to neutralize the opposition.[40] "Of course," Wood conceded, "the usual opposition party will gradually develop, but I shall endeavor to give them as slender a foundation as possible to stand on."[41]

Wood's disappointment in June 1900 was twofold. First, he was unhappy over the outcome of the balloting—effectively, a popular repudiation of his candidates, those men publicly identified with the United States. Secondly, and in his mind related, conservatives' poor showing at the polls signified poor performance as candidates. Conservatives ran lackluster campaigns, many withdrawing their candidacy at the first signs of defeat, thereby guaranteeing the opposition victory. Wood attributed the conservatives' weak showing to inexperience and political pusillanimity. The time had arrived, Wood concluded, for the United States to move out from behind the shadows of Cuban politics and take an active and public part in promoting the political fortunes of the "better classes."

Only weeks after the elections, the military government called for new elections in September, these to choose delegates for a constituent assembly. The convention was scheduled to convene in Havana on the first Monday of November "to frame and adopt a constitution for the people of Cuba, and, as a part thereof, to provide for and agree with the government of the United States upon the relations to exist between that Government and the Government of Cuba."[42]

Disappointed at the results of the municipal elections, Wood decided to participate more actively in the new campaign in behalf of conservative candidates. He plunged into the thick of late summer politics with the zeal of a candidate himself seeking public office. In August, he undertook an arduous tour of the island to campaign for the election of the "better classes." "I leave tonight," he cabled Root on August 13, "for a trip around the east end of the Island for . . . purpose of telling the leaders of all parties that they must not trifle with this Constitutional Convention and that if they send a lot of political jumping-jacks as delegates they must not expect that their work will be received very seriously."[43] In Santiago, Wood publicly appealed for election of the "best men:"

I beg you as a personal favor to me and to the United States Government to sink your political differences and passions and to send men to the convention who are renowned for honor and capacity, so that the convention may mean more than the Cubans even now anticipate. Again, I say send the best men. The work before your representatives is largely legal work. . . . For the present party considerations must be suspended for the sake of the greater end in view. . . . Bear in mind that no constitution which does not provide for a stable government will be accepted by the United States. I wish to avoid making Cuba into a second Haiti.[44]

In Puerto Príncipe, Wood warned Camagüeyans that if Cubans elected delegates who failed to provide for stability and order, the United States would not withdraw its military forces.[45] From Cienfuegos, he could report confidently that the "better class of men [were] coming to the front daily for candidates to the convention."[46] In the preelection final report to the White House, Wood detailed the achievements of his travels around the island. "I have seen most of the prominent men," he explained, "using every effort to have them send the best and ablest men to the Constitutional Convention without consideration to political parties. Some of the men nominated are excellent, others are rather bad. I hope, however, that the latter will be defeated." Nevertheless, he struck a note of caution and appealed to President McKinley to proceed slowly with plans for evacuation "until we see what class are coming to the front for the offices called for under the Constitution."[47] A week before the elections, he predicted confidently that "a very good class of men" appeared "to be coming to the front in most provinces." To be sure, a "good many undesirable individuals" would probably be elected as delegates. But, "on the whole," Wood concluded optimistically, "I think we will come out fairly successfully."[48]

17 From Amendment to Appendix

If it is our business to see that the Cubans are not destroyed by any foreign power, is it not our duty to see that they are not destroyed by themselves?
—Senator Albert J. Beveridge, April 1901

The third clause in the amendment, giving to the American Government the power to intervene in our country, is most serious, because, under its shadow, it is impossible to establish here any Cuban government, stable, strong, and orderly. Should we concede this, there will be born a government resting upon a supposition of incapacity.
—Domingo Méndez Capote, February 1901

The Cuban government, launched by the United States with an expression of contempt for its capacity, will inevitably be embarrassed by our mistrust: Stigmatized as an object of suspicion, is it not likely to lack the self-reliance essential to administration, and to lack the self-reliance essential to administration, and to fail in the end, if only because failure was taken for granted?
—Columbia Law Review, June 1901

We are asked to give the United States the key to our house, with the right to come in whenever they choose.
—Juan Gualberto Gómez, February 1901

I "I regret to inform you," a disheartened Wood wrote Senator Orville H. Platt in December 1900, "that the dominant party in the convention to-day contains probably the worst political element in the Island and they will bear careful watching." He continued his lament:

The men whom I had hoped to see take leadership have been forced into the background by the absolutely irresponsible and unreliable element. . . . There are a number of excellent men in the Convention; there are also some of the most unprincipled rascals who walk the Island. The only fear in Cuba to-day is not that we shall stay, but that we shall leave too soon. The elements desiring our immediate departure are the men whose only capacity will be demonstrated as a capacity for destroying all hopes for the future. I do not mean to say that the people are not capable of good government; but I do mean to say, and emphasize it, that the class to whom we must look for the stable government in Cuba are not as yet sufficiently well represented to give us that security and confidence which we desire.[1]

Wood also shared his despair with the secretary of war. "I am disappointed in the composition of the Convention," he confided ruefully to Root. The important responsibility of framing a new constitution had fallen to some of the "worst agitators and political radicals in Cuba." Wood expressed too his disappointment and bafflement at the poor voter turnout—not more than 30 percent of the qualified voters had participated in the elections. The implications were sobering. Once again he questioned the wisdom of Washington's decision to proceed with preparations for self-government. "None of the more intelligent men claim that the people are yet ready for self-government," Wood wrote plaintively.[2] "In case we withdraw," he warned, the convention represented "the class to whom Cuba would have to be turned over . . . for the highly intelligent Cubans of the land owning, industrial and commercial classes are not in politics."[3] Two-thirds of the convention were "adventurers pure and simple," not "representatives of Cuba" and "not safe leaders."[4] Two months later, Wood drew the obvious moral: "To abandon this country to the control of the element now very largely influencing the Convention . . . would, in my opinion, destroy all immediate hopes for the future advancement and development of the Island and its people."[5]

316   Wood was not alone in his generally bleak assessment of Cuban political

developments. Robert P. Porter found the absence of the "more intelligent and farseeing Cuban planters" an ominous portent.[6] "That assemblage is nothing short of a conundrum," an army chaplain in Cuba complained. "There are four niggers in it, and the rest of the gang is on the par with them. Talk about making a Constitution! They have no idea, conception, or even a faint discernment of what they are expected to do."[7] The poor showing of the "better classes," an American correspondent wrote from Havana after the election, served to underscore obvious hazards attending the establishment of self-government in Cuba: "The absence of a well-organized Conservative party, is doubtless a serious menace to successful government." Without effective opposition from the stable forces on the island, radicals would have an unlimited opportunity to establish a "rapacious" regime.[8] From Washington, Senator Orville H. Platt agreed. The convention represented the "most radical element of the Cuban electorate," he despaired, "irresponsible as children, jealous of outside influences, dazzled with the prospects of at last being their own masters."[9]

II American apprehensions notwithstanding, deliberations proceeded uneventfully. In early January 1901, the assembly finished the final draft of the new constitution. But the work of the convention remained incomplete. On the issue of relations with the United States, the second part of the American charge to the convention, the Cubans remained silent.

The future of relations between the United States and Cuba had long been the subject of discussions within the American policy officialdom. As early as the first months of the occupation, the exact nature of relations was a source of lively official correspondence.[10] Elihu Root's policy formulations, later to emerge as the operational clauses of the Platt Amendment, represented the cumulative counsel and recommendations of many men, including James H. Wilson, John R. Brooke, Leonard Wood, Joseph B. Foraker, and Orville H. Platt.[11]

By early January 1901, Root had outlined in draft form those features of Cuban-American relations deemed essential in Washington. The United States, he explained to Secretary of State John Hay, desired the right of intervention for the preservation of Cuban government and "the maintenance of a stable government, adequately protecting life, property, and individual liberty." Nor could Washington allow Cuba the authority to negotiate any treaty or concede to a foreign country special privileges without prior approval of the United States. Cuba, lastly, would be expected to cede to the United States several sites for the establishment of naval stations. Root acknowledged that his formulations owed some inspiration to England's relations with Egypt—relations that seemed to allow "England to retire and still maintain her moral control."[12]

The need to define the precise nature of Cuban-American relations while at the same time holding the future Cuban government to some standard of performance and accountability, subject to American review and restraints, assumed a new urgency after 1900. In early 1901 Washington found itself moving ineluctably toward the establishment of self-government in Cuba without having successfully mobilized those sectors of the Cuban polity to which it had hoped to entrust political leadership. Efforts to promote the ascendancy of pro-American parties through the electoral system, and institutionalizing that ascendancy during the occupation, had failed. A review of the political panorama in early 1901 offered Americans bleak prospects for rule by the "better classes." Even under controlled and favorable circumstances, supported by the occupation government and appealing to a comparatively exclusive electorate, pro-American conservatives had fared poorly at the polls. Nor could the United States reasonably expect the political fortunes of conservatives to improve at the end of the occupation. On the contrary, with the Cuban constituent assembly contemplating a liberal franchise, the "better classes" had a dim electoral future indeed.

In Havana, Wood continued his passive resistance to self-government for Cuba. "These men," he insisted, "are all rascals and political adventurers whose object is to loot the Island."[13] He once again proposed the disavowal of the Joint Resolution. "You can be assured," he sought to persuade Washington, "that the real interests and the real people of Cuba will support any reasonable demands and if the rascals in the Convention who are attempting to make trouble succeed even to a small extent they will, before the world, absolve us from any reference to the [Teller] resolution. I do not contemplate anything of this sort, but it is better to have it than to destroy the island by surrendering it . . . to the class of people whom I have always characterized as unprincipled and irresponsible."[14]

III   The decision to press for binding relations while the island was under military rule signified an admission of Washington's inability to orchestrate Cuban political developments to its satisfaction. There was never much question that the United States intended to establish close relations with the island—"ties of singular intimacy," McKinley had suggested to Congress in December 1898.[15] If these ties could not find immediate fruition in annexation, they would then be established by treaty. Indeed, the Joint Resolution had made this a necessary if only—in the minds of policymakers—a temporary half-way measure pending annexation. Washington believed, too, that the matter of binding relations between the United States and Cuba belonged properly on an agenda negotiated later by the diplomatic representatives of both countries—not something imposed on occupied Cuba by the threat of continued deferral of independence. But this was before developments in Cuba had shaken American confidence in the political solvency of its local allies. To pass up the opportunity to wrest from Cubans during the occupation the guarantees necessary to American interests would have forced the United States to negotiate later with Cuba on a parity of sovereignty. This, Americans feared, would foreclose any reasonable prospect that Cuba, once independent, would accede voluntarily to the types of limitations that Washington planned to impose on Cuban sovereignty. The "most obvious meaning" of the Joint Resolution, Root conceded privately in early 1901 to a friend, called for the establishment first of an independent government in Havana, to be followed in the ordinary course of events with the negotiation of a treaty of relations between Cuba and the United States. "Yet," Root hastened to add, "it is plain that such a course would leave the United States in a worse position as to its own interests than she was when Spain held sovereignty of Cuba and would be an abandonment of both our interests and Cuba herself." The "obvious terms" of the Joint Resolution had tied the hands of the president, Root insisted, and unless the Cubans could be "induced to do voluntarily whatever we think they ought to do," the United States would find itself forced to "abandon American interests" or engage Cubans in a controversy in which they would shelter themselves "under the resolution of Congress against the Executive." It was necessary, during the drafting of the Cuban constitution, to secure from the convention those guarantees deemed vital to American interest, no matter what the disposition of the Cubans.[16] Senator Orville H. Platt similarly predicted that to delay the matter of relations until the establishment of a Cuban government would effectively result in the American "surrender [of] any right to be heard as to what relations shall be," and run the risk of having to be "contented with nothing at all."[17] Indeed, by early 1901, the American definition of "pacification" had undergone the final transfiguration. "All that we have asked," Senator Platt argued in a published article, "is that the mutual relation shall be defined and acknowledged coincidently with the setting up of Cuba's new government. In no other way could a stable government be assured in Cuba, and until such assurance there could be no complete 'pacification' of the island, and no surrender of its control."[18]

The imposition of binding relations as a condition for evacuation, moreover, promised to have a salutary effect on the "better classes." Leonard Wood had given much thought to the inability of what he called the "natural governing class" to assert its proper political prominence in Cuba. The uncertainty surrounding Cuba's future, Wood reasoned, and, more specifically, the American failure to give public form to the nature of Cuba's future relationship to the United States, had sapped conservative morale and discouraged the "better classes" from asserting their "natural governing" role on the island. As early as 1899, a conservative political tract had appealed to the United States for a statement of future policy. "The conservative element of Cuba," the petition indicated, "composed of property owners, holders of mortgages, etc., require to be assured in the most emphatic manner that they have due protection, from whatever Government that may be established finally in the island. At present they think themselves on the verge of a precipice and all their hopes of salvation are fixed on the United States."[19] For Wood, the question of relations was strategically linked to the issue of political leadership in Cuba. In January 1901, Wood urged Elihu Root to submit the matter of Cuban-American relations to Congress. "I think Congress should be told very plainly," the military governor counseled, "that the men who have been elected to positions of authority in Cuba are in no way competent to protect the present interests or develop the future prosperity of the island." He continued:

The situation is vexatious and annoying, but we should not
commit ourselves to actions which, like some of those of '98, will
give us cause for regret and annoyance. Let Congress tell these
people frankly that we are going to establish a government here
if they want it, but that we will not turn the island over until
competent men come to the front, men whose ability and
character give reasonable guarantee of stability of the coming
government. The men on top now are, politically speaking, a
danger to the Island and its future.[20]

In early 1901 American authorities discerned a relationship between the poor political performance of conservatives in Cuba, on one hand, and the lack of a public policy in Washington on the other. "Our policy towards Cuba," Wood complained, "has rendered it impossible for business and conservative elements to state frankly what they desire, they fearing to be left in the lurch by our Government's sudden withdrawal." Wood again returned to his enduring concern:

It must not be forgotten for a moment that the present dominant political elements are not representative of the Cuban people as a whole. In general terms they are a lot of adventurers and to turn the country over before a better element has come to the front will be nothing more or less in effect than turning the island over to spoilation. It would be a terrific blow to civilization here. I believe in establishing a government of and by the people of Cuba and a free government, because we have promised it, but I do not believe in surrendering the present Government to the adventurers who are now in the Convention and in many of the municipalities. Let Congress set a definite date of withdrawal provided a suitable government exists and I will make every effort to bring the conservative and representative elements to the front, . . . I have started the new year with a systematic policy of urging and encouraging by all proper means, the conservative element to come forward and interest themselves in the political situation.[21]

"Our best friends," Wood reminded Senator Joseph B. Foraker, "are the country people, the planters and the commercial classes. Our enemies are the groups of political agitators who want to get their fingers into the treasury and pay themselves their real and fictitious claims." To the point, Wood concluded: "No one wants more than I a good and stable government, of and by the people here, but we must see that the right class are in office before we can turn the government over."[22] A month later, Wood welcomed Washington's decision to move ahead with the proposed statement of relations. "We must find some way of getting the representative people to the front." The proposed relations promised to accomplish these goals. The "more intelligent, well educated Cuban," Wood complained, however privately displeased with the quality of elected officials, continued to show some reluctance about entering national politics. "It is going to take a little time to bring him out," he conceded. However—"with a definite policy announced this class will come forward in self-protection. . . . To go further without giving them time to organize and get rid of the adventurers who are now on top simply means to ruin the whole proposition of any

Cuban Government." Within a year, Wood predicted confidently, with Cuba bound to the United States by formal political ties, Washington could end the military government and reduce the American military presence to several regiments. "What is wanted," he wrote, echoing Root's analogy with Egypt, "is the moral force to hold these people up to their work until the decent element assumes its normal position in the government of this island."[23]

The choices before Washington were now clear. The failure of conservatives to assert their assigned political role made it necessary for the United States to retain some form of institutionally sanctioned control over the Cuban national system before withdrawing American military forces from the island. The specific features of Cuban-American relations outlined earlier by Root were not negotiable. "The political element are an ungrateful lot," Wood insisted, "and they appreciate only one thing, which is, the strong hand of authority and if necessary *we must show it*." He dismissed opposition to the proposed relations as the reactions of "emotional and hysterical" men. The "great mass of intelligence and material interests," on the other hand, "cordially supported" the relations proposed by Washington. Wood counseled Washington to ignore Cuban opposition. Support for binding relation by the "better classes" was silent, he divined, while the "ultra-radical element representing perhaps ten percent of the people are going to make a great deal of noise."[24]

IV   Unable to prolong the military occupation interminably, but unwilling to relinquish the government of the island to the "ultra-radical" Cubans immediately, Washington settled on the third course. Yes—concede to Cubans self-government but deny them sovereignty. Political developments during the occupation had underscored the inefficacy of entrusting American interests to the vagaries of Cuban electoral politics. If extenuating circumstances prohibited immediate annexation, political consideration precluded complete independence. The proposed relations, attached directly as the appendix to the organic act creating the republic, would institutionalize American control over the Cuban national system. Root warned Cubans that the appended articles represented the "extreme limit of this country's indulgence in the matter of the independence of Cuba." Root was blunt: simply stated, the political leadership emerging in Havana did not inspire American confidence. "The character of the ruling class is such that their administration of the affairs of the island will require the restraining influence of the United States government for many years influence of the United States government for many years to come, even if it does not eventually become necessary for this government to take direct and absolute control of Cuban affairs."[25] Senator Platt concurred. The United States had an obligation to protect Cuba from both external and internal threats. "The United States of right may, and must, insist," Platt wrote, "that before it will withdraw from the military occupation of Cuba there shall be a friendly government established there."[26]

In late February, Platt gave legislative form to administration policy in an amendment to the 1901 army appropriations bill.[27] By the terms of Platt's amendment, the president was authorized to "leave the government and control of the island of its people"—an artful link to the Joint Resolution—as

soon as a government shall have been established in said island under a constitution which, either as part thereof or in an ordinance appended thereto, shall define the future relations of the United States with Cuba, substantially as follows:

1. That the government of Cuba shall never enter into any treaty or other compact with any foreign power or powers which will impair or tend to impair the independence of Cuba, or in any manner authorize or permit any foreign power or powers to obtain by colonization or, for military or naval purposes or otherwise, lodgment in or control over any portion of said island.

2. That said government shall not assume or contract any public debt, to pay the interest upon which, and to make reasonable sinking fund provision for the ultimate discharge of which, the ordinary revenues of the island, after defraying the current expenses of government, shall be inadequate.

3. That the government of Cuba consents that the United States may exercise the right to intervene for the preservation of Cuban independence, the maintenance of a government adequate for the protection of life, property, and individual liberty, and for discharging the obligations with respect to Cuba imposed by the Treaty of Paris on the United States, now to be assumed and undertaken by the government of Cuba.

4. That all Acts of the United States in Cuba during its military occupancy thereof are ratified and validated, and all

lawful rights acquired thereunder shall be maintained and
protected.

5. That the government of Cuba will execute and as far as
    necessary extend, the plans already devised or other plans
    to be mutually agreed upon, for the sanitation of the cities
    of the island, to the end that a recurrence of epidemic and
    infectious diseases may be prevented, thereby assuring pro-
    tection to the people and commerce of Cuba, as well as to
    the commerce of the southern ports of the United States
    and the people residing therein.

6. That the Isle of Pines shall be omitted from the proposed
    constitutional boundaries of Cuba, the title thereto being
    left to future adjustment by treaty.

7. That to enable the United States to maintain the indepen-
    dence of Cuba, and to protect the people thereof as well as
    for its own defence, the government of Cuba will sell or
    lease to the United States land necessary for coaling or
    naval stations at certain specified points, to be agreed upon
    the President of the United States.

8. That by way of further assurance the government of Cuba
    will embody the foregoing provisions in a permanent treaty
    with the United States.[28]

Even as Congress completed the final details of the Platt Amendment,
Wood was communicating its substance to members of constituent assembly.[29] News of the proposed relations stunned Cubans and precipitated
protests and anti-American demonstrations across the island. On the evening of March 2, a torchlight demonstration converged on Wood's residence to protest the proposed amendment. In Santiago, speakers at public
rallies alluded to the necessity of returning to arms to redeem national
honor. Across the island municipalities, civic associations, and veterans'
organizations cabled protests to Havana.[30] On March 2, Wood cabled
Washington that the "intelligent classes" had endorsed the proposed relations, but the "extreme element" was seeking to persuade the convention
to reject the Platt Amendment and dissolve in protest. A visit from the
American naval squadron stationed in the Florida Keys, Wood suggested
to Washington, would have a calming effect in Havana.[31]

Supported by public opinion and encouraged by the press, the convention balked at the proposed relations. Throughout early spring, Cuban

representatives refused to act on American instructions.[32] "Can you indicate our action in case Convention should refuse to accept Platt Amendment," an anxious Wood queried Secretary Root. The military governor urged Washington to give thought to dissolving the convention and organizing new elections later that spring for another and presumably more sympathetic assembly. The "irresponsible people" of the convention, Wood insisted, had to realize that American policy was "fixed and that they are confronting a serious responsibility."[33]

Cuban resistance to proposed relations angered Americans. This lack of regard for American requests, this manifest refusal to accommodate American national interests, was seen as one more example of the general thanklessness with which the Cubans had repaid American generosity. "These people are base ingrates," former Consul Walter B. Barker complained to Senator John T. Morgan. "I pity this people for . . . they are incapacitated for self-government. With "minds of no greater scope than children," Barker asserted, "how could they be expected to conduct successfully a Government of their own."[34]

In Washington, a determined administration defined a policy with which there would be neither compromise nor concession. The members of the convention, Root informed Wood, "cannot escape their responsibility except by a refusal to act, which will necessarily require the convening of another Convention which will act." Root was adamant—and blunt. Cubans could not have any government other than American military government until they acted favorably on the proposed relations. "No constitution can be put into effect in Cuba," he emphasized, "and no government can be elected under it, no electoral law by the Convention can be put into effect, and no election held under it until they have acted upon this question of relations in conformity with this act of Congress." To the point: "There is only one possible way for them to bring about the termination of the military government and make either the constitution or electoral law effective; that is to do the whole duty they were elected for." Continued resistance to American demands, the secretary of war warned ominously, would have dire consequences. "If they continue to exhibit ingratitude and entire lack of appreciation of the expenditure of blood and treasure of the United States to secure their freedom from Spain, the public sentiment of this country will be more unfavorable to them."[35] Senator Francis M. Cockrell summed up the administration's position succinctly: either the Cubans accept the Platt Amendment or accommodate themselves to indefinite American military occupation.[36]

But all this hard talk during the early months of spring was still private and confined largely to the upper reaches of the American policy official-dom. Publicly, Washington was prepared to proffer ceremonial concessions to mollify Cuban sensibilities. In April, the constituent assembly dispatched a commission to meet with ranking American officials in Washington. The real purpose of the visit, Wood informed Root, was to provide the Cubans a face-saving way out of the political impasse. Made up of "good representative men," Wood assured Washington, the commission ostensibly sought clarification of several articles of the Platt Amendment. In fact, however, the visit was preliminary to acceptance of the proposed relations. "This must not be even intimated," Wood cautioned Root. "Everything depends upon this being unknown."[37]

For three days in April 1901 Leonard Wood chaperoned the Cuban commissioners through the Washington offices of senior American officials. On April 25, the Cuban delegates met President McKinley socially. A day later the commission conferred with Root and was assured that the Platt Amendment would in no manner interfere with the independence of the Cuban government.[38] Senator Platt also reassured the Cubans that he did not intend the proposed relations to "result in the establishment of a protectorate or suzerainty or in any way interfere with the independence or sovereignty of Cuba."[39]

The commission also sought American commitment to favorable commercial relations, specifically a treaty of reciprocity between Cuba and the United States. On this point, too, Americans were unanimous: the settlement of economic issues would have to await the resolution of political matters. As soon as the Cubans constituted their government, Root promised the delegation, Washington would move immediately toward the negotiation of a reciprocity treaty with Havana. First, however, the Cubans had to accede to American demands as a precondition to independence.[40]

American officials were confident that the Cuban visit would have a salutary effect on deliberations in Havana. Much had been done, a self-satisfied Root noted, to disabuse the commission that the Platt Amendment "concealed a real purpose to make their independence merely nominal and really fictitious." Root also believed that discussions with senior American officials provided the Cubans the "material" with which to "meet the arguments of the irreconciliables." A "feeling of kindliness towards the United States" had also emerged from the meetings, a feeling, Root hoped, that would have the effect of carrying the convention toward ratification of the Platt Amendment.[41]

For the better part of the following months, the debate in Havana continued. In April, the Círculo de Hacendados and the Sociedad Económica endorsed the Platt Amendment as a necessary safeguard for prosperity and stability.[42] In early June, impatient with the convention's delay in ratifying proposed relations, Wood asked Washington for authority to issue an ultimatum announcing that there would be "no further reconsideration or discussion."[43]

This proved unnecessary, however. By mid-June, the Cubans had capitulated and reconciled themselves to American demands. Opponents to the proposed relations conceded defeat and announced their intention to vote for the amendment. The choice before the assembly, Manuel Sanguily concluded ruefully, was limited sovereignty or none at all. "Independence with restrictions is preferable to the military regime," he announced as he cast his vote to accept.[44] "There is no use objecting to the inevitable," Enrique Villuendas conceded. "It is either annexation or a Republic with an Amendment. I prefer the latter."[45] Cuba's rejection of the Platt Amendment, Domingo Méndez Capote feared, would be interpreted by the Americans as "tacit acquiescence to an indefinite protectorate."[46] Máximo Gómez, too, reconciled himself to the inevitable. "The Republic will surely come," a disconsolate Gómez wrote to a friend, "but not with the absolute independence we had dreamed about." It was enough now to accept the restrictions imposed by the Americans. To fail in this, Gómez warned, alluding to annexation, would someday result in a future generation of children, having lost even the language, alienated from the traditions of the past generation and fully imbued with the "Yankee spirit." "We must make great efforts to remain always Cubans."[47] On June 12, by a ballot of sixteen to eleven and four abstentions, the convention voted to accept the Platt Amendment as an appendix to the new constitution.

18 The Construction of a Colonial Army

I think the reported plan . . . to replace American troops on the island by Cuban soldiers with American officers entirely impracticable. Soldiers without drill or discipline are valueless. How could such instruction be imparted by officers who do not understand the language of their men; and where is the authority to organize a Cuban army with U.S. officers?
—Fitzhugh Lee, November 1899

The insurgent army should disband. So long as it is held together, it is merely a political factor with which we should have nothing to do. When disbanded, we can get such men as we may require.
—General James Wade, U.S. Commission for Evacuation of Cuba, November 1898

I When the war ended in August 1898, three armies shared control of Cuba: Spaniards in the western cities, Americans in the eastern cities, and Cubans encircling both in the surrounding countryside. There was more than symbolic significance to this military landscape, for in a very real sense the midway position occupied by armed Cubans threatened to obstruct the completion of American rule over all of the island. The continued presence of armed Cubans after the war, organized in regiments and battalions under the independent control of *insurrecto* chieftains, had an enormously unsettling effect on the American army command in Cuba. But it was also true that units of the Liberation Army had provided valuable assistance to American military forces immediately after the war. Cubans had served American commanders through the period of transition in the fall of 1898, supporting American forces in maintaining order and peace in the countryside and upholding the authority of municipal government in the towns.[1]

However useful Cuban soldiers may have been during the early period of the occupation, Americans were not insensitive to the potential peril posed by this body of armed Cubans. The Liberation Army possessed at once the capacity to dispute militarily American claims of "conquered territory" in Cuba and contest U.S. political authority. By preserving its organization into the period of transition, the Liberation Army emerged as a de facto military co-occupier of the island. Units of the insurgent army remained intact. Many continued to administer towns and cities captured earlier in the war—vivid reminder that American control in Cuba was incomplete.

The survival of insurgent military organizations after 1899, the period of formal American rule in Cuba, compounded the anomaly. Indeed, the transfer of authority from Spain to the United States on January 1, 1899, immediately transformed the nature of Cuban-American relations. The establishment of an American government in Cuba converted the erstwhile allies into subjects of the United States, transforming the Liberation Army into a potentially hostile body of armed Cubans in a country occupied by American military forces. As long as the Liberation Army maintained its armed unity, the spectre of armed resistance overshadowed the military government. Americans looked upon the insurgent army with a mixture of suspicion and apprehension. Just as the Assembly sought to eliminate the army in order to establish its authority over the separatist polity, so too did the Americans, in order to remove the challenge to U.S. administration of the island.

Early in the occupation, as part of the larger effort to attract Cubans out of the ranks of the insurgent army, American authorities recruited Cuban veterans to serve in informal auxiliary military units under the command of American officers. Initial efforts were in large measure a variant of the "jobs for guns" policy, a way to facilitate the demobilization of the Liberation Army while permitting veterans to continue to bear arms in the service of Cuba. These early projects, however, were motivated more by the necessity to dissolve the potentially hostile Liberation Army than by a conscious effort to create a politically useful military organization. General J. C. Bates, the first military governor of Santa Clara, expressed the attitude of many provincial commanders in early 1899: "I deem it a matter of the utmost importance that a system of rural guards be organized. . . . We should give employment to about two thousand Cubans, many of whom are in my opinion very liable to give us serious trouble unless we take care of them; and I believe any other means would be more expensive."[2]

But the successful dissolution of the Liberation Army that following spring did not solve all the problems associated with the Cuban armed forces. The sudden release of forty thousand soldiers into a devastated economy, searching fruitlessly for work, aroused considerable misgivings in American policy circles. "Unless employed in some manner," Major John A. Logan, provost marshall in Santa Clara, warned in early 1899, "many of the Cuban troops themselves will soon be turned loose to find existence as best they can. That there is not sufficient employment this year in the agricultural districts or in the cities for even fifty percent of them, is evident. . . . If allowed to wander aimlessly about many of them will soon take to lawlessness and brigandage."[3] Similar conditions were reported by the department commander in Pinar del Río. "They are absolutely destitute," General George W. Davis wrote in January 1899, "and have no property of any kind except a rifle or machete or both, and no means for procuring the work cattle and farming implements needed in cultivating tobacco. The sugar estates, only found in the eastern part of the Province, are nearly all destroyed and the owners of these estates cannot give employment." Davis warned that dissolving the army without providing employment would result "in turning loose upon the community some thousands of armed men who would in many cases resort to highway robbery and pillage as a means of support."[4] In Washington, proposals to organize a local constabulary received additional support as a palliative to relieve the employment pressures attending the entry of these veterans into a glutted labor market. The threat of violence, even after the demobilization of the Liberation Army, was underscored by President McKinley's secretary, John Addison Porter, who warned the War Department:

Even though without arms it would be extremely dangerous to cast thousands of men on the mercy of the community absolutely penniless and without resources. They would have to continue to live on the country in large numbers, and some might be driven by the extremity of their wants to take food and clothing by stealth and force. With such men wandering aimlessly about, the planters would not dare buy the cattle necessary to begin the operation of their plantations, and even those disposed to work would thus not find the opportunity of doing so. Unless this element of danger is entirely removed, a large American military force will be necessary to guarantee peace, involving a great expenditure of money. . . . The proper disbandment of the Cuban Army is the best guarantee of peace; mere disorganization would be a constant menace and peril to the community.[5]

The idea of permanent Cuban military units, acting in conjunction with and under the command of American officers, soon captured the policy imagination of officials in Washington. In a White House cabinet meeting in October 1898, the McKinley administration approved plans to recruit Cuban veterans for a "native gendarme" in order to employ those "who might otherwise in the absence of individual employment, drift into evil course or become a dissatisfied and dangerous element in the community."[6] Several weeks later, the War Department authorized Governor General Brooke to prepare for the enlistment of Cubans starting at the company level.[7]

By late 1898, the White House advocated outright the establishment in Cuba of some type of local military force. Discussing the dissolution of the Liberation Army with the Cuban Assembly commission visiting Washington in December 1898, President McKinley expressed interest in establishing a "colonial army" for the island. This military force, McKinley suggested, would be organized principally from the ranks of the Liberation Army. It would be developed to a full strength of 10,000 officers and men, serve with the American army of occupation, and be paid by the United States. Such an armed force, the president predicted, would be invaluable to the military government in Cuba as well as absorb thousands of Cubans who would otherwise encounter difficulty finding employment.[8]

Nor was the appeal of a "colonial army" confined to Americans. Rafael M. Portuondo, the former secretary of war in the provisional government and chairman of the Assembly's Executive Committee, urged Brooke to organize a "rural constabulary guard" recruited principally from the ranks of military veterans. "The measure," Portuondo stressed, "would satisfy the Cuban people who would look upon it as proof of confidence that the interventionist power has in us." Such a force would, further, produce jobs, increase rural security, and "bring about a renewal of confidence so that the little remaining capital that planters have or can secure would be invested in the betterment of their estates."[9] Máximo Gómez, too, proposed in October 1898 the creation of a "native civil guard" as one measure through which to facilitate the disbandment of the Liberation Army.[10] In his meeting with Robert P. Porter in February 1899, Gómez again urged the Americans to establish in Cuba an armed force consisting of army veterans. Later that month, he appealed to Brooke to organize a new Cuban army under the military government as evidence of American confidence in Cubans.[11] Some weeks later, the insurgent army chieftain addressed his argument directly to President McKinley. The imminent disbandment of the Liberation Army, he warned, promised to create conditions of "misery and desperation" that would lead "to pauperism, if not to the abyss of demoralization and disorder." Gómez called for the creation of an army of 10,000 Cuban soldiers, "without distinction of race," to serve under the American officers.[12] In May, he directed a public manifesto to the Liberation Army in which he detailed his efforts to persuade the United States to create a Cuban army to serve under the occupation government. "I proposed," he recounted, "the creation of a corps of national militia in which, without distinction of race, at least 10,000 men could enlist and of which our Army would furnish the largest and best contingent." The American president had expressed interest in the project, Gómez disclosed, but the uncertainty caused by separatist politics had delayed implementation of his proposal. "These efforts," Gómez indicated, "which were being made with every promise of success were suspended when, against public opinion, I bowed to the decree removing me from the command of the army."[13]

Gómez was only partially correct, however. The uncertainty produced by internal strife in the separatist polity, climaxed by Gómez's ouster and later the dissolution of the Assembly, had, to be sure, delayed American plans to organize a "colonial army." But other factors contributed to the delay. Throughout the better part of Brooke's year as governor general, the development of a "colonial army" remained essentially the undertaking of provincial department commanders. In Havana, Brooke had expressed reservations about the projected army, fearing that the organization of a colonial military force would create suspicions about American intentions among Cubans.[14] But Brooke was not one to oppose actively policy injunctions from Washington. While outlining his misgivings, he also communicated his willingness to conform to the instructions from Washington and awaited only the directives detailing the manner in which he should proceed with the funding and organization of the proposed army.[15] Such instructions were not forthcoming, however. As with so many other matters during the first year, the administration failed to formulate a coherent policy. The "colonial army" project languished.

II　In Cuba, what steps had been taken to organize a local constabulary were principally in response to the need to disband the Liberation Army and create employment for the discharged jobless veterans. These were immediate needs, and largely local. But, as early as the autumn of 1898, a new purpose for Cuban army units, one of a more enduring utility, had become obvious to American provincial commanders in Cuba. Americans sensitive to the subtleties attending colonial administration detected in Cuban veterans one means by which to bridge the distance between the government of the occupation and society of the occupied. Whatever apparent dangers attended the existence of a formal insurgent army functioning as co-occupier, independent of American control, it was equally apparent that the United States lacked the resources and personnel to patrol every village, garrison every estate, pursue every highwayman, and arrest every law offender. Very early in the occupation, American officials perceived in the island's veteran ranks an efficacious and comparatively unobtrusive way of consolidating U.S. authority over Cuba. An accommodation was devised in which armed Cubans, separated from the allegiance system of the Liberation Army, would serve as an adjunct force of the occupation. American policy planners sought to dissolve the Liberation Army and rebuild around the discharged insurgent veterans a new Cuban armed force, one aligned with the American mission in Cuba and attuned to the requirements of American policy objectives.[16]

The local needs of American provincial administration, in fact, had early inspired the creation of Cuban rural guard units to assist department commands. Well before senior officials in Washington had arrived at some consensus about the policy efficacy of a colonial military institution, a Cuban armed force, independently organized by American provincial department heads, and no less "colonial" in organization, sentiment, and mission than the project contemplated earlier in Washington, was at the service of the military government. Throughout late 1898 and early 1899, American department chiefs reported considerable early success with the *ad hoc* organization of local Cuban military units. Fitzhugh Lee in Pinar del Río, L. H. Carpenter in Camagüey, and Leonard Wood in Santiago had successfully organized local rural guard units recruited principally from among the veterans of the Liberation Army.[17] Wood, the first department commander to recruit insurgent veterans, endorsed the organization of Cuban military units enthusiastically. The creation of the rural guard in Oriente had greatly facilitated the disbandment of the insurgent army corps of the east. Once organized into a provincial rural guard, moreover, Cubans had provided valuable assistance in preserving peace and order in the countryside. The performance of the rural guard, Wood stressed to Cuban recruits, served as a measure of Cuba's ability for self-government. Support for and enforcement of American authority became the central criteria by which Cubans would be selected and their performance evaluated. "In appointing these men," Wood informed McKinley in November 1898, "I have impressed upon them the fact that their duty is a very important one, and if they fail to maintain civil order, to arrest all offenders against the law, and to conduct themselves with propriety, that the failure will be, not a failure for them personally, but a failure for civil law in Cuba, and an advertisement to the world that they are unable to control and govern themselves."[18]

Throughout the early months, American authorities were singularly preoccupied with establishing administrative agencies, organizing provincial government, reorganizing the municipalities, and improving health and sanitation facilities. However vital to the success of the occupation order and stability may have been, the military government was loathe to employ American troops to enforce the law.[19] Even if American officials had desired to assume such a role, provincial commanders simply lacked the resources to extend adequate security to the interior rural districts.[20] And even possessed with the means, provincial commanders correctly sensed the perils of using American soldiers as law enforcement agents. Strangers in the land, Americans were unfamiliar with the surrounding countryside and ignorant of local customs. The need to recruit locally and organize Cuban military units familiar with interior became manifestly clear early in the occupation. "Knowing the physical character of the remote parts of this Province as I do," Major John A. Logan in Santa Clara acknowledged in February 1899, "I can easily see that a great amount of men and money would be necessary to apprehend the smallest kind of band of . . . outlaws. That this can be done by our troops, is impossible;. . . in the end natives will have to be employed."[21] In Pinar del Río, General George W. Davis arrived at similar conclusions: "It seems to me the time is favorable for organizing a necessary adjunct, a Rural Guard composed of native population. . . . I would have a small detachment in each municipality employed as patrols, covering the whole country in their daily or weekly rounds; every man perfectly familiar with the country, acquainted with every inhabitant, knowing every trail, path or mountain pass, speaking the language of the country and used to its manner, custom and laws. . . . This force to be selected largely from the Cuban Army, for the men know every rod of ground over which they have been fighting Spain for years."[22]

Concerns well founded, events elsewhere would prove. In February 1899, the second month of American rule in Havana, official Washington was jolted by news of armed rebellion in the Pacific. The outbreak of local resistance to U.S. rule in the Philippines underscored in dramatic terms the necessity of American sensitivity to the nature of its relations with the people of occupied Cuba. The implications of the Filipino war were readily apparent in Washington. The "President and everybody," Henry Adams wrote from the capital in late February, were as "eager to get out of Cuba as they were a year ago to get into it." The "thought of another Manila at Havana," Adams mused, "sobers even an army contractor."[23]

Larger political considerations, reflecting in part developments in the Pacific, required solicitude to the sensibilities of the occupied population. The use of Cubans spared American troops from the necessity of acting directly against the population while couching the authority of American rule behind a Cuban military organization. As governor in Santiago de Cuba, Wood steadfastly refused to permit Americans to patrol the interior countryside unaccompanied by Cubans. Whatever outlawry existed in the interior, Wood insisted, would be met with Cuban rural guards—organized, drilled, and armed specifically for this purpose. "Let the Cubans kill their own rats," Wood prescribed tersely.[24] More to the point, armed Cubans imbued with a sense of respect for and loyalty to American rule, would be freer to act in behalf of the military government with fewer attending risks to American rule. "The Cubans," Wood suggested in a published article in 1899, "are perfectly willing to accept the acts of their own civil officers, which, if performed by soldiers of the United States, would give rise to a great deal of bad feeling and friction."[25]

Developments in the Pacific made the obvious obligatory. The organization of Cuban armed forces had the manifest virtue of minimizing the likelihood of conflict between American soldiers and Cuban civilians. Ranking American officials had drawn the correct moral from the Filipino insurrection. Cultural differences, language misunderstandings, and threat of racial conflict served as constant reminders of the anomalous circumstances surrounding the American presence in Cuba. A conflict in Cuba would have disastrous consequences. Indeed, on few other issues during the first year of the occupation was the official consensus either as immediate or as complete. "In my opinion," Senator Joseph B. Foraker wrote from Washington, "the moment the American soldiers pull the trigger on the Cubans, if they ever do, the—well, the mischief will be to pay generally, and the administration at Washington will have to pay it, and I predict there won't be funds enough for the purpose."[26] General Fitzhugh Lee, writing from Pinar del Río, concurred. "If by accident or bad management," Lee warned, "an exchange of shots took place anywhere between the Cubans and American soldiers, resulting in many of the former falling into ranks again, the country might have a guerrila war on its hands and our troubles [would] multiply."[27] In Santiago, Leonard Wood expressed fear that the deployment of American troops in the pursuit of outlaws would lead inevitably to a disaster of far graver proportions than the conflict in Manila.[28] "The American private soldier," Wood explained to President McKinley, "ignorant of the language and susceptible to all the diseases incident to the climate is not available for many duties which can be performed successfully by men speaking the language, belonging to the country and immune to the climate. The average American soldier does not understand the customs of the people, his amusements and recreations are few; the result is many small misunderstandings with the natives, not all of them serious, but sufficient to keep up slight irritation."[29]

Wood's review of conditions in Cuba touched upon one other American concern: the effects of tropical climate on American troops. From the outset of the occupation, the military government had endeavored to employ where possible troops recruited locally for duty in regions hazardous to the health of American soldiers.[30] "The maintenance of non-immune American troops in Cuba . . . ," Wood advised the War Department in late 1899, "will nevertheless always be attended with a loss of life much greater than would occur among troops immune to the climate and its diseases, especially yellow fever." Wood recommended to Washington the organization of a body of "native troops" under the command of American officers to garrison the more inhospitable regions of eastern Cuba. "This policy,"

Wood reminded Washington, "has been followed by all nations maintaining troops in tropical countries and I believe it would be especially advantageous here. In addition to giving us a body of troops which can be maintained at less cost and with less loss of life it will also give us men who are part and parcel of the people of the Island, connected with them by every tie, largely immune to its diseases and spending their wages in the Island in the maintenance of their families."[31]

By mid-1899, pressures of a new sort heightened the need to release American troops from service in Cuba. Fighting in the Philippines had strained American military forces, requiring the War Department to deploy troops stationed in Cuba for duty in the Pacific. The quicker Cubans replaced Americans, Washington pressed, the sooner relief could be provided to the beleaguered expeditionary forces in Manila.[32]

III It was not until Elihu Root assumed charge of the War Department in August and Leonard Wood became governor-general of Cuba in December that American military policy received a measure of coherence and purpose. "The matter of recruiting in Cuba," President McKinley explained to his newly appointed secretary of war in August 1899, "has been under consideration ever since our occupation of the island. I have wanted to organize a regiment in that island, but the time has never yet seemed to be opportune, and those in command have not advised it or have rather advised against it. The time may be ripe for it now."[33] Indeed, it was.

Whatever the immediate utility of the rural guard in the provinces, and however useful Cubans may have been in assisting department commanders with the needs peculiar to the day-to-day local governance of the island, more visionary American officials detected in a Cuban army an agency through which to promote American influence and consolidate American control. By recruiting separatist leaders of the Cuban armed struggle against Spain, many of whom had achieved senior ranks in the Liberation Army, and appointing them to positions of command in an American-organized constabulary, officials in Washington reasoned, the United States would establish considerable influence and control over a key sector of the old revolutionary polity. A new military organization offered an opportunity to teach Cubans American methods; American values would be diffused through a strategic sector of the population, having the net effect of further Americanizing Cubans. The organization of a Cuban armed force in the service of the United States promised to create the institutional structure through which to obtain the loyalty of an uncertain sector of the old separatist polity. "It is our mission to establish good government and instruct the people in the qualifications of good citizenship," Major John A. Logan wrote in early 1899. "I have found in my contact with Cuban forces that as a rule they are honest, faithful, patient and long-suffering. . . . They have to be guided and instructed like children . . . and for these reasons I believe that an organization based on a military foundation will be more effective than any other."[34]

Secretary of War Root early contemplated recruiting a Cuban regiment modeled on the plan adopted by the British in Egypt, commanded by American field officers, Cuban captains and lieutenants, and American sergeants. A colonial army would "dispose of a lot of men most likely to make trouble in Cuba," Root mused, "turn them from possible bandits, and educate them into Americans."[35] Leonard Wood, too, saw a long-term value to a colonial army. In August 1899, Wood proposed to Theodore Roosevelt the establishment of three "native regiments" under the command of American officers. The Cubans, he wrote, "are all enthusiastic to become American soldiers and we could get as many thousands as we want at short notice. It would have a wonderfully good effect in Americanizing the people also."[36] Some weeks later, he wrote again at length about virtues of the proposed Cuban army and recommended organizing three regiments of Cuban cavalry under American officers. The three regiments, each 1200 strong with 600 men distributed in every province, would replace the rural guard. Agreeing with Root, Wood recommended the appointment of Cubans to the rank of lieutenant with the expectation that, through promotions, Cubans would over time occupy senior grades and, ultimately, full command of the military establishment. "These native regiments," Wood predicted, "would embody the restless and wild spirits which have been engaged in the recent war." The "native regiments" also offered the United States an ideal control agency. "Anyone at all familiar with people of this sort," Wood stressed, "understand fully how much more readily and gracefully they submit to authority enforced by their own people than by a people of absolutely alien blood." One last consideration was noted in passing: "These Cuban regiments will become intensely loyal to us and our methods."[37]

This was a theme to which Wood would return frequently. In October 1899, as the military governor of Santiago was readying himself to assume his new position in Havana, he drafted a lengthy personal memorandum to President McKinley, outlining the broader policy imperatives for the organization of "native regiments." Cubans were "thoroughly amenable to discipline, take kindly to the service and are proud of and delight in good uniform and equipment." Above all, "they are faithful and reliable." The organization of Cuban regiments, Wood predicted, "will do more to unify the sentiment of our people and Cubans in the island than anything we can do." He continued:

Again, there is no single means which presents itself to me as a more feasible one for binding the people of the Island closely to us and obliterating the differences of opinion which now exist. . . . Every native soldier, well paid, well uniformed and well taken care of, forms a friendly bond between ourselves and all his relatives and indirectly to support many of them. Again, a force of this description, recruited from different parts of the Island, would bring us through them, in direct contact with al-most every family in the Island. . . . They would be of immense value in building up American sentiment, and respect for American institutions and American officials.[38]

Several weeks later, Wood reiterated these points directly to the War Department. "Such action would be pleasing to the people of the Island and . . . it would do much to draw the two races together and obliterate many of the misunderstandings which arise from the presence of soldiers foreign in language and sentiment, and totally ignorant of the customs and prejudices of the people."[39]

As governor-general, Wood moved immediately toward the establish-ment of a rural guard under a unified command. Within a year of his appointment, he ordered the organization of the provincial rural guard unit into national companies, the first step toward establishing the haphazardly organized service on a proper island-wide military basis.[40] In January 1901, the military government summoned provincial rural guard chiefs to Havana to participate in a sweeping reorganization of the service. After several months of deliberations, the military government issued the Or-ganic Law of the Rural Guard. Henceforth, four provincial chiefs exercised control over the island's six provinces. The distribution of rural guard units conformed to provincial needs, the relative proportion of the rural and urban population, the efficiency of communications, and the extent of ag-ricultural property. The military government also created an artillery corps to assume command of coastal fortifications. In April 1902, General

Alejandro Rodríguez, a veteran officer of the war against Spain from Santa Clara, assumed unified command of the rural guard.[41]

IV   From the outset, the military government allied the rural guard directly with property owners and the "better classes"—precisely those sectors of Cuban society the Americans had summoned to lead the new republic. In still one more fashion, the United States reaffirmed its commitment to the well-being of the propertied classes. The principal responsibility of the rural guard consisted of protecting property interests in the interior. Land owners frequently donated to the rural guard rent-free land contiguous to or directly on their property. Owners often included in the offer land sufficient to permit maneuvers and drill, grazing land for livestock, free building material, access to drinking water, free construction of roads serving the detachment, and the establishment of a communications network, at the owner's expense, to connect the smaller posts with provincial headquarters.[42] In Cienfuegos, planters and land owners supplied free telephone communication connecting all sugar estates and rural guard stations with the provincial capital headquarters. All this, the provincial commander reported with some satisfaction in 1900, "without entailing any disbursement to the present or future government of the Island."[43] The rural guard was assigned more frequently, as one Cuban official urged it should be, to "the country properties situated at strategic places, in order that it may be enabled to attend with more efficiency and activity to that which constitutes its main duty, which is no other than giving to agriculture, to cattle-raising, and to all other branches of wealth, defense and assistance."[44] By 1905, the vast majority of the rural guard's outposts were located on privately owned property: of 288 stations, only 28 were owned outright by the state; the remainder were either privately rented or donated rent-free by municipalities and business enterprises, including the Chaparra Sugar Company, Juraguá Iron Company, and the United Fruit Company.[45]

The link between property and the rural guard was further strengthened by the recruitment system adopted by the military government. Enlistment qualifications included literacy, good character, and excellent standing in the community. In addition, applicants were required to provide letters of recommendation from at least two well-known citizens of good repute, "preferably property owners."[46] In preparation for the formal organization of the rural guard, American military authorities insisted that recruits "must present certificates of good character from individuals—preferably plantation owners; well known to be men of un-questioned integrity. . . . It would be advisable to obtain as many of the men as possible from those recommended by plantation owners as it is for the protection of rural estates and maintenance of order in rural districts that this guard is being organized."[47] Planters frequently interceded directly with government officials to secure the appointment or reappointment of particular officers who had been uncommonly solicitous of the needs of local property owners.[48]

V   By 1902, the military government had created one more institution to serve American interests. Not only had the military government purged the *independentista* sentiment from the Cuban military establishment, but it also eliminated from the newly organized rural guard the social diversity that had characterized the Liberation Army. In no other separatist institution had blacks won more positions of authority than in the commissioned ranks of the old insurgent army. In the rural guard, black recruits not excluded by virtue of practice were barred by policy. The exclusion of non-white officers was particularly apparent in all the various branches of Cuban armed services. Literacy requirements, the necessity of recruits to pay for their uniforms and mounts upon enlistment, and the need for recommendations from property owners all but formally barred Afro-Cubans from commissioned ranks.[49] Blacks were also woefully underrepresented in municipal police departments. One American traveling in Cuba noted that most patrolmen seemed to be "members of the best Cuban families. Some of them had been wealthy, some looked like former prosperous business men."[50] Where mobility was not restricted by literacy requirements, individual expenses, and personal contacts, it was restricted by official policy. In the Artillery Corps organized in 1901, American military advisors insisted that all Cuban "officers will be white."[51] The call for volunteers for the new service specifically enjoined only white Cubans to apply.[52]

From the outset, a new system of allegiance was subsumed into the rural guard. Recruitment enforced institutional loyalty and assured American control. Cuban recruits took oaths of allegiance to the United States. The officer corps consisted largely of Cubans sympathetic to American policy and quickly took to American methods—"obedient and faithful," in Wood's terms.[53] Officers and men were selected carefully from the "best material" of the Liberation Army and awarded ranks commensurate with grades attained during the war.[54]

Dependence upon the American presence was basic to the rural guard. Cuban officers were selected by and responsible to American commanders; the military government defined the nature of the rural guard's mission on the island. The officers and men of the rural guard, Captain H. J. Slocum, the American advisor to the Cuban armed force wrote, had "gradually stiffened up to their work, protecting life and property, as they came to realize that they were backed by a powerful Government." Cubans were made to understand from the outset, Slocum stressed, "that the strong arm of the Government of the Intervention was supporting them."[55]

In every essential aspect, the rural guard was an institution born of the occupation and developed in conformity with American needs—traits it would retain for the next sixty years. The conditions under which the rural guard emerged, the nature of its mission in occupied Cuba, and, particularly, the relation of Cubans to the American army of occupation, transformed the rural guard into something of a police agency of the United States rather than a national army of Cuba. The Platt Amendment conferred on Washington ultimate responsibility for the external security and internal order. Cuba had no need for a formal army, Senator Orville Platt insisted, for Washington guaranteed an "independent . . . stable republic government" against "foreign aggression or domestic disorder."[56] Secretary of State Elihu Root similarly suggested that the Platt Amendment served to counteract "such revolutions as have afflicted Central and South America," for it was "known to all men that an attempt to overturn the foundations of that government will be confronted by the overwhelming power of the United States."[57]

The rural guard emerged as a surrogate local force of American authority. Nor would this relationship change significantly at the end of the occupation. By the very setting against which the force emerged, and the mission to which it was assigned, the rural guard had acquired its institutional personality around the premise of American hegemony. The rural guard served a foreign government. Its authority did not rest on a national mandate or the legitimacy attending service of a national government, but rather found sanction in American rule—directly during the occupation and indirectly after the evacuation through the Platt Amendment. The circumstances under which the rural guard emerged made a "national" relation—national in the sense of a common and autonomous nation-building relationship—between the Cuban armed forces and the body social impossible. The rural guard was, from its inception, alienated from its national context and deprived of a sense of national mission; it lacked historicity and was bereft of any relevance to the national experience. The occupation experience bestowed upon it a mission and a set of loyalties not consistent with the national needs of the republic—certainly not consistent with the republic envisioned by the old insurgent polity. Armed Cubans in the service of the American military government, subordinate to American commanders, acquired a mission distinct from that inherent in the Liberation Army. Indeed, the central institutional expression of Cuban nationalism had been dissolved and replaced with an agency Leonard Wood hoped would "have a wonderfully good effect in Americanizing" Cubans.

19 Sugar, Reciprocity, and the Reconstruction of the Colonial Economy

Once assured of peace, [Cuba] will be magical. Millions of American money will flow into the island. Under a protectorate, such as will exist for some time, a reciprocity in trade will doubtless be sanctioned and all the riches of the most fruitful and productive bit of ground on the globe will flow into our markets. Cuba will become a source of great profit to the people of the United States. This is not the motive for intervention, but it will be a very gratifying result.
—Vice Consul Joseph A. Springer, April 1898

Suppose prohibitory measures are adopted which cause the enforced sale of Cuban sugar and tobacco at a loss. It means immediate bankruptcy for the country. It means general discouragement and apathy, and a dislike of Americans which may lead to future uprisings against this country. . . . The effect of what has already been accomplished by the United States at such cost of life and money will soon be lost.
—Leonard Wood, January 1902

Cuba is our first and most necessary strategic position in the commercial struggle which must come for trade supremacy in the countries lying to the south of us, with the population of between 60,000,000 to 70,000,000 people and an annual trade, inward and upward of about $1,000,000,000. With the certainty of remunerative cargos both to and from Cuba our merchant marine can afford to venture further and take the initial charges in carrying our products to more and more remote ports of the continent. We shall thus gain the advantage of direct trade at minimum rates, which now enable Europe to control the commerce of those countries.
—Tasker H. Bliss, May 1902

I In early 1896, on any clear day, *habaneros* could look toward the interior horizon and see in the still morning air columns of dark smoke rising from the outlying countryside—vivid reminder of the war raging in the interior. Actually, in 1896, this was the only indication residents of the capital had of the war. It was perhaps fitting that Havana, the loyal center of the rebellious colony, remained during the early years an enclave of peace set starkly against a landscape of war. Surely *habaneros*' expectation of security in return for loyalty to Spain was not an unreasonable exchange. And, indeed, Havana did remain remarkably untouched by the conflict playing havoc elsewhere on the island. Until 1897. The impact of insurgent strategy took a little longer to affect the residents of the capital, but eventually the war reached Havana. In the end, the war against property and the attending destruction of the principal means of production would leave no community in Cuba unaffected.[1]

It was a brutal war, one in which the opposing armies seemed determined more to punish the land than pursue the enemy. For three and a half years, insurgent armies laid siege on the bounty of the land, preying upon its resources, consuming or destroying cultivation and livestock; pillage of all kinds was practiced by both sides as a normal method of war. In the western provinces, the *Ejército Invasor* had destroyed tobacco *vegas*. In central Cuba, the insurgent torch reduced lush *cañaverales* (cane fields) to barren fields of charred cane stalks. In the east, insurgent forces scattered the vast livestock herds formerly roaming the expanses of Camagüey and Las Villas; coffee production halted and the mines closed.

But Cubans had assistance. Spanish commanders, too, contributed to the general desolation of the countryside. Any resource—human and material—of any potential use to insurgent armies was destroyed when it could not be removed. What the Cubans spared, the Spaniards destroyed. Armies swept back and forth across the land, leaving in their wake a devastated countryside all but totally despoiled of its productive capabilities.

Insurgent strategy had been vindicated. The destruction of the colonial economy announced the end of Spanish sovereignty and foretold the passing of the colony. But the price of independence was incalculable. The war of liberation had left Cuba a wasteland. Travelers to the island that first autumn of peace could not suppress their horror at the sights in the interior. "I saw neither a house, nor a cow, calf, sheep or goat, and only two chickens," one reporter wrote from Camagüey. "The country there is wilderness," a "desert," another correspondent wrote from Las Villas. In some regions of Pinar del Río, Fitzhugh Lee later reported, the countryside "resembled an ash pile, in others the dreary desert." Robert P. Porter described Oriente as "a wilderness." The "desolation is scarcely conceivable," General James H. Wilson wrote from Matanzas.[2]

These impressions actually understated the postwar reality. Previously prosperous agricultural regions were now scenes of desolation and depopulation, with nothing to export and barely the means to meet subsistence needs. The pastures were vacant, the fields were barren, and the fruit trees bare. War consumption reduced livestock. The once-prosperous cattle ranches of eastern and central Cuba lay prostrate. Of the three million head of cattle roaming Cuban pastures in 1895, only some 10 percent remained in 1898. In some provinces, including Matanzas and Las Villas, the loss of work cattle and breeding stock was almost complete. Poultry had fared no better.[3] The reconcentration policy dealt a body blow to Cuban agriculture. The rural population during its internment lost crops, livestock, tools, and homes. Over one hundred thousand small farms, three thousand livestock ranches, twenty-two thousand stores, eight hundred tobacco *vegas*, and seven hundred coffee *fincas* (farms), perished during the war. Tobacco fields and coffee estates not destroyed or abandoned were paralyzed by the dispersal of labor. Roads, bridges, and railroads were in a state of complete disrepair. Commerce was disrupted. Property owners were in debt and lacked either access to capital or sources of credit. The total urban indebtedness, some $100 million, represented more than three-quarters of the declared property value of $139 million. A similar pattern existed in rural real estate, where some $107 million was owed on $185 million worth of property.[4]

But it was for sugar that Cubans reserved the greatest punishment. And not surprisingly: sugar, the principal subsidy of imperial rule and the source of colonial inequity. The destruction of sugar was the cornerstone of Cuban strategy. By 1898 insurgent armies had totally disrupted and all but completely destroyed the foundations of the colonial economy. Of the 70 sugar mills in Pinar del Río in 1894, only 7 survived the war. Of the 166 *centrales* in operation in 1894 in Havana province, only 20 participated in the 1899 harvest. Of the 434 *centrales* located in Matanzas, only 62 survived. The 332 *centrales* in Las Villas were reduced to 73. Of the estimated total 1,100 sugar mills registered in Cuba in 1894, only 207 survived the war and not all these mills contributed either to the 1899/1900 harvest or the 1900/1901 crop.[5]

II Cubans understood well the political economy of colonialism. Nothing had perpetuated Cuba's colonial status as completely as its dependency on sugar. A complex and mutually reinforcing institutional order had emerged around the sugar system, one in which social and political structures served to underwrite internally the colonial export economy. The genius of insurgent strategy had been its ability to identify the primary internal structures supporting the colonial regime and successfully mount a revolutionary challenge against Spain's local collaborators and their sources of power on the island. The destruction of the sugar system precipitated the downfall of Spain's local collaborators and announced the end of the colony.

If Cubans recognized that the road to independence was paved over the wreckage of the colonial economy, Americans, for their part, recognized that hegemonial relations with Cuba depended on reconstructing the sugar system. Neo-colonial economic relationships, leading ultimately to the absorption of the island, rested directly on the reestablishment of the colonial export economy. The state of the Cuban economy, and the place of that economy in United States-Cuban relations, was key to annexationist calculations. Indeed, no strategy was so central to the goals of annexationists as the reconstruction of the sugar export economy.

In the most immediate sense, the restoration of sugar production to prewar levels promised to restore the propertied classes to positions of privilege—the very elites from which Americans were seeking to recruit allies. From the very outset, Americans were most solicitous of the needs of the planters. On January 1, 1899, Governor-General Brooke pledged the resources of the military government "to build up wasted plantations."[6] In Matanzas, General James H. Wilson urged the extension of liberal credit terms to allow planters to rebuild the damaged estates and repair or replace damaged machinery and equipment.[7] "Everything that can be done in Cuba to assist the producers of sugar and tobacco has been done," Wood informed Elihu Root in late 1901. Export duties were abolished and internal taxes eliminated. Import duties on agricultural equipment and railroad machinery were reduced to 5 percent ad valorem. Similarly, the organization and distribution of the rural guard conformed to planter needs. Nor did Americans remain passive to the threat of strikes and labor protests. Strikes were broken by force and strikers replaced by workers brought in from the interior and Puerto Rico.[8] "The policy of the Military Government," Adjutant General Hugh L. Scott announced in 1901, "is to give in every way the greatest security and protection to the planters and others engaged in the reconstruction of the country."[9] Now, Wood counseled Washington, it was necessary for the administration in Washington to participate directly in the revival of Cuban agriculture. "In short," he suggested, "all that could be done here has been done, and appeal is now made to the United States to give such reduction of duties on the staple products of this Island, on which its commercial life and prosperity depend, as will render the continuance of these industries possible and their growth probable."[10]

Americans singled out sugar and tobacco. On the twin pillars of the island's historic colonial crops, the United States proceeded to reconstruct the foundations of a new colonial system. The reconstruction of the sugar system in particular, Americans divined, leading ultimately to the integration of the Island's principal export crop into the American market system, promised to provide the economic basis upon which to secure entry for American exports and lead ultimately to political union. Sugar would serve as the wedge to open the island's economy to American investment and deliver Cuban products to the United States.

For the architects of annexation, close economic relationships were the necessary foundations for achieving over the long run what the Teller Amendment prohibited in the short term. "This is a natural sugar and tobacco country," Wood advised President McKinley, "and as we must in any case, control its destinies, and will probably soon own it, I believe it sound policy to do what we can to develop it and make it prosperous." The Platt Amendment, Wood wrote with satisfaction, had effectively blocked Cuban independence and prepared the way for annexation; all that remained to consummate the union was to promote close economic ties. He added:

There is, of course, little or no independence left in Cuba under the Platt Amendment. The more sensible Cubans realize this and feel that the only consistent thing to do now is to seek annexation. This, however, will take some time, and during the period which Cuba maintains her own government, it is most desirable that she should be able to maintain such a one as will tend to her advancement and betterment. With control which we have over Cuba, a control which will soon undoubtedly become a possession, combined with the other sugar producing lands we now own, we shall soon practically control the sugar trade of the world, or at least a very large part of it. . . . I believe Cuba to be the most desirable acquisition for the United States. She is easily worth any two southern states, probably any three with the exclusion of Texas.[11]

No less an expansionist and advocate of the annexation of Cuba, General James H. Wilson also detected in the close economic ties the basis of political union. "Inasmuch as we are, for the present, prohibited by the Joint Resolution from taking Cuba into the Union . . . it would seem to be but natural that we should seek some other way to take care of her, and safeguard our own interests in respect to her."[12] It was crucial to settle first the "sugar question," Wilson counseled. He advocated the establishment of a special trade relationship—a "zollverein" he called it—to provide for free trade between the United States and Cuba. This arrangement, Wilson predicted, "would put matters on the best possible footing for the ultimate absorption of the latter into the Union by natural voluntary and progressive steps honorable alike to both parties."[13] "I am trying," Wilson wrote to a Washington lawmaker, "to find a practicable road by which the Congress can make it easy for Cuba to come into the Union. This I conceive to be her ultimate and highest destiny. . . . Every state . . . had from the start the advantage of absolutely free trade with the older states of the Union, without which it would not have been possible for them ever to reach the dignity of statehood. . . . Cuba is entitled to be placed upon the same footing."[14] The relationship between free trade and "dignity," on one hand, and eventual statehood, on the other, was central to Wilson's calculations. He claimed to have studied the history of colonialism and it had revealed to him that the "great mistake" of all colonial powers was their uniform tendency to give their "colonial subjects different and less advantageous commercial privileges from those enjoyed by the home subjects."[15] Under Wilson's plan, Cuba, over a period of time, would become wholly integrated into the American economic system so that it would be all but impossible for Cuba to resist the inevitable. The adoption of his recommendation, Wilson was certain, would place "Cuba in a position to become self-supporting, and also to become rapidly Americanized."[16] "In my judgment," Wilson exulted, "it would not be ten years before the Cuban Republic would become afraid of the termination of this temporary arrangement and would be knocking at the door for permanent admission into the Union."[17]

Wilson was not alone in his belief that economic considerations generally and reciprocal trade relations specifically would lead ultimately to annexation. "It will not be long," Senator Joseph Benson Foraker predicted confidently, "until Cuba will appeal for annexation just as Hawaii has done. . . . She cannot afford to stay out with Hawaiian and Puerto Rican sugar, tobacco and coffee products in possession of the United States."[18] Wood, too, was confident that preferential tariff treatment of Cuban products would lead ultimately to permanent acquisition of the island. "The whole future of Cuba rests on the duties of sugar and tobacco," Wood explained to Roosevelt in 1901. "With a thirty percent reduction of the duties on these two articles there will be no Cuban question in the future. Trade relations will shortly draw the two countries together and place them not only upon a footing of commercial friendship and confidence but, I believe, also, upon a political one."[19]

It was not so much that the United States required access to Cuban sugar on terms substantially different from those existing before the war. In fact, powerful economic and political opposition to reciprocity in the United States successfully delayed a reciprocal trade agreement until 1903.[20] Rather, access to sugar through reciprocity was designed to serve as the fulcrum upon which to tilt irrevocably the political balance against Cuban independence. Reciprocity served as the principal means by which the United States sought to secure claim over Cuba's primary export staple exclusively for the American market, restrict Cuban participation in international trade, and thereby perpetuate and deepen Cuban dependency upon one crop for one market. Reciprocal trade arrangements, in turn, promised also to favor American exports in Cuban markets. Under reciprocity the Cuban national system would be fully integrated into the American political economy. In the end, Cuba's economic independence as both a seller and buyer under reciprocal trade arrangements would be as restricted as its political sovereignty under the Platt Amendment.

The closer the United States moved toward evacuation, the louder became the calls for reciprocity. The revival of a Cuban sugar system linked to and dependent on American markets was perceived essential to the stability of the island. As early as 1899, General James H. Wilson warned that without a "speedy recovery of prosperity," one organized around sugar, Cuba would be threatened with a "spirit of disorder and violence."[21] For American officials in both Havana and Washington, the future stability of Cuba depended directly on contended producers and a prosperous economy. The success of a stable government in Cuba, Wood insisted in a published article in December 1901, was "predicted primarily upon the establishment and the maintenance of business confidence among the producers and traders of the island. And if a government of this type be not established—and well established—we shall speedily find the conditions in Cuba . . . reverting to what they were when first we went there."[22] Privately, Wood was more emphatic. "We are going to turn these people loose," he wrote to Root, "knowing that they cannot establish a well ordered and stable government under present trade conditions. The fact is so patent and apparent that as a nation we may be criticized for it."[23]

Reciprocity also had far-reaching political implications in Cuba. The failure to secure reciprocal trade concessions from Congress, Wood feared, threatened to deal a body blow to American efforts to promote the political leadership of the "better classes." Without preferential access to American markets, property owners would lack the economic base from which to assert political leadership in the republic. Reviewing the island's recent history, Wood reminded Washington that political agitation against Spain in 1895 had resulted directly from adverse American tariff measures against Cuban sugar.[24] This was also the theme of General Tasker H. Bliss, the American director of the Cuban customs service. It was a "noteworthy fact," Bliss suggested, that the Cuban insurrection began only six months after the abrogation of the reciprocal trade agreement of 1892. The relationship was clear. "This merely emphasizes the fact," Bliss generalized a bit carelessly, "that the insurrection was inspired, upon the part of Cuba, solely for commercial reasons." Bliss concluded: "With the termination of the treaty of 1891, all hope of reciprocity was lost, and the only hope left was commercial annexation, with or without political annexation, with the United States. To secure this sovereignty of Spain, otherwise not objectionable, had to be thrown off. Unfortunately, however, the successful insurrection has not been followed by the commercial annexation which was hoped with the United States. Therefore . . . the conditions which caused the late insurrection remain unchanged after it."[25] The moral of these history lessons was not lost on Secretary of War Root. In the War Department annual report of 1901, Root emphasized the relationship between sugar and politics. If efforts to revive the sugar industry failed due to American unwillingness to offer Cuba tariff concessions, Root predicted soberly, "we may expect that the fields will again become waste, the mills will again be dismantled, the great body of laborers will be thrown out of employment, and that poverty and starvation, disorder and anarchy will ensue."[26]

The existence of a prosperous and contented planter class with ready access to American markets, predisposed to function politically to promote those class interests, promised to align the "better classes" on the side of the United States in the manner they had allied themselves to Spain before 1895. The denial of reciprocity, Americans feared, would undermine the economic base of responsible political leadership if not alienate altogether

that segment of the Cuban elite that had a natural interest in close relations with the United States. The resulting conditions would likely preclude the political ascendency of the "better classes" and do great damage
to that sector to whom the Americans hoped to entrust the republic. "The
planters and the commercial class are those to whom the United States
must look for a conservative, stable government in Cuba," Wood insisted,
"and, to the justice and reasonableness of their demands, from an economical and commercial standpoint, should be added the important, far reaching political effect of prosperity and good economical relations in the Island." He continued:

The United Sates, generally speaking, has the good will and
support of the planters and commercial class and this good will
and support should be retained. . . . Cuba finds herself at a dis-
advantage, economically and commercially, and the United
States cannot expect the support of the producers and manufacturers, unless they see some positive advantage accruing from
the United States control. They are fully appreciative of the advantage of a good order existing under the present military
government, but they foresee that, if Cuba is going to prosper,
she must receive certain commercial considerations and concessions and favorable action in the way of a reduction of the present duties paid by her products on entering the United States.
Under the present policy we are liable to lose the support and
sympathy of the only class which can build up and render profitable the standard industries of the Island, and the only class to
whom we can look for these elements of stability and
strength. . . . Now is the time to make the Cubans appreciate
the advantages of being under the protection and control of our
government.[27]

The fate of annexation, Americans argued, depended directly on preferential tariff concessions for Cuban products and the attending political ascendency of the "better classes." A mere 25 percent tariff reduction, Wood
insisted in 1901, would make the United States master in Cuba. "Our
supporters are the producers and the merchants," he reminded Senator
Joseph B. Foraker in January 1901. "Destroy them and you have the conditions which made the last war possible. . . . There is going to be no fighting
in Cuba, but we may have a great deal of disgust and discontentment

unless we show these people that it means something for them to be under the protection of the United States."[28] It was no easy task, Wood complained to Senator Orville H. Platt, "to instill wild enthusiasm into the people over the advantages of American protection" without support from Washington in the form of tariff reduction. To the point—"We do not want to get the *real Cuban people*, I mean the producers and merchants, against us."[29] In a similar tone, Wood complained to Senator Redfield Proctor that it was no "easy matter to convince people of the unlimited benefits that are to be derived from our control" as long as the United States insisted on maintaining heavy import duties on Cuba's principal products. "The producers and merchants are all our friends and we ought to make a sincere and strong effort to do something which will retain their good will."[30] The refusal to reduce the import duties on Cuban products, Wood warned in December 1900, was "short sighted and destined to make trouble."[31] "Let the planters lose confidence and cease planting," Wood predicted soberly a year later, "such a condition of affairs will soon arise as will compel us to either let Cuba go the way of Haiti and Santo Domingo or require another intervention."[32]

Wood carried his case directly to the American public. In an article published in January 1902, he drew an oblique parallel to the experience of Spanish administration of Cuba and recalled the disastrous consequences of American tariff policies of 1894. A similar policy in 1901, with Cuba under American control, Wood warned, could not fail to produce similar economic distress and political dislocation. The refusal to reduce import duties on Cuban products "means immediate bankruptcy for the country. It means general discouragement and apathy, and a dislike of Americans which may lead to future uprisings against this country. Such uprisings may not be serious in the near future, but with the steady increase in population . . . they may become serious in a few years."[33]

The value of planters as allies, and the strategic relationship of reciprocity to that alliance, was set in dramatic relief during the Cuban debates over the Platt Amendment. Throughout early 1901, planters pursued a shrewd and calculated strategy, one designed to secure trade concessions from the United States in return for their support of the proposed political relations. Throughout the early years of the occupation, planters had appealed unsuccessfully for tariff concession for Cuban products.[34] By mid-1900, one discouraged planter spoke of "a feeling of doubt and disappointment" settling over the Cuban property classes as the belief spread that there was "no hope of relief" forthcoming from the United States.[35] Planters shrank in horror at the spectre of independence without reciprocity. Few Cubans who had lived through the depression of 1884 and crisis of 1894 needed any reminder of the effects of a protective tariff on the island's economy.[36]

The debate in 1901 over the Platt Amendment offered planters the opportunity to parlay their influence in Havana in exchange for favorable tariff consideration from Washington. The question of reciprocity quickly emerged as a central if not publicly discussed issue. For Washington, the promise of tariff reductions for Cuban products, concessions based on formal and binding trade relations, offered an incentive to induce the constituent assembly to accept the proposed relations. For planters, preferential access to American markets was their price for endorsement of the Platt Amendment. In late March, the Círculo de Hacendados recommended to the convention acceptance of the Platt Amendment contingent on a 50 percent reduction of American import duties.[37] Charles Pepper, the resident *Washington Star* correspondent in Havana, reported in April 1901 that the delay in securing the convention's endorsement of the Platt Amendment was the failure of the "great banking and mercantile houses in Havana closely identified with sugar and tobacco" to exert their influence—something, Pepper noted, these sectors would not do until having received assurances of tariff preferential.[38] By early 1901, Wood could informally suggest to Cuban planters that influential congressional leaders in Washington were committed to reciprocal trade arrangements once Cuba had endorsed the proposed relations.[39] The Cuban commission visiting Washington in April 1901 also received assurances that tariff consideration would be forthcoming upon the convention's acceptance of the Platt Amendment. Root pledged that the establishment of the republic on the basis proposed by the United States would be followed immediately with formal tariff concessions for Cuban products. "To give effect to such a treaty," Root suggested as a final reminder, "the consent of the Senate will be necessary and an acceptance of the political relations which the Senate desires cannot fail to create a favorable disposition in that body."[40]

By the spring of 1901, planters, merchants, and businessmen, assured of American intentions, endorsed the Platt Amendment. In late April, the Círculo de Hacendados, the Junta de los Comerciantes e Industriales, and the Sociedad Económica de Amigos del País organized a sustained campaign in Cuba to urge the convention to accept the proposed basis of relations. "The most pressing necessity felt by this Island," Narciso Gelats, executive director of the Junta de Comerciantes e Industriales, wrote to the president of the constituent assembly, "is that of insuring a remunerative market for its products; and, if to attain this end, it becomes necessary to make sacrifices let it be done for we will very soon be amply compensated."[41]

III   Nor were Americans unmindful of the economic benefits for the United States resulting from reciprocal trade with Cuba. United States customs receipts, to be sure, American advocates of reciprocity conceded, would suffer a slight decline. And, no doubt, too, American domestic sugar producers would experience some early dislocation attending the importation of Cuban sugar at preferential tariff rates. These losses were inconsequential, however, and would be more than adequately compensated by preferential access to the Cuban market. "A few million lost to the United States now," Wood argued, "may save hundreds of millions later on in the avoidance of all sorts of petty complications."[42] The island had been thoroughly devastated by the war, and the first essential step toward reconstruction lay in reviving the languishing estates by providing incentives to Cuban planters in the form of tariff preferentials. The revival of the estates, in turn, would have a generally salutary effect on both the Cuban economy and American trade with Cuba. Wood predicted confidently in late 1901:

The people of Cuba will spend for many years all the money they can get from the sale of their products in rebuilding their industries, their homes and supplying them with the thousand and one things which they now lack. The Island has been so thoroughly devastated by war that it is practically barren of works of art, articles of luxury, etc., etc., and with a tariff which would render possible a continuance and increase of the sugar and tobacco industries of the Island, Cuba would be importing in four or five years not less than 150 to 160 million dollars per year, most of which should come from our own country.[43]

The United States, Wood estimated, had lost some $40 million worth of trade as a result of "unnecessarily oppressive and burdensome" duties. Any hope of close political relations with Cuba, he reminded Washington, depended on close economic relations with the island. Indeed, control of Cuban commerce was essential. As matters stood in late 1901, Wood warned, the "commerce of Cuba is falling into the hands of other nations than our own."[44] Several months later he entered another plea for reciprocity. By modifying the existing tariff schedule, some $34 million of the $37 million of Cuban trade with Europe would be redirected toward the United States. "It may take some time to break up old trade relations with Europe," Wood calculated, "but under the pressure of a tariff favorable to purchase in the United States the work will surely be accomplished."[45] The idea of monopolizing Cuban trade struck the official fancy of many Americans. In early 1902, General Tasker H. Bliss thought it unreasonable to ask the Cuban government to forego vitally needed customs receipts that would follow tariff reductions on American imports. To compensate for the loss, Bliss recommended that Cuba raise the tariff against world trade. This would make up the differential for the Cuban treasury, deal a body blow to European competitors, and lead to complete dependency on the United States.[46]

IV   The decision to revive the sugar system as the principal means of promoting Cuba's economic recovery rested on two central assumptions: first, that Cuban sugar would secure preferential access to American markets; and second, that capital existed in sufficient quantity to rebuild the estates. The importance of preferential access to U.S. markets was self-evident. What was not as clear, however, not at least to Cuban planters, was the means by which the sugar revival would be financed. Planters expected government assistance. But for all the official talk about reconstructing Cuban agriculture, American authorities opposed direct government subsidies to planters. To be sure, John R. Brooke and James H. Wilson recommended on several occasions, without results, a system of low interest government loans and credits to encourage Cuban planters to rebuild their farms and estates.[47] Leonard Wood openly opposed public credit for planters. "There has been considerable thoughtless talk in Cuba about making loans to aid agriculturalists," he complained in 1902. "It is not believed that any such policy is either wise or desirable." It was enough, Wood insisted, that planters secure preferential access to American markets to insure their prosperity.[48]

But, in fact, capital-starved and credit-hungry Cuban planters could not return to prewar production levels unassisted and unaided—which was exactly what Wood counted on. Denied public credit, destitute planters had one of two choices: borrow from American creditors or sell out completely to American buyers. In either case, Wood's credit policy contributed to creating the conditions that promoted American control over Cuba's principal export product. The reconstruction of the Cuban economy would be dependent on a foreign market and foreign capital; the revival of the sugar system offered the opportunity to extend American control over this key sector of the Cuban economy.

Preferential tariffs, as Wood privately knew, offered little by way of permanent relief to Cuban planters. Reciprocity assured the revival of Cuban sugar system, but it promised to be a revival in which Cuban planters would not participate. Wood's refusal to sanction government credit dealt the latest in a series of body blows to Cuban planters. The outbreak of the separatist war only months after the expiration of the Foster-Cánovas agreement found many planters hopelessly in debt and at the brink of collapse. Planters had borrowed money at enormous rates of interest, with many loans at 20 to 40 percent not uncommon. The war dealt hapless planters one more setback. Indeed, ownership of many encumbered estates would have been long transferred if it had not been for repeated prorogations of mortgage regulations between 1895 and 1899.

After 1899, Cuban planters needed credit—extensive credit, from new sources, at reasonable rates of interest. Even a 25 percent profit return would have proved inadequate to permit many planters to pay the interest on their mortgages. The military government's refusal to provide loans and easy long-term credit sealed their fate.

Reciprocity as a source of relief for the beleaguered Cuban planters was little more than a hoax. Many planters, no doubt, stood to benefit, especially a few of the larger solvent estates. For many more, however, reciprocity offered too little too late. If reciprocity failed to provide planters sufficient assistance, it did succeed in creating favorable conditions to enable Cubans to sell their damaged and unproductive estates, so long a millstone around planters' necks. Nor was this either unforeseen or unintended. "All that reciprocity can do for the [planters]," Tasker H. Bliss predicted correctly in early 1902, "will be that, by an improvement of the general conditions of the country, and by a restoration of confidence, they will be able to sell their mortgaged estates for enough, possibly, to pay their debts." Bliss continued: "But all these estates must go into the market; they must be acquired by individuals or companies who will consolidate them, and who will work them on a modern basis. But the present owners are ruined, and will stay ruined reciprocity or no reciprocity. . . . Reciprocity will merely enable, at the best, a large number of planters to gracefully withdraw from business, leaving their estates in the hands of new men who will work them on modern conditions." He concluded: "The first consequence of reciprocity will be a complete upheaval of the sugar industry in Cuba, with the consolidation of many estates into one, with one mill doing the work that several do even now, with the consequent reduction in the cost of producing raw sugar, and with the continued administration of the business on the most modern and economical lines."[49]

Wood not only refused to sanction government loans to Cuban bankrupt planters, he also tilted government policy to favor American capital. Civil Order No. 34 in February 1902 removed existing obstacles for establishing private railroads, thereby facilitating the concentration of property by large companies.[50] Civil Order No. 62 later that year, promulgated for the purpose of "cleaning up the mess of titles that has entangled the properties" of communal farms, also gave impetus for concentration.[51] The 90,960 plantations and farms in Cuba before the war diminished to 60,710 after 1899.[52] Many of the titles of these smaller properties were hopelessly tied up in confused ownership and unclear possession. Wood's decrees facilitated real estate transactions leading toward a renewed growth of land concentrations. Years later, the Foreign Policy Association would conclude that the policy of the military government had established "the foundation for modern corporate development, and the present *latifundia* system which would not have been possible had the old system of land tenure remained in effect."[53]

Bliss's observation in January 1902 was not as much prophetic as it was perceptive. Even as the *Ejército Invasor* blazed its way westward in 1896, American investors were purchasing the charred remains of defunct sugar estates. In mid-1897, Cuban planters, alarmed by the loss of their property, decried the sale of estates to Americans and petitioned General Weyler to decree a moratorium on all real estate transactions involving foreigners.[54] At the end of the war, with Cuban agriculture in ruin, American real estate investors moved quickly to acquire title to damaged estates. In September 1898, the Island of Cuba Real Estate Company opened an office in Havana to purchase ruined sugar estates. Numerous real estate transactions in Santiago de Cuba signaled the transfer of land to American buyers.[55] Political uncertainty and economic distress early in the occupation further contributed to conditions favoring American purchase of sugar property. "The Spaniards want to sell because they want to get out," one American writer reported in January 1899. "The Cubans must sell because they cannot afford to keep."[56]

Large-scale American investment in Cuban sugar property, however, did not commence until the onset of formal American military rule. In 1899, former Texas Congressman R. B. Hawley organized the Cuban-American Sugar Company and established the Chaparra sugar mill around 70,000 acres of land in Puerto Padre on the Oriente north coast. Later that year, he acquired and restored the 7,000 acre Tinguaro estate in Perico, Matanzas. He also purchased the defunct Merceditas mill in Cabañas Bay in Pinar del Río. In 1901, the Cuban-American Sugar Company acquired control of the last remaining sugar refinery at Cárdenas. In that same year, the United Fruit Company acquired 200,000 acres on Nipe Bay in northern Oriente. Only a year earlier, the Nipe Bay Company, a subsidiary of United Fruit, had purchased 40,000 acres in the same region. In 1899, a group of Philadelphia investors had organized the Francisco Sugar Company and purchased the 80,000 acre Francisco estate in southern Camagüey province. Two years later, the old Constancia mill in Las Villas passed wholly under American control. Several other American companies, including the Cuba Company and the American Sugar Company, acquired sugar estates during the military government but delayed the development of their property until the following decade.[57] In 1899, Edwin F. Atkins purchased two neighboring estates to round off his property in Las Villas.[58]

The infusion of American capital during the occupation and the introduction of new organization into the languishing estates foreshadowed the revival of the sugar system around the expansion of land concentration and consolidation under foreign control. When Chaparra commenced operations in 1900, it was the largest mill ever built in Cuba, the first *central* to employ twelve rollers and boast of an initial capacity of 200,000 bags of sugar. Chaparra represented 10 percent of the 1900 harvest.[59] By 1902, of the 223 *centrales* in operation, Americans owned 55, representing some 40 percent of the island's total sugar production.[60] More dramatically than ever before, the new corporate latifundia signaled the restoration of the colonial economy.[61]

V Reciprocity was the final link of the annexationist chain the United States was uncoiling as it prepared to evacuate Cuba. Reciprocal trade was to establish in economic relations what the Platt Amendment achieved in political relations. By establishing trade relations with Cuba as if it were "an integral part of our own territory," one journal editorialized, "the question of political annexation of Cuba can be safely left to the future."[62] Francis B. Thurber, appointed by Secretary Root in 1901 as special agent of the military government to study the benefits of reciprocity, predicted that economic conditions favored reciprocity, and "annexation later on, at the request of the Cubans."[63] As early as 1900, George B. Hopkins, an American businessman with close relations to the administration, was confident that felicitous economic conditions would lead inevitably to annexation. "Commercial interests now and must always favor annexation," Hopkins predicted to annexationist Senator John H. Spooner. "Carry the present conditions or any decent conditions along for comparatively a short time and commercial interests will have become so powerful that they can dictate the final policy of the whole people."[64] Senator Henry Cabot Lodge, too, saw reciprocity paving the way to annexation. "The truth is," Lodge wrote in 1901, "that the hope of Cuba lies in annexation which would give her immediate entrance into our markets, and it is amazing to me that the real interests of the island are not awakened to this fact and do not exert all their influence to bring it about."[65]

In fact, the "real interests" of Cuba had long awakened to their interests and pursued annexation through reciprocity as vigorously as their American counterparts. "As a Cuban," planter representative Luis V. Placé explained to Tasker H. Bliss, "looking to the future and for the happiness of my countrymen, I want Cuba annexed to the United States, through commercial advantages if possible. Make a commercial union,—the rest will follow." Placé chided the Americans for their shortsightedness in adopting the Teller Amendment, thereby foreclosing the immediate annexation of Cuba. "Strike the iron while it is hot," Placé counseled. "Don't put all the blame of our present situation on our politicians, for the commercial element of Cuba is now and always has been anxious to get in touch with the United States Government. The 'joint resolution' was the error of yourselves and we are suffering the consequences."[66] Within a year, Placé predicted to Bureau of Insular Affairs Chief Clarence Edwards that the United States would have the Cuban government "begging you to take them in under your own conditions."[67] William O. McDowell and Antonio A. Aguirre, president and secretary respectively of the Cuban American League, expected confidently that the elimination of existing tariff barriers would facilitate the fulfillment of Cuba's destiny to "become and continue a permanent part of the United States."[68] Settle the economic questions, one planter advised Robert P. Porter, and "all other questions (political and social) would be naturally and easily resolved."[69] B. W. Merrill, a Cuban-American Sugar Company representative in Havana, wrote to R. B. Hawley that planters and merchants in the capital perceived reciprocity as the prelude to annexation. "They believe," Merrill wrote, "that . . . the people will readily see the advantages of a close connection with the United States and that thus 'baited' they will cry for more, upon any terms, in a voice that will drown opposition. In a word, they are working like beavers for annexation at the earliest possible moment."[70] "There is every reason to believe," Leonard Wood predicted in his final report in 1902, "that, with the increase of American capital and interests in Cuba, those relations which we desire to see established between the two countries will be established, strengthened and extended."[71]

VI In December 1902, the six-month old Cuban republic approved its first treaty—a reciprocal trade convention with the United States. Cuban legislators, however, proved more tractable on the issue of reciprocity than their American counterparts. Almost twelve months before the formal signing in Havana, during hearings in Washington before the House Ways and Means Committee, formidable domestic sugar interests opposed proposed reciprocal relations with Cuba. Led by the powerful American Beet Sugar Association, opponents to reciprocity included the American Cane Growers' Association, the League of American Producers, and several tobacco and fruit producing associations.[72] In June, Theodore Roosevelt, now president, intervened personally to secure congressional approval of Cuban-American reciprocity. In a special message to Congress, Roosevelt reminded lawmakers of his deceased predecessor's past commitment to reciprocal trade relations with Cuba. Invoking the responsibilities attending the growing American presence in the circum-Caribbean region, Roosevelt stressed the "special" quality of Cuban-American relations. "We expect Cuba to treat us on an exceptional footing politically, and we should put her in the same exceptional position economically."[73]

Congress remained unmoved. Continued legislative opposition to reciprocity did not, however, deter the White House from pressing forward with negotiations for a treaty. When Roosevelt submitted his annual message to Congress on December 2, Cuban and American negotiators had completed all but the formal signing of the treaty. With the signing ceremonies in Havana imminent, Roosevelt appealed again for congressional support in his annual message of 1902. "In a sense," the president noted, "Cuba has become a part of our international political system. This makes it necessary that in return she should be given some of the benefits of becoming part of our economic system."[74] A fortnight later, Roosevelt submitted the treaty to Congress for Senate ratification.

In the meantime, political opposition to reciprocity developed in Cuba. Many Cubans shrank in horror at the treaty's terms. The proposed tariff schedule conceded Cuban agricultural exports a 20 percent tariff reduction. In return, Cuba granted the United States a 20 percent concession on most items with 24, 30, and 40 percent on selected categories. Most items placed on the 20 percent schedule included American products already controlling a large share of the Cuban market, so that a tariff reduction would not likely have any effect on trade. Most articles falling into the higher tariff reduction categories, however, competed directly with either national industry or, in most cases, European imports. A concession of merely 20 percent, Americans believed, would have little effect on enabling American products to overtake Cuban and European producers. The 25 percent category included iron and steel products (except machinery and cutlery), glassware, preserved fish, and earthen and stone ware. Items receiving a 30 percent reduction included cotton goods, boots and shoes, chemicals, paper and cardboard, dyes, linen goods, corn and corn meal, soap, butter, and canned vegetables. Reductions of 40 percent were conceded to wool, rice, luxury items, perfumes, preserved fruits, and cheese.[75]

"This is not a Treaty of Reciprocity—it lacks much of being such!" Manuel Sanguily decried in the Cuban Senate. "The United States has substituted our old mother country; they have put the problem on a basis identical with that which existed here during that memorable epoch, converting Cuba into a mercantile colony and the United States into its mother country." The treaty had one objective, Sanguily charged: "It will close our market to the world in order that it may be solely at the mercy of the United States. And the balance will come—that is, the commercial control always carries with it the political control."[76] Gonzalo de Quesada, the new Cuban minister in Washington, expressed privately his reservations about the proposed tariff schedule. Quesada feared the long-term adverse effects on Cuba, predicting that the treaty in "some cases would kill Cuban industries." The Cuban government, he complained, was being asked to underwrite the cost of reciprocity by forfeiting in advance the revenue otherwise generated by import duties. "The Customs Revenues," Quesada noted, "which are the foundation of the income budget and indispensable to meet the obligations of the country, would decrease."[77]

The delay in ratifying the treaty in Washington in early 1902 allowed political opposition to reciprocity in Havana to gain momentum. More important, in March 1902, European economic ministers met in Brussels and agreed to end the traditional state subsidies for beet sugar production. Scheduled to end the following year, the suspension of the artificial bounty system promised to curtail European sugar production drastically, reduce overall production, and increase the price of sugar for remaining producers. Suddenly, Havana acquired a new-found bargaining power. In August 1902, a resolution introduced into the Cuban House of Representatives urged the government to seek new markets for Cuban products and establish reciprocal trade agreements with other countries. Before the end of the year, England and Germany had dispatched trade agents to Havana to discuss future commercial relations with Cuba. These representatives, American Minister in Havana Herbert G. Squiers reported anxiously to Washington, were pressing the Cubans for commercial trade agreements. "Cuba will soon commence," Squires warned, "if our Congress affords her no relief, the negotiation of commercial treaties with these as well as other European powers."[78] Squiers also detected a growing restlessness among Cuban planters and mounting impatience in Havana with the United States. In a meeting with Fermín Goicochea, the director of the Círculo de Hacendados, Squiers learned that pro-American sentiment among Cuban planters had waned considerably as a result of Washington's failure to deliver the much-promised reciprocity. European events, moreover, were not without their consequences in Havana. "Now that the future appears much brighter," Squiers informed the State Department after his meeting with Goicochea, "owing partially to the possible abolition of beet sugar bounties next September, they are unwilling to accept the reduction they would gladly accept some months ago; that a treaty has been offered them from which they can expect little benefit . . . while the United States demands in exchange the whole Cuban market." Squiers could not suppress his ire at planter opportunism: "They were annexationists, not because they admired our institutions and desired to join our political body, but because they thought they could make more money as part of the United States. . . . They are devoid of gratitude, devoid of any feeling other [than] mercenary."[79]

The increase in Cuba's bargaining power, the sudden appearance of alternative and potentially profitable markets for Cuban products, together with signs of growing disaffection among planters and rising opposition from politicians, increased pressure on the White House to secure quick passage of the proposed reciprocity treaty. The process required another six months. In November 1903, Roosevelt convened a special session of Congress and exhorted legislators to ratify the treaty.[80] A year after the completion of negotiations for the treaty, and a year after extraordinary pressure from the White House, the Senate approved the convention on December 16.[81]

"I congratulate you and your fellow sugar growers in the ratification of the reciprocity treaty," General James H. Wilson wrote planter Edwin F. Atkins a day after the Senate endorsement of the treaty. "I am persuaded that the agitation in a quiet way should begin shortly for annexation." Annexation, Wilson asserted confidently, "is the great cure all and it can now be resorted to as an independent measure, completely justified by the commercial, strategic and international relations between Cuban and the United States."[82]

20 A General Understanding

We have arrived.
—Máximo Gómez, May 20, 1902

The day is not far distant when Cuba, resembling the United States in its constitution, laws and liberties—and in all which a country desirable to live in for people brought up and educated as Americans—will have from five to six million people who are educated upon American lines and worthy of all the rights of American citizenship. Then, with the initiative from Cuba, we can welcome another star to our flag.
—Senator Chauncey Depew, February 1903

I May 20, 1902. Noon. "My heart was swelling so that I thought it would burst with pride," Don Tomás remembered wistfully. The passing of seventy-four years had not, it seemed, diminished in the slightest the emotional rushes of that moment long past. With an aroused exuberance, Tomás Mayet recalled May 20, 1902, the day the Cuban flag was raised over El Morro to announce the birth of the republic. At fourteen years of age, Don Tomás was one of the many tens of thousands of Cubans who pressed themselves along the Malecon to bear witness to the moment—the inauguration of the republic. It was said that tears streamed down the face of Máximo Gómez as he raised the Cuban flag. He was not alone. Tomás Mayet recalled his father's pride beaming through his tears.[1] Federico Villoch also recalled May 20—"a day with a splendid blue sky, almost as if God himself had come down to participate in the ceremony." Street dancing, strolling musicians, and everyone dressed formally for the occasion, Villoch remembered. "There wasn't a window, a door, a roof, a balcony, or lamp post without a Cuban flag."[2]

Two months later, a thousand miles away, Leonard Wood completed his last official report. "I regret to state that a large portion of the conservative element," he wrote with unrelieved dissappointment in Washington, "composed of property owners, business and professional men, etc., did not take such an interest in the [presidential] elections as proper regard for the welfare of the country required." The former governor-general continued:

Consequently the representation of this element among the officials elected has not been proportionately as large as the best interests of the Island demand. It has been and continues to be difficult to interest to a desirable extent the property holding element in the conduct of the Island's political affairs, and until this class awake to their full responsibility and manifest a proper interest in public affairs of the Island, they cannot have the representation in her councils which the Island's welfare demands.[3]

It is possible that Leonard Wood's regrets extended beyond those expressed in his last report of July 1902. Measured against his goals, he could not have looked back on his achievements of two-and-a-half years in Havana without some disappointment. He acknowledged—to the end—his frustration at getting "the better classes" to assume their "full responsibility" in affairs of state. As Wood wrote in July 1902, reciprocity languished in Congress. May 20 must have been especially painful. Even as Wood the soldier officially prepared to relinquish control of the island to the Cubans, Wood the person privately resisted the fate that would leave Cuba outside the American union. To the end, he continued to summon the spectre of annexation. "The feeling and talk for annexation grows rapidly," Wood confided mischievously to Root in October 1901, "and the coming Congress may possibly find itself with this issue."[4] Three months later: "We shall find it embarrassing to get out of here, as the chaotic business condition, accompanied by a lack of employment, might result in such a condition of affairs as to render our presence here desirable."[5]

Wood's enduring lament may not have been entirely justified, however. True, the United States had failed to forge the "better classes" into an effective political force on the island. But that had never been a realistic objective. That the representatives of the "better classes" fared poorly in political competition after the war represented nothing less than popular repudiation of their politics during the war. Electoral mandates after 1898 represented typically popular certification of revolutionary antecedents. Indeed, the principal source of political legitimacy, a candidate's most compelling claim to electoral support during the occupation—and continuing thereafter—derived from participation in the war of liberation. Manipulation of suffrage requirements and American exhortations in behalf of candidates from the "better classes" could not adequately compensate office seekers who lacked separatist credentials.

Not until 1901 did American authorities recognize the futility of efforts to promote the political ascendancy of the "better classes." In early 1901 the military government announced plans to proceed with municipal elections. Wood again committed the military government to a policy designed to "encourage the most conservative and representative element to come to the front" and alerted Washington to the probability of hearing "more or less criticism from the office-seeking contingent." But, he added reassuringly, "I believe the good people of the country are back of the movement."[6] And, indeed, the military government was driven to employ extraordinary measures to promote the election of the "conservative and representative element." An unusual—some charged illegal—convocation of two separate registration periods lengthened time for enrollments. Wood to Root: "It is of vital importance so that the better elements should be given ample time to prepare for the coming contest."[7] Wood also encouraged American officials in the provinces to use their influence locally to secure the election of the "conservative and representative element." In early spring, Wood summoned Edwin F. Atkins to Havana to ask the American planter to use his influence in behalf of a "very respectable man" the military governor wanted elected mayor of Cienfuegos. Atkins later recalled the election: "I sent for one of the *alcaldes de barrios* and told him my wishes. He told me to have no anxiety; the man I suggested would be elected. I asked him how he proposed to do it. He said it was a simple matter; they would take possession of the ballot box and destroy the ballots of the opposition candidates. I told him that was a magnificent idea and worthy of Tammany Hall. Needless to say, this candidate was elected."[8]

II　The military government enjoyed no more success at political midwifery in 1901 than it had in its previous two efforts. Despite the extended registration period, American endorsement of select candidates, and official sanction of widespread electoral fraud, the military government proved incapable of generating a popular mandate for candidates without revolutionary antecedents.[9]

The results of the June 1901 elections disabused American authorities of whatever hopes remained that the "better classes" could successfully compete against the revolutionary element in national politics. The election confirmed what many Americans had long suspected, namely, that the tide of separatist political leadership, temporarily stemmed by the intervention, was inexorable. That the political leadership of the future republic appeared ebbing ineluctably toward the former separatist leaders had far-reaching implications for American policy. Most immediately, it signaled the futility of American attempts to recruit political allies from the "better classes." The continued political solvency of separatism during the occupation, further, forced American policymakers to acknowledge the enduring potency of its popular appeal. By 1901, this issue had assumed some urgency. Washington had made the decision to end the occupation in 1902 and was in need of a president of the new republic. If, indeed, separatist antecedents served as the principal legitimizing factor of successful political competition, it behooved the United States to align itself with the most congenial sector of the most politically solvent force in Cuba. Early preoccupation with cultivating the "better classes" had committed the United States to supporting a class politically insolvent, a sector of the population that even with the advantage of American endorsement could not overcome the liability of having spent the war years in exile. More important, this strategy tended to blind American officials to the moderates existing with the separatist polity, those individuals more or less politically compatible with the United States in possession of the necessary political credentials. By supporting the traditional conservative elite, American policy all but guaranteed the success of the most intransigent sector of the old revolutionary coalition. This confirmed the worst American misgivings about separatist leadership, further committing the United States to seek allies capable of thwarting the ascendency of separatists. By 1901, however, their continuing success obligated the United States to acknowledge the necessity of separatist credentials as the entry requirement for national leadership. The focus of American strategy, hence, centered on finding allies within the old revolutionary coalition, individuals politically compatible with the United States in possession of separatist antecedents.

III Preparations for the December 1901 presidential elections delineated again the contradictions of the wartime coalition. In many ways, the struggle for the presidency was as much a function of the old divisions within the separatist polity as it was the result of American policy. If U.S. policy succeeded in further fracturing the old revolutionary polity, it did so only along pre-existent stress lines.

The trail of the American search for presidential candidate led back to the United States, to the ranks of the expatriate sector. As early as February 1901, Wood conferred with Máximo Gómez to discuss the upcoming presidential elections. And as early as February 1901, a tentative agreement had been reached to seek the candidacy of the former PRC chief, Tomás Estrada Palma.[10] In July, only weeks after the municipal elections, Gómez traveled to the United States to persuade Estrada Palma to serve as the republic's first president.[11]

In Tomás Estrada Palma, the United States had found an ideal candidate for the Cuban presidency. Estrada Palma possessed impeccable separatist credentials. During the Ten Years' War, he had served a term as provisional president of the insurgent republic. In 1895, Estrada succeeded José Martí as head of the PRC, a position he held through the war. Of more direct concern to American officials, however, were his politics. The PRC chief was as unabashed in his pro-American sympathies as he was unequivocal in his annexationist aspirations. Estrada shared with American policymakers the belief that Cuba's ultimate fate lay in union with the United States. Like Wood, he believed that annexation should and would come about by acclamation after only a brief period of independence.

"What do I believe will be the natural destiny of Cuba?" Estrada responded rhetorically in an interview in July 1901. "Why, to be part of the United States, of course. There is no other alternative in the end, but for the present . . . the Cubans want to taste what they have been fighting and dying for just for once, even if for a little while—and that is Cuba Libre."[12] A naturalized American citizen, a converted Quaker, the sixty-six-year-old Estrada had passed the last thirty years of the nineteenth century entirely in exile. He had supported the American intervention in 1898, endorsed the Platt Amendment in 1901, and lobbied for reciprocity in 1902.[13]

Estrada's candidacy did not pass unchallenged, however. In late summer of 1901, Bartolomé Masó announced his candidacy for the presidency. Also a former president of the provisional government (1897–1898), Masó in every important respect represented the antithesis of Estrada. An outspoken nationalist, he campaigned against limited suffrage, against the Platt Amendment, and in behalf of complete and unfettered independence for Cuba.[14]

Masó was also an anathema to the United States. Wood wrote to the White House in October that Masó "has gathered about him the radical and discontented element." He characterized him as "an old man already in his second childhood and particularly susceptible to flattery." "I should fear very much for the new government under his control," he concluded somberly.[15]

IV   By early fall, the resources and authority of the military government had been arrayed against Masó. This was an election the Americans could not lose. Wood campaigned vigorously, seeking to mobilize the "better element" behind the Estrada candidacy.[16] The alternative, Wood reminded the Cuban elite, was bleak indeed. Mayors who openly supported the Masó candidacy were displaced by the military government. Miguel Gener Rincón (Havana), Eloy Zapico (Mariel), Rosendo Torrent (Mayarí), Juan Lorente (San Luis), and Emilio Giró (Guantánamo), all *masoístas*, were fired early in the election campaign.[17] In determining the representation on the Junta Central, the body charged with supervising election procedures and counting the ballots, Wood appointed all partisans of Estrada Palma. The entire five-man board—Alfredo Zayas, Domingo Méndez Capote, Martín Morúa Delgado, Diego Tamayo, and Enrique Villuendas—also served on the Estrada Palma Executive Campaign Committee and were themselves candidates for national office on the Estrada ticket.

Masoístas reacted immediately. "The facts . . . indicate," Eusebio Hernández, chief of the Masó coalition, complained to Wood, "if not a deliberate purpose, at least a very marked tendency to favor one presidential candidate and one group of political interests at the expense of the other presidential candidate and the political elements allied to him." Under such circumstances, Hernández concluded, it was "idle to expect a fair and honest election." He appealed to Wood to reorganize the Junta Central and include at least one supporter of Masó.[18] Wood rejected the request, whereupon *masoístas* appealed directly to Washington for a one-month postponement of elections to permit a reorganization of the Junta Central.[19] "The effect of granting the application," Secretary Root responded in rejecting the appeal, "would be to prolong the American occupation and postpone the independence of Cuba and the control of the Island by the government of her own people."[20] On December 23, a week before the scheduled elections, Masó withdrew his candidacy.

V On December 31, 1901, Tomás Estrada emerged victorious in the uncontested election. Candidate Estrada never left his residence in upstate New York; the successful candidate did not a make a single campaign appearance on the island. "The election of Mr. Palma," Wood exulted, "in my opinion, has defeated the infamous plan to wreck the Island government."[21] To be sure, Wood continued to despair over his earlier inability to forge the "better classes" into successful political contenders. The election of Estrada Palma, however, brought some consolation.[22] He grudgingly resigned himself to the "revolutionary element predominating." This "must be expected for some time yet," he conceded philosophically.[23]

In fact, as the military occupation drew to an end, the political success of the "revolutionary element" may not have much mattered. An annexationist occupied the Presidential Palace. More important, the occupation had created the institutional structures that fixed the island on an annexationist orbit. Annexationist expectations after Estrada's election ran high in both Cuba and the United States. Estrada Palma's task, in the end, may have consisted of presiding over Cuban independence long enough to achieve annexation. "It is generally understood," Francisco Gamba, president of a Cuban business commission in the United States, suggested in November 1901, "that if the candidate of the businessmen Palma is elected President next month the annexation will be favored by our government."[24]

21 Postscript to the Colony— Prologue to the Republic

The Cuban republic arose in a night, on soil owned by others than its electors, swarming with a bureaucracy these foreigners and producing Cubans have had to support ever since. There it stands, tottering, and pregnant with militant trouble as was the Trojan horse of old; when finally it collapses to its inevitable destruction let Americans on hearing the crash recall distinctly, that this republic is not a creature of the Cubans,—it was neither fashioned by them nor by them upheld,—but on the contrary, it is of all-American manufacture. Americans built it. Americans set it up again when once it fell flat. American influence is all that sustains it to this moment. If they discover anything to criticise in it, or its failure, let Americans remember in so criticising that they are dealing with the work of their own hands.
—Irene Wright, *Cuba* (1910)

I Cuban separatism was a fragile force, a delicate balance of divergent interests organized around ambiguous and often incompatible objectives. Separatism could at times seem to mean nothing, because potentially it could mean anything or everything. This was the source of its appeal as a revolutionary ideal and its weakness as the basis for programmatic action. It possessed a capacity to obscure alignment and interest groupings within a coalition organized around armed struggle. The requirements of the war demanded the participation of a wide range of political actors—people skilled in violence, diplomacy, propaganda, fund-raising, and administration. Accordingly, a heterogeneous revolutionary polity formed during the war, one that contained as many differences within itself as it did with its opposition. These contradictions mattered little during the war, however, for issues far more urgent than internal inconsistencies preoccupied Cuban attention. The unanimity of purpose around the goal of independence from Spain transcended all other sources of disagreement. Whatever else may have divided Cubans, they were uncommonly united around a determination to expel Spain by force. This consensus served them well. Indeed, for the duration of the war, it was enough, for in the end this unanimity provided the moral subsidy to sustain Cuban resolve over three decades of armed struggle.

But Cuban success against Spain did not produce independence. Instead, it precipitated the intervention of the United States, a power Cubans were ill-prepared to resist. Weakened by internal conflict, exhausted by the revolutionary struggle against Spain, the old separatist coalition proved ill-matched to the new foreign presence in Havana. The separatist consensus unraveled, and the contradictions muted earlier by the exigencies of war surfaced with devastating consequences for the revolutionary coalition. Cubans turned on each other with a wrath previously reserved for Spaniards. It was certainly possible if not altogether probable that the contradictions inherent in wartime separatism would have been resolved in the ordinary course of postwar developments. Whatever its outcome, it would have been a Cuban solution. But the denouement of the war was extraordinary. Confronted with the American presence, competing wings of the revolutionary polity maneuvered for position and showed no reluctance to enlist foreign support to advance their ascendancy. In appealing for American assistance, separatists introduced into an internal struggle one more power contender—a superior power contender—who took advantage of discord in Cuban ranks to pursue ends of an entirely different character.

Cuban separatism collapsed from within, under the weight of internal conflict and contradiction. After the defeat of the common enemy, a confrontation between the contradictory forces of the revolution ensued, and precisely their diversity of origin and purpose contributed to the collapse of the old wartime coalition. The failure of separatists to resolve among themselves conflicting definitions of Cuba Libre left Cubans without a common purpose. Conflicting separatist goals were compounded by blurred separatist authority. If there was no common purpose, neither was there common leadership. Cuban separatism spoke with too many voices. No single person, no single institution, could speak authoritatively for the diverse groupings that had gathered under the banner of Cuba Libre. It was inevitable, too, that separatist structures would reflect as well as contribute to these difficulties. The various centers of revolutionary authority pulled in too many different directions in pursuit of too many different goals. Separatist agencies had attracted quite different sectors of Cuban society at different times for quite different purposes. The revolution not only perpetuated old antagonisms but also created new sources of tension within the separatist coalition. At times it seemed that the PRC, the provisional government, and the Liberation Army were opposed as much to each other as they were to Spain. And, indeed, at times, they were.

Having defeated Spain, a fragmented separatist polity faced a new adversary, one no less opposed to Cuban independence than the Iberian metropolis. In their struggle for independence, Cubans had confronted two metropolitan centers—Spain and the United States. Martí understood this. It appears that Maceo did too. But after 1895, Cuban determination to defeat Spain so exhausted the separatist fund that insurgent leaders rarely looked much beyond the expulsion of the old colonial regime. To be sure, Máximo Gómez, Calixto García, and Bartolomé Masó, among others, warned from time to time of the perils the United States posed to Cuban independence. But Cubans failed to transform these occasional forebodings into coherent political formulations. The leadership proved incapable of transferring the prevailing agreement on the desirability of separation from Spain into a comparable postwar consensus about independence from the United States. By 1898, moreover, the centrifugal forces of race, regionalism, economic interests, generations, and class proved stronger than the centripetal power of nationalism, cultural identification, and revolutionary fervor. The insurrection grounded in so anomalous and tenuous a social organization, basing its appeal largely on a war against Spain, could not reorganize itself in sufficient time or with sufficient strength to resist the imposition of the rule of a new metropolis.

By 1898, separatists had established effective governance over much of Cuba. But it was a costly triumph. The defeat of Spain resulted in the enfeeblement of the revolutionary forces. Cubans had thrown everything into the campaign against Spain; nothing was spared, and nothing was left in reserve. Victory over Spain left them exhausted, weak—and vulnerable.

Cubans emerged from the war victorious, but only over one metropolis. The defeat of one simply provided the opportunity for the other to expand its control over the island. It was one of the supreme ironies of the conflict that Cubans themselves served as the unwitting agents of U.S. hegemony, creating in three years the conditions that three generations of American statesmen believed necessary to allow the United States to assert claim over the island: the extinction of Spanish sovereignty.

The American intervention crushed the revolution. Indeed, in many important ways the intervention of 1898 represented the first of a twentieth-century genre of American military intervention in the circum-Caribbean: a counterrevolutionary intervention to rescue a dependent socio-economic system threatened by indigenous revolutionary forces.

But it was not certain that awareness of American designs would have evoked universal misgiving from the heterogeneous sectors of the separatist coalition. The American intervention was preceded by almost half a century of growing intimacy between Cuba and the United States. Even before American troops had arrived in El Caney and Siboney, the United States had powerful allies in and out of Cuba, as well as in and out of the separatist coalition. Two generations of Cubans had been educated in the United States and had taken a fancy to American institutions. Many Cubans looked upon the United States as an agent of modernity and progress. American institutions, economic development, and political democracy offered dissident Cubans an attractive model around which to contemplate the organization of the future republic. And, for many, if Cuba were to become part of the North American union, well, so much the better. Others on the island, particularly, the old colonial elite, *peninsular* and Creole alike, saw in the United States the salvation of tradition. The growing spectre of separatist revolution awoke the propertied elite to the necessity of shedding traditional, if not unrequited, loyalties, devotions that by 1898 were propelling the traditional order ineluctably toward its own destruction. Spain was now a liability to the colonial system. If the colonial institutions were to survive, a new metropolis was necessary. The colonial elite permitted its fear of separatism to surrender the Spanish system and allowed it to be replaced by American rule, rather than risk the unknown perils of Cuban political ascendancy. The American intervention in 1898, and the subsequent years of occupation, gave renewed institutional vitality to a colonial system brought to the brink of destruction by separatist arms. The American intervention redeemed the threatened colonial system; the occupation reoriented the orbit of the colony around a new metropolis.

II   That Cubans proved incapable of resisting American designs after 1898 said as much about the weakness of separatist structures as it did about the contradictions of the separatist purpose. The absence of anything like organized Cuban resistance to the American occupation was one of the striking features of postwar Cuba. The *independentista* ideal survived the war and persisted into the period of occupation intact, but without either an institution or a person to give independence sentiment political focus. The corporate expressions of Cuban separatism, those institutions summoned into existence to secure independence, failed to survive the early months of the occupation. Successively, the PRC, the Assembly, and, lastly, the bastion of *independentista* sentiment, the Liberation Army, disappeared within six months of the intervention. Postwar separatism found itself bereft of leadership. The separatist chieftains most conspicuously associated with the ideal of independence, leaders of national stature capable of giving *independentismo* postwar purpose, did not live into the period of the military government. José Martí, Antonio Maceo, and Calixto García died before the formal organization of the military government. There was, to be sure, some continuity from the Cuban Assembly in 1899 to the Constituent Assembly of 1901. Fully a third of the latter, eleven out of thirty-one, had served in the Cuban Assembly of 1899. But here, too, this continuity was not necessarily a source of strength for *independentismo*. Indeed, during peace Cuban nationalists continued to fracture along the old stress lines of the war. Of the eleven delegates voting against the Platt Amendment in June 1901, seven had also voted for the ouster of Máximo Gómez in February 1899. The nationalist anti-American vote remained in conflict with the *independentista* wing of the army command.

Other factors induced Cuban acquiescence to the occupation. The failure of Cubans to seize the apparatus of state contributed powerfully to weakening separatist corporate affiliation. The victors had little to show for their hard-won triumph, nothing with which to give the amorphous coalition of war an enduring institutional structure in peace. The end of the war found the *libertadores*, from senior generals to privates, impoverished and in desperate personal crisis. This single development, set against the backdrop of a devastated economy, converted separatists into supplicants and transformed separatist credentials from a collective national movement into criteria for individual advancement. That the source of patronage was now the United States necessarily induced many Cubans to conform with the American purpose on the island. A pressing need for employment and livelihood, as much as anything else, contributed to the rapid thinning of separatist ranks. Then, too, many Cubans believed the American statement of purpose for the intervention. In April 1898, the Teller Amendment allayed separatist suspicions and persuaded many Cubans that they did indeed have an ally in the United States. Cubans erred, Domingo Méndez Capote acknowledged years later, for having failed to "perceive with clarity" the distinction between public opinion and official policy, confusing popular support of the Cuban cause with official endorsement.[1] By the time American policy became suspect among Cubans, the old separatist polity had so fragmented that Cubans were incapable of reviving anything that faintly resembled the wartime coalition. By this time, too, the insurgent leadership had in one way or another reconciled itself to the American presence. In this sense, Máximo Gómez's support of the United States exerted a powerful influence on the course *independentismo* would take after 1899. As defined by the Dominican army chieftain, collaboration with the United States emerged as a policy of singular patriotic virtue. Resistance to the American presence threatened to jeopardize the independence to which the Cubans believed the United States had already pledged itself. This was Gómez's fear: that Cuban resistance would be seized by the United States to abrogate the pledge of the Joint Resolution and provide the pretext for annexation.[2] Separatists feared the charge of incapacity of self-government so much that they did nothing that would lend credence to that allegation—not even defend the gains of their three-year struggle.

A corollary habit emerged out of the occupation experience. Cubans were not slow to perceive that opposition to the United States jeopardized political—and, inevitably, economic—mobility. Succeeding generations of Cuban politicians came to see collaboration with American authorities as the surest means of political success and personal prosperity. Opposition to the United States was often associated with a barrier to patriotic aspiration and always a bane to political ambitions.

III   Thirty years of struggle had lasting effects on the republic. Between 1868 and 1898, the separatist elite took on its definitive characteristics, organizing not around the acquisition and expansion of control over the means of production, but, rather, around the cause of independence. In the course of thirty years of intermittant war, Creoles' hold over the sources of wealth grew increasingly tenuous. By the end of the nineteenth century, much of the island's traditional sources of wealth had slipped beyond the possession of the separatist elite and passed under the control of non-Cubans. Other means of acquiring wealth, prestige, and power were severely limited. Without resources with which to revive moribund agriculture, without positions from which to aggregate capital, the impoverished *libertadores* came to constitute an elite organized around the quest of public office as the principal means to economic well-being. This central reality gave Cuban political culture its definitive characteristic. Wealth would be derived from political power, it would not create it. Political office symbolized opportunity. Politics in the republic acquired a particular distributive quality. With so much of the national wealth passing into the hands of non-Cubans, political office guaranteed the victorious candidate and his immediate constituency access to the lever of resource and benefit allocation in the only enterprise wholly Cuban—government.

The havoc befalling the Cuban class structure was not confined to the impoverishment of Creole separatists. The Cuban bourgeoisie never quite recovered from the effects of the war. The appointment of Weyler announced the demise of their political fortunes, the invasion signaled the ruin of their economic condition. By 1898, the old planter elite had become irrelevant to the colonial crisis; it was now facing extinction. The American intervention restored the beleaguered bourgeoisie to its position of local preeminence, but at a price. This was now a captive bourgeoisie, a class that had no function other than to serve American needs as a means to guarantee its own survival. It would remain an estranged elite, artificial in some ways, superfluous in others, and always subservient to interests from abroad and vulnerable to forces at home. It would not become necessary for local elites to justify their prominence or defend their interests—the United States would always do so. The Cuban bourgeoisie was doomed by 1898; it would remain for the next sixty years functionally inert in every important respect save one—providing legitimacy for American hegemony in Cuba.

IV   Fragile separatism produced a fragile republic. The republic collapsed in almost shorter time than it took the Americans to fashion it. Four years after the end of the occupation, an armed rebellion protesting fraud in the re-election of Tomás Estrada Palma toppled the government of the first Cuban president. "The truth is," Secretary of War William Howard Taft concluded ruefully from Havana in 1906, "that the Cuban government has proven to be nothing but a house of cards."[3]

And so it was. But if, indeed, the Cuban government was a "house of cards," it was one stacked during the first military occupation. The Americans had fixed the orbit of the republic on a collision course with itself, a republic organized around planned impermanence. The institutions of the republic were not designed to endure independence but to induce annexation.

During the years of the Estrada Palma administration, Americans waited patiently for the occasion that would produce the expected "annexation by acclamation." The U.S. minister in Havana, Herbert G. Squiers, was unabashedly public in his anticipation of annexation. The American Legation became a center of annexationist activity, with scores of visitors seeking daily information about the current status of annexation plans. "I invariably tell them," Squiers reported to the State Department in 1902, "that the safest and surest way is to give their best, active, and moral support to this Government and in a comparatively short time Cuba will drift into the Union without causing a ripple; that annexation accompanied by the necessity of a single soldier is not desirable and ought not to be."[4]

That Squiers could urge Cubans to support the Estrada Palma government was in no small measure due to Estrada's known sympathy for the United States and support of annexation. Ten years, Estrada Palma predicted confidently to the American minister in 1902, would be a sufficient period of independence, after which Cuba would be ready for annexation.[5] "I do not believe there is a more devoted friend of the United States than he, or a firmer believer in ultimate annexation and the benefit which will accrue to Cuba," Squiers wrote enthusiastically of Estrada in 1902. "But," the American minister cautioned, "not now."[6] The time would be right in a decade or so. In 1905 Estrada had won a disputed re-election for a second four-year term. Political protest produced armed rebellion, and in August 1906, the Estrada government fell.

The August revolution against Estrada Palma, and the subsequent United States intervention, put to rest all reasonable prospects for annexation. The organization of the new Cuban government in 1902, the last year of the American military occupation, had provided for the political ascendancy of the pro-American wing of the old separatist coalition. The old expatriate sector, the most conservative wing of the revolutionary polity, assumed political control of the republic under the protective auspices of the United States. The establishment of a national government headed by Tomás Estrada Palma, the former head of the expatriate sector, and the exclusion of *independentista* representatives from either the old provisional government or the Liberation Army, was one of the striking results of the four-year military occupation. The new government was dominated by the old PRC leadership. Vice-President Luis Estévez Romero had spent the war years in Paris. Eduardo Yero, secretary of public works, had served as Estrada Palma's secretary in New York during the war. But more striking than the expatriate composition of the new Cuban government was the source of expatriation. More than half of the Estrada cabinet consisted of old Autonomists who had sought refuge in separatist ranks after 1896. Emilio Terry, secretary of agriculture, a wealthy Las Villas planter, had served as an autonomist deputy in the Spanish *cortes* before joining the PRC junta in Paris. Carlos de Zaldo (minister of justice and state), Diego Tamayo (minister of government), and José María García Montes (minister of finance), had all served on the Junta Central of the Autonomist party before joining the PRC in the United States in 1896.

The August revolution represented more than a protest against the re-election frauds of an incumbent president. The revolution dealt a body blow to annexationist plans. In a very real sense, the rebellion symbolized an *independendista* reaction to a regime of old expatriate conservatives and autonomists. Led by former insurgent army chieftains, the successful revolution eventually catapulted into power former insurgent military leaders. If there was indeed a ten-year time schedule for annexation, as Estrada suggested, it was short-circuited by the August revolution. The 1906 revolution, General Enrique Collazo wrote a year later, was the necessary destruction of a government imposed on Cuba by the United States against the will of the Cuban people.[7]

But in 1906 annexationism was also an idea that had outlived its time. The annexation of Cuba had been a nineteenth-century policy formulation, one resting on an expanding but yet undefined American policy for the circum-Caribbean. In the eight years between the intervention of 1898 and the one of 1906, much had changed in American policy approaches to the

Caribbean. United States hegemony in the Caribbean had moved from the understood to the underscored. The United States had achieved formal control over an Isthmian canal. The Roosevelt Corollary, moreover, had given definite expression to American policy assumptions for the region. Accordingly, acquisition of Cuba lost momentum in official circles in Washington. Not that annexation had lost its appeal altogether but, rather, it was no longer so urgent an issue. American interests in the Caribbean had been defined in broad geo-political terms for the whole region. Cuba was simply a part of the area.

In the end, both the Teller and Platt Amendments proved instrumental in preserving Cuban independence. The Teller Amendment, in the short run, blocked the surge of postwar annexationist sentiment. It was a gesture that Americans a generation or two later would single out as evidence of the selflessness of the American purpose in April 1898, but one that many contemporaries soon came to regret bitterly. Even the most zealous and unabashed advocate of annexation recognized the necessity of acknowledging the constraints of this congressional commitment. "However great may be the temptation, the Great Republic always keeps faith with itself and the world!" General James H. Wilson had exclaimed in 1899. Its interpretation could be manipulated, its application could be capricious, but its intent could not be entirely negated. Without it, the annexationist tide would have proved to be a swell difficult to resist.

Over the longer run, the Platt Amendment met all the traditional American demands. To be sure, it had placed severe restraints on Cuban sovereignty. But the illusion of independence survived, enough to preserve in Cuba the ideal of independence and, with it, an enduring commitment to redeem in full the *independentista* vision. The real choice in 1901 was not between the Platt Amendment and complete independence but, rather, between no independence and limited independence. The Platt Amendment guaranteed at least the form if not the substance of sovereignty, thereby propelling subsequent generations of Cubans into the struggle to redeem the nineteenth-century ideal of independence. This process, too, was vastly facilitated by the Platt Amendment. Nothing served to arouse Cuban indignation more than the "Enmienda Platt." A source of enduring injury to Cuban national sensibilities, it quickly became the focal point of growing nationalism—something Cubans would neither forgive nor forget.

The nineteenth-century separatist struggle cast a shadow across twentieth-century Cuba. The grievances that propelled Cubans to arms in the colony persisted unresolved in the republic. Inspired by the republican vision of José Martí, nurtured by the aspirations of thousands of Cubans who responded to the separatist summons, the insurrection left a legacy of expectations unfulfilled and promises unkept. The war was always more than a struggle for the independence. In the most exalted view of the revolutionary struggle, independence was the means. The end was a new social order. The insurrection against Spain was always as much a rebellion against the colonial system as it was a reaction against colonial rule, containing from the outset a revolution within the revolution. This was the essence of Martí's call to arms. It was the compelling premise of the land reform decree of 1896. It was the inspiration for the countless thousands of the poor, the dispossessed, the landless, who responded to the call of the "redemptive revolution."

The republic rested on a foundation of broken commitments, defaulting on every substantive revolutionary promise—real or implied. Separatists had summoned Cubans to dramatic action but failed to produce dramatic change. Cuban independence was incomplete. Social inequities and racial injustice persisted. Indeed, the issue of racism had long preoccupied the separatist leadership. A commitment to its elimination in Cuban society had moved into a position of central importance in the insurgent vision of Cuba Libre. And, in fact, Afro-Cubans had secured key positions in a variety of separatist organizations, most notably the Liberation Army. The American intervention arrested and reversed these developments and strengthened the institutional foundations of racism on the island. The vast preponderance of Cuban officeholders in occupied Cuba were white. In dissolving the Liberation Army, moreover, the United States destroyed the one national institution in which Cubans of color and modest social origins had achieved status and power. Instead of the Liberation Army, a microcosm of the ideological undercurrents and social composition of the revolution, there emerged the rural guard—white, pro-American, devoted to serving property. The land distribution decree of 1896 was forgotten. The armed struggle, too, had destroyed the basis of the colonial economy. Not since the eighteenth century had Cuba been in a better position to pursue diversified economic development than it was in 1898–1899. The very foundations of the monoculture system had been shaken. Although economic diversification had not occupied a position of central importance in separatist thought, separatist leaders had come during the war to identify the evils of the latifundia system and re-examine the efficacy of an economy organized around one crop for one market. The American occupation ended these prospects. In reconstructing the sugar system, the United States revived the foundations of the colonial economy. The reciprocity treaty locked the colonial product into one market. More important, reciprocity guaranteed that earlier political ties would not be challenged by Cuban economic relations with other countries.

What remained of the separatist experience was the ideal, and this ideal became the cornerstone of republican politics and a clarion call to revolution for the next sixty years. The symbols and texts of the "redemptive revolution" provided the inspiration and articles of faith for every revolutionary movement in the twentieth century. Indeed, the redemption of the "redemptive revolution" served as the recurring theme of the republic. It produced the political idiom that became the stock in trade of national politics. In many important ways, much of Cuban politics, revolutionary as well as institutional, turned on who most faithfully interpreted and most zealously pursued the ideals of Martí's "redemptive revolution." The unfinished revolution of 1895–1898 gave decisive shape and content to republican politics, a legacy that served as a mandate to revolution for the next three generations of Cubans.

Notes

Bibliography

Index

Notes

Chapter 1. The Fateful Interlude

1. The literature on the Ten Years' War is voluminous. See Collazo, *Desde Yara hasta El Zanjón. Apuntaciones históricas*; Blanco Herrero, *Política de España en ultramar*; Fernando Figueredo Socarrás, *La revolución de Yara, (1868–1878)* (Havana: Instituto Cubano del Libro, 1972); LeRiverend Brusone, "Cuba: la revolución de 1868 como transición ideológica"; Sergio Aguirre, "Problemas de interpretación de la guerra de los diez años," *Islas* XI (May–Aug. 1970):26–49; Besada Ramos, "Antecedentes económicos de la guerra de los diez años"; Caballero, "Aspectos fundamentales sobre análisis de clases en la guerra de 1868"; Ministerio de las Fuerzas Armadas Revolucionarias, Dirección Política de las Fuerzas Armadas Revolucionarias, *Historia Militar de Cuba: La guerra de los diez años, 1868–1878* (Havana: Ministerio de las Fuerzas Armadas Revolucionarias, n.d.). For the most complete bibliographical guide to the literature of the Ten Years' War see Aleida Plasencia, ed., *Bibliografía de la guerra de los diez años* (Havana: Biblioteca Nacional "José Martí," 1968).

2. Reverter Delmas, *Cuba española: Reseña histórica de la insurrección cubana en 1895*, I: 15–16.

3. Guerra y Sánchez, *Historia de la nación cubana*, V: 252–60; Figueredo Díaz, *La guerra de Cuba en 1878: La protesta de Baraguá*; Franco, *Antonio Maceo: apuntes para una historia de su vida*, I: 132–58.

4. Guerra y Sánchez, *Historia de la nación cubana*, VI:77–82.

5. *Diario de la Marina*, Aug. 2, 1878, pp. 1, 2. See also Infiesta, *El autonomismo cubano: su razón y manera*; Conte, *Las aspiraciones del Partido Liberal de Cuba*; Eliseo Giberga, "La ideas políticas en Cuba en el siglo XIX," *Cuba Contemporánea* X (Apr. 1916): 347–81. For one of the most complete studies on the Autonomist party see Rafael Montoro, *El ideal autonomista*.

6. Fabié, *Mi gestión ministerial respecto a la isla de Cuba*, p. 21; García Escudero, *De Cánovas a la República*, p. 107; Cueto, *Origen y desarrollo del pensamiento cubano*, II: 371–72.

7. Raúl Cepero Bonilla, *Azúcar y abolición* (Havana: Instituto Cubano del Libro, 1971), pp. 268–76.

8. Lamar Schweyer, *La crisis del patriotismo*, pp. 141–42.

9. Hernández y Pérez, *El período revolucionario de 1879 a 1895*, pp. 11, 30; Llano, *Los partidos de Cuba y la normalidad política*, pp. 9–16.

10. Hernández y Pérez, *El período revolucionario de 1879 a 1895*, pp. 9–10.

11. See Francisco Barrero to Calixto García, Sept. 26, 1879, in Manuel Pérez Cabrera, ed., *Documentos para servir a la historia de la Guerra Chiquita*. 3 vols. (Havana: Archivo Nacional de Cuba, 1950). II: 239–40, and Carlos Roloff to Mariano I. Prado, n.d., ibid, III: 195–96.

12. Castellanos García, "Raíces históricos del Partido Revolucionario Cubano," pp. 8–9; Guerra y Sánchez, *Historia de la nación cubana*, V: 357–58.

13. See Lizaso, *Martí: Martyr of Cuban Independence*, pp. 3–165; Mañach, *Martí, Apostle of Freedom*, pp. 1–192; Carbonell, "La lucha por la independencia en Cuba (1810–1898)," pp. 348–49.

14. José Martí, "Las elecciones del 10 de abril," Apr. 16, 1893, in Martí, *Obras completas*, I, pt. 1, p. 329.

15. José Martí to Máximo Gómez, July 20, 1882, Ibid., p. 74.

16. José Martí to Máximo Gómez, July 20, 1882, Ibid., pp. 72–76. See also Pedro Pablo Rodríguez, "La idea de liberación nacional en José Martí."

17. José Martí to Máximo Gómez, Oct. 20, 1884, in Martí, *Obras completas*, I, pt. 1, pp. 78–81.

18. See Alvarez, "El Partido Revolucionario Cubano y los militares mambises del '68."

19. Máximo Gómez, *Diario de campaña del mayor general Máximo Gómez*, p. 238. See also Castellanos García, *Un paladín (Serafín Sánchez)*, pp. 85–93.

20. Martí, *Obras completas*, I, pt. 1, p. clxiii.

21. Perera and Acosta, "La campaña anti-Martí"; Trujillo, *Apuntes históricos*, p. 31; Lizaso, *Martí*, pp. 197–99, and Mañach, *Martí*, pp. 241–43.

22. José Martí, "Discurso conmemorativo," Nov. 27, 1891, in Martí, *Obras completas*, I, pt. 1, p. 40.

23. Out of this community of expatriate cigarworkers emerged Diego Vicente Tejera, founder of the Cuban Socialist Party, and Carlos Baliño, organizer of the Cuban communist party. See Pedro Luis Padrón, "Carlos Baliño," *Granma*, Feb. 16, 1967, p. 2, and Bueno, "Diego Vicente Tejera." See also García Hernández, "Movimiento obrero y liberación nacional," and Hidalgo, "El movimiento obrero cubano y el primer partido antimperialista de la historia"; Pedro Pablo Rodríguez, "Caracter popular del P.R.C."

24. As early as 1869, cigarworkers had organized revolutionary clubs in exile to support the armed struggle in Cuba. See Castañeda, *Martí, los tabaqueros y la revolución de 1895*, pp. 20–21; Pedro Pablo Rodriguez, "La idea de liberación nacional en José Martí," pp. 136–39, 146–47; Portuondo, "Ideología del Partido Revolucionario Cubano," p. 65.

25. Horrego Estuch, "Martí: su ideología." See also Ayon, "Martí y los trabajadores"; Morales, "Origen y caracter del partido fundado por Martí."

26. Jorge Ibarra, "Hacia la organización revolucionaria," *Bohemia* LXXI (Jan. 26, 1979): 88–91; Mencia, "Martí: la unidad revolucionaria"; Román Hernández, "Consideración sobre la obra unificadora de Martí y el Partido Revolucionario Cubano"; Vitier, *Martí, estudio integral*, pp. 21–25.

27. See "Resoluciones tomadas por la emigración cubana de Tampa, el dia 28 de noviembre de 1891," in Martí, *Obras completas*, I, pt. 2, pp. 298–99.

28. See José Martí, "El Partido Revolucionario Cubano," Apr. 3, 1892, in Martí, *Obras completas*, I, pt. 2, pp. 303–07, and "La proclamación del Partido Revolucionario Cubano, el 10 de Abril," in ibid., I, pt. 2, pp. 307–13. See also Portuondo del Prado, "Martí y el Partido Revolucionario Cubano."

29. Friedlander, *Historia económica de Cuba*, p. 432.

30. Alvarez Díaz, *A Study on Cuba*, pp. 91–92; Ramiro Guerra y Sánchez, *Sugar and Society in the Caribbean* (New Haven: Yale University Press, 1964), p. 63; Guerra y Sánchez, *Historia de la nación cubana*, VII, p. 153; Friedlander, *Historia económica de Cuba*, p. 432.

31. Guerra y Sánchez, *Historia de la nación cubana*, VII, p. 165.

32. Alvarez Díaz, *A Study on Cuba*, p. 93.

33. Jenks, *Our Cuban Colony*, p. 27.

34. Thomas, *Cuba, The Pursuit of Freedom*, p. 272.

35. For the impact of abolition on sugar production see Corwin, *Spain and the Abolition of Slavery in Cuba, 1817–1886*, pp. 293–313.

36. Adam Badeau, "Report on the Present Condition of Cuba," February 7, 1884, Despatches from United States Consuls in Havana, 1783–1906, General Records of the Department of State, Record Group 59, National Archives, Washington, D.C. (Hereafter cited as Despatches/Havana.)

37. David Vickers to Assistant Secretary of State John Davis, October 24, 1883, Despatches from United States Consuls in Matanzas, 1820–1889, General Records of the Department of State, Record Group 59, National Archives, Washington, D.C. (Hereafter cited as Despatches/Matanzas.)

38. Ibid.

39. Guerra y Sánchez, *Historia de la nación cubana*, VII, pp. 155, 163; Friedlander, *Historia económica de Cuba*, p. 422.

40. William P. Pierce to Assistant Secretary of State John Davis, August 10, 1883, Despatches from United States Consuls in Cienfuegos, 1876–1906, General Records of the Department of State, Record Group 59, National Archives, Washington, D.C. (Hereafter cited as Despatches/Cienfuegos.)

41. See Edwin F. Atkins, *Sixty Years in Cuba*, pp. 48–137.

42. Froude, *The English in the West Indies*, pp. 301, 304, 306.

43. Davey, *Cuba, Past and Present*, p. 137.

44. Ballou, *Due South, or Cuba Past and Present*, pp. 39, 43, 45, 49, 51, 168.

45. Adam Badeau to Department of State, March 6, 1884, Despatches/Havana.

46. Adam Badeau, "Report on the Present Condition of Cuba," February 7, 1884, Despatches/Havana.

47. Alvarez Díaz, *A Study on Cuba*, p. 71; Thomas, *Cuba, The Pursuit of Freedom*, p. 285.

48. Merchan, *Cuba, justificacion de sus guerras de independencia*, p. 38; Duvon C. Corbitt, "Immigration in Cuba," *Hispanic American Historical Review* XXII (May 1942): 302–08.

49. See Montejo, *Diary of a Runaway Slave*, pp. 63–73. See also Davey, *Cuba, Past and Present*, pp. 177, 208.

50. *Diario de la Marina*, Nov. 24, 1888, enclosure in Ramon O. Williams to George L. Rives, November 24, 1888, Despatches/Havana.

51. Guerra y Sánchez, *Sugar and Society in the Caribbean*, pp. 61–67.

52. See Guerra y Sánchez, *Historia de la nación cubana*, VII, pp. 192–94; Friedlander, *Historia económica de Cuba*, pp. 436–38.

53. For a general discussion of social banditry see Eric Hobsbawm, *Primitive Rebels* (New York: Norton, 1965) and *Bandits* (New York: Delacorte Press, 1969). See also Enrique José Varona, "El bandolerismo en Cuba," in Estévez Romero, *Desde el Zanjón hasta Baire*, II, pp. 243–47.

54. For the complete text of this decree see Estévez Romero, *Desde el Zanjón hasta Baire*, II, pp. 1–2. See also *La Lucha*, Apr. 17, 1888, enclosure in Ramon O. Williams to assistant secretary of state, April 18, 1888, Despatches/Havana and *La Voz de Cuba*, Apr. 8, 1888, enclosure in Ramon O. Williams to assistant secretary of state, April 12, 1888, Despatches/Havana.

55. López Leiva, *El bandolerismo en Cuba (contribución al estudio de esta plaga social)*, pp. 22–25.

56. By the early 1890s, ranking members of the planter elite had acquired American citizenship, including Juan Pedro Baró, Perfecto Lacosta, Andrés Terry, Arturo Averhoff, Francisco J. Cazares, Francisco D. Duque, Carlos Manuel García y Ruiz, Alberto V. de Goicuría, José González, Domingo González y Alfonso, Cristóbal N. Madan, Antonio A. Martínez, Federico P. Montes, Luis Felipe Morejón y Marquez, Joaquín Pérez Cruz, Manual A. Recio, José Rafael de los Reyes y García, Juan Rossell, Francisco Soria y Díaz, Manuel de la Torres, José Ignacio Toscano, Manuel de la Vega, and José Antonio Yznaga.

57. Ramon O. Williams to Assistant Secretary of State James N. Porter, December 28, 1886, Despatches/Havana.

58. See *La Unión Constitucional*, June 23, 1891, enclosure in Ramon O. Williams to William F. Wharton, June 23, 1891, Despatches/Havana, and *Boletín de la Cámara Oficial de Comercio, Industria y Navegación de La Habana*, June 30, 1891, enclosure in Ramon O. Williams to William F. Wharton, June 18, 1891, Despatches/Havana.

59. "El Manifiesto Económico," *La Discusión*, July 22, 1891, enclosure in Ramon O. Williams to William F. Wharton, July 28, 1891, Despatches/Havana.

60. Ramon O. Williams to William F. Wharton, June 23, 1891, Despatches/Havana.

61. Alvarez Díaz, *A Study on Cuba*, pp. 133–36 and Thomas, *Cuba, The Pursuit of Freedom*, p. 289.

62. Pulaski F. Hyatt to Department of State, October 12, 1894, Despatches from U.S. Consuls in Santiago de Cuba, 1799–1906, General Records of the Department of State, Record Group 59, National Archives, Washington, D.C. (Hereafter cited as Despatches/Santiago de Cuba).

63. *La Lucha*, Dec. 1, 1894, p. 1.

64. *Diario de la Marina*, Dec. 19, 1894, p. 2. See also Nichols, "Domestic History of Cuba During the Insurrection, 1895–1898", (unpublished M.A. Thesis), pp. 29–30, 32.

65. Ramon O. Williams to Assistant Secretary of State Edwin F. Uhl, January 5, 1895, Despatches/Havana.

66. Pulaski F. Hyatt to Department of State, October 12, 1894, Despatches/Santiago de Cuba.

67. *La Lucha*, Dec. 19, 1894, p. 2.

68. See Ramon O. Williams to Assistant Secretary of State Edwin F. Uhl, January 3, 1895, Despatches/Havana, and Joseph Hance to Assistant Secretary of State Edwin F. Uhl, October 9, 1894, Despatches from U.S. Consuls in Cárdenas, 1843–1849, 1879–1898, General Records of the Department of State, Record Group 59, National Archives. (Hereafter cited as Despatches/Cárdenas.)

69. *La Lucha*, Jan. 3, 1895, p. 2.

70. Pulaski F. Hyatt to Department of State, October 12, 1894, Despatches/Santiago de Cuba.

71. *La Lucha*, Jan. 3, 1895, p. 2.

72. *Diario de la Marina*, Dec. 19, 1894, p. 2.

73. Casas y González, *La guerra separatista de Cuba*, p. 115.

74. Ibid., p. 119.

75. Costa y Blanco, *Juan Gualberto Gómez: una vida sin sombra*, pp. 118–19. See also Pirala, *España y la regencia: Anales de diez y seis años (1885–1902)*, I, pp. 247–53.

76. Reverter Delmas, *Cuba española. Reseña de la insurrección cubana en 1895*, I, p. 31; p. 247.

77. At the outbreak of the war for independence, Lino Mirabal in Camagüey, Nicasio Matos in Santa Clara, José "Matagás" Alvarez in Matanzas, and Manuel García and Gallo Sosa in Havana immediately seconded the separatist cause. Bandit forces provided the separatist cause with the early core of insurgent units in the Cuban interior. The followers of Nicasio Matos ultimately passed into the ranks of the separatist armies led by Roloff, Lacret, Sánchez, Zayas, Rego, and Alemán. See Morales Patiño, *El capitán chino*, p. 131, and Varona Guerrero, *La guerra de independencia de Cuba, 1895–1898*, 3 vols. (Havana: Editorial Lex, 1946), II, p. 836.

78. In Mañach, *Martí, Apostle of Freedom*, p. 261.

79. Estévez Romero, *Desde el Zanjón hasta Baire*, II, p. 55.

80. Ibid., p. 57.

81. Raimundo Cabrera, *Cuba and the Cubans*. pp. 172–73, 193; Guiteras, *Free Cuba*, pp. 228, 230–31; 329–39. See also Zayas, "The Causes of the Present War in Cuba," p. 812.

Chapter 2. From Reconciliation to Reconcentration

1. See Roberto Pavón Tamayo, "Aquel primer domingo de Carnaval de 1895," *Verdo Olivo*, VII (Feb. 27, 1966): 4–10; Franco and Cabrera Alvarez, "¿Que pasó en La Habana el 24 de febrero?"

2. See Ojeda, "Antecedentes de la guerra de 1895 en Oriente," pp. 157–77.

3. David Vickers to John Davis, July 2, 1884, Despatches/Matanzas.

4. See *Los preparativos de la revolución y el general Calleja, 1893–1895* (Havana: Imprenta del Avisador Comercial, 1896), pp. 26–96.

5. See José Martí, "El tercer año del Partido Revolucionario Cubano," in Martí, *Obras completas,* I, pt. 2, pp. 348–53, and Martí, *El Partido Revolucionario Cubano y la guerra,* pp. 169–74.

6. During the early years, the PRC depended primarily on weekly donations from cigar-workers in Florida and other modest contributions from Cubans in exile. "Colectas del Club 24 de febrero, desde el 25 de agosto," unpublished ledger, Club Maceo-Marti, Tampa, Florida. Photocopy in author's possession.

7. José Martí to Máximo Gómez, Sept. 13, 1892, in Martí, *Obras completas,* I, pt. 1, pp. 99–102.

8. See Collazo, *Cuba independiente,* p. 33; Rousset, *Historial de Cuba,* II, p. 170.

9. José Martí, José María Rodríguez, and Enrique Collazo, "Al ciudadano Juan Gualberto Gómez, y en él a todos los grupos de Occidente," Jan. 29, 1894, in Martí, *El Partido Revolucionario Cubano y la guerra,* p. 249; Estela Izquierdo, "La orden de alzamiento para la guerra del '95," *Granma,* Feb. 5, 1973, p. 2; Rebeca Rosell Planas, *Las claves de Martí y el plan de alzamiento para Cuba,* (Havana: Archivo Nacional de Cuba, 1948), pp. 3–30.

10. Gutiérrez, *Oriente heroico,* p. 15; Lagomasino Alvarez, *Reminiscencias patriotas,* pp. 107–44. For a general survey of the February 24 uprising across the island see Boti, "El 24 de febrero de 1895."

11. Arnao, *Páginas para la historia de la isla de Cuba,* p. 266.

12. Fernández Almagro, *Historia política de la España contemporánea,* II, p. 244.

13. Giberga, *Obras de Eliseo Giberga,* III, pp. 184–85.

14. Rafael María de Labra to José María Gálvez, June 18, 1895, *Boletín del Archivo Nacional* XXVI (Jan.–Dec., 1927): 240–43. See also "Exposición dirigida al gobierno de S. M. por la Junta Central del Partido Liberal," Sept. 18, 1895, enclosure in Ramon O. Williams to Edwin F. Uhl, October 18, 1895, Despatches/Havana.

15. Manuel Ortiz de Pinedo to José María Gálvez, Mar. 2, 1895, *Boletín del Archivo Nacional* XXVI (Jan.–Dec., 1927): 209–11.

16. Collazo, *Cuba independiente,* pp. 93–97; Reverter Delmas, *Cuba española: Reseña histórica de la insurrección cubana en 1895.* 1, p. 215; Leiseca, *Historia de Cuba,* p. 314.

17. *Diario de la Marina,* April 5, 1895, p. 1; Varona, *De la colonia a la república,* p. 78.

18. Pulaski F. Hyatt to Edwin F. Uhl, May 11, 1895, Despatches/Santiago de Cuba.

19. Fabié, *Cánovas del Castillo,* pp. 319–20, 325; Ortega Rubio, *Historia de la regencia de María Cristina Habsbourg-Lorena,* III, p. 137.

20. Arsenio Martínez Campos to Tomás Castellanos, July 8, 1895, in Ortega Rubio, ibid., II, pp. 466–67. *La Lucha,* Oct. 28, 1895, enclosure in Ramon O. Williams to Edwin F. Uhl, October 31, 1895, Despatches/Havana.

21. See Arsenio Martínez Campos to Antonio María Fabié, May 12, 1895, in Fabié, *Cánovas del Castillo,* pp. 324–25; Arsenio Martínez Campos to José de Castro, June 1895, in ibid., p. 325. See also Flores, *La guerra de Cuba (apuntes para la historia),* pp. 529–42.

22. See Antonio Maceo to Jesús Rabí, Apr. 21, 1896, in Maceo, *Antonio Maceo. Ideología política. Cartas y otros documentos,* II: 27. (Hereafter cited as *Cartas y otros documentos.*) See also Collazo, *Cuba independiente,* p. 141; Portillo, *La guerra de Cuba (el primer año). Apuntes,* p. 68; Angel E. Rosende y de Zayas, *Con sombrero de yagua* (Havana: Molina y Cía, 1932), pp. 98–99.

23. See Arsenio Martínez Campos to Tomás Castellanos, July 8, 1895, in Ortega Rubio,

Historia de la regencia de María Cristina Habsbourg-Lorena, II. 466–67; A & B, *Apuntes en defensa del honor del ejército*, p. 37. Portillo, *La guerra de Cuba*, pp. 54–55; Reverter Delmas, *Cuba española. Reseña histórica de la insurrección cubana en 1895*, III: 72–73; Martin, "El combatiente cubano en función de pueblo," pp. 37–38.

24. Academia de la Historia de Cuba, *Crónicas de la guerra de Cuba* pp. 38–39, 123.

25. Arsenio Martínez Campos to Tomás Castellanos, July 8, 1895, in Ortega Rubio, *Historia de la regencia de María Cristina Habsbourg-Lorena*, II: 467.

26. In Conangla Fontanilles, *Cuba y Pi y Margall*, p. 378.

27. *La Lucha*, Oct. 28, 1895, enclosure in Ramon O. Williams to Edwin F. Uhl, October 31, 1895, Despatches/Havana.

28. Arsenio Martínez Campos to Antonio Cánovas del Castillo, 25 de julio de 1895, in Ortega Rubio, *Historia de la regencia de María Cristina Habsbourg-Lorena*, II: 473.

29. Enrique Gay-Calbó, "En los finales de la guerra de independencia," p. 59.

30. Arsenio Martínez Campos to Antonio Cánovas del Castillo, July 25, 1895, in Ortega Rubio, *Historia de la regencia de María Cristina Habsbourg-Lorena*, II: 473.

31. Arsenio Martínez Campos to Antonio Cánovas del Castillo, July 25, 1895, in O'Donnell y Abreu, *Apuntes del ex-Ministro de Estado Duque de Tetuán*, II: 115–17.

32. *Gaceta de La Habana*, Jan. 3, 1896, enclosure in Ramon O. Williams to Department of State, January 4, 1896, Despatches/Havana.

33. Ortega Rubio, *Historia de la regencia de María Cristina Habsbourg-Lorena*, III: 9. Varona, *De la colonia a la república*,, p. 80; Villoch, *Viejas postales descoloridas. La guerra de independencia*, pp. 95–102.

34. García Escudero, *De Cánovas a la República*, p. 109.

35. In Miró Argenter, *Crónicas de la guerra*, I: 361.

36. *El Boletín Comercial*, Sept. 2, 1895, enclosure in Ramon O. Williams to Alvey A. Adee, September 12, 1895, Despatches/Havana.

37. *El Avisador Comercial*, Nov. 14, 1895, enclosure in Ramon O. Williams to Edwin F. Uhl, November 20, 1895, Despatches/Havana.

38. *Diario de la Marina*, Oct. 27, 1895, enclosure in Ramon O. Williams to Edwin F. Uhl, October 28, 1895, Despatches/Havana.

39. Meléndez Meléndez, *Cánovas y la política exterior española*, pp. 345–46; Fabié, *Cánovas del Castillo*, pp. 330–31.

40. Fernández Almagro, *Historia política de la España contemporánea*, II: 274–75; Armiñán, *Weyler*, pp. 163–65; Fernando Gómez, *La insurrección por dentro. Apuntes para la historia*, p. ix.

41. Meléndez Meléndez, *Cánovas y la política exterior española*, pp. 345–46; Fabié, *Cánovas del Castillo*, pp. 330–31.

42. In Ortega Rubio, *Historia de la regencia de María Cristina Habsbourg-Lorena*, III, p. 11; León y Castillo, *Mis tiempos*, II: p. 89.

43. In Guiteras, *Free Cuba*, p. 526.

44. Weyler, *Mi mando en Cuba*, I, p. 128; Roig de Leuchsenring, *Weyler en Cuba*, pp. 71–72. For the best discussion of Spain's *trocha* strategy see Murviedro, *Bosquejo de un plan de campaña en la isla de Cuba*, pp. 6–51.

45. Weyler, *Mi mando en Cuba*, I, pp. 128–29; Romano, *Weyler, el hombre de hierro*, p. 97; Weyler y López de Pugna, *En el archivo de mi abuelo. Biografía del Capitán General Weyler*, pp. 100, 104–05.

46. Weyler, *Mi mando en Cuba*, I: 170; Carlos Muecke Bertel, *Patria y libertad*, trans. Walfredo J. Rodríguez y Rodríguez (Camagüey: Ramentol y Boan, 1928), pp. 150–51, 155; Roig de Leuchsenring, *1895 y 1898. Dos guerras cubanas. Ensayo de revaloración*, pp. 48–49.

47. Castellano García, *Aranguren (del ciclo mambí)*, pp. 156–57; Díaz Benzo, *Pequeñaces de la guerra de Cuba por un español*, pp. 99–108.

48. Weyler, *Mi mando en Cuba*, I: 128–29.

49. See Sanjenís, *Memorias de la revolución de 1895 por la independencia de Cuba*, pp. 117–18.

50. See Weyler's reconcentration order for Pinar del Río, October 21, 1896, in Fernández Almagro, *Historia política de España contemporánea*, II, pp. 306–07 and Weyler, *Mi mando en Cuba*, II: 427–28.

51. Estimates of the number of people who perished in reconcentration camps vary. Most writers agree, however, that several hundred thousand Cubans lost their lives in Spanish reconcentration centers. See Varona Guerrero, *La guerra de independencia de Cuba, 1896–1898*, II, p. 780; Cabrera, *Episodios de la guerra. Mi vida en la manigua*, pp. 265–70; Roig de Leuchsenring, *Weyler en Cuba*, pp. 90–102; José Antonio Medel, *La guerra hispano-americana y sus resultados* (2nd ed., La Habana: P. Fernández y Ca., 1932), pp. 110–11; Gómez, *La insurrección por dentro. Apuntes para la historia*, pp. 19–20; Trelles y Govín, *Bibliografía cubana del siglo XIX*, VIII, p. 202; Francisco de P. Machado, *¡Piedad! Recuerdos de la reconcentración*, (Havana: Imprenta y Papelería de Rambla, Bouza y Ca., 1927), pp. 20–22.

Chapter 3. Intuitive Certainty

1. *New York Times*, December 7, 1896, p. 4.

2. Grover Cleveland, "Fourth Annual Message," December 7, 1896, in Richardson, ed., *A Compilation of the Messages and Papers of the Presidents, 1789–1902*, IX, pp. 716–22.

3. *New York Times*, December 8, 1896, p. 1.

4. *New York Times*, December 8, 1896, p. 4. See also Wisan, *The Cuban Crisis as Reflected in the New York Press (1895–1898)*, pp. 237–45.

5. Robert F. Kelley, *The Cultural Pattern in American Politics* (New York: Knopf, 1979), p. 265.

6. John Quincy Adams to Hugh Nelson, April 28, 1823, U.S. Congress, House of Representatives, 32nd Congress, 1st Session, House Document No. 121, Ser. 648, p. 7. (Hereafter cited as House Document No. 121.)

7. See Albert K. Weinberg, *Manifest Destiny* (Baltimore: John Hopkins University Press, 1935), pp. 233–35.

8. "In the hands of a powerful and active nation," American Minister in Spain Alexander H. Everett noted in 1825, "[Cuba] would carry with it complete control over the commerce of the Gulph [sic] of Mexico, and over the navigation of the River Mississippi, as to endanger very much the intercourse of our country in that quarter. Our safety from this danger has, I believe, long been considered as resulting wholly from the feebleness and insufficiency of Spain; and it has been viewed by all as a settled point that the American Government could not consent to any change in the political situation of Cuba other than one which should place it under the jurisdiction of the United States." Alexander H. Everett to the President, November 30, 1825, Everett, *The Everett Letters on Cuba*, p. 6.

9. For a general discussion of the "no transfer" principle see John A. Logan, Jr., *No Transfer*.

10. Thomas Jefferson to James Monroe, June 11, 1823, in Ford, ed., *The Writings of Thomas Jefferson*, XII: 293.

11. John Forsyth to secretary of state, November 20, 1822, House Document 121, p. 4. Several months later, Forsyth reiterated this position: "We desire . . . no other neighbor in Cuba but Spain. . . . The United States would do everything in their [sic] power, consistent with their [sic] obligations to prevent Cuba from being wrested from Spain." See John Forsyth to John Quincy Adams, February 10, 1823, ibid., p. 5.

12. Thomas Jefferson to James Monroe, October 24, 1823, U.S. Congress, Senate, Senate

Document No. 26, 57th Congress, 1st Session. Ser. 4220, pp. 3–4. James Buchanan echoed similar sentiments three years later: "I would not agree that any nation on earth should wrest those islands [Cuba and Puerto Rico] from the dominion of Spain." James Buchanan, "Remarks, March 27, 1826, on Mr. Poinsett's Negotiations With Mexico," John Bassett Moore, ed., *The Works of James Buchanan*, 12 vols. (New York: Antiquarian Press, Ltd., 1960), I: 181.

13. John Forsyth to Aaron Vail, July 15, 1840, House Document No. 121, pp. 36–37.

14. John M. Clayton to Daniel M. Barringer, August 2, 1849, Manning, ed., *Diplomatic Correspondence of the United States: Inter-American Affairs, 1831–1860*, XI: 70. (Hereafter cited as *Diplomatic Correspondence*.)

15. Langley, *The Cuban Policy of the United States*, p. 5.

16. Martin Van Buren to Cornelius P. Van Ness, October 2, 1829, House Document No. 121, p. 26.

17. John Quincy Adams to Hugh Nelson, April 28, 1823, House Document No. 121, p. 8.

18. Henry Clay to Alexander H. Everett, April 26, 1825, House Document No. 121, pp. 17–18.

19. Nevins, *Hamilton Fish*, I: 180.

20. Hamilton Fish Diary, April 6, 1869, Box 314, Hamilton Fish Papers. See also Nevins, *Hamilton Fish*, I: 192–200.

21. Ulysses S. Grant, "Annual Message to Congress," December 7, 1875, in Richardson, *A Compilation of the Messages and Papers of the Presidents, 1789–1902*, IX: 4293–94.

22. James Buchanan to Romulus M. Saunders, June 17, 1848, *Diplomatic Correspondence*, XI, p. 58, and James Buchanan to Romulus M. Saunders, June 9, 1848, ibid, p. 53. This expectation was suggested as early as 1825 by the American minister to Spain: "[I am] authorized to declare to Spain the repugnance with which the United States would see these islands [Cuba and Puerto Rico] transferred to any other power; that they [sic] prefer to see the connexion between Spain and these islands continued, to their severance from Spain and junction to any such power who might be desirous of acquiring these rich possessions . . . [I am] authorized, unequivocally, to disclaim all views of aggrandizement . . . to declare the exemption of [my] government from all connivance at, or countenance of, internal dissension, or at expeditions, or equipments, having in view either the disturbance of the internal repose of these islands, or the dismemberment of the Spanish empire. The undersigned was also instructed to say that the government of the United States expected, from the friendship and good understanding subsisting between the two governments, that Spain would not conceal from them a measure of this sort, should they at any time contemplate the transfer of these islands, so contiguous to the territory of the United States." See Hugh Nelson to first secretary of state, June 22, 1825, House Document No. 121.

23. John Forsyth to Aaron Vail, July 15, 1840, House Document No. 121, pp. 36–37.

24. A. Stevenson to John Forsyth, June 16, 1837, House Document No. 121, p. 34. Italics in original.

25. For a general review of American efforts to purchase Cuba see Langley, *The Cuban Policy of the United States*, pp. 21–81; Guerra y Sánchez, *La expansión territorial de los Estados Unidos*.

26. Richard B. Olney to Grover Cleveland, September 25, 1895, Grover Cleveland Papers.

27. Richard B. Olney to Enrique Dupuy de Lôme, April 4, 1896, U.S. Department of State, *Papers Relating to the Foreign Relations of the United States: 1897*, p. 541. (Hereafter cited as *FRUS:1897*.)

28. Fitzhugh Lee to Richard B. Olney, June 27, 1896, Despatches/Havana.

29. Richard B. Olney to Grover Cleveland, September 25, 1895, Cleveland Papers.

30. Grover Cleveland, "Third Annual Message," December 2, 1895, in Richardson, *A Compilation of the Messages and Papers of the Presidents, 1789–1902*, IX: 636.

31. Langley, *The Cuban Policy of the United States*, pp. 94–95.

32. See Charles F. Rand to Richard B. Olney, April 8, 1896, Richard B. Olney Papers, and Alexander C. Brice to Ramon O. Williams, November 11, 1895, Despatches/Havana.

33. Grover Cleveland, "Fourth Annual Message," December 7, 1896, in Richardson, *A Compilation of the Messages and Papers of the Presidents, 1789–1902*, IX: 719.

34. Richard B. Olney to Enrique Dupuy de Lôme, April 4, 1896, *FRUS: 1897*, p. 543.

35. *New York Journal*, January 1, 1897, p. 1. See also Ortega Rubio, *Historia de la regencia de María Cristina Habsbourg-Lorena*, II: 307; Henry Adams to Brooks Adams, February 7, 1896, in Henry Adams, *Letters of Henry Adams*, ed. Worthington Chauncey, 2 vols. (Boston: Houghton-Mifflin, 1930–1938), II: 96.

36. U.S. Congress, Senate, Report of the Committee on Foreign Relations, *Affairs in Cuba*, 55th Congress, Report No. 885, Ser. 3624, p. 74. (Hereafter cited as *Affairs in Cuba*.)

37. See Juan B. Spotorno to Oscar B. Stillman, January 4, 1896, and Edwin F. Atkins to Richard B. Olney, December 16, 1896, Olney Papers.

38. Enrique Dupuy de Lôme to Antonio Canovas del Castillo, March 20, 1895, in Ferrara y Marino, *The Last Spanish War, Revelations in 'Diplomacy,'* pp. 15–16. A slightly different translation of this memorandum appears in May, *Imperial Democracy*, pp. 91–92.

39. Richard Olney to Enrique Dupuy de Lôme, April 14, 1896, *FRUS: 1897*, pp. 543–44.

40. Grover Cleveland, "Third Annual Message to Congress," December 2, 1895, in Richardson, *A Compilation of the Messages and Papers of the Presidents, 1789–1902*, IX: 636.

41. Grover Cleveland, "Fourth Annual Message," December 7, 1896, in ibid., p. 718.

42. Ortega Rubio, *Historia de la regencia María Cristina Habsbourg-Lorena*, II: 295.

43. Samuel Flagg Bemis, ed., *The American Secretaries of State and Their Diplomacy*, 18 vols. (New York: Pageant Book Company, 1958–1970), VIII: 286; Morgan, *William McKinley and His America*, p. 329. See also Gage, "Work of the Treasury Department," and Wilkie, "The Secret Service in the War." In fact, by late 1895, separatist leaders despaired over Cuban losses at the hands of American customs authorities. See Tomás Estrada Palma to Antonio Maceo, Oct. 17, 1895, in Julián Martínez Castells, ed., *Antonio Maceo: documentos para su vida* (La Habana: Archivo Nacional de Cuba, 1945), p. 152; and Tomás Estrada Palma to Ramón Emeterio Betances, Nov. 27, 1896, in Llaverías y Martínez, ed., *Correspondencia de la delegación cubana en Nueva York durante la guerra de 1895 a 1898*, I: 95.

44. Grover Cleveland, "Fourth Annual Message," December 7, 1896, in Richardson, *A Compilation of the Messages and Papers of the Presidents, 1789–1902*, IX: 720.

45. Duke of Tetuán to Enrique Dupuy de Lôme, May 22, 1896, in Spain, Ministerio de Estado, *Spanish Diplomatic Correspondence and Documents, 1896–1900*, pp. 10–11.

46. Hannis Taylor to Richard Olney, January 8, 1897, Despatches from United States Ministers to Spain, 1792–1906, General Records of the Department of State, Record Group 59, National Archives, Washington, D.C. (Hereafter cited as Despatches/Spain.)

47. Fitzhugh Lee to Richard Olney, June 24, 1896, and Fitzhugh Lee to Richard Olney, July 22, 1896, Olney Papers.

48. Grover Cleveland, "Fourth Annual Message," December 7, 1896, in Richardson, *A Compilation of the Messages and Papers of the Presidents, 1789–1902*, IX: 719.

49. Grover Cleveland to Richard Olney, July 16, 1896, in Allen Nevins, ed., p. 448.

50. Robert McElroy, *Grover Cleveland*, II: 250–52. See also Nevins, *Grover Cleveland*, pp. 718–19 and Farquhar, "Intimate Recollections of Grover Cleveland," p. 15.

51. Grover Cleveland, "Fourth Annual Message," December 7, 1896, in Richardson, *A Compilation of the Messages and Papers of the Presidents, 1789–1902*, IX: 721–22.

Chapter 4. Exhaustion of the Passions

1. Gallego, *La insurrección cubana*, p. 257.

2. See José Conangla Fontanilles, *Cuba y Pi y Margall* (La Habana: Editorial Lex, 1947), p. 292; *El Avisador Comercial*, I, June 10, 1895, p. 1.

3. Portillo, *La guerra de Cuba (el primer año). Apuntes*, p. 44.

4. Valeriano Weyler to Ministro de la Guerra, Sept. 20, 1897, in Weyler, *Mi mando en Cuba*, V, p. 113; Isern, *Del desastre nacional y sus causas*, p. 289.

5. Payne, *Politics and the Military in Modern Spain*, p. 76; Reverter Delmas, *Cuba española. Reseña histórica de la insurrección cubana en 1895*, VI, p. 138.

6. Corral, *¡El desastre! Memorias de un voluntario en la campaña de Cuba*, pp. 124–26, 128–29; Isern, *Del desastre nacional y sus causas*, p. 285. See also Walter B. Barker to William R. Day, June 2, 1897, Despatches from U.S. Consuls in Sagua la Grande, 1878–1900, General Records of the Department of State, Record Group 59, National Archives, Washington, D.C. (Hereafter cited as Despatches/Sagua la Grande.)

7. See Reverter Delmas, *Cuba española. Reseña histórica de la insurrección cubana en 1895*, VI: 190–91.

8. Brunner, "Morbidity and Mortality in the Spanish Army in Cuba During the Calendar Year 1897," pp. 411–12; Corral, *¡El desastre! Memorias de un voluntario en la campaña de Cuba*, pp. 124–26.

9. Reverter Delmas, *Cuba española. Reseña histórica de la insurrección cubana en 1895*, VI, p. 192; Souza y Rodríguez, "Triunfo de la revolución cubana," pp. 28–29; "Las bajas del ejército español," *Patria*, Aug. 6, 1898, p. 2.

10. Burguete, *¡La guerra! Cuba. (Diario de un testigo)*, p. 109; Reparaz, *La guerra de Cuba*, pp. 186–97, 197–99; Reverter Delmas, *Cuba española. Reseña histórica de la insurrección cubana en 1895*, II: p. 58.

11. León Aldama del Monte, "The Cuban Insurrection," *Pall Mall Magazine* XII (May, 1897): 118.

12. Souza y Rodríguez, *Máximo Gómez, el generalísimo*, pp. 228–29; Duarte Oropesa, *Historiología cubana*, IV: 229.

13. See Weyler, *Mi mando en Cuba*, II: 55–58; Juan I. Casanova to William R. Rockhill, October 12, 1896, Despatches/Cienfuegos. Walter B. Barker to William R. Day, June 17, 1897, Despatches/Sagua la Grande. See also Bonsal, *The Real Condition of Cuba Today*, pp. 11–12, and Díaz Benzo, *Pequeñeces de la guerra de Cuba por un español*. pp. 56–57.

14. Valeriano Weyler to Ministro de la Guerra, Sept. 20, 1897, in Ortega Rubio, *Historia de la regencia de María Cristina Habsbourg Lorena*, III: 409; Guerra y Sánchez, *Por las veredas del pasado, 1880–1902*, p. 87; Corral, *¡El desastre! Memorias de un voluntario en la campaña de Cuba*, p. 97; El Capitán Verdades, *Historia negra: relato de los escándalos ocurridos en nuestras excolonias durante las últimas guerras* (Barcelona: Casa Editorial Maucci, 1899), pp. 140–41, 245–47.

15. Charles Morris, *The War With Spain*, p. 88.

16. Souza y Rodríguez, *Ensayo histórico sobre la invasión*, p. 186. See also Reparaz, *La guerra de Cuba*, pp. 105–06 and Diaz Benzo, *Pequeñeces de la guerra de Cuba por un español*, pp. 65–70.

17. Estimates of Spanish forces available for field operations vary. Spanish observers estimated about fifty-two thousand; Cubans believed the number to be closer to fifty thousand, while the American Consul in Sagua la Grande estimated "an active available force" of some fifty-seven thousand. See Reverter Delmas, *Cuba española. Reseña histórica de la insurrección cubana en 1895*, VI, p. 155; II: 434; Guerrero, *Crónica de la guerra de Cuba y de Filipinas*, V: 243; Walter B. Barker to William R. Day, September 20, 1897, Despatches/Sagua la Grande.

18. Recent studies of counterinsurgency suggest the need for a vast superiority of conventional military forces over insurgent armies. Estimates vary, but most writers agree that a 25:1 ratio is a necessary minimum, with conventional forces possessed of the capacity to suffer a 15:1 fatality ratio. See John S. Pustay, *Counterinsurgency Warfare* (New York: The Free Press, 1965), pp. 86–87. See also N. I. Klonis, *Guerrilla Warfare: Analysis and Projections* (New York: Robert Speller & Sons, Inc., 1972), pp. 368–77; Julian Paget, *Counter-Insurgency Operations: Techniques of Guerrilla Warfare* (New York: Walker and Company, 1967), pp. 167–68; Napoleon D. Valeriano and Charles T. R. Bohannan, *Counter-Guerrilla Operations* (New York: Frederick A. Praeger, 1962), p. 24; John J. McCuen, *The Art of Counter-Revolutionary War* (Harrisburg, Penn.: Stackpole Books, 1966), p. 124.

19. *London Times*, October 15, 1897, p. 4.

20. Fitzhugh Lee to William R. Day, July 14, 1897, Despatches/Havana.

21. Edwin F. Uhl to assistant secretary of state, July 1, 1895, Despatches from U.S. Consuls in Puerto Rico, 1821–1899, General Records of the Department of State, Record Group 59, National Archives, Washington, D.C. (Hereafter cited as Despatches/Puerto Rico.) See also Isern, *Del desastre nacional y sus causas*, pp. 255–56; Corral, *¡El desastre! Memorias de un voluntario en la campaña de Cuba*, pp. 34–35; Ortega Rubio, *Historia de la regencia de María Cristina Habsbourg-Lorena*, III, p. 199.

22. Montejo, *The Autobiography of a Runaway Slave*, pp. 177–78; Guerrero, *Crónica de la guerra de Cuba y de Filipinas*, V, p. 627.

23. Payne, *Politics and the Military in Modern Spain*, p. 72. See also Walter B. Barker to secretary of state, September 15, 1897, Despatches/Sagua la Grande.

24. Payne, *Politics and the Military in Modern Spain*, p. 76.

25. One soldier later wrote that he served on some twelve different estates during his tour of duty in Cuba. See Corral, *¡El desastre! Memorias de un voluntario en la campaña de Cuba*, pp. 66–67.

26. Isern, *Del desastre nacional y sus causas*, p. 319; Corral, *¡El desastre! Memorias de un voluntario en la campaña de Cuba*, pp. 87–88; Morris, *The War With Spain*, pp. 89–90.

27. Corral, *¡El desastre! Memorias de un voluntario en la campaña de Cuba*, pp. 101–02, 106, 110–12, 115–16, 194–95; Fitzhugh Lee to William Day, June 9, 1897, Despatches/Havana; Cruz, *Estudios históricos*, pp. 80–81.

28. Walter B. Barker to Secretary of State, September 15, 1897, Despatches/Sagua la Grande, and "Statement of Frederick W. Lawrence," May 20, 1896, in U.S. Congress, Senate, *Affairs in Cuba*, pp. 328–29.

29. *London Times*, August 29, 1896, p. 6.

30. Arsenio Martínez Campos to Tomás Castellanos, n.d. [received August 21, 1895], in Ortega Rubio, *Historia de la regencia de María Cristina Habsbourg-Lorena*, II: 475.

31. Souza y Rodríguez, "Triunfo de la revolución cubana," p. 27; *London Times*, August 29, 1896, p. 6.

32. Corral, *¡El desastre! Memorias de un voluntario en la campaña de Cuba*, pp. 56–59. See also Alvarez Díaz, *A Study on Cuba*, pp. 36–38.

33. *New York Journal*, May 26, 1897, p. 7.

34. Walter B. Barker to William R. Day, June 17, 1896, Despatches/Sagua la Grande. See also Portillo, *La guerra de Cuba (el primer año). Apuntes*, p. 140; Muecke Bertel, "Diario de operaciones," p. 132.

35. *New York World*, April 25, 1897, p. 52. See also Bacardí y Moreau, *Crónicas de Santiago de Cuba*, IX, pp. 327–28; Weyler y López de Pugna, *En el archivo de mi abuelo. Biografía del Capitán General Weyler*, p. 97; *New York Journal*, January 5, 1898, p. 7. By mid-1896, the insurgent provisional government was encouraging Spanish officers and soldiers to desert. Soldiers deserting with their arms and ammunition received ten *pesos* in gold. Officers' ranks would be honored in the Liberation Army. All would be compensated after the

war with an allocation of land, with their families to be later transported to Cuba at the republic's expense. See Máximo Gómez to Tomás Estrada Palma, Mar. 23, 1897, *Boletín del Archivo Nacional*, XXX (Jan.–Dec., 1931). 54.

36. Fitzhugh Lee to William R. Day, July 14, 1897, Personal Correspondence, General Lee to the secretary of state, 1897–1898, John Bassett Moore Papers.

37. Antonio Maceo to María Cabrales de Maceo, Aug. 20, 1895, in Cabrales, ed., *Espistolario de heroes. Cartas y documentos históricos*, p. 80. (Hereafter cited as *Cartas y documentos históricos.*)

38. Antonio Maceo to María Cabrales de Maceo, Nov. 20, 1895, *Cartas y documentos históricos*, pp. 84–85.

39. Antonio Maceo to José Maceo, Nov. 30, 1895, in Maceo, *Cartas y otros documentos*, II: 173.

40. Llorens y Maceo, *Con Maceo en la invasión*, p. 71. See also Piedra Martel, *Memorias de un mambí*, p. 104; Valeriano Weyler to ministro de la guerra, Sept. 20, 1896, in Weyler, *Mi mando en Cuba*, V: 113; Fernando Gómez, *La insurrección por dentro. Apuntes para la historia*, p. xxvi; Corona Ferrer, *De la manigua (ecos de la epopeya)*, pp. 42–43.

41. Pérez Abreú, *En la guerra con Máximo Gómez*, pp. 17–106. See also Manuel Bueno y Javaloyes, *El 1er batallón de María Cristina en el Camagüey*, pp. 19–80.

42. Richard Harding Davis, *A Year From a Reporter's Notebook*, p. 120. See also Gonzales, *In Darkest Cuba*, p. 233, and Batrell Oviedo, *Para la historia. Apuntes autobiográficos*, pp. 45–53.

43. Walter B. Barker to William R. Day, June 17, 1897, Despatches/Sagua la Grande.

44. Fitzhugh Lee to William R. Day, August 25, 1897, Personal Correspondence, General Lee to the secretary of state, 1897–1898, Moore Papers.

45. The guerrilla assault on the cities, as well as the increase in formal military engagements, by which time guerrilla columns have captured heavy arms, has been the hallmark of a successful insurgency entering the final stages of military operations. See Ernesto Che Guevara, *Guerrilla Warfare* (New York: Monthly Review Press, 1961), pp. 73–75; Vo Nguyen Giap, *People's War, People's Army* (New York: Praeger, 1962), pp. 90–97. Mao Tse-Tung spoke of the "encirclement of the cities" as the final stage of a people's war. See William J. Pomeroy, ed., *Guerrilla Warfare and Marxism* (New York: International Publishers, 1968), p. 198.

46. The insurgent conquest of Victoria de las Tunas sent shock waves across the Atlantic and led many in Spain to believe that the eastern half of the island had fallen fully to the insurgent armies. For a discussion of the impact of Las Tunas in Spain see Maura y Gamazo, *Historia crítica del reinado de Don Alfonso XIII durante su menoridad bajo la regencia de su madre Doña María Cristina de Austria*, I: 332–33; Reverter Delmas, *Cuba española. Reseña histórica de la insurrección cubana en 1895*, V: 834–35; Fernández Almagro, *Historia política de la España contemporánea*, II: 425–26; *New York Journal*, September 13, 1897, p. 4.

47. Luis Miranda y de la Rúa, *Con Martí y con Calixto García (recuerdos de un mambí del 95)*, p. 77; Gutiérrez, *Oriente heroico*, p. 62; Lores y Llorens, *Relatos históricos de la guerra del 95*, pp. 41–51.

48. "José Fernández Lozada, Inspector General de Sanidad Militar, explicando el estado en que había quedado el Ejército de Cuba al dejar el mando General Weyler," Dec. 5, 1897, in Amblard, *Notas coloniales*, pp. 150–51.

49. *New York Times*, September 20, 1897, p. 1.

50. Harrison, "Catalan Business and the Loss of Cuba, 1898–1914," p. 433; Houghton, "The Political Condition of Spain," p. 182; Carrera Pujal, *Historia política de Cataluña en el siglo XIX*, VI: 179–95.

51. *New York Times*, July 11, 1898, p. 2. See also Pi y Margall and Pi y Arsuaga, *Historia de España en el siglo XIX*, VII: 567.

52. *London Times*, August 24, 1896, p. 3. See also Vladimirov, *La diplomacia de los Estados Unidos durante la guerra hispano-americana*, p. 40.

53. See "Discurso del Excelentísimo D. Práxedes Mateo Sagasta ante los minorías liberales," 19 de mayo de 1897, in O'Donnell y Abreu, *Apuntes del ex-Ministro de Estado Duque de Tetuán*, II, p. 32, and Figueroa y Torres, *Obras completas del Conde de Romanones*, I: 112–13.

54. Carrera Pujal, *Historia política de Cataluña en el siglo XIX*, V, pp. 184–85; Ortega Rubio, *Historia de la regencia de María Cristina Habsbourg-Lorena*, III: 62–63.

55. *La Discusión*, Apr. 11, 1896, enclosure in Ramon O. Williams to William R. Rockhill, April 13, 1896, Despatches/Havana.

56. Conangla Fontanilles, *Cuba y Pi y Margall*, p. 284.

57. Reverter Delmas, *Cuba española. Reseña histórica de la insurrección cubana en 1895*, II: 236–39; Conangla Fontanilles, *Cuba y Pi y Margall*, p. 284.

58. Ramón Emeterio Betances to Tomás Estrada Palma, Sept. 18, 1896, Llaverías y Martínez, ed., *Correspondencia de la delegación*, III: 70.

59. Interview with Angel Fernández, Tampa, Florida, February 19, 1974. Angel Fernández, ninety-two years of age at the time of this interview, left Galicia at the age of fifteen to avoid "belonging to the King." He arrived at Tampa and found a community of compatriots who had earlier fled Spain and Cuba to avoid military service.

60. Ortega Rubio, *Historia de la regencia de María Cristina Habsbourg-Lorena*, III: 62–63; *Washington Post*, October 27, 1897, p. 1.

61. Pi y Margall and Pi y Arguaga, *Historia de España en el siglo XIX*, VII, pp. 902–03; Reverter Delmas, *Cuba española. Reseña histórica de la insurrección cubana en 1895*, VI: 148–49.

62. Emilio Castelar to Adolfo Calzado, Oct. 12, 1895, in Castelar, *Correspondencia de Emilio Castelar, 1868–1898*, pp. 357–60.

63. Melchor Ferrer, *Historia del tradicionalismo español*, XXVIII, p. 201–38; Miguel M. Cuadrado, *Elecciones y partidos políticos de España*, 2 vols. (Madrid : Taurus Ediciones, S.A., 1969), II, pp. 575–612; Martín, *Veinte años con Don Carlos*, pp. 214–17.

64. Ramón Emeterio Betances to Tomás Estrada Palma, Sept. 9, 1897, *Correspondencia de la delegación*, III: 108.

65. Fernández Almagro, *Historia política de la España contemporánea*, II: 389.

66. Ortego Rubio, *Historia de la regencia de María Cristina Habsbourg-Lorena*, III: 38–39; Pi y Margall and Pi y Arsuaga, *Historia de España en el siglo XIX*, VII: 281; Maura y Gamazo, *Historia crítica del reinado de Don Alfonso XIII durante su menoridad bajo la regencia de su madre*, I: 298–99.

67. Hannis Taylor to Richard Olney, January 8, 1897, Despatches/Spain.

68. See Valdés Domínguez, *Diario de soldado* III: 253.

69. Fitzhugh Lee to William R. Day, July 14, 1897, Despatches/Havana.

70. William Woodford to William McKinley, October 20, 1897, Despatches/Spain. See also Dillon, "The Ruin of Spain," pp. 876–907 and Conangla Fontanilles, *Cuba y Pi y Margall*, pp. 101–02.

Chapter 5. An Imperfect Consensus

1. José Martí to Federico Henríquez y Carbajal, Mar. 25, 1895, in Martí, *Obras completas*, I: 248.

2. See "Resoluciones tomadas por la emigración cubana de Tampa," Nov. 28, 1891, in José

Martí, *El Partido Revolucionario Cubano y la guerra*, pp. 1–3; "Bases del Partido Revolucionario Cubano," Jan. 5, 1892, in ibid., pp. 3–4; "El Manifiesto de Montecristi," Mar. 25, 1895, in ibid, pp. 263–70. See also José Martí, "La guerra," Jan. 9, 1892, in Martí, *Obras completas*, I: 2, pp. 431–33; José Martí, "La revolución," Mar. 16, 1894, in ibid., pp. 459–64. For further discussions of Martí's view of armed struggle see Mario Mencia, "La concepción de la guerra en Martí," *Bohemia*, LXVII (Feb. 21, 1975): 4–9; Sergio Aguirre "El concepto de la revolución de Martí," *Juventud Rebelde*, Nov. 19, 1975, p. 3, and Nov. 20, 1975, p. 3; Maldonado Denis, "Martí y su concepto de la revolución"; Francisco Pividal Padrón, "Martí: la guerra justa y la emigración," *Granma*, Jan. 25, 1974, p. 2; Samuel Feijoo, "La guerra culta de José Martí," *Bohemia* LV (May 16, 1963): 26–27; Estela Izquierdo, "La necesidad de la lucha armada en la obra de José Martí," *Granma*, Mar. 8, 1973, p. 3; Marcos Llanos, "Creación e intención del Partido Revolucionario Cubano," pp. 206–07.

3. Ponte Domínguez, *Historia de la guerra de los diez años*, pp. 27–29, 184–89; Rodríguez, *Estudio histórico sobre el origen, desenvolvimiento y manifestaciones prácticas de la idea de la anexión de la isla de Cuba a los Estados Unidos de America*, pp. 220–335.

4. Herminio Portell Vilá, "Anexionismo," *Humanismo* VII (Jan.–Apr. 1959): 28–42. García Valdés, *La idea de la anexión de Cuba a los Estados Unidos*, pp. 39–40; Ibarra, *Ideología mambisa*, pp. 44–50.

5. A Cuban, "A Plea for the Annexation of Cuba," *Forum* XXX (October, 1900): 204–07.

6. Figueras, "Cuba Libre, Independence or Annexation," p. 424.

7. Roig de Leuchsenring, *La guerra libertadora cubana de los treinta años, 1868–1898: razón de su victoria*, p. 173.

8. Luis Placé to Richard Olney, March 20, 1896, Richard Olney Papers.

9. Tomás Estrada Palma to Benigno and Plácido Gener, Jan. 13, 1878, in Estrada Palma, *Desde el Castillo de Figueras. Cartas de Estrada Palma (1877–1878)*, pp. 72–75; Camacho, *Estrada Palma, el gobernante honrado*, p. 93; Carlos Márquez Sterling, *Don Tomás (biografía de una época)*, p. 147.

10. Tomás Estrada Palma to Andrés Moreno de la Torre, Feb. 1, 1898, in Manuel Sanguily, "Sobre la génesis de la Enmienda Platt."

11. José Martí to Gonzalo de Quesada, Nov. 12, 1889, in Martí, *Obras completas*, III: 190.

12. José Martí to Serafín Bello, Nov. 16, 1889, in ibid., I, pt. 2, p. 392.

13. José Martí to Ricardo Rodríguez Otero, May 16, 1886, in ibid., I, pt. 2, p. 410.

14. José Martí to Gonzalo de Quesada, Oct. 19, 1889, in ibid., I, pt. 2, p. 655.

15. José Martí to Ricardo Rodríguez Otero, May 16, 1886, in ibid., I, pt. 2, p. 410.

16. José Martí to Máximo Gómez, Dec. 16, 1887, in ibid., I, pt. 1, pp. 91–92.

17. José Martí to Gonzalo de Quesada, Dec. 14, 1889, in ibid., III, p. 97.

18. José Martí to Gonzalo de Quesada, Oct. 19, 1889, in ibid., I, pt. 2, p. 656. See also Roig de Leuchsenring, *Martí anti-imperialista*, pp. 8–9.

19. Ibarra, *Ideología mambisa*, p. 65; Roig de Leuchsenring, "Ideario de la revolución"; idem, *1895 y 1898. Dos guerras cubanas. Ensayo de revaloración*, p. 87.

20. Núñez de Villavicencio, *Aventuras emocionantes de un emigrado revolucionario cubano*, p. 85.

21. Portuondo del Prado, *Historia de Cuba*, p. 438.

22. George W. Van Vleck, *The Panic of 1857* (New York: Columbia University Press, 1943), p. 104.

23. LeRiverend Brusone, *Historia económica de Cuba*, pp. 167–196.

24. For the early antecedents of cigar manufacturing in Key West see Castellanos García, *Motivos de Cayo Hueso (contribución a la historia de las emigraciones revolucionarias cubanas en los Estados Unidos)*.

25. Deulofeo y Lleonart, *Heroes del destierro. La emigración*, pp. 11–15.

26. Thomas, *Cuba, the Pursuit of Freedom*, p. 291.

27. Jefferson B. Browne, *Key West: The Old and The New* (St. Augustine: 1912), pp. 117–18. See also Leon, "The Cigar Industry and Cigar Leaf Tobacco in Florida During the Nineteenth Century" (unpublished M.A. thesis).

28. Rivero Muñiz, "Los cubanos en Tampa," pp. 29–35.

29. See José Luciano Franco, "Panamá: refugio de la rebeldía cubana en el siglo XIX"; Clara del Claro Valle, "Los exiliados en Honduras, *El Mundo*, June 29, 1967, p. 40.

30. *New York Herald*, December 16, 1897, p. 11.

31. *The State*, July 29, 1898, p. 2.

32. Flint, *Marching with Gómez*, p. 226.

33. Bonsal, *The Fight for Santiago*, pp. 532–33.

34. Hernández Corujo, *Organización civil y política de las revoluciones cubanas de 1868 y 1895*, pp. 75–86; "Constitución de la República de Cuba," in Cuba, Consejo de Gobierno, *Recopilación de las leyes, reglamentos, decretos y demas disposiciones dictadas por el Consejo de Gobierno de la República de Cuba*, pp. 9–12.

35. Collazo, *La guerra en Cuba*, pp. 19–20; Rey, *Recuerdos de la guerra. 1895–1898*, pp. 15–16; Ramiro Cabrera, *A sitio Herrera*, pp. 198–99; Rubens, "The Insurgent Government in Cuba." For representative civil ordinances see "Ley para el gobierno civil de la República de Cuba," in Cuba, Consejo de Gobierno, *Recopilación de las leyes, reglamentos, decretos y demas disposicions dictadas por el Consejo de Gobierno de la República de Cuba*, pp. 15–27; "Ley para la hacienda pública de la República de Cuba," ibid., pp. 31–32; and "Ley de matrimonio," in ibid., pp. 35–42.

36. For various accounts of the conference at La Mejorana see Griñán Peralta, *Antonio Maceo, análisis caracterológico*, pp. 57–58; Collazo, *Cuba independiente*, pp. 137–39; Castellanos García, *Resplandores epicos*.

37. José Martí, "Diario," in Martí, *Obras completas*, I, pt. 2, pp. 285–87.

38. José Martí to Manuel Mercado, May 18, 1895, in Martí, *Obras completas*, I, pt. 2, p. 273.

39. See Azcuy Alón, *El Partido Revolucionario y la independencia de Cuba*, pp. 112–13.

40. See Máximo Gómez, *Diario de campaña de mayor general Máximo Gómez*, pp. 352–60.

41. In Raúl Aparicio, *Hombradía de Antonio Maceo* (Havana: Editorial Unión, 1967), pp. 486–87.

42. In Griñán Peralta, *El carácter de Máximo Gómez*, pp. 150–68. See also Costa y Blanco, *Perfil político de Calixto García*, pp. 19–24. See also Ramón de Armas, *La revolución pospuesta* (Havana: Editorial de Ciencias Sociales, 1975), pp. 82–91.

43. See Valdés Domínguez, *Diario de soldado*, I, pp. 144–45.

44. Llaverías y Martínez and Santovenia, eds., *Actas de las Asambleas de Representantes y del Consejo de Gobierno durante la guerra de independencia*, I: 68. See also Hernández Corujo, *Historia constitucional de Cuba*, I, pp. 315–16.

45. The most controversial case involved General José María ("Mayía") Rodríguez who, relieved of his command in the west by Gómez, was subsequently reinstated by the Council of Government. See Horrego Estuch, *Máximo Gómez, libertador y ciudadano*.

46. *Actas de las Asambleas*, II, p. 23.

47. Ibid., III: 64–65.

48. Hernández Corujo, *Historia constitucional de Cuba*, I: 315–16; Horrego Estuch, *Máximo Gómez, libertador y ciudadano*, pp. 189–90. See also Reyna Cossio, *Estudios histórico-militares sobre la guerra de independencia de Cuba*, p. 88; Rubens, *Liberty, The Story of Cuba*, pp. 270–74.

49. In Despradel, "Máximo Gómez y la campaña del 97," p. 313. See also Varona Guerrero, *La guerra de independencia de Cuba, 1895–1899*, III: 1700–01, and Collazo, *La guerra en Cuba*, pp. 3–5.

50. Hastings, "With Gómez in the Cuban Skirmishes," p. 157.

51. In Flint, *Marching with Gómez*, p. 195.

52. Rea, *Facts and Fakes About Cuba*, pp. 258–59.

53. Armas, *La revolución pospuesta*, pp. 94–101; "La guerra de 1895," pp. 554–55.

54. Rubens, *Liberty, The Story of Cuba*, p. 113.

55. Máximo Gómez, *Revoluciones . . . Cuba y hogar*, p. 13; José Manuel Carbonell, "La lucha por la independencia de Cuba (1810–1898)," in Ricardo Levene, *Historia de América*, 10 vols. (Buenos Aires: W.M. Jackson, Inc., 1940), VII: 363.

56. Antonio Maceo to Angel del Castillo, Nov. 11, 1895, in Souza y Rodríguez, *Ensayo histórico sobre la invasión*, p. 89; Antonio Maceo to Francisco Estrada, Dec. 4, 1895, in Maceo, *Cartas y otros documentos*, II: 44. Carbonell y Rivero, *Resumen de una vida heroica*, p. 35. Academia de la Historia de Cuba, *Crónicas de la guerra de Cuba*, p. 50; Llorens y Maceo, *Con Maceo en la invasión*, p. 65.

57. Matías Duque, *Nuestra patria* (Havana: Imprenta Montalvo, Cárdenas & Ca., 1923), p. 144; Kunz, *La guerra hispano-americana*, p. 12; Kiple, *Blacks in Colonial Cuba, 1774–1899*, p. 81; Fermoselle, *Política y color en Cuba*, p. 26.

58. One of the central purposes of the PRC, Martí insisted, was to prevent patrician ascendency within separatist ranks, as had occurred in 1868. "Under no circumstances," Martí explained in 1892, "do we want to inaugurate either a partial war from above, that leaves the popular elements without sufficient representation and without whose participation in Cuba and abroad the revolution is impossible, or a partial war from below, which to win converts makes immoral and lamentable commitments with some classes of society against others." See José Martí to Gerardo Castellanos, Aug. 4, 1892, in Martí, *Obras completas*, I, pt. 2, p. 575.

59. José Martí to Gonzalo de Quesada, July 6, 1885, in Martí, *Obras completas*, I, p. 2, p. 503.

60. José Martí, "Nuestras ideas," Mar. 14, 1892 in Martí, *El Partido Revolucionario Cubano y la guerra*, pp. 12–13.

61. José Martí to Antonio Maceo, July 20, 1882, in Martí, *Obras completas*, I, pt. 1, p. 77.

62. José Martí to Rafael Serra, March, 1891, in True, "Revolutionaries in Exile: The Cuban Revolutionary Party, 1891–1898" (unpublished Ph.D. Dissertation), p. 60.

63. José Martí, "Nuestras ideas," Mar. 14, 1897, in Martí, *El Partido Revolucionario Cubano y la guerra*, p. 19. See also José Martí to Máximo Gómez, Sept. 13, 1892, in Martí, *Obras completas*, I, pt. 1, p. 99.

64. José Martí, "Con todos y para el bien de todos," Nov. 26, 1891, in Martí, *Obras completas*, I, pt. 2, p. 705.

65. José Martí, "Guatemala," in Martí, *Obras completas*, III: 220.

66. José Martí, "El Partido Revolucionario a Cuba," May 27, 1893, in Martí, *Obras completas*, I: 345. See also Manuel Navarro Luna, "Martí y la reforma agraria," *Hoy Domingo*, May 20, 1962, p. 2, and Pedro Pablo Rodríguez, "La idea de liberación nacional en José Martí," pp. 160–65.

67. José Martí, "Con todos y para el bien de todos," Nov. 26, 1891, in Martí, *Obras completas*, I, pt. 2, pp. 697–706.

68. José Martí, "Nuestra America," Sept. 27, 1889, in Martí, *Obras completas*, III: 109.

69. Torres-Cuevas, "La revolución necesaria," pp. 87–88; Matías Duque, *Nuestra patria*, p. 144; Delahoza, "Los comienzos del 95," p. 341: Raúl Roa, *Aventuras, venturas, y desventuras de un mambí*, p. 254.

Chapter 6. Convergence and Divergence in Cuban Separatism

1. José Martí, "El Partido Revolucionario a Cuba," May 27, 1893, in Martí, *Obras completas*, I, pt. 2, pp. 336–44.

2. José Martí, "La crisis y el Partido Revolucionario Cubano," Aug. 19, 1893, in Martí,

Obras completas, I, pt. 2, p. 667. See also José Martí, "Las expediciones, y la revolución," Aug. 6, 1892, in Martí, *El Partido Revolucionario Cubano y la guerra*, pp. 64–66.

3. See Varona, "El objetivo fundamental de servicio exterior," p. 2; Guerra y Sánchez, *Historia de la nación cubana*, VI: 365–405; Luz León, *La diplomacia de la manigua: Betances*, pp. 253–64. In Europe, "consular" agencies were established in France, Italy, England, Germany, Austria, Belgium, and Russia. In Latin America, agents operated in Mexico, Central America, Santo Domingo, Haiti, Venezuela, Colombia, Bolivia, Ecuador, Peru, Chile, Argentina, Uruguay, and Brazil. In the United States, Cuban "consulates" were established in virtually every major city east of the Mississippi River. See Estrada Palma, "The Work of the Cuban Delegation," pp. 403–21; Casasús, *La emigración cubana y la independencia de la patria* pp. 264–65; Raymond A. Detter, "The Cuban Junta and Michigan, 1895–1898," *Michigan History*, LVIII (March, 1964): 35–46.

4. See Tomás Estrada Palma to Editor, *New York Journal*, January 8, 1896, p. 1.

5. Tomás Estrada Palma to Antonio Maceo, Dec. 10, 1895, in Maceo, *Antonio Maceo: Documentos para su vida*, pp. 158–59. (Hereafter cited as *Documentos*.)

6. *New York Journal*, May 14, 1897, p. 4.

7. *New York Herald*, January 14, 1898, p. 3. See also Carlos Márquez Sterling, *Don Tomás (biografía de una época)*, p. 282. See also Juan Gualberto Gómez, "La revolución del '95," in *La lucha anti-imperialista en Cuba*, 2 vols. (Havana: Editora Popular de Cuba y del Caribe, 1960), I: 10–12; True, "Revolutionaries in Exile: The Cuban Revolutionary Party, 1891–1898" (unpublished Ph.D. diss.), p. 229.

8. Antonio Maceo to Federico Pérez Carbó, July 14, 1896, in Maceo, *El pensamiento vivo de Maceo*, p. 94. See also Antonio Maceo to Diego González, June 12, 1896, in Maceo, *Cartas y otros documentos*, ed. II:269.

9. Calixto García to Gonzalo de Quesada, May 13, 1897, in Roig de Leuchsenring, *La guerra libertadora cubana de los treinta años, 1868–1898: razón de su victoria*, p. 186.

10. Antonio Maceo to Alberto J. Díaz, July 15, 1896, *Cartas y otros documentos*, II:304–05.

11. Máximo Gómez to Tomás Estrada Palma, Nov. 8, 1895, in Máximo Gómez, *Ideario cubano*, p. 41. See also Roig de Leuchsenring, *Tradición antimperialista de nuestra historia*, p. 60.

12. Máximo Gómez to Tomás Estrada Palma, Mar. 19, 1896, in Gómez, *Ideario cubano*, p. 51.

13. In Flint, *Marching With Gómez* p. 189. See also Hernández y Pérez, *Dos conferencias históricas*, p. 68. Maceo also characterized himself as "one of those who says if it comes fine, if not, fine, too." See Antonio Maceo to Tomás Estrada Palma, Nov. 21, 1895, *Cartas y otros documentos*, II:154. See also Miró Argenter, *Crónicas de la guerra*, III:46–48.

14. Antonio Maceo to José Dolores Poyo, July 16, 1896, *Cartas y otros documentos*, II:306.

15. *New York Journal*, March 8, 1897, p. 5.

16. In Foner, *The Spanish-Cuban-American War and the Birth of American Imperialism*, I:147.

17. Valdés Domínguez, *Diario de soldado*, III:209.

18. Boza, *Mi diario de la guerra*, I:270–71; Roig de Leuchsenring, *Máximo Gómez: el libertador de Cuba y el primer ciudadano de la república*, pp. 42–44; Horrego Estuch, *Máximo Gómez, libertador y ciudadano*, p. 198.

19. Richardson, ed., *A Compilation of the Messages and Papers of the Presidents, 1789–1902*, IX:591.

20. *New York Tribune*, April 9, 1898, p. 6.

21. Rubens, *Liberty, The Story of Cuba*, p. 188. See also O'Brien, *A Captain Unafraid*, pp. 36–80.

22. José Martí to Gonzalo de Quesada and Benjamín Guerra, Apr. 26, 1895, in Martí, *El Partido Revolucionario Cubano y la guerra*, pp. 278–79.

23. Francisco Palomares to Benjamín Guerra, Oct. 31, 1895, in Primelles, ed., *La revolución del 95 según la correspondencia de la delegación cubana en Nueva York*, II:69. (Hereafter cited as *Correspondencia de la delegación.*)

24. Valdés Domínguez, *Diario de soldado*, I:197–98.

25. José María Rodríguez to Gonzalo de Quesada, Mar. 29, 1896, in Quesada, *Archivo de Gonzalo de Quesada*, II:189.

26. José Maceo to Benjamín Guerra, June 23, 1895, *Correspondencia de la delegación*, I:160.

27. Antonio Maceo to Tomás Estrada Palma, Mar. 21, 1896, III:357.

28. Antonio Maceo to Tomás Estrada Palma, Apr. 14, 1896, *Boletín del Archivo Nacional* XXII (Jan.–Dec., 1923): 226–27. See also Antonio Maceo to José María Rodríguez, July 17, 1896, in Acosta León, *La revolución en Camagüey (1895–1896). Ruta y anecdotario de Máximo Gómez*, p. 114.

29. Antonio Maceo to Máximo Gómez, June 27, 1896, in Griñán Peralta, *Antonio Maceo, análisis caracterológico*, p. 191. See also Zarragoita Ledesma, *Biografía de Antonio Maceo*, p. 102.

30. *New York World*, January 18, 1897, pp. 1, 2. The correspondent interviewing General Rius Rivera added: "The boat which brought the *The World* correspondent to this coast might have landed a cargo of arms and ammunition if that had been the purpose of the expedition. But the Cubans in New York on whom the war so much depends, do not seem to be able to do what *The World* has done." Ibid. For insurgent accounts of the shortages during the western campaign see Llorens y Maceo, *Con Maceo en la invasión*, pp. 122–23; Rosell, "Diario de operaciones del comandante Eduardo Rosell, jefe de Estado Mayor del Brigadier Pedro Betancourt," pp. 171–72; Piedra Martel, *Memorias de un mambí*, pp. 101–03; Nestor Carbonell y Rivero, *Resumen de una vida heroica* (Havana: Imprenta "El Siglo XX," 1945), pp. 35–36; Pedro G. Subirats, *Un mensaje a Estrada Palma. Episodio de la guerra de independencia de Cuba* (Havana: Editorial Guerrero, 1937).

31. See Trelles y Govín, *Matanzas en la independencia de Cuba*, pp. 55–81; Souza y Rodríguez, *Biografía de un regimiento mambí: el regimiento 'Calixto García.' Discurso*, pp. 113–33; Santovenia, *Pinar del Río*, pp. 184–86; José Rivero Muñiz, *Vereda Nueva* (La Habana: Instituto de Historia, 1964), pp. 84–85; Guerra y Sánchez, *Por las veredas del pasado, 1880–1902*, pp. 37–38; Miró Argenter, *Crónicas de la guerra*, II:25.

32. Antonio Maceo to director, *Washington Star*, Jan. 27, 1896, in Maceo, *El pensamiento vivo de Maceo*, p. 57. This estimate was corroborated by Spanish military officials. See Fernández Almagro, *Historia política de la España contemporánea*, II:260. Fernando Gómez, *La insurección por dentro. Apuntes para la historia*, pp. 195–96, 210.

33. See Souza y Rodríguez, *Ensayo histórico sobre la invasión*, pp. 76–77.

34. Giberga, *Obras de Eliseo Giberga*, III:236–37.

35. Raimundo Cabrera to José Ignacio Rodríguez, Jan. 21, 1896, José Ignacio Rodríguez Papers.

36. Camacho, *Marta Abreu, una mujer comprendida*, pp. 173–95; M. García Garofalo y Mesa, *Marta Abreu Arencibia y el Dr. Luis Estévez y Romero* (La Habana: Imprenta y Librería "La Moderna Poesía," 1925), pp. 129–30; Pérez Cabrera, *Una cubana ejemplar: Marta Abreu de Estévez*, pp. 20–21; Veitia Ferrer, *Marta G. Abreu, la cubana excelsa*, pp. 121–22; Estrade, "L'emigration cubaine de Paris (1895–1898)."

37. Giberga, *Obras de Eliseo Giberga*, III:241–43; Portillo, *La guerra de Cuba (el primer año). Apuntes*, p. 203; Roig de Leuchsenring, *Weyler en Cuba* p. 54; Rivero Muñiz, "Los cubanos en Tampa," p. 89; Reverter Delmas, *Cuba española*, III:454–60; Harris, "Some Economic Aspects of the Cuban Insurrection," p. 441.

38. Fitzhugh Lee to William Rockwell, July 3, 1896, Despatches/Havana.

39. Francisco Pi y Margall and Francisco Pi y Arsuaga, *Historia de España en el siglo XIX*,

VII:362; Conangla Fontanilles, *Cuba y Pi y Margall*, pp. 309–10; Marcos García, *Carta-folleto a José Gálvez*, p. 57.

40. Bashkina, "A Page From the Cuban People's Heroic History," p. 122.

41. Willets, *The Triumph of Yankee Doodle*, pp. 171–72.

42. In Havana, the Autonomist party leadership in the *Junta Central* warned Spanish authorities that local excesses would serve only to weaken the party and drive autonomists into separatist ranks. For accounts of local harassment of Autonomists see Antonio de Castineyra to José María Gálvez, Apr. 11, 1895, *Boletín del Archivo Nacional*, XXVI (Jan.–Dec., 1927), pp. 224–25; Antonio de Castineyra to José María Gálvez, May 4, 1895, Ibid., pp. 229–30; Emilio Rodríguez y Abreu to José María Gálvez, June 23, 1895, ibid., p. 243; Francisco Sánchez to José María Gálvez, Aug. 9, 1895, ibid., pp. 251–52.

43. A. M. Zamora to José María Gálvez, Feb. 28, 1895, ibid., p. 208.

44. Varona, *De la colonia a la república*, p. 157.

45. Antonio Maceo derived great pleasure at seeing Autonomists of such stature turn "separatists from night to morning." See Antonio Maceo to Diego González, June 24, 1896, *Cartas y otros documentos*, II:283.

46. See "Discurso del Señor Gabriel Camps," in *Propaganda cubana. Por la independencia*, p. 52.

47. Cristóbal N. Madan to Ramon O. Williams, January 24, 1896, Despatches/Havana.

48. Ramon O. Williams to Edwin F. Uhl, January 28, 1896, Despatches/Havana.

49. Juárez y Cano, *Apuntes de Camagüey*, p. 208; Avelino Sanjenís, *Mis cartas, memorias de la revolución de 1895 por la independencia de Cuba* (Sagua la Grande: Imprenta "El Comercio," 1900), pp. 184–85; 203–08.

50. These developments conform generally to the conditions that Barrington Moore suggests precipitate peasant revolution. "What infuriates peasants," Moore suggests, ". . . is a new and sudden imposition or demand that strikes many people at once and that is a break with accepted rules and customs. . . . Under these conditions individual grievances in a flash, become apparent as collective ones. If the impact is of the right kind (sudden, widespread, yet not so severe as to make collective resistance seem hopeless from the start), it can ignite the solidarity of rebellion or revolution in any kind of peasant society." See Barrington Moore, Jr., *Social Origins of Dictatorship and Democracy* (Boston: Beacon Press, 1966), pp. 474–75.

51. José María Rodríguez to Gonzalo de Quesada, Mar. 20, 1896, in Quesada, *Archivo de Gonzalo de Quesada*, II:188. See also Antomarchi, *Life with the Cubans*, p. 17; Máximo Gómez, "Las tres faces principales de la guerra de Cuba," in Máximo Gómez, *Papeles dominicanos de Máximo Gómez*, p. 67.

52. Antonio Maceo to Federico Pérez Carbó, Nov. 19, 1896, *Cartas y otros documentos*, II:350–51. See also Salvador Cisneros Betancourt to Miguel Betancourt, Mar. 3, 1896, *Correspondencia de la delegación*, III: 164.

53. Valdés Domínguez, *Diario de soldado*, I:209.

54. Fitzhugh Lee to William R. Day, June 12, 1897, Personal Correspondence, General Lee to the secretary of state, 1897–1898, John Bassett Moore Papers.

55. See Sánchez, *Julián Sánchez cuenta su vida*, pp. 27–37, 50–51.

56. Valdés Domínguez, *Diario de Soldado*, I:197. See also Sanjenís, *Mis cartas, memorias de la revolución de 1895 por la independencia de Cuba*, p. 123; "It is necessary that the Revolution be felt everywhere," Colonel Fermín Valdés Domínguez wrote in his diary. "This is a measure that affects Spanish commerce in Guantánamo and Santiago de Cuba. To those wretched people it is necessary to wage war against their pockets." See Valdés Domínguez, *Diario de soldado*, II:68.

57. José María Rodríguez, José Martí, and Enrique Collazo, "Plan de alzamiento," Dec. 8, 1895, in Martí, *El Partido Revolucionario Cubano y la guerra*, pp. 235–37 and José Martí and Máximo Gómez, "El Manifiesto de Montecristi," Mar. 25, 1895, ibid., pp. 263–70.

58. José Martí and Máximo Gómez, "Circular a los jefes," Apr. 26, 1895, in Martí, *El Partido Revolucionario Cubano y la guerra*, pp. 282–83.

59. José Martí and Máximo Gómez, "Circular: la política de la guerra," Apr. 28, 1895, in ibid., pp. 286–87.

60. Antonio Maceo to Secretario de la Guerra, Nov. 26, 1895, *Cartas y otros documentos*, II:170–72. See also Lateulade, *Apuntes de la Delegación de Hacienda del distrito de Guantánamo*, passim.

61. Ojeda, "Antecedentes de la guerra de 1895 en Oriente," and Gutiérrez Fernández, *Los heroes de 24 de febrero*, p. 5.

62. Máximo Gómez to Tomás Estrada Palma, Aug. 22, 1895, *Boletín del Archivo Nacional* XXI (Jan.–Dec., 1922): 173–74.

63. Máximo Gómez to Tomás Estrada Palma, Nov. 25, 1895, *Boletín del Archivo Nacional* XXII (Jan.–Dec., 1923): 222.

64. Santovenia, *Gómez el máximo*, pp. 16–17; Ponte Domínguez, "La invasión," p. 349; Giberga, *Obras de Eliseo Giberga*, III: 233–34; Miró Argenter, *Crónicas de la guerra*, I:30.

65. Carlos M. Trelles, "El azúcar y la independencia," *Patria*, Mar. 20, 1897, p. 2.

66. Antonio Maceo to Tomás Estrada Palma, Mar. 24, 1896, *Cartas y otros documentos*, II:222–23 and Antonio Maceo to Tomás Estrada Palma, Apr. 14, 1896, *Documentos*, pp. 137–38.

67. In Souza y Rodríguez, *Ensayo histórico sobre la invasión*, pp. 75–76.

68. In Barquín, *Las luchas guerrilleras en Cuba. De la colonia a la Sierra Maestra*, I:22.

69. Máximo Gómez, "Circular del General en Jefe del Ejército Libertador dirigido a los hacendados y ganaderos," July 1, 1895, in Máximo Gómez, *Algunos documentos políticos de Máximo Gómez*, p. 16. (Hereafter cited as *Algunos documentos políticos*.)

70. Máximo Gómez, "Circular," Nov. 6, 1895, *Algunos documentos políticos*, p. 16. See also Horrego Estuch, *Máximo Gómez, libertador y ciudadano*, pp. 158–59; idem, "Máximo Gómez: el militar y el ciudadano," p. 94; Souza y Rodríguez, *Ensayo histórico sobre la invasión*, pp. 75–76.

71. Máximo Gómez, "Orden General del dia 21 de febrero de 1897," in Valdés Domínguez, *Diario de soldado*, III:64.

72. Maxímo Gómez, "Circular," Nov. 6, 1895, *Algunos documentos políticos*, p. 16.

73. Tomás Estrada Palma to Carlos Roloff, Nov. 16, 1895, *Correspondencia de la delegación cubana*, II:179.

74. Antonio Maceo, "Relación de las cantidades recaudades en el Departamento Oriental por concepto de contribución de guerra," Nov. 14, 1895, *Cartas y otros documentos*, pp. 136–38; Ramón Emeterio Betances to Tomás Estrada Palma, Sept. 19, 1895, Llaverías y Martínez, ed., *Correspondencia diplomática*, III:9–10.

75. "Libro de caja del Partido Revolucionario Cubano (1893–1895)," Cuba, Archivo Nacional, *El Archivo Nacional en la conmemoración del centenario del natálico de José Martí y Pérez, 1853–1953*, pp. 349–90.

76. Tomás Estrada Palma to Máximo Gómez, Aug. 15, 1895, *Correspondencia de la delegación cubana*, I:38–39.

77. Ramón Emeterio Betances to Tomás Estrada Palma, Sept. 19, 1895, *Correspondencia diplomática*, III:9–10.

78. "Extract From a Letter Received February 22, 1896," Philip Phillips Family Papers.

79. See Miró Argenter, *Crónicas de la guerra*, I:299–300.

80. See Tomás Estrada Palma to Salvador Cisneros Betancourt, May 30, 1895, *Correspondencia de la delegación cubana*, V:18; Tomás Estrada Palma to Salvador Cisneros Betancourt, July 30, 1896, ibid., VI:43–44.

81. Valdés Domínguez, *Diario de soldado*, II:139–40.

82. Juan Guiteras to Tomás Estrada Palma, Oct. 20, 1895, *Correspondencia de la delegación cubana*, II:74; Tomás Estrada Palma to Antonio Maceo, Oct. 23, 1895, ibid., II:93.

83. Tomás Estrada Palma to Salvador Cisneros Betancourt, Jan. 3, 1896, *Correspondencia de la delegación cubana*, III:21–22.

84. Tomás Estrada Palma to Salvador Cisneros Betancourt, Mar. 11, 1896, *Correspondencia de la delegación cubana*, III:216–318.

85. Tomás Estrada Palma to Salvador Cisneros Betancourt, May 30, 1896, *Correspondencia de la delegación cubana*, V:16.

86. In Edwin F. Atkins, *Sixty Years in Cuba*, p. 214. This meeting is also recounted in Rubens, *Liberty, The Story of Cuba*, p. 208.

87. In Valdés Domínguez, *Diario de soldado*, III:93–94.

88. Ibid., II:231.

89. Tomás Estrada Palma to Máximo Gómez, July 29, 1896, *Correspondencia de la delegación cubana*, V:40–41.

90. Máximo Gómez to Tomás Estrada Palma, July, 1897, *Boletín del Archivo Nacional* XXX (Jan.–Dec., 1931): 71–72.

91. Máximo Gómez to Tomás Estrada Palma, Aug. 15, 1897, ibid., p. 76, and Máximo Gómez to Tomás Estrada Palma, September 1897, in Nichols, "Domestic History of Cuba During the War of the Insurrectos, 1895–1898" (unpublished masters thesis), p. 76.

92. Máximo Gómez to Tomás Estrada Palma, Nov. 8, 1895, *Boletín del Archivo Nacional* XXII (Jan.–Dec., 1923):218.

93. Máximo Gómez to Tomás Estrada Palma, August 11, 1896, in Nichols, "Domestic History of Cuba During the War of the Insurrectos, 1895–1898," p. 75.

94. Máximo Gómez to Tomás Estrada Palma, Dec. 8, 1895, *Boletín del Archivo Nacional* XXII (Jan.–Dec., 1923):223. See also Máximo Gómez, "A los hombres honrados víctimas de la tea," Nov. 11, 1895, in Castillo, *Autobiografía del general José Rogelio Castillo*, p. 236.

95. Tomás Estrada Palma to Salvador Cisneros Betancourt, December 23, 1895, in U.S. Congress, Senate, *Affairs in Cuba*, p. 16. The Marquis of Apetzeguía, arch-enemy of Cuban independence and owner of "Constancia," one of the largest sugar estates in Cuba, had transferred title to his property to an American corporation.

96. Horrego Estuch, *Máximo Gómez, libertador y ciudadano*, pp. 158–59; Edwin F. Atkins to Edwin F. Uhl, December 12, 1895, U.S. Department of State, *FRUS: 1895*, p. 1217.

97. *The World*, January 28, 1897, p. 1.

98. In Roig de Leuchsenring, *La guerra libertadora cubana de los treinta años, 1868–1898: razón de su victoria*, pp. 212–13.

99. Cuba, Consejo de Gobierno, *Recopilación de las leyes, reglamentos, decretos y demás disposiciones dictadas por el Consejo de Gobierno de la República de Cuba*, pp. 49–51.

100. Hernández y Pérez, *Dos conferencias históricas*, pp. 72–73, and Angel Carbonell, *Eusebio Hernández*, II:37–41.

101. Fermín Valdés Domínguez to Andrés Moreno de la Torre, Feb. 9, 1897, in Valdés Domínguez, *Diario de soldado*, II:142–46.

102. Máximo Gómez, "Carta al presidente del Club 'Obreros de la Independencia,' " n.d., *Casa de las Américas* IX (Sept.–Oct., 1968): 123.

103. Máximo Gómez to Andrés Moreno de la Torre, Feb. 6, 1867, Máximo Gómez, *Recuerdos y previsiones*, pp. 130–37.

104. Roig de Leuchsenring, *Máximo Gómez: el libertador de Cuba y el primer ciudadano de la república*, p. 30; Horrego Estuch, *Máximo Gómez, libertador y ciudadano*, pp. 167–95; Jorge Castellanos, "El pensamiento social de Máximo Gómez."

105. Headquarters of the Army Liberation, "Proclamation," July 4, 1896, *Correspondencia diplomática*, V:176–77.

106. Raimundo Cabrera to José Ignacio Rodríguez, Sept. 18, 1896, Rodríguez Papers.

Chapter 7. Rebellion of the Loyal

1. The Democratic platform in 1896 extended formal "sympathy to the people of Cuba in their heroic struggle for liberty and independence." The Republicans, too, for their part, proclaimed in their platform "sympathy [with] the struggles of other American peoples to free themselves from European domination. . . . We believe that the government of the United States should actively use its influence and good offices to restore peace and give independence to the Island." The Populist party also announced its sympathy for the Cubans' "heroic struggle for political freedom and independence" and urged that the United States recognize "that Cuba is, and of right ought to be, a free and independent state." See Porter and Johnson, eds., *National Party Platforms, 1840–1968*, pp. 97–111.

2. In Frederick H. Gillett, *George Frisbie Hoar* (Boston: Houghton Mifflin Company, 1934), p. 196.

3. Henry Cabot Lodge to Theodore Roosevelt, December 2, 1896, in Henry Cabot Lodge, *Selections from the Correspondence of Theodore Roosevelt and Henry Cabot Lodge*, I:240. To which Roosevelt responded: "I am delighted at what you say about McKinley. I do hope he will take a strong stand both about Hawaii and Cuba. I do not think a war with Spain would be serious enough to cause much strain on the country, or much interruption to the revival of prosperity; but I certainly wish the matter could be settled this winter." Theodore Roosevelt to Henry Cabot Lodge, December 4, 1896, in ibid., I:243.

4. *The World*, July 10, 1897, p. 7.

5. *The World*, May 19, 1897, p. 2; *William McKinley and His America*, pp. 333–34.

6. John Sherman to Stewart L. Woodford, July 16, 1897, U.S. Department of State, *FRUS: 1898*, p. 560.

7. *New York Journal*, June 23, 1897, p. 6.

8. *New York Journal*, January 17, 1897, p. 6.

9. Henry Cabot Lodge to Theodore Roosevelt, December 2, 1896, in Lodge, *Selections from the Correspondence of Theodore Roosevelt and Henry Cabot Lodge*, I:246.

10. Whitelaw Reid to William McKinley, December 5, 1896, William McKinley Papers.

11. John Sherman to Stewart L. Woodford, July 16, 1897, *FRUS: 1898*, pp. 558–61.

12. Ibid.

13. Morgan, *William McKinley and His America*, pp. 344–45; May, *Imperial Democracy*, p. 125.

14. Fabié, *Canovas del Castillo*, pp. 353–54.

15. Stewart L. Woodford to John Sherman, September 20, 1897, *FRUS: 1898*, pp. 566–67.

16. "Note of the United States to Spain," September 23, 1897, *FRUS: 1898*, p. 572.

17. Ortega Rubio, *Historia de la regencia de María Cristina Habsbourg-Lorena*, III:90; Reverter Delmas, *Cuba española. Reseña histórica de la insurrección cubana en 1895*, VI:63, 72, 83, 110–12.

18. Ortega Rubio, *Historia de la regencia de María Cristina Habsbourg-Lorena*, II:186.

19. "Reply of the Duke of Tetuán to Mr. Woodford's Note of September 23, 1897," October 23, 1897, *FRUS: 1898*, pp. 586–87.

20. Stewart L. Woodford to John Sherman, November 13, 1897, ibid., pp. 600–01. See also Stewart L. Woodford to William McKinley, January 7, 1898, Despatches/Spain.

21. Stewart L. Woodford to William McKinley, January 17, 1898, Despatches/Spain; *The World*, October 13, 1897, p. 7.

22. Stewart L. Woodford to John Sherman, November 13, 1897, *FRUS: 1898*, p. 601.

23. Stewart L. Woodford to Pio Gullon, December 20, 1897, Despatches/Spain.

24. Fitzhugh Lee to William R. Day, November 17, 1897, Personal Correspondence, General Lee to the secretary of state, 1897–1898, John Bassett Moore Papers.

25. John Sherman to Stewart L. Woodford, November 20, 1897, *FRUS: 1898*, pp. 603–06.

26. "Note of the United States to Spain," September 23, 1897, *FRUS: 1898*, pp. 568–73, and John Sherman to Stewart L. Woodford, November 20, 1897, ibid., pp. 603–11.

27. William McKinley, "First Annual Message," December 6, 1897, in Richardson, ed., *A Compilation of the Messages and Papers of the Presidents, 1789–1902*, X:32, 37–38.

28. Stewart L. Woodford to William McKinley, November 7, 1897, Despatches/Spain. See also Stewart L. Woodford to William McKinley, November 17, 1897, Despatches/Spain.

29. Stewart L. Woodford to William McKinley, November 14, 1897, Despatches/Spain.

30. The most noteworthy instance was the appointment of Marcos García, a ranking insurgent officer during the Ten Years War, as governor of Santa Clara. See Borrero Pérez, *La cubanía aniquilada por la Enmienda Platt*, pp. 113–14.

31. Máximo Gómez to John R. Caldwell, December 5, 1897, *New York Herald*, December 29, 1897, p. 3.

32. *The World*, January 27, 1897, p. 3.

33. *The World*, February 10, 1897, pp. 1–2.

34. *The World*, March 6, 1897, p. 4.

35. *New York Journal*, January 17, 1897, p. 6.

36. Máximo Gómez to Tomás Estrada Palma, Enero de 1898, *Boletín del Archivo Nacional* XXXI (Jan.–Dec., 1932):91. For other military views see General Pedro Díaz to editor, Nov. 19, 1897, *Patria*, Dec. 8, 1897, and General Pedro Betancourt to Tomás Estrada Palma, Aug. 10, 1897, *Patria*, Sept. 1, 1897, p. 2.

37. *New York Herald*, December 8, 1896, p. 8.

38. *New York Journal*, February 6, 1897, p. 14. Nor was this position new. See Estrada Palma, *Petition of Tomás Estrada Palma for the Belligerency of the Cubans*, p. 36.

39. *Tampa Tribune*, November 11, 1897, p. 1; *Washington Post*, November 5, 1897, p. 1.

40. Tomás Estrada Palma to John Sherman, December 1, 1897, Notes from the Cuban Legation in the United States to the Department of State, 1844–1906, General Records of the Department of State, Record Group 59, National Archives, Washington, D.C. (Hereafter cited as Notes from the Cuban Legation.)

41. Gonzalo de Quesada to John Sherman, January 13, 1898, in Llaverías y Martínez, ed., *Correspondencia de la delegación cubana en Nueva York durante la guerra de 1895 a 1898*, V:227. See also "Manifiesto de la Revolución rechazando la autonomía," Oct. 26, 1897, in Méndez Capote, *Trabajos*, I:139–43.

42. See Máximo Gómez to Francisco Carrillo, Dec. 25, 1897, in Máximo Gómez, *Cartas a Francisco Carrillo*, pp. 191–92; Raúl Roa, *Aventuras, venturas y desventuras de un mambí* p. 273; Pérez Abreu, *En la guerra con Máximo Gómaz*, p. 178.

43. The most notable insurgent chieftain to surrender was General Juan Masó Parra, who led his battalion to a separate peace with Spain. Ubieta, *Efemérides de la revolución cubana*, pp. 129–32; Bacardí y Moreau, *Crónicas de Santiago de Cuba*, IX:267.

44. Calixto García, "Al Departamento Militar de Oriente," Nov. 1897, in Calixto García *Palabras de tres guerras*, pp. 79–80.

45. *New York Journal*, February 24, 1898, p. 12.

46. Calixto García to editor, December 28, 1897, *New York Journal*, January 5, 1898, p. 7.

47. Máximo Gómez to Francisco Gregorio Billini, Feb. 6, 1898, in Máximo Gómez, *Papeles dominicanos de Máximo Gómez*, pp. 428–30. See also Landa, *Bartolomé Masó y Márquez. Estudio biográfico documentado*, p. 208; Ferrar, *Con el rifle al hombro*, p. 129; Tirado, "Apuntes de un corresponsal (II)," p.1 32.

48. Walter B. Barker to William R. Day, October 18, 1897, Despatches/Sagua la Grande.

49. Weyler, *Mi mando en Cuba*, I:407.

50. Fitzhugh Lee to William R. Rockhill, July 3, 1896, Despatches/Havana; Pulaski F.

Hyatt to William R. Rockhill, March 14, 1896, Despatches/Santiago de Cuba. See also *The World*, March 28, 1897, p. 7; *New York Journal*, May 16, 1897, p. 1; *The London Times*, June 6, 1896, p. 8.

51. For one such incident see *New York Journal*, May 26, 1897, p. 7.

52. See García, *Carta-folleto a José María Gálvez*, pp. 41–42.

53. *Avisador Comercial*, Apr. 13, 1896, enclosure in Ramon O. Williams to William R. Rockhill, April 20, 1896, Despatches/Havana.

54. Fitzhugh Lee to William R. Rockhill, July 3, 1896, Despatches/Havana.

55 .*The World*, March 22, 1897, p. 7.

56. Walter B. Barker to William R. Day, June 19, 1897, Despatches/Sagua la Grande.

57. *London Times*, October 15, 1897, p. 4.

58. *New York Journal*, May 15, 1897, p. 5.

59. Walter B. Barker to department of state, June 19, 1897, Despatches/Sagua la Grande. See also *The Washington Post*, October 21, 1897, p. 2.

60. "To the President of the Republic of the United States of America," enclosure in Fitzhugh Lee to Richard Olney, June 24, 1896, Richard Olney Papers. The petitioners included: Eduardo Ferrer y Picabia, ex-partner of Perseverancia sugar plantation and owner of Magdalena sugar plantation; Juan Pablo Tonarely, lawyer, proprietor and provincial representative for Havana; José González Lanuza, lawyer, justice of the Supreme Court and professor of the University of Havana; Dr. Emiliano Núñez, director of the civil hospital Reina Mercedes; Pedro P. Garmendía, lawyer and municipal judge of Pinar del Río; José María Aguirre, lawyer and proprietor; Santiago Labarrere, owner of Bramales sugar plantation; Mariano Artis, owner of Narcisa sugar plantation (Santa Clara); José María Espinosa, owner of Fe sugar plantation (Santa Clara); Perfecto Lacoste, owner of Central Lucía sugar plantation (Havana); Francisco Casuso, owner of San Agustín sugar plantation; Dr. Gabriel Casuso, physician and proprietor; Gabriel Camps, owner of Mi Rosa sugar plantation (Havana); Francisco Rosell, owner of Aguedita and Dolores sugar plantations (Matanzas); Eduardo Delgado, owner of San Claudio sugar plantation (Pinar del Río); Abelardo Ledesma, owner of Tomasita sugar plantation (Pinar del Río); Ernesto Desvernine, proprietor; Marquis of the Real Campina, proprietor; Marquis of La Real Proclamación, first land owner in Cuba; Samuel T. Tolón, boiler, wholesaler—molasses dealer, lumber yard, and merchant (Cárdenas); Gaston Rabel Cárdenas, banker, sugar warehouses, exporter and sugar refinery; Julio B. Hamel, merchant (Cárdenas); Gabriel Carol, owner of Aguada sugar plantation (Cárdenas); Joaquín de Rojas y Bacet, banker and sugar exporter; Francisco Larrieu, partner of Precioso sugar plantation (Matanzas); Ernesto Castro, lawyer, partner of Precioso sugar plantation, and owner of Gascajal sugar plantation (Cárdenas); Carlos Alberto Smith, lawyer and proprietor; Rafael Reynaldos, lawyer and owner of Perseverancia sugar plantation (Cárdenas); Porfirio Pascual, lawyer and proprietor; Dr. Joaquín Otazo, proprietor and physician; Dr. Alejandro Neyra, proprietor and physician; Dr. José María Verdeja, proprietor and physician; Dr. José María Verdeja, proprietor and physician; Dr. José Martíinez Moreno, physician and owner of the Luisa sugar plantation (Matanzas); Feliciano Richet, attorney and heir of Mr. Antonio Gomez Araujo, owner of Nena sugar plantation (Matanzas), and owner of 100 houses in Cárdenas; Dr. Daniel Gutiérrez, physician and proprietor; Dr. Carlos Pascual (Cárdenas), owner of drug stores; Dr. Enrique Pascual, proprietor and physician; Dr. Juan M. Sáez, owner of La Central drug store; Dr. Pedro de Jongh, owner of La Marina drug store; Dr. Octavio Smith, director of the hospital and San Luis Gonzaga College; Juan Neyra, proprietor; Agustín Mederos, owner of Ohucha sugar plantation (Matanzas); José B. Rodríguez Maribana, lawyer and proprietor of Chorot sugar plantation; Eduardo Catá, merchant; Miguel Lluria, molasses and sugar warehouses; Dr. Octavio Pimienta, chemist and manager of the gas company; Juan M. Fazi, board of directors of the gas company; Joaquín Robleno, owner of Los Indios sugar plantation (Matanzas); Enrique and Emilio

Vilá, members of Vila Hermanos, lumber yard and ice manufacturers; Joaquín Tellado and Eusebio Mayol, members of Tellado, Mayol and Company, merchants and owners of Cabo Micacos salt works; Ventura Fernández de Castro, sugar broker and owner of Santa Ysabel sugar plantation (Matanzas); Juan D. Argüelles, owner of Destino sugar plantation (Matanzas); Juan Alvarez Celis, merchant; Ricardo Lombard, merchant; Septimio Sardina, owner of Reglita sugar plantation (Cárdenas); Enrique Segrera y Herrero, lawyer and secretary of the Junta del Puerto (Cárdenas); Patricio Ponce de León, owner of Ponces sugar plantation (Matanzas); Cirilo Ponce de León, owner of Indio sugar plantation (Santa Clara); Jorge Deschapelles, merchant; Eduardo de Zaldo, druggist; Francisco Marchena, druggist; Guillermo Scott, proprietor, Marquis de Casa Negra, proprietor; Patricio Ballester, proprietor.

61. A Planter in Cuba, "The Argument for Autonomy," p. 1012.

62. *The World*, March 22, 1897, p. 7.

63. William J. Calhoun to William McKinley, June 22, 1897, Special Agents, General Records of the Department of State, Record Group 59, Vol. XLVIII. National Archives, Washington, D.C. See also *New York Journal*, June 6, 1897, p. 1.

64. See Vesa y Fillart, *Voluntarios de Isla de Cuba. Historial del Regimiento Caballería de Jaruco y de su estandarte*, pp. 218–19.

65. Fitzhugh Lee to William R. Day, November 27, 1897, Despatches/Havana.

66. *Washington Post*, December 8, 1897, pp. 1, 3. See also Bonsal, *The Real Condition of Cuba To-Day*, pp. 35–35, and Fernández Almagro, *Historia política de la España contemporanea*, II:455.

67. Fitzhugh Lee to William R. Day, November 17, 1897, Despatches/Havana.

68. *Washington Post*, December 22, 1897, p. 1; H. White, "After Intervention—What?" See also Bonsal, *The Real Condition of Cuba To-day*, pp. 35–36.

69. See Fitzhugh Lee to William R. Day, February 15, 1898, Despatches/Havana, and Máximo Gómez to Tomás Estrada Palma, Feb. 12, 1898, *Boletín del Archivo Nacional*, XXXI (Jan.–Dec., 1932):96.

70. Serra Orts, *Recuerdos de las guerras de Cuba. 1868–1898*, p. 75. See also A & B, *Apuntes en defensa del honor del ejército*, pp. 106–07.

71. Alexander C. Brice to William R. Day, November 17, 1897, Despatches/Matanzas. See also Morales y Morales, *Nociones de historia de Cuba*, p. 368; *New York Herald*, January 9, 1898, p. 5; *Washington Evening Star*, January 22, 1898, p. 1.

72. Alexander C. Brice to William R. Day, November 17, 1897, Despatches/Matanzas. See also the *Washington Post*, October 19, 1897, p. 2.

73. Pulaski F. Hyatt to William R. Day, March 24, 1898, United States Congress, Senate, *Consular Correspondence Respecting the Conditions of the Reconcentrados in Cuba, the State of the War in that Island, and the Prospects of the Projected Autonomy*, 55th Congress, 2nd. Session, Senate Document No. 230 (Washington, D.C.: Government Printing Office, 1898), p. 44.

74. Fitzhugh Lee to William R. Day, November 23, 1897, Despatches/Havana.

75. Fitzhugh Lee to William R. Day, January 8, 1898, Personal Correspondence, General Lee to the secretary of state, 1897–1898, John Bassett Moore Papers.

76. *New York Herald*, December 14, 1897, p. 9; *Washington Evening Star*, February 11, 1898, p. 1; Charles M. Pepper, *To-morrow in Cuba*, p. 96.

77. *New York Herald*, December 9, 1897; p. 3. See also Colonel Manuel del Valle, Corps of Volunteers, to Fitzhugh Lee, June 20, 1896, Despatches/Havana.

78. Martínez Arango, *Cronología crítica de la guerra hispano-cubano-americana*, p. 24; Piñeyro, *Como acabó la dominación de España en América*, pp. 163–64.

79. Alvey A. Adee to William R. Day, January 12, 1898, General Records of the Department of State, Reports of Bureau Officers, Vol. IX, 1895–1898, Record Group 59.

80. Fitzhugh Lee to William R. Day, January 13, 1898, *FRUS: 1898*, p. 1025.

Chapter 8. The Passing of Spanish Sovereignty

1. Pulaski F. Hyatt to William R. Day, February 1, 1898, Despatches/Santiago de Cuba.
2. Walter B. Barker to William R. Day, November 11, 1897, Despatches/Sagua la Grande.
3. Fitzhugh Lee to William R. Day, November 17, 1897, Despatches/Havana.
4. John Sherman to William McKinley, December 15, 1897, Miscellaneous Archives, Relations With Spain, General Records of the Department of State, Record Group 59, National Archives, Washington, D.C. (Hereafter cited as Miscellaneous Archives/Spain.)
5. Fitzhugh Lee to William R. Day, January 18, 1898, Despatches/Havana.
6. Fitzhugh Lee to William R. Day, January 8, 1898, Personal Correspondence, General Lee to the secretary of state, 1897–1898, John Bassett Moore Papers.
7. *New York Times*, March 22, 1898, p. 1. See also Conangla Fontanilles, *Cuba y Pi y Margall*, pp. 422–23.
8. *El Nuevo Régimen*, Dec. 25, 1897, enclosure in Fitzhugh Lee to William R. Day, January 2, 1898, Despatches/Havana.
9. *La Epoca*, Jan. 8, 1898, enclosure in Stewart L. Woodford to Alvey A. Adee, January 8, 1989, Despatches/Spain. See also Polavieja, *Relación documentada de mi política en Cuba*, pp. 344–52; Pi y Margall and Pi y Arsuaga, *Historia de España en el siglo XIX*, VII:103, 575–76; Martínez Arango, *Cronología crítica de la guerra hispano-cubano-americana*, p. 42.
10. *The World*, January 2, 1898, p. 3.
11. Presidente de la República, "Manifiesto al pueblo de Cuba," Oct. 27, 1897, enclosure in Fitzhugh Lee to William R. Day, November 1, 1897, Despatches/Havana.
12. Máximo Gómez to Tomás Estrada Palma, July 30, 1897, *Boletín del Archivo Nacional* XXX (Jan.–Dec., 1930):74; Souza, *Máximo Gómez el generalísimo*, p. 231.
13. José Miguel Gómez to Tomás Estrada Palma, June 14, 1897, *Patria*, July 21, 1897, p. 2; Calixto García to Gonzalo de Quesada, May 29, 1897, in Quesada, *Archivo de Gonzalo de Quesada*, I:173; Máximo Gómez, *Diario de campaña del mayor general Máximo Gómez*, p.333; Nestor Aranguren to Benito Aranguren, Aug. 4, 1897, in Castellanos García, *Aranguren (del ciclo mambí)*, pp. 185–86; Máximo Gómez to Francisco Gregorio Billini, Feb. 8, 1897, in Máximo Gómez, *Papeles dominicanos de Máximo Gómez*, pp. 50–51; Despradel, "Máximo Gómez y la campaña del 97," p. 298.
14. See Guillermo R. Torres to Tomás Estrada Palma, Jan., 1898, *Patria*, Feb. 16, 1898, p. 2; Luis Rodolfo Miranda to Benjamín Guerra, Feb. 4, 1898, *Patria*, Mar. 2, 1898, p. 2.
15. Máximo Gómez to Gonzalo de Quesada, March 10, 1898, *New York Daily Tribune*, April 10, 1898, p. 3.
16. Máximo Gómez to Tomás Estrada Palma, Jan., 1898, *Boletín del Archivo Nacional* XXXI (Jan.–Dec., 1932):90.
17. Máximo Gómez to Tomás Estrada Palma, Jan., 1898, *Boletín del Archivo Nacional* XXXI (Jan.–Dec., 1932):90; Máximo Gómez to Ernesto Fonts Sterling, Mar. 1, 1898, in Máximo Gómez, *Algunos documentos políticos*, pp. 20–21.
18. Máximo Gómez to Tomás Estrada Palma, Apr. 11, 1898, *Patria*, Apr. 30, 1898, p. 2; Máximo Gómez to Tomás Estrada Palma, Feb. 26, 1898, *Boletín del Archivo Nacional* XXXI (Jan.–Dec., 1932):97; Calixto García to Tomás Estrada Palma, Feb. 18, 1898, in Casasús, *Calixto García (el estratega)*, p. 249; Máximo Gómez to Francisco Gregorio Billini, Jan. 17, 1898, in Máximo Gómez, *Cartas de Máximo Gómez*, pp. 41–42, 61–62; Máximo Gómez to Tomás Estrada Palma, Sept. 5, 1897, *Boletín del Archivo Nacional* XXX (Jan.–Dec., 1930):77–78; "Juicios del General Gómez," *Patria*, Apr. 30, 1898, p. 1; Máximo Gómez to Tomás Estrada Palma, Nov. 25, 1897, *Boletín del Archivo Nacional* XXX (Jan.–Dec., 1930):88.
19. Taylor, "A Review of the Cuban Question in Its Economic, Political, and Diplomatic Aspects," p. 610.

20. *The World*, August 7, 1897, p. 2.

21. William R. Day to Stewart L. Woodford, March 26, 1898, U.S. Department of State, *FRUS: 1898*, p. 704.

22. William R. Day, "Recognition of Independence," n.d., William R. Day Papers.

23. *The State*, April 16, 1898, p. 4.

24. Fitzhugh Lee to William R. Day, December 13, 1897, Despatches/Havana. See also U.S. Congress, Senate, *Affairs in Cuba*, pp. 544–45. American travelers to Cuba arrived at similar conclusions. See Musgrave, *Under Three Flags in Cuba*, p. 206; Akers, "The Cuban Revolt," p. 115; Pagliuchi, "A Glimpse of the Cuban War."

25. Walter B. Barker to William R. Day, January 10, 1898, Despatches/Sagua la Grande; May, *Imperial Democracy*, pp. 126–27. See also interview with the former American Minister to Spain Hannis Taylor in *New York Journal*, January 14, 1898, p. 2.

26. Stewart L. Woodford to John Sherman, September 13, 1897, *FRUS: 1898*, p. 565. See also Fitzhugh Lee to John Sherman, April 20, 1897, Despatches/Havana, and William J. Calhoun to William McKinley, Special Agents, Department of State, vol. XLVII, General Records of the Department of State, Record Group 59; Stewart L. Woodford to William McKinley, November 7, 1897, Despatches/Spain.

27. Grover Cleveland, "Fourth Annual Message," December 7, 1896, Richardson, ed., *A Compilation of the Messages and Papers of the Presidents, 1789–1902*, IX:719–22.

28. Ibid., p. 722.

29. William McKinley, "First Annual Message," December 6, 1897, Richardson, ed., *A Compilation of the Messages and Papers of the Presidents, 1789–1902*, X:38.

30. Stewart L. Woodford to William McKinley, February 26, 1898, Despatches/Spain. See also Charles S. Olcott, *William McKinley*, 2 vols. (Boston: Houghton Mifflin, 1916) I:17.

31. Stewart L. Woodford to William McKinley, November 14, 1897, Despatches/Spain.

32. Stewart L. Woodford to William McKinley, March 17, 1898, private correspondence, General Woodford to the president, August 1897 to May 1898, John Bassett Moore Papers.

33. Stewart L. Woodford to William McKinley, March 9, 1898, private correspondence, General Woodford to the president, August 1897 to May 1898, ibid.

34. Stewart L. Woodford to William McKinley, March 17, 1898, Despatches/Spain.

35. Stewart L. Woodford to William McKinley, March 17, 1898, private correspondence, General Woodford to the president, August 1897 to May 1898, Moore Papers.

36. *Washington Post*, February 20, 1898, p. 4.

37. See Cortissoz, *The Life of Whitelaw Reid*, II:219–20, and Morgan, *William McKinley and His America*, p. 340.

38. Stewart L. Woodford to William McKinley, March 17, 1898, Despatches/Spain.

39. Stewart L. Woodford to William McKinley, March 17, 1898, private correspondence, General Woodford to the president, August 1897 to May 1898, Moore Papers.

40. Stewart L. Woodford to McKinley, March 18, 1898, private correspondence, General Woodford to the president, ibid.

41. Stewart L. Woodford to William McKinley, March 19, 1898, private correspondence, General Woodford to the president, ibid.

42. Marcus M. Wilkerson, *Public Opinion and the Spanish-American War*, pp. 54–120; Wisan, *The Cuban Crisis as Reflected in the New York Press (1895–1898)*, pp. 227–421. For the published text of the de Lôme letter see *New York Journal*, February 9, 1898, p. 1.

43. Olcott, *William McKinley*, II:28. Hobart, *Memories*, p. 61. See also *Washington Evening Star*, March 29, 1898, p. 1.

44. *Chicago Tribune*, February 27, 1898, p. 30.

45. Henry Cabot Lodge to William McKinley, March 21, 1898, McKinley Papers.

46. In Acheson, *Joe Bailey, The Last Democrat*, p. 103.

47. Hobart, *Memories*, p. 60.

48. Dawes, *A Journal of the McKinley Years*, p. 149.

49. Stewart L. Woodford to William McKinley, March 23, 1898, private correspondence, General Woodford to the president, August 1897 to May 1898, Moore Papers.

50. Maura y Gamazo, *Historia crítica del reinado de Don Alfonso XIII durante su menoridad bajo la regencia de su madre Doña María Cristina de Austria*, I:359–61; Guerra y Sánchez, *En el camino de la independencia*, pp. 161–62; Guerra y Sánchez, *La expansión territorial de los Estados Unidos*, pp. 340–42; Pabón y Suárez de Urbina, *El 98, acontecimiento internacional*, pp. 23–24, 72–73.

51. See Stewart L. Woodford to William McKinley, March 24, 1898, and Stewart L. Woodford to William McKinley, March 25, 1898, private correspondence, General Woodford to the president, August 1897 to May 1898, Moore Papers.

52. Stewart L. Woodford to William McKinley, March 25, 1898, private correspondence, General Woodford to the president, ibid.

53. William R. Day to Stewart L. Woodford, March 27, 1898, *FRUS: 1898*, pp. 711–12. See also Robinson, *Cuba and the Intervention*, pp. 67–68.

54. William R. Day to Stewart L. Woodford, March 28, 1898, *FRUS: 1898*, p. 713.

55. William R. Day to Stewart L. Woodford, March 29, 1898, ibid., p. 718.

56. William R. Day to Stewart L. Woodford, March 30, 1898, ibid., p. 721.

57. Stewart L. Woodford to William R. Day, March 31, 1898, ibid., p. 726.

58. Stewart L. Woodford to William R. Day, March 30, 1898, ibid., p. 723. See also interview with Prime Minister Práxedes M. Sagasta in *New York Tribune*, April 4, 1898, p. 1.

59. Stewart L. Woodford to William McKinley, April 1, 1898, private correspondence, General Woodford to the president, August 1897 to May 1898, Moore Papers.

60. R. MacArthur to Stewart L. Woodford, April 2, 1898, ibid.

61. Stewart L. Woodford to William McKinley, April 5, 1898, private correspondence, General Woodford to the president, August 1897 to May 1898, Moore Papers.

62. *New York Daily Tribune*, April 6, 1898, p. 6. See also LaFeber, *The New Empire*, p. 402.

63. Luis Polo de Bernabé to secretary of state, April 10, 1898, Spain, Ministerio de Estado, *Spanish Diplomatic Correspondence and Documents, 1896–1900, Presented to the Cortes by the Minister of State*, p. 121; William R. Day, "Interview With Spanish Minister," April 10, 1898, Day Papers; Dawes, *A Journal of the McKinley Years*, p. 149.

64. Ramón Blanco, "Suspension of Hostilities," April 10, 1898 in *FRUS: 1898*, p. 750.

65. Stewart L. Woodford to William McKinley, April 10, 1898, ibid., p. 747.

66. Rubens, *Liberty, The Story of Cuba*, pp. 326–27. See also Carlos Márquez Sterling, *Don Tomás (biografía de una época)*, p. 283. Tomás Estrada Palma later wrote that "enormous pressure was brought to bear on the Delegation to persuade the Cubans to accept an armistice." See Estrada Palma, "The Work of the Cuban Delegation," pp. 419–20.

67. Bartolomé Masó, "Manifiesto," Apr. 24, 1898, in Cuba, Secretaria de Gobernación, *Documentos históricos*, pp. 165–66. (Hereafter cited as *Documentos historicos*.) See also Máximo Gómez to Francisco Carrillo, Apr. 20, 1898, in Máximo Gómez, *Cartas a Francisco Carrillo*, p. 212; Llaverías y Martínez and Santovenia, eds., *Actas de las Asambleas de Representantes y del Consejo de Gobierno durante la guerra de independencia*, IV: 35. (Hereafter cited as *Actas de las Asambleas*.)

68. Calixto García to Mario G. Menocal, Apr. 18, 1898, in Calixto García, *Palabras dé tres guerras*, pp. 143–44; Casasús, *Calixto García (el estratega)*, p. 251.

69. Maximo Gómez, *Diario de campaña del mayor general Máximo Gómez*, p. 354. See also Consejo de Gobierno, "Manifiesto," Apr. 24, 1898, *Documentos históricos*, pp. 165–66.

70. Stewart L. Woodford to William McKinley, March 26, 1898, Despatches/Spain.

71. John Davis Long to editor, *Boston Globe*, April 15, 1898 in Mayo, ed., *America of Yesterday as Reflected in the Journal of John Davis Long*, pp. 179–.

72. *New York Times*, September 1, 1912, p. 2. See also Heath, "The Work of the President," p. 282; Pritchett, "Some Recollections of President McKinley and the Cuban Intervention," p. 400.

Chapter 9. Shades of a Shadow

1. Wilkerson, *Public Opinion and the Spanish American War*, pp. 91–107; Auxier, "Propaganda Activities of the Cuban Junta in Precipitating the Spanish-American War, 1895–1898."

2. Mayo, ed., *America of Yesterday as Reflected in the Journal of John Davis Long*, pp. 174–75; Holbo, "Presidential Leadership in Foreign Affairs: William McKinley and the Turpie-Foraker Amendment," pp. 1323–25.

3. Richardson, ed., *A Compilation of the Messages and Papers of the Presidents, 1789–1902*, X:67.

4. Alvey A. Adee to John Sherman, August 19, 1897, McKinley Papers.

5. Nor was the proposition of an American intervention to assist Spain entirely ruled out. The *Journal of Commerce* insisted that if the insurgents did not accept the compromise arranged by Madrid and Washington, "we should have no excuse for expending any further sympathy upon them." See *Journal of Commerce*, April 1, 1898, p. 6. Separatists feared that Cuban rejection of autonomy and armistice would lead to United States to intervene in behalf of Spain. Indeed, in March 1898 a special Spanish envoy Juan M. Ceballos arrived in the United States to propose joint Spanish-American operations against Cubans. "If, unfortunately," Estrada Palma announced in disbelief, "this incredible proposal be carried into effect, and American bayonets arrayed against us in our struggle for freedom and in aid of the Spanish monarchy, we will fight on, sadly but determined, and let history judge whether the vanquished had not a purer ideal of free institutions than the victors." *New York Times*, March 18, 1898, p. 2.

6. William McKinley, "First Annual Message," December 6, 1897, Richardson, ed., *A Compilation of the Messages and Papers of the Presidents, 1789–1902*, X:33.

7. Ibid., X:64.

8. Alvey A. Adee to William R. Day, April 7, 1898, William R. Day Papers.

9. *Washington Evening Star*, April 5, 1898, p. 1. See also Orville Platt to John H. Flagg, April 7, 1898, in Coolidge, *An Old-Fashioned Senator: Orville H. Platt of Connecticut*, p. 278.

10. *New York Daily Tribune*, April 7, 1898, p. 6. This theme was the subject of similar editorial in the *Journal of Commerce*, April 13, 1898, p. 6.

11. John Sherman to William McKinley, February 15, 1897, McKinley Papers.

12. *The Washington Post*, April 6, 1898, p. 1.

13. *New York Daily Tribune*, April 6, 1898, p. 2. See also *New York Times*, April 6, 1898, p. 2.

14. Richardson, ed., *A Compilation of the Messages and Papers of the Presidents, 1789–1902*, X:63–64.

15. Dawes, *A Journal of the McKinley Years*, p. 154. See also *Washington Evening Star*, April 14, 1898, p. 1.

16. *New York Times*, April 5, 1898, p. 5.

17. *Washington Evening Star*, April 6, 1898, p. 1.

18. "Borrador relacionado con la Resolución Conjunta," Abril de 1898, Gonzalo de Quesada, *Documentos históricos*, p. 409.

19. *The State*, April 8, 1898, p. 3. See also the *Washington Evening Star*, April 6, 1898, p. 1, and "Bulletin," April 6, 1898, Day Papers. The State Department feared this reaction. On March 24, Assistant Secretary of State Day indicated that unless the United States recognized the Cubans, "or make some arrangement with them when we intervene, we will have to

overcome both the Spaniards and Cubans." See "Memorandum," March 24, 1898, Day Papers. Rubens, long devoted to Cuban independence and suspicious of administration policy, made these comments without prior authorization from the leadership of the New York junta. He was subjected in the days that followed to enormous pressure from the Cuban junta to retract his statement. "I will not modify what I have said," Rubens countered. "I do not consider that you spoke for or represent the real Cubans, the Cubans in arms . . . you do not represent those who risk their lives for liberty. I am sure they will ratify and applaud my attitude." See Rubens, *Cuba, The Story of Liberty*, p. 340.

20. Was it the intention of the administration, Virginia Senator John W. Daniel asked rhetorically, "to send the American Army to Cuba for the purpose of turning their guns into the face of Maximo Gomez and crushing the glorious revolution there?" See *Congressional Record*, XXXI (April 15, 1898), pt. IV, p. 3882.

21. *Congressional Record*, XXXI (April 16, 1898): 3988–89. For the best single account of the details of the congressional debate see Holbo, "Presidential Leadership in Foreign Affairs: William McKinley and the Turpie-Foraker Amendment," pp. 1321–35.

22. Leech, *In the Days of McKinley*, p. 188.

23. *New York Herald*, February 24, 1907, II:3; *Washington Post*, February 28, 1907, p. 1. See also Ogden, "Light from the Junta"; Portell Vilá, *Historia de Cuba en sus relaciones con los Estados Unidos y España*, III:356–64.

24. *Willett and Gray's Weekly Statistical Sugar Trade Journal*, March 3, 1898 and March 24, 1898.

25. Leonard J. Arrington, *Beet Sugar in the West* (Seattle: University of Washington Press, 1966), p. 12.

26. Baker, "How the Beet-Sugar Industry is Growing," p. 325; Roy G. Blakey, *The United States Beet-Sugar Industry and the Tariff* (New York: Columbia University Press, 1912), p. 38; *The Sugar Beet*, XX (August, 1898):109.

27. Olmstead, "Some Economic Consequences of the Liberation of Cuba," p. 174.

28. *Sugar* X (January 15, 1898):1. See also *The Sugar Beet* XIX (October, 1898):99–100.

29. *Deseret Evening News*, February 19, 1898, p. 2.

30. *Congressional Record*, XXVI (January 29, 1894), pt. II, p. 1578.

31. *Congressional Record*, XXXVIII (December 8, 1903), pt. I, pp. 39–40.

32. See Welliver, "The Annexation of Cuba by the Sugar Trust," pp. 385–86.

33. Holbo, "Presidential Leadership in Foreign Affairs: William McKinley and the Turpie Foraker Amendment," p. 1333.

34. See Emilio Núñez to Tomás Estrada Palma, Apr. 30, 1898, in Arce, *Emilio Núñez (1875–1922): historiografía*, p. 180; Costa y Blanco, *Manuel Sanguily*, pp. 61–62.

35. *Washington Evening Star*, April 19, 1898, p. 2.

36. Tomás Estrada Palma to William McKinley, Apr. 26, 1898, in *Actas de las Asambleas*, IV:56; Castellanos García, *Tierras y glorias de Oriente (Calixto García Iñiguez)*, pp. 316–17.

37. Bartolomé Masó to Román Betances, Mar. 1898, in Pardo Llada, *Bartolomé Masó: el presidente que vetaron los yanquis*, p. 13; Roig de Leuchsenring, *Máximo Gómez: el libertador de Cuba y el primer ciudadano de la República*, p. 45.

38. José Miró Argenter to Bartolomé Masó, June 3, 1898, Pérez Landa, *Bartolomé Masó y Márquez. Estudio biográfico documentado*, p. 244; Piedra Martel, *Mis primeros treinta años: memorias*, p. 487; Rodolfo Bergés, *Cuba y Santo Domingo. Apuntes de la guerra de Cuba de mi diario de campaña 1895–96–97–98* (La Habana: Imprenta "El Score," 1905), p. 148; Escalante Beatón, *Calixto García, su campaña en el 95*, pp. 408–09; Castillo, *Autobiografía del general José Rogelio Castillo*, pp. 253–54; Infiesta, *Máximo Gómez*, pp. 203–04.

39. See Modesto A. Tirado, "Apuntes de un corresponsal (IV)," p. 434.

40. See Tomás Estrada Palma to William McKinley, Apr. 26, 1898, in *Actas de las*

Asambleas, IV:55–56; Carlos Márquez Sterling, *Don Tomás (biografía de una época)*, pp. 293–94; Méndez Capote, *Trabajos*, II:73–74.

41. Andrés Moreno de la Torre to Tomás Estrada Palma, May 10, 1898, *Actas de las Asambleas*, IV:61–62. See also Méndez Capote, *Trabajos*, III:74.

42. *Actas de las Asambleas*, IV:62–63; Méndez Capote, *Trabajos*, III:74–75; Santovenia, *Armonías y conflictos en torno a Cuba*, p. 276; Hernández Corujo, *Historia constitucional de Cuba*, II, pp. 42–45.

43. Domingo Méndez Capote to Calixto García, May 12, 1898, in Casasús, *Calixto García (el estratega)*, p. 261; *Actas de las Asambleas*, IV:56–57.

44. Collazo, *La guerra en Cuba*, pp. 96–97.

45. Máximo Gómez to Domingo Méndez Capote, May 14, 1898, in Máximo Gómez, *Algunos documentos políticos* pp. 31–32.

46. Máximo Gómez to Tomás Estrada Palma, June 1896, in Máximo Gómez, *Ideario cubano*, pp. 102–03.

47. Calixto García to Tomás Estrada Palma, June 27, 1898, *Boletín del Archivo Nacional* XXXV (Jan.–Dec. 1936):109–10; Martínez Arango, *Cronología crítica de la guerra hispano-cubano-americana*, pp. 70–71; Torriente y Peraza, *Calixto García cooperó con las fuerzas armadas de los EE. UU. en 1898 cumpliendo órdenes del gobierno cubano*, pp. 28–30.

48. Calixto García to Consejo de Gobierno, June 27, 1898, Casasús, *Calixto García (el estratega)*, p. 300. See also Calixto García to Manuel Ramón Silva, May, 1898, *Boletín del Archivo Nacional* XXXV (Jan.–Dec., 1936):106–07, and Calixto García to Domingo Méndez Capote, May 1, 1898, Calixto García, *Palabras de tres guerras*, pp. 83–85.

49. Calixto García to Domingo Méndez Capote, May 1, 1898, in Casasús, *Calixto García (el estratega)*, p. 199; Costa y Blanco, *Perfil político de Calixto García*, pp. 24–25; Calixto García to Tomás Estrada Palma, June 27, 1898, *Boletín del Archivo Nacional* XXXV (Jan.–Dec., 1936):110–11.

50. Calixto García to Tomás Estrada Palma, June 27, 1898, *Boletín del Archivo Nacional* XXXV (Jan.–Dec., 1936):110–11).

51. Emilio Núñez to Gonzalo de Quesada, May 16, 1898, in Quesada, *Archivo de Gonzalo de Quesada*, II:114.

52. Calixto García to Tomás Estrada Palma, n.d., in Pérez Cabrera, *Calixto García*, p. 63; Bartolomé Maso to Gonzalo de Quesada, May 11, 1898, in Quesada, *Archivo de Gonzalo de Quesada*, II:82; Arbelo, *Recuerdos de la última guerra por la independencia de Cuba. 1896 a 1898*, pp. 303–05; Torriente y Peraza, *Cuarenta años de mi vida, 1898–1938*, p. 5–10; Guerra y Sánchez, *Por las veredas del pasado, 1880–1902*, pp. 176–77.

53. Méndez Capote, *Trabajos*, III:76–77. See also interview with Méndez Capote in *New York Times*, September 23, 1898, p. 4.

54. Gonzalo de Quesada to Máximo Gómez, Apr. 30, 1898, in Quesada, *Documentos históricos*, p. 278.

55. Calixto García to Tomás Estrada Palma, Apr. 26, 1896, in Martínez Arango, *Cronología crítica de la guerra hispano-cubano-americana*, p. 44.

Chapter 10. The Infelicitous Alliance

1. Tomás Estrada Palma to Máximo Gómez, May 27, 1898, in Torriente y Peraza, *Calixto García cooperó con las fuerzas armadas de los EE. UU. cumpliendo órdenes del gobierno cubano*, pp. 38–39.

2. Rowan, *How I Carried the Message to Garcia*, pp. 26–27. Tosquella, *The Truth About the Message to García;* Elbert Hubbard, *A Message to Garcia*, pp. 2–11.

3. Máximo Gómez to Tomás Estrada Palma, June, 1898, *Boletín del Archivo Nacional*

XXXI (Jan.–Dec., 1932):108; Pérez Abreu, *En la guerra con Máximo Gómez*, pp. 389–90.

4. Alger, *The Spanish-American War*, pp. 85–86; J.M. Miley, "Notes on Conference Between General Shafter and General García," June 20, 1898, in ibid., pp. 90–91; Cuba, Ejército Libertador, *Parte oficial del lugarteniente general Calixto García al General en Jefe Máximo Gómez el 15 de julio de 1898 sobre la campaña de Santiago de Cuba*, p. 5; Corona Ferrer, *De la manigua (ecos de la epopeya)*, pp. 92–93. Shafter later denied having promised to concede control of Santiago to the Cubans. García and several other participants, however, insisted that, indeed, such a commitment had been made. General Joaquín del Castillo, the official interpreter, later recalled that General Shafter, "of his own accord, promised García that on the surrender of the city it would be turned over to him." See *New York Herald*, August 24, 1898, p. 6. Hermann Hagedorn, the biographer of Leonard Wood, years later acknowledged that "in an unguarded moment Shafter told García that the Cubans should direct the civil government of the province." See Hagedorn, *Leonard Wood, A Biography*, I:199. See also Casasús, *Calixto García (el estratega)*, p. 310; Escalante Beatón, *Calixto García, su campaña en el 95*, p. 453.

5. See W. A. Swanberg, *Citizen Hearst* (New York: Charles Scribner's Sons, 1961), p. 108; Butler, *Cuba Must Be Free*, pp. 4–5; "The Thanks of the Cuban Junta," *Leslie's Weekly*, LXXXIV (January 14, 1897):18. This was the view, too, of many ranking American officers. See William Ludlow to Henry C. Corbin, June 5, 1898, Henry C. Corbin Papers.

6. *Congressional Record*, XXVIII (February 28, 1896), pt. III, p. 2244.

7. Ibid., XXVIII (March 2, 1896), pt. III, pp. 2344, 2349.

8. Ibid., XXXI (April 15, 1898), pt. IV, pp. 3885, 3887.

9. Ibid., XXXI (April 15, 1898), pt. IV, p. 3891.

10. Ibid., XXVIII (March 2, 1896), pt. III, p. 2349.

11. Hall, *The Fun and Fighting of the Rough Riders*, p. 114.

12. Roosevelt, *The Rough Riders*, p. 75.

13. George Kennan, *Campaigning in Cuba*, p. 92.

14. Tingley, "The Cuban Diary of Edwin M. Lacey," p. 24; McIntosh, *The Little I Saw of Cuba*, p. 74.

15. Stephen Crane, *Wounds in the Rain*, p. 220; Horton, "The Battle of San Juan," pp. 413–14; Miller, *Rough Rider. His Diary as A Soldier*, p. 126; Bookmiller, "The Ninth U.S. Infantry in the Santiago Campaign," p. 61; Howard Chandler Christy, "The Story of the War," *Leslie's Weekly* LXXXVII (September 1, 1898):174; Kennan, *Campaigning in Cuba*, pp. 91–92; Brown, *The Correspondents' War. Journalists in the Spanish-American War*, p. 332; Graham, *Schley and Santiago*, p. 2.

16. *New York Evening Post*, July 21, 1898, p. 2.

17. In Steffy, "The Cuban Immigrants of Tampa, Florida, 1866—1898" (unpublished M. A. thesis), p. 118.

18. Moss, *Memories of the Campaign of Santiago*, pp. 15, 17.

19. Theodore Roosevelt, "The Fifth Corps at Santiago," in Fitzhugh Lee, *Cuba's Struggle Against Spain*, p. 645.

20. Parker, *History of the Gatling Gun Detachment, Fifty Army Corps, at Santiago, With a Few Unvarnished Truths Concerning That Expedition*, pp. 76–77.

21. Sargent, *The Campaign of Santiago de Cuba*, II:43.

22. *New York Evening Post*, July 21, 1898, p. 2.

23. Roosevelt, *The Rough Riders*, p. 75.

24. Frank R. McCoy to parents, n.d., Frank R. McCoy Papers.

25. Lieutenant J. W. Heard to Adjutant General Henry C. Corbin, August 21, 1898, U.S. War Department, *Annual Report of the War Department: Report of the Major-General Commanding the Army, 1898*, House of Representatives, House Document No. 2, 55th Congress, 3rd Session, Ser. 3745, p. 343; Richard Harding Davis to Charles Belmont Davis,

June 26, 1898, in Charles Belmont Davis, ed., *Adventures and Letters of Richard Harding Davis*, p. 249; Bonsal, *The Fight for Santiago*, pp. 379–80; Stratemeyer, *A Young Volunteer in Cuba*, pp. 171, 194; *New York Times*, July 23, 1898, p. 1.

26. Sargent, *The Campaign of Santiago de Cuba*, II:164–66.

27. *New York Tribune*, August 5, 1898, p. 3.

28. *New York Times*, August 7, 1898, p. 2.

29. U.S. Congress, Senate, *Report of the Commission Appointed by the President to Investigate the Conduct of the War Department in the War with Spain*, V:1954.

30. Roosevelt, "The Fifth Corps at Santiago," p. 645.

31. General William R. Shafter to Adjutant General Henry C. Corbin, July 31, 1898, File 110293, Records of the Adjutant General's Office, 1780s–1917, National Archives, Record Group 94. (Hereafter cited as AGO/RG 94.)

32. Draper, *The Rescue of Cuba*, p. 176.

33. General Samuel B.M. Young to Adjutant General Henry C. Corbin, June 29, 1898, Correspondence File, General Joseph Wheeler Papers.

34. Stallman and Hageman, eds., *The War Despatches of Stephen Crane*, pp. 181–82.

35. General William R. Shafter, "Operations at Santiago," September 13, 1898, in U.S. Department of War, *Annual Report of the War Department Report of the Major-General Commanding the Army, 1898*, p. 149. Miley, *In Cuba With Shafter*, p. 58; Wheeler, *The Santiago Campaign, 1898*, p. 250.

36. See Nelson A. Miles to Calixto García, June 2, 1898, in U.S. Department of War, *Annual Report of the War Department: Report of the Major-General Commanding the Army, 1898*, p. 16. General Miles later wrote that "General García regarded my requests *as his orders* and promptly took steps to execute the plan of operation." See Miles, *Serving the Republic*, p. 280.

37. Adjutant General Henry C. Corbin to General William R. Shafter, May 31, 1898, in Lee, *Cuba's Struggle Against Spain*, p. 33.

38. Wagner, *Report of the Santiago Campaign, 1898*, p. 14. See also Miles, "The Work of the Army as a Whole," pp. 523–24, and Gay Calbó, "Los últimos tiempos del 95 y la guerra hispanoamericana," p. 355. "It is our war," *The Nation* insisted, "and we must depend upon ourselves to conduct it." See *The Nation* LXII (May 12, 1898):354.

39. Calixto García to Tomás Estrada Palma, June 27, 1898, in Torriente y Peraza, *Calixto García cooperó con las fuerzas armadas de los EE. UU. cumpliendo órdenes del gobierno cubano*, p. 32.

40. *The New York World*, July 27, 1898, p. 3.

41. *New York Tribune*, August 5, 1898, p. 3.

42. *Chicago Daily News*, July 15, 1898, p. 3. See also Morris, *The War With Spain*, p. 310, and Wheeler, *The Santiago Campaign 1898*, p. 294. The Cubans made a much more powerful enemy of the American press corps. The arrival of American forces brought to Cuba some 150 reporters and writers, all of whom descended on Cuban command headquarters demanding translators, scouts, assistants, and horses. García refused to fulfill these requests and recommended they take their requests to General Shafter. Muecke Bertel, *Patria y libertad*, p. 36; Corona Ferrer, *De la manigua (ecos de la epopeya)* pp. 100–01; Carlos García Vélez, son of Calixto, later charged that the Cubans "were slandered bitterly by the war-correspondents . . . who, in their wrath against us for not furnishing them servants and horses as they expected we would, wrote down statements that only existed in their excited imagination." See García Vélez, "Cuba Against Spain, 1895–1898," pp. 67–68.

43. Parker, *History of the Gatling Gun Detachment*, p. 78.

44. McIntosh, *The Little I Saw in Cuba*, p. 74. This view persisted into the twentieth century. "Americans, when they rushed to the aid of Free Cuba in 1898," Irene Wright wrote in 1910, "supposed that they were intervening in behalf of an oppressed people struggling for

justice. The truth is, they championed a horde of disgruntled political aspirants after 'jobs.' "
Wright, *Cuba*, p. 167.

45. George Edward Graham, "The Truth About the Insurgents," *Leslie's Weekly*
LXXXVII (July 28, 1898):74. See also McCurdy, ed., *Two Rough Riders: Letters from F.
Allen McCurdy and J. Kirk McCurdy*, p. 30, and Wright, *Cuba*, p. 168.

46. Draper, *The Rescue of Cuba*, p. 176.

47. *New York Times*, August 9, 1898, p. 2.

48. *New York Times*, July 28, 1898, p. 4.

49. George Kennan, "Cuban Character," p. 960.

50. *New York Times*, July 24, 1898, p. 2.

51. *New York Times*, July 29, 1898, p. 4.

52. *New York Times*, August 7, 1898, p. 2.

53. Hastings, "With Gomez in the Cuban Skirmishes," p. 158; Flint, *Marching With Gomez*,
p. 189; Hernández y Pérez, *Dos conferencias históricas*, p. 68.

54. Máximo Gómez to Secretario de la Guerra, Apr. 29, 1898, in Torriente, *Calixto García
cooperó con las fuerzas armadas de los EE. UU. compliendo órdenes del gobierno cubano*, p.
25; *The Nation* LXII (May 12, 1898):354.

55. See Adolfo del Castillo to Jorge León Mendoza, Feb. 2, 1897, in Castellanos García,
Adolfo del Castillo en la paz y en la guerra, pp. 91–92; Bergés, *Cuba y Santo Domingo.
Apuntes de la guerra de mi diario de campaña. 1895–96–97–98*, p. 150; José Miguel Gómez to
Tomás Estrada Palma, June 14, 1897, *Patria*, June 21, 1897, p. 2.

56. *Washington Evening Star*, February 12, 1898, p. 1; Horton, "The Battle of San Juan,"
pp. 413–14.

57. Stallman and Hageman, *The War Dispatches of Stephen Crane*, p. 4.

58. *New York Times*, July 28, 1898, p. 4; *Chicago Tribune*, July 13, 1898, p. 3.

59. *The New York World*, July 14, 1898, p. 3.

60. Dawley, Jr., "With Our Army at Tampa" (unpublished ms.), p. 146.

61. Lieutenant Colonel Clinton Smith to Colonel Augustus R. Francis, July 31, 1898, in *New
York Times*, August 12, 1898, p. 1.

62. *New York Times*, July 20, 1898, p. 1.

63. *New York Evening Post*, July 21, 1898, p. 2; *The State*, July 28, 1898, p. 1; *New York
Tribune*, August 5, 1898, p. 1.

64. Parker, *History of the Gatling Gun Detachment*, p. 76.

65. *The New York World*, July 14, 1898, p. 3.

66. Howard, *Fighting for Humanity*, pp. 53–84; Moss, *Memories of the Campaign of
Santiago*, p. 53; Morris, *The War With Spain*, pp. 295–97.

67. Vivian, *The Fall of Santiago*, pp. 124–25.

68. Theodore Roosevelt to Henry Cabot Lodge, July 3, 1898, Henry Cabot Lodge, ed.,
Selections From the Correspondence of Theodore Roosevelt and Henry Cabot Lodge, I:317.

69. Theodore Roosevelt to Henry Cabot Lodge, July 7, 1898, ibid., I:321–22. See also
Keeler, *The Journal of Frank Keeler. 1898*, p. 21.

70. For an account of conditions in Santiago de Cuba during the siege see Ramsden, "Diary
of the British Consul at Santiago During Hostilites"; Medel, *La guerra hispano-americana y
sus resultados*, pp. 75–76; Rodríguez Martínez, *Los desastres y regeneración de España.
Relatos e impresiones*, pp. 8–9.

71. General William A. Shafter to Adjutant General Henry C. Corbin, July 14, 1898, in
Carter, *The Life of Lieutenant General Chaffee*, p. 149; General William R. Shafter to Adjutant General Henry C. Corbin, July 15, 1898, in U.S. Congress, Senate, *Report of the Commission Appointed by the President to Investigate the Conduct of the War Department in the
War with Spain*, II:1014; General William R. Shafter to Adjutant General Henry C. Corbin,

July 16, 1898, in Wheeler, *The Santiago Campaign*, pp. 139–46; *The New York World*, July 9, 1898, p. 2.

72. General Nelson A. Miles to Secretary of War Russell A. Alger, July 13, 1968, in U.S. Congress, Senate, *Report of the Commission Appointed by the President to Investigate the Conduct of the War Department in the War With Spain*, II:1001. See also Dierks, *A Leap to Arms: The Cuban Campaign of 1898*, pp. 171–84.

73. José Müeller y Tejeiro, *Battles and Capitulations of Santiago de Cuba*, p. 145; William McKinley to secretary of war, July 18, 1898, Day Papers.

74. For a detailed account of this meeting see Stanhope Sams, "Trouble with Cubans," *New York Times*, August 5, 1898, p. 2, and "El General Shafter y los cubanos," *Patria*, Aug. 27, 1898, p. 2. At the almost same time in Washington, Vice President Domingo Méndez Capote learned from Attorney General John Griggs that the McKinley administration considered the American army in Cuba as an "invading army that would carry with it American sovereignty wherever it went." See Domingo Méndez Capote, *Trabajos*, III:78.

75. Calixto García to Pedro Pérez, Aug. 12, 1898, in Casasús, *Calixto García (el estratega)*, p. 284.

76. William R. Shafter to adjutant general, July 23, 1898, in U.S. Congress, Senate, *Report of the Commission Appointed by the President to Investigate the Conduct of the War Department in the War With Spain*, II:1042; *Washington Evening Star*, July 19, 1898, p. 1; *Chicago Tribune*, July 25, 1898, p. 1; Bonsal, *The Fight For Santiago*, pp. 441–42.

77. Arbelo, *Recuerdos de la última guerra por la independencia de Cuba. 1896 a 1898*, pp. 307–08; García Vélez, "Cuba Against Spain, 1895–1898," pp. 88–89; *Chicago Tribune*, July 25, 1898, p. 1.

78. Calixto García to William R. Shafter, July 17, 1898, in Calixto García, *Palabras de tres guerras*, pp. 107–10.

79. Ibid. See also Cuba, Ejército Libertador, *Parte oficial del lugarteniente general Calixto García al General en Jefe Máximo Gómez 15 de Julio de 1898 sobre la campaña de Santiago de Cuba*, pp. 22–23.

80. Calixto García, "Circular," July 17, 1898, in García, *Palabras de tres guerras*, pp. 110–11.

81. Ricardo Díaz-Albertini to Tomás Estrada Palma, Aug. 12, 1898, in Llaverías y Martínez, ed., *Correspondencia de la delegación cubana en Nueva York durante la guerra de 1895 a 1898*, V:21–22.

82. Tomás Estrada Palma to Domingo Méndez Capote, Aug. 15, 1898, *Actas de las Asambleas*, IV:126–27; Rubens, *Liberty, The Story of Cuba*, pp. 380–81.

83. Collazo, *La guerra en Cuba*, pp. 35–36; Carlos González Palacio, *Exaltación a la fe* (La Habana: Editorial "Alfa," 1941), pp. 61–62.

Chapter 11. From Allies to Adversaries

1. *The State*, July 28, 1898, p. 1.

2. *New York Evening Post*, July 21, 1898, p. 2.

3. Lieutenant Colonel Clinton H. Smith to Colonel Augustus T. Francis, July 31, 1898, in *New York Times*, August 12, 1898, p. 1.

4. Ibid.

5. Chamberlain, "Spanish Bravery at Caney."

6. See Wheeler, *The Santiago Campaign, 1898*, pp. 140–76, and Sargent, *The Campaign of Santiago de Cuba*, III:51.

7. Watterson, *History of the Spanish-American War*, p. 353. See also Linderman, *The Mirror of War*, pp. 144–46.

8. Pierce, *Reminiscences of the Experiences of Company L, Second Regiment Massachusetts Infantry, U.S.V., in the Spanish American War*, p. 67. See also Stewart, *The N'th Foot in War*, pp. 151–53.

9. *New York Times*, July 21, 1898, p. 2. See also Gauvreau, *Reminiscences of the Spanish-American War*, p. 48; Miley, *In Cuba With Shafter*, p. 224; Shafter, "Address of Major General William R. Shafter, U.S. Army, Before the Chamber of Commerce, Los Angeles, California," p. 262; Alger, *The Spanish-American War*, p. 279.

10. *New York Times*, July 19, 1898, p. 4.

11. *The Philadelphia Inquirer*, July 22, 1898, p. 5. See also *New York Times*, July 29, 1898, p. 4.

12. *New York Tribune*, August 7, 1898, II, p. 1.

13. Pedro López de Castillo to soldiers of the American Army, August 21, 1898, in U.S. War Department, Adjutant General, *Correspondence Relating to the War With Spain*, p. 250.

14. George Edward Graham, "The Truth About the Insurgents," *Leslie's Weekly* LXXXVII (July 28, 1898):74.

15. *New York Times*, July 29, 1898, p. 4.

16. Martel, *Memorias de un mambí*, p. 142; Muecke Bertel, *Patria y libertad*, pp. 255–58.

17. Montejo, *The Autobiography of a Runaway Slave*, p. 216. See also Matthews, *The New-Born Cuba*, p. 38.

18. Frank Burns to editor, *Illinois Record*, n.d., in Willard B. Gatewood, Jr., *"Smoked Yankees" and the Struggle for Empire: Letters From Negro Soldiers, 1898–1902* (Urbana: University of Illinois Press, 1971), p. 205.

19. *New York Tribune*, August 16, 1898, p. 3. These developments made a similar impression on the *Philadelphia Inquirer* correspondent: "Sentiment throughout the American army is vastly more favorable to the Spaniards than to the Cubans." *Philadelphia Inquirer*, July 21, 1898, p. 5. The editorial writer for *The State* also noted: "The people of the city of Santiago have apparently nothing to regret in the change of masters. They welcomed the American troops warmly; they saw without regret the Spanish depart; no doubt the people of Santiago know a good thing when they see it." *The State*, July 30, 1898, p. 6.

20. *New York Tribune*, August 7, 1898, II, p. 1.

21. *New York Times*, December 19, 1898, p. 2.

22. *The State*, July 30, 1898, p. 4.

23. *New York Times*, August 5, 1898, p. 2. See also Howard, *Fighting for Humanity*, p. 79.

24. *New York Times*, July 19, 1898, p. 6.

25. William R. Shafter to Henry C. Corbin, July 29, 1898, U.S. War Department, *Correspondence Relating to the War With Spain*, p. 186; *New York Times*, July 31, 1898, p. 2, and *New York Times*, August 5, 1898, p. 2.

26. *New York Tribune*, August 9, 1898, p. 3.

27. *Washington Post*, October 8, 1898, p. 2.

28. "Statement of Marquis of Apezteguía," September 9, 1898, in U.S. Department of Treasury, *Appendix to the Report on the Commercial and Industrial Condition of the Island of Cuba* (Washington, D.C.: Government Printing Office, 1899), pp. 332–33.

29. *New York Times*, July 20, 1898, p. 1.

30. Draper, *The Rescue of Cuba*, pp. 176–79.

31. "General García and Cuban Conduct," p. 124.

32. Parker, *History of the Gatling Gun Detachment, Fifth Army Corps, at Santiago, With a Few Unvarnished Truths Concerning That Expedition*, p. 78.

33. James Harrison Wilson, *Under the Old Flag*, II, p. 490.

34. Leonard Wood to secretary of war, September 9, 1898, File 139813, AGO/RG 94; *Washington Post*, October 1, 1898, p. 2.

35. *New York Times*, December 24, 1898, p. 9.

36. *The State*, December 19, 1898, p. 1; *New York Times*, December 19, 1898, p. 2.

37. In Millis, *The Martial Spirit. A Study of Our War With Spain*, p. 362.

38. *New York Times*, July 22, 1898, p. 2.

39. *New York Times*, July 29, 1898, p. 4.

40. *New York Times*, August 1, 1898, p. 6.

41. *New York Times*, July 29, 1898, p. 4. See also *The State*, July 20, 1898, p. 1, and Morris, *The War With Spain*, p. 312.

42. *New York Tribune*, August 14, 1898, p. 6.

43. Ogden, "Multiplying Difficulties in Cuba," p. 84.

44. *New York Herald*, August 16, 1898, p. 6.

45. *New York Times*, August 1, 1898, p. 6.

46. Hazeltine, "What is to be Done With Cuba?" pp. 320–21.

47. *New York Times*, August 24, 1898, p. 4.

48. Hazeltine, "What is to be Done with Cuba?" pp. 322–23.

49. *New York Evening Post*, July 21, 1898, p. 2.

50. Robinson, *Thomas B. Reed, Parliamentarian*, p. 369; McElroy, *Grover Cleveland*, p. 274; Johnson, *William Allen White's America*, p. 110.

51. In "General García and Cuban Conduct," pp. 122–23.

52. *Washington Evening Star*, July 30, 1898, p. 2.

53. *New York Times*, August 12, 1898, p. 6.

54. *New York Tribune*, August 7, 1898, p. 6.

55. *New York Tribune*, August 17, 1898, p. 6.

56. *Philadelphia Inquirer*, August 6, 1898, p. 6.

57. Richardson, ed., *A Compilation of the Messages and Papers of the Presidents, 1789–1902*, X:67.

58. Draper, *The Rescue of Cuba*, pp. 178–79.

59. *New York Times*, July 19, 1898, p. 6.

60. *New York Times*, July 23, 1898, p. 1.

61. "Statement of Commissioner Robert P. Porter, Given Before the United States Commission for the Evacuation of Cuba," September, 1898, in U.S. Department of Treasury, *Appendix to the Report on the Commercial and Industrial Condition of the Island of Cuba*, p. 147.

62. Howard, *Fighting for Humanity*, p. 20.

63. Dawes, *A Journal of the McKinley Years*, p. 165. See also Ellis, *Henry Moore Teller, Defender of the West*, p. 341.

64. *New York Times*, July 30, 1898, p. 1.

65. *The State*, July 18, 1898, p. 2. See also Gonzales, *In Darkest Cuba* pp. 54–55.

66. Máximo Gómez to Tomás Estrada Palma, Aug. 26, 1898, in Máximo Gómez, *Ideario cubano*, p. 104.

67. See Máximo Gómez, *Diario de campaña del mayor general Máximo Gómez*, pp. 363–64; Castillo, *Autobiografía del general José Rogelio Castillo*, pp. 265–66; Arbelo, *Recuerdos de la última guerra por la independencia de Cuba. 1896 a 1898*, pp. 315–16; Tirado, "Apuntes de un corresponsal (VI)," p. 464.

68. Calixto García to Tomás Estrada Palma, Aug. 23, 1898, *Boletín del Archivo Nacional* XXXV (Jan.–Dec., 1936), pp. 124–25.

69. William R. Shafter to Adjutant General Henry C. Corbin, July 23, 1898, in U.S. War Department, *Correspondence Relating to the War With Spain*, p. 175.

70. William R. Shafter to Russell A. Alger, July 29, 1898, U.S. Congress, Senate, *Report of the Commission Appointed by the President to Investigate the Conduct of the War Department in the War With Spain*, II:1052.

71. William R. Shafter to Adjutant General Henry C. Corbin, August 16, 1898, U.S. Con-

gress, Senate, *Report of the Commission Appointed by the President to Investigate the Conduct of the War Department in the War With Spain*, II:1102.

72. *New York Herald*, August 10, 1898, p. 5.

73. Horacio Ferrer, *Con el rifle al hombro*, pp. 135–37; Collazo, *Los americanos en Cuba*, pp. 189–90; Cañizares y Quirós, "Diario de operaciónes del teniente coronel Rafael M. Cañizares y Quirós," pp. 147–48; *The State*, November 19, 1898, p. 3.

74. William R. Shafter to Adjutant General Henry C. Corbin, July 31, 1898, File 110293, AGO/RG 94.

75. J. W. Heard to adjutant general, August 21, 1898, U.S. War Department, *Annual Reports of the War Department: Report of the Major-General Commanding the Army, 1898*, p. 376.

76. William R. Shafter to Adjutant General Henry C. Corbin, August 17, 1898, U.S. Congress, Senate, *Report of the Commission Appointed by the President to Investigate the Conduct of the War Department in the War With Spain*, II, p. 1102.

77. *New York Herald*, August 16, 1898, p. 6.

78. See Jenks, *Our Cuban Colony*, p. 320.

Chapter 12. Peace Without Victory

1. Esteban Borrero E. to Tomás Estrada Palma, Sept. 29, 1898, in Llaverías y Martínez, ed., *Correspondencia de la delegación cubana en Nueva York durante la guerra de 1895 a 1898*, II:251. See also Rafael M. Merchán to Tomás Estrada Palma, June 11, 1898, ibid., II:143–44; Rivero Muñiz, "Los cubanos en Tampa," pp. 110–11; *Chicago Tribune*, July 15, 1898, p. 7; *New York Times*, July 19, 1898, p. 1; *New York Journal*, August 3, 1898, p. 2.

2. José Dolores Poyo to Tomás Estrada Palma, Aug. 31, 1898, in Azcuy Alón, *El Partido Revolucionario y la independencia de Cuba*, p. 125; Esteban Borrero E. to Tomás Estrada Palma, Aug. 14, 1898, *Correspondencia de la delegación cubana*, II:248–49; Lola R. de Tío, "Club 'Caridad': acta final," Oct. 24, 1898, *Patria*, Nov. 5, 1898, p. 3.

3. Emilio Núñez, "A los jefes y oficiales del Departamento de Expediciones," Oct. 15, 1898, *Patria*, Oct. 19, 1898, p. 1; Luis A. de Arce, *Emilio Núñez (1875–1922): historiografía* (La Habana: Editorial "Niños," 1943), pp. 192–94. See also Tomás Estrada Palma to Emilio Núñez, Oct. 8, 1898, *Patria*, Oct. 15, 1898, p. 1.

4. Tomás Estrada Palma, "A los clubs, cuerpos de consejos y agentes del Partido Revolucionario Cubano," *Patria*, Dec. 21, 1898, pp. 1–2.

5. Horacio Ferrer, *Con el rifle al hombro*, p. 129; Espinosa y Ramos, *Al trote y sin estribos (recuerdos de la guerra de independencia)*, pp. 249–51.

6. Pelayo García to Rafael Lubián, Sept. 8, 1898, in Lubián, *El Club Revolucionario Juan Bruno Zayas*, pp. 215–15; Cañizares y Quirós, "Diario de operaciones del teniente coronel Rafael M. Cañizares y Quirós," p. 147; M. García Garofalo y Mesa, *Como acabó la dominación de España en Villaclara* (Villaclara: n.p., 1944), p. 24; Bergés Tabares, *Cuba y Santo Domingo. Apuntes de la guerra de Cuba de mi diario de campaña 1895–96–97–98*, p. 164.

7. Enrique Callazo, *Los americanos en Cuba* (La Habana: Instituto Cubano del Libre, 1972), p. 232.

8. Piedra Martel, *Mis primeros treinta años: memorias*, p. 496; Conill, *Enrique J. Conill, soldado de la patria*, p. 21; *The State*, September 27, 1898, p. 1; *London Times*, December 2, 1898, p. 32.

9. Lieutenant Colonel Edgar Carbonne to Gonzalo de Quesada, October 29, 1898, in *New York Times*, November 5, 1898, p. 4.

10. "Statement of Antonio Caballero," n.d., in U.S. Department of the Treasury, *Appendix to the Report on the Commercial and Industrial Condition of the Island of Cuba, June 15, 1899*, p. 243.

11. *New York Times*, September 24, 1898, p. 2. See also José M. Rodríguez to Bartolomé Masó, n.d., in Llaverías y Martínez and Santovenia, eds., *Actas de las Asambleas de Representantes y del Consejo de Gobierno durante la guerra de independencia*, IV:151; Sergio Aguirre, "La desaparición del Ejército Libertador," p. 51; Ferrara y Marino, *Mis relaciones con Máximo Gómez*, p. 220; Varona Guerrero, *La guerra de independencia de Cuba, 1898–1898*, III:1704–06; Berges Taberes, *Cuba y Santo Domingo. Apuntes de la guerra de Cuba de mi diario de campaña 1895–96–97–98*, p. 167.

12. Lieutenant Edward P. Mahony to J. Nelson Polhamus, n.d., *The Daily Picayune* (New Orleans), October 29, 1898, p. 11.

13. Francisco Díaz Silveira to Gualterio García, Aug. 31, 1898, in Quesada, *Documentos históricos*, p. 486.

14. *Actas de las Asambleas*, IV:120–21; Casasús, *Calixto García (el estratega)*, pp. 305–07; Torriente y Peraza, *Calixto García cooperó con las fuerzas armadas de los EE. UU. en 1898, cumpliendo órdenes del gobierno cubano*, p. 35.

15. Francisco Sánchez to Calixto García, Sept. 4, 1898, in Castellanos García, *Tierras y glorias de Oriente (Calixto García Iñiguez)*, pp. 361–62; Collazo, *Los americanos en Cuba*, p. 229.

16. Domingo Méndez Capote to Generals Pedro A. Pérez and Agustín Cebreco, Sept. 19, 1898, *Actas de las Asambleas*, IV:138.

17. The appointees were all lawyers, engineers, and physicians, and included Manuel Despaigne, Eugenio Sánchez Agramonte, Octavio Giberga y Galí, and Fernando Freyre de Andrade. See *Actas de las Asambleas*, IV:131–32.

18. Ibid., IV:134–36.

19. Ibid., V:27.

20. In Castellanos García, *Tierras y glorias de Oriente (Calixto García Iñiguez)*, p. 370. See also Casasús, *Calixto García (el estratega)*, p. 314.

21. *Actas de las Asambleas*, VI:11–29.

22. See Infiesta, *Historia constitucional de Cuba*, pp. 291–92; *Actas de las Asambleas*, V:43–62.

23. Slightly varying versions of this interview appeared in the *New York Herald*, September 25, 1898, p. 3, *The Philadelphia Inquirer*, September 25, 1898, and *The State*, September 28, 1898, p. 4. Several days after this interview, an aide to García acknowledged to the *Herald* correspondent: "So long as the Spaniards ruled the island we had to calm our feelings and present a united front to our enemies. Now it is better to reveal publicly the dissensions among us, which have excited us for years." *New York Herald*, September 28, 1899, p. 10.

24. Ferrara y Marino, *Mis relaciones con Máximo Gómez*, p. 193.

25. See Máximo Gómez to Tomás Estrada Palma, Aug. 26, 1898, *Boletín del Archivo Nacional*, XXXII (Jan.–Dec., 1933), p. 92. See also *Patria*, Sept. 28, 1898, p. 2.

26. Máximo Gómez to Francisco Carrillo, Sept. 2, 1898, in Máximo Gómez, *Cartas a Francisco Carrillo*, p. 240.

27. Fernandy Gómez, *La insurrección por dentro. Apuntes para la historia*, p. 185; Céspedes y de Quesada, *Un instante de la maravillosa carrera de Máximo Gómez*, p. 21; Aguirre, "La desaparición del Ejército Libertador," p. 57.

28. Máximo Gómez, "Carta abierta a Bernarda Toro de Gómez y a los dominicanos," n.d., in Máximo Gómez, *Cartas de Máximo Gómez*, pp. 50–51.

29. Máximo Gómez to Francisco Gregorio Billini, Nov. 15, 1898, in Máximo Gómez, *Papeles dominicanos de Máximo Gómez*, p. 76.

30. Muecke Bertel, *Patria y libertad*, pp. 227–28; Torriente, *Mi casa en la tierra*, p. 18; Morales Patiño, *El capitán chino. Teniente coronel Quirino Zamora. Historia de un mambí en la provincia de La Habana*, p. 110; Aguirre, "La desaparición del Ejército Libertador," pp. 53–54.

31. *Patria*, Oct. 1, 1898, p. 2. See also Emilio Núñez to Gonzalo de Quesada, in Quesada, *Archivo de Gonzalo de Quesada*, II:123.

32. Ferrara y Marino, *Mis relaciones con Máximo Gómez*, pp. 223–24.

33. Infiesta, *Máximo Gómez*, p. 205; *The State*, October 31, 1898, p. 7; Ferrara y Marino, *Mis relaciones con Máximo Gómez*, pp. 193–95, 216.

34. Ferrara y Marino, *Mis relaciones con Máximo Gómez*, pp. 220–21. See also Collazo, *La guerra en Cuba*, pp. 39–40, 100.

35. Máximo Gómez, *Diario de campaña del mayor general Máximo Gómez*, p. 366. See also Máximo Gómez, "Carta abierta a Bernarda Toro de Gómez y a los dominicanos," n.d., in Gómez, *Cartas de Máximo Gómez*, pp. 51–52.

36. Ferrara y Marino, *Mis relaciones con Máximo Gómez*, p. 220.

37. *New York Herald*, September 30, 1898, p. 9.

38. Duarte Oropesa, *Historiología cubana*, IV:361–62; Ferrara y Marino, *Mis relaciones con Máximo Gómez*, pp. 193–94.

39. Ferrara y Marino, *Mis relaciones con Máximo Gómez*, pp. 219–21.

40. Máximo Gómez, *Diario de campaña del mayor general Máximo Gómez*, pp. 367–68.

41. Conill, *Enrique J. Conill, soldado de la patria*, pp. 22–27; Portell Vilá, *Historia de Cuba en sus relaciones con los Estados Unidos y España*, IV:36.

42. For biographies of Calixto García see Casasús, *Calixto García (el estratega)*, and Castellanos García, *Tierras y glorias de Oriente (Calixto García Iñiguez)*.

43. William R. Shafter to Henry C. Corbin, August 16, 1898, U.S. War Department, Adjutant General, *Correspondence Relating to the War With Spain*, p. 232.

44. H. W. Lawton to Henry C. Corbin, August 16, 1898, File 116542, AGO/RG 94.

45. Henry C. Corbin to H. W. Lawton, August 16, 1898, Letters Sent, File 282, Department of Santiago de Cuba, Records of the U.S. Army Overseas Operations and Commands, 1898–1945, Record Group 395, National Archives, Washington, D.C. (Hereafter cited as AOOC/RG 395.)

46. Leonard Wood to Russell A. Alger, September 9, 1898, File 139813, AGO/RG 94.

47. *New York Herald*, September 28, 1898, p. 10.

48. H. W. Lawton to Henry C. Corbin, September 27, 1898, File 132232, AGO/RG 94. See also Bail, "The Military Government of Cuba, 1898–1902" (unpublished ms.), p. 7.

49. Calixto García to Tomás Estrada Palma, Aug. 22, 1898, *Boletín del Archivo Nacional* XXXV (Jan.–Dec., 1936):122.

50. *The Philadelphia Inquirer*, September 28, 1898, p. 8.

51. H. C. Lawton to Agustín Cebreco, September 5, 1898, File 186, Letters Sent, Department of Santiago de Cuba, AOOC/RG 395. See also *New York Times*, September 6, 1898, p. 3.

52. In Hagedorn, *Leonard Wood, A Biography*, I:255.

53. Leonard Wood to William McKinley, November 27, 1898, Leonard Wood Papers.

54. Leonard Wood, "The Military Government of Cuba," p. 2; *New York Times*, October 24, 1898, p. 5; *The Washington Post*, October 25, 1898, p. 4.

Chapter 13. Dissent and Dissolution

1. Collazo, *Los americanos en Cuba*, pp. 229–30.

2. Ibid., p. 229.

3. Octavio Ramón Costa y Blanco, *Perfil político de Calixto García*, p. 30; Duarte Oropesa, *Historiología cubana*, IV:307–08.

4. Emilio Núñez to Gonzalo de Quesada, Nov. 19, 1899, in Quesada, *Archivo de Gonzalo de Quesada*, II:128.

5. Emilio Núñez to Gonzalo de Quesada, Jan. 2, 1899, in ibid., II:127–28.

6. Emilio Núñez to Gonzalo de Quesada, Jan. 27, 1899, in ibid., II:131–32. See also Rodríguez Altunaga, *El general Emilio Núñez*, pp. 343–44.

7. Calixto García to Tomás Estrada Palma, Aug. 22, 1898, *Boletín del Archivo Nacional* XXXV (Jan.–Dec., 1936):122, and Calixto García to Gonzalo de Quesada, Aug. 24, 1898, in Quesada, *Archivo de Gonzalo de Quesada*, II:176–77.

8. Máximo Gómez to Gonzalo de Quesada, Sept. 29, 1898, in Quesada, Archivo de Quesada, II:230; Máximo Gómez to Gonzalo de Quesada, October 19, 1898, *The Washington Post*, November 6, 1898, p. 5; Máximo Gómez to Tomás Estrada Palma, Oct. 29, 1898, *Boletín del Archivo Nacional* XXXII (Jan.–Dec., 1933):94–95.

9. Máximo Gómez to Tomás Estrada Palma, Nov. 14, 1898, *Boletín del Archivo Nacional* XXXII (Jan.–Dec., 1933):96.

10. Calixto García to Tomás Estrada Palma, June 27, 1898, *Boletín del Archivo Nacional* XXXV (Jan.–Dec., 1936):111. See also Máximo Gómez to Tomás Estrada Palma, June, 1898, *Boletín del Archivo Nacional* XXXI (Jan.–Dec., 1932):108.

11. Rubens, *Liberty, The Story of Cuba*, pp. 388–89.

12. "Memoria de la primera comisión enviada a Wáshington," in Llaverías y Martínez and Santovenia, eds., *Actas de las Asambleas*, V:149–52.

13. Rubens, *Liberty, The Story of Cuba*, p. 389. See also "Memoria de la primera comisión enviada a Wáshington," p. 149–52; *La Lucha*, Feb. 27, 1899, p. 2; Octavio Costa y Blanco, *Manuel Sanguily*, pp. 65–66; Guerra y Sánchez, *Historia de la nación cubana* VII:13–14.

14. *The Washington Post*, December 30, 1898, p. 1. See also William Ludlow, "Report of Brigadier General William Ludlow, Commanding Department of Havana and Military Governor of the City of Havana, Cuba," August 1, 1898, U.S. War Department, *Annual Report of the War Department: Report of the Major-General Commanding the Army, 1899*, p. 221; Ludlow, "The Transition in Havana," p. 866.

15. *New York Times*, December 14, 1898, p. 1.

16. Raúl Roa, *Aventuras, venturas y desventuras de un mambí*, pp. 314–15; Healy, *The United States in Cuba, 1898–1902*, pp. 70–71.

17. *The State*, December 10, 1898, p. 4.

18. Leonard Wood, "Report of General Leonard Wood," United States Department of War, I:63.

19. *Washington Daily Star*, June 20, 1899, p. 11. See also Hagedorn, *Leonard Wood, A Biography*, I:256; E. G. Rathbone, "Memoranda for Senator Hanna," n.d. Roswell R. Hoes Papers.

20. Leonard Wood, "Report of Brigadier Leonard Wood," in U.S. War Department, *Annual Reports of the War Department: Report of the Major-General Commanding the Army, 1899*, pp. 302–03.

21. James Harrison Wilson to R. Suydam Grant, September 14, 1899, Letterbook, James Harrison Wilson Papers.

22. Máximo Gómez to Federico Henríquez y Carjaval, Oct. 14, 1898, in Máximo Gómez, *Cartas de Máximo Gómez*, pp. 30–31.

23. Máximo Gómez, "Al pueblo cubano y al Ejército," Dec. 29, 1898, *Boletín del Archivo Nacional* XXXII (Jan.–Dec., 1933):97–98. See also Griñán Peralta, *El caracter de Máximo Gómez*, p. 159.

24. Máximo Gómez to the executive commission, Jan. 6, 1898, *Actas de las Asambleas*, VI:34–35.

25. Executive commission to Máximo Gómez, n.d., ibid., VI:35–37.

26. *New York Times*, February 4, 1899, p. 6.

27. James Harrison Wilson to adjutant general, February 16, 1899, in U.S. War Department, *Annual Report of the War Department: Report of the Major-General Commanding the Army, 1899*, p. 156.

28. Fitzhugh Lee, "Special Report of Brigadier General Fitzhugh Lee, U.S.V.," September 18, 1899, in John R. Brooke, *Civil Report of Major-General John R. Brooke, U.S. Army, Military Governor of Cuba, 1899*, p. 343.

29. H. L. Carpenter, "Report of L. H. Carpenter, Commanding Department of Puerto Príncipe," July 10, 1899, in U.S. War Department, *Annual Report of the War Department, 1899*, Series 3899–904 I, pt. 1, p. 331.

30. H. L. Lawton to adjutant general, September 3, 1898, File 174, Letters Sent, Department of Santiago, AOOC/RG 395.

31. Máximo Gómez, *Diario de campaña del mayor general Máximo Gómez*, pp. 371–72.

32. Tomás Estrada Palma to Máximo Gómez, Jan. 26, 1899, in Quesada, *Documentos históricos*, p. 8; Portell Vilá, *Historia de Cuba en sus relaciones con los Estados Unidos y España*, IV:34; Raúl Roa, *Adventuras, venturas y desventuras de un mambí*, pp. 315–16. On January 12, the Washington *Evening Star* reported that Gómez "is understood to be hurt at the fact that the United States government officials are not noticing him and are not inviting him to Havana. Although he says nothing on the subject himself regarding his feelings, his intimate friends are aware that he expected different treatment." See *Evening Star*, January 12, 1899, p. 2.

33. Thompson, "How Porter Carried a Message to Gómez," p. 2.

34. Healy, *The United States in Cuba, 1898–1902*, p. 69. Porter arrived in Havana, one correspondent learned, "clothed with absolute authority." See *New York Tribune*, February 3, 1898, p. 1.

35. Robert P. Porter to Lyman J. Gage, February 6, 1899, File 328/1, Records of the Bureau of Insular Affairs, Record Group 350, National Archives, Washington, D.C. (Hereafter cited as BIA/RG 350.) See also Brooke, *Civil Report of Major-General John R. Brooke, U.S. Army, Military Governor of Cuba, 1899*, p. 16.

36. *La Lucha*, Feb. 3, 1899, p. 2.

37. Robert P. Porter to Lyman J. Gage, February 6, 1899, File 328/1, BIA/RG 350. See also Robert P. Porter, *Report on the Commercial and Industrial Condition of Cuba. Special Report on the Commissioner's Visit to General Gómez, and in Relation to the Payment and Disbandment of the Insurgent Army*, pp. 226–27.

38. Robert P. Porter to William McKinley, February 2, 1899, William McKinley Papers.

39. Gonzalo de Quesada, "Cuba Libre, By Gómez," *New York Journal Magazine*, February 26, 1899, p. 26.

40. Máximo Gómez, "Carta abierta a Bernarda Toro de Gómez y a los dominicanos," n.d., in Gómez, *Cartas de Máximo Gómez*, pp. 53–54. See also Ferrara y Marino, *Mis relaciones con Máximo Gómez*, pp. 221–27; Griñán Peralta, *El caracter de Máximo Gómez*, pp. 167–68.

41. C. M. Cohen to Cuban Assembly, n.d., in *Actas de las Asambleas*, V:92–93; Costa y Blanco, *Manuel Sanguily*, pp. 66–68.

42. *La Discusión*, Mar. 13, 1899, p. 2.

43. *La Lucha*, Feb. 4, 1899, p. 4.

44. Rafael Martínez Ortiz, *Cuba: los primeros años de independencia*, 2 vols., 3rd ed. (Paris: Editorial "Le Livre Libre," 1929), I:56; Castellanos García, *Legado mambí*, pp. 21–22.

45. *La Discusión*, March 13, 1899, p. 2.

46. *Actas de las Asambleas*, V:108.

47. Asamblea de Representantes, "Al pueblo y al ejército cubano," Mar. 14, 1899, in *Actas de las Asambleas*, V:119–20; *La Lucha*, Mar. 15, 1899, p. 2.

48. *La Lucha*, Mar. 14, 1899, p. 2; *Actas de las Asambleas*, V:113; Rodríguez Altunaga, *El general Emilio Núñez*, p. 101.

49. John R. Brooke to Henry C. Corbin, February 20, 1899, Letters Sent, File 808, Division of Cuba, Headquarters, AOOC/RG 395.

50. Russell A. Alger to John R. Brooke, March 6, 1899, Letters Received, File 2360, Division of Cuba, Headquarters, AOOC/RG 395.

51. Henry C. Corbin to John R. Brooke, March 17, 1899, Letters Received, File 2360, Division of Cuba, Headquarters, AOOC/RG 395. See also Russell A. Alger to John R. Brooke, March 13, 1899, McKinley Papers.

52. "Notes of Interview Between General Gómez and Major Kennon," March 14, 1899, John R. Brooke Papers.

53. John R. Brooke to Henry C. Corbin, May 24, 1899, Letters Sent, File 2532, Division of Cuba, Headquarters, AOOC/RG 395.

54. See "El viaje del General Gómez en febrero de 1898," in Máximo Gómez, *El general Máximo Gómez y su política de paz, unión y concordia*, pp. 37–44.

55. See *La Lucha*, Mar. 13, 1899, p. 2.

56. Sergio Aguirre, "La desaparición del Ejército Libertador," p. 59; Raúl Roa, *Aventuras, venturas y desventuras de un mambí*, pp. 331–32; Martínez Ortiz, *Cuba: los primeros años de independencia*, I:58–59.

57. John R. Brooke to Russell A. Alger, n.d., McKinley Papers.

58. *Actas de las Asambleas*, V:138–48.

59. See Paradela, "La paga del Ejército Libertador y la economía cubana," and Aguirre, "La desaparición del Ejército Libertador."

Chapter 14. Purpose Without Policy

1. John R. Brooke, *Civil Report of Major-General John R. Brooke, U.S. Army, Military Governor of Cuba: 1900* p. 7; *New York Times*, January 1, 1899, p. 5.

2. William McKinley to John R. Brooke, December 22, 1898, John R. Brooke Papers.

3. James Harrison Wilson, *Under the Old Flag*, II: 479–80.

4. Ibid. II:482. See also U.S. Congress, Senate, Committee on Relations With Cuba, *Conditions in Cuba*, p. 1.

5. Joseph Benson Foraker to James H. Wilson, May 22, 1899, James Harrison Wilson Papers.

6. Henry Adams to Elizabeth Cameron, January 22, 1899, in Henry Adams, *Letters of Henry Adams*, II:206.

7. Henry Adams to Elizabeth Cameron, February 19, 1899, in ibid., II:218–19.

8. Walter B. Barker to John Addison Porter, November 28, 1899, William McKinley Papers.

9. Platt, "The Pacification of Cuba," p. 1466.

10. In George Kennan, "Cuban Character," pp. 1021–22. Both Frantz Fanon and O. Mannoni speak at length of the phenomenon of "infantilization," a common practice in colonial domination in which colonial powers seek to reduce their subjects to a state of childlike helplessness and thereby justify the tutelage of a distant "adult" authority and perpetuate a dependency relationship. See Frantz Fanon, *The Wretched of the Earth*, trans. Constance Farrington (New York: Grove Press, 1968), and O. Mannoni, *Prospero and Caliban: The Psychology of Colonization*, trans. Pamela Powesland (2nd ed., New York: Frederick A. Praeger, 1964).

11. *Washington Daily Star*, June 20, 1899, p. 11.

12. Leonard Wood to William McKinley, April 12, 1900, Leonard Wood Papers.

13. John R. Brooke to Thomas H. Carter, October 21, 1899, Brooke Papers. See also W. W. Wright to E. G. Rathbone, October 3, 1899, Records of the Post Office Department, Record Group 28, National Archives, Washington, D.C. (Hereafter cited as RPO/RG 28.)

14. *New York Evening Post*, November 17, 1899, p. 7.

15. *New York Times*, June 29, 1899, p. 4.

16. In "The Future of Cuba," *The World's Work* I (January, 1901):362.

17. See Foraker, *Notes of a Busy Life*, II:39–40; James H. Wilson to Joseph K. McCammon, February 11, 1900, Letterbook, Wilson Papers. "I think annexation is absolutely out of the question," Senator Orville H. Platt, chairman of the Senate Committee on Relations with Cuba, wrote from Washington. "The Teller resolution stands not only in the way of that, but all other actions which we might take if it had never been passed. I think I know enough of congressional sentiment to know that it is regarded as a pledge of the Government against annexation." See Orville H. Platt to Edwin F. Atkins, June 11, 1901, in Coolidge, *An Old-Fashioned Senator, Orville H. Platt of Connecticut*, p. 314. From Cuba, General Wilson wrote to Theodore Roosevelt: "I am very sure that the 4th Paragraph of the Joint Resolution was a very bad piece of legislation, but doubtless it was rendered necessary by the conditions then existing, and it must be, in my judgement, honestly and faithfully adhered to. However great may be the temptation, the Great Republic always keeps faith with itself and with the world!" See James H. Wilson to Theodore Roosevelt, July 5, 1899, Roosevelt Papers.

18. Muecke Bertel, *Patria y libertad*, pp. 203–04.

19. "Notes of an Interview Between General Wilson and General Bartolomé Massó," November 30, 1899, Speech and Article File, Wilson Papers.

20. Theodore Roosevelt to John Hay, July 1, 1899, Wood Papers.

21. Burt A. Miller to Charles R. Miller, November 4, 1899, McKinley Papers.

22. Leonard Wood to Louise Wood, October 4, 1899, Wood Papers.

23. John R. Brooke to secretary of war, November 30, 1899, File 293936/B, AGO/RG 94.

24. For excellent accounts of this incident see Healy, *The United States in Cuba, 1898–1902*, pp. 116–21, and Foner, *The Spanish-Cuban-American War and the Birth of American Imperialism*, II:514–33. General James H. Wilson, a year later, wrote Whitelaw Reid that Wood had acknowledged that the administration "never intended to live up to the pledge contained in the Joint Resolution." See James H. Wilson to Whitelaw Reid, August 3, 1900, General Correspondence, Wilson Papers.

25. *The Statutes at Large of the United States*, XXX:1755.

26. In Coolidge, *An Old-Fashioned Senator: Orville H. Platt of Connecticut*, p. 331.

27. Mayo W. Hazeltine, "What Is to be Done With Cuba?" p. 321.

28. Richardson, ed., *A Compilation of the Messages and Papers of the Presidents, 1789–1902*, X:152.

29. *New York Journal*, February 27, 1899, p. 12.

30. Whelpley, "Cuba of To-Day and To-Morrow," p. 48.

31. U.S. Congress, Senate, Committee on Relations With Cuba, *Conditions in Cuba*, pp. 17–18.

32. *New York Tribune*, August 26, 1898, p. 6.

33. Williams, "The Outlook in Cuba," p. 833.

34. Leonard Wood, "The Need for Reciprocity With Cuba," p. 2928; Leonard Wood to Elihu Root, January 13, 1900, Wood Papers.

35. Leonard Wood to William Mckinley, February 6, 1900, Special Correspondence, Elihu Root Papers.

36. *Washington Evening Star*, November 9, 1899, p. 1.

37. *La Lucha*, Apr. 4, 1899, p. 1.

38. Whitelaw Reid to James H. Wilson, March 17, 1900, General Correspondence, Wilson Papers.

39. Platt, "The Pacification of Cuba," pp. 1466–67. See also Platt, "The Solution to the Cuban Problem," p. 734.

40. Hagedorn, *Leonard Wood, A Biography*, I:371.

41. Theodore Roosevelt to Henry Cabot Lodge, July 21, 1899, Theodore Roosevelt Papers.

42. Leonard Wood to Theodore Roosevelt, April 20, 1900, Roosevelt Papers.

43. This was attributed to Root by General James H. Wilson. See James H. Wilson to Joseph K. McCammon, February 11, 1900, Letterbooks, Wilson Papers.

44. James H. Wilson to Henry Cabot Lodge, November 1, 1899, General Correspondence, Wilson Papers.

45. James H. Wilson to Elihu Root, November 3, 1899, General Correspondence, Wilson Papers.

46. James H. Wilson to Augustine P. Gardner, February 11, 1900, Letterbooks, Wilson Papers.

47. James H. Wilson to Henry Cabot Lodge, November 1, 1899, General Correspondence, Wilson Papers. Such "a treaty," Wilson wrote a friend, "would give us indirectly, if not directly, absolute control over the internal conditions affecting the peace of the island, over its revenue, sanitary and postal services, and over at least two of its principal sea ports." See James H. Wilson to Charles Emory Smith, September 7, 1899, General Correspondence, Wilson Papers.

48. James H. Wilson, "Special Report of James H. Wilson," September 7, 1899, in Brooke, *Civil Report of Major-General John R. Brooke, U.S. Army, Military Governor of Cuba: 1900*, p. 339.

49. James H. Wilson to Augustine P. Gardner, February 11, 1900, Letterbooks, Wilson Papers.

50. James H. Wilson, "Supplemental Report—Confidential," September 7, 1899, File 995/48, BIA/RG 350.

51. James H. Wilson to Theodore Roosevelt, July 5, 1899, Roosevelt Papers.

Chapter 15. Collaboration and Conflict

1. James H. Wilson to Charles Emory Smith, May 29, 1899, General Correspondence, James Harrison Wilson Papers.

2. Leonard Wood to Theodore Roosevelt, August 18, 1899, Theodore Roosevelt Papers.

3. William McKinley to James F. Wade, William T. Sampson, and Matthew C. Butler, August 26, 1898, William McKinley Papers.

4. William McKinley to John R. Brooke, December 22, 1898, John R. Brooke Papers.

5. John R. Brooke to William McKinley, September 26, 1899, McKinley Papers.

6. Matthews, *New Born Cuba*, pp. 42–43.

7. Varona Guerrero, *La guerra de independencia de Cuba, 1895–1898*, p. 1680; Rubens, *Liberty, The Story of Cuba*, p. 384.

8. See Gerardo Machado to Gonzalo de Quesada, Feb. 10, 1899, in Quesada, *Archivo de Gonzalo de Quesada*, II:49–50; José Miguel Tarafa to Gonzalo de Quesada, Feb. 14, 1899, in ibid., II:279; José de Jesús Monteagudo to Gonzalo de Quesada, Feb. 17, 1899, ibid., II:91.

9. "The Spanish element," Leonard Wood's biographer wrote "—having nowhere else to go—had . . . ranged itself behind the Americans." Hagedorn, *Leonard Wood, A Biography*, I:208.

10. Edwin F. Atkins, *Sixty Years in Cuba*, pp. 294–319.

11. In Matthews, *The New-Born Cuba*, p. 314; See also *The State*, June 4, 1899, p. 1.

12. Hagedorn, *Leonard Wood, A Biography*, I:256–59.

13. L. H. Carpenter to adjutant general's office, Division of Cuba, July 10, 1899, in U.S. War Department, *Annual Report of the War Department: Report of the Major-General Commanding the Army, 1899*, pp. 313–16.

14. See Henry C. Corbin to Francis V. Greene, December 5, 1898, File 243553.

15. Leonard Wood to William McKinley, November 27, 1898, Wood Papers. See also Holme, *Life of Leonard Wood*, pp. 74–75.

16. James H. Wilson to Edwin H. Atkins, May 31, 1899, Letterbooks, Wilson Papers.

17. James H. Wilson, "Supplemental Report—Confidential," September 7, 1899, File 995/48, BIA/RG 350.

18. See General George Davis, "Memorandum: Notes on the Industrial Condition of the Inhabitants of the Province of Pinar del Río, Cuba," December 30, 1898, File 984, Letters Received, Division of Cuba, Headquarters, AOOC/RG 395.

19. William Ludlow, "Report of Brigadier General William Ludlow, Commanding Department of Havana and Military Governor of the City of Havana, Cuba," August 1, 1899, in U.S. War Department, *Annual Report of the War Department: Report of the Major-General Commanding the Army, 1899*, pp. 231–32.

20. See War Department to John R. Brooke, January 18, 1899, File 195/1, BIA/RG 350.

21. See *The Washington Post*, November 7, 1898, p. 3 and *New York Times*, November 7, 1898, p. 7.

22. An estimated twenty thousand Cubans returned to the island as naturalized American citizens. See *The Washington Evening Star*, February 16, 1901, p. 10.

23. *New York Times*, October 2, 1898, p. 2.

24. *New York Herald*, August 13, 1898, p. 4. See also Tomás Estrada Palma to William R. Day, August 11, 1898, Notes From the Cuban Legation/RG 59.

25. *Washington Evening Star*, October 15, 1898, p. 1.

26. *The Philadelphia Inquirer*, September 18, 1898, p. 28.

27. See Tasker H. Bliss, "Annual Report of the Collector of Customs for Cuba, Fiscal Year Ending June 30, 1899," in John R. Brooke, *Civil Report of Major-General John R. Brooke, U.S. Army, Military Governor of Cuba, 1900*, pp. 374–75.

28. Fred E. Bach to James H. Wilson, September 10, 1901, General Correspondence, Wilson Papers.

29. For the organization of local government see García y Castañeda, *La municipalidad holguinera. Comentario histórico, 1898–1953*, pp. 1–10; Miranda, *La emigración al Caney*, pp. 99–105.

30. See José María Rodríguez to Gonzalo de Quesada, Sept. 22, 1898, in Quesada, *Archivo de Gonzalo de Quesada*, II:189; José Lacret Morlot to Gonzalo de Quesada, Oct. 15, 1898, in ibid., II:32; Emilio Núñez to Gonzalo de Quesada, Sept. 29, 1898, in ibid., II:123; Nestor L. Carbonell to Gonzalo de Quesada, Jan. 12, 1899, in ibid., I:65; Gualterio García to Gonzalo de Quesada, June 26, 1898, in ibid., I:186. "If I have accomplished any good," Tasker H. Bliss, head of Havana customs, wrote to Gonzalo de Quesada in mid-1899, "I am specially grateful to you for the assistance which you have given me, both by your recommendation of deserving men for employment, and for your messages of commendation and encouragement." See Tasker H. Bliss to Gonzalo de Quesada, ibid., I:52.

31. U.S. Congress, Senate, Committee on Relations with Cuba, *Conditions in Cuba*, p. 4.

32. Leonard Wood to Elihu Root, February 6, 1900, Special Correspondence, Elihu Root Papers.

33. Llaverías y Martínez and Santovenia, eds., *Actas de las Asambleas*, VI:33, 38–39, 47–48.

34. See John L. Logan to John C. Bates, February 3, 1899, File 294/10, BIA/RG 350; *New York Times*, January 16, 1899, p. 5.

35. *New York Times*, August 16, 1898, p. 2. See also *La Lucha*, Jan. 24, 1898, p. 5, and Carlos B. Trujillo to John C. Bates, n.d., Letters Received, File 738, Records of the Military Government of Cuba, Record Group 140, National Archives, Washington, D.C. (Hereafter cited as MGC/RG 140.)

36. See Máximo Gómez to Francisco Javier Balmaseda, Feb. 4, 1899, in *La Discusión*, Feb. 12, 1899, p. 1.

37. Giberga, *Obras de Eliseo Giberga*, III:743–44.

38. In Martínez Ortiz, *Cuba: los primeros años de independencia*, I:41; Varona Guerrero, *La guerra de independencia de Cuba*, III:1711.

39. Máximo Gómez, "Proclama del general Gómez al pueblo cubano," June 5, 1899, in Máximo Gómez, *El general Máximo Gómez y su política de paz, union y concordia*, pp. 75–77. See also Máximo Gómez to Bernabé Boza, Aug. 21, 1901, in Boza, *Mi diario de guerra*, II:326.

40. Roig de Leuchsenring, *Máximo Gómez: el libertador de Cuba y el primer ciudadano de la República*, p. 51; Iraizoz y de Villar, *Lecturas cubanas*, pp. 107–09.

41. "Notes of Conversation Between General Gómez and Major Kennon," March 5, 1899, Brooke Papers.

42. Catá, *Cuba y la intervención*, p. 49. See also Gonzalo de Quesada's interview of Máximo Gómez in *New York Journal Magazine*, February 26, 1899, p. 26.

43. Walter B. Booker to William R. Day, May 24, 1899, William R. Day Papers.

44. John D. Logan to John C. Bates, January 22, 1899, File 294/4, Letters Received, BIA/RG 350.

45. *The State*, June 26, 1899, p. 1.

46. See General Rafael M. Portuondo to John R. Brooke, January 24, 1899, File 504, Letters Received, MGC/RG 140; *Actas de las Asambleas*, IV:38–39. See also Antonio González de Mendoza to José Ignacio Rodríguez, May 3, 1899, José Ignacio Rodríguez Papers.

47. Tasker H. Bliss, "Annual Report of the Collector of Customs for Cuba, Fiscal Year Ending June 30, 1899," in Brooke, *Civil Report of Major-General John R. Brooke, U.S. Army, Military Governor of Cuba, 1900*, pp. 374–75.

48. See "Confidential Report Province of Santiago de Cuba," n.d., RPO/RG 28.

49. R. Muñoz to Military Governor, File 2870, Letters Received, MGC/RG 140.

50. José Antonio González Lanuza to Robert Porter, n.d., *Actas de las Asambleas*, V:167.

51. John R. Brooke to Adjutant General, June 2, 1899, File 248666, AGO/RG 94.

52. Rubens, *Liberty, The Story of Cuba*, p. 397.

53. James H. Wilson, "Special Report of Brigadier General James H. Wilson," September 7, 1899, in Brooke, *Civil Report of Major-General John R. Brooke, U.S. Army, Military Governor of Cuba, 1900*, p. 330.

54. Tasker H. Bliss, "Annual Report of the Collector of Customs for Cuba," Fiscal Year Ending June 30, 1899," in ibid., p. 375.

55. Fred E. Bach to James H. Wilson, September 10, 1901, General Correspondence, Wilson Papers.

56. José Antonio González Lanuza to Robert Porter, n.d., *Actas de las Asambleas*, VI:167.

57. Carlos Roloff to Gonzalo de Quesada, Apr. 10, 1899, in Quesada, *Archivo de Gonzalo de Quesada*, II:205.

58. Alejandro Rodríguez to Gonzalo de Quesada, June 13, 1899, in ibid., II:180.

59. Céspedes, "Empleo-manía." See also Figueras, *La intervención y su política*, pp. 18–22; Mario Guiral Moreno, "El problema de la burocracia en Cuba," *Cuba Contemporánea* II (Aug. 1913):262–63.

60. Cisneros y Betancourt, *Appeal to the American People on Behalf of Cuba*, p. 10.

61. *The State*, February 5, 1899, p. 1. See also Enrique Collazo to Leonard Wood, December 28, 1899, File 568, BIA/RG 350. "We made politics our only industry," Miguel de Carrión wrote twenty years later, "and administrative fraud the only road open to the well being of our countrymen." See Miguel de Carrión, "El desenvolvimiento social de Cuba en los últimos veinte años," p. 20.

62. *La Lucha*, Apr. 11, 1899, p. 2; *La Discusión*, Sept. 23, 1900, p. 1; "Confidential Report: Province of Santiago de Cuba," n.d., RPO/RG 28.

63. See "Oath of Office," Letters Received, Segregated Correspondence and Related Documents, MGC/RG 140.

64. See Gus O'Brien to E. T. Rathbone, December 5, 1902, Roswell R. Hoes Papers.

65. Elihu Root to Charles Emory Smith, August 19, 1899, Philip C. Jessup Papers.

66. E. T. Rathbone to Charles Emory Smith, February 6, 1899, RPO/RG 28.

67. John R. Brooke to John Hay, July 17, 1899, Brooke Papers. See also John R. Brooke to Máximo Gómez, May 24, 1899, File 1066, Letters Sent, MGC/RG 140.

68. Harry C. Lewis, "Memorandum for Colonel Edwards," June 1902, File 3438/1, BIA/RG 350.

69. *New York Times*, June 17, 1902, p. 1.

70. Leonard Wood to Elihu Root, December 30, 1899, Wood Papers.

Chapter 16. The Electoral Imperative

1. Leonard Wood to William McKinley, April 27, 1899, McKinley Papers.

2. Leonard Wood to William McKinley, September 26, 1899, McKinley Papers. See also Philip C. Jessup, *Elihu Root*, 2 vols. (New York: Dodd, Mead and Company, Inc., 1938), I:307.

3. William Ludlow, "The Transition in Havana," *The Independent* LII (April 12, 1900):868.

4. Whelpley, "Cuba of To-Day and To-Morrow," p. 46.

5. Leonard Wood to Elihu Root, January 19, 1900, Wood Papers.

6. Leonard Wood to William McKinley, February 6, 1900, Special Correspondence, Root Papers.

7. Leonard Wood to William McKinley, September 26, 1899, McKinley Papers.

8. Williams, "The Outlook in Cuba," pp. 835–36.

9. In Hagedorn, *Leonard Wood, A Biography*, p. 261.

10. John R. Brooke to Henry A. Castle, September 6, 1899, Brooke Papers.

11. Leonard Wood to Elihu Root, February 23, 1900, Special Correspondence, Root Papers.

12. Leonard Wood to Elihu Root, February 23, 1900, Wood Papers.

13. *New York Evening Post*, November 17, 1899, p. 7.

14. *New York Tribune*, August 5, 1898, p. 4.

15. *New York Times*, June 24, 1899, p. 1.

16. T. Bently Mott, "The Social Life of Havana," *Scribner's Magazine* XXXVI (February, 1900):183.

17. Williams, "The Outlook in Cuba," p. 835.

18. John R. Brooke to adjutant general, June 2, 1899, File 248666, AGO/RG 94.

19. A. P. Berry to adjutant general, Department of Matanzas and Santa Clara, August 26, 1899, File 995/24, BIA/RG 350.

20. *New York Times*, August 7, 1899, p. 4.

21. *Washington Evening Star*, January 19, 1899, p. 3. See also *The State*, August 7, 1899, p. 1.

22. Leonard Wood to Elihu Root, February 23, 1900, Wood Papers.

23. William Ludlow to chief of staff, Division of Cuba, October 4, 1898, File 287874, AGO/RG 94.

24. James H. Wilson to Bluford Wilson, June 24, 1899, Letterbooks, Wilson Papers. Two months later, Wilson urged limiting "suffrage by an intelligence test." See James H. Wilson to Anthony Higgins, August 14, 1899, Letterbooks, Wilson Papers.

25. Leonard Wood to Elihu Root, January 13, 1900, Wood Papers.

26. Elihu Root to Paul Dana, January 15, 1900, Personal Correspondence, Root Papers. See also Theodore P. Wright, Jr., "United States Electoral Intervention in Cuba," *Inter-American Economic Affairs* XIII (Winter, 1959):54.

27. Leonard Wood to Elihu Root, February 23, 1900, Wood Papers.

28. Ibid.

29. See "Order of the Military Governor of Cuba Relative to the Municipal Elections to be Held Throughout the Island of Cuba on June, 1900," May 12, 1900, File 1305, Letters Received, MGC/RG 140, and U.S. Congress, Senate, *Qualification of Voters at Coming Elections in Cuba*, p. 2.

30. Partido Republicano Democrático, "Protesta," Mar. 24, 1900, File 1305, Letters Received, MGC/RG 140.

31. Thomas P. Orum, "The Politics of Color: The Racial Dimension of Cuban Politics During the Early Republican Years, 1900–1912" (unpublished Ph.D. diss.), pp. 68–69. See also Manuel Linares to José María Rodríguez, June, 1900, in Linares, *Un libro más: fragmentos de 1881 a 1906*, pp. 264–66. For correspondence, cables, and petitions from *ayuntamientos* and municipalities protesting suffrage restrictions see File 1305, Letters Received, MGC/RG 140.

32. Elihu Root to Leonard Wood, April 14, 1900, File 1327–3, BIA/RG 350. See also J. P. Sanger to Elihu Root, April 14, 1900, General Correspondence, Root Papers; James H. Hitchman, *Leonard Wood and Cuban Independence, 1898–1902* (The Hague: Martinus Nijhoff, 1971), p. 79.

33. Leonard Wood to Elihu Root, May 1, 1900, Wood Papers.

34. Robert Matthews to Henry W. Peabody, January 17, 1902, File 102, Letters Received, MGC/RG 140.

35. Elihu Root to Leonard Wood, June 20, 1900, Correspondence Between General Leonard Wood and Secretary of War, 1899–1902, BIA/RG 350.

36. Leonard Wood to Elihu Root, June 21, 1900, Wood Papers. See also Mario Averhoff Purón, *Los primeros partidos políticos* (Havana: Instituto Cubano del Libro, 1971), pp. 26–36.

37. U.S. War Department, *Civil Report of Brigadier General Leonard Wood, Military Governor of Cuba, for the Period From December 20, 1899 to December 31, 1900*, I, pt. 1, p. 52.

38. Alejandro Rodríguez to William McKinley, June 21, 1900, McKinley Papers.

39. Leonard Wood to Elihu Root, February 16, 1900, Wood Papers.

40. Leonard Wood to William McKinley, February 6, 1900, Special Correspondence, Root Papers. See also Figueras, *La intervención y su política*, pp. 6–8.

41. Leonard Wood to Elihu Root, January, 1900, in Hagedorn, *Leonard Wood, A Biography*, I:267.

42. Healy, *The United States in Cuba, 1898–1902*, p. 147.

43. Leonard Wood to Elihu Root, August 13, 1900, Wood Papers.

44. *New York Times*, August 27, 1900, p. 7. See also B. D. Washburn to H. C. Cortelyou, September 10, 1900, File 331–24, BIA/RG 350; Fitzgibbon, *Cuba and the United States, 1900–1935*, p. 72.

45. Currier, "Why Cuba Should be Independent," pp. 145–46.

46. Leonard Wood to adjutant general, September 1, 1900, File 340125/B, AGO/RG 94.

47. Leonard Wood to William McKinley, August 31, 1900, Wood Papers.

48. Leonard Wood to Elihu Root, September 8, 1900, Special Correspondence, Root Papers.

Chapter 17. From Amendment to Appendix

1. Leonard Wood to Orville H. Platt, December 6, 1900, Wood Papers.

2. Leonard Wood to Elihu Root, March 4, 1901, in Hagedorn, *Leonard Wood, A Biography*, I:359.

3. Leonard Wood to Elihu Root, September 26, 1900, Wood Papers.

4. Leonard Wood to Elihu Root, January 12, 1901, Wood Papers.

5. Leonard Wood to Elihu Root, March 4, 1901, Special Correspondence, Elihu Root Papers. There were "too many patriots and too few businessmen in the Convention," one foreign

investor complained to Root. See C. Van Horne to Elihu Root, General Correspondence, March 11, 1901, Root Papers.

6. Robert P. Porter to editor, *New York Times*, February 11, 1901, p. 6.

7. *New York Times*, December 12, 1900, p. 3.

8. Robinson, "Cuban Constitution Making," p. 437.

9. In Coolidge, *An Old-Fashioned Senator: Orville H. Platt of Connecticut*, p. 337.

10. See James H. Wilson, "Supplemental Report—Confidential," September 7, 1899, File 995/48, BIA/RG 350; Augustus P. Gardner to James H. Wilson, October 23, 1899, General Correspondence, Wilson Papers; Leonard Wood to Theodore Roosevelt, April 20, 1900, Roosevelt Papers; James H. Wilson to Elihu Root, November 3, 1899, General Correspondence, Wilson Papers; Joseph Benson Foraker to James H. Wilson, May 22, 1899, General Correspondence, Wilson Papers.

11. See "Platt Amendment: Talk With Mr. Root," January 4, 1939, Correspondence, Leonard Wood Book, 1928–1931, Hermann Hagedorn Papers. See also Wilson, *Under the Old Flag*, II:502; Foraker, *Notes of a Busy Life*, II:60; Cummins, "The Formulation of the 'Platt' Amendment"; Gay-Calbó, "Génesis de la Enmienda Platt."

12. Elihu Root to John Hay, January 11, 1901, Root Papers.

13. Leonard Wood to Elihu Root, December 23, 1900, Special Correspondence, Root Papers.

14. Leonard Wood to Elihu Root, February 27, 1901, File 331–71, BIA/RG 350. See also Rubens, *Liberty, The Story of Cuba*, p. 426.

15. Richardson, ed., *A Compilation of the Messages and Papers of the Presidents, 1789–1902*, X:152.

16. Elihu Root to Albert Shaw, February 23, 1901, File 331–71, BIA/RG 350. "It would be a most lame and impotent conclusion," Root explained to Wood, "if, after all the expenditure of blood and treasure by the people of the United States for the freedom of Cuba . . . we should, through the constitution of the new government, by inadvertence or otherwise, be placed in a worse condition in regard to our vital interests than we were while Spain was in possession." See Elihu Root to Leonard Wood, February 14, 1901, Correspondence Between General Leonard Wood and Secretary of War, 1899–1902, BIA/RG 350.

17. Platt, "The Solution of the Cuban Problem," pp. 730–31.

18. Platt "The Pacification of Cuba," pp. 1466–67. See also Foraker, *Notes of a Busy Life*, II:51–52.

19. "Cosas de Cuba," n.d., File 294/24, BIA/RG 350.

20. Leonard Wood to Elihu Root, January 19, 1901, Wood Papers.

21. Ibid.

22. Leonard Wood to Joseph Benson Foraker, January 11, 1901, Wood Papers.

23. Leonard Wood to Elihu Root, February 8, 1901, Wood Papers. See also *Washington Evening Star*, February 11, 1901, p. 3.

24. Leonard Wood to Elihu Root, February 27, 1901, File 331–71, BIA/RG 350.

25. *Washington Evening Star*, June 1, 1901, p. 1.

26. Platt, "The Solution of the Cuban Problem, p. 734. See also Platt, "Our Relation to the People of Cuba and Puerto Rico"; idem, "Cuba's Claim Upon the United States"; idem, "The Pacification of Cuba"; Coolidge, *An Old-Fashioned Senator: Orville H. Platt of Connecticut*, p. 331.

27. William Eaton Chandler, "Senator Platt and the Platt Amendment," April 21, 1905, William Eaton Chandler Papers. See also Coolidge, *An Old-Fashioned Senator: Orville H. Platt of Connecticut*, pp. 348–350; Foraker, *Notes of a Busy Life*, II:51–52.

28. *The Statutes at Large of the United States*, XXI:897–98.

29. Leonard Wood to Elihu Root, February 19, 1901, File 331–72, BIA/RG 350. See also Bravo y Correoso, *Como se hizo la constitución de Cuba*, pp. 80–81.

30. File 568 of BIA/RG 350 and Files 1400, 3051, and 4000 of MGC/RG 140 contain hundreds of protests from Cubans across the island. See also "Our Demands on Cuba"; Robinson, "Some Cuban Opinions"; Salvador Cisneros Betancourt, *Appeal to the American People on Behalf of Cuba*, p. 120.

31. Leonard Wood to Elihu Root, March 2, 1901, Root Papers.

32. Cuba, Convención Constituyente, *Opinión sobre las relaciones entre Cuba y los Estados Unidos*, pp. 5–20.

33. Leonard Wood to Elihu Root, March 20, 1901, Special Correspondence, Root Papers.

34. Walter B. Barker to John T. Morgan, April 2, 1901, Philip C. Jessups Papers.

35. Elihu Root to Leonard Wood, March 2, 1901, File 331–71, BIA/RG 350; Jessup, *Elihu Root*, I:316.

36. *Washington Evening Star*, April 17, 1901, p. 2; Portell Vilá, "La intervención militar norteamericana," pp. 34, 36; Philip G. Wright, *The Cuban Situation and Our Treaty Relations*, p. 23.

37. Leonard Wood to Elihu Root, April 5, 1901, File 331–74, BIA/RG 350.

38. "Informe de la Comisión designada para avistarse con el gobierno de los Estados Unidos, dando cuenta del resultado de sus gestiones," May 6, 1901, in Cuba, Senado, *Memoria de los trabajos realizados durante las cuatro legislaturas y sesión extraordinaria del primer período congresional, 1902–1904. Mención histórica. Documentación relacionada con los acontecimientos que dieron, como resultado definitivo, la independencia y el establecimiento en república de Cuba, 1892–1902* (Havana: Imprenta y Papelería de Rambla, Bouza y Ca., 1918), pp. 468–79.

39. Orville H. Platt to Elihu Root, April 26, 1901, General Correspondence, Root Papers. See also Infiesta, *Historia constitucional de Cuba*, pp. 327–28.

40. Elihu Root, "Statement to Cuban Committee Regarding Reciprocity Treaty," April 26, 1901, Jessup Papers; Orville H. Platt to Leonard Wood, n.d., in Coolidge, *An Old-Fashioned Senator: Orville H. Platt of Connecticut*, p. 371; "Informe de la Comisión," pp. 466–67, 474.

41. Elihu Root to Orville H. Platt, May 9, 1901, Personal Correspondence, Root Papers.

42. *La Lucha*, Apr. 20, 1901, p. 2.

43. Leonard Wood to Elihu Root, June 9, 1901, Correspondence Between General Leonard Wood and Secretary of War, 1899–1902, BIA/RG 350.

44. See Martínez Ortiz, *Cuba: los primeros años de independencia*, I:287; Costa y Blanco, *Manuel Sanguily*, p. 91; Miguel Angel Carbonell, *Sanguily*, p. 28; Cortina, *Manuel Sanguily en la evolución de Cuba*, pp. 24–25.

45. In Robinson, *Cuba and the Intervention*, p. 270.

46. Renée Méndez Capote, *Domingo Méndez Capote, el hombre civil del 95*, p. 141.

47. Máximo Gómez to Sotero Figueroa, May 8, 1901, in Máximo Gómez, *Papeles dominicanos de Máximo Gómez*, pp. 396–97.

Chapter 18. The Construction of a Colonial Army

1. See John C. Bates to adjutant general, Division of Cuba, March 11, 1899, AOOC/RG 395.

2. John C. Bates to adjutant general, Division of Cuba, January 28, 1899, File 196, Letters Sent, Santa Clara, AOOC/RG 395.

3. John A. Logan, provost marshall, to adjutant general, Department of Santa Clara, February 3, 1899, File 294/11, BIA/RG 350.

4. George W. Davis to Adna R. Chaffee, January 15, 1899, File 297, Letters Received, MGC/RG 140.

5. John Addison Porter to Adjutant General Henry C. Corbin, September 29, 1898, File 132052, AGO/RG 94.

6. *Washington Evening Star*, November 1, 1898, p. 2.

7. Henry C. Corbin to John R. Brooke, November 16, 1898, Brooke Papers.

8. "Memoria de la primera comisión enviada a Wáshington," n.d., Llaverías y Martínez and Santovenia, eds., *Actas de las Asambleas*, V:152–53; Miguel Angel Carbonell, *Sanguily*, pp. 48–49.

9. Rafael M. Portuondo to John R. Brooke, January 2, 1899, Letters Received, Segregated Correspondence and Related Documents, MGC/RG 140.

10. Máximo Gómez to Gonzalo de Quesada, October 20, 1898, *The Washington Post*, November 6, 1898, p. 5.

11. *La Lucha*, Mar. 2, p. 2.

12. Máximo Gómez to William McKinley, March 25, 1899, Brooke Papers. A slightly different version of this letter dated March 4, 1899, appears in Infiesta, *Máximo Gómez*, pp. 226–28.

13. Máximo Gómez, "Al Ejército Libertador de Cuba," May 18, 1899, in Máximo Gómez, *El general Máximo Gómez y su política de paz, unión y concordia*, pp. 69–70; *La Lucha*, May 19, 1899, p. 5.

14. Healy, *The United States in Cuba, 1898–1902*, p. 105. See also John R. Brooke to Henry C. Corbin, January 18, 1899, File 243531, AGO/RG 94. Other ranking American officials in Cuba also opposed the organization of locally-recruited armed forces, fearing that Cuban guns could just as easily be trained on American soldiers. See James H. Wilson to Charles Emory Smith, May 29, 1899, General Correspondence, Wilson Papers; E. G. Rathbone to Elihu Root, December 4, 1899, General Correspondence, Root papers.

15. John R. Brooke to Henry C. Corbin, January 18, 1899, File 243531, AGO/RG 94.

16. See Major General J. Wade, "Memorandum," November 30, 1898, File 243551, AGO/RG 94.

17. See Fitzhugh Lee to W. V. Richards, n.d., File 2123, MGC/RG 140; Fitzhugh Lee to John R. Brooke, April 19, 1899, File 3200½, MGC/RG 140; Leonard Wood to William McKinley, November 27, 1898, Wood Papers; Frank Steinhart, "Memorandum," December 28, 1928, Correspondence, Leonard Wood Book, 1928–1931, Hagedorn Papers; L. H. Carpenter to adjutant general, Division of Cuba, July 10, 1899, in U.S. War Department, *Annual Report of the War Department: Report of the Major-General Commanding the Army, 1899*, pp. 311–12.

18. Leonard Wood to William McKinley, November 27, 1898, Wood Papers.

19. See Captain H. J. Slocum, "Report of H. J. Slocum, 7th U.S. Cavalry, Superintendent of the Rural Guard and the Cuerpo de Artilleria of the Island of Cuba, for the Period of January 1st, 1902 to May 20th, 1902," July 2, 1902, in U.S. War Department, *Civil Report of Brigadier General Leonard Wood, Military Governor of Cuba, January 1st to May 20th, 1902*, III:67.

20. William Ludlow, "Report of Brigadier General William Ludlow, Commanding Department of Havana and Military Governor of the City of Habana, Cuba," August 1, 1899, in U.S. War Department, *Annual Report of the War Department, 1899*, Ser. 3899–3904, I, pt. 1, p. 228. See also "Report of Havana Police and Rural Guards," n.d., File 331-16, BIA/RG 350.

21. John A. Logan to adjutant general, Department of Santa Clara, February 3, 1899, File 294/11, BIA/RG 350.

22. George W. Davis to Adna R. Chaffee, chief of staff, Division of Cuba, January 16, 1899, File 2551, Letters Received, MGC/RG 140.

23. Henry Adams to Elizabeth Cameron, February 28, 1899, in Henry Adams, *Letters of Henry Adams*, II:20.

24. In Holme, *The Life of Leonard Wood* pp. 77–78.

25. Wood, "The Existing Conditions and Needs in Cuba," p. 600.

26. Joseph Benson Foraker to James H. Wilson, May 22, 1899, General Correspondence, Wilson Papers.

27. Fitzhugh Lee to Joseph Benson Foraker, November 29, 1899, in Foraker, *Notes on a*

Busy Life, II:48; Francis Green to adjutant general, November 19, 1898, File 243549, AGO/RG 94.

28. Hagedorn, *Leonard Wood, A Biography*, I:213–14.

29. Leonard Wood, "Memorandum," enclosure in Leonard Wood to William McKinley, October 27, 1899, Wood Papers.

30. See Russell A. Alger to William McKinley, November 12, 1898, McKinley Papers; Russell A. Alger to Francis V. Greene, November 12, 1898, File 243548, AGO/RG 94.

31. Leonard Wood to adjutant general, November 11, 1899, File 2594, MGC/RG 140.

32. Henry C. Corbin to John R. Brooke, June 8, 1899, Brooke Papers. See also John R. Brooke to Henry C. Corbin, n.d., File 2594, MGC/RG 140.

33. William McKinley to Elihu Root, August 19, 1899, General Correspondence, Root Papers.

34. John A. Logan to adjutant general, Department of Santa Clara, February 3, 1899, File 294/11, BIA/RG 350.

35. Elihu Root to William McKinley, August 17, 1899, Semi-Official Correspondence, Root Papers.

36. Leonard Wood to Theodore Roosevelt, August 3, 1899, Wood Papers.

37. Leonard Wood to Theodore Roosevelt, August 18, 1899, Roosevelt Papers. See also Hagedorn, *Leonard Wood, A Biography*, I:256.

38. Leonard Wood, "Memorandum," enclosure in Leonard Wood to William McKinley, October 27, 1899, Wood Papers.

39. Leonard Wood to adjutant general, November 11, 1899, File 2594, MGC/RG 140.

40. Leonard Wood, "Civil Report of Major General Leonard Wood, U.S. Volunteers, Military Governor of Cuba," in U.S. War Department *Civil Report of Brigadier General Leonard Wood, Military Governor of Cuba, for the Period of December 20, 1899 to December 31, 1900*, pt. 1, pp. 63–64.

41. Slocum, "Report of H. J. Slocum . . . for Period of January 1st, 1902 to May 20th, 1902," III:67–70. See also H. J. Slocum to adjutant general, Late Department of Cuba, July 2, 1902, MGC/RG 140.

42. Comandante B. Peña, Guardia Rural de Puerto Príncipe, to C. A. P. Hatfield, February 3, 1901, File 879, MGC/RG 140; J. F. Craig, president, Francisco Sugar Company, to Leonard Wood, February 2, 1901, File 879, ibid.; W. I. Consuegra, acting chief of Rural Guard, "Monthly Report for November, 1900," File 6105, ibid.

43. José de Jesús Monteagudo, chief of the Rural Guard, to Fitzhugh Lee, October 31, 1900, File 138, MGC/RG 140.

44. Leopoldo Figueroa, president of the municipality of Cienfuegos, to Leonard Wood, January 24, 1901, File 138, ibid.

45. Cuba, Guardia Rural, *Memoria explicativa de los trabajos realizados por el cuerpo durante el año fiscal 1905*, (Havana: n.p., 1906), pp. 89–95.

46. H. J. Slocum to Adjutant General, Late Department of Cuba, July 2, 1902, MGC/RG 140.

47. Hugh L. Scott to C. B. Hoppin, December 6, 1900, File 5165, Letters Sent, ibid.

48. See Eduardo Usabiega to Leonard Wood, May 26, 1901, File 194, MGC/RG 140; Colonel Pío Domínguez to Leonard Wood, May 16, 1901, File 194, ibid.; García, Llana and Company to Leonard Wood, January 18, 1901, File 138, ibid.

49. For complete enlistment requirements for the Rural Guard see Cuba, Camagüey, *Reglamento para el gobierno interior del Cuerpo de Guardia Rural*.

50. Matthews, *The New-Born Cuba*, pp. 386–87.

51. Captain Dwight Aultman, "Project for Combining the Cuerpo do Artilleria with the Rural Guard," enclosure in Dwight Aultman to adjutant general, Department of Cuba, January 25, 1902, File 2, MGC/RG 140.

52. Frank R. McCoy to Hugh L. Scott, July–December 1901 folio, McCoy Papers; *New York Times*, August 9, 1901, p. 2; Fermoselle, *Política y color en Cuba*, pp. 28–29. For an excellent general treatment of racist practices during the occupation see Orum, "The Politics of Color: The Racial Dimension of Cuban Politics During the Early Republican Years, 1900–1912" (unpublished Ph.D. diss.) pp. 58–64.

53. See Leonard Wood, "The Existing Conditions and Needs in Cuba," p. 600; Portell Vilá, "La intervención militar norteamericana, 1899–1902," p. 34, and H. J. Slocum to adjutant general, Department of Havana and Pinar del Río, May 16, 1900, File 1392, MGC/RG 140.

54. Leonard Wood, "The Existing Conditions and Needs in Cuba," p. 600; Slocum, "Report of H. J. Slocum . . . for Period of January 1st, 1902 to May 20th, 1902," III:67.

55. H. J. Slocum to Adjutant General, Late Department of Cuba, July 2, 1902, MGC/RG 140.

56. Platt, "The Solution of the Cuban Problem," p. 732.

57. Root, *The Military and Colonial Policy of the United States*, p. 100.

Chapter 19. Sugar, Reciprocity, and the Reconstruction of the Colonial Economy

1. For a detailed account of Havana and the war see Francisco Pérez, *La guerra en La Habana, desde enero de 1896 hasta el combate de San Pedro* (Havana: Instituto Cubano del Libro, 1974), pp. 7–64.

2. *The State*, November 5, 1898, p. 5; *Washington Evening Star*, September 24, 1898, p. 21; Fitzhugh Lee, "Special Report of Brigadier General Fitzhugh Lee," September 19, 1899, in Brooke, *Civil Report of Major-General John R. Brooke, U.S. Army, Military Governor of Cuba, 1900*, p. 342; U.S. Department of Treasury, *Report on the Commercial and Industrial Condition of Cuba. Special Report on the Commissioner's Visit to General Gomez, and in Relation to the Payment and Disbandment of the Insurgent Army of Cuba*, p. 8.

3. Foreign Policy Association, *Problems of the New Cuba* (New York: Foreign Policy Association, 1935), p. 43. James H. Wilson, "Special Report of Brigadier General James H. Wilson," September 7, 1899, in Brooke, *Civil Report of Major-General John R. Brooke, U.S. Army, Military Governor of Cuba, 1900*, pp. 334, 337.

4. U.S. War Department, *Informe sobre el censo de Cuba, 1899*, pp. 44–45. See also Pazos, "La economia cubana en el siglo XIX," pp. 105, 106; and Edmund Wood, "Can Cubans Govern Cuba?" p. 70.

5. Alvarez Díaz et al., *A Study on Cuba* pp. 96–97; LeRiverend Brusone, *La Habana (biografía de una provincia)*, pp. 458–59; U.S. War Department, *Informe sobre el censo de Cuba, 1899*, pp. 551, 563–64; Rea, "The Destruction of Sugar Estates in Cuba"; Abad, "The Cuban Problem"; Hinton, "Cuban Reconstruction"; Matthews, "The Reconstruction of Cuba"; Quintana, "Lo que costó a Cuba la guerra de 1895."

6. Brooke, *Civil Report of Major-General John R. Brooke, U.S. Army, Governor of Cuba, 1899*, p. 7.

7. See James H. Wilson to adjutant general's office, Division of Cuba, June 20, 1899 in U.S. War Department, *Annual Reports of the War Department: Report of the Major-General Commanding the Army, 1899*, pp. 183–85.

8. See Hugh L. Scott to Lieutenant Stokes, January 3, 1901, File 38, MGC/RG 140, and Hugh L. Scott to customs collector, Santiago, February 25, 1901, File 1062, ibid.

9. Hugh L. Scott to civil governor of Matanzas, January 4, 1901, File 68, ibid. For a general study of the Cuban labor movement during the occupation see Rivero Muñiz, *El movimiento obrero durante la primera intervención: apuntes para la historia del proletariado de Cuba*, and Foner, *The Spanish-Cuban-American War and the Birth of American Imperialism*, II:484–513.

10. Leonard Wood to Elihu Root, October 18, 1901, Letters Sent, File 4754, MGC/RG 140.

11. Leonard Wood to William McKinley, October 28, 1901, Wood Papers.

12. James H. Wilson to Henry Cabot Lodge, November 1, 1899, General Correspondence, Wilson Papers. See also James H. Wilson to Elihu Root, November 3, 1899, General Correspondence, ibid.

13. James H. Wilson, "Supplemental Report—Confidential," September 7, 1899, File 995/48, BIA/RG 350.

14. James H. Wilson to John Dalzell, November 23, 1901, General Correspondence, Wilson Papers. See also James H. Wilson, "Special Report of James H. Wilson, September 7, 1899, in Brooke, *Civil Report of Major-General John R. Brooke, U.S. Army, Military Governor of Cuba, 1900*, p. 339.

15. James H. Wilson to William B. Allison, April 16, 1900, General Correspondence, Wilson Papers.

16. James H. Wilson to William S. Opdyke, January 30, 1900, Letterbooks, Wilson Papers.

17. James H. Wilson, "An Address on Our Trade Relations with the Tropics," November 9, 1901, File C–705/163, BIA/RG 350. See also Wilson, "Cuba Revisited," p. 905.

18. In Walters, *Joseph Benson Foraker*, p. 153.

19. Leonard Wood to Theodore Roosevelt, May 9, 1901, Roosevelt Papers.

20. See Welliver, "The Annexation of Cuba By the Sugar Trust," pp. 385–87.

21. James H. Wilson, "Report of Brigadier General James H. Wilson," September 7, 1899, in Brooke, *Civil Report of Major-General John R. Brooke, U.S. Army, Military Governor of Cuba, 1900*, pp. 336–37.

22. Leonard Wood, "The Need for Reciprocity with Cuba," p. 2928.

23. Leonard Wood to Elihu Root, October 22, 1901, Wood Papers.

24. Leonard Wood to Elihu Root, January 4, 1901, ibid.

25. Tasker H. Bliss, "Report of Brigadier General Tasker H. Bliss, Chief of the Cuban Customs Service, for the Period of January 1, 1902–May 12, 1902," in U.S. War Department, *Civil Report of Brigadier General Leonard Wood, Military Governor of Cuba, for the Period from January 1 to May 20, 1902* III:21–22.

26. Root, *The Military and Colonial Policy of the United States*, pp. 216–17.

27. Leonard Wood to Elihu Root, January 4, 1901, Letters Sent, File 96, MGC/RG 140.

28. Leonard Wood to Joseph B. Foraker, January 11, 1901, Wood Papers. See also Leonard Wood to Henry Cabot Lodge, May 12, 1900, ibid.

29. Leonard Wood to Orville H. Platt, January 12, 1901, Wood Papers. See also Leonard Wood to Orville H. Platt, December 19, 1900, Wood Papers.

30. Leonard Wood to Redfield Proctor, January 18, 1901, Wood Papers. See also Leonard Wood, "Report of General Leonard Wood," July 5, 1901, U.S. War Department, *Civil Report of Brigadier General Leonard Wood, Military Governor of Cuba, For the Period from January 1 to May 20, 1902*, I:11.

31. Leonard Wood to Orville H. Platt, December 19, 1900, Wood Papers.

32. Leonard Wood to Elihu Root, October 11, 1901, Letters Sent, File 4754, MGC/RG 140.

33. Leonard Wood, "The Future of Cuba," p. 194. See also Leonard Wood, "Report of Brigadier General Leonard Wood," July 5, 1902, in U.S. War Department, *Civil Report of Brigadier General Leonard Wood, Military Governor of Cuba, For the Period from January 1 to May 20, 1902*, I:11.

34. See M. F. Cuervo to Robert P. Porter, September 21, 1898, in U.S. Department of Treasury, *Report on the Commercial and Industrial Conditions of Cuba* (Washington, D.C.: Government Printing Office, 1899), pp. 101–102; William O. McDowell and Antonio A. Aguirre to William McKinley, June 2, 1899, File 273/9, BIA/RG 350.

35. Adolpho Muñoz to Robert P. Porter, April 4, 1900, William McKinley Papers.

36. See General Society of Merchants and Businessmen of the Island of Cuba, "Petition,"

September 20, 1901, Letters Received, File 3759, MGC/RG 140; Arturo de Vegas, president, Centro de Propiedad Urbana, to Leonard Wood, December 7, 1900, Letters Received, File 96, MGC/RG 140; "Petition of the Planters Association," June 25, 1902, enclosure in Herbert G. Squiers to John Hay, June 25, 1902, Despatches from U.S. Ministers to Cuba, 1902–1906, General Records of the Department of State, Record Group 59, National Archives, Washington, D.C. (Hereafter cited as Despatches/Cuba).

37. *La Lucha*, Apr. 2, 1901, p. 1.

38. *Washington Evening Star*, April 29, 1901, p. 11.

39. Henry Cabot Lodge to Leonard Wood, January 15, 1902, Wood Papers; Orville H. Platt to Leonard Wood, January 18, 1901, ibid.

40. Elihu Root, "Statement to Cuban Committee Regarding Reciprocity Treaty," April 26, 1901, Jessup Papers. See also "Informe de la Comisión designada para avistarse con el gobierno de los Estados Unidos, dando cuenta del resultado de sus gestiones," May 6, 1901, in Cuba, Senado, *Memoria de los trabajos realizados durante las cuatro legislaturas y sesión extraordinaria del primer período congresional, 1902–1904. Mención histórica. Documentación relacionada con los acontecimientos que dieron, como resultado definitivo, la independencia y el establecimiento en república de Cuba, 1892–1902* (Havana: Imprenta y Papelería de Rambla, Bouza y Ca., 1918) pp. 466–67, 474. See also Márquez Sterling, *Proceso histórico de la Enmienda Platt (1897–1934)*, p. 241; Orville H. Platt to Leonard Wood, January 18, 1901, in Coolidge, *An Old-Fashioned Senator: Orville H. Platt of Connecticut*, p. 371.

41. Narciso Gelats to president, Constituent Assembly, Apr. 17, 1901, Letters Received, File 409, MGC/RG 140.

42. Leonard Wood to Orville H. Platt, January 12, 1901, Wood Papers.

43. Leonard Wood to Elihu Root, October 18, 1901, Letters Sent, File 4754, MGC/RG 140.

44. Ibid.

45. Leonard Wood to Elihu Root, January 2, 1902, Letters Sent, File 75, MGC/RG 140.

46. Tasker H. Bliss to James H. Wilson, January 12, 1902, General Correspondence, Wilson Papers.

47. See Wilson, "Special Report of Brigadier General James H. Wilson," September 7, 1898, in Brooke, *Civil Report of Major-General John R. Brooke, U.S. Army Military Governor of Cuba, 1900*, pp. 13–14.

48. Leonard Wood, "Report of Brigadier General Leonard Wood," July 5, 1902, in U.S. War Department, *Civil Report of Brigadier General Leonard Wood, Military Governor of Cuba, For the Period from January 1 to May 20, 1902*, I:13.

49. Tasker H. Bliss to James H. Wilson, January 12, 1902, General Correspondence, Wilson Papers.

50. "Civil Order No. 34," February 7, 1902, in Cuba, Military Governor, 1899–1902, *Civil Orders and Proclamations of the Department of Cuba*, II, n.p.

51. "Civil Order No. 62", March 5, 1902, in Ibid., n.p.

52. U.S. War Department, *Informe sobre el censo de Cuba, 1899*, p. 554.

53. Foreign Policy Association, *The Problems of the New Cuba*, p. 52.

54. *New York Journal*, June 29, 1897, p. 7.

55. *The State*, September 28, 1898, p. 5; Robinson, "Industrial and Commercial Conditions in Cuba," p. 199.

56. Gilson Willets, "Business Opportunities in Our New Colonies," *Leslie's Weekly* LXXXVIII (January 5, 1899):12.

57. See Hitchman, "U.S. Control Over Cuban Sugar Production, 1898–1902"; Thomas, *Cuba, The Pursuit of Freedom*, pp. 466–70; Arredondo, *Cuba: tierra indefensa*, pp. 155–56. Julio LeRiverend Brusone, "La penetración económica extranjera en Cuba," *Revista de la Biblioteca Nacional "José Martí"* III (Jan.–Mar., 1966):11–13.

58. Edwin F. Atkins, *Sixty Years in Cuba* p. 299.

59. Jenks, *Our Cuban Colony*, p. 131.

60. U.S. Congress, Senate, *Cuba Sugar Sales: Testimony Taken By Committee on Relations with Cuba*, pp. 332, 339–41.

61. Raúl Maestri, *El latifundismo en la economía cubana*, pp. 29–68; Ramiro Guerra y Sánchez, *Sugar and Society in the Caribbean* (New Haven: Yale University Press, 1964), passim.

62. "The True Line of Policy," *Review of Reviews* XXV (February, 1902):133. See also Jenks, *Our Cuban Colony*, p. 136.

63. Francis B. Thurber to Elihu Root, October 18, 1901, File 3759, Letters Received, MGC/RG 140.

64. George B. Hopkins to John H. Spooner, March 14, 1900, John C. Spooner Papers.

65. Henry Cabot Lodge to Leonard Wood, January 15, 1901, Wood Papers.

66. Luis V. Placé to Tasker Bliss, November 6, 1900, File C–705/21, BIA/RG 350.

67. Luis V. Placé to Clarence Edwards, January 29, 1902, File C–705/185, BIA/RG 350.

68. William O. McDowell and Antonio A. Aguirre to William McKinley, June 2, 1899, File 273/9, BIA/RG 350.

69. Adolpho Muñoz to Robert P. Porter, April 4, 1900, McKinley Papers.

70. B. W. Merrill to R. B. Hawley, July 25, 1901, File 273/35, BIA/RG 350. See also Martínez Ortiz, *Cuba: los primeros años de independencia*, I:335; Bustamante y Sirvén, *Discursos*, I:116–17.

71. Leonard Wood, "Report of Brigadier General Leonard Wood," July 5, 1902, in U.S. War Department, *Civil Report of Brigadier General Leonard Wood, Military Governor of Cuba for the Period From January 1 to May 20, 1902*, I:11–12.

72. U.S. Congress, House, *Reciprocity With Cuba, Hearings Before the Committee on Ways and Means*, 57th Congress, 1st Session (Washington, D.C.: Government Printing Office, 1902), pp. 17–24. See also Philip C. Jessup, "Conversation with Mr. Root in His Apartment," December 16, 1929, Jessup Papers.

73. U.S. Congress, Joint Committee on Printing, *A Compilation of the Messages and Papers of the Presidents*, 18 vols. New York: Bureau of National Literature, Inc., n.d.), XV:6683.

74. U.S. Congress, Joint Committee on Printing, *A Compilation of the Messages and Papers of the President*, XV:6717.

75. U.S. Tariff Commission, *Effects of the Cuban Reciprocity Treaty*, p. 2.

76. "Discussion of the Reciprocity Treaty in the Cuban Senate," in Herbert G. Squiers to John Hay, March 23, 1903, Despatches/Cuba. See also Costa y Blanco, *Manuel Sanguily*, p. 107.

77. Gonzalo de Quesada, "Memorandum," November 18, 1902, Notes/Cuban Legation. See also Gonzalo de Quesada to secretary of state, October 22, 1902, File C–705/237, BIA/RG 350, and José Antonio González Lanuza to José María Lasa, Oct. 9, 1901, in Luis Gardel, ed., *Tres cartas del doctor González Lanuza*, pp. 32–33. Nor were these concerns unfounded. In 1904, the Cuban Treasury Department reported a loss of some $1.8 million in custom revenues as a result of the reciprocity arrangements with the United States. See Henry L. James to Elihu Root, December 5, 1905, Despatches/Cuba.

78. Herbert G. Squiers to John Hay, June 23, 1902, Despatches/Cuba.

79. Herbert G. Squiers to John Hay, October 23, 1902, Despatches/Cuba.

80. U.S. Congress, Joint Committee on Printing, *A Compilation of the Messages and Papers of the Presidents*, XV:6741–43.

81. For a detailed account of the politicking and manuevering to secure passage of the treaty see Healy, *The United States in Cuba, 1898–1902*, pp. 189–206, and Foner, *The*

Spanish-Cuban American War and the Birth of American Imperialism, II:633–54.

82. James H. Wilson to Edwin F. Atkins, December 17, 1903, General Correspondence, Wilson Papers.

Chapter 20. A General Understanding

1. Interview with Tomás Mayet, February 20, 1973, West Tampa, Florida.

2. Federico Villoch, *Viejas postales descoloridas. La guerra de independencia* (Havana: Imprenta P. Fernández y Cía., 1946), pp. 221–28.

3. Leonard Wood, "Report of Brigadier General Leonard Wood," July 5, 1902, in U.S. War Department, *Civil Report of Brigadier General Leonard Wood, Military Governor of Cuba, for the Period From January 1 to May 20, 1902*, I:3–4.

4. Leonard Wood to Elihu Root, October 22, 1901, Wood Papers.

5. Leonard Wood to Elihu Root, January 16, 1902, Wood Papers.

6. Leonard Wood to Elihu Root, January 12, 1901, Wood Papers.

7. Leonard Wood to Elihu Root, March 7, 1901, Special Correspondence, Elihu Root Papers. See also *New York Times*, April 9, 1901, p. 6.

8. Edwin F. Atkins, *Sixty Years in Cuba*, p. 322. Nor was this the first act of coercion and intimidation sanctioned under the auspices of the military government in behalf of pro-American candidates. See Carlos de Pedroso to José Ignacio Rodríguez, June 1, 1901, José Ignacio Rodríguez Papers.

9. For a detailed account of the June 1901 municipal elections see Mario Riera Hernández, *Cuba política, 1899–1955* (Havana: Impresora Modelo, 1955), pp. 31–41.

10. Leonard Wood to Elihu Root, February 27, 1901, File 331–71, BIA/RG 350; Perdomo, *Máximo Gómez*, p. 24; Ferrara y Marino, *Mis relaciones con Máximo Gómez*, 1942), p. 250.

11. Griñán Peralta, *El caracter de Máximo Gómez*, p. 79; Figueras, *La intervención y su política*, p. 9; *New York Times*, July 7, 1901, p. 2.

12. *New York Times*, July 7, 1901, p. 2.

13. See Estrada Palma, *Carta-programa;* Tomás Estrada Palma to Juan Rius Rivera, Sept. 7, 1901, in Iznaga, *Tres años de República*, p. 13; Tomás Estrada Palma to James H. Wilson, January 11, 1902, General Correspondence, Wilson Papers; Carlos Márquez Sterling, *Don Tomás (biografía de una época)*, p. 339.

14. Pérez Landa, *Bartolomé Masó y Márquez. Estudio biográfico documentado* pp. 313–14; Santovenia, *Bartolomé Masó*, pp. 14–16; Pardo Llada, *Bartolomé Masó: el presidente que vetaron los yanquis* pp. 10–11; Martínez Ortiz, *Cuba: los primeros años de independencia*, I:348–49.

15. Leonard Wood to Theodore Roosevelt, October 28, 1901, Wood Papers.

16. Leonard Wood to Elihu Root, October 2, 1901, Special Correspondence, Root Papers.

17. Pardo Llada, *Bartolomé Masó: el presidente que vetaron los yanquis*, pp. 18–19; Riera Hernández, *Cuba política, 1899–1955*, pp. 34–35.

18. Eusebio Hernández to Leonard Wood, December 4, 1901, File 1327–36, BIA/RG 350.

19. See Eusebio Hernández to Elihu Root, December 3, 1901, File 1327–32, ibid; Fidel G. Pierra to Elihu Root, December 23, 1901, File 1327–32, ibid.

20. Elihu Root to Fidel G. Pierra, December 16, 1901, File 1327–35, ibid. BIA/RG 350.

21. Leonard Wood to Theodore Roosevelt, January 4, 1901, Wood Papers.

22. Leonard Wood to Elihu Root, January 4, 1902, ibid.

23. Leonard Wood to John Kendrick Bangs, February 18, 1902, McCoy Papers.

24. *New York Times*, November 22, 1901, p. 16. See also Casuso, *Política cubana y sistema americano*, pp. 33–37.

Chapter 21. Postscript to the Colony—Prologue to the Republic

1. Méndez Capote, *Trabajos*, III:56.

2. Cubans were not the only ones who feared that resistance would have grave repercussions. General James H. Wilson, suspicious of administration designs, warned Cubans against disorders. Otherwise, Wilson indicated, Cubans would "be guilty of just enough violence to play into the President's hand, and cause an indefinite postponement of the return of our forces to the United States." See James H. Wilson to Goldwyn Smith, December 27, 1899, Wilson Papers; Foner, *The Spanish-Cuban-American War and the Birth of American Imperialism*, II:526.

3. William Howard Taft to Elihu Root, September 14, 1906, William Howard Taft Papers.

4. Herbert G. Squiers to John Hay, July 4, 1902, Despatches/Cuba.

5. Herbert G. Squiers to John Hay, June 16, 1902, Despatches/Cuba.

6. Herbert G. Squiers to John Hay, July 4, 1902, Despatches/Cuba.

7. Collazo, *La revolución de agosto de 1906*, pp. 7–11.

Bibliography

Unpublished Material

Archival Sources

National Archives of the United States. Records of the Post Office Department. Record Group 28.
——. General Records of the Department of State. Record Group 59.
——. Records of the Adjutant General's Office, 1780s–1917. Record Group 94.
——. Records of the Bureau of Insular Affairs. Record Group 350.
——. Records of the Military Government of Cuba. Record Group 140.
——. Records of the War Department General and Special Staffs. Record Group 165.
——. Records of the United States Army Overseas Operations and Commands, 1898–1942. Record Group 395.

Manuscript Collections

Juan and Nicolás Arnao Papers. Miscellaneous Manuscripts Collection. Library of Congress. Washington, D.C.
John R. Brooke Papers. Historical Society of Pennsylvania. Philadelphia, Pennsylvania.
William Eaton Chandler Papers. Library of Congress. Washington, D.C.
Grover Cleveland Papers. Library of Congress. Washington, D.C.
Henry C. Corbin Papers. Library of Congress. Washington, D.C.
William R. Day Papers. Library of Congress. Washington, D.C.
Hamilton Fish Papers. Library of Congress. Washington, D.C.
Hermann Hagedorn Papers. Library of Congress. Washington, D.C.
Roswell R. Hoes Papers. Library of Congress. Washington, D.C.
Philip C. Jessup Papers. Library of Congress. Washington, D.C.
Frank R. McCoy Papers. Library of Congress. Washington, D.C.
William McKinley Papers. Library of Congress. Washington, D.C.
John Bassett Moore Papers. Library of Congress. Washington, D.C.
John Tyler Morgan Papers. Library of Congress. Washington, D.C.
Richard B. Olney Papers. Library of Congress. Washington, D.C.
Philip Phillips Family Papers. Library of Congress. Washington, D.C.
José Ignacio Rodríguez Papers. Library of Congress. Washington, D.C.
Theodore Roosevelt Papers. Library of Congress. Washington, D.C.
Elihu Root Papers. Library of Congress. Washington, D.C.
John C. Spooner Papers. Library of Congress. Wahsington, D.C.
William Howard Taft Papers. Library of Congress. Washington, D.C.
Joseph Wheeler Papers. Alabama Department of Archives and History. Montgomery, Alabama.
James Harrison Wilson Papers. Library of Congress. Washington, D.C.
Leonard Wood Papers. Library of Congress. Washington, D.C.

Theses and Unpublished Manuscripts

Bail, Hamilton, V. "The Military Government of Cuba, 1898–1902." Unpublished manuscript, Hoover Institution on War and Peace, Stanford, California, 1943.
Cuba—Miscellaneous Records, File 215–2807. Library of Congress. Washington, D.C.

Dawley, Thomas R., Jr. "With Our Army At Tampa." Unpublished manuscript, P.K. Yonge Library, University of Florida, Gainesville, Florida, 1898.

Leon, Joseph M. "The Cigar Industry and Cigar Leaf Tobacco in Florida During the Nineteenth Century, M.A. thesis, Florida State University, Tallahassee, Florida, 1962.

Miscellaneous Manuscript Collection. Círculo Cubano. Tampa, Florida.

Miscellaneous Records. Club Martí-Maceo. Tampa, Florida.

Nichols, Lawrence R. "Domestic History of Cuba During the War of the Insurrectos, 1895–1898." Masters thesis, Duke University, Durham, North Carolina, 1951.

Orum, Thomas T. "The Politics of Color: The Racial Dimension of Cuban Politics During the Early Republican Years, 1900–1912." Ph.D. diss., New York University, New York, 1975.

Steffy, Joan Marie. "The Cuban Immigrants of Tampa, Florida, 1886–1898." Masters thesis, University of South Florida, Tampa, Florida, 1975.

True, Marshall MacDonald, "Revolutionaries in Exile: The Cuban Revolutionary Party, 1891–1898." Ph.D. diss., University of Virginia, Charlottesville, Virginia, 1965.

Published Material

Documents

Academia de la Historia de Cuba. *Crónicas de la guerra de Cuba.* Ed. Enrique Gay-Calbó. Havana: Imprenta "El Siglo XX," 1957.

Adams, Henry. *Letters of Henry Adams.* Ed. Worthington Chauncey Ford. 2 vols. Boston: Houghton Mifflin Company, 1930–1938.

Brooke, John R. *Civil Report of Major-General John R. Brooke, U.S. Army, Military Governor of Cuba: 1900.* Washington, D.C.: Government Printing Office, 1900.

Cabrales, Gonzalo, ed. *Epistolario de heroes. Cartas y documentos históricos.* Havana: Imprenta "El Siglo XX," 1922.

Carbonell, Nestor L. *Resonancias del pasado.* Havana: Imprenta "La Prueba," 1916.

Castelar, Emilio. *Correspondencia de Emilio Castelar, 1868–1908.* Madrid: Establecimiento Tipográfico "Sucesores de Rivadeneyra," 1908.

Cervera y Topete, Pascual. *The Spanish-American War. A Collection of Documents Relative to the Squadron Operations in the West Indies.* Office of Naval Intelligence, War Notes No. VII, Washington, D.C.: Government Printing Office, 1899.

Cisneros Betancourt, Salvador. *Tras la bandera.* Havana: Imprenta "La Prueba," 1916.

Cuba. Archivo Nacional. *El Archivo Nacional en la conmemoración del centenario del natálico de José Martí y Pérez, 1853–1953.* Havana: Archivo Nacional de Cuba, 1953.

———. Camagüey. *Reglamento para el gobierno interior del Cuerpo de la Guardia Rural.* Camagüey: n.p., 1899.

———. Consejo de Gobierno. *Recopilación de las leyes reglamentos, decretos y demás disposiciones dictadas por el Consejo de Gobierno de la República de Cuba.* New York: Imprenta "América," 1897.

———. Convención Constituyente. *Opinión sobre las relaciones entre Cuba y los Estados Unidos.* Havana: Imprenta y Papelería "La Universal" de Ruiz y Hermano, 1901.

———. Ejército Libertador. *Parte oficial del lugarteniente general Calixto García al General en Jefe Máximo Gómez el 15 de abril de 1898 sobre la campaña de Santiago de Cuba.* Havana: Academia de la Historia de Cuba, 1953.

———. Guardia Rural. *Memoria explicativa de la fundación y reorganización del Cuerpo y de los trabajos realizados por el mismo durante el año fiscal 1904.* Havana: n.p. 1904.

———. Military Governor, 1899–1902. *Civil Orders and Proclamations of the Department of Cuba.* 2 vols. Havana: n.p., n.d.

————. Secretaria de Gobernación. *Documentos históricos*. Havana: Imprenta y Papelería de Rambla, Bouza y Cía., 1912.

Davis, Charles Belmont, ed. *Adventures and Letters of Richard Harding Davis*. New York: Charles Scribner's Sons, 1917.

Estrada Palma, Tomás. *Desde el Castillo de Figueras. Cartas de Estrada Palma (1877–1878)*. Ed. Carlos de Velasco. Havana: Sociedad Editorial Cuba Contemporánea, 1918.

Everett, Alexander H. *The Everett Letters on Cuba*. Boston: George H. Ellis, 1897.

Ford, Paul L., ed. *The Writings of Thomas Jefferson*. 10 vols. New York: G. P. Putnam's Sons. 1898.

García, Marcos. *Carta-folleto a José María Gálvez*. Havana: Imprenta "La Universal" de Ruiz y Hermano, 1899.

Gardel, Luis D., ed. *Tres cartas del doctor González Lanuza*. Rio de Janeiro: n.p., 1959.

Gómez, Máximo. *Algunos documentos políticos de Máximo Gómaz*. Ed. Amalia Rodríguez Rodríguez. Havana: Biblioteca Nacional "José Martí," 1962.

————. *Archivo del mayor general Máximo Gómez*. Havana: Oficina del Historiador de la Ciudad de La Habana, 1959.

————. *Cartas a Francisco Carrillo*. Ed. Hortensia Pichardo Viñals. Havana: Instituto Cubano del Libro, 1971.

————. *Cartas de Máximo Gómez*. Ed. Emilio Rodríguez Demorizi. Ciudad Trujillo: Imprenta de J. R. Vda. García, 1936.

————. *El general Máximo Gómez y su política de paz, unión y concordia*. Havana: Tipografía "Los Niños Huérfanos," 1900.

————. *Ideario Cubano*. Ed. Emilio Roig de Leuchsenring. Havana: Municipio de La Habana, 1936.

————. *Papeles dominicanos de Máximo Gómez*. Ed. Emilio Rodríguez Demorizi. Ciudad Trujillo: Editora Montalvo, 1954.

Lee, Fitzhugh. *Annual Report of Brigadier General Fitzhugh Lee, Commanding the Department of the Province of Havana and Pinar Del Río*. Quemados, Cuba: n.p. 1899.

————. *Special Report of Brigadier General Fitzhugh Lee on the Industrial, Economic and Social Conditions Existing in the Province of Havana and Pinar del Río*. Quemados, Cuba: n.p., 1899.

Llaverías y Martínez, Joaquín, ed. *Correspondencia de la delegación cubana en Nueva York durante la guerra de 1895 a 1898*. 5 vols. Havana: Imprenta del Archivo Nacional, 1943–1946.

Llaverías y Martínez, Joaquín and Santovenia, Emeterio Santiago, eds. *Actas de las Asambleas de Representantes y del Consejo de Gobierno durante la guerra de independencia*. 6 vols. Havana: Imprenta y Papelería de Rambla, Bouza y Cía, 1927–1933.

Lodge, Henry Cabot, ed. *Selections From the Correspondence of Theodore Roosevelt and Henry Cabot Lodge*. 2 vols. New York: Charles Scribner's Sons, 1925.

Maceo, Antonio. *Antonio Maceo: documentos para su vida*. Ed. Julián Martínez Castells. Havana: Archivo Nacional de Cuba, 1945.

————. *Antonio Maceo. Ideología política. Cartas y otros documentos*. Ed. Sociedad Cubana de Estudios Históricos e Internacionales. 2 vols. Havana: Cárdenas y Compañía, 1950–1952.

————. *Ideario Cubano*. Ed. Emilio Roig de Leuchsenring. Havana: Municipio de La Habana. 1946.

————. *El pensamiento vivo de Maceo*. Ed. José Antonio Portuondo. Havana: Consejo Nacional de Cultura, 1962.

McCurdy, J. M., ed., *Two Rough Riders: Letters from F. Allen McCurdy and J. Kirk McCurdy*. New York: F. Tennyson Neely, 1903.

Manning, William Roy, ed. *Diplomatic Correspondence of the United States: Inter-American Affairs, 1831-1860.* 12 vols. Washington, D.C.: Carnegie Endowment, 1932-1939.

Martí, José. *Ideario cubano.* Ed. Emilio Roig de Leuchsenring. Havana: Municipio de La Habana, 1936.

————. *Ideario separatista.* Ed. Félix Lizaso. Havana: Publicación del Ministerio de Educación, 1947.

————. *Obras completas.* Ed. Jorge Quintana. 5 vols. Caracas: n.p., 1964.

————. *El Partido Revolucionario Cubano y la guerra.* Ed. Pedro Pablo Rodríguez López. Havana: Editorial de Ciencias Sociales, 1978.

Masó, Bartolomé. *En días grandes.* Havana: Imprenta "La Preuba," 1916.

Mayo, Lawrence Shaw, ed. *America of Yesterday As Reflected in the Journal of John Davis Long.* Boston: The Atlantic Monthly Press, 1923.

Müeller y Tejeiro, José. *Battles and Capitulations of Santiago de Cuba.* Office of Naval Intelligence. War Notes No. 1, Information from Abroad. U.S. Cong. Senate. Notes on the Spanish-American War. 56th Cong. 1st session, Document No. 388, Ser. 3876, Washington, D.C.: Government Printing Office, 1900.

Nevins, Allan, ed. *Letters of Grover Cleveland.* Boston: Houghton Mifflin, 1933.

Parker, Captain Frank. *Informe anual del instructor de la Guardia Rural sobre la instrucción militar durante el año académico que expiró en 30 de junio de 1912.* Havana: n.p., 1912.

Pérez Cabrera, Manuel, ed. *Documentos para servir a la historia de la Guerra Chiquita.* 3 vols. Havana: Archivo Nacional de Cuba, 1950.

Porter, Kirk H., and Donald Bruce Johnson, eds. *National Party Platforms, 1840-1968.* Urbana: University of Illinois, 1970.

Porter, Robert P. *Report on the Commercial and Industrial Condition of Cuba. Special Report on the Commissioner's Visit to General Gomez, and in Relation to the Payment and Disbandment of the Insurgent Army of Cuba.* Washington, D.C.: Government Printing Office, 1899.

Primelles, León, ed. *La revolución del 95 según la correspondencia de la delegación cubana en Nueva York.* 5 vols. Havana: Editorial Habanera, 1932-1937.

Quesada, Gonzalo de. *Archivo de Gonzalo de Quesada.* Ed. Gonzalo de Quesada y Miranda. 2 vols. Havana: Imprenta "El Siglo XX," 1948-1951.

————. *Documentos históricos.* Havana: Editorial de la Universidad de La Habana, 1965.

Richardson, James D., ed. *A Compilation of the Messages and Papers of the Presidents, 1789-1902.* 10 vols. Washington, D.C.: Library of Congress, 1896-1902.

Spain. Ministerio de Estado. *Spanish Diplomatic Correspondence and Documents, 1896-1900, Presented to the Cortes by the Minister of State.* Washington, D. C.: Government Printing Office, 1905.

Stallman, R. W., and E. R., Hageman, eds. *The War Dispatches of Stephen Crane.* New York: New York University Press, 1964.

United States Congress. House. *Affairs in Cuba.* 54th Congress, 1st Session, Document No. 224, Ser. 3425, Washington, D.C.: Government Printing Office, 1896.

————. Senate. *Affairs in Cuba.* 56th Congress, 2nd Session, Ser. 4053. Washington, D.C.: Government Printing Office, 1901.

————. Senate. *Consular Correspondence Respecting the Conditions of the Reconcentrados in Cuba, the State of the War in that Island, and the Prospects of the Projected Autonomy.* 55th Congress, 2nd Session, Senate Document, No. 230. Washington, D.C.: Government Printing Office, 1898.

————. Senate. *Cuban Sugar Sales: Testimony Taken by Committee on Relations with Cuba.* 57th Congress, 1st Session, Washington, D.C.: Government Printing Office, 1902.

————. Senate. *The Establishment of Free Government in Cuba.* 58th Congress, 2nd Session, Senate Document No. 312, Ser. 4592. Washington, D.C.: Government Printing Office, 1904.

———. Senate. *Qualifications of Voters at Coming Elections in Cuba*. 56th Congress, 2nd Session, Senate Document No. 243, Ser. 3867. Washington, D.C.: Government Printing Office, 1900.

———. Senate. *Report of the Committee on Foreign Relations: Affairs in Cuba*. 55th Congress, 2nd Session, Report No. 885, Ser. 3624. Washington, D.C.: Government Printing Office, 1898.

———. Senate. Committee on Relations with Cuba. *Conditions in Cuba*. Washington, D.C.: Government Printing Office, 1900.

———. Senate. *Report of the Commission Appointed by the President to Investigate the Conduct of the War Department in the War With Spain*. 56th Congress, 1st Session, 8 vols., Ser. 3859–66. Washington, D.C.: Government Printing Office, 1900.

———. Senate. *Report of the Committee on Relations: Affairs in Cuba*. 55th Congress, 2nd Session, Report No. 885, Ser. 3654, Washington, D.C.: Government Printing Office, 1898.

United States Department of State. *Papers Relating to the Foreign Relations of the United States*. 1895–1898. Washington, D.C.: Government Printing Office, 1896–1901.

United States Department of the Treasury. *Report on the Commercial and the Industrial Condition of Cuba. Special Report. The Province of Santiago de Cuba and the Internal Revenue of the Island of Cuba*. Washington, D.C.: Government Printing Office, 1899.

———. *Report of the Commercial and Industrial Condition of the Island of Cuba*. Washington, D.C.: Government Printing Office, 1898.

United States Tarriff Commission. *Effects of the Cuban Reciprocity Treaty*. Washington, D.C.: Government Printing Office, 1929.

United States War Department. Adjutant General's Office. *Correspondence Relating to the War With Spain*. Washington, D.C.: Government Printing Office, 1902.

———. Adjutant General's Office. Military Information Division. *Military Notes on Cuba*. Washington, D.C.: Government Printing Office, 1898.

———. Oficina del Director del Censo de Cuba. *Informe sobre el censo de Cuba, 1899*. Washington, D.C.: Government Printing Office, 1900.

———. *Annual Report of the War Department, 1899*. House of Representatives. 56th Congress, 1st Session, House Document No. 2, 3 vols. Washington, D.C.: Government Printing Office, 1899.

———. *Annual Reports of the War Department: Report of the Major-General Commanding the Army, 1899*. House of Representatives. 56th Congress, 1st Session, House Document No. 2, Ser. 3901. Washington, D.C.: Government Printing Office, 1899.

———. *Civil Report of Brigadier General Leonard Wood, Military Governor of Cuba, for the Period from December 20, 1899 to December 31, 1900*. 12 vols. Washington, D.C.: Government Printing Office, 1900.

———. *Civil Report of Brigadier General Leonard Wood, Military Governor of Cuba, for the period from January 1 to May 20, 1902*. 6 vols. Washington, D.C.: Government Printing Office, 1902.

———. *Annual Reports of the War Department: Report of the Major-General Commanding the Army, 1898*. House of Representatives. 55th Congress, 3rd Session, House Document No. 2, Ser. 3745. Washington, D.C.: Government Printing Office, 1898.

Newspapers

El Avisador Comercial
Chicago Daily News

Chicago Tribune
The Daily Picayune
Deseret Evening News
Detroit Free Press
Diario de la Marina
La Discusión
Journal of Commerce
London Times
La Lucha
The Morning Tampa Tribune
El Mundo
New York Daily Tribune
New York Evening Post
New York Journal
New York Herald
New York Times
New York World
Patria
Philadelphia Enquirer
The State
Washington Evening Star
Washington Post

Memoirs, Autobiographies, and Reminiscences

Acosta León, Raúl D. *La revolución en Camagüey (1895–1896). Ruta y anecdotario de Máximo Gómez.* Camagüey: Imprenta "El Camagüeyano," 1950.

Alger, Russell A. *The Spanish-American War.* New York: Harper & Brothers, 1901.

Amblard, Arturo. *Notas coloniales.* Madrid: Ambrosio Pérez y Cía., 1904.

Anillo Rodríguez, Eduardo. *Cuatro siglos de vida.* Havana: Imprenta "Avisador Comercial," 1919.

Antomarchi, Jean. *Life With the Cubans.* Trans. J. L. Moreau. New York: Brooklyn Eagle, 1898.

Aranguren y Martínez, Benito. *Recuerdos.* Havana: Imprenta Librería "Nueva," 1934.

Arbelo, Manuel. *Recuerdos de la última guerra por la independencia de Cuba. 1896 a 1898.* Havana: Imprenta "Tipografa Moderna," 1918.

Atkins, Edwin F. *Sixty Years in Cuba.* Cambridge, Mass.: Riverside Press, 1926.

Atkins, John Black. *The War in Cuba.* London: Smith, Elder & Co., 1899.

Ballou, Maturin M. *Due South, or Cuba Past and Present.* Boston: Houghton, Mifflin, and Company, 1886.

Basail, Tomás. *En poder de españoles.* Sagua la Grande: Imprenta "La Epoca," 1898.

Basulto de Montoya, Flora. *Una niña bajo tres banderas (memorias).* Havana: Compañía Editoria de Libros y Folletos, 1954.

Batrell Oviedo, Ricardo. *Para la historia. Apuntes autobiográficos.* Havana: Seoane y Alvarez, 1912.

Bergés Tabares, Rodolfo. *Cuba y Santo Domingo. Apuntes de la guerra de Cuba, de mi diario de campaña 1895–96–97–98.* Havana: Imprenta "El Score," 1905.

Bonsal, Stephen. *The Fight For Santiago.* New York: Doubleday & McClure Company, 1899.

Boza, Bernabé. *Mi diario de la guerra.* 2 vols. Havana: Librería Cervantes, 1924.

Bravo y Correoso, Antonio. *Como se hizo la constitución de Cuba.* Havana: Rambla, Bouza y Cía., 1928.

Bueno y Javaloyes, Manuel. *El ler. batallón de María Cristina en el Camagüey*. Matanzas: Imprenta, Librería y Papelería "La Propaganda," 1897.

Burguete, Ricardo. *¡La guerra! Cuba (diario de un testigo)*. Barcelona: Casa Editorial Maucci, 1902.

Cabrera, Raimundo. *Desde mi sitio*. Havana: Imprenta "El Siglo XX," 1911.

———. *Episodios de la guerra. Mi vida en la manigua (relato del coronel Ricardo Buenamar)*. 3rd ed. Philadelphia: La Compañía Levytype, 1898.

Cabrera, Ramiro. *¡A Sitio Herrera!* Havana: Imprenta y Papelería de Rambla, Bouza y Cía., 1922.

Camps y Feliu, Francisco de. *Españoles e insurrectos. Recuerdos de la guerra de Cuba*. 2nd ed. Havana: Imprenta de A. Alvarez y Compañía, 1890.

Cañizares y Quirós, Rafael M. "Diario de operación del teniente coronel Rafael M. Cañizares y Quirós," *Boletín del Archivo Nacional* XLVIII (Jan.–Dec., 1949), 104–51.

El Capitán Verdades. *Historia negra: relato de los escándalos ocurridos en nuestras excolonias durante las últimas guerras*. Barcelona: Casa Editorial Maucci, 1899.

Carrillo, Mario. *In the Saddle With Gómez*. London: F. Tennyson Neely, 1898.

Castillo, José Rogelio. *Autobiografía del general José Rogelio Castillo*. 2nd ed. Havana: Instituto Cubano del Libro, 1973.

Concas y Palau, Víctor, M. *La escuadra del almirante Cervera*. 2nd ed. Madrid: Librería de San Martín, n.d.

Conill, Enrique J. *Enrique J. Conill, soldado de la patria*. Ed. Gaspar Carbonell Rivero. Havana: Imprenta de P. Fernández y Cía., 1956.

Consuegra y Guzmán, Israel. *Mambiserías. Episodios de la guerra de independencia. 1895–1898*. Havana: Imprenta del Ejército, 1930.

Corona Ferrer, Mariano. *De la manigua (ecos de la epopeya)*. Santiago de Cuba: Imprenta de "El Cubano Libre," 1900.

Corral, Manuel. *¡El desastre! Memorias de un voluntario en la campaña de Cuba*. Barcelona: Alejandro Martínez, 1899.

Corvisón, Segundo. *En la guerra y en la paz*. Havana: Cultural, S. A., 1939.

Crane, Stephen. *Wounds in the Rain*. New York: Alfred A. Knopf, 1900.

Creelman, James. *On the Great Highway*. Boston: Lothrop Publishing Company, 1901.

Davis, Richard Harding. *The Cuban and Porto Rican Campaigns*. New York: Charles Scribner's Sons, 1898.

———. *Notes of a War Correspondent*. New York: Charles Scribner's Sons, 1910.

———. *A Year From a Reporter's Note-Book*. New York: Harper & Brothers, 1898.

Dawes, Charles G. *A Journal of the McKinley Years*. Chicago: The Lakeside Press, 1950.

Díaz Benzo, Antonio. *Pequeñeces de la guerra de Cuba por un español*. Madrid: Imprenta de los Hijos de M. G. Hernández, 1897.

Espinosa Betancourt, Arístides. *Recuerdos e impresiones*. Mexico: Imprenta de Eduardo Dublán, 1902.

Espinosa y Ramos, Serafín. *Al trote y sin estribos (recuerdos de la guerra de independencia)*. Havana: Jesús Montero, 1946.

Fabié, Antonio María. *Mi gestión ministerial respecto a la isla de Cuba*. Madrid: Imprenta del Asilo de Huérfanos del Sagrado Corazón de Jesús, 1898.

Fernández de Castro, Rafael. *Para la historia de Cuba*. Havana: "La Propaganda Literaria," 1899.

Fernández Máscaro, Guillermo. *Ecos de la manigua (el Maceo que yo conocí)*. Havana: Imprenta de P. Fernández y Cía., 1950.

Ferrara y Marino, Orestes. *Memorias: Una mirada sobre tres siglos*. Madrid: Colección Plaza Mayor, 1975.

———. *Mis relaciones con Máximo Gómez*. 2nd ed. Havana: Molina y Compañía, 1942.

Ferrer, Horacio. *Con el rifle al hombro*. Havana: Imprenta "El Siglo XX," 1950.

Ferrer Díaz, Virgilio. *Diario de campaña de un estudiante mambí*. Ed. Virgilio Ferrer Gutiérrez. Havana: Ediciones de la Revista "Indice," 1945.

Flint, Grover. *Marching With Gómez*. Boston: Lamson, Wolffe and Company, 1898.

Flores, Eugenio Antonio. *La guerra de Cuba (apuntes para la historia)*. Madrid: Tipografía de los Hijos de M. G. Hernández, 1895.

Foraker, Joseph Benson. *Notes of a Busy Life*. 2 vols. 3rd ed. Cincinnati: Steward & Kidd Company, 1917.

Froude, John Anthony. *The English in the West Indies*. London: Longmans, Green, and Company, 1888.

Fuller, Charles. *What a New York Trooper Saw of the War*. New York: A Mackel & Company, 1900.

Funston, Frederick. *Memories of Two Wars*. New York: Charles Scribner's Sons, 1914.

Gálvez, Wen. *Tampa. Impresiones de un emigrado*. Ibor City: Establecimiento Tipográfico "Cuba," 1897.

García, Calixto. *Palabras de tres guerras*. Havana: Instituto Cívico Militar, 1942.

Gauvreau, Charles F. *Reminiscences of the Spanish-American War*. Rouses Point, N.Y.: The Authors Publishing Co., 1915.

Gómez, Juan Gualberto. *Por Cuba Libre*. Havana: Oficina del Historiador de la Ciudad de La Habana, 1954.

Gómez, Máximo. *Diario de campaña del mayor general Máximo Gómez*. Havana: Centro Superior Tecnológico, 1940.

———. *Horas de tregua*. Havana: Imprenta Artística "Comedia," 1916.

———. *Recuerdos y previsiones*. Havana: Publicaciones de la Secretaria de Educación, 1935.

———. *Revoluciones . . . Cuba y hogar*. ed. Bernardo Gómez Toro. Havana: Imprenta y Papelería de Rambla, Bouza y Cía., 1927.

Gonzales, N. G. *In Darkest Cuba*. Columbia, S. C.: The State Company, 1922.

Granda, Manuel J. de. *Memoria revolucionaria*. Santiago de Cuba: Tipografía Arroyo Hermanos, 1926.

Guerra y Sánchez, Ramiro. *Por las veredas del pasado, 1880–1902*. Havana: Editorial Lex, 1957.

Hall, Thomas Winthrop. *The Fun and Fighting of the Rough Riders*. New York: Frederick A. Stokes Company, 1899.

Hancock, Irving. *What One Man Saw, Being the Personal Impressions of a War Correspondent in Cuba*. New York: Street & Smith, 1898.

Hernández Guzmán, José. *Memorias tristes*. Havana: Imprenta "Heraldo Cristiano," 1934.

Hobart, (Mrs.) Garrett A. *Memories*. Mount Vernon, N.Y.: William Edwin Rudge, 1930.

Howard, Oliver Otis. *Fighting For Humanity*. New York: F. Tennyson Neely, 1898.

Keeler, Frank. *The Journal of Frank Keeler, 1898*. Ed. Carolyn A. Tyson. Quantico, Va.: Marine Corps Museum, n.d.

Kennan, George. *Campaigning in Cuba*. New York: Century Company, 1899.

Knight, E. F. *Reminiscences*. London: Hutchinson and Company, 1923.

Lagomasino Alvarez, Luis. *Reminiscencias patriotas*. Manzanillo: Tipografía "El Reporter," 1902.

León y Castillo, F. de. *Mis tiempos*. 2 vols. Madrid: Librería de los Sucesores de Hernando, 1921.

Llorens y Maceo, José Silviera. *Con Maceo en la invasión*. Havana: n.p., 1928.

Lodge, Henry Cabot. *The War With Spain*. New York: Arno Press, 1970.

Lores y Llorens, Eduardo F. *Relatos Históricos de la guerra del 95*. Havana: Imprenta "El Siglo XX," 1955.

McCutcheon, John T. *Drawn From Memory*. Indianapolis: Bobbs-Merrill, n.d.

Machado, Francisco de P. *¡Piedad! Recuerdos de la reconcentración.* Havana: Imprenta y Papelería de Rambla, Bouza y Cía., 1927.

McIntosh, Burr, *The Little I Saw of Cuba.* New York: F. Tennyson Neely, 1899.

Martín, Francisco. *Veinte años con Don Carlos.* Madrid: Espasa-Calpa, S. A., 1940.

Medel, José Antonio. *La guerra hispano-americana y sus resultados.* 2nd ed. Havana: Imprenta de P. Fernández y Cía., 1932.

Méndez Miranda, Fernando. *Historia de los servicios prestados en la guerra de independencia.* Havana: Editorial Alberto Soto, 1928.

Miles, Nelson A. *Serving the Republic.* New York: Harper & Brothers, 1911.

Miley, John D. *In Cuba With Shafter.* New York: Charles Scribner's Sons, 1899.

Miller, Theodore W. *Rough Rider. His Diary as a Soldier.* Ed. George E. Vincent. Akron, Ohio: n.p., 1899.

Miranda, Luis Rodolfo. *Diario de campaña del comandante Luis Rodolfo Miranda.* Ed. Manuel I. Mesa Rodríguez. Havana: Oficina del Historiador de la Ciudad de La Habana, 1954.

———. *Recuerdos de Oriente (Bayamo, Banes y Santiago de Cuba).* Havana: Imprenta de P. Fernández y Cía., 1942.

Miranda y de la Rua, Luis. *Con Martí y con Calixto García (recuerdos de un mambí del 95).* Havana: Imprenta de P. Fernández y Cía., 1943.

Miró Argenter, José. *Crónicas de la guerra.* 3 vols. Havana: Librería e Imprenta "La Moderna Poesía," 1909.

Montejo, Esteban. *The Autobiography of a Runaway Slave.* Ed. Miguel Barnet, Trans. Jocasta Innes. London: The Bodley Head, 1968.

Moss, James A. *Memories of the Campaign of Santiago.* San Francisco: The Mysell-Rollins Company, 1899.

Muecke Bertel, Carlos. *Patria y libertad.* Trans. Walfredo J. Rodríguez y Rodríguez. Camagüey: Ramentol y Boan, 1928.

Munroe, Kirk. *Forward March. A Tale of the Spanish-American War.* New York: Harper & Brothers, 1899.

Musgrave, George C. *Under Three Flags in Cuba.* Boston: Little, Brown, and Company, 1899.

Núñez de Villavicencio, Ricardo. *Aventuras emocionantes de un emigrado revolucionario cubano.* Havana: Maza, Caso, y Ca., 1929.

O'Brien, John. *A Captain Unafraid.* New York: Harper & Brothers, 1912.

O'Donnell y Abreu, Carlos (Duke of Tetuán). *Apuntes del ex-Ministro de Estado Duque de Tetuán para la defensa de la política internacional y gestión diplomática del gobierno Liberal-Conservador.* 2 vols. Madrid: Tipografía y Litografía de Raoul Peant, 1902.

Parker, John H. *History of the Gatling Gun Detachment, Fifth Army Corps, at Santiago, With a Few Unvarnished Truths Concerning that Expedition.* Kansas City: Hudson-Kimberly Publishing Company, 1898.

Pérez Abreu, Gustavo. *En la guerra con Máximo Gómez.* Havana: Editorial "Carbonell," 1952.

Piedra Martel, Manuel. *Memorias de un mambí.* Havana: Instituto Cubano del Libro, 1968.

———. *Mis primeros treinta años: memorias.* Havana: Editorial Minerva, 1944.

Pierce, Frederick E. *Reminiscences of the Experiences of Company L, Second Regiment Massachusetts Infantry, U.S.V., in the Spanish-American War.* Greenfield, Mass.: Press of E.A. Hall & Co., 1900.

Polaviejo, Camilo G. *Relación documentada de mi política en Cuba.* Madrid: Imprenta de Emilio Minuesa, 1898.

Quesada, Gonzalo de. *Páginas escogidas.* Havana: Instituto Cubano del Libro, 1968.

Radillo y Rodríguez, Luis de. *Autobiografía del cubano Luis Radillo y Rodríguez. Episodios de su vida histórico-político-revolucionario desde el 24 de febrero de 1895 hasta el 1 de enero de 1899*. Havana: Imprenta de R. Santana Rodríguez, 1899.

Rey, Santiago C. *Recuerdos de la guerra. 1895–1898*. Havana: Imprenta de P. Fernández y Cía., 1931.

Roa, Raúl. *Aventuras, venturas y desventuras de un mambí*. Havana: Instituto Cubano del Libro, 1970.

Rodríguez Martínez, J. *Los desastres y la regeneración de España. Relatos e impresiones*. La Coruña: Est. Tipográfico "La Gutenberg," 1899.

Roosevelt, Theodore. *An Autobiography*. New York: The Macmillan Company, 1913.

———. *The Rough Riders*. New York: Charles Scribner's Sons, 1920.

Rosell y Malpica, Eduardo. *Diario del teniente coronel Eduardo Rosell y Malpica*. 2 vols. Havana: Academia de la Historia de Cuba, 1949–1950.

Rosende y de Zayas, Angel E. *Memorias de la guerra, 1895–1898*. Havana: n.p., 1928.

Rowan, Andrew Summers. *How I Carried the Message to Garcia*. San Francisco: Walter D. Harney Publishers, n.d.

Rubens, Horatio S. *Liberty, The Story of Cuba*. New York: Warren and Putnam, Inc., 1932.

Sánchez, Julián. *Julián Sánchez cuenta su vida*. Ed. Erasmo Dumpierre. Havana: Instituto Cubano del Libro, 1970.

Sanjenís, Avelino. *Memorias de la revolución de 1895 para la independencia de Cuba*. Havana: Imprenta y Papelería de Rambla, Bouza y Cía., 1913.

———. *Mis cartas. Memorias de la revolución de 1895 por la independencia de Cuba*. Sagua la Grande: Imprenta "El Comercio," 1900.

Sargent, Herbert H. *The Campaign of Santiago de Cuba*. 3 vols. Chicago: A.C. McClurg & Co., 1907.

Schley, Winfield Scott. *Forty-Five Years Under the Flag*. New York: Appleton and Company, 1904.

Serra Orts, Antonio. *Recuerdos de las guerras de Cuba. 1868 a 1898*. Santa Cruz de Tenerife: A. J. Benítez, 1906.

The Spanish-American War. The Events of the War Described by Eye Witnesses. Chicago: Herbert S. Stone & Company, 1899.

Steward, M. B. *The N'th Foot in War*. Kansas City: Hudson Press, 1906.

Stratemeyer, Edward. *A Young Volunteer in Cuba*. Boston: Lee and Shepard Publishers, 1900.

Torriente, Loló de la. *Mi casa en la tierra*. Havana: Imprenta Ucar, García, S. A., 1956.

Torriente y Peraza, Cosme de la. *Cuarenta años de mi vida, 1898–1938*. Havana: Imprenta "El Siglo XX," 1939.

Valdés Domínguez, Fermín. *Diario de soldado*. 4 vols. Havana: Universidad de La Habana, 1972–1974.

Vesa y Fillart, Antonio. *Voluntarios de la Isla de Cuba. Historial del Regimiento Caballería de Jaruco y de su estandarte*. Barcelona: Imprenta y Litografía de la Viuda de José Cunill, 1908.

Vivian, Thomas J. *The Fall of Santiago*. New York: R. F. Fenno & Company, 1898.

Wagner, Arthur L. *Report of the Santiago Campaign, 1898*. Kansas City, Mo.: Franklin Hudson Publishing Co., 1908.

Weyler, Valeriano. *Mi mando en Cuba*. 5 vols. Madrid: Imprenta de Felipe González Rojas, 1910–1911.

Wheeler, Joseph. *The Santiago Campaign 1898*. Port Washington, N. Y.: Kennikat Press, 1971.

Willets, Gilson. *The Triumph of Yankee Doodle*. New York: F. Tennyson Neely, 1896.

Wilson, James Harrison. *Under the Old Flag*. 2 vols. New York: D. Appleton and Company, 1912.

Woodward, Frank R. E. *With Maceo in Cuba*. Minneapolis: The Scarlett Printing Company, 1896.

Books

A & B. *Apuntes en defensa del honor del ejército*. Madrid: Est. Tipográfico de Ricardo Fe., 1898.

Abreu Licairac, Rafael. *Mi obolo a Cuba* New York: Imprenta "Patria," 1897.

Acheson, Sam Hanna. *Joe Bailey, The Last Democrat*. New York: The MacMillan Company, 1932.

Alienes y Urosa, Julián. *Características fundamentales de la economía cubana*. Havana: Banco Nacional de Cuba, 1950.

Allen, Benjamin. *A Story of the Growth of E. Atkins & Co. and the Sugar Industry in Cuba*. New York: n.p., 1925.

Alonso, Aurelio Martín, *Diez y seis años de regencia: María Cristina de Hapsburgo-Lorena (1885–1902)*. Barcelona: Casa Editorial Vda. de Luis Tasso, 1914.

Alvarez Conde, José. *Homenaje del Archivo Nacional a su primer director Nestor Ponce de León, el emigrado intransigente*. Havana: Archivo Nacional, 1955.

Alvarez Díaz, José R., et al. *A Study on Cuba*. Coral Gables: University of Miami Press, 1965.

Alzola y Minondo, Pablo de. *El problema cubano*. Bilbao: Imprenta de Andrés P. Cardenal, 1898.

Arce, Luis A. de. *Emilio Núñez (1875–1922): historiografía*. Havana: Editorial "Niños," 1943.

Armiñán, Luis de. *Weyler*. Madrid: Editorial "Gran Capitán," 1946.

Arnao, Juan. *Páginas para la historia de la Isla de Cuba*. Havana: Imprenta "La Nueva," 1900.

Arredondo, Alberto. *Cuba: tierra indefensa*. Havana: Editorial Lex, 1945.

Austin, Oscar Phelps. *Uncle Sam's Soldiers. A Story of the War with Spain*. New York: D. Appleton and Company, 1899.

Azcuy Alón, Fanny. *El Partido Revolucionario y la independencia de Cuba*. Havana: Molina y Compañía, 1930.

Bangs, John Kendrick. *Uncle Sam Trustee*. New York: Riggs Publishing Company, 1902.

Barcardí y Moreau, Emilio. *Crónicas de Santiago de Cuba*. Ed. Amalia Bacardí Cape. 10 vols. 2nd ed. Madrid: Breogan, I.G.S.A., 1973.

Barquín, Ramón M. *Las luchas guerrilleras en Cuba. De la colonia a la Sierra Maestra*. 2 vols. Madrid: Colección Plaza Mayor, 1975.

Barras y Prado, Antonio de las. *La Habana a mediados del siglo XIX*. Madrid: Imprenta de la Ciudad Lineal, 1926.

Beck, Henry Houghton. *Cuba's Fight for Freedom and the War with Spain*. Philadelphia: Globe Bible Publishing Company, 1898.

Benton, Elbert J. *International Law and Diplomacy of the Spanish-American War*. Baltimore: Johns Hopkins Press, 1908.

Blanco Herrero, Miguel. *Política de España en ultramar*. 2nd ed. Madrid: Imprenta de Francisco G. Pérez, 1890.

Bonsal, Stephen. *The Real Condition of Cuba To-day*. New York: Harper & Brothers, 1897.

Borrero Pérez, Juan G. *La cubanía aniquilada por la Enmienda Platt*. Sancti-Spíritus: Imprenta "Iris," 1958.

Bowers, Claude G. *Beveridge and the Progressive Era*. Cambridge, Massachusetts: The Riverside Press, 1932.

Brown, Charles H. *The Correspondents' War. Journalists in the Spanish-American War.* New York: Charles Scribner's Sons, 1967.

Bustamante y Montoro, Antonio S. de. *La ideología autonomista.* Havana: Imprenta Molina y Cía., 1933.

Bustamante y Sirvén, Antonio S. de. *Discursos.* 2 vols. 2nd ed. Havana: Cultural , S.A., 1932–1933.

Butler, Charles Henry. *Cuba Must Be Free.* New York: n.p., 1898.

Buttari Gaunaurd, J. *Boceto crítico histórico.* Havana: Editorial Lex, 1954.

Cabrera, Raimundo. *Cuba and the Cubans.* Philadelphia: The Levytype Company, 1896.

———. *Los partidos coloniales.* Havana: Imprenta "El Siglo XX," 1914.

Callahan, James Morton. *Cuba and International Relations.* Baltimore: Johns Hopkins Press, 1899.

Camacho, Panfilo D. *Enrique Collazo, libertador e historiografo.* Havana: Imprenta "El Siglo XX," 1948.

———. *Estrada Palma, el gobernante honrado.* Havana: Editorial Trópico, 1938.

———. *Marta Abreu, una mujer comprendida.* Havana: Editorial Trópico, 1947.

Candamo, Víctor G. *Weyler. La insurrección de Cuba.* Puerto Rico: Imprenta de Francisco J. Marxuach, 1897.

Cánovas del Castillo, Emilio. *Cánovas del Castillo.* Madrid: M. Romero, 1901.

Un caracter. Tomás Estrada Palma. Un detalle de su vida. Havana: n.p., 1901.

Carballal, Rodolfo Z. *El general José Gómez.* Havana: Imprenta de Rambla, Bouza y Compañía, 1913.

Carbonell, José Manuel. *Manuel Sanguily. Adalid, tribuno y pensador.* Havana: Imprenta "El Siglo XX," 1925.

Carbonell, Miguel Angel. *Eusebio Hernández.* 2 vols. Havana: Editorial Guáimaro, 1939.

———. *Sanguily.* Havana: Editorial Guáimaro, 1938.

Carbonell y Rivero, Nestor. *Elogio del coronel Fernando Figueredo Socarrás.* Havana: Imprenta "El Siglo XX," 1935.

———. *En torno a una gran vida.* Havana: Imprenta "El Siglo XX," 1948.

Cárdenas, Raúl de. *Cuba no puede invocarse en testimonio del imperialismo norteamericano.* Havana: Imprenta "El Siglo XX," 1917.

———. *La política de los Estados Unidos en el continente americano.* Havana: Sociedad Editorial Cuba Contemporánea, 1921.

Carrera Pujal, Jaime. *Historia política de Cataluña en el siglo XIX.* 7 vols. Barcelona: Bosch, 1957–1958.

Carrillo Morales, Justo. *Expediciones cubanas.* 2 vols. Havana: Imprenta de P. Fernández y Ca., 1936.

Carter, William Harding. *The Life of Lieutenant General Chaffee.* Chicago: University of Chicago Press, 1917.

Casas y González, Juan Bautista. *La guerra separatista de Cuba.* Madrid: Tipográfico de San Francisco de Sales, 1896.

Casasús, Juan J. E. *Calixto García (el estratega).* 2nd ed. Havana: Oficina del Historiador de la Ciudad de La Habana, 1962.

———. *La emigración cubana y la independencia de la patria.* Havana: Editorial Lex, 1953.

———. *La Invasión. Sus antecedentes, sus factores, su finalidad. Estudio crítico-militar.* Havana: Imprenta Habana, 1950.

Castañeda, Orlando. *Martí, los tabaqueros y la revolución de 1895.* Havana: Editorial Lex, 1946.

Castañeda, Tiburcio P. *La explosión del Maine y la guerra de los Estados Unidos con España.* Havana: Librería e Imprenta "La Moderna Poesía," 1925.

Castellanos García, Gerardo. *Adolfo del Castillo en la paz y en la guerra*. Havana: Editorial "Hermes," 1922.

————. *Aranguren (del ciclo mambí)*. Havana: Editorial "Hermes," n.d.

————. *Francisco Gómez Toro: en el surco del generalísimo*. Havana: Imprenta Seone y Fernández, 1932.

————. *Legado mambí: formación, odisea y agonía del archivo del general Máximo Gómez*. Havana: Ucar, García y Cía., 1940.

————. *Motivos de Cayo Hueso (contribución a la historia de las emigraciones revolucionarias cubanas en los Estados Unidos)*. Havana: Ucar, García y Cía., 1935.

————. *Un paladín (Serafín Sánchez)*. Havana: Editorial "Hermes," 1926.

————. *Panorama histórico*. Havana: Ucar, García y Cía., 1934.

————. *Relieves*. Havana: Imprenta de P. Fernández y Cía., 1910.

————. *Resplandores épicos*. Havana: Ucar, García y Cía., 1942.

————. *Soldado y conspirador*. 3rd ed. Havana: Editorial "Hermes," 1930.

————. *Sondeo histórico: Máximo Gómez y su diario de campaña*. Havana: Ucar, García y Cía., 1941.

————. *Tierras y glorias de Oriente (Calixto García Iñiguez)*. Havana: Editorial "Hermes," 1927.

Casuso, Enrique. *Política cubana y sistema americano*. Havana: Imprenta Avisador Comercial, 1901.

Catá, Alvaro. *Cuba y la intervención*. Havana: Imprenta "El Fígaro," 1899.

————. *De guerra a guerra*. Havana: Imprenta "La Razón," 1906.

Céspedes y de Quesada, Carlos Manuel. *Un instante de la maravillosa carrera de Máximo Gómez*. Havana: Imprenta "El Siglo XX," 1932.

Chadwick, French Ensor. *The Relations of the United States and Spain: Diplomacy*. New York: Russell & Russell, 1968.

————. *The Relations of the United States and Spain: The Spanish-American War*. 2 vols. New York: Russell & Russell, 1968.

Chicago Record. *The Chicago Record's War Stories*. Chicago: The Chicago Record, 1898.

Cisneros y Betancourt, Salvador. *Appeal to the American People on Behalf of Cuba*. New York: The Evening Post Job Printing House, 1900.

Collazo, Enrique. *Los americanos en Cuba*. Havana: Instituto Cubano del Libro, 1972.

————. *Cuba heroica*. Havana: Imprenta "La Mercantil," 1912.

————. *Cuba independiente*. Havana: La Moderna Poesía, 1900.

————. *Desde Yara hasta Zanjón. Apuntaciones históricas*. 2nd ed. Havana: Tipografía de "La Lucha," 1893.

————. *La guerra en Cuba*. Havana: Librería "Cervantes," 1926.

————. *La revolución de agosto de 1906*. Havana: Casa Editorial C. Martínez y Ca., 1907.

Conangla Fontanilles, José. *Cuba y Pi y Margall*. Havana: Editorial Lex, 1947.

Congreso Nacional de Historia. X. *En el cincuentenario de la República*. Havana: Oficina del Historiador de la Ciudad de La Habana, 1953.

————. XII. *La lucha por la independencia de Cuba*. Havana: Oficina del Historiador de la Ciudad de La Habana, 1957.

————. XIII. *Historia de Cuba republicana y sus antecedentes favorables y adversos a la independencia*. Havana: Oficina del Historiador de la Ciudad de La Habana, 1960.

Consejo Nacional de Veteranos de la Independencia de Cuba. *Máximo Gómez*. Havana: Imprenta y Papelería de Rambla, Bouza y Cía., 1935.

Conte, F. A. *Las aspiraciones del Partido Liberal de Cuba*. Havana: Imprenta de A. Alvarez y Compañía, 1892.

Coolidge, Louis A. *An Old-Fashioned Senator: Orville H. Platt of Connecticut*. New York: C. P. Putnam's Sons, 1910.

Córdova, Federico. *Flor Crombet (el Sucre cubano)*. Havana: Cultural, S.A., 1939.

------. *Manuel Sanguily*. Havana: Seoane, Fernández y Cía., 1942.

Cortina, José Manuel. *Calixto García*. Havana: Imprenta "El Siglo XX," 1929.

------. *Manuel Sanguily en la evolución de Cuba*. Havana: Imprenta "El Siglo XX," 1929.

Cortissoz, Royal. *The Life of Whitelaw Reid*. 2 vols. London: T. Butterworth, 1921.

Corwin, Arthur F. *Spain and the Abolition of Slavery in Cuba, 1817–1886*. Austin: University of Texas, 1969.

Corzo Pi, Daniel. *Historia de Antonio Maceo (el Aníbal cubano)*. Havana: Imprenta de Díaz y Castro, n.d.

------. *Historia de Don Tomás Estrada Palma*. Havana: Imprenta de Díaz y Castro, n.d.

Costa y Blanco, Octavio Ramón. *Juan Gualberto Gómez: una vida sin sombra*. Havana: Imprenta "El Siglo XX," 1950.

------. *Manuel Sanguily*. Havana: Editorial Unidad, 1950.

------. *Pérfil político de Calixto García*. Havana: Imprenta "El Siglo XX," 1948.

Cruz, Manuel de la. *Episodios de la revolución cubana*. Havana: Miranda, López Sena y Cía., 1911.

------. *Estudios históricos*. Havana-Madrid: Aldus, S.A., 1926.

Cuban Delegation in Atlanta. *Cuba and the United States*. Atlanta: Charles P. Byrd Printing Company, 1897.

Cuevas, Ernesto de la. *Narraciones históricas de Baracoa*. 3 vols. Baracoa: Taller Tipográfico "La Crónica," 1919–1920.

Davey, Richard. *Cuba, Past and Present*. New York: Charles Scribner's Sons, 1898.

Deulofeo y Lleonart, Manuel. *Héroes del destierro. La emigración*. Cienfuegos: Imprenta de M. Mestre, 1904.

------. *Martí, Cayo Hueso y Tampa. La emigración. Notas históricas*. Cienfuegos: Imprenta de Antonio Cuevas y Hermano, 1902.

Dierks, Jack Cameron. *A Leap to Arms: The Cuban Campaign of 1898*. Philadelphia: J. B. Lippincott, 1970.

Dihigo y Mestre, Juan Miguel. *El mayor general Pedro E. Betancourt y Dávalos en la lucha por la independencia de Cuba*. Havana: Imprenta "El Siglo XX," 1934.

------. *Pi y Margall y la revolución cubana*. Havana: Imprenta "El Siglo XX," 1928.

Domingo, Marcelino. *Libertad y autoridad*. Madrid: Javier Morata, 1927.

Draper, Andrew S. *The Rescue of Cuba*. New York: Silver, Burdett and Company, 1899.

Duarte Oropesa, José A. *Historiología cubana*. 5 vols. n.p., 1969–1970.

Duque, Francisco M. *Historia de Regla*. Havana: Imprenta y Papelería de Rambla, Bouza y Cía. 1925.

Duque, Matías. *El comandante Antonio Duque*. Havana: Imprenta Compostela y Chacón, 1928.

Edo, Enrique. *Memoria histórica de Cienfuegos y su jurisdicción*. 3rd ed. Havana: Ucar, García y Cía., 1953.

Eggert, Gerald C. *Richard Olney*. University Park: The Pennsylvania State University Press, 1974.

Ellis, Elmer. *Henry Moore Teller, Defender of the West*. Caldwell, Idaho: The Caxton Printers, 1941.

Escalante Beatón, Aníbal. *Calixto García, su campaña en el 95*. Havana: Editorial Caribe, 1946.

Estévez Romero, Luis. *Desde el Zanjón hasta Baire*. 2 vols. Havana: Editorial de Ciencias Sociales, 1975.

Estrada Palma, Tomás. *Carta-programa*. Santiago de Cuba: Imprenta de "El Cubano Libre," 1901.

————. *Petition of Tomás Estrada Palma for the Belligerency of the Cubans.* New York: n.p. 1896.

Fabié, Antonio María. *Cánovas del Castillo.* Barcelona: Gustavo Gili, 1928.

Falco, Francesco Federico. *El jefe de los mambises.* 3rd ed. Havana: Imprenta "El Fígaro," 1898.

————. *.Veinte años después del grito de Bayre.* Genova: R. Instituto Sordomuti, 1915.

Fermoselle, Rafael. *Política y color en Cuba.* Montevideo: Ediciones Geminis, 1974.

Fernández Almagro, Melchor. *Historia política de la España contemporánea.* 2 vols. Madrid: Ediciones Pegaso, 1956–1959.

Ferrand Latoison D'or, Angel. *Rasgos biográficos del mayor general José Miguel Gómez.* Guantánamo: Medrano y Ricardo, 1925.

Ferrara y Marino, Orestes. *Las enseñanzas de una revolución.* Havana: Imprenta de P. Fernández y Cía., 1932.

————. *The Last Spanish War. Revelations in "Diplomacy."* Trans. William C. Shea. New York: The Paisley Press, Inc., 1937.

Ferrer, Melchor. *Historia del tradicionalismo español.* 30 vols. Sevilla: Editorial Católica Española, S.A., 1941–1959.

Ferrer Gutiérrez, Virgilio. *Luperón: brida y espuela.* Havana: Imprenta de F. Verduge, 1940.

Figueras, Francisco. *Cuba Libre: independencia o anexión.* New York: Alfred W. Howe, 1898.

————. *Cuba y su evolución colonial.* Havana: Imprenta Avisador Comercial, 1907.

————. *La intervención y su política.* Havana: Imprenta Avisador Comercial, 1906.

Figueredo Díaz, Félix. *La guerra de Cuba en 1878: La protesta de Baraguá.* Havana: Editorial Organismos 1973.

Figueroa y Torres, Alvaro (Conde de Romanones). *Obras completas del Conde de Romanones.* 3 vols. Madrid: Editorial Plus Ultra, n.d.

Fitzgibbon, Russel H. *Cuba and the United States, 1900–1935.* Menasha, Wisconsin: George Banta Publishing Company, 1935.

Foner, Philip S. *Antonio Maceo.* New York: Monthly Review Press, 1977.

————. *The Spanish-Cuban-American War and the Birth of American Imperialism, 1895–1902.* 2 vols. New York: Monthly Review Press, 1972.

Franco, José Luciano. *Antonio Maceo: apuntes para una historia de su vida.* 3 vols. Havana: Instituto Cubano del Libro, 1973.

Friedlander, H. E. *Historia económica de Cuba.* Havana: Jesús Montero, 1944.

Gallego, Tesifonte. *La insurrección cubana.* Madrid: Imprenta Central de los Ferrocarriles, 1897.

García Escudero, José María. *De Cánovas a la República.* 2nd ed. Madrid: Ediciones Rialp, S.A., 1953.

García Garofalo y Mesa, M. *Como acabó la dominación de España en Villaclara.* Villaclara: n.p., 1944.

————. *Marta Abreu Arencibia y el Dr. Luis Estévez y Romero.* Havana: Imprenta y Librería "La Moderna Poesía," 1925.

García Valdés, Pedro. *La idea de la anexión de Cuba a los Estados Unidos.* Pinar del Río: Imprenta "La Nacional," 1947.

García y Castañeda, José A. *La municipalidad holguinera. Comentario histórico, 1898–1953.* Holguín: Imprenta Hermanos Legra, 1955.

Garrigo, Roque E. *América. José Martí.* Havana: Imprenta y Papelería de Rambla y Bouza, 1911.

Gatewood, Willard B. Jr., *"Smoked Yankees" and the Struggle for Empire: Letters from Negro Soldiers, 1898–1902.* Urbana: University of Illinois Press, 1971.

Giberga, Eliseo. *Obras de Eliseo Giberga.* 4 vols. Havana: Imprenta y Papelería de Rambla, Bouza y Cía., 1930–1931.

Gómez, Fernando. *La insurrección por dentro. Apuntes para la historia.* Havana: M. Ruiz y Cía., 1897.

Gómez, Herminia. *Al paso de la vida.* Havana: Imprenta Seone y Fernández, 1916.

Gómez, Juan Gualberto. *Juan Gualberto Gómez: su labor patriótica y sociológica.* Havana: Imprenta y Papelería de Rambla, Bouza y Cía., 1934.

Gómez Núnez, Severo. *La guerra hispano-americana.* 5 vols. Madrid: Imprenta del Cuerpo de Artillería, 1899–1902.

González Valdés, José. *Episodios de la guerra de independencia.* Havana: Imprenta "El Siglo XX," 1919.

Graham, George Edward. *Schley and Santiago.* Chicago: W. B. Conkey Company, 1902.

Green, Nathan C. *Story of Spain and Cuba.* Baltimore: International News and Book Company, 1898.

Griñán Peralta, Leonardo. *Antonio Maceo, análisis caracterológico.* Havana: Editorial Trópico, 1936.

———. *El carácter de Máximo Gómez.* Havana: Jesús Montero, 1946.

Guerra y Miranda, Wáshington. *Panchito Gómez, su vida y su obra.* Havana: Imprenta "La Propagandista," 1931.

Guerra y Sánchez, Ramiro. *En el camino de la independencia.* Havana: Cultural, S.A., 1930.

———. *La expansión territorial de los Estados Unidos.* 2nd ed. Havana: Editorial del Consejo Nacional de Universidades, 1964.

Guerra y Sanchez, Ramiro, et al. *Historia de la nación cubana.* 10 vols. Havana: Editorial Historia de la Nación Cubana, S.A., 1951.

Guerrero, Rafael. *Crónica de la guerra de Cuba y de Filipinas.* 5 vols. Barcelona: Casa Editorial Maucci, 1895–1897.

Guiteras, John. *Free Cuba.* Philadelphia: Publisher's Union, 1896.

Gutiérrez, Rafael. *Oriente heroico.* Santiago de Cuba: Tipografía el "Nuevo Mundo," 1915.

Gutiérrez Fernández, Rafael. *Los heroes del 24 de febrero.* Havana: Carasa y Cía., 1932.

Hagedorn, Hermann. *Leonard Wood, A Biography.* 2 vols. New York: Harper and Brothers, 1931.

———. *That Human Being, Leonard Wood.* New York: Harcourt, Brace, and Haw, 1920.

Hall, A. D. *Cuba, Its Past, Present, and Future.* New York: Street and Smith, 1898.

Havana. Oficina del Historiador de la Ciudad de La Habana. *Cosme de la Torriente en la revolución libertadora y en la Repúblic.* Havana: Municipio de La Habana, 1951.

Healy, David F. *The United States in Cuba, 1898–1902. Generals, Politicians, and the Search for Policy.* Madison: The University of Wisconsin Press, 1963.

Hernández Corujo, Enrique. *Los fundamentos históricos y filosóficos de la constitución de 1901.* Havana: Editorial Lex, 1953.

———. *Historia constitucional de Cuba.* 2 vols. Havana: Campañía Editora de Libros y Folletos, 1960.

———. *Organización civil y política de las revoluciones cubanas de 1868 y 1895.* Havana: Imprenta y Papelería de Rambla, Bouza y Cía., 1929.

Hernández y Pérez, Eusebio. *Dos conferencias históricas.* Havana: Cultural, S.A., n.d.

———. *El Período revolucionario de 1879 a 1895.* Havana: Imprenta "El Siglo XX," 1914.

Hitchman, James H. *Leonard Wood and Cuban Independence, 1898–1902.* The Hague: Martinus Nijhoff, 1971.

Hobbs, William Herbert. *Leonard Wood.* New York: G. P. Putnam's Sons, 1920.

Holme, John G. *The Life of Leonard Wood.* New York: Doubleday, Pagé & Company, 1920.

Horrego Estuch, Leopoldo. *Juan Gualberto Gómez, un gran inconforme.* 2nd ed. Havana: Editorial La Milagrosa, 1954.

————. *Máximo Gómez, libertador y ciudadano.* Havana: Imprenta de P. Fernández y Cía., 1948.

Hubbard, Elbert. *A Message to García.* East Aurora, New York: The Roycroft Shop, 1899.

Ibarra, Jorge. *Ideología mambisa.* Havana: Instituto Cubano del Libro, 1967.

Inclán Lavastida, Fernando. *Historia de Marianao.* Marianao: Editorial "El sol," 1943.

Infiesta, Ramón. *El autonomismo cubano: su razón y manera.* Havana: Jesús Montero, 1939.

————. *Historia constitucional de Cuba.* Havana: Editorial Selecta, 1942.

————. *Máximo Gómez.* Havana: Imprenta "El Siglo XX," 1937.

Iraizoz y de Villar, Antonio. *Lecturas cubanas.* Havana: Editorial "Hermes," 1939.

Isern, Damián. *Del desastre nacional y sus causas.* Madrid: Imprenta de la Viuda de M. Minuesa de los Ríos, 1899.

Iznaga, R. *Tres años de República.* Havana: Imprenta y Papelería de Rambla y Bouza, 1905.

James, Henry. *Richard Olney and His Public Service.* Boston: Houghton Mifflin, 1923.

Jenks, Leland Hamilton. *Our Cuban Colony.* New York: Vanguard Press, 1928.

Jerez Villarreal, Juan. *Oriente (biografía de una provincia).* Havana: Imprenta "El Siglo XX," 1960.

Jessup, Philip C. *Elihu Root.* 2 vols. New York: Dodd, Mead and Company, Inc., 1938.

Jiménez Pastrana, Juan. *Los chinos en las luchas por la liberación cubana (1847–1930).* Havana: Instituto Cubano del Libro, 1963.

Johnson, Walter. *William Allen White's America.* New York: Henry Holt and Company, 1947.

Juárez y Cano, Jorge. *Apuntes de Camagüey.* Camagüey: Imprenta "El Popular," 1929.

Justiz y del Valle, Tomás. *Historia documentada de la isla de Cuba.* Havana: n.p., 1945.

King, W. Nephew. *The Story of the Spanish-American War and the Revolt of the Philippines.* New York: Peter Fenelon Collier and Sons, 1898.

Kiple, Kenneth F. *Blacks in Colonial Cuba, 1774–1899.* Gainesville: The University Presses of Florida, 1976.

Kirchner, Adelaide Rosalind. *A Flag for Cuba.* New York: The Mershon Company, 1897.

Kunz, Hermann. *La guerra hispano-americana.* Trans. Manuel Martínez. Barcelona: Imprenta Vda. D. Casanovas, 1909.

Labra, Rafael M. de., et al. *El problema colonial contemporáneo.* 2 vols. Madrid: Victoriano Suárez, n.d.

LaFeber, Walter. *The New Empire.* Ithaca: Cornell University Press, 1963.

Lagomasino Alvarez, Luis. *La guerra de Cuba.* Vera Cruz: Imprenta "Las Selvas," 1897.

————. *Patricios y heroínas.* 3 vols. Havana: Tipografía del "Boletín Nacional de Historia y Geografía," 1912–1917.

Lamar Schweyer, Alberto. *La crisis del patriotismo.* Havana: Editorial Martí, 1929.

Lambert, Oscar Doane. *Stephen Benton Elkins.* Pittsburgh: University of Pittsburgh Press, 1955.

Langley, Lester D. *The Cuban Policy of the United States.* New York: John Wiley and Sons, Inc., 1968.

Lateulade, Emilio. *Apuntes de la delegación de hacienda del distrito de Guantánamo.* Guantánamo: Imprenta "El Arte," 1930.

Lee, Fitzhugh. *Cuba's Struggle Against Spain.* New York: The American Historical Press, 1899.

Leech, Margaret. *In the Days of McKinley.* New York: Harper & Brothers, 1959.

Leiseca, Juan M. *Historia de Cuba.* Havana: Librería "Cervantes," 1925.

LeRiverend Brusone, Julio E. *La Habana (biografía de una provincia).* Havana: Imprenta "El Siglo XX," 1960.

————. *Historia económica de Cuba.* 2nd ed. Havana: Editora del Consejo Nacional de Universidades, 1965.

Linares, Manuel. *Un libro más: fragmentos de 1881 a 1906.* Havana: Imprenta Mercantil, 1906.

Linderman, Gerald F. *The Mirror of War.* Ann Arbor: University of Michigan Press, 1974.

Lizaso, Félix. *Martí, Martyr of Cuban Independence.* Trans. Esther Elise Shuler. Albuquerque, N.M.: University of New Mexico Press, 1953.

Llano, Sergio del. *Los partidos de Cuba y la normalidad política.* Havana: Imprenta "El Aerolito," 1893.

Logan, John A., Jr. *No Transfer.* New Haven: Yale University Press, 1961.

López Leiva, Francisco. *El bandolerismo en Cuba (contribución al estudio de la plaga social)* Havana: Imprenta "El Siglo XX," 1930.

Lubián, Silvia. *El Club Revolucionario Juan Bruno Zayas.* Santa Clara: Universidad Central de Las Villas, 1961.

La lucha anti-imperialista en Cuba. 2 vols. Havana: Editora Popular de Cuba y del Caribe, 1960.

Lufriu, René. *El impulso inicial.* 2 vols. Havana: Imprenta "El Siglo XX," 1930.

Luz León, José de la. *La diplomacia de la manigua: Betances.* Havana: Editorial Lex, 1947.

McElroy, Robert. *Grover Cleveland.* 2 vols. New York: Harper and Brothers, 1923.

Machado y Ortega, Luis. *La Enmienda Platt.* Havana: Imprenta "El Siglo XX," 1922.

Maestri, Raúl. *El latifundismo en la economía cubana.* Havana: Editorial "Hermes," n.d.

Mañach, Jorge. *Martí, Apostle of Freedom.* Trans. Coley Taylor. New York: The Devin-Adair Company, 1950.

Márquez Sterling, Carlos. *Don Tomás (biografía de una época).* Havana: Editorial Lex, 1953.

Márquez Sterling, Manuel. *La diplomacia en nuestra historia.* Havana: Imprenta Avisador Comercial, 1909.

―――. *Proceso histórico de la Enmienda Platt (1897–1934).* Havana: Imprenta "El Siglo XX," 1941.

Martínez Arango, Felipe. *Cronología crítica de la guerra hispano-cubano-americana.* Santiago de Cuba: Universidad de Oriente, 1960.

―――. *Próceres de Santiago de Cuba.* Havana: Imprenta de la Universidad de La Habana, 1946.

Martínez de Campos, Carlos. *España bélica.* Madrid: Aguilar, 1968.

Martínez Fraga, Pedro. *El general Menocal (apuntes para su biografía).* Havana: Editorial "Tiempo," 1941.

Martínez Ortiz, Rafael. *Cuba: los primeros años de independencia.* 2 vols. 3rd ed. Paris: Editorial "Le Livre Libre," 1929.

―――. *General Leonard Wood's Government in Cuba.* Paris: Imprimerie Dubois et Bauer, 1920.

Matthews, Franlkin. *The New-Born Cuba.* New York: Harper and Brothers, 1899.

Maura y Gamazo, Gabriel. *Historia crítica del reinado de Don Alfonso XIII durante su menoridad bajo la regencia de su madre Doña María Cristina de Austria.* 2 vols. Barcelona: Montaner y Simón, 1919–1925.

May, Ernest R. *Imperial Democracy.* New York: Harcourt, Brace & World, Inc., 1961.

Meléndez Meléndez, Leonor. *Cánovas y la política exterior española.* Madrid: Instituto de Estudios Políticos, 1944.

Méndez Capote, Domingo. *Trabajos.* 3 vols. Havana: Molina y Cía., 1929–1930.

Méndez Capote, Renée. *Domingo Méndez Capote. El hombre civil del 95.* Havana: Ucar, García, S.A., 1957.

Menocal y Cueto, Raimundo. *Origen y desarrollo del pensamiento cubano.* 2 vols. Havana: Editorial Lex, 1947.

Merchán, Rafael María. *Cuba, justificación de sus guerras de independencia.* Havana: Imprenta Nacional de Cuba, 1961.

Mesa, Roberto. *El colonialismo en la crisis del XIX español*. Madrid: Editorial Ciencia Nueva, 1967.

Miranda, Fernando E. *La emigración al Caney*. Santiago de Cuba: Imprenta de Juan E. Ravelo, 1899.

Miranda, Rodolfo. *Calixto García Iñiguez, estratega*. Havana: Academia de la Historia de Cuba, 1951.

Montesinos y Salas, Enrique. *Los yankees in Manzanillo*. Manzanillo: Imprenta Guttenberg, 1898.

Montoro, Rafael. *El ideal autonomista*. Havana: Editorial Cuba, 1936.

———. *Obras*. 3 vols. Havana: Cultural, S.A., 1930.

Morales Patiño, Oswaldo. *El capitan Chino. Teniente coronel Quirino Zamora: historia de un mambí en la provincia de La Habana*. Havana: Municipio de La Habana, 1953.

Morales y Coello, Julio. *La importancia del poder naval—positivo y negativo—en el desarrollo y en la independencia de Cuba*. Havana: Imprenta "El Siglo XX," 1950.

———. *Los presidentes de la república de Cuba y la organización del estado cubano*. Havana: n.p., 1955.

Morales, y Morales, Vidal. *Nociones de historia de Cuba*. Havana: Cultural, S.A., 1938.

Morgan, H. Wayne. *America's War to Empire: The War with Spain and Overseas Expansion*. New York: John Wiley and Sons, Inc., 1965.

———. *William McKinley and His America*. Syracuse: Syracuse University Press, 1963.

Morote, Luis. *Sagasta. Melilla. Cuba*. Paris: Sociedad de Ediciones Literarias y Artísticas, 1908.

Morris, Charles. *The War with Spain*. Philadelphia: J. B. Lippincott Company, 1899.

Murviedro, J. J. de. *Bosquejo de un plan de campaña en la isla de Cuba*. Madrid: Tipografía de los Hijos de M.G. Hernández, 1896.

Musick, John Roy. *Lights and Shadows of Our War with Spain*. New York: J. S. Ogilvie Publishing Company, 1898.

Nevins, Allen. *Hamilton Fish*. 2 vols. New York: Frederick Ungar Publishing Company, 1957.

Olcott, Charles, S. *William McKinley*. 2 vols. Boston: Houghton Mifflin, 1916.

Orizondo Siverio. Sergio. *Episodios de ayer y exaltación de la personalidad del general Máximo Gómez*. Havana: n.p., 1960.

Ortega Rubio, Juan. *Historia de la regencia de María Cristina Habsbourg Lorena*. 5 vols. Madrid: Imprenta, Litografía y Casa Editorial de Felipe González Rojas, 1905–1906.

Pabon y Suárez de Urbina, Jesús. *El 98, acontecimiento internacional*. Madrid: Imprenta del Ministerio de Asuntos Exteriors, 1952.

Padrón Valdes, Abelardo. *El generál Jose. Apuntes biográficos*. Havana: Instituto Cubano del Libro, 1973.

Pardo Llada, José. *Bartolomé Masó: el presidente que vetaron los yanquis*. Havana: n.p., 1960.

Payne, Stanley G. *Politics and the Military in Modern Spain*. Stanford: Stanford University Press, 1967.

Pepper, Charles M. *To-morrow in Cuba*. New York Harper & Brothers, 1899.

Peraza y Sarausa, Fermín. *Un hombre del 95: el general Peraza*. Havana: Imprenta "El Siglo XX," 1950.

Perdomo, José, E. *Máximo Gómez*. Havana: Imprenta "El Siglo XX," 1952.

Pérez Cabrera, José Manuel. *Calixto García*. Havana: Imprenta "El Siglo XX," 1942.

———. *El cincuentenario del Partido Revolucionario Cubano*. Havana: Imprenta "El Siglo XX," 1942.

———. *Una cubana ejemplar: Marta Abreu de Estévez*. Havana: Imprenta "El Siglo XX," 1945.

Pérez Landa, Rufino. *Bartolomé Masó y Márquez. Estudio biográfico documentado.* Havana: Imprenta "El Siglo XX," 1947.

Pérez Rioja, Antonio. *La invasión norteamericana en Cuba.* Havana: Imprenta "El Fígaro," 1898.

———. *Los yankees en Cuba. Pro-patria.* Havana: Tip. "Los Niños Huérfanos," 1897.

Pi y Margall, Francisco, and Pi y Arsuaga, Francisco. *Historia de España en el siglo XIX.* 7 vols. Barcelona: Miguel Seguí, 1902.

Piedra-Bueno, Andrés de. *Mayía.* Havana: n.p., 1957.

Piedra Martel, Manuel. *Juan Ruis Rivera y la independencia de Cuba.* Havana: Imprenta "El Siglo XX," 1945.

Piloto, Jorge H. *Mayor General James Harrison Wilson, el buen amigo de los cubanos.* Matanzas: Imprenta "Estrada," 1934.

Piñeyro, Enrique. *Como acabó la dominación de España en América.* Paris: Garnier Hermanos, 1908.

Pirala, Antonio. *España y la regencia: Anales de diez y seis años (1885–1902).* 3 vols., Madrid: Librería de Victoriano Suárez, 1904—1907.

Ponte Domínguez, Francisco José, *Historia de la guerra de diez años.* Havana: Imprenta "El Siglo XX," 1948.

Portell Vilá, Herminio. *Historia de Cuba en sus relaciones con los Estados Unidos y España.* 4 vols. Havana: Jesús Montero, 1938–1941.

———. *Historia de la guerra de Cuba y los Estados Unidos contra España.* Havana: Oficina del Historiador de la Ciudad de La Habana, 1949.

———. *Los periodistas norteamericanos y la independencia de Cuba.* Havana: Sociedad Colombista Panamericana, 1952.

Portillo, Lorenzo G. del. *La guerra de Cuba (el primer año). Apuntes.* Key West: Imprenta "La Propaganda," 1896.

Portuondo, José. *La historia y las generaciones.* Santiago de Cuba: Tipografía San Román, 1958.

Portuondo del Prado, Fernando. *Estudios de historia de Cuba.* Havana: Instituto Cubano del Libro, 1973.

———. *Historia de Cuba.* 6th ed. Havana: Ediciones Minerva, 1957.

Post, Charles Johnson. *The Little War of Private Post.* New York: The New American Library, 1960.

Pozo Arjana, Alejandro del. *Páginas de sangre o el libro del cubano. Relación de los caudillos cubanos muertos en la actual campaña (1895 a 1898).* Havana: Imprenta "La Juventud," 1898.

Los preparativos de la revolución y el general Calleja, 1893–1895. Havana: Imprenta del Avisador Comercial, 1896.

Propaganda cubana. Por la independencia. New York: Imprenta de Alfred W. Howes, n.d.

Quesada, Gonzalo de. *Cuba.* Washington, D.C.: Government Printing Office, 1905.

Quesada, Gonzalo de, and Northrop, Henry Davenport. *Cuba's Great Struggle for Freedom.* New York: n.p., 1898.

Raggi Ageo, Carlos M. *Condiciones económicas y sociales de la república de Cuba.* Havana: Editorial Lex, 1944.

Rea, George Bronson. *Facts and Fakes About Cuba.* New York: George Munro's Sons, 1897.

Reparaz, Gonzalo de. *La guerra de Cuba.* Madrid: La España Editorial, 1896.

Reverter Delmas, Emilio. *Cuba española. Reseña histórica de la insurrección cubana en 1895.* 6 vols. Barcelona: Centro Editorial de Alberto Martín, 1897–1899.

Reyna Cossío, René E. *Estudios histórico-militares sobre la guerra de independencia de Cuba.* Havana: Impresora Modelo, S.A., 1954.

————. *El lazo de la invasión*. Havana: Oficina del Historiador de la Ciudad de La Habana, 1956.

Rhodes, James Ford. *The McKinley and Roosevelt Administrations, 1897–1909*. Port Washington, New York: Kennikat Press, 1965.

Richardson, Leon Burr. *William E. Chandler, Republican*. New York: Dodd, Mead & Company, 1940.

Rivero Muñiz, José. *El movimiento obrero durante la intervención*. Havana: Ucar, García, S.A., 1961.

————. *Vereda Nueva*. Havana: Instituto de Historia, 1964.

Roa, Ramón. *Con la pluma y el machete*. 3 vols. Havana: Ministerio de Educación, 1950.

Robinson, Albert Gardner. *Cuba and the Intervention*. London: Longsmans, Green, and Company, 1905.

Robinson, William A. *Thomas B. Reed, Parliamentarian*. New York: Dodd, Mead & Company, 1930.

Roches, V. de. *Cuba Under Spanish Rule*. New York: Great American Engraving and Printing Company, n.d.

Rodríguez, José Ignacio. *Estudio histórico sobre el origen, desenvolvimiento y manifestaciones prácticas de la idea de la anexión de la isla de Cuba a los Estados Unidos de América*. Havana: Imprenta La Propaganda Literaria, 1900.

Rodríguez Abascal, Pedro. *Un español que llegó a coronel por sus hazañas en Cuba*. 2nd ed. Havana: Impresa ASPA, 1953.

————. *El mayor general Pedro E. Betancourt (estratega y táctico militar del Ejército Libertador)*. Havana: Asociación Nacional de Veteranos de la Independencia de Cuba, 1956.

Rodríguez Altunaga, Rafael. *El general Emilio Núñez*. Havana: Sociedad Colombista Panamericana, 1958.

————. *Historia de Trinidad*. Havana: Jesús Montero, 1945.

————. *Las Villas (biografía de una provincia)*. Havana: Imprenta "El Siglo XX," 1955.

Rodríguez García, José A. *De la revolución y de las cubanas en la época revolucionaria*. Havana: Imprenta "El Siglo XX," 1930.

————. *Manuel Sanguily*. Havana: "Cuba Intelectual," 1926.

Rodríguez Morejón, Gerardo. *Menocal*. Havana: Cárdenas y Compañía, 1941.

Roig de Leuchsenring, Emilio. *Análisis y consecuencias de la intervención norteamericana en los asuntos interiores de Cuba*. Havana: Imprenta "El Siglo XX," 1923.

————. *Cuba no debe su independencia a los Estados Unidos*. 3rd ed. Havana: Edición la Tertulia, 1960.

————. *Cuba y los Estados Unidos, 1805–1898*. Havana: La Sociedad Cubana de Estudios Históricos e Internacionales, 1949.

————. *Los Estados Unidos contra Cuba Libre*. Havana: Oficina del Historiador de la Ciudad de La Habana, 1960.

————. *Los Estados Unidos contra Cuba republicana*. 2 vols. Havana: Consejo Nacional de Cultura, n.d.

————. *Los grandes movimientos políticos cubanos en la colonia*. 2 vols. Havana: Oficina del Historiador de la Ciudad de La Habana, 1943.

————. *La guerra hispano-cubanoamericana fué ganada por el lugarteniente general del Ejército Libertador Calixto García Iñiguez*. Havana: Oficina del Historiador de la Ciudad de La Habana, 1955.

————. *La guerra libertadora cubana de los treinta años, 1868–1898: razón de su victoria*. Havana: Oficina del Historiador de la Ciudad de La Habana, 1952.

————. *Historia de la Enmienda Platt*. 2 vols. 2nd ed. Havana: Oficina del Historiador de la Ciudad de La Habana, 1961.

——. *Juan Gualberto Gómez, paladín de la independencia y la libertad de Cuba*. Havana: Oficina del Historiador de la Ciudad de La Habana, 1954.

——. *La Habana, apuntes históricos*. 2nd ed. 3 vols. Havana: Oficina del Historiador de la Ciudad de La Habana, 1963–1964.

——. *La lucha cubana por la República, contra la anexión y la Enmienda Platt, 1899–1902*. Havana: Oficina del Historiador de la Ciudad de La Habana, 1952.

——. *Martí anti-imperialista*. Havana: Instituo Cubano del Libro, 1967.

——. *Máximo Gómez: el libertador de Cuba y el primer ciudadano de la República*. Havana: Oficina del Historiador de la Ciudad de La Habana, 1959.

——. *1895 y 1898. Dos guerras cubanas. Ensayo de revaloración*. Havana: Cultural, S.A., 1945.

——. *Por su propio esfuerzo conquistó el pueblo cubano su independencia*. Havana: Oficina del Historiador de la Ciudad de La Habana, 1957.

——. *El presidente McKinley y el gobernador Wood máximos enemigos de Cuba Libre*. Havana: Oficina del Historiador de la Ciudad de La Habana, 1960.

——. *Revolución y república en Maceo*. Havana: Imprenta de P. Fernández y Cía., 1945.

——. *Tradición antimperialista de nuestra historia*. Havana: Oficina del Historiador de la Ciudad de La Habana, 1962.

——. *Weyler en Cuba*. Havana: Editorial Páginas, 1947.

Romano, Julio. *Weyler, el hombre de hierro*. Madrid: Espasa-Calpe, S.A., 1934.

Root, Elihu, *The Military and Colonial Policy of the United States*. Ed. Robert Bacon and James Brown Scott. Cambridge, Mass.: Harvard University Press, 1916.

Rousset, Ricardo V. *Historial de Cuba*. 2 vols. Havana: Librería "Cervantes," 1918.

Saíz de la Mora, Jesús. *Consideraciones alrededor del generalísimo Máximo Gómez*. Havana: Imprenta y Papelería "El Dante," 1927.

Salazar Carrera, A. *Cuba en su última etapa revolucionaria*. Havana: Cultural, S.A., 1936.

Sanguily, Manuel. *Defensa de Cuba*. Ed. Emilio Roig de Leuchsenring. Havana: Oficina del Historiador de la Ciudad de La Habana, 1948.

——. *Discursos y conferencias*. Havana: Ministerio de Educacion, 1949.

——. *Obras de Manuel Sanguily*. 6 vols. Havana: A. Dorrbecker, 1929.

——. *Victoria de Las Tunas*. New York: Alfred W. Howes, 1897.

Santovenia, Emeterio Santiago. *Armonías y conflictos en torno a Cuba*. México: Fondo de Cultura Económica, 1956.

——. *Bartolomé Masó*. Havana: Imprenta "El Siglo XX," 1930.

——. *Gómez el Máximo*. Havana: Imprenta "El Siglo XX," 1936.

——. *Pinar del Río*. México: Fondo de Cultura Económica, 1946.

——. *Theodore Roosevelt y la soberanía de Cuba*. Havana: Imprenta "El Siglo XX," 1958.

Schriftgiesser, Karl. *The Gentleman from Massachusetts: Henry Cabot Lodge*. Boston: Little, Brown and Company, 1944.

Souza y Rodríguez, Benigno. *Biografía de un regimiento mambí: el regimiento 'Calixto García.' Discursos*. Havana: Imprenta "El Siglo XX," 1939.

——. *Esayo histórico sobre la invasión*. Havana: Imprenta del Ejército, 1948.

——. *Máximo Gómez, el generalísimo*. Havana: Editorial Trópico, 1936.

Thayer, William Roscoe. *John Hay*. 2 vols. Boston: Houghton Mifflin, 1908.

Thomas, Hugh. *Cuba, The Pursuit of Freedom*. New York: Haper & Row, 1971.

Tithertington, Richard H. *A History of the Spanish-American War of 1898*. New York: D. Appleton and Company, 1900.

Torriente y Peraza, Cosme de la. *Calixto García cooperó con las fuerzas armadas de los EE. UU. en 1898, cumpliendo órdenes del gobierno cubano*. Havana: Imprenta "El Siglo XX," 1952.

————. *La Enmienda Platt y el Tratado Permanente.* Havana: Imprenta y Papelería de Rambla, Bouza y Cía., 1930.

————. *Fin de la dominación de España en Cuba (12 de agosto de 1898).* Havana: Imprenta "El Siglo XX," 1948.

Tosquella, Max. *The Truth About the Message to García.* Trans. I. F. Berndes and Charles Pujol. Havana: José A. López, 1955.

Trelles y Govín, Carlos M. *Bibliografía cubana del siglo XIX.* 8 vols. Matanzas: Imprenta de Quirós y Estrada, 1915.

————. *Bibliografía de la segunda guerra de independencia cubana y de la hispano-yankee.* Havana: n.p., 1902.

————. *Matanzas en la independencia de Cuba.* Havana: Imprenta Avisador Comercial, 1928.

Trujillo, Enrique. *Apuntes históricos. Propaganda y movimientos revolucionarios cubanos en los Estados Unidos desde enero de 1880 hasta febrero de 1895.* New York: Tipografía de "El Porvenir," 1896.

Ubieta, Enrique. *Efemérides de la revolución cubana.* 2 vols. Havana: "La Moderna Poesía," 1911.

Varona, Enrique José. *De la colonia a la república.* Havana: Sociedad Editorial Cuba Contemporánea, 1919.

Varona Guerrero, Miguel Angel. *La guerra de independencia de Cuba, 1895–1898.* 3 vols. Havana: Editorial Lex, 1946.

————. *Máximo Gómez Báez. Generalísimo del Ejército Libertador visto por uno de sus ayudantes.* Havana: Escuela Tipográfica M. Inclán, 1951.

Veitia Ferrer, Agustín. *Marta G. Abreu, la cubana excelsa.* Havana: Editorial Lex, 1947.

Velasco, Carlos de. *Estrada Palma, contribucion histórica.* Havana: Imprenta y Papelería "La Universal," 1911.

Verrill, A. Hyatt. *Cuba Past and Present.* New York: Dodd, Mead & Company, 1914.

Villoch, Federico. *Viejas postales descoloridas. La guerra de independencia.* Havana: Imprenta de P. Fernández y Cía., 1946.

Vitier, Medardo. *Martí, estudio integral.* Havana: Publicaciones de la Comisión Nacional Organizador de los Actos y Ediciones del Centenario y del Monumento de Martí, 1954.

Vladimirov, L. *La diplomacia de los Estados Unidos durante la guerra hispano-americana.* Moscow: Ediciones en Lenguas Extranjeras, 1958.

Walters, Everett. *Joseph Benson Foraker.* Columbus, Ohio: Ohio State Archaeological and Historical Society, 1948.

Watterson, Henry. *History of the Spanish-American War.* Boston: Home Library Association, 1898.

Weyler y López de Pugna, Valeriano. *En el archivo de mi abuelo. Biografía del Capitán General Weyler.* Madrid: Industrias Gráficas, 1946.

White, Trumbull. *United States in War with Spain and the History of Cuba.* Chicago: International Publishing Co., 1898.

Wilkerson, Marcus M. *Public Opinion and the Spanish-American War.* Baton Rouge: Louisiana State University Press, 1932.

Wilson, James H. *Our Relations With Cuba.* Wilmington, Del.: The John M. Rogers Press, 1902.

Wisan, Joseph E. *The Cuban Crisis as Reflected in the New York Press (1895–1898).* New York: Columbia University Press, 1934.

Wright, Irene A. *Cuba.* New York: The MacMillan Company, 1910.

Wright, Philip G. *The Cuban Situation and Our Treaty Relations.* Washington, D.C.: The Brookings Institution, 1931.

Yero Buduén, Eduardo. *Voz de Caín*. New York: n.p., 1896.

Zámora, Juan Clemente. *Derecho constitucional: Cuba*. Havana: Imprenta "El Siglo XX," 1925.

Zarragoitia Ledesma, L. *Biografía de Antonio Maceo*. Havana: Editorial Lex, 1945.

Articles

Abad, L. V. de. "The Cuban Problem." *Gunton's Magazine* XXI (Dec., 1901): 515–25.

Aguirre, Sergio. "La desaparición del Ejército Libertador." *Cuba Socialista* III (Dec., 1963):51–68.

Akers, C.E. "The Cuban Revolt." *Harper's Weekly* XLI (Jan.30, 1897):114–15.

Alavez, Elena. "Máximo Gómez, maestro y protagonista de dos guerras." *Bohemia* LVIII (June 11, 1976):88–93.

Aldama del Monte, León. "The Cuban Insurrection." *Pall Mall Magazine* XII (May, 1897):115–27.

Alvarez, Rolando. "El Partido Revolucionario Cubano y los militares mambises del '68." *Granma* (May 31, 1968):p. 2.

Alvord, Thomas Gold, Jr. "Is the Cuban Capable of Self-Government?" *Forum* XXIV(Sept., 1898):119–28.

Appel, John C. "The Unionization of Florida Cigarmakers and the Coming of the War with Spain." *The Hispanic American Historical Review* XXXVI (Feb., 1956):38–49.

Arduro, Ernesto. "Manuel Sanguily, el estadista precursor." *Revista Cubana* XXIX (Jan.–June, 1949):349–74.

Armas, Ramón de. "La revolución pospuesta: destino de la revolución martiana de 1895." *Pensamiento Crítico* 49–50 (Feb.–Mar., 1971):8–119.

Arredondo, Alberto. "La ocupación militar norteamericana." In Emilio Roig de Leuchsenring, ed., *Curso de introducción a la historia de Cuba*. La Habana: Municipio de La Habana, 1938, pp. 359–70.

Auxier, George W. "Propaganda Activities of the Cuban Junta in Precipitating the Spanish-American War, 1895–1898." *The Hispanic American Historical Review* XIX (August, 1939):286–305.

Ayón, Maria, "Martí y los trabajadores." *El Caimán Barbudo* IV (Jan., 1972):9–11.

Banga, Henry. "What Form of Government Should Cuba Libre Adopt?" *The Independent* LII (Aug. 9, 1900):1893–96.

Baker, Ray Stannard. "How the Beet-Sugar Industry is Growing." *Review of Reviews* XXIII (March, 1901):324–28.

Barquín, Ramón M. "El Ejército Libertador: génesis, organización y tácticas de lucha." In Vicente Báez, ed. *La enciclopedia de Cuba*. 8 vols. Madrid: Enciclopedia y Clásicos Cubanos, 1974. Vol. IV, pp. 654–74.

Bashkina, N. "A Page from the Cuban People's Heroic History." *International Affairs* (Moscow) (March 1964):117–24.

Besada Ramos, Benito. "Antecedentes económicos de la guerra de los diez años." *Economía y Desarrollo* XIII (Sept.–Oct., 1972):155–62.

Beveridge, Albert J. "Cuba and Congress." *North American Review* CLXXII (April, 1901):535–50.

Bookmiller, Edwin V. "The Ninth U. S. Infantry in the Santiago Campaign." In Society of Santiago de Cuba, *The Santiago Campaign: Reminiscences*. Richmond, Va.: Williams Printing Company, 1927, 58–65.

Boti, Regino E. "El 24 de febrero de 1895." *Anales de la Academia de la Historia* IV (Jan.–June, 1922):69–143.

Brownell, Atherton. "The Commercial Annexation of Cuba." *Appleton's Magazine* VIII (Oct., 1906):406–11.

Brunner, W. F., "Morbidity and Mortality in the Spanish Army in Cuba During the Calendar Year 1897." *Public Health Reports* XIII (April 29, 1898):409–12.

Bueno, Salvador. "Diego Vicente Tejera." *Bohemia* LV (Aug. 2, 1963):19–21, 82.

Caballero, Iván. "Aspectos fundamentales sobre análisis de clases en la guerra de 1868." *Santiago* XIII (Dec. 1973–Mar. 1974):229–40.

Cañizares y Quirós, Rafael M. "Diario de operaciones del teniente coronel Rafael M. Cañizares y Quirós." *Boletín del Archivo Nacional* XLVIII (Jan.–Dec., 1949):104–51.

Capó-Rodríguez, Pedro. "The Platt Amendment." *American Journal of International Law,* XVII (Oct., 1923):761–65.

Carbonell, José Manuel. "La lucha por la independencia en Cuba (1810–1898)." In Ricardo Levene, ed. *Historia de América.* 10 vols. Buenos Aires: W. M. Jackson, Inc., 1940. Vol. VII, pp. 267–380.

Carrión, Miguel de. "El desenvolvimiento social de Cuba en los últimos veinte años." *Cuba Contemporánea* XXVII (Sept., 1921):5–27.

Castellanos, Jorge. "El pensamiento social de Máximo Gómez." *América* (Havana), (Feb.–Mar., 1946), 22–28.

Castellanos García, Gerardo, "Raíces históricos del Partido Revolucionario Cubano." *Cuadernos de Historia Habanera* XXII (1942):7–44.

Céspedes, José María. "Empleo-manía." *Cuba y América* III (Apr. 20, 1899):6–8.

Chamberlin, Joseph Edgar. "Spanish Bravery at Caney." *Review of Reviews* XVIII (Sept., 1898):325.

Corbitt, Duvon C. "Immigration in Cuba," *Hispanic American Historical Review.* XXII (May, 1942):280–308.

"Cuba for Cubans," *Review of Reviews* XIX (Feb., 1899):134–35.

A Cuban. "A Plea for the Annexation of Cuba." *Forum* XXX (Oct., 1900):202–14.

"The Cuban Commission at Washington." *The Independent* LIII (May 2, 1901):981–82.

"The Cuban Constitutional Convention." *The World's Work* I (Dec., 1900):131.

"Cuba's Future Relations to the United States." *Literary Digest* XXII (Feb. 9, 1901):152–53.

Cummins, Lejuene. "The Formulation of the 'Platt' Amendment." *The Americas* XXIII (Apr., 1967):370–89.

Currier, Charles Warren. "Why Cuba Should Be Independent." *Forum* XXX (Oct., 1900):139–46.

Daniel, J. W. "War Legislation of the Senate." *The American-Spanish War. A History by the War Leaders.* Norwich Conn.: Charles C. Haskell & Son, 1899, pp. 299–324.

Dawley, Thomas Robinson, Jr., "With the Cuban Insurgents: In Search of Gomez." *Harper's Weekly* XLI (May 15, 1897):491.

Delahoza, Enrique. "Los comienzos del 95." In Emilio Roig de Leuchsenring, ed. *Curso de introducción a la historia de Cuba.* Havana: Municipio de La Habana, 1938, pp. 333–41.

Despradel, Lorenzo. "Máximo Gómez y la campaña del 97." In Orestes Ferrara, *Mis relaciones con Máximo Gómez.* 2nd ed. Havana: Molina y Companía, 1942, pp. 281–314.

Dillon, E.J. "The Ruin of Spain." *The Contemporary Review* LXXIII (June, 1898):876–907.

"The Effect of the Cuban Commission's Visit." *Literary Digest* XII (May 4, 1901):531–32.

Estrada Palma, Tomás. "The Future of Cuba." *The Independent* LIV (Apr. 3, 1902):789–91.

———. "The Work of the Cuban Delegation." *The American Spanish War. A History by the War Leaders.* Norwich, Conn.: Charles C. Haskell & Son, 1899, pp. 403–21.

Estrade, Paul. "Cuba en 1895: las tres vías de la burguesía insular." *Casa de las Américas* XIII (Sept.–Oct., 1972):55–65.

———. "L'emigration cubaine de Paris (1895–1898)." *Caravelle* XVI (1971):33–53.

Falco, Francesco Federico. "La representación de Cuba Libre en Italia durante la última guerra de independencia." *Cuba Contemporánea* XIX (Feb., 1919):120–48.

Farquhar, Q. F. "Intimate Recollections of Grover Cleveland." *Harper's Weekly* LII (Aug. 1, 1908):14–15.

Figueras, Francisco. "Cuba Libre, Independence or Annexation." *The Journal of American History* II (July–Aug.–Sept., 1908):411–40.

Foraker, Joseph B. "Our War with Spain: Its Justice and Necessity." *The Forum* XXV (June, 1898):385–95.

Franco, José Luciano. "Introducción al 68." *Casa de las Américas* IX (Sept.–Oct., 1968):4–30.

———. "Panamá: refugio de la rebeldía cubana en el siglo XIX." *Casa de las Américas* XV (July–Aug., 1974):16–26.

Franco, José Luciano, and Cabrera Alvarez, Guillermo. "¿Que Pasó en La Habana el 24 de febrero?" *Juventud Rebelde*, Feb. 24, 1969, p. 2.

Gage, Lyman J. "Work of the Treasury Department." *The American-Spanish War. A History by the War Leaders*. Norwich, Conn.: Charles C. Haskell & Son, 1899, pp. 367–91.

"García and the Insurgent Attitude," *Review of Reviews*. XVIII (Sept., 1898):250–51.

García Hernández, Adrián. "Movimiento obrero y liberación nacional." *Trabajo* I (June, 1960):38–43.

García Vélez, Carlos. "Cuba Against Spain, 1895–1898." *The American-Spanish War. A History by the War Leaders*. Norwich, Conn.: Charles C. Haskell & Son, 1899, pp. 45–90.

Gay-Calbó, Enrique. "En los finales de la guerra de independencia: recuerdos de la niñez." In Congreso Nacional de historia. XII. *La lucha por la independencia de Cuba*. Havana: Oficina del Historiador de la Ciudad de La Habana, 1957, pp. 59–61.

———. "Génesis de la Enmienda Platt." *Cuba Contemporánea* XLI (May, 1926):47–63.

———. "Los últimos tiempos del 95 y la guerra hispanoamericana." In Emilio Roig de Leuchsenring, ed. *Curso de introducción a la historia de Cuba*. Havana: Municipio de La Habana, 1938, pp. 351–58.

"General García and Cuban Conduct." *Literary Digest* XVII (July 30, 1898):121–24.

Giberga, Eliseo. "Las ideas políticas en Cuba en el siglo XIX." *Cuba Contemporánea* X (Apr., 1916):347–81.

González, Miriam, and Ravelo, Aloima. "La guerra del 95: la invasión." In *La invasión: estrategia fundamental en nuestras guerras revolucionarias*. Havana: Instituto Cubano del Libro, 1972, pp. 150–261.

"La guerra de 1895." In Vicente Báez, ed. *La enciclopedia de Cuba*. 8 vols. Madrid: Enciclopedia y Clásicos Cubanos, 1974, IV, pp. 511–600.

Harris, C. Alexander. "Some Economic Aspects of the Cuban Insurrection." *The Economic Journal* VII (September, 1897):435–43.

Harrison, R. J. "Catalan Business and the Loss of Cuba, 1898–1914." *The Economic History Review*. 2nd Series, XXVII (August, 1974):431–41.

Hastings, Elbert G. "With Gómez in the Cuban Skirmishes." *National Magazine* XIV (1898):150–60.

Hazeltine, Mayo W. "What Is to Be Done with Cuba?" *The North American Review* CLXVII (Sept., 1898):318–25.

Heath, Perry S. "The Work of the President." *The American-Spanish War. A History by the War Leaders*. Norwich, Conn.: Charles C. Haskell & Son, 1899, pp. 281–95.

Hidalgo, Ariel. "El movimiento obrero cubano y el primer partido antimperialista de la historia." *El Caimán Barbudo* VI (Jan., 1974):3–8.

Hinton, Richard J. "Cuban Reconstruction." *North American Review* CLXIV (Jan., 1899):93–102.

Hitchman, James L. "The American Touch in Imperial Administration: Leonard Wood in Cuba, 1898–1902." *The Americas* XXIV (Apr. 1968):394–403.

———. "U.S. Control Over Cuban Sugar Production, 1898–1902." *Journal of Inter-American and World Affairs* XII (Jan., 1970):90–106.

Holbo, Paul S. "Presidential Leadership in Foreign Affairs: William McKinley and the Turpie-Foraker Amendment." *The American Historical Review* LXXII (July, 1967):1321–35.

Horrego Estuch, Leopoldo. "Máximo Gómez: el militar y el ciudadano." *Revista de la Biblioteca Nacional.* 2nd series, VII (July–Sept., 1956):87–101.

———. "Antonio Maceo, el heroe." *Bohemia* LIII (Dec. 3, 1961):4–15, 127.

———. "Martí: su ideología." *Bohemia* LVII (Jan.22, 1965):99–101.

———. "El sentido revolucionario de la guerra grande." *Bohemia* LV (Oct. 11, 1963):73–75.

Horton, William E. "The Battle of San Juan." In Society of Santiago de Cuba, *The Santiago Campaign: Reminiscences.* Richmond, Va.: Williams Printing Company, 1927. 413–20.

Houghton, Arthur, "The Political Condition of Spain." *Harper's Weekly* XLI (Feb. 20, 1897):179–83.

James, Joel. "La primera instancia agrupadora." *Santiago* XVII (Mar., 1975):7–41.

Jorge, Gaspar. "Influencia del tabaquero en la trayectoría revolucionaria de Cuba." *Revista Bimestre Cubana* XXXIX (First Sem., 1937):100–21.

Kennan, George. "Cuban Character." *The Outlook* LXIII (Dec. 23, 1899):959–65.

King. Clarence. "Fire and Sword in Cuba." *Forum* XXII (Sept., 1896):31–52.

Lane, Jack C. "Instrument for Empire: The American Military Government in Cuba, 1899–1902." *Science and Society* XXXVI (Fall, 1972):314–30.

Latane, John H. "Intervention of the United States in Cuba." *North American Review* CCCCXCVI (Mar., 1898):350–61.

Lee, Fitzhugh. "Cuba and Her Struggle for Freedom." *Fortnightly Review* LXIII (June, 1898):855–66.

———. "Cuba Under Spanish Rule." *McClure's Magazine* XI (June, 1898):99–114.

LeRiverend Brusone, Julio E. "Cuba: la revolución de 1868 como transición ideológica." *Casa de las Américas* XIV (May–June, 1974):3–18.

———. "Raíces del 24 de febrero: la economía y la sociedad cubana de 1878 a 1895." *Cuba Socialista* V (Feb., 1965):1–17.

Lewis, Henry Harrison. "The Truth About Cuba." *The World's Work* IV (June, 1902):2217–21.

Llaguno y de Cárdenas, Pablo. "Campaña del mayor general Antonio Maceo en la provincia de Pinar del Río, enero 8 de 1896 a diciembre 4 de 1896." *Boletín del Archivo Nacional* XLVIII (Jan.–Dec., 1949):81–98.

Llanos, Marcos. "Creación e intención del Partido Revolucionario Cubano." *Santiago* XX (Dec., 1975):203–36.

Ludlow, William "The Transition in Havana." *The Independent* LII (Apr. 12, 1900):866–68.

McCreary, George D. "Cuba's Commercial Future." *The Independent* LIII (Apr. 25, 1901):957–58.

McDonald, Timothy G. "McKinley and the Coming of the War with Spain." *The Midwest Quarterly* VII (Spring, 1966):225–39.

McDowell, William Osborne. "Secret Story of American Interference in Cuba." *The Journal of American History* II (July–Aug.–Sept., 1908): 405–07.

Maldonado Denis, Manuel. "Martí y su concepto de la revolución." *Casa de las Américas* XX (July–Aug., 1971):3–12.

Marriott, Crittenden, "The Character of the Cubans." *Review of Reviews* XIX (Feb., 1899):176–78.

Martín, Juan Luis. "El combatiente cubano en función de pueblo." *Cuadernos de Historia Habanera* XXX (1945):25–64.

Matheson, Fred J. "The United States and Cuban Independence." *Fortnightly Review* LXIII (May, 1898):816–32.

Matthews, Franklin. "The Reconstruction of Cuba." *Harper's Weekly* XLIII (July 15, 1899):700–01.

Meitín, Enríquez. "De los partidos en la primera etapa de la Cuba neocolonial." *Bohemia* LXVII (Jan. 24, 1975):88–92.

Mencia, Mario. "Martí: la unidad revolucionaria." *Bohemia* LXVIII (Jan. 30, 1976):88–93.

Miles, Nelson A. "The Work of the Army as a Whole." *The American-Spanish War. A History by the War Leaders.* Norwich, Conn.: Charles C. Haskell & Son, 1899, pp. 509–40.

Morales, Salvador. "Origen y caracter del partido fundado por Martí." *Granma*, Jan. 28, 1975, p. 2.

Moreno Pla, Enrique H. "Genealogía y proyecciones de las ideas del Manifiesto de Monte-cristi." *Universidad de La Habana,* no. 179 (May–June, 1966), pp. 57–78.

Muecke Bertel, Carlos. "Diario de operaciones." *Revista Bimestre Cubana* XLII (Second); 126–53.

Musgrave, G. C. "The Cuban Insurrection," *The Contemporary Review* LXXIV (July, 1898):1–19.

———. "The Government of 'Free Cuba.' " *Review of Reviews* XVIII (August, 1898):208–09.

A Native Cuban. "The Cuban Revolt: Its Causes and Effects." *Engineering Magazine* (October, 1895):9–16.

Ogden, Rollo. "Light from the Junta." *Nation* LXVI (Apr. 14, 1898):278.

———. "Multiplying Difficulties in Cuba." *Nation* LXVI (August 4, 1898):84–85.

Ojeda, Dolores Bessy. "Antecedentes de la guerra de 1895 en Oriente." *Santiago* XX (Dec., 1975):157–79.

Olmstead, G. Kingsley. "Some Economic Consequences of the Liberation of Cuba." *Yale Review* VII (August, 1898):168–79.

Olney, Richard. "Growth of Our Foreign Policy." *The Atlantic Monthly* LXXXV (March, 1900):289–301.

Osa, Enrique de la. "Una interpretación materialista de la guerra de los diez años." *Bohemia* LIII (Oct. 8, 1961):54–56, 79–80.

"Our Demands on Cuba." *The Literary Digest* XXII (March 9, 1901):273.

Pagliuchi, F.D. "A Glimpse of the Cuban War." *Harper's Weekly* XLII (Feb. 19, 1898):174.

Paradela, Francisco de. "La paga del Ejército Libertador y la economía cubana." *Revista Bimestre Cubana* XLVII (May–June, 1941):431–44.

Pazos, Felipe. "La economía cubana en el siglo XIX." *Revista Bimestre Cubana* XLVII (Jan.-Feb., 1941):83–106.

Perera, Virgilio, and Acosta, Leonardo. "La campaña anti-Martí." *El Caimán Barbudo* V (Feb., 1973):19–24.

Pérez, Antonio Gonzalo. "Cuba for the Cubans." *Contemporary Review* LXXIV (Nov., 1898):692–701.

———. "The Independence of Cuba." *The Contemporary Review* LXXVI (July, 1899):118–31.

A Planter In Cuba. "The Argument for Autonomy." *The Outlook* LVIII (April 23, 1898):1012–14.

Platt, Orville H. "Cuba's Claim Upon the United States." *North American Review* CLXXV (Aug., 1902):145–51.

———. "Our Relations to the People of Cuba and Porto Rico." *The Annals of the American Academy of Political and Social Science* XVIII (July, 1901):145–59.

———. "The Pacification of Cuba." *The Independent* LIII (June 27, 1901):1464–68.

———. "The Solution of the Cuban Problem." *The World's Work* II (May 1901):729–35.

Ponte Domínguez, Francisco J. "La invasión." In Emilio Roig de Leuchsenring, ed., *Curso de introducción a la historia de Cuba*. Havana: Municipio de La Habana, 1938, pp. 343–50.

Portell Vilá, Herminio. "Anexionismo." *Humanismo* VII (Jan.–Apr., 1959):28–42.

———. "La intervención militar norteamericana." *El Mundo*, May 20, 1952, 34–36.

———. "El Senador Teller y los derechos de Cuba." In Congreso Nacional de Historia. XII. *La lucha por la independencia de Cuba*. Havana: Oficina del Historiador de la Ciudad de La Habana, 1957, pp. 76–78.

Portuondo, José Antonio. "Ideología del Partido Revolucionario Cubano." *Cuadernos de Historia Habanera* XXII (1942):63–70.

Portuondo del Prado, Fernando. "Martí y el Partido Revolucionario Cubano." *Islas* XI (Oct.–Dec., 1968):171–74.

Poumier, María. "La vida cotidiana en la ciudades cubanas en 1898." *Universidad de La Habana*, 196–97 (Feb.–Mar., 1972), 170–209.

"Primera intervención de los Estados Unidos." In Vicente Báez, ed. *La enciclopedia de Cuba*. 8 vols. Madrid: Enciclopedia y Clásicos Cubanos, 1974, IV, pp. 601–53.

Pritchett, Henry S. "Some Recollections of President McKinley and the Cuban Intervention." *The North American Review* CLXXXIX (Mar., 1909):397–403.

Quesada y Miranda, Gonzalo. "Labor del Partido Revolucionario Cubano." *Cuadernos de Historia Habanera* XXII (1942):45–61.

Quintana, Jorge. "Lo que costó a Cuba la guerra de 1895." *Bohemia* LII (Sept. 11, 1960):4–6, 107–08.

Ramsden, Frederick W. "Diary of the British Consul at Santiago During Hostilities." *McClure's Magazine* XI (Oct., 1898) 580–90.

Randolph, Carman F. "The Joint Resolution of Congress Respecting Relations Between the United States and Cuba." *Columbia Law Review* I (June, 1901):352–76.

Rea, George B. "The Destruction of Sugar Estates in Cuba." *Harper's Weekly* XLI (Oct. 16, 1897):10–34.

Reno, George. "Operating an 'Underground' Route to Cuba." *Cosmopolitan* XXVII (Aug., 1899):431–40.

Reyna, René E. "La campaña de la invasión en la guerra de independencia." *Revista Bimestre Cubana* XXIII (May–June, 1928):344–77.

Rivero Mūniz, José. "Los cubanos en Tampa." *Revista Bimestre Cubana* LXXIV (First Sem., 1958):5–140.

Robinson, Albert Gardner. "Cuban Constitution Making." *The Independent* LIII (Feb. 21, 1901):435–38.

———. "Cuban Self-Government." *The Independent* LII (Dec. 18, 1900):2968–71.

———. "Cuba's Cause of Offense." *The Independent* LIII (Mar. 21, 1901):671–74.

———. "Industrial and Commercial Conditions in Cuba." *Review of Reviews* XXVI (Aug. 1902):195–201.

———. "Our Legacy to the Cuban Republic." *Forum* XXXIII (June, 1902):450–58.

———. "The Real Cuban." *The Independent* LII (Dec. 20, 1900):3030–34.

———. "Some Cuban Opinions." *The Independent* LIII (May 9, 1901):1055–61.

Rodríguez, José Ignacio. "Can There Ever Be a Cuban Republic?" *Forum* XXX (Dec., 1900):436–41.

Rodríguez, Pedro Pablo. "Caracter popular del P. R. C." *Bohemia* LXVII (Nov. 21, 1975):88–93.

———. "La idea de liberación nacional en José Martí." *Pensamiento Crítico* 49–50 (Feb.–Mar., 1971):120–69.

Roig de Leuchsenring, Emilio. "Cuatro hechos ejemplares en la vida de Cosme de la Torriente." In *Cosme de la Torriente en la revolución libertadora y en la República*. Havana: Oficina del Historiador de la Ciudad de La Habana, 1951, pp. 47–84.

————. "La Enmienda Platt, consecuencia y ratificación de la inalterable política seguida por el estado norteamericano contra Cuba desde 1805." *Universidad de La Habana* VII (Jan.–Feb., 1935):119–47.

————. "Ideario de la Revolución." *Cuadernos de Historia Habanera* XXIX (1945):42–58.

————. "Independentismo de 1868 a 1901." *Humanismo* VII (Jan.–Apr., 1959):79–104.

————. "Proceso evolutivo y revolucionario forjador de la nación cubana." *Cuadernos de Historia Habanera* XL (1948):37–56.

Román Hernández, Jorge. "Consideración sobre la obra unificadora de Martí y el Partido Revolucionario Cubano." *Anuario Martiano* VII (1977):241–51.

Rosell, Eduardo. "Diario de operaciones del comandante Eduardo Rosell, jefe de Estado Mayor del Brigadier Pedro Betancourt." In Carlos M. Trelles y Govín, *Matanzas en la independencia de Cuba.* Havana: Imprenta Avisador Comercial, 1928, pp. 142–74.

Rubens, Horatio S. "The Insurgent Government in Cuba." *North American Review* CCCXCVIII (May, 1898):560–69.

Rutter, Frank R. "The Sugar Question in the United States." *Quarterly Journal of Economics* XVII (Nov., 1902):44–81.

Sanguily, Manuel. "Sobre la génesis de la Enmienda Platt." *Cuba Contemporánea* XXX (Oct., 1922):117–25.

Santovenia, Emeterio Santiago. "Como contribuyeron los Estados Unidos de América a la independencia de Cuba." *Revista Bimestre Cubana* XXI(July–Aug., 1926): 481–95.

Scott, James B. "The Origin and Purpose of the Platt Amendment." *American Journal of International Law* (July, 1914):585–91.

"Secretary Root Talks About Cuba." *The Independent* LII (Mar. 22, 1900): 689.

Shafter, William R. "Address of Major General William R. Shafter, U.S. Army, Before the Chamber of Commerce, Los Angeles, California." In Society of Santiago de Cuba, *The Santiago Campaign: Reminiscences.* Richmond, Va.: Williams Printing Company, 1927, pp. 246–63.

————. "The Santiago Campaign." *The American-Spanish War. A History by the War Leaders.* Norwich, Conn.: Charles C. Haskell & Son, 1899, pp. 180–98.

"Situation in Cuba." *The Independent* LII (March 8, 1900):575–76.

Souza, Benigno. "Triunfo de la revolución cubana." *Cuadernos de Historia Habanera* XL (1948):15–35.

Steep, Thomas W. "A Cuban Insurgent Newspaper." *National Magazine* VIII (May, 1898):147–49.

Taylor, Hannis. "A Review of the Cuban Question in Its Economic, Political and Diplomatic Aspects." *North American Review* CCCCXCII (Nov., 1897):610–35.

"Technically We Annex Cuba." *Review of Reviews* XVIII (September, 1898): 252.

Thompson, Winfield M. "How Porter Carried a Message to Gomez." *Spare Moments* (Rochester, N.Y.) I (Mar., 1905):1–2, 12–13.

Tingley, Donald F. "The Cuban Diary of Edwin M. Lacey." *Journal of the Illinois State Historical Society* LVI (Spring, 1963):20–35.

Tirado, Modesto A. "Apuntes de un corresponsal (I)." *Revista Bimestre Cubana* XXXXVII (July–Aug., 1941):94–114.

————. "Apuntes de un corresponsal (II)." *Revista Bimestre Cubana* IL (Jan.–Feb., 1942):123–36.

————. "Apuntes de un corresponsal (III)." *Revista Bimestre Cubana* (May–June, 1942):283–302.

————. "Apuntes de un corresponsal (IV)." *Revista Bimestre Cubana* L (First Sem., 1943):418–49.

———. "Apuntes de un corresponsal (V)." *Revista Bimestre Cubana* LI (Second Sem., 1943):107–36.

———. "Apuntes de un corresponsal (VI)." *Revista Bimestre Cubana* LII (Second Sem., 1943):464–67.

Torres-Cuevas, Eduardo. "Génesis, estructura y función del primer partido para la revolución cubana." *Bohemia* LXVII (Oct. 17, 1975):4–9.

———. "El Partido Autonomista: la traición permanente." *Bohemia* LXVII (Feb. 14, 1975):88–93.

———. "La revolución necesaria." *Bohemia* LXIX (Jan. 28, 1977):84–89.

Torriente, Loló de la. "Baraguá: la resistencia maceísta." *Bohemia* LVI (Mar. 13, 1964):100–01, 109.

Varona, Enrique José. "Los Estados Unidos y la asamblea cubana." *Cuba y América* III (Apr. 5, 1899):6–8.

Varona Guerrero, Miguel. "Operaciones militares cubanas." *Cuadernos de Historia Habanera* XXIX (1945):59–77.

Vázquez Candela, Euclides. "El 'Baraguá' que no tuvimos." *Bohemia* LVII (May 21, 1965):106–07, 113.

Velasco, Carlos de. "La obra de la revolución cubana." *Cuba Contemporánea* V (July, 1914):273–83.

"The War Spirit of the People." *Harper's Weekly* XLII (Apr. 16, 1898):362–63.

Welliver, Judson C. "The Annexation of Cuba by the Sugar Trust." *Hampton Magazine* XXVI (Mar. 1910):375–88.

Wellman, Walter. "The Cuban Republic—Limited." *Review of Reviews* XXII (Dec., 1900):708–12.

Welsh, Osgood. "Cuba As Seen from the Inside." *The Century Magazine* LVI (Aug., 1898):586–93.

Whelpley, J. D. "Cuba of To-Day and To-Morrow." *The Atlantic Monthly* LXXXVI (July, 1900):45–52.

White, H. "After Intervention—What?" *The Nation*. LXVI (March 17, 1898):199.

Whitney, Caspar. "Conference at Aserradero." *Harper's Weekly* XLII (July 9, 1898):661.

Wilcos, Marrion. "Our Honor and Cuba's Need." *The Forum* XXXII (Jan. 1902):623–28.

Wilkie, John E. "The Secret Service in the War." *The American-Spanish War. A History by the War Leaders*. Norwich, Conn.: Charles C. Haskell & Son, 1899, pp. 423–36.

Willets, Gilson, "Business Opportunities in Our New Colonies." *Leslie's Weekly* LXXXVIII (Jan.5, 1899):9–12.

Williams, Herbert Pelham. "The Outlook in Cuba." *The Atlantic Monthly* LXXXIII (June, 1899):827–36.

Willis, H. Parker, "Reciprocity with Cuba." *The Annals of the American Academy of Political and Social Science* XXII (July, 1903):129–47.

Wilson, James H. "Cuba Revisited." *The Independent* LV (Apr. 16, 1903):903–06.

Wood, Edmund. "Can Cubans Govern Cuba?" *Forum* XXXII (Sept., 1901):66–73.

Wood, Leonard. "The Cuban Convention." *The Independent* LII (Nov. 1, 1900):2605–06.

———. "The Existing Conditions and Needs in Cuba." *North American Review* CLXVIII (May, 1898):593–601.

———. "The Future of Cuba." *The Independent* LIV (Jan. 23, 1902):193–94.

———. "The Military Government of Cuba." *The Annals of the American Academy of Political and Social Science* XXI (March, 1903):1–30.

———. "The Need for Reciprocity with Cuba." *The Independent* LII (Dec. 12, 1901):2927–29.

———. "U.S. Military Government of Santiago." *The American Spanish War. A History by the War Leaders*. Norwich, Conn.: Charles C. Haskell & Son, 1899, pp. 393–401.

Woodford, Steward L. "Introduction." *The American-Spanish War. A History by the War Leaders*. Norwich, Conn.: Charles C. Haskell & Son, 1899, pp. 4–13.

Wooley, Robert Wicklife. "America's Bad Faith Toward Cuba." *Pearson's Magazine* XXIII (June, 1910):715–24.

Wright, Theodore P., Jr. "United States Electoral Intervention in Cuba." *Inter-American Economic Affairs* XIII (Winter, 1959):50–71.

Yznaga, Fernando A. "The Wanton Destruction of American Property in Cuba." *The Forum* XXII (Jan., 1897):571–74.

Zayas, Henry Lincoln de. "The Causes of the Present War in Cuba." *Catholic World* LXII (Mar., 1896):807–16.

Index

PITT LATIN AMERICAN SERIES

Cole Blasier, Editor